American Folk Poetry

An Anthology

Books by Duncan Emrich

IT'S AN OLD WILD WEST CUSTOM

COMSTOCK BONANZA

THE COWBOY'S OWN BRAND BOOK

THE LUCIUS BEEBE READER
(Co-Editor)

THE FOLKLORE OF LOVE AND COURTSHIP

THE FOLKLORE OF WEDDINGS AND MARRIAGE

THE NONSENSE BOOK

THE BOOK OF WISHES AND WISHMAKING

FOLKLORE ON THE AMERICAN LAND

THE HODGEPODGE BOOK

AMERICAN FOLK POETRY
An Anthology

American Folk Poetry

An Anthology

Duncan Emrich

Little, Brown and Company — Boston — Toronto

Third Printing

T 08/74

Acknowledgments of permission to reprint excerpted material, as noted in the source notes, appear on pages xxiii–xxiv.

Most of the illustrations in this book are from the collections of the Prints and Photographs Division of the Library of Congress.

LIBRARY OF CONGRESS CATALOGING IN PUBLICATION
Emrich, Duncan, 1908–   comp.
    American folk poetry: an anthology.

    "A bibliography of American folksong," compiled by
J. C. Hickerson: p.
        1. American ballads and songs.   2. Folk–songs,
American.   I. Title.
    PS593.L8E5   811:04   74-3499
    ISBN 0-316-23722-1

MV

Published simultaneously in Canada by Little, Brown & Company (Canada) Limited

PRINTED IN THE UNITED STATES OF AMERICA

This book is dedicated
with affection and respect to

Harold Spivacke

Chief of the Music Division — The Library of Congress
from 1937 to 1972
who nursed the fledgling archive of folk song
into the great and magnificent collection
which it now is

Contents

CONTENTS

PLAY-PARTY SONGS, GAMES AND DANCES

Play-Party, Courting, and Kissing Games and Songs   27

Square Dance Calls   51

Banjo and Fiddle Pieces   58

LOVE

Family Opposition to Love   75

Love's Laments   96

CONTENTS

CONTENTS

CHILD BALLADS

CONTENTS

CONTENTS

HYMNS, RELIGIOUS PIECES, CAROLS

Selections from *The Original Sacred Harp* and *The Social Harp*   355

Hymns and Religious Pieces   371

WARS AND OTHER DISASTERS

CONTENTS

The Assassination of Presidents   459

Disasters and Tragedies   464

SONGS OF OCCUPATIONS AND SEA, FOREST, MINES

Sea Shanties   479

Forecastle Songs of the Sea and Sailors and Wrecks and
Disasters at Sea   489

Lumbering   530

CONTENTS

SONGS OF A GROWING NATION: COWBOYS, MORMONS, OUTLAWS, AND OTHERS

CONTENTS

Miscellaneous Pieces and Pieces Relating to the American Land
and to Events on the American Land, Regional and Historical   755

A Bibliography of American Folksong
    Compiled by Joseph C. Hickerson   775

Index of Titles   819

Index of First Lines   825

Acknowledgments

It is my pleasure and privilege to express my appreciation for the helpfulness of the staff of the Library of Congress, and particularly to Alan Jabbour (Head of the Archive of Folk Song) and Joseph Hickerson (Reference Librarian of the Archive), in the preparation of this book. Alan Jabbour reviewed the contents and made valuable suggestions; Joseph Hickerson prepared the excellent basic bibliography, which adds to the usefulness of the work for librarians and students.

In the note to each song-text I have cited the collector, the singer or informant, and the place and date of collection, as well as the Library of Congress archive number for recordings drawn from its collections. To each collector and every informant I am greatly indebted. I should like, however, to express my special thanks to Professor Bertrand Harris Bronson of the University of California, who read and commented on the introduction to the section on the Child ballads; to Anne and Frank Warner, who freely gave me half a dozen or more song-texts from their important collection — which deserves independent publication; to Mrs. Rae Korson, wife of George Korson, the great collector of coal mining songs and coal mining folklore, for permission to draw from his classic *Minstrels of the Mine Patch;* to Professor George Boswell of the University of Mississippi (whose collection of Tennessee folksong is most valuable and hopefully may be published shortly) for the inclusion of a rare Child ballad; to Alan Lomax, whose collection of folksong touched a high-water mark in the preservation

ACKNOWLEDGMENTS

of this material in the United States; to Vance Randolph of Missouri and Arkansas for the same reason; to Professor Alton Morris of the University of Florida, whose book on Florida folksongs deserves reprinting; to Professor Herbert Halpert, now of the University of Newfoundland, who collected in Kentucky, New Jersey, Montana, and all over the lot; to Professor Austin E. Fife and his wife, Alta, of Utah, for their collection and preservation of an enormous body of traditional Mormon material; and, again, to all the collectors and scholars — past and present — named in the source notes.

I am grateful also to the editors and secretary-treasurers of various folklore societies for their willingness to permit the inclusion here of texts first published in their journals, all of which are noted throughout the book: the *Journal of American Folklore* (*JAF*), the *Southern Folklore Quarterly* (*SFQ*), the *California Folklore Quarterly* (*CFQ*) (now *Western Folklore*), the *Kentucky Folklore Record* (*KFR*), the *New York Folklore Quarterly* (*NYFQ*), *Hoosier Folklore* (*HF*), and the *Publications of the Texas Folklore Society* (*PTFS*).

For permission to reprint selected material in copyright, as detailed in the notes, I acknowledge the courtesy of the following presses and publishers: Columbia University Press, Yale University Press, Harvard University Press, Duke University Press, the University of Michigan Press, the University of Florida Press, Dover Publications, W. W. Norton & Company, and Folk Legacy Records.

Introduction

THIS IS A COLLECTION of American folk poetry with an indication of the types of that poetry. The selections are representative, but they are not exhaustive — any more than any anthology is exhaustive. I have attempted to include the best, just as any anthologist would do. The choice, of course, is personal.

Folk poetry should not and cannot be judged on the aesthetic scales used to weigh the poetry of great literature (learned or academic literature): Shakespere, Donne, Marvell, Dante, Santa Teresa, San Juan de la Cruz, Shelley, Ronsard, Yeats, Dickinson, Herrick, Marlowe, Whitman, Virgil, Catullus, and so on down the lists in every land of those who have, with absolute control of the language and with genius and the sweat of midnight oil, given to us the perfection of form and thought, emotion and spirit, which will make their names live forever as long as language is alive. "As long as the iron of English shall ring from the tongue . . ." "*Quand vous serez bien vieille* . . ." "Was this the face that launched a thousand ships/ And burnt the topless towers of Ilium . . ." "Death, be not proud . . ." "But at my back I always hear/Time's winged chariot hurrying near . . ." "*Arma virumque cano* . . ." "I could not love thee, dear, so much . . ." "O wild West Wind, thou breath of Autumn's being . . ." "*Da mi basia mille, deinde centum* . . ." "When in disgrace with fortune and men's eyes . . ." "*Nel mezzo del cammin di nostra vita* . . ."

INTRODUCTION

The literary poet has been trained in the schools, has learned his art there, or sought after it consciously elsewhere. He is aware of his individualism, his personality, his name. ("When you are old and gray and full of sleep . . .") He is projecting his special message and his gift *in his name* to those who will listen.

Not so the folk poet. He often does not know the word "poet" or the word "poetry." Rarely uses them. And, if strong Kentucky or Tennessee male, would be horrified that he should be so named or categorized.

I had a piece of pie and a little piece of puddin'.
I'd give it all to hug Sally Goodin.
Night's so dark, road's so muddy,
I'm so drunk I can't walk steady.

The folk poet is not conscious of form. He knows nothing of and is totally unconcerned about sonnets, madrigals, epics, quatrains, hexameters, free or blank verse, couplets, or whatever. And fortunately.

The simple point is: if someone is happily barefoot, why force shoes on him? "My aunt, who was fifty-six years old and had never worn shoes in her life, put shoes on, and in three months she was dead."

There are various touchstones to folk poetry.

One, the language. It is not the language of the schools, of Oxford, of Magdalen, of Christ Church, of Edinburgh, of Harvard, of Virginia. But it still is the great and powerful language of England, and an America born of England. It is Chaucer and Shakespere, and the Kentucky and Tennessee hills, the coast of Maine and the towns of Massachusetts, Georgia, and the Carolinas. It is the spoken language of the streets of London, with its signboards, because no man could read: the Three Squirrels, Hand and Star, Royal Oak, Goose and Gridiron, Cheshire Cheese, Running Footman, Hat and Beaver, the Poet's Head, the Mermaid. It is the language of England, some of it retained with incredible toughness in the Ozarks, in back-country Connecticut, in the Berkshires, in Alabama. The language is free and moves easily: it is not penned and trapped. It has no use for the schools. It is not

Rose Aylmer, whom these wakeful eyes
May weep, but never see,
A night of memories and sighs
I consecrate to thee.

It is

> *Eyes like the morning star,*
> *Cheek like the rose,*
> *Laura was a pretty girl,*
> *God Almighty knows. . . .*
> *Weep, all you little rains,*
> *Wail, winds, wail,*
> *All along, along, along*
> *The Colorado Trail.*

It is

> *Yes, I am sick and very sick,*
> *And death upon me crawlin'.*

It is

> *She went on a little piece further and what did she spy,*
> *A new duggen grave and a spade layin' by.*

And

> *When the moon and the stars enters in yonders green*
> *And the sky, it shall shed no more rain . . .*

It is a language that has nothing to do with the brittle and self-conscious poets who strive with terrible concentration to be unique. It is natural and of the earth. You will find it on most pages of this book. On some pages a little less perhaps than on others. But always there. The poetry of those who have a great and innate sense of poetry, but who do not know the firm meaning of the word.

We are very fortunate (those of us who know great literature) to have this "literature." We are perhaps the only ones who can fully and totally appreciate it. Certainly the mass or popular segment of our society cannot understand or appreciate it: the sophisticated and the folk are here brought together, wittingly and unwittingly.

Two, the anonymity. In sophisticated and literary poetry, the names again ring like bells: Suckling, Milton, Herbert, Herrick, Jonson, Spenser, Raleigh.

In folk poetry there are no such names. There are few names. One or two maybe out of ten thousand. And those by accident.

INTRODUCTION

Folk poets are essentially anonymous. And the reason, of course, lies in the transmission of this poetry. It moves from one person to another without any attribution of source. There is no findable or fixable source. One individual may sing it at a certain point (and it may be caught and recorded), but there is no source there: any more than there is a source of the river for the individual standing by the Mississippi at Natchez. The river is there and moving, moving, moving, but there is no sense or question of source. As a song or playground-chant moves from one person to another and another and another, all possibility of tracing it to an individual source is lost. It is a waste of time even to consider doing so. Catch it as you see it (the river) and hear it as you may (the song). In effect, folk poetry on all levels is as totally anonymous as a bawdy joke.

Three, carry the foregoing a step further. A poem in the literary world is fixed. It cannot be changed or altered. Any persons reading or reciting

> *Seven weeks of sea, twice seven days of storm*
> *Upon the huge Atlantic, and once more*
> *We ride into still water and the calm*
> *Of a sweet evening, screen'd by either shore*
> *Of Spain and Barbary. . . .*
>   *Ay, this is the famed rock which Hercules*
> *And Goth and Moor bequeath'd us. At this door*
> *England stands sentry. . . .*

must read or recite it precisely as Wilfred Scawen Blunt wrote it. He cannot alter it. He has no right to do so. It is Blunt's poem: fixed in the writing, fixed in print, fixed in precise quotation. Unchangeable. The same is true of any printed song, ranging from "Jeanie with the Light Brown Hair" to the "Lullaby of Broadway" to all the "Alma Maters" which were once so pleasantly sung at chapel and on college steps, and some of which — moving and tied to our history — still are: as at Annapolis, the Navy Hymn:

> *Eternal Father! strong to save,*
> *Whose arm hath bound the restless wave,*
> *Who bidd'st the mighty ocean deep*
> *Its own appointed limits keep;*
> *O, hear us when we cry to Thee*
> *For those in peril on the sea.*

and, skipping two stanzas, the last:

> *O, Trinity of love and power!*
> *Our brethren shield in danger's hour*
> *From rock and tempest, fire and foe,*
> *Protect them wheresoe'er they go;*
> *Thus evermore shall rise to Thee*
> *Glad hymns of praise from land and sea.**

No word can be altered.

But with folk poetry it is precisely the reverse. If any folk poem were to become *irrevocably* fixed — by way of print or record — it would cease to be folk, and become part of the popular or mass culture, destroying the folk poem: eliminating its natural manner of folk transmission, killing it with a fixative.

I need not belabor the point here. It is self-evident throughout the book. Each song changes as it moves from one person to another and is "re-created" in the process. Changed. Turn the pages to "Lady Alice" where, purely for example of this, I have given a few variants.

Four, the aesthetic standards again: the folk have none except as these standards stem from the group to which they belong, and the folk poet has none except as he satisfies with his product the group to which he belongs. His material is drawn from his milieu and given back to his milieu, which understands it at once. He does not attempt to set himself apart or separate himself from his group. He does not, for example, attempt to build a sur-realistic fence or weathervane on his property, totally out of keeping with his neighbor's fences and weathervanes — and with those of his father. No. He stands within a tradition, and in that tradition lie — for him and the members of his group — the aesthetics of his poetry. One person may produce a better and more beautiful weathervane than the next, but they are within the same tight tradition — and within yelling distance. There is no such thing here as a search for special identity, for ivory-tower art. The folk poet (and transmitter of folk poetry) lives within the group and is bound by the group: it cannot be otherwise: if it were so he would be removing

---

* The words were written by the Reverend William Whiting, clergyman of the Church of England, after he had come through a terrible storm in the Mediterranean Sea. Every service at the Naval Academy is closed with the first stanza, the entire congregation kneeling or seated with bowed heads. From the Academy the custom has spread to ships of the Fleet.

himself from the group and ceasing to be a member of it: ceasing to be a folk poet accepted naturally and easily by his fellows.

I have not included in this selection sentimental songs, tear-jerker, anti-tobacco and anti-drinking songs, blackface minstrel songs, vaudeville songs, pro-tobacco and pro-drinking songs, college and community songs, songs sung on the Chautauqua circuit, contrived "humorous" songs, and the like. They belong in a separate book beginning with "Gaudeamus Igitur" and winding up, perhaps, with "Who Shot Maggie in the Freckle?" The majority of songs in these groupings have not had folk circulation, but have been passed on or "taught" within a glee club tradition. Not that they are not good. They are wonderfully good. But they do not belong within the purer folk tradition. They are on the popular, rather than folk, side. A distinction to be noted and understood. Put it more plainly: all the songs (with a few exceptions) reported here come clearly from oral tradition. All of the songs which I have excluded in the categories listed above (with some few exceptions) come from print. The ones circulated one way, the others another. That has been a basis of selectivity, a demarking line: the folk as over against the popular, the oral as over against print, the untutored as over against the tutored. "Gaudeamus Igitur" I sang with classmates on the steps of Sayles Hall at Brown University in 1932. "I've Got No Use For the Women" I heard casually from an eight-year-old child at a ranch school outside of Mesa, Arizona, in 1928. The first had to be "learned," since it was Latin. The second came out of the traditions of the Southwest: unlearned (in an academic sense), but heard — against the natural background of desert and mesquite and cholla and the dry winds. And a child singing. Where he had learned it, and enough of it to make a full story-sense, God knows. It is in this collection: "Gaudeamus Igitur," for the preceding reasons, is not.

The majority of these ballads and songs and chants come from Library of Congress recordings, a great many of them transcribed here for the first time. I have given the Library (or Archive of Folk Song) record number in the footnotes. Those which are designated with an "LP" number (as LP26 for "Sea Songs and Shanties") are available on long-playing records from the Recording Laboratory of the Library of Congress, Washington, D.C., 20540. A brief catalog listing the sixty or more LPs may be had from the Recording Laboratory. Each LP sells for $4.95, tax and shipment included. Very, very good buys for those interested in the pure tradition. Those songs designated with an "AFS" number refer to the basic collections of the Archive of Folk Song, and these songs — not available on LPs — must be specially ordered on tapes or discs from the Recording Laboratory. They cost a bit more.

Just as the words of a song vary from singer to singer, and also from one rendition by a singer to a second or third rendition by the same singer, so the music changes. Within any one song, an informant's singing of the first stanza may differ considerably from his singing of the third or sixth or last. The music changes to fit the altered lines — some longer, some shorter than those in a neighboring stanza. Consequently, musical transcription of the songs — in single stanza form — would necessarily have to be arbitrary. The best way of approaching the music is to hear it: to transcribe the full music as one transcribes the full text would be next to impossible except in the study or attention one might give to a single song and its variants. I recommend the recordings.

It has been a pleasure gathering this material, listening hours on end to the recordings, and putting the words to paper. They are good words. I hope you enjoy the reading of them.

Duncan Emrich

The American University
Washington, D.C.

CHILDREN'S SONGS

*Lullabies and Songs
for Very Little Children*

Cumulative Songs

Nonsense Songs

Lullabies and Songs for Very Little Children

Hush up, baby,
Don't say a word,
Papa's going to buy you
A mocking bird.

ALL THE PRETTY LITTLE HORSES

Go to sleep, go to sleepy,
Go to sleepy, little baby,
Mammy and Daddy they went to town
To see the pretty little horses.

Go to sleep, go to sleepy,
Go to sleepy, little baby,
When you wake you'll have a cake
And all the ponies in the stable.

White and gray, black and bay,
All the ponies in the stable,
So hush, li'l baby, and don't you cry,
Go to sleepy, little baby.

Go to sleep, go to sleepy,
Go to sleepy, little baby,
Mammy went away, Daddy wouldn't stay,
Left nobody but the baby.

"All the Pretty Little Horses" was recorded by John A. Lomax from the singing of Aunt Florida Hampton, Livingston, Alabama, 1937. Library of Congress AFS record 1324 A2 and A3; stanzas 2 and 3 from current tradition.

THE MOCKING BIRD

Hush up, baby,
Don't say a word,
Papa's going to buy you
A mocking bird.

If it can't whistle
And it can't sing,
Papa's going to buy you
A diamond ring.

If that diamond ring
Turns to brass,
Papa's going to buy you
A looking-glass.

If that looking-glass
Gets broke,
Papa's going to buy you
A Billy-goat.

If that Billy-goat
Runs away,
Papa's going to buy you
Another today.

And some added gentle stanzas:

If that Billy-goat
Won't pull,
Papa's going to buy you
A cart and bull.

If that cart and bull
Turn over,
Papa's going to buy you
A dog named Rover.

If that dog named Rover
Won't bark,
Papa's going to buy you
A horse and cart.

If that horse and cart
Fall down,
You'll still be the sweetest little
Baby in town.

"The Mocking Bird" was collected by Cecil Sharp from the singing of Mrs. Julia Boone, Micaville, North Carolina, 1918. In Sharp, *English Folksongs from the Southern Appalachians*, (Oxford) New York, 1932, p. 342. With music.

"The Mocking Bird" additional stanzas are from Mrs. Margaret Lovel, ca. 1939, who learned it from her mother, Evelyn Hodgin, of Columbus, Indiana.

GO TELL AUNT RHODY

Go tell Aunt Rhody,
Go tell Aunt Rhody,
Go tell Aunt Rhody
The old gray goose is dead.

The one she was saving,
The one she was saving,
The one she was saving
To make a feather bed.

The old gander is mourning,
The old gander is mourning,
The old gander is mourning
Because his wife is dead.

The little goslings are weeping,
The little goslings are weeping,
The little goslings are weeping
Because their mammy's dead.

The whole family's weeping,
The whole family's weeping,
The whole family's weeping
Because the mama's dead.

LULLABY

I wish to God my child was born
And sitting on its dada's knee,
While I, poor girl, was in my grave
And the tall green grass growing over me.
    La la la, la la lee,
    La la la, la la lee low,
While I, poor girl, was in my grave
And the tall green grass growing over me.

La la la, la la lee,
I wish I was in the bottom of the sea,
My soul to God, my body in the sea,
And the dark blue waves rolling over me.
    La la la, la la lee,

"Go Tell Aunt Rhody" text from current tradition.

"Lullaby" is from Carrie B. Grover, *A Heritage of Songs* (privately printed, Gould Academy, Bethel, Maine, n.d.), p. 24.

La la la, la la lee low,
My soul to God, and my body in the sea,
And the dark blue waves rolling over me.

THE LOST BABY

How can you set to the table a-dining?
My poor babe's in the woods a-starving,
Poor little lost baby, baby, poor little lost babe!

Don't you hear that rain a-falling?
My little babe's in the woods a-squalling,
Poor little lost baby, baby, poor little lost babe!

Don't you hear them wolves a-howling?
My little babe's in the woods a-roving,
Poor little lost baby, baby, poor little lost babe!

Don't you hear them horns a-blowing?
They have found it and I'm a-going.
Poor little lost baby, baby, poor little lost babe!

BAA, BAA, BLACK SHEEP

Baa, baa, black sheep, where'd you leave your lamb?
Way down yonder in the valley,
The birds and the butterflies a-picking out its eyes
And the poor little thing cried, "Ma-a-amy."

Mammy told me before she went away
To take good care of the baby.

"The Lost Baby" was recorded by John A. Lomax and Laurence Powell from the singing of Mrs. Emma Dusenbury, Mena, Arkansas, 1936. Library of Congress AFS record 876 A1.

"Baa, Baa, Black Sheep" was recorded by Artus M. Moser from the singing of Bascom Lamar Lunsford of South Turkey Creek, North Carolina, at Swannanoa, North Carolina, 1946. Library of Congress record LP20.

But then I went away and the baby ran away,
And the poor little thing cried, "Ma-a-amy."

The birds and the butterflies a-flying all around,
And the poor little thing was crying, "Ma-a-amy."

WHO KILLED POOR ROBIN?

Who killed poor robin?
Who killed poor robin?
"It was I," said the sparrow,
"With my little bow and arrow,
It was I, it was I."

Who seen him dying?
Who seen him dying?
"It was I," said the fly,
"With my little teenty eye,
It was I, it was I."

Who laid him out?
Who laid him out?
"It was I," said the raven,
"Just as straight as I could lay him,
It was I, it was I."

Who made his coffin?
Who made his coffin?
"It was I," said the crane,
"With my little saw and plane,
It was I, it was I."

Who made his shroud?
Who made his shroud?
"It was I," said the eagle,
"With my thimble and my needle,
It was I, it was I."

Who dug his grave?
Who dug his grave?
"It was I," said the crow,
"With my little garden hoe,
It was I, it was I."

Who hauled him over?
Who hauled him over?
"It was I," said the lark,
"With my little horse and cart,
It was I, it was I."

Who let him down?
Who let him down?
"It was I" said the crane,
"With my little silver chain,
It was I, it was I."

Who covered him up?
Who covered him up?
"It was I," said the duck,
"With my big splatter foot,
It was I, it was I."

Who preached his funeral?
Who preached his funeral?
"It was I," said the owl,
"Just as loud as I could howl,
It was I, it was I."

"Who Killed Poor Robin?" was recorded by Sidney Robertson Cowell from the singing of Mrs. Emma Dusenbury, Mena, Arkansas, 1936. Library of Congress AFS record 3229 B1.

SQUAT DOWN, JOSEY

A very simple game for little children, who form a ring, singing and suiting their action to the words, repeating over and over again.

— JOHN HARRINGTON COX

> Ring around a rosey,
> Pocket full of posey,
> One for me, one for you,
> One for uncle Josey.
> Squat, little Josey!

LITTLE SALLY WATERS

I

A girl sits in the center of the ring, her face in her hands. At the word "rise," she chooses anyone whom she pleases.

> Little Sally Waters,
> Sitting in the sun,
> Crying and weeping
> For a young man.
>
> Rise, Sally, rise,
> Dry your weeping eyes,
> Fly to the East,
> Fly to the West,
> Fly to the one you love best.

"Squat Down, Josey" was collected by Miss Alicia Barnes, Bruceton Mills, Preston County, West Virginia, 1916, and reported in John Harrington Cox, "Singing Games," *SFQ*, 6 (1942):205. With music.

Version 1 of "Little Sally Waters" is from W. W. Newell, *Games and Songs of American Children*, 2nd ed., New York, 1903 (Dover reprint, 1963), p. 70.

II

Little Sally Ann,
Sitting in the sand,
Weeping and crying,
For her young man.

Rise, Sally, rise,
Wipe your dirty eyes,
Turn to the East,
Turn to the West,
Turn to the one you love the best.

MISS JENNIAN JONES

Newell points out that this childish drama was originally a love-tale, in which the young lady died of blighted affection and the prohibition of cruel parents: "You can't come in today." Jennian Jones was, in the Scotch, *Jenny jo*. "Jo" is an old English and Scotch word for sweetheart, a corruption of *joy*, itself from the French *joie*, a term of endearment, *Jenny my joy* becomes Miss Jennian (a contraction for Virginia) Jones! Folk transmission at work.

I've come to see Miss Jennian Jones,
Miss Jennian Jones, Miss Jennian Jones,
I've come to see Miss Jennian Jones,
And how is she today?

Today she is washing,
Washing, washing,
Today she is washing,
You can't come in today.

I'm sorry to say she's sick, sir,
Sick, sir, sick, sir,
I'm sorry to say she's sick, sir,
You can't come in today.

Version II of "Little Sally Waters" is from my wife, Sally Richardson Emrich, who was taught the chant by her grandmother in Wheeling, West Virginia, ca. 1921. The children — in this case, all little girls — played it sitting in a sandbox.

"Miss Jennian Jones" is from W. W. Newell, *Games and Songs of American Children*, 2nd ed., 1903 (Dover reprint, 1963), pp. 63–66. See also John Harrington Cox, "Singing Games," *SFQ*, 6 (1942):190.

What shall we dress her in,
Dress her in, dress her in,
What shall we dress her in,
Red, white, or blue?

Red is for soldiers,
Soldiers, soldiers,
Red is for soldiers,
And that will never do.

Blue is for sailors,
Sailors, sailors,
Blue is for sailors,
And that will never do.

White is for dead people,
Dead people, dead people,
White is for dead people,
And that will do.

Where shall we bury her,
Bury her, bury her,
Where shall we bury her?
Under the apple tree.

After Miss Jennian Jones has been buried, her ghost suddenly rises and ghoulishly chants:

I dreamt I saw a ghost last night,
Ghost last night, ghost last night,
I dreamt I saw a ghost last night
Under the apple tree!

The ring of children breaks up with shrieks, with the ghost of Miss Jones chasing them. The first one caught in turn becomes Miss Jennian Jones, and the game continues.

Cumulative Songs

I had a goose and the goose pleased me,
And I fed my goose under yonder tree,
And the goose went (honk)
And the duck went (quack)
And the dog went (woof)
And the cat went (meow)
And the bird went (whistle).

THE TREE IN THE WOOD

On the ground there was a tree,
The prettiest little tree you ever did see.
The tree's on the ground
And the green grass growing all around-round-round,
And the green grass growing all around.

On the tree there was a limb,
The prettiest little limb you ever did see.
The limb's on the tree
And the tree's on the ground
And the green grass growing all around-round-round,
And the green grass growing all around.

On that limb there was a nest,
The prettiest little nest you ever did see.
The nest's on the limb
The limb's on the tree
And the tree's on the ground
And the green grass growing all around-round-round,
And the green grass growing all around.

On that nest there was a bird,

"The Tree in the Wood" was recorded by Vance Randolph from the singing of Doney
Hammontree at Farmington, Arkansas, 1941. Library of Congress record LP12.

The prettiest little bird you ever did see.
The bird's on the nest
And the nest's on the limb
And the limb's on the tree
And the tree's on the ground
And the green grass growing all around-round-round,
And the green grass growing all around.

On that bird there was a wing,
The prettiest little wing you ever did see.
The wing's on the bird
And the bird's on the nest
And the nest's on the limb
And the limb's on the tree
And the tree's on the ground
And the green grass growing all around-round-round,
And the green grass growing all around.

On that wing there was a flea,
The prettiest little flea you ever did see.
The flea's on the wing
And the wing's on the bird
And the bird's on the nest
And the nest's on the limb
The limb's on the tree
The tree's on the ground
And the green grass growing all around-round-round,
And the green grass growing all around.

On that flea there was a mosqueetee,
The prettiest little mosqueetee you ever did see.
The mosqueetee's on the flea
And the flea's on the wing
And the wing's on the bird
And the bird's on the nest
And the nest's on the limb
And the limb's on the tree
And the tree's on the ground
And the green grass growing all around-round-round,
And the green grass growing all around.

FIDDLE-I-FEE

Had me a cat, the cat pleased me,
I fed my cat in yonders tree,
Cat went fiddle-i-fee.

Had me a hen, and the hen pleased me,
I fed my hen in yonders tree,
Hen went kaa-kaa-kaa,
And the cat went fiddle-i-fee.

Had me a pig and the pig pleased me,
And I fed my pig on yonders tree,
Pig went krucy-krucy,
The hen went kaa-kaa-kaa,
And the cat went fiddle-i-fee.

Had me a dog and the dog pleased me,
And I fed my dog in yonders tree,
Dog went boo-boo-boo,
The pig went krucy-krucy,
The hen went kaa-kaa-kaa,
And the cat went fiddle-i-fee.

Had me a sheep, the sheep pleased me,
I fed my sheep in yonders tree,
Sheep went baa-baa-baa,
The dog went boo-boo-boo,
The pig went krucy-krucy,
The hen went kaa-kaa-kaa,
And the cat went fiddle-i-fee.

"Fiddle-I-Fee" was recorded by Artus M. Moser from the singing of Mrs. Maud Long at Hot Springs, North Carolina, 1946. A last stanza in another variant ends the song with:

Had me a wife, and my wife pleased me,
I fed my wife in yonders tree,
Wife went honey-honey,
The horse went neigh-neigh-neigh. . . .

Library of Congress record LP14.

Had me a guinea and the guinea pleased me,
I fed my guinea in yonders tree,
Guinea went poterack-poterack,
The sheep went baa-baa-baa,
The dog went boo-boo-boo,
The pig went krucy-krucy,
The hen went kaa-kaa-kaa,
And the cat went fiddle-i-fee.

Had me a cow, the cow pleased me,
Fed my cow on yonders tree,
Cow went moo-moo-moo,
The guinea went poterack-poterack,
The sheep went baa-baa-baa,
The dog went boo-boo-boo,
The pig went krucy-krucy,
The hen went kaa-kaa-kaa,
And the cat went fiddle-i-fee.

Had me a horse, the horse pleased me,
I fed my horse in yonders tree,
Horse went neigh-neigh-neigh,
The cow went moo-moo-moo,
The guinea went poterack-poterack,
The sheep went baa-baa-baa,
The dog went boo-boo-boo,
The pig went krucy-krucy,
The hen went kaa-kaa-kaa,
And the cat went fiddle-i-fee.

THE BARNYARD

Oh, I had a bird and the bird pleased me,
And I fed my bird under yonder tree,
And the bird went (whistle).

"The Barnyard" was recorded by Duncan Emrich from the singing of Sam Hinton of La Jolla, California, at Washington, D.C., 1947. Library of Congress record LP21.

I had a cat and the cat pleased me,
And I fed my cat under yonder tree,
And the cat went (meow)
And the bird went (whistle).

I had a duck and the duck pleased me,
And I fed my duck under yonder tree,
And the duck went (quack)
And the cat went (meow)
And the bird went (whistle).

I had a dog and the dog pleased me,
I fed my dog under yonder tree,
And the dog went (woof)
And the duck went (quack)
And the cat went (meow)
And the bird went (whistle).

I had a goose and the goose pleased me,
And I fed my goose under yonder tree,
And the goose went (honk)
And the duck went (quack)
And the dog went (woof)
And the cat went (meow)
And the bird went (whistle).

I had a turkey and the turkey pleased me,
And I fed my turkey under yonder tree,
And the turkey went (gobble)
And the goose went (honk)
And the duck went (quack)
And the dog went (woof)
And the cat went (meow)
And the bird went (whistle).

Nonsense Songs

As I went down to Derby Town
All on a summer's day,
It's there I saw the finest ram
That was ever fed on hay.

And if you don't believe me
And think I tell a lie,
Just you go down to Derby
And you'll see the same as I!

NOTTINGHAM FAIR

As I was a-walking to Nottingham Fair,
A-riding on horseback all on a gray mare,
With a white tail and mane and streak down her back
But darn' a hair on her but what was coal black.

My mare she stood still, threw me off in the ditch,
My skin she did dab and my shirt she did bruise;
With my foot in my stirrup I mounted again
And on my ten toes rode over the plain.

I met a king and a queen and a company more,
All riding on horseback, all walking before,
With a stark naked drummer a-beating the drum,
With his heels in his pockets before them did run.

I pulled my head off, the majest' to greet,
I asked him the road though I knew not the place,
But with gladness he could scarcely look down
To tell me the road to fair Nottingham Town.

When I came into town not a soul could I see,
Though the streets were all lined a-gazy at me;
I set myself down on a hot frozen stone,
Ten thousand around me, and me all alone.

"Nottingham Fair" was recorded by Vance Randolph from the singing of Charles Ingenthron at Walnut Shade, Missouri, 1941. Library of Congress record LP20.

I called for a glass to drive gladness away,
I stifled with dust though it rained all the day,
It rained and it hailed and I stood in the storm
With my hat in my hand to keep my head warm.

THE DERBY RAM

George Washington enjoyed singing this song of wild exaggeration, and tradition has it that he sang it to the children of the Chief Justice of the United States.

Oh, as I went down to Derby Town
All on a summer's day,
It's there I saw the finest ram
That was ever fed on hay.

"The Derby Ram" was recorded by Vance Randolph from the singing of Charles Ingenthron, Walnut Shade, Missouri, 1941. Library of Congress record LP12.

And if you don't believe me
And think I tell a lie,
Just you go down to Derby,
And you'll see the same as I!

Oh, the wool upon this ram's back
It drug to the ground,
And I hauled it to the market,
And it weighed ten thousand pounds.

Oh, the horns upon this ram's head
They reached to the moon,
For the butcher went up in February
And never got back till June.

Oh, the ears upon this ram's head
They reached to the sky,
And the eagle built his nest there
For I heard the young ones cry.

Oh, every tooth this ram had
Would hold a bushel of corn,
And every foot he stood on
Would cover an acre of ground.

And if you don't believe me
And think I tell a lie,
Just you go down to Derby,
And you'll see the same as I!

An added stanza from another variant:

Oh, the man that owned this ram, sir,
He must have been awful rich,
And the boy who wrote this song, sir,
Was a lying son of a bitch.

ON A BRIGHT AND SUMMER'S MORNING

On a bright and summer's morning, the ground all covered with snow,
I put my shoulder to my gun, and a-hunting . . .
A-hunting I did go.

I went up on the mountain, beyond yon high hill,
And fifteen or twenty, ten thousand . . .
Ten thousand I did kill.

The money that I got for the venison skin, I hauled it to my daddy's barn,
And it wouldn't half go i — . . .
It wouldn't half go in.

Some boys and girls were skating, on a bright and summer's day,
The ice broke through, they all fell in, the rest they run . . .
The rest they run away.

I went up on the mountain, beyond the peak so high,
The moon come round with lightning speed. "I'll take a ride," says . . .
"I'll take a ride," says I.

The moon come around the mountain, it took a sudden whirl,
My feet slipped and I fell out, and landed in this . . .
And landed in this world.

The man that made this song tune, his name was Benny Young,
If you can tell a bigger lie, I'll say you ought to be . . .
I'll say you ought to be hung.

OLD HUMPY

Old Humpy he died and he rose again, and he rose again,
Hey, hey, and he rose up again.

"On a Bright and Summer's Morning" was recorded by Artus M. Moser from the singing, with banjo, by Bascom Lamar Lunsford of South Turkey Creek, North Carolina, at Swannanoa, North Carolina, 1946. Library of Congress record LP21.

"Old Humpy" was recorded by Charles Todd and Robert Sonkin from the singing of Vernon Allen, Shafter, California, 1941. Library of Congress AFS record 5101 A1.

They placed on his grave a horse-apple tree, a horse-apple tree,
Hey, hey, a horse-apple tree.

The apple tree grew and it grew, and it grew,
Hey, hey, and the horse-apple grew.

The apples got ripe and began to fall, began to fall,
Hey, hey, and began to fall.

An old woman went out to gather them all, to gather them all,
Hey, hey, to gather them up.

Old Humpy he rose and he gave her a knock, and he gave her a knock,
Hey, hey, and he gave her a knock.

The old woman went off ti-hippity-hop, ti-hippity-hop,
Hey, hey, ti-hippity-hop, ti-hippity-hop.

THE SKIN-AND-BONE LADY

The last note of the music is very high and followed by a shriek, whereupon the skin-and-bone lady presumably faints away.

There was a lady all skin and bone,
And such a lady was never known.

This lady took a walk one day,
This lady rested on the way.

This lady came to a church stile,
And there she rested a little while.

This lady came to a church door,
And there she rested a little more.

She looked up and she looked down,
And spied a corpse upon the ground;

"The Skin-and-Bone Lady" was communicated to John Harrington Cox by Miss Lily Hagans, Morgantown, Monongalia County, West Virginia, 1916, who had obtained it from Mrs. Julia McGrew. In Cox, *Folksongs of the South* (Harvard) Cambridge, 1925 (Dover reprint, New York, 1967), p. 483. Without music.

And from the crown and to the chin,
The worms crept out and the worms crept in.

This lady to the parson said,
"Will I look so when I am dead?"

The parson to the lady said,
"You will look so when you are dead,
You will look so when you are dead."

FROGGIE WENT A-COURTING

"Froggie" can be traced with certainty to England of the sixteenth century. According to an entry in the Stationers' Hall Registry for 1580, Edward White was given permission to print and sell "A Moste Strange Weddinge of the ffrogge and the mowse." Almost four centuries later it is still fresh and alive, and has been found in virtually every section of the United States with innumerable variant stanzas. Mobley's hesitation at the end is due not to any forgetfulness on his part, but to chuckling good humor at the nonsense of the song. It is a favorite of children.

Well, Froggie went a-courting and he did ride,
  Uh-uh!
Froggie went a-courting and he did ride,
Sword and pistol by his side,
  Uh-uh!

He took little Mousie on his knee,
  Uh-uh!
He took little Mousie on his knee,
Saying, "Mousie, won't you marry me?"
  Uh-uh!

Little Mousie said, "No, couldn't do that,"
Little Mousie said, "I couldn't do that
Unless you ask old Uncle Rat."

"Froggie Went A-Courting" was recorded by Artus M. Moser from the singing of Pleaz Mobley of Manchester, Kentucky, at Harrogate, Tennessee, 1943. Library of Congress record LP12.

Well, the old Rat said it'd be all right,
Well, the old Rat said it'd be all right,
Set that wedding for Tuesday night.

Where shall the weddin' supper be?
Where shall the weddin' supper be?
Way down yonder in a hollow tree.

Well, what shall the weddin' supper be?
What shall the weddin' supper be?
Two big beans and a goober pea.

Well, the first come in was a bumble bee,
     Z-z-z-z!
First come in was a bumble bee
Tuning his fiddle on his knee
     Uh-uh!

Well, the next come in was a big black snake,
     Zip!
The next come in was a big black snake,
Asked for that wedding cake,
     Uh-uh!

Well, the next come in was a big old ram,
     B-a-a-a!
Well, the next come in was a big old ram,
Hope, by Ned, he didn't give a ——
Pharaoh shot old Combo. Combo! Tum-a-rap-trap-feeney-winkle-plennle-
    doodle-yalla-bugga-rap-trap-barney, Mister Combo.

(PLEAZ MOBLEY: "You can sing the rest of it now, professor.")
(ARTUS MOSER: "No, you go ahead . . . go ahead . . .")

Well, Mousie got scared and ran up the wall,
     Uh-uh!
Mousie got scared and ran up the wall,
Said, "The devil take the Froggie — house and all!"
     Uh-uh!

JINNIE JINKINS

"Will you wear white, my dear, oh my dear,
Oh, will you wear white, Jinnie Jinkins?"
"I won't wear white, for the color's too bright,
I'll buy me a foldy-roldy, tildy-toldy, seek a double
Use-a-cause-a, roldy binding."
Roll, Jinnie Jinkins, roll!

"Will you wear red, my dear, oh my dear,
Oh, will you wear red, Jinnie Jinkins?"
"I won't wear red, for it's the color on my head,
I'll buy me a foldy-roldy, tildy-toldy, seek a double
Use-a-cause-a, roldy binding."
Roll, Jinnie Jinkins, roll!

"Will you wear green, my dear, oh my dear,
Oh, will you wear green, Jinnie Jinkins?"
"I won't wear green, for it's a shame to be seen,
I'll buy me a foldy-roldy, tildy-toldy, seek a double
Use-a-cause-a, roldy binding."
Roll, Jinnie Jinkins, roll!

"Will you wear black, my dear, oh my dear,
Oh, will you wear black, Jinnie Jinkins?"
"I won't wear black, for it's the color on my back,
I'll buy me a foldy-roldy, tildy-toldy, seek a double
Use-a-cause-a, roldy binding."
Roll, Jinnie Jinkins, roll!

"Jinnie Jinkins" was recorded by Alan and Elizabeth Lomax from the singing of Mrs. E. C. Ball, Rugby, Virginia, 1941. Library of Congress record LP2.

PARTY SONGS, GAMES AND DANCES

Play-Party, Courting,
and Kissing Games and Songs

Square Dance Calls

Banjo and Fiddle Pieces

Play-Party, Courting, and Kissing Games and Songs

Here we march all around in a ring,
One will choose while others sing,
Choose the one that you love best,
And I'm sure you will please the rest.

Geeminny jinkins, what a choice you've made!
Better in your grave be laid!
Kiss her slow and let her know
How you come to love her so.

The happiest possible way of introducing these play-party songs and games is to quote in full Emma M. Backus's introduction to her article "Song-Games from Connecticut" in the *Journal of American Folklore*, 14 (1901): 295. We move back nostalgically to a wonderful country-America that was: simple, honest, lovely. Those *were* the good old days, and the poetry of youth was part and parcel of them.

The games below communicated were played and sung in the back country towns of Connecticut as late as the year 1870, at the so-called "Evening Party." In the center of the house was usually found a large and old chimney, and the rooms were connected by doors, so that it was possible to march round. In each cosy corner was stationed one to choose from the players, who moved marching and singing; at the proper time in the game the chooser took a sounding kiss, and left his choice to continue in the same manner. About midnight were passed refreshments of several kinds, "frosted cake," apples, popped corn, walnuts and butternuts already cracked, a pitcher of cider, and another of cold water; no napkins were thought of. Each guest was seated and given an empty plate, after which the young men handed the good things on large waiters. The singing and marching was resumed, and kept up until about four o'clock in the morning, when the young men issued and huddled about the door, and as the girls came out, each stepped forward, and offered his arm to his choice, with the words: "Can I see you home?" after which they separated, and went in the dark, often across fields, to their scattered homes, perhaps two miles away; at the door of the fair one (which often was the back door, when snow lay on the ground, and no path had been shovelled to the front entrance), there was always a final hug and kiss. Chaperones were unknown in those neighborhoods; thus did our rural Puritan mothers trust to the inherited honor and good sense of their daughters, and all was right and pure and good. Of flirting there was not much; each girl had one young man, whom, as she would have said, she "liked," and cared nothing for the admiration of the others. When any girl in the community had acquired the name of "liking the boys" (which meant receiving questionable attentions from more than one), she was dropped from the kissing party, and the young men who would "wait upon her" were considered as of doubtful character, and no longer accepted as escorts by those on whose name no stain of reproach had rested.

These games I saw played in the hill towns of Ashford and Eastford, in the year 1865.

OLD MAIDS

All you that are single and wild in your ways,
Come sow your wild oats in your youthful days,
And you shall live happy,
You shall live happy when you grow old.
The day is far spent and the night's coming on,
So give us your arm and go jogging along;
And you shall be happy,
You shall be happy when you grow old.

At the words: "So give us your arm," the couples which are marching change off, and each girl tries to get a boy's arm, and escape being left over for the old maid, the number of players being so arranged that the girls make one more than the young men.

THE RICH WIDOW

I am a rich widow, I live all alone,
I have but one daughter and she is my own.
Go, daughter, go, daughter, and choose you a one,
Go choose you a good one, or else choose none.
I've married off my daughter, I've given her away,
I've married off my daughter, she's bound to obey,
She's bound to obey and to never disagree,
So as you go round, kiss her one, two, three.

KING WILLIAM WAS KING GEORGE'S SON

In this play a young man stands with a broad-brimmed hat in his hand. While the song proceeds, he puts it on a girl's head, after which they march arm in arm, and finally she in turn puts it on the head of a young man, to continue as before:

> *King William was King George's son,*
> *And from the royal blood he sprung;*
> *Upon his breast he wore a star,*
> *And it was called the sign of war.*
> *Say, young lady, will you 'list* and go?*
> *Say, young lady, will you 'list and go?*
> *The broad-brimmed hat you must put on,*
> *And follow on to the fife and drum.*

The play continues until all have been crowned with the hat and march round the chimney in couples, singing with a will the words over and over. And with each crowning, of course, there is a kiss.

ROSE IN THE GARDEN

> *Sailing in the boat when the tide runs high,*
> *Sailing in the boat when the tide runs high,*
> *Sailing in the boat when the tide runs high,*
> *Waiting for the pretty girl to come by 'm by.*
> *Here she comes so fresh and fair,*
> *Sky-blue eyes and curly hair,*
> *Rosy in cheek, dimple in her chin,*
> *Say, young men, but you can't come in.*
>
> *Rose in the garden for you, young man,*
> *Rose in the garden for you, young man,*
> *Rose in the garden, get it if you can,*
> *But take care and don't get a frost-bitten one.*
>
> *Choose your partner, stay till day,*
> *Choose your partner, stay till day,*
> *Choose your partner, stay till day,*
> *Never, never mind what the old folks say.*
>
> *Old folks say 'tis the very best way,*

* Enlist.

29

Old folks say 'tis the very best way,
Old folks say 'tis the very best way,
To court all night and sleep all day.

MARRIAGE

Here we go around this ring,
For you to choose while others sing;
Choose the one that you love best,
And I'll be bound 't will suit the rest.
Now you're married you must be good,
Be sure and chop your husband's wood;
Live together all your life,
And be a good and faithful wife.

OLD GRANDPAW YET

Old Grandpaw Yet, not a soul can he get,
And he's tired of living here alone, here alone,
And he's tired of living here alone.

Some of you girls, have pity on his case,
And make him a wife of his own, of his own,
And make him a wife of his own.

You can rise to your feet and kiss the first you meet,
There's plenty all around the chair, chair, chair,
There's plenty all around the chair.

Old Grandmaw Yet, not a soul can she get,
And she's tired of living here alone, here alone,
And she's tired of living here alone.

Some of you boys, have pity on her case,
And make her a husband of her own, of her own,
And make her a husband of her own.

You can rise to your feet and kiss the first you meet,
There's plenty all around the chair, chair, chair,
There's plenty all around the chair.

"Old Grandpaw Yet" was recorded by Alan Lomax from the singing of Mrs. Nell Hampton, Saylersville, Kentucky, 1937. Library of Congress AFS record 1585 B2.

RISE YOU UP, MY TRUE LOVE

Rise you up, my true love, present to me your hand,
For I want a wife, and I know you want a man.

Now we'll travel on together till we two must part,
For I've lost my true love and it almost breaks my heart.

I'll weep and I'll mourn and this will be my cry,
'I've lost my true love and sure I will die.'

Oh, yonder she comes and it's, "Honey, howdy-do,
How have you been since I last saw you?"

Now we'll travel on together, I know we can agree,
We'll hug and kiss each other and a-married we will be.

HERE WE MARCH ALL AROUND IN A RING

Here we march all around in a ring,
One will choose while others sing,
Choose the one that you love best,
And I'm sure you will please the rest.

Geeminny jinkins, what a choice you've made!
Better in your grave be laid!
Kiss her slow and let her know
How you come to love her so.

"Rise You Up, My True Love" was recorded by Herbert Halpert from the singing of Mrs. Ina Jones, Iuka, Mississippi, 1939. Library of Congress record 2991 B2.

"Here We March All Around in a Ring" was collected by the Federal Music Project, Works Progress Administration (WPA), Boyd County, Kentucky, ca. 1937. Jean Thomas, Supervisor for Boyd County. Ms., with music, in the Archive of Folk Song, Library of Congress.

WALKING ON THE GREEN GRASS

Walking on the green grass,
Walking side by side,
Walking with a pretty girl,
She shall be my bride.

And now we form a round ring,
The girls are by our sides,
Dancing with the pretty girls
Who shall be our brides.

And now the king upon the green
Shall choose a girl to be his queen,
Shall lead her out his bride to be,
And kiss her, one, two, three.
Now take her by the hand, this queen,
And swing her 'round and 'round the green.

And now we'll go around the ring,
And every one we'll swing.
    Oh, swing the king and swing the queen,
    Oh, swing the king and swing the queen,
    Oh, swing 'em 'round and 'round the green,
    Oh, swing 'em 'round the green.

LAZY MARY

In this game Lazy Mary lies down in the center of a ring with her mother kneeling beside her, attempting to persuade her to get up. Butter and bread is not much of an inducement, but a young man with rosy cheeks is quite a

"Walking on the Green Grass" appears in W. W. Newell, *Games and Songs of American Children*, New York, 1883 (Dover reprint, New York, 1963), p. 228.

"Lazy Mary" was collected by Maude Minish Sutton from Nell Searcy, Chimney Rock, North Carolina, ca. 1927. In the "Games and Rhymes" section (ed. Paul G. Brewster) of *The Frank C. Brown Collection of North Carolina Folklore* (Duke University Press) Durham, North Carolina, I, 55. Without music.

different matter. Again, this is a pairing game with a kiss to seal the getting up.

> Lazy Mary, will you get up,
> Will you, will you, will you get up?
> Lazy Mary, will you get up,
> Will you get up today?
>
> What will you give me for my breakfast,
> For my breakfast, for my breakfast,
> What will you give me for my breakfast
> If I'll get up today?
>
> (*spoken*) Butter and bread.
>
> No, mother, I won't get up,
> I won't get up, I won't get up,
> No, mother, I won't get up,
> I won't get up today.
>
> Lazy Mary, will you get up,
> Will you, will you, will you get up?
> Lazy Mary, will you get up,
> Will you get up today?
>
> What will you give me for my dinner,
> For my dinner, for my dinner,
> What will you give me for my dinner
> If I'll get up today?
>
> (*spoken*) Peas and cornbread.
>
> No, mother, I won't get up,
> I won't get up, I won't get up,
> No, mother, I won't get up,
> I won't get up today.
>
> Lazy Mary, will you get up,
> Will you, will you, will you get up?
> Lazy Mary, will you get up,
> Will you get up today?
>
> What will you give me for my supper,

For my supper, for my supper,
What will you give me for my supper
If I'll get up today?

(*spoken*) Nice young man with rosy cheeks.

Yes, mother, I will get up,
I will get up, I will get up,
Yes, mother, I will get up,
I will get up today.

THE KEYS OF CANTERBURY

"The Keys of Canterbury" is a delightful game-song and appears not to
have been collected, other than this unique version, in the United States.
The gifts are quite charming: "the keys of Canterbury," "boots of cork,
one made in London, the other in York," "a little golden bell," "a gallant
silver chest," and finally "a broidered silken gownd, with nine yards a-drooping and trailing on the ground." I wonder what children in Kentucky made
of these? I only know that I thank them for their gift of them to us. Once
you have read these, you cannot forget them: how can you forget "the boots
of cork?" "One made in London . . ."

O madam, I will give to you the keys of Canterbury,
And all the bells in London shall ring to make us merry,
    If you will be my joy, my sweet and only dear,
    And walk along with me anywhere.

I shall not, sir, accept of you the keys of Canterbury,
Nor all the bells in London shall ring to make us merry,
    I will not be your joy, your sweet and only dear,
    Nor walk along with you anywhere.

O madam, I will give to you a pair of boots of cork,
The one was made in London, the other made in York.

"The Keys of Canterbury" was "taken from a manuscript song book compiled by Miss
Camilla Dennis from the singing of schoolchildren at Hindman, Knott County, Kentucky,
1922–1923." Reported in John Harrington Cox, "Singing Games," *SFQ*, 6 (1942):230–231.
No music. Cecil Sharp, however, in *One Hundred English Folk Songs*, p. 148, prints a tune
and a version in ten stanzas very much like the one given here from Kentucky.

I shall not, sir, accept of you a pair of boots of cork,
Though both were made in London or both were made in York.

O madam, I will give to you a little golden bell,
To ring for all your servants and make them serve you well.

I shall not, sir, accept of you a little golden bell,
To ring for all my servants and make them serve me well.

O madam, I will give to you a gallant silver chest,
With a key of gold and silver and jewels of the best.

I shall not, sir, accept of you a gallant silver chest,
A key of gold and silver nor jewels of the best.

O madam, I will give to you a broidered silken gownd,
With nine yards a-drooping and trailing on the ground.

O sir, I will accept of you a broidered silken gownd,
With nine yards a-drooping and trailing on the ground,
    If you will be my joy, my sweet and only dear,
    And walk along with you anywhere.

PAPER OF PINS

"I'll give to you a paper of pins,
For that's the way that love begins,
If you will marry me, me, me,
If you will marry me."

"I won't accept your paper of pins
If that's the way that love begins,
And I'll not marry you, you, you,
And I'll not marry you."

"I'll buy for you a pair of gloves,
Inside silk and outside love,
If you will marry me, me, me,
If you will marry me."

"I won't accept your pair of gloves,
Inside silk and outside love,
And I'll not marry you, you, you,
And I'll not marry you."

"Paper of Pins" is from a compilation by Miriam M. Sizer, *Folk Songs to Sing* (mimeographed), Virginia Writers' Project and Virginia Music Project, sponsored by the Virginia State Board of Education, 1942, p. 24. The informants were Anne Corbin Ball of Richmond; Mrs. Winfred Hollyfield and Barbara Davis of Wise County; Mrs. Dicie Roberts of Big Laurel; Mrs. M. S. Jones of Pittsylvania County; and Alice Wagener of Franklin County.

"I'll give to you a little black dog,
To run by your side as you go
   abroad,
If you will marry me, me, me,
If you will marry me."

"I won't accept your little black
   dog,
To run by my side as I go abroad,
And I'll not marry you, you, you,
And I'll not marry you."

"I'll buy you a little gray mule,
Jump on his back and ride to
   school,
If you will marry me, me, me,
If you will marry me."

"I won't accept your little gray
   mule,
Jump on his back and ride to
   school,
And I'll not marry you, you, you,
And I'll not marry you."

"I'll give to you an easy chair,
To sit and comb your golden hair,
If you will marry me, me, me,
If you will marry me."

"I'll not accept your easy chair,
To sit and comb my golden hair,
And I'll not marry you, you, you,
And I'll not marry you."

"I'll give to you a dress of blue,
With blue shoestrings to tie your
   shoe,
If you will marry me, me, me,
If you will marry me."

"I'll not accept your dress of blue,
With blue shoestrings to tie my
   shoe,
And I'll not marry you, you, you,
And I'll not marry you."

"I'll give to you a dress of brown,
All stitched with thread at a dollar
   a pound,
If you will marry me, me, me,
If you will marry me."

"I'll not accept your dress of
   brown,
All stitched with thread at a dollar
   a pound,
And I'll not marry you, you, you,
And I'll not marry you."

"I'll give to you the key to my
   heart,
That we may lock and never part,
If you will marry me, me, me,
If you will marry me."

"I'll not accept the key to your
   heart,
That we may lock and never part,
And I'll not marry you, you, you,
And I'll not marry you."

"I'll give to you the key to my chest,
That you may have money at your
   request,
If you will marry me, me, me,
If you will marry me."

"I will accept the key to your chest,
That I may have money at my
   request,
And I will marry you, you, you,
And I will marry you."

"You would not accept my hand
  and heart,
That we might lock and never part,
And I'll not marry you, you, you,
And I'll not marry you."

"For now I see that money is all,
And woman's love is nothing at all,
So I'll not marry you, you, you,
So I'll not marry you.

"I am determined to be an old
  maid,
I'll take my stool and sit in the
  shade,
If you won't marry me, me, me,
If you won't marry me."

"Ha, ha, ha, and that's enough,
For you're not worth a pinch of snuff,
And I'll not marry you, you, you,
And I'll not marry you."

SKIP TO MY LOU

The verses to the ring-game, "Skip to My Lou," are endless and as readily created and tossed together as verses are for "Cindy," "Weevily Wheat," or "The Old Chisholm Trail." Authorship of any verse is, of course, unknown, and will forever be. Piper says: "The ease with which anyone could fashion the nonsense line quickly gave satisfying length to the song. It was this feature, I believe, which made it so widely popular." I would add, as reasons for its popularity, the happy and catchy repetition of the first three lines, the standard and unchanging coda of the last line, and a lively tune which virtually sings itself. The lines all deal with country things.

> I lost my pardner, what'll I do?
> I lost my pardner, what'll I do?
> I lost my pardner, what'll I do?
> Skip to my Lou, my darling!
>
> Gone again, skip to my Lou!
> Gone again, skip to my Lou!
> Gone again, skip to my Lou!
> Skip to my Lou, my darling!

"Skip to My Lou" texts were collected by Edwin F. Piper (Western Nebraska, 1888), "Some Play-Party Games of the Middle West," *JAF*, 28 (1915):276–277, and Leona Nessly Ball (Idaho, ca. 1891), "The Play-Party in Idaho," *JAF*, 44 (1931):20–21. The latter with music. Numerous Library of Congress recordings.

The cat's in the buttermilk, skip to my Lou,
Cat's in the buttermilk, skip to my Lou,
Cat's in the buttermilk, skip to my Lou,
Skip to my Lou, my darling!

Flies in the sugarbowl, skip to my Lou,

Mama churns the butter in Grandpa's boot,

Mice in the cream jar, what'll I do?

Chickens in the haystack, shoo, shoo, shoo,

Pigs in the 'tater patch, two by two,

Gone again, and I don't care,

I'll get another one better than you,

Rats in the bread-pan, chew, chew, chew,

Little red wagon painted blue,

Hair in the biscuit, two by two,

Pretty as a blackbird, and prettier too,

If I can't get a blackbird, a white bird'll do,

Gone again, what'll I do?

I'll get another one sweeter than you,

I'll get her back again, you bet you!

When I go courting, I take two,

My Ma says, I can have you,
My Ma says, I can have you,
My Ma says, I can have you,
Skip to my Lou, my darling!

    Gone again, skip to my Lou!
    Gone again, skip to my Lou!
    Gone again, skip to my Lou!
    Skip to my Lou, my darling!

MARCHING 'ROUND THE LEVEE

With the first stanza, the children march around in a ring formation, with the one who has been chosen as "It" standing in the center. With the second stanza, the children in the ring drop hands, and "It" goes in and out the open "windows," alternately passing in front of one player and behind another. With the third stanza he begins singing himself and acts out the words, ending with a kiss.

We're marching 'round the levee,
We're marching 'round the levee,
We're marching 'round the levee,
For we have won the day.

Go in and out the windows,
Go in and out the windows,
Go in and out the windows,
For we have gained the day.

Go forth and choose your lover,
Go forth and choose your lover,
Go forth and choose your lover,
For we have gained the day.

I kneel because I love you,
I kneel because I love you,
I kneel because I love you,
For we have gained the day.

I measure my love to show you,
I measure my love to show you,
I measure my love to show you,
For we have gained the day.

One kiss before I leave you,
One kiss before I leave you,
One kiss before I leave you,
For we have gained the day.

WEEVILY WHEAT

Oh, Charlie's sweet and Charlie's neat,
And Charlie he's a dandy,

"Marching 'Round the Levee" was collected by Leona Nessly Ball, and reported, with music, in "The Play-Party in Idaho," *JAF* 44 (1931):12.

The first five stanzas of "Weevily Wheat" were recorded by John A. Lomax and Laurence Powell from the singing of Mrs. Emma Dusenbury, Mena, Arkansas, 1936. Library of Congress AFS record 863 A4. Remaining stanzas drawn from Leona Nessly Ball, "The Play-Party in Idaho," *JAF*, 44 (1931):16–17; from John Harrington Cox, "Singing Games," *SFQ*, 6 (1942):200, who was given stanzas by Miss Frances Sanders, Morgantown, West Virginia, 1914, as collected by her from Mr. Carey Woofter of Gilmer County; and from Edwin F. Piper, "Some Play-Party Games of the Middle West," *JAF*, 28 (1915):279 for stanzas 11 and 12.

Charlie he's the very lad
That feeds the girls on candy.

Come over here, we'll trip together
In the morning early,
Here we'll take the parting hand,
It's true I love you dearly.

I don't want no more of your weevily wheat,
Nor I don't want none of your barley,
But I want some more of your pretty white flour
To bake a cake for Charlie.

Oh, Charlie he's a handsome man,
Charlie, he's a dandy,
Charlie he's the very lad
That stoled all Daddy's brandy.

Oh, five times five is twenty-five,
And six times five are thirty,
Seven times five are thirty-five,
And eight times five are forty.

Charlie, barley, wheat, and rye,
Kissed the girls and made them cry,
I'll jump over your weevily wheat,
And you'll jump over the barley.

I'll step her to your weevily wheat,
I'll step her to your barley,
I'll step her to your weevily wheat,
I'll step away to Charlie.

The higher up the cherry tree,
The riper grow the cherries,
The sooner the boy courts the girl,
The sooner they will marry.

The higher up the cherry tree,
The redder grow the cherries,
The more you hug and kiss the girl,
The sooner they will marry.

Come down this way with your weevily wheat,
Come down this way with your barley,
Come down this way with your weevily wheat
To make a cake for Charlie.

Christmas comes but once a year,
Why not all be merry?
Sitting around the old log fire,
A-drinking Tom and Jerry.

O don't you see that pretty little girl?
Don't you think she's clever?
Don't you think that I and her
Would make a match forever?

Up the river, skip together,
In the morning early,
Join with me your heart and hand,
For I do love you dearly.

Oh, Charlie he's a nice young man
Charlie he's a dandy,
Charlie hugs and kisses the girls,
For he knows they taste like candy.

MRS. VICKERS' DAUGHTER

Johnny Thomson, so they say,
Goes a-courting every day,
Sword and pistol by his side,
Lizzie Vickers for his bride.

Oh, dear doctor, can you tell
What will make poor Lizzie well?
She is sick and she may die,
That would make poor Johnny cry.

Johnny here and Johnny there,
Johnny o'er the water,
Johnny's got the sweetest girl,
Mrs. Vickers' daughter.

"Mrs. Vickers' Daughter." Maine: from the WPA manuscript collection, Archive of Folk Song, Library of Congress.

THE NEEDLE'S EYE

The needle's eye it doth supply the thread that runs so true,
There's many a beau that I've let go because I wanted you,
You, oh, you, because I wanted you.

The needle's eye, it doth combine the threads you love so true,
Many a beau have I let go because I wanted you,
You, oh, you, because I wanted you.

OLD LADY SITTING IN THE DINING ROOM

Old lady sitting in the dining room,
Sitting by the fi-re,
Her foot slipped and she fell down,
Raise up higher and high-er.

Choose the one the ring go round,
Choose the one in the morning,
Choose the one with coal-black hair,
Kiss her and call her honey.

MARCHING TO QUEBEC
or *Quebec Town*

As we were marching to Quebec,
The drums were loudly beating;
The Americans have won the day,
The British are retreating.
March! march! march! march!
(*Philadelphia, prior to 1883*)

"The Needle's Eye" was recorded by Herbert Halpert from the singing of Mrs. Ollie Womble, Banner, Mississippi, 1939. Library of Congress AFS record 3031 B3 and 3032 A1.

"Old Lady Sitting in the Dining Room" was recorded by Herbert Halpert from the singing of schoolchildren, Brandon, Mississippi, 1939. Library of Congress AFS record 3050 A3.

All the "Marching to Quebec" above was reported in W. W. Newell, *Games and Songs of American Children*, 2nd ed., New York, 1903 (Dover reprint, 1963), pp. 125 and 246.

We were marching to Quebec,
The drums were loudly beating;
America has gained the day,
The British are retreating.

The war is o'er, and they are turned back,
For evermore departed;
So open the ring, and take one in,
For they are broken-hearted.

Oh, you're the one that I love best,
I praise you high and dearly;
My heart you'll get, my hand I'll give,
The kiss is most sincerely.
                    (*Massachusetts and Maine, prior to 1883*)

We are marching down to Quebec Town,
Where the drums and fifes are beating;
The Americans have gained the day,
The British are retreating.

The war's all over; we'll turn back
To friends, no more to be parted:
We'll open our ring, and receive another in,
To relieve this broken-hearted.

   This last song was sung by the whole company as it marched around one
person, who was blindfolded and seated in a chair. He or she selected a
partner by touching one of the ring with a long stick held for the purpose.
The game concluded:

Put a hat on her head to keep her warm,
And a loving, sweet kiss will do her no harm.
                    (*North Carolina, prior to 1883*)

MY PRETTY PINK

My pretty little pink, I once did
   think
That you and I would marry,
But now I've lost all hopes of that,
I can no longer tarry.

I've got my knapsack on my back,
My musket on my shoulder,
To march away to Quebec Town,
To be a gallant soldier.

Where coffee grows on a white-oak tree,
And the rivers flow with brandy,
Where the boys are like a lump of gold,
And the girls as sweet as candy.

THIS LADY SHE WEARS A DARK GREEN SHAWL

I saw in Southern Georgia a number of ring-games which I believe are peculiar to the colored children of that region. . . . Perhaps the most charming of all is "This Lady She Wears a Dark Green Shawl." The action is carried out by two children in the center, each choosing in turn, as in the other games.

— LORAINE DARBY

This lady she wears a dark green shawl,
A dark green shawl, a dark green shawl,
This lady she wears a dark green shawl,
I love her to my heart.

Now choose for your lover, honey, my love,
Honey, my love, honey, my love,
Now choose for your lover, honey, my love,
I love her to my heart.

Now dance with your lover, honey, my love,
Honey, my love, honey, my love,

"My Pretty Pink" was collected from East Tennessee prior to 1883 and reported in W. W. Newell, *Games and Songs of American Children*, 2nd ed., New York, 1903 (Dover reprint, 1963), p. 245.

"This Lady She Wears a Dark Green Shawl" was collected by Loraine Darby and reported in "Ring-Games from Georgia," *JAF*, 30 (1917):221. With music.

Now dance with your lover, honey, my love,
I love her to my heart.

Throw your arms 'round your lover, honey, my love,
Honey, my love, honey, my love,
Throw your arms 'round your lover, honey, my love,
I love her to my heart.

Farewell to your lover, honey, my love,
Honey, my love, honey, my love,
Farewell to your lover, honey, my love,
I love her to my heart.

TOM JONES'S PLUM TREE
(*The Juniper Tree*)

Oh, sister Phoebe, how merry were we
The night we took plums from Tom Jones's plum tree,
Tom Jones's plum tree, hi-o, hi-o,
Tom Jones's plum tree, hi-o.

Tom Jones he took down his old rifle shotgun,
He swore he would shoot us if we didn't run,
And he made us scratch gravel, by Jo, by Jo,
And he made us scratch gravel, by Jo.

Come take this hat on your head, keep your head warm,
And take a sweet kiss, it'll do you no harm,
No harm in kisses, I know, I know,
No harm in kisses, I know.

"Tom Jones's Plum Tree" was recorded by John A. Lomax and Laurence Powell from the singing of Mrs. Emma Dusenbury, Mena, Arkansas, 1933. Library of Congress AFS record 865 A.

PA, PA, BUILD ME A BOAT

Pa, Pa, build me a boat,   Pa, Pa, build me a boat,
Pa, Pa, build me a boat,   Pa, Pa, build me a boat,
Pa, Pa, build me a boat   Pa, Pa, build me a boat
To sail across the ocean.   To sail across the ocean.

Come, my love, set by me,   Come, my love, and go along,
Come, my love, set by me,   Come, my love, and go along,
Come, my love, set by me,   Come, my love, and go along,
And sail across the ocean.   Go along with me.

Pa, Pa, build me a boat,
Pa, Pa, build me a boat,
Pa, Pa, build me a boat
To sail across the ocean.

THE CHIMNEY SWEEPER

Here goes a poor old chimney sweeper,
He has but one son and he cannot keep him,
He says he will and must get married,
Go choose you one and do not tarry.

Here stands one of your own choosing,
We have no time for to be losing,
Join your right hands, this broom step over,
And kiss the lips of your own true lover.

"Pa, Pa, Build Me a Boat" was recorded by Margot Mayo from the singing of Rufus Crisp, Allen, Kentucky, 1946. Library of Congress AFS record 8495 B2.

"The Chimney Sweeper" was recorded by Laurence Powell from the singing of Mrs. Emma Dusenbury, Mena, Arkansas, Library of Congress AFS record LC 869 B1.

LONDON'S BRIDGE IS A-BURNING DOWN

London's bridge is a-burning down,
Oh, girls, remember me,
London's bridge is a-burning down,
For the prettiest girl I know.

Choose you one as we march around,
Oh, girls, remember me,
Choose you one as we march around,
Of the prettiest girls I know.

Hug her neat and kiss her sweet,
Oh, girls, remember me,
Hug her nice and kiss her twice
For the prettiest girl I know.

London's bridge is a-burning down,
Oh, girls, remember me,
London's bridge is a-burning down,
For the prettiest girl I know.

Choose you one as we march around,
Oh, girls, remember me,
Choose you one as we march around,
Of the prettiest girls I know.

Take her by the right hand, tell her how you love her,
Oh, girls, remember me,
Take her by the right hand, tell her how you love her,
For the prettiest girl I know.

Hug her neat and kiss her sweet,
Oh, girls, remember me,
Hug her nice and kiss her twice
For the prettiest girl I know.

"London's Bridge Is A-Burning Down" was recorded by John A. Lomax and Laurence Powell from the singing of Mrs. Emma Dusenbury, Mena, Arkansas. Library of Congress AFS record 865 A1.

HOG DROVERS

"Hog drovers, hog drovers, hog drovers we are,
A-courting your daughter so neat and so fair.
Can we get lodging here, oh here?
Can we get lodging here?"

"I shall have but one daughter and she sits by my side,
And none of you hog drovers can get her for bride,
And you can't have lodging here, oh here,
And you can't get lodging here."

"Care nothing for your daughter, much less for yourself,
We'll travel on further and seek better wealth,
And we don't want lodging here, oh here,
And we don't want lodging here, oh here,
And we don't want lodging here."

"I have but one daughter and she sits by my knee,
And Mr. _____ can get her from me
By bringing a prettier one here, oh here,
By bringing a prettier one here."

WHISTLE, DAUGHTER, WHISTLE

The manner of play is implicit in the words, the daughter making matters difficult for her mother, but suddenly able to whistle superbly. The mother roundly scolds her, but the daughter presumably marches off happily with a young man of her choosing from the company playing the game and observing the family squabble.

"Hog Drovers" was recorded by Herbert Halpert from the singing of Mrs. Birmah Hill Grissom, Saltillo, Mississippi, 1939. Library of Congress AFS record 2965 B1.

"Whistle, Daughter, Whistle" was "taken from a manuscript song book compiled by Miss Camilla Dennis from the singing of schoolchildren at Hindman, Knott County, Kentucky, 1922–1923." Reported by John Harrington Cox, "Singing Games," *SFQ*, 6 (1942):256–257.

"Mother, I long to get married,
   I long to be a bride,
I long to be with that young man,
   Forever by my side.
Forever by my side,
   Oh, how happy I should be, should be,
For I'm young and merry and almost weary
   Of my vir-gin-i-ty."

"Daughter, I was twenty
   Before that I was wooed,
And many a long and lonesome mile
   I carried my maidenhood."
"Oh, Mother, that may be,
   But it's not the case with me,
For I'm young and merry and almost weary
   Of my vir-gin-i-ty."

"Whistle, Daughter, whistle,
   And you shall have a sheep."
"I can not whistle, Mother,
   But I can sadly weep.
My maidenhood does grieve me,
   It fills my heart with fear,
For it's a burden, a heavy burden,
   It's more than I can bear."

"Whistle, Daughter, whistle,
   And you shall have a cow."
"I can not whistle, Mother,
   Indeed I know not how.
My maidenhood does grieve me,
   It fills my heart with fear,
For it's a burden, a heavy burden,
   It's more than I can bear."

"Whistle, Daughter, whistle,
   And you shall have a man."
"I can not whistle, Mother,
   But I'll do the best I can."

[*The daughter whistles with no trouble.*]

"You nasty impudent jade,
   What makes you whistle now?"
"Oh, I'd rather whistle for a man
   Than either sheep or cow."

"You nasty, impudent jade,
   I will put your courage down,
Take off your silks and satins,
   Put on your working gown.
I'll send you to the fields,
   A-tossing of the hay,
With your fork and rake the hay to make,
   And then hear what you say."

"Mother, don't be so cruel
   To send me to the field
Where young men will entice me
   And to them I may yield.
Fah, Mother, it's quite well known
   I am not too young grown,
And it is a pity a maid so pretty,
   As I should live alone."

Square Dance Calls

Oh, that girl, that pretty little girl,
The girl I left behind me,
I'll weep and I'll cry till the day I die
For the girl I left behind me.

SALUTE YOUR PARTNER

Salute your partner! Let her go!
Balance all and do-si-do!
Swing your gal, and all run away!
Right and left, and gents sashay!
Gents to right and swing or cheat!
On to the next gal and repeat!
Balance to the next and don't be shy!
Swing your partner and swing her high!
Bunch the gals and circle around!
Whack your feet until they sound!
Form a basket! Break away!
Swing and kiss and all git gay!
All gents to the left and balance all!
Lift your hoofs and let 'em fall!
Swing your opp'sites! Swing again!
Kiss the sage-hens if you can!
Back to your partners, do-si-do!
Gents salute your little sweets!
Hitch up and promenade to your seats!

"Salute Your Partner" was collected from Elza White, Roswell, New Mexico, in the WPA collections of the Library of Congress: "Here's a little set I used to like to call to my crowd of girls and cowboys at Midland, Texas, in the 80's."

MISSISSIPPI SAWYER

Eight hands across, form a ring.
Everybody dance, everybody swing.
Turn down, right back, Indian style.
Swing corner, two-hand swing,
Honor partners, promenade the ring.

First couple lead.
Ring up four, in the middle of the floor.
Right hand across, how d'you do?
Left hand back and-a how are you?
Swing your corner by the right,
Partner by the left.
Balance all, all night long.
Same four, middle of the floor.
Do-si, boys, you all know.
Chicken in the bread pan, picking up dough.
Come on, boys, don't be so slow.
Swing your partner, and around you go.
Same four, the middle of the floor.
Change, six and two.
Ring up six till you get fixed
Gents swing right, leads pass back.
Do-si round, swing your corner till you come around.
Honor partners, balance all.
Ring up six till you get fixed.
Gents swing right, leads pass back.
Do-si round.
Swing your corners till you come around.
Honor partners, balance all.
Same six till you get fixed.
Change, six and two.
Ring up eight till you get straight.

"Mississippi Sawyer" was recorded by John A. Lomax from the calling of S. C. Simon at Lubbock, Texas, 1936, with instrumental accompaniment by J. C. Fowler, Elic Buckner, and Alva Ruffner. Library of Congress record LP9.

Right hand across and how d'you do?
Left hand back and-a how are you?
Swing corner by the right,
Partner by the left.
Balance all, all night long.
Ring up eight till you get straight.
Swing your corner by the right,
Partner by the left.
Pass right along, all night long.
Come on, boys, don't be so lazy.
Dip that hunk in a whole lot of gravy.
Swing that corner like swinging on a gate.
Honor partner, and pull your freight.
Same eight till you get straight.
Four ladies change
Change once more.
Change this time, you all know.
Change this time and no more.
Honor your partners and boy, balance all.
First gent lead.
Ring up four in the middle of the floor.
Right hand across and-a how d'you do?
Left hand back and-a how are you?
Swing corner by the right,
Partner by the left.
Balance all, all night long.
Same four, middle of the floor.
Swing corner by the right, half way around;
Back to the left and all the way around;
Promenade the corner, you come around.
Same four, middle of the floor.
Ring up six till you get fixed.
Gents pass left, to the right, leads pass back.
Do-si round and swing your corner, you come around.
Honor partners, balance all, all night long.
Ring up six till you get fixed
Do-si, boys, you all know.
Chicken in the bread pan picking up dough.
Come on, boys, I see you're so slow.

Swing your corner, round you go.
Ring up eight till you get straight.
Swing corner by the right,
Partner by the left.
Pass right along — all night long.
Come on, boys, don't be so lazy.
Dip that hunk in a whole lot of gravy.
Rope the bell, bell the calf.
Swing your corner once and a half.
Treat 'em all alike.
Come on, boys, don't be so slow.
Whip the babe, and around you go.
Honor partners, balance all.

THE GIRL I LEFT BEHIND ME

Break and trail home,
Lady in the lead and the gents follow up.
Circle eight and you'll all get straight,
And everybody dance.
Don't be lazy, do-si-do, and a little more dough.
Chicken in the bread tray scratchin' out dough.
Granny, will your dog bite? No, child, no.
And everybody dance.
Swing your partners, promenade,
And-a home you go and you meet your taw.
Everybody dance just as pretty as you can.

Four young gents swing out to the right,
And swing them by the right hand.
Swing your partners by the left
And promenade the girl behind you.
Oh, that girl, that pretty little girl,
The girl I left behind me,
With the rosy cheeks and the curly hair,

"The Girl I Left Behind Me" was recorded by John A. Lomax from the calling of Bob McClary at Dallas, Texas, 1942, with instrumental accompaniment by Oscar Harper, Harman Clem, Homer Peters, and Ray Hanby. Library of Congress record LP9.

Oh, the girl I left behind me.
Everybody rest.

Four young gents swing out to the right,
And swing them by the right hand.
Swing your partners by the left
And promenade the girl behind you.
Oh, that girl, that pretty little girl,
The girl I left behind me,
With the rosy cheeks and the curly hair,
Oh, the girl I left behind me.
Four young gents swing out to the right.

Four young gents swing out to the right,
And swing them by the right hand.
Swing your partners by the left
And promenade the girl behind you.
Oh, that girl, that pretty little girl,
The girl I left behind me.
I'll weep and cry till the day I die
For the girl I left behind me.
Circle eight and you'll all get straight,
And everybody dance.
Don't be lazy, do-si-do, and a little more dough. . . .

SALLY GOODIN

Four gents up and swing Sally Goodin with the old right hand,
Now your taw with your left hand,
Now the old lady with your right hand,
Now your taw with your left hand.
Don't forget that girl from Arkansas.
Two-hand swing,
Everybody dance.
Partners to the left, and the left all around.

"Sally Goodin" was recorded by John A. Lomax from the calling of Bob McClary at Dallas, Texas, 1942, with instrumental accompaniment by Oscar Harper, Harman Clem, Homer Peters, and Ray Hanby. Library of Congress record LP9.

Promenade your corner as you come down.
One foot up and the other one down,
Make that big foot jar the ground.
Amazing grace, how sweet it sounds.
The jaybird kicked the snowbird down.
Everybody rest.

Four gents up and swing Sally Goodin with the old right hand,
Now your taw with your left hand,
Now the old lady with your right hand,
Now your taw with your left hand.
Don't forget to swing grandmaw.
Two-hand swing.
Everybody dance just as pretty as you can.
Partners to the left, and the left all around.
Promenade your corner as you come down.
One foot up and the other one down,
Make that big foot jar the ground.

Four gents up and swing Sally Goodin with the old right hand,
Now your taw with your left hand,
Now the old lady with your right hand,
Now your taw with your left hand.
Don't forget that girl from Arkansas.
Two-hand swing.
Everybody dance just as pretty as you can.
Amazing grace, how sweet it sounds.
The jaybird kicked the snowbird down.
One foot up and the other one down,
Make that big foot jar the ground.
Everybody dance.

Do-si, around your corner.
Back around your partner.
Corner left with the old left hand,
Partner right with the grand right and left.
Everybody dance.
Watch your partner and-a watch her close.
You meet her on the corner, double the dose.
Once and a half and treat 'em all alike

If it takes all night, and everybody dance.
Get hot!
Everybody dance just as pretty as you can.

Hooray! boys. Swing your taw.
Swing your partner and promenade the hall.
Everybody dance.
Circle eight and you'll all get straight.
And everybody dance.
Don't be lazy, do-si-do, and a little more dough.
Chicken in the bread tray scratchin' out dough.
Granny, will your dog bite? No, child, no.
And everybody dance.
Swing your partner and promenade,
And-a home you go, the old last time,
And you know where.

Banjo and Fiddle Pieces

Wish I was in Tennessee,
Sitting in an easy chair,
My true-love along my side
A-combing her yellow hair.

    I shoo, old lady, shoo,
    I shoo, old lady, shy,
    Shoo, old lady, shoo, my love,
    And I'm going to Tennessee.

SOURWOOD MOUNTAIN

I'se got a gal in the Sourwood Mountain,
She's so good and kind,
She's broke the heart of a many poor fellow
But she's never broke this-un of mine.

I'se got a gal in the Sourwood Mountain,
Hey-tank-toodle all the day,
I'se got a gal in the Sourwood Mountain,
Hey-tank-toodle all the day.

I'se got a gal in the buffalo hollow,
A hey-tank-toodle all the day,
Oh, she won't come and I won't follow,
And a hey-tank-toodle all the day.

Some of these days before very long,
And a hey-tank-toodle all the day.
I'll get my gal and home I'll run her,
And a hey-tank-toodle all the day,

Now my love's gone a-floating down the river,
Hey-tank-toodle all the day,
If I had my boat I'd go along with her,
A hey-tank-toodle all the day.

"Sourwood Mountain" was recorded by Duncan Emrich from the singing (with dulcimer accompaniment) of I. G. Greer of Thomasville, North Carolina, at Washington, D.C., 1945. Library of Congress record LP12.

An old grey goose went swimming down the river,
A hey-tank-toodle all the day,
If I was a gander, I'd go along with her,
A hey-tank-toodle all the day.

Chickens a-crowing in the Sourwood Mountain,
Chickens a-crowing for day,
Oh, come, my love, and it's time for to go,
And a hey-tank-toodle all the day.

I'se got a gal in the Sourwood Mountain,
Hey-tank-toodle all the day,
I'se got a gal in the Sourwood Mountain,
Hey-tank-toodle all the day.

DARLING CORY

Wake up, wake up, darlin' Cory,
What makes you sleep so sound
When the revenooers are comin',
Goin' to tear your still house down?

Go away, go away, darlin' Cory,
Stop hangin' around my bed.
Bad liquor destroyed my body,
Pretty women's gone to my head.

Don't you hear those bluebirds a-singin'.
Don't you hear their mournful sound?
They are preachin' Cory's funeral
In some lonesome graveyard ground.

The last time I saw darlin' Cory
She was sittin' on the bank of the sea,
With a jug of liquor in her arm
And a .45 across her knee.

"Darling Cory" was recorded by Artus M. Moser from the singing of Pleaz Mobley of Manchester, Kentucky, at Renfro Valley, Kentucky, 1946. Library of Congress record LP14.

DOGGET GAP

Walnut bark, walnut sap,
Colors all the stockings in the Dogget Gap.

Breaking up ground and I'm a-going to pitch a camp,
I'm getting something started in the Dogget Gap.

Jerked on my boots and pulled on the strap
With both socks missing in the Dogget Gap.

They went to the buggy and they raised up the flap,
Stole all my liquor in the Dogget Gap.

Oh, they took off a wheel and throwed away a tap
When I went a-courting in the Dogget Gap.

I reined up my filly and I give a little slap,
And I run like the devil through the Dogget Gap.

I shot about twice and I fetched a little yell,
And the boys all run like a bat out of hell.

I've got a girl in the Dogget Gap,
She don't mind sitting in her sweetheart's lap.

Ask your pappy to send you back,
Send all the children to the Dogget Gap.

BLUE-EYED GIRL

Fare you well, my blue-eyed girl,
Fare you well, my daisy,
Fare you well, my blue-eyed girl,
You almost run me crazy.

Apples in the summertime,
Peaches in the fall,
If I don't get the girl I want,
Don't want none at all.

"Dogget Gap" was recorded by Artus M. Moser from the singing of Bascom Lamar Lunsford of South Turkey Creek, North Carolina, at Swannanoa, North Carolina, 1946. Library of Congress AFS record 7962 A2.

"Blue-Eyed Girl" was recorded by Margot Mayo, Stuart Jamieson, and Freyda Simon from the singing of Rufus Crisp, with banjo, at Allen, Kentucky, 1946. Library of Congress record LP20.

Fare you well, my blue-eyed girl,
Fare you well, my dandy,
Fare you well, my blue-eyed girl,
Going up Big Sandy.

Blue-eyed girl is mad at me,
And black-eyed one won't have me,
If I don't get the girl I want
Single I will tarry.
           I won't neither.

Oh, fare you well, my blue-eyed girl,
Fare you well, my daisy,
Fare you well, my blue-eyed girl,
Almost drives me crazy.

You stay up on the mountain top,
And I'll live in town,
Boarding at the same hotel,
Courting Betty Brown.

Fare you well, my blue-eyed girl,
Fare you well, my daisy,
Fare you well, my blue-eyed girl,
Almost drive me crazy.

Remember what you told me last,
Remember what you said,
Said you wouldn't marry me
If all the rest was dead.

Going away to leave you now,
Baby, don't you cry,
Long days are rolling 'round,
I'll be back and die.

Fare you well, my blue-eyed girl,
Fare you well, my dandy,
Fare you well, my blue-eyed girl,
I'm going up Big Sandy.

When I was a single boy,
Happy I would be,
Now I am a great big boy,
Happy do I feel.

When she saw me coming,
She threw up her hands and cried,
"Yonder comes the ugliest thing
That ever lived or died."

ROLL ON THE GROUND

Work on the railroad,
Sleep on the ground,
Eat sody crackers
And the wind blow 'em around.

    Roll on the ground, boys,
    Roll on the ground;
    Roll on the ground, boys,
    Roll on the ground.

Work on the railroad,
Work all the day,
Eat sody crackers
And the wind blow 'em away.

    Roll on the ground, boys,
    Roll on the ground;
    Roll on the ground, boys,
    Roll on the ground.

"Roll on the Ground" was recorded by Herbert Halpert from the singing of Thaddeus C. Willingham, with banjo accompaniment, at Gulfport, Mississippi, 1939. Library of Congress record LP2.

BILE THEM CABBAGE DOWN

The hardest work I ever did
Was pulling potato vines,
The easiest thing I ever did
Was handing ladies wine.

I wish I was in Heaven,
Sitting in a chair,
With a glass of wine in one hand
And an arm around my dear.

Bile them cabbage down,
Bile them cabbage down,
Stop that fooling, pretty little girl,
And bile them cabbage down.

SHOUT, LITTLE LULU

A whole heap of nickels and a whole heap of dimes,
A-going to see my Lulu gal a whole heap of times.

Shout, little Lulu, shout your best,
Your old grandmother's in hell, I guess.

I'd give a nickel and I'd give a dime,
To see my Lulu gal cut a monkeyshine.

OLD KIMBALL

Old Kimball was a gray nag,
Old Nellie was a brown,
Old Kimball beat old Nellie
On the very first go-round.

"Bile Them Cabbage Down" was recorded by Herbert Halpert from the singing of Austin Harmon, Maryville, Tennessee, 1939. Library of Congress AFS record 2884 A2 and B1.

"Shout, Little Lulu" was recorded by Alan and Elizabeth Lomax from the singing, with banjo accompaniment, by Pete Steele at Hamilton, Ohio, 1938. Library of Congress record LP21.

"Old Kimball" was recorded by Alan and Elizabeth Lomax from the singing of Mrs. Texas Gladden, Salem, Virginia, 1941. Library of Congress record LP1.

And I see, and I see,
And I see on the fourth day of July.

His bridle made of silver,
His saddle made of gold,
And the value of his harness
It has never been told.

I'll get up in my buggy
With my lines in my hand.
"Good morning, young lady."
"Good morning, young man."

I often have wondered
What makes women love men,
Then looked back and wondered
What makes men love them.

And I see, and I see,
And I see on the fourth day of July.

BLACK-EYED SUSIE

All I want in this creation's
A pretty little wife and a big plantation.

Hey, pretty little black-eyed Susie,
Hey, pretty little black-eyed Susie.

I love my wife, I love my baby,
I love my biscuits sopped in gravy.

All I want to make me happy,
Two little boys to call me pappy.

All I want in this creation's
A pretty little wife and a big plantation.

Hey, pretty little black-eyed Susie,
Hey, pretty little black-eyed Susie.

"Black-Eyed Susie" was recorded by Herbert Halpert from the singing of Thaddeus C. Willingham, Gulfport, Mississippi, 1939. Library of Congress AFS record 3114 B3.

FOD

As I went down to the mowin' field,
Hu-rye, tu-rye, fod-a-link-a-dye-do,
As I went down to the mowin' field,
Fod!
As I went down to the mowin' field,
A big black snake got me by the heel.
Tu rolly day.

Well, I fell down upon the ground,
Hu-rye, tu-rye, fod-a-link-a-dye-do,
Well, I fell down upon the ground,
Fod!
Well, I fell down upon the ground,
I shut both eyes and looked all around
Tu rolly day.

I set upon a stump to take my rest;
It looked like a woodchuck on his nest.

The woodchuck grinned a banjo song,
And up stepped a skunk with the britches on.

The woodchuck and skunk got into a fight;
The fume was so strong it put out the light.

They danced and they played till the chimney begin to rust,
Hu-rye, tu-rye, fod-a-link-a-dye-do,
They danced and they played till the chimney begin to rust,
Fod!
They danced and they played till the chimney begin to rust,
It was hard to tell which smelt the worst.
Tu rolly day.

"Fod" was recorded by Charles Todd and Robert Sonkin from the singing of Henry King (of Arkansas) at Visalia, California, 1941. Library of Congress record LP2.

GIT ALONG DOWN TO TOWN

"Folks, this is the King Family playing 'Git Along Down to Town.'"

Boss he had a yaller gal,
He brought her from the South,
She had her hair done up so tight
Couldn't hardly shut her mouth.

> Git along down to town,
> Git along down to town,
> Git along down to Little Rock town,
> Gonna set my banjo down.

Her head looked like a coffee pot,
Her nose looked like the spout,
Her mouth looked like the fireplace
With the ashes all raked out.

I wouldn't have a yaller gal,
Now here's the reason why,
Her neck's so long and scrangy
She'd make them biscuits fly.

Boss he had an old gray mare,
He rode her down in town,
Before he got his trading done,
The buzzards had her down.

Boss he had an old gray mare,
Her name was Brindly Brown,
Every tooth in that mare's head
Had sixteen inches 'round.

Well I hopped upon that old gray mare,
I rode her through the town,
I sold that mare for fifteen cents
And I got my money down.

"Git Along Down to Town" was recorded by Charles Todd and Robert Sonkin from the singing of Henry King and family at Visalia, California, 1941. Library of Congress record LP20.

Git along down to town,
Git along down to town,
Git along down to Little Rock town,
Gonna push my 'bacco 'round.

Boss he had a big white house
Sixteen stories high,
Well every story in that house
Was lined with chicken pie.

Git along down to town,
Git along down to town,
Git along down to Little Rock town,
Gonna push my 'bacco 'round.

Whiskey by the gallon
And sugar by the pound,
A great big bowl to pour it in
And a pretty girl to carry it around.

Git along down to town,
Git along down to town,
Git along down to Little Rock town,
Gonna set my banjo down.

THE KICKING MULE

"Folks, this is the King Family playing 'The Kicking Mule' with a tenor banjo lead."

As I went down to the huckleberry picnic,
Dinner all over the ground,
Skippers in the meat was nine foot deep
And the green flies walking all around.
The biscuit in the oven was a-baking,
Was a beefsteak frying in the pan,
Pretty gal sitting in the parlor,
Lord God a'mighty, what a hand I stand!

"The Kicking Mule" was recorded by Charles Todd and Robert Sonkin from the singing of Henry King and family at Visalia, California, 1941. Library of Congress record LP20.

Whoa there, mule, I tell you,
Miss Liza, you keep cool,
I ain't got time to kiss you now,
I'm busy with this mule.

My uncle had an old mule,
His name was Simon Slick,
'Bove anything I ever did see
Was how that mule could kick.
Went to feed that mule one morning
And he met me at the door with a smile,
He backed one ear and he winked one eye
And he kicked me a half a mile.

Well, whoa there, mule, I tell you,
Miss Liza, you keep cool,
I ain't got time to kiss you now,
I'm busy with my mule.

That mule he am a kicker,
He's got an iron jaw,
He's the very thing to have about
To tame your mother-in-law
This mule he am a kicker,
He's got a iron back,
He headed off a Texas railroad train
And kicked it clear o' the track.

Whoa there, mule, I tell you,
Well whoa there, mule, I say,
Just keep your seat, Miss Liza Jane,
And hold on to that sleigh.

He kicked a feather from a goose,
He pulverized a hog,
He kicked up three dead chinymans
And swatted him a yellow dog.

Well, whoa there, mule, I tell you,
Miss Liza, you keep cool,
I ain't got time to kiss you now,
I'm busy with that mule.

When I seen Miss Dinah the other day,
She was bent all over her tub,
And the more I'd ask her to marry me,
Well, the harder she would rub.

Well, whoa there, mule, I tell you,
Whoa there, mule, I say,
Just keep your seat, Miss Liza Jane,
And hold on to that sleigh.

You see that mule a-coming,
He's got about a half a load,
When you see a roomy mule,
Better give him all the road.

Whoa there, mule, I tell you,
Miss Liza, you keep cool,
I ain't got time to kiss you now,
I'm busy with this mule.

CRIPPLE CREEK

"Folks, this number is 'Cripple Creek' . . ."

Goin' down to Cripple Creek, goin' at a run,
Goin' down to Cripple Creek to have some fun.
Roll my britches to my knees,
Wade old Cripple Creek when I please!
Goin' down to Cripple Creek, goin' at a run,
Goin' down to Cripple Creek to have some fun.

Goin' down to Cripple Creek, goin' in a whirl,
Goin' down to Cripple Creek to see my girl.
Roll my britches to my knees,
Wade old Cripple Creek when I please!
Goin' down to Cripple Creek, goin' in a whirl,
Goin' down to Cripple Creek to see my girl.

"Cripple Creek" was recorded by Charles Todd and Robert Sonkin from the singing of Henry King and family at Visalia, California, 1941. Library of Congress record LP20.

TENNESSEE

Wish I was in Tennessee,
Sitting in an easy chair,
My true-love along my side
A-combing her yellow hair.

> I shoo, old lady, shoo,
> I shoo, old lady, shy,
> Shoo, old lady, shoo, my love,
> And I'm going to Tennessee.

Jay birds up in the acorn tree,
Shaking acorns down,
My true-love in the sugar tree,
Shaking sugar down.

Went up on the hillside
And I give my horn a blow,
I thought I heard birds a-singing,
"Yonder comes my beau!"

> I shoo, old lady, shoo,
> I shoo, old lady, shy,
> Shoo, old lady, shoo, my love,
> And I'm going to Tennessee.

THE SUN SHINES OVER THE MOUNTAIN

The sun shines over the mountain, the fog hangs over the lake,
The devil never can catch me, for I'm too wide awake.
> Who-ay hay-ay-hay, who-ay hay-e-o,
> Who-ay hay-ay-hay, for yonder comes my beau.

I went over the mountain, I gave my horn a blow,
I thought I see'd my true love a-standing in the door.
> Who-ay hay-ay-hay, who-ay hay-e-o,
> Who-ay hay-ay-hay, for yonder comes my beau.

As I went over the mountain, I gave my horn a toot,
I thought I see'd my true love's head a-sticking out of my boot.

"Tennessee" was recorded by Alan and Elizabeth Lomax from the singing of J. M. Mullins, Floress, Kentucky, 1937. Library of Congress AFS record 1590 B2, 1591 A.

"The Sun Shines over the Mountain" was recorded by John A. Lomax and Laurence Powell from the singing of Mrs. Emma Dusenbury, Mena, Arkansas, 1936. Library of Congress AFS record 865 B1.

Who-ay hay-ay-hay, who-ay hay-e-o,
Who-ay hay-ay-hay, for yonder comes my beau.

STAY ALL NIGHT, STAY A LITTLE LONGER

You ought to see my blue-eyed Sally,
She lives away down in Chin Bone Alley,
Number on the gate and number on the door,
The next house over by the grocery store.

   Stay all night, stay a little longer,
   Dance all night, dance a little longer,
   Pull off your coat and throw it in the corner,
   I don't see why you don't stay a little longer.

Hey, old man, you can't get to the mill,
'Cause the bridge washed out at the foot of the hill;
Big creek's up and big creek's level,
I plow my corn with a double shovel.

Standing by the window talking to my love,
A water bucket fell from a window up above.
Mule on the grass over eating ice cream,
And the mule got sick and I laid him on the beam.

Pat your girl and pat her on the head,
If she won't eat biscuits, feed her cornbread,
A girl don't jig until she's about half gone,
Then she'll jump on a man like a dog on a bone.

   Stay all night, stay a little longer,
   Dance all night, dance a little longer,
   Pull off your coat and throw it in the corner,
   I don't see why you don't stay a little longer.

"Stay All Night, Stay a Little Longer" was recorded by Margot Mayo, Stuart Jamieson, and Freyda Simon from the singing, with guitar, of Palmer Crisp, Allen, Kentucky, 1946. Fiddle accompaniment also by Sam Leslie. Library of Congress AFS record 8482 B1.

BUFFALO GIRLS

Buffalo girls, ain't you coming out tonight,
Ain't you coming out tonight, ain't you coming out tonight,
Buffalo girls, ain't you coming out tonight,
To dance by the light of the moon?

> You bet your socks I'm a-coming out tonight,
> I'm a-coming out tonight, I'm a-coming out tonight,
> You bet your socks I'm a-coming out tonight
> To dance by the light of the moon.

As I was a-walking down the street,
Down the street, down the street,
I passed my girl and she looked so neat
Under the light of the moon.

> You bet your socks I'm a-coming out tonight,
> I'm a-coming out tonight, I'm a-coming out tonight,
> You bet your socks I'm a-coming out tonight
> To dance by the light of the moon.

JACK OF DIAMONDS

Jack o' Diamonds, Jack o'
    Diamonds
I've known you of old,
You've robbed my poor pockets
Of silver and gold.

Whiskey, you villain,
You've been my downfall,
You've kicked me, you've cuffed
    me,
But I love you for all.

"Buffalo Girls" was recorded by Vance Randolph from the singing of Mrs. May Kennedy McCord, Springfield, Missouri, 1941. Library of Congress AFS record 5301 B2.

"Jack of Diamonds" was recorded by Artus M. Moser from the singing, with guitar, of Bill Nicholson, accompanied by Zane Shrader with steel guitar, both of New Albany, Indiana, at Renfro Valley, Kentucky, 1946. Library of Congress record LP14.

They say I drink whiskey,
My money's my own,
And them that don't like it
Can leave me alone.

'Cause I'll eat when I'm hungry,
I'll drink when I'm dry,
And when I get thirsty
I'll lay down and die.

H-e-e-c! Oh, lordy,
How bad I do feel!
H-e-e-c! Oh, lordy,
How bad I do feel!

If the ocean was whiskey
And I was a duck,
I'd dive to the bottom
And never come up.

Whiskey, rye whiskey,
Rye whiskey I cry,
If I don't get my whiskey
I surely will die.

It's beefsteak when I'm hungry,
Rye whiskey when I'm dry,
The greenbacks when I'm hard up
And heaven when I die.

Whiskey, rye whiskey,
Rye whiskey, I cry,
If I don't get my whiskey
I surely will die.

Jack o' Diamonds, Jack o'
  Diamonds,
I've known you of old,
You've robbed my poor pockets
Of silver and gold.

Whiskey, you villain,
You've been my downfall,
You've kicked me, you've cuffed
  me,
But I love you for all.

H-e-e-c! Oh, lordy,
How bad I do feel!
H-e-e-c! Oh, lordy,
How bad I do feel!

PHILADELPHIA

Philadelphia is a handsome town
And so is Cincinnati,
The streets are lined with dollar bills,
And the pretty girls are plenty.

"Philadelphia" was collected by Cecil J. Sharp from the singing of Mr. Hillard Smith, Hindman, Knott County, Kentucky, 1917. Text with music in Sharp, *English Folk Songs from the Southern Appalachians* (Oxford) New York, 1932, II, 374.

LOVE

Family Opposition to Love

Then he being close unto a thicket,
He thought he heard a female's voice;
He run to her like one distracted,
And said, "Oh, true love, I'm forever lost."

Then she lay fainting by his feetside,
Her cold dark eyes like stars they shine,
Saying, "Prepare to meet me on Mount Zion,
Where all true loves in peace shall meet."

Then she pulled out a silver dagger,
She pierced it through her snow-white breast,
Saying, "Adieu, adieu, I'm gone forever,
I'm gone forevermore to rest."

THE SILVER DAGGER

Young man and maid, pray lend attention,
And of the story I'll relate,
Of the young man who I will mention,
That courted fair a pretty girl.

And when his parents came to know this,
They strove against it night and day,
And said, "Oh, son, don't be so foolish,
For she's too poor for to marry you."

Down on his bended knees a-crying,
Saying, "Cruel parents, pity me;
Don't keep me from my own dear Julie,
What's all this world without her to me."

He wandered off by flowing waters,
He taken his seat by a shady tree.
He set and said, "Oh, shall I ever,
Ever any more my true love see."

"The Silver Dagger" was recorded by John A. Lomax and Laurence Powell from the singing of Mrs. Emma Dusenbury at Mena, Arkansas, 1936. Library of Congress AFS record 866 B3. Laws, G21.

Then he being close unto a thicket,
He thought he heard a female's voice;
He run to her like one distracted,
And said, "Oh, true love, I'm forever lost."

Then she lay fainting by his feetside,
Her cold dark eyes like stars they shine,
Saying, "Prepare to meet me on Mount Zion,
Where all true loves in peace shall meet."

Then she pulled out a silver dagger,
She pierced it through her snow-white breast,
Saying, "Adieu, adieu, I'm gone forever,
I'm gone forevermore to rest."

Then he picked up this bloody weapon,
He pierced it through his tender heart,
Saying, "Leave this as a dreadful token
To those that keep me and Julie apart."

COME ALL YE FAIR AND TENDER LADIES

Come all ye fair and tender ladies,
And hear this story I am going to tell;
A couple as true as ever was spoken
At last, at last, engaged themselves,
A couple as true as ever was spoken
At last, at last, engaged themselves.

And when his parents came to know this,
They tried, they tried, to break it up.
"O son, O son, don't be so foolish,
She is too poor for you a bride!
O son, O son, don't be so foolish,
She is too poor," they often cried.

"Come All Ye Fair and Tender Ladies" was collected by Harvey H. Fuson from Lizzie Dills. In Fuson, *Ballads of the Kentucky Highlands*, London, 1931, p. 71. Without music. Laws, G21.

Falling on his bended knees before them,
"O parents, O parents, pity me!
Don't keep me from my heart's jewel,
For she is all the world to me;
Don't keep me from my heart's jewel,
For she is all the world to me!"

And when this lady came to know this,
She walked the meadows and fields around;
Until she came to a place of beauty,
And there she cried and there sat down;
Until she came to a place of beauty,
And there she cried and there sat down.

And as she sat there broken-hearted,
She pierced herself through the snow-white breast;
And here she reeled and there she staggered;
"Oh, at last, at last, I am gone to rest!"
And here she reeled and there she staggered;
"Oh, at last, at last, I am gone to rest!"

And her true, true-love being on the ocean,
He heard her struggling and her groans.
He ran like one that were distracted;
"I am lost, I am ruined, I am left alone!"
He ran like one that were distracted;
"I am lost, I am ruined, I am left alone."

Then he picked up her bleeding body,
And turned her over in his arms;
"Is there no one, no doctor, can save you?
Don't you want to die in your true-love's arms?
Is there no one, no doctor, can save you?
Don't you want to die in your true-love's arms?"

She walled her dying eyes up toward him;
"Oh, at last, at last, you have come to me;
You are all the one could have killed or cured me;
At last, too late, you have come to me!
You are all the one could have cured or killed me;
At last, too late, you have come to me!"

"Prepare to meet me on Mount Zion,
Up there, where true-lovers never part!"
And then he drew the bloody dagger,
And pierced it through his tender heart.
Says: "Let this be a faithful warning
For those who keep true-lovers apart."

THE SILK WEAVER'S DAUGHTER

As down through Moore's field one evening I went,
I heard a fair damsel a-making sad lament;
By the wringing of her hands and the tearing of her hair,
Crying, "O cruel parents, you've been too severe.

"You banished my true love quite away from me
Which causes me in Bedlam to weep bitterly.
May all tortures and torments attend in your breast
And partake of my sorrow and never find rest.

"Was it because he a 'prentice boy were
You banished my true love and left me in despair?
But while my jolly sailor goes plowing o'er the main
I'll go picking my straws and a-rattling my chains."

As down to Bedlam this sailor drew nigh,
He saw through the window a dark rolling eye.
He went unto the porter and to him he did say,
"Can you show me the place where my true love doth lay?

"A silk weaver's daughter in Bedlam doth lie,
And all for the love that she bore unto me."
He gave unto the porter a broad piece of gold
For to show him the way to the joy of his soul.

It's when in Bedlam his true love he did see,
He kissed her and embraced her and took her on his knee.

"The Silk Weaver's Daughter" was recorded by Sidney Robertson Cowell from the singing of Mrs. Carrie Grover of Gorham, Maine, at Teaneck, New Jersey, 1941. Library of Congress AFS record 4696 B1. Text with music also in Carrie B. Grover, *A Heritage of Songs* (privately printed, Gould Academy, Bethel, Maine, n.d.), p. 8.

"Here's adieu to my sorrows; away from me they've fled.
Here's adieu to my chains and my cold strawy bed."

JOHNNY DYERS

It happened, it happened all on a Saturday night
That I and Johnny Dyers was talking of a flight;
My watching girl stood near-by, so plainly I could see,
She run to my mother, and told her on me.

My mother concealed me all in a room so high
That no one could see me or scarcely pass me by.
She bundled up my clothing and bid me put them on,
So slowly and so sorrowfully I did put them on.

My father provided for me one thousand pounds,
Besides a horse and saddle for me to ride upon,
And four brave horsemen to ride by my side
In order to make me young Samuel Moore's bride.

We rode and we rode until we came to his town,
At old Squire Myer's, and there we all lit down;
And then upon the floor she forced me to stand
In order to give young Samuel Moore my hand.

About the time I should have answered, I scarcely could stand,
The thought of Johnny Dyers came fresh into my mind.
The rings upon my fingers around them turned blue,
I thought in my soul my poor heart would break in two.

Then behind my oldest brother then I rode home,
My mother conveyed me into a silent room;
And there upon the bedside I laid my body down.
So slowly and so sorrowfully I laid my body down.

"Johnny Dyers" was recorded by Laurence Powell and John A. Lomax from the singing of Mrs. Emma Dusenbury, Mena, Arkansas, 1936. Library of Congress AFS record 872 A2, Laws, M2.

"Oh, mother dear, oh, mother, please fasten to the door
And don't let Samuel Moore in until the break of day;
For he shall never enjoy me or call me his bride:
Before the morning's light grim death will end the strife."

"Oh, daughter, dear daughter, we'll send for Johnny Dyers."
"To send for Johnny Dyers, it isn't worth your while,
For you have enjoyed the pleasure while I have borne the grief.
There's more grief at my heart than my poor heart can bear.

"Oh, Johnny, oh, Johnny, my love, so fare you well,
There's more grief at my heart than my poor tongue can tell."

A LOVER'S LAMENT

I once did court a damsel most beautiful and bright.
I thought of her by day and I dreamed of her by night.
I courted her for love and her love I did obtain.
She vowed that she did love me and constant would remain.

Oh then we did plan that together we would go,
But when her old father these tidings came to know,
He shut her up so tight and he kept her so severe
That I never once after caught sight of my dear.

Oh then to the wars, to the wars I did go
To see if I could forget my true love or no.
Three years I served my king, then homeward did steer.
My heart was filled with longing for a sight of my dear.

Oh when I returned, to her father I did go
To see if my true love had forgot me or no.
He met me at the door and he made me this reply,
"My daughter loved you dearly, and for your sake she died."

"A Lover's Lament" was recorded by Alan Lomax from the singing of Mrs. Carrie Grover of Gorham, Maine, at Washington, D.C., 1941. Library of Congress AFS record 4458 B3. Text with music also in Carrie B. Grover, *A Heritage of Songs* (privately printed, Gould Academy, Bethel, Maine, n.d.), p. 99. Laws, M3.

Oh then I sank down like one that was slain,
Saying, "I'll never, no I'll never see my true love again."
Crying, "Oh dear! oh dear! this grief I cannot bear;
My true love's in her grave and I wish I was there."

Charming Beauty Bright

How I go courting a charming beauty bright,
Joy of my love and my whole heart's delight,
I courted her for love, and love I did obtain,
And don't you think I had a good reason to complain.

When her father and mother came to know
Me and my love was together to go,
They locked her in a room, and kept her so severe
I never did but once more get sight of my dear.

She was standing in the window with tears in her eyes
Said "I love the man that loves me,
I'll love him till I die."

Then to the army I thought I would go
To see if I could forget my lover or no;
I was standing in the ring, my armor shining bright,
I always was a-thinking of my whole heart's delight.

Six long months I served my king.
At the end of the seventh I returned home again.
Her mother saw me coming, she wrung her hands and cried,
"My daughter loved you dearly, and for your sake she died."

There I stood like a man to be slain,
Tears were a-falling like whosers* of rain.
Come all you weary lovers, come pity, pity me,
Come and pity my misfortune and sad miser-ee.

---

* How "showers" becomes "whosers" is a happy wonder. It has been retained for your enjoyment.

"Charming Beauty Bright" was collected by the Federal Music Project, Works Progress Administration (WPA), Boyd County, Kentucky, ca. 1937. Jean Thomas, Supervisor for Boyd County. Ms., with music, in the Archive of Folk Song, Library of Congress. Laws, M3.

LOVE

I'm troubled out of reason,
It's more than I can bear,
My true love is in her grave,
And I wish I were there.

The Fair Beauty Bride*

Once I courted a fair beauty bride;
I courted her by day and I courted her by night.
Her father found I was courting her and caring for her love;
He locked her in the dining-room and strowed the keys above.

She rapped on the window, she answered me and cried;
She rapped on the window, she answered me and mourned;
She rapped on the window and she said,
"True-love, I love you dearly, and shall until I die."

Away to the army, away I did go,
To see if I could forget the love I know.
When I got there, the army shone so bright.
It put me in the mind of my own heart's delight.

For seven long years I served under the king,
For seven long years before I came home again.
Her father saw me coming; he wrung his hands and cried,
"My daughter loved you dearly, and for your sake she died."

There he stood like a man ready to be slain;
He could not keep back his tears, it was so great a pain.
Let the angels above come down and pity me,
My true-love is dead and in her grave, and it's there I long to be.

* This probably should be "bright."

"The Fair Beauty Bride" was collected by Harvey H. Fuson from Myrtle Hayes. In Fuson, *Ballads of the Kentucky Highlands*, London, 1931, p. 136. Without music. Laws, M3.

AWAKE, ARISE, YOU DROWSY SLEEPER

"Awake, arise, you drowsy sleeper,
Awake, arise, 'tis almost day,
And open wide your bedroom window
Hear what your true love has to say.

"Oh, Mary dear, go ask your father,
Whether you my bride may be,
And if he says no, love, come and tell me,
It's the very last time I'll trouble thee."

"I dare not go to ask my father,
For he lies on his couch of rest,
And by his side he keeps a weapon
To slay the one that I love best."

"Oh, Mary dear, go ask your mother,
Whether you my bride may be,
And if she says no, love, come and tell me,
It's the very last time I'll trouble thee."

"I dare not go to ask my mother,
To let her know my love is near,
But dearest dear, go court some other,"
She gently whispered in my ear.

"Oh, Mary dear, oh dearest Mary,
It is for you my heart will break.
From North to South to Pennsylvania,
I'll roam the ocean for your sake."

"And now I'll go down by some silent river,
And there I'll spend my days and years,
And there I'll plant a weeping willow;
Beneath its shade I'll shed my tears."

"Awake, Arise, You Drowsy Sleeper" was recorded by Aubrey Snyder and Phyllis Pinkerton from the singing of Lester A. Coffee, Harvard, Illinois, 1946. Library of Congress record LP55. Laws, M4.

"Come back, come back, my wounded lover,
Come back, come back to me, I pray,
And I'll forsake both father, mother,
And with you I'll run away."

THE 'PRENTICE BOY

As down through Cupid's garden for pleasure I did walk,
I heard two loyal lovers most sweetly for to talk.
It being an honored lady and her apprentice boy,
And in secret they were talking, for he was all her joy.

He says, "Dear honored lady, I am your 'prentice boy.
How can I e'er expect a fair lady to enjoy?"
With cheeks as red as roses, her manner kind and free,
She says, "Dear lad, if e'er I wed, I will surely marry thee."

But when her father came to know, the same to understand,
He had this young man banished unto a foreign land.
And, as she lay broken-hearted, these words was heard to say,
"For my honest charming 'prentice, a maid I'll live and die."

This young man to a merchant a waiting-man was bound,
And by his good behavior great fortune there he found.
Soon he became a butler, which prompted him to fame,
And by his careful conduct his steward he became.

For a ticket in a lottery the money he paid down,
And there he gained a fortune of full five thousand pounds.
With store of gold and silver he packed his clothes indeed,
And to England he returned to his own true love with speed.

He offered kind embraces, but she flew from his arms,
Saying, "No lord or nobleman shall e'er enjoy my charms;
The love of gold is cursed, great riches I decry,
For my honest charming 'prentice, a maid I'll live and die."

"The 'Prentice Boy" was recorded by Sidney Robertson Cowell from the singing of Mrs. Carrie Grover of Gorham, Maine, at Teaneck, New Jersey, 1941. Library of Congress AFS record 4695 B. Text with music also in Carrie B. Grover, *A Heritage of Songs* (privately printed, Gould Academy, Bethel, Maine, n.d.), p. 5. Laws, M12.

He says, "Dear honored lady, you have been in these arms,
This is the ring I gave you in token of your charms;
You vowed if e'er you married, your charms I should enjoy,
Your father did me banish, I am your 'prentice boy."

When she beheld his features, she flew into his arms;
With kisses and embraces she did enjoy his charms,
And then through Cupid's garden a road to church they found,
And there in virtuous pleasure in Hymen's chains were bound.

THE SERVANT MAN
(*The Iron Door*)

'Tis of a lady both fair and handsome,
A merchant's daughter as I've been told;
On the banks of Shannon a lofty mansion,
Her father had great stores of gold.

Her hair was black as a raven's feather,
Her form and feature describe who can;
But youth and folly belong to nature,
She fell in love with her servant man.

When her father found out her intention,
He like a lion loud did roar,
Saying, "From Ireland I'll have you banished,
Or with my broadsword I'll spill your gore."

To build a dungeon was his intention,
Three flights of stairs it was underground;
The food he gave her was bread and water,
The only cheer for her to be found.

Three times a day he so cruelly beat her,
Till to her father she thus began:

"The Servant Man" was recorded by Alan Lomax from the singing of Mrs. Carrie Grover of Gorham, Maine, at Washington, D.C., 1941. Library of Congress AFS record 4461 A. Laws, M15.

"My own dear father, I have transgressed thee,
But I'll live and die for my servant man."

When Edmund found out her habitation,
It was well secured by an iron door;
He swore in spite of all the nation
He'd release his true love or be no more.

So at his leisure he toiled with pleasure
To find releasement for his Mary Ann,
And when she saw him in the dungeon
She cries, "My faithful servant man!"

When the old man came with his bread and water,
He to her father thus began:
"I freed your daughter, I own I love her;
The one at fault is your servant man."

He fell a-fainting on the dungeon floor,
Saying, "True lovers should ne'er be parted,
Since love's broke through an iron door."

THE BANKS OF SWEET DUNDEE

A farmer had a daughter whose beauty ne'er was told.
Her parents died and left her five hundred pounds in gold.
She lived with her uncle, who caused her all her woe,
And if you'll but list to this pretty fair miss, I'll prove it all to you.

Her uncle had a plowboy that Mary loved so well,
The way she loved that plowboy, no human tongue could tell.
There was a wealthy squire came Mary for to see,
But she loved her uncle's plowboy on the banks of the Sweet and Dee.

A press-gang came to Willie when he was all alone,
He bravely fought for liberty, but they were six to one.

"The Banks of Sweet Dundee" was collected by Asher E. Treat and reported in "Kentucky Folksong in Northern Wisconsin," *JAF*, 52 (1939):9. With music. Laws, M25.

LOVE

His blood it flowed in torrents. "Pray kill me now!" said he,
"For I'd rather die for Mary on the banks of the Sweet and Dee."

One day while she was walking, lamenting for her love,
She spied this wealthy squire down in her uncle's grove.
He took a step toward her. "Stand back, young man!" said she,
"For you've banished the only one I love on the banks of the Sweet and Dee."

He threw his arms around her and strove to set her down.
She spied a sword and pistol beneath his morning gown.
She drew the pistol from its belt, the sword she used so free;
The pistol fired and the squire fell on the banks of the Sweet and Dee.

Her uncle heard the noise and hastened to the ground,
Saying, "Now you've killed my squire, I'll give you your death wound."
"Stand back! Stand back!" said Mary, "Stand back! Stand back!" said she.
The sword she drew, and her uncle slew on the banks of the Sweet and Dee.

A doctor was sent for, a man of note and skill,
And also a lawyer, that he might write his will.
He willed his gold to Mary, who fought so manfully,
Then he closed his eyes, no more to rise on the banks of the Sweet and Dee.

THE GREEN BRIAR SHORE

At the foot of yonders mountain where the fountains do flow,
Red roses and branches and pleasant gales blow,
I spied a fair damsel and her I adore,
I spied my own true love on the green briar shore.

I stepped up to her, says, "Miss, won't you fancy me?
My portion is small . . ." "But it's nothing," said she,
"Your beauty does please me, alas, nothing more,
And I never will deny you on the green briar shore."

As soon as her old parents came this for to know,
They swore they'd separate her from her dearest dear;

"The Green Briar Shore" was recorded by Herbert Halpert from the singing of Joe Hubbard, Hamiltontown, Virginia, 1939. Library of Congress AFS record 2826 A1. Third line of first stanza lacking and supplied from Cecil J. Sharp, *English Folk Songs from the Southern Appalachians* (Oxford) New York, 1932, II, 188. Laws, M26.

They gathered an army, fully twenty or more,
To fight her own true love on the green briar shore.

He pulled out his sword and it glittered all 'round,
Not very long after some fell dead on the ground;
The rest was all wounded and that very sure,
And he gained his own true love on the green briar shore.

Hard is the fortune of all womankind,
They're forever controlled, they're forever confined;
They're controlled by their parents until they're married wives,
And slave for their husbands all the rest of their lives.

Oh, I can love light love, or I can love long,
I can love an old sweetheart till a new one comes on;
I can court them and kiss them and gain their hearts kind,
And turn my back upon them and alter my mind.

THE SOLDIER'S WOOING

I will tell you of a gallan soldier
Who lately came from sea:
He courted a lady,
A lady said to be.

The old man said unto her,
"This I here complain:
If you marry a gallan soldier,
It will be all in vain.

"Since you have been so foolish
To be a soldier wife,
Down in some lonesome valley
I will take your pleasant life."

He drew his swords and pistols
And hung them to his side —
Swore that he would be married
Whatever may betide.

She jumped on a milk-white steed
And he jumped on another one;
Off to church they rode
Just like a sister and brother.

They had been to church
And just returning;
Then she said, "I see my father,
With twenty well-armed men."

He drew his swords and pistols
And caused them to rattle;

"The Soldier's Wooing" was collected by Mellinger E. Henry from the singing of Mrs. Samuel Harmon of Cade's Cove, Tennessee, at Varnell, Georgia, October 1930. See Mellinger E. Henry, "Ballads and Folk-Songs from the Southern Highlands," *JAF*, 45 (1932):114–116. Laws, M27.

The lady helt the horse,
While the soldier fought the battle.

The first one that tackled him
He soon had him slain;
And the next one that tackled him
He served him the same.

"Let's run," said the balance,
"For fear we will be slain,
To fight a gallan soldier,
For it is all in vain."

"Hold your arm," said the old man,
"And pray spare my life;
You can have my daughter
To be your loving wife.

"Hold your arm," said the old man,
"And don't you strike so bold;
You can have my daughter,
And a thousand pounds of gold."

"Fight on," said the lady,
"The portion is too small."
"Hold your arm," said the old man,
"And you can have it all."

He took them home with him
And pronounced them his heirs.
It was not the good will of the old
man,
But it was all through dread and
fears.

The Jolly Soldier

'Tis of a jolly soldier that lately came from war,
He loved a young damsel, a damsel so fair;
Her fortune was so great it could scarcely be told,
And she loved a jolly soldier because he was so bold.

"Oh," then said the lady, "I fain would be your wife,
But my father he is cruel and he'd surely end my life."
He drew out his sword and pistol, and he hung them by his side,
And he swore that he would marry her, let what would betide.

So they went and they got married, and as they were coming home
They met her old father with seven armed men.
"Let us flee," cried the lady, "or we both will be slain."
"Fear nothing, dear charmer," the soldier said again.

Then up came the old man and unto her did say,
"It's for your disobedience to me this very day.

"The Jolly Soldier" was recorded by Alan Lomax from the singing of Mrs. Carrie Grover of Gorham, Maine, at Washington, D.C., 1941. Library of Congress AFS record 4452 A2. Laws, M27.

Since you have been so mean as to be a soldier's wife,
Down in this lonely valley I will surely end your life."

"Oh," then said the soldier, "I do not like your prattle,
For although I am a bridegroom, I am well prepared for battle."
He drew out his sword and pistol and he caused them for to rattle,
The lady held the horse while the soldier fought the battle.

The first one he came to, he run him through amain,
The second one he came to, he served him the same.
"Let us flee," cried the rest, "or we all will be slain."
"Fight on, my brave soldier," the lady said again.

"Stay your hand," cried the old man, "you make my blood run cold.
And you shall have my daughter and five thousand pounds in gold."
"Fight on," cried the lady, "for my fortune is too small."
"Stay your hand," cried the old man, "and you shall have it all."

So he took them both home; he made them his heirs,
It was not for love but it was through dread fear,
For there never was a soldier ever carried a gun
Who would ever flinch or budge an inch till the battle he had won.

So don't despise a soldier because he is poor,
He's happy on the battlefield as at the barrack door;
For they are the lads to be jovial, brisk and free,
And they'll fight for the pretty girls, for rights and liberty.

THE JEALOUS BROTHERS

There sits a fair couple courting,
Two brothers for to overhear,
They were determined all in their mind
To put a stop to their design.
They were determined all in their mind
To put a stop to their design.

So they rose the very next morning

"The Jealous Brothers" was recorded by Vance Randolph from the singing of Doney Hammontree, Farmington, Arkansas, 1941. Library of Congress AFS record 5382 A1. Laws, M32.

LOVE

A game of hunting for to go,
The brothers saying they were both insisting
That this young man should go along.
The brothers saying they were both insisting
That this young man should go along.

They traveled over hills and mountains
And many other places where they were unknown,
Until they came to the lonesome valley,
And there they killed him and left him alone.

And when the brothers were returning,
The sister asked where her lover were.
"We lost him in the game of hunting,
No more of him we ne'er could find."

That night the sister lay early dreaming,
Her true love appeared by her bedside,
Saying, "Your brothers killed me both rash and cruel
And wallowed me in a gore of blood."

She arose the very next morning
And dressed as fine as she could be,
Says, "I'll go hunt for my own true lover,
He's a darling bosom friend to me."

She traveled over hills and mountains
And many other places where she were unknown,
Until she came to the lonesome valley
And there she found him all alone.

His rosy cheeks they had all faded,
His lips were white as any snow,
She kissed them over and over, crying,
"You're a darling friend to me, I know."

And when the sister were returning,
The brothers asked where she had been.
"Hush your tongues, hush your tongues, you deceitful villyans,
Not one alone, you both shall hang."

So they arose the very next morning,
A trip across the raging sea;

It rained and it hailed and a storm o'ercame them,
Both a watery grave all in the sea.
It rained and it hailed and a storm o'ercame them,
Both a watery grave all in the sea.

EDWIN IN THE LOWLANDS LOW

Young Edward came to Emily his gold all for to show,
That he had made upon the lands, upon the lowlands low.
"My father keeps a rooming house, all down by yonder lee,
And you go there this night, and until morning be."

Young Emily in her chamber, she dreamed an awful dream,
She dreamed she saw young Edward's blood go flowing like a stream.
She rose so early in the morning, and dressed herself as though
For to go and see young Edward, who ploughed the lowlands low.

"Oh, father, where's that stranger came here last night to dwell?"
"His body's in the ocean and you no tales must tell."
"Oh, father, oh, father, you'll die a public show
For the murdering of young Edward, who ploughed the lowlands low."

Away she went to some councillor to let the deed be known,
The jury found him guilty his trial to come on;
The jury found him guilty, and hanged was he to be
For the murdering of young Edward, who ploughed the lowlands low.

"The fish that's in the ocean swims over young Edward's breast.
While his body's in the ocean, I know his soul's at rest,
While his body's in the ocean, I know his soul's at rest,
For his name it is young Edward, who ploughed the lowlands low."

"Edwin in the Lowlands Low" was recorded by Duncan Emrich from the singing of Mrs. Maud Long of Hot Springs, North Carolina, at Washington, D.C., 1947. Library of Congress AFS record 9152 B2. Laws, M34.

LOVELYE WILLIAM

"There's a tree in father's garden, lovelye William," says she,
"Where young men and young maidens they wait there for me,
And it's while they are sleeping at their own silence rest,
Meet me there, lovelye William, you're the one I love best."

Her mother standing near her these words she did hear,
And cursed be the moments they fell on her ear;
Now her father lies in lust, brave deeds for to do,
With a long and silver dagger he pierced her love through.

"Oh, father, cruel father, since this be your will
The innocent blood of poor William to spill,
I will set me down beside him, since you've him destroyed.
Oh, William, lovelye William, you're my own darling boy.

"Now I'll go to some foreign country, a strange people to see,
Where it's I know no one and no one knows me.
May the grave be got ready since in death we must part,
Oh, William, lovelye William, you're the joy of my heart.

"Oh, it's green grow the rushes, and the tops of them small,
For it's death is a rout that can conquer us all;
And love lies our waiting like a stone on my breast,
And the grave is the first place I expect to find rest."

"Lovelye William" was collected from Mr. Chauncey Leach, Kalkaska, Michigan, 1934, who learned it from his mother, ca. 1890. In Emelyn Elizabeth Gardner and Geraldine Jencks Chickering, *Ballads and Songs of Southern Michigan* (University of Michigan Press) Ann Arbor, 1939, p. 103. A tune is recorded by Vance Randolph from the singing of Mrs. May Kennedy McCord, Springfield, Missouri, 1941. Library of Congress AFS record 5300 A1. The two opening lines above and the last two lines of stanza 2 are from Mrs. McCord's singing. Laws, M35.

Willie

Oh last Thursday morning while playing at ball,
I met my dear Willie, the fairest of them all.
I asked him to take a walk with me a piece down the road.
I'd show him my father's garden and the place of my abode.

"There's a tree in my father's garden, dear Willie," said she,
"Where my young men and maidens they wait upon me.
When my young men and maidens are at their own silent rest,
Meet me there, my dearest Willie; you're the lad I love best."

Now when her old father the truth came to know
He swore to prove his downfall and fatal overthrow.
Her father lay in ambush this deed for to do
And with a rusty broadsword he pierced her love through.

"Oh father, dearest father, is this your good will
The blood of my own precious Willie to spill?"
She threw herself down on the ground where he lay,
"May the heavens shine upon him; he's my own darling boy."

Oh the grave it was made ready and Willie laid in.
"Oh Willie, dear Willie, you're the joy of my soul.
Oh I'll go away to some far country
Where there I know no one and no one knows me.

"Oh green grows the rushes and the tops of them small,
But love is a root that will conquer them all.
Oh love is a burden like a load on my breast
And the grave it is the first place I expect to find rest."

"Willie" is from Carrie B. Grover, *A Heritage of Songs* (privately printed, Gould Academy, Bethel, Maine, n.d.), p. 101. Laws, M35.

Love's Laments

Oh, don't you see that little dove
A-fluttering from her nest?
She sounds so clear in the morning
With the dew all on her breast.

So lonesome was her music,
So mournful was her tune,
She sung so clear in the morning
On the twenty-ninth of June.

I wish I were ten thousand miles,
Or on some lonely shore,
Or on top of the Rocky Mountains
Where the wild beasts howls and roars.

THE MOURNFUL DOVE
(*The False True-Lover*)

"Oh, who will shoe your feet, my love,
And who will glove your hands,
And who will kiss your red rosie lips
Till I return again?"

"My papa will shoe my feet, my love,
My mamma will glove my hand,
No one will kiss my red rosie lips
Till you return again.

"Oh, who will take care of the red rosebush,
Plant out the willow tree,
For it is plain-ly to be seen
By this wide world around
That you have forsaken me."

"If I have forsaken you, my love,
If I've forsaken you,
The fire will freeze to a solid block of ice,
And the raging sea will burn."

"The Mournful Dove" was collected by the Federal Music Project, Works Progress Administration (WPA), Boyd County, Kentucky, ca. 1937. Jean Thomas, Supervisor for Boyd County. Ms., with music, in the Archive of Folk Song, Library of Congress.

"Oh, don't you see that little turtle-dove,
It's flying from pine to pine,
It's mourning for its lost true love
Just like I've mourned for mine."

"As long as the stars hang up above,
And the burning sun does shine,
There's a curley headed girl just a-roaming in the world,
I'll always call her mine."

TEN THOUSAND MILES

"O fare you well, my darling,
O fare you well, my dear,
O fare you well, my darling;
I'm going to volunteer.

"I'm going to the army
To stay for a while,
So far from you, my darling;
It's about ten thousand miles.

"I will see the cannon
As they roll the wheels around;
I will fight for my country,
To the army I am bound.

"O do not wring your lily-white hands,
O mournfully do not cry;
I'm going to the army,
Perhaps in the army die.

"I ask you not to grieve for me
And give your poor heart pain,
For if I live, my darling,
I'll return to you again.

"Ten Thousand Miles" was recorded by Alan Lomax from the singing of Aunt Molly Jackson of Clay County, Kentucky, at New York City, 1939. Library of Congress record LP2.

LOVE

"I'll return to you again, my love,
If I keep my life;
I'll come back to you, my love,
And you shall be my wife.

"Well-uh who will shoe your feet, my love?
Now who will glove your hand?
And who will kiss your rosy lips
While I'm in a distant land?"

"My father will shoe my feet, my love;
My mother will glove my hand,
And as for kissing my rosy lips,
There'll be no other man."

"O fare you well, my darling,
O fare you well, my dear.
Be true to me, my own sweetheart,
I'm bound to leave you here."

WHEN YOU AND I MUST PART

Times are swiftly drawing nigh
When you and I must part,
But little do you think or care
For the great wish of my heart.

Your eyes are of some sparkling
    blue,
Like diamonds they do shine;
Your teeth they are so pearly white,
They charm this heart of mine.

The crow that is so very black
It surely will turn white;
If I ever turn false-hearted to you
Bright days will turn to night.

The sky may roar, my own true-
    love,
The sea may howl and whine,
If I ever prove false-hearted to you
The rocks will melt and run to
    wine.

I wish I were ten thousand miles,
Ten thousand miles or more,
On the top of some high mountain
Where the high blasts howl and
    roar.

I wish I were ten thousand miles
In some big western town;
I'd set my foot on some fine ship
And sail the ocean around.

"When You and I Must Part" was collected by Harvey H. Fuson from Mary Carr. In Fuson, *Ballads of the Kentucky Highlands*, London, 1931, p. 112. Without music.

THE ROCKY MOUNTAINS

I've been in jail from slander
For seven long years or more;
I lived a bold commander
Where the gun and cannon roar.

I can build a ship, my love,
Without the wood of trees;
This ship will burst asunder, love,
If I prove false to thee.

If I prove false to you, my love,
The rocks will melt and run,
Your fire will freeze throughout, my love,
The raging sea will burn.

Oh, don't you see that little dove
A-fluttering from her nest?
She sounds so clear in the morning
With the dew all on her breast.

So lonesome was her music,
So mournful was her tune,
She sung so clear in the morning
On the twenty-ninth of June.

I wish I were ten thousand miles,
Or on some lonely shore,
Or on top of the Rocky Mountains
Where the wild beasts howls and roars.

"The Rocky Mountains" was recorded by Herbert Halpert from the singing of Finley Adams, Dunham, Kentucky, 1939. Library of Congress AFS record 2770 A2.

NO CHANGE IN ME

If there is no change in the ocean,
There is no change in the sea;
If there be no change in you, my
   love,
There'll be no change in me.

   The storms are on the ocean;
   The sea begins to roar;
   The world shall lose its motion,
   If I prove false to you.

I asked your mama for you;
She said you was too young;
I wish I never had seen you,
Nor love had never been born.

Oh! It is sad to leave you, dear;
Oh! It is sad to part.
It's sad to leave you, darling;
It almost breaks my heart.

I have a ship on the ocean,
All lined with silver and gold;
Before my love shall suffer,
I'll have it anchored and sold.

If I prove false to you, my love,
The rocks will melt and run,
The fire will freeze and be like ice,
And the raging sea will burn.

LONESOME DOVE

Down in some lonesome piney grove,
Down in some lonesome piney grove,
Down in some lonesome piney grove,
My little dove she sets and moans.

My little dove, you're not by yourself,
My little dove, you're not by yourself,
My little dove, you're not by yourself,
For my dear Polly is by your side.

"No Change in Me" was collected by Mellinger E. Henry from Ray Bohanan, Indian Gap, Sevierville, Sevier County, Tennessee, 1929. In Henry, *Folksongs from the Southern Highlands*, New York, 1938, p. 272. Without music.

"Lonesome Dove" was collected by Mrs. Mellinger Henry from the singing of Mrs. Samuel Harmon, Cade's Cove, Blount County, Tennessee, August 1930. See Mellinger E. Henry, "Ballads and Folk-Songs from the Southern Highlands," *JAF*, 45 (1932):83–85.

LOVE

I once, like you, I had a mate,
I once, like you, I had a mate,
I once, like you, I had a mate,
But now, like you, I'm disalayed.*

Consumption seized my love so dear,
Consumption seized my love so dear,
Consumption seized my love so dear,
And preyed on her for seven long years.

Her red rosy cheeks, her pretty blue eyes,
Her red rosy cheeks, her pretty blue eyes,
Her red rosy cheeks, her pretty blue eyes,
Just like a rose that blooms and dies.

God bless them arms that bounds me round,
God bless them arms that bounds me round,
God bless them arms that bounds me round,
Lie mouldering away in the cold ground.

The Little Dove

As I sat in a lonesome grove,
Sat o'er my head a little dove.
For its lost mate began to coo;
It made me think of my mate too.

"O little dove, you're not alone,
I was once like you constrained to mourn,
Once like you I had a mate,
But now like you I'm desolate.

"Consumption seized my lover dear
And lingered on for one long year,
Till death came at the break of day
And lovely Mary him† did slay.

* Desolate.
† This word should be "he."

"The Little Dove" was recorded by Alan Lomax from the singing of Aunt Molly Jackson of Clay County, Kentucky, at New York City, 1939. Library of Congress record LP2.

"O death, grim death, did not stop there,
I had a babe to me most dear;
Death like a virtue* came again
And took from me my little Jane.

"She said to me: 'My dearest friend,
Go on, prove faithful to the end
And soar on high to that blessed shore,
There we will meet to part no more.'

"O hasten on the happy day,
When I must leave this clod of clay
And soar on high to that blessed plain;
There I'll meet Mary and my Jane."

Newberry
(*Lonesome Dove*)

One day, while in a lonesome grove,
Sat o'er my head a little dove;
For her lost mate began to coo,
Which made me think of my mate too.

Ah! little dove, you're not alone,
For I, like you, can only mourn;
I once, like you did have a mate
But now, like you, am desolate.

Consumption seized my love severe,
And preyed upon her one long year,
Till death came at the break of day,
And my poor Mary he did slay.

Her sparkling eyes, and blooming cheeks
Withered like the rose, and died;
The arms that once embraced me round,
Lie mouldering under the cold ground.

* Vulture.

"Newberry." *The Social Harp*, 1855, p. 131.

LOVE

But death, grim death, did not stop here;
I had one child, to me most dear;
He, like a vulture, came again,
And took from me my little Jane.

But, bless the Lord, his Word is given,
Declaring babes are heirs of heaven;
Then cease, my heart, to mourn for Jane,
Since my small loss is her great gain.

I have a hope that cheers my breast,
To think my love has gone to rest;
For, while her dying tongue could move,
She praised the Lord for pardoning love.

Shout on, ye heavenly powers above,
While I this lonesome desert rove;
My master's work will soon be done,
And then I'll join you in your song.

O, hasten on that happy day,
When I must leave this clod of clay,
And soar aloft o'er yon blest plain,
And there meet Mary and my Jane.

THE GREENBACK DOLLAR

I don't want your greenback dollar,
I don't want your silver chain;
All I want is your heart, darling,
To say you'll take me back again.

Won't you love me, little darling,
Just to give my poor heart ease?
When my back is turned on you, darling,
You can court just who you please.

"The Greenback Dollar" was recorded by Alan Lomax from the singing of George Turner, Middlesborough, Kentucky, 1937. Library of Congress AFS record 1404 A2.

You have wronged me, little darling,
But I'll always wish you well.
My love for you, my little darling,
There's no tongue can ever tell.

You slighted me, my little darling,
You have also broke my heart.
I love you more than ever, darling,
Oh, how can I from you depart?

When I'm dead and in my coffin,
And they've laid me down to rest,
Won't you one time, little darling,
Think of the one that loves you best?

When they've laid me down to rest, dear,
Neath the weeping willow tree,
As I slumber on in silence,
Won't you shed one tear for me?

I will soon be with the angels
On that bright and peaceful shore,
Soon my heart will close in slumber,
Then my heart will ache no more.

But I don't want your greenback dollar,
I don't want your silver chain,
But I trust we'll meet up in heaven,
Where the heart will know no pain.

FORSAKEN

(*He Once Did Love with Fond Affection*)

He once did love with fond affection
And his heart was all for me,
Until a dark-haired girl proclaimed him,
And now he cares no more for me.

"Forsaken" was collected by Mellinger E. Henry from Miss Mary E. King, Gatlinburg, Sevier County, Tennessee, 1930, and reported, without music, in Henry, "Ballads and Folk-Songs from the Southern Highlands," *JAF*, 45 (1932):70–71.

LOVE

So go and leave me if you wish to;
Never let me cross your mind;
For if you think me so unworthy,
Go and leave me, never mind.

It's many a night with him I wandered;
It's many an evening with him I spent;
I thought his heart was mine forever,
But I found I was only lent.

It's many a night while you lie sleeping,
Dreaming out your sweet repose;
While I, poor girl, I'm broken-hearted,
Listening to the wind that blows.

So go and leave me, if you wish to,
And from me you will be free,
For in your heart you love another
And in my grave I'd rather be.

There's only three things that I wish for:
That is my coffin, shroud and grave;
And when I'm dead, love, come and see me,
And kiss the heart you once betrayed.

PRETTY SARO

Way down in yonders low valley, in some lonesome place,
Where the small birds doth whisper, their notes do increase,
And I'll think on pretty Saro, her ways are complete,
And I want no better pastime than to be with my sweet.

It's fare you well, Father, likewise and Mother, too,
I'm going to travel this country all through,
And when I get tired, I'll sit down and weep,
And I'll think on pretty Saro, my darling and sweet.

"Pretty Saro" was recorded by Alan and Elizabeth Lomax from the singing of M. J. Mullins, Floress, Kentucky, 1937. Library of Congress AFS record 1592 A.

It's not this long journey I'm a-dreading to go,
Nor the country I'm leaving, but the debts that I owe.
There ain't but one thing that grieves me or troubles my mind,
That's leaving pretty Saro, my darling, behind.

My true lover won't have me, as I understand,
She wants a freeholder and I have no land,
But I can maintain her on silver and gold
And as many of the fine things as my love's house can hold.

I came into this country in eighteen and forty-nine,
I saw many true lovers here, but I never saw mine.
I looked all around me and I were alone,
And me a poor soldier and a long ways from home.

I wish I were a good poet, could write a fine hand,
I would write my love a letter that she could understand,
And I'd send it by the water where the highways doth flow.
And I'll think on pretty Saro wherever I go.

I wish I were a little dove, had wings and could fly,
All through my love's dwelling, it's right there I'd draw near,
And in her lily-white arms all night long I'd lie,
And watch out some little window till the dawning of day.

I've strove on the old Gauley, I've strove on the main,
It was for to get to pretty Saro, but it were all in vain.
I've strove on the old Gauley, on the mountain's set brow,
And I once loved pretty Saro, and I loved her till now.

THYME

When I was young and in my prime,
I flourished like a vine.
There came along a young man

"Thyme" was recorded by Alan Lomax from the singing of Mrs. Carrie Grover of Gorham, Maine, at Washington, D.C., 1941. Library of Congress AFS record 4460 A. Text with music also in Carrie B. Grover, *A Heritage of Songs* (privately printed, Gould Academy, Bethel, Maine, n.d.), p. 103.

And stole away my thyme, thyme,
And stole away my thyme.

Come, all you pretty fair maids
Who flourish in your prime,
Be sure to keep your garden clear,
Let no man steal your thyme, thyme,
Let no man steal your thyme.

GREEN WILLOW, GREEN WILLOW

Come all you pretty fair maids
Who flourish in your prime,
Be sure to keep your garden clean,
Let no one take your thyme.

My thyme it is all gone away,
I cannot plant anew,
And in the place where my thyme stood
It's all growed up in rue.

Stand up, stand up, you pretty hope,
Stand up and do not die,
And if your lover comes to you,
Pick up your wings and fly.

The pink it is a pretty flower,
But it will bud too soon,
I have a posy of my own,
I'm sure 'twill wait till June.

In June comes in the primrose flower,
But it is not for me,
I will pull up my primrose flower
And plant a willow tree.

Green willow, green willow,
With sorrow mixed among,

"Green Willow, Green Willow" was recorded by Vance Randolph from the singing of Mrs. May Kennedy McCord, Springfield, Missouri, 1938. Library of Congress AFS record 8931 A6.

To tell all the wide world
I loved a false young man.

IBBY DAMSEL

Some "old Robin Down" they call me,
But I'm a weaver by my trade,
In this fair berth, in which I'm dwelling,
And Ibby Damsel my heart betrayed.

Her hair's as black as a raven's feather,
That do sit on yon willow tree,
Her sparkling eyes they're so enticing,
But from her chamber I can't get free.

Her heart as sweet as any posy,
Her cheeks are of the rosy red,
Her sparkling eyes are so enticing,
Her eyebrows wove with a golden thread.

KITTY KLINE

Do you ever think of me, Kitty Kline?
Do you ever think of me, darling one?
Do you ever think of me
When I'm sailing on the sea,
Do you ever think of me, darling one?

"Ibby Damsel" was collected by Cecil J. Sharp from the singing of Mrs. Rose Hensley, Carmen, North Carolina, 1916. See his *English Folksongs from the Southern Appalachians*, II, 137.

Alan Jabbour of the Library of Congress has cogently pointed out that "Ibby" is not part of any name and that Sharp did not understand its use: it is a descriptive diminutive, like "itty bitty baby" or "itsy bitsy." The line should properly read "And ibby damsel . . ." The damsel is an "ibby" one, but beautifully ibby enough in this instance to have turned a man's heart and given us this wonderful lyric.

"Kitty Kline" was collected by the Federal Music Project, Works Progress Administration (WPA), Boyd County, Kentucky, ca. 1937. Jean Thomas, Supervisor for Boyd County. Ms., with music, in the Archive of Folk Song, Library of Congress.

LOVE

Sometimes I wish I were dead
And buried on the banks of the sea
Where all of my friends could gather around
And see the last of me.

   Oh how I love Kitty Kline, Kitty Kline,
   Oh how I love that girl,
   I love her so well no human tongue can tell,
   Oh how I love that girl.

If I were a bird, a little bird,
I would never build on the ground.
I would build my nest in some high oak tree
Where the bad boys could not tear me down.

If I were a bee, a little bee,
I would never steal the honey from a rose;
I would steal one kiss from my true love's lips
And back to the hive I would go.

   Oh how I love Kitty Kline, Kitty Kline,
   Oh how I love that girl,
   I love her so well no human tongue can tell,
   Oh how I love that girl.

FREE LITTLE BIRD

I'm as free a little bird as I can be;
I'm as free a little bird as I can be;
I'm as free a little bird as ever spoke a word;
I'm as free a little bird as I can be.

Go bring me a chair and set me down;
Go bring me a pen and ink to write it down;
And at the end of every line that I write down
The tears will come falling to the ground.

"Free Little Bird" was collected by Harvey H. Fuson from Laura Lawson. In Fuson, *Ballads of the Kentucky Highlands*, London, 1931, p. 130. Without music.

If I were a little fish,
I would never bite the hook any more;
I would fly away down in the middle of the sea,
Where the bad boys cannot bother me.

If I were a little dove,
I would fly from vine to vine,
And let you weep for your true-love,
Just as I weep for mine.

If I were a little bird,
I would never build my nest on the ground;
I would build my nest in sweet Kitty's breast,
Where the bad boys cannot tear it down.

If I were a honey bee,
I would never steal the honey from the cup;
I would steal one kiss from my sweet Kitty's lips,
And I'd fly away to old Tennessee.

I cried all day like a child,
And I cried all day the day before;
And I ain't going to cry any more.

IN THE PINES

True love, true love, what have I done
That you should treat me so?
You've caused me to weep, you've caused me to mourn,
You've caused me to leave my home.

In the pines, in the pines, where the sun never shines,
I'll shiver when the cold wind blows,
In the pines, in the pines, where the sun never shines,
I'll shiver when the cold wind blows.

"In the Pines" was recorded by Artus M. Moser from the singing of June Ebbs and Laura Dixon, Hot Springs, North Carolina, 1946. Library of Congress AFS record 7925 A1.

LOVE

"Little girl, little girl, where'd you stay last night?
Not even your mother knows."
"I stayed in the pines where the sun never shines,
And shiver when the cold wind blows."

The longest train I ever saw,
Was fourteen coaches long,
The only boy I ever loved
Is on that train and gone.

In the pines, in the pines, where the sun never shines,
I'll shiver when the cold wind blows,
In the pines, in the pines, where the sun never shines,
I'll shiver when the cold wind blows.

WALY, WALY

When cockle shells turn silver bells
And mussels grow on every tree,
When blooms the rose 'neath wintry snows,
Then will my false love be true to me.

Oh, waly, waly, but love is bonny
A little while when it is new,
But when it's old, it groweth cold
And fades away like morning dew.

Oh, had I wist before I kissed
That love had been so ill to win,
I'd locked my heart in case of gold
And pinned it with a silver pin.

Oh, waly, waly, but love is bonny
A little while when it is new,
But when it's old, it groweth cold
And fades away like morning dew.

"Waly, Waly" was recorded by Duncan Emrich from the singing of Eugenia Blount Anderson of Ruxton, Maryland, at Washington, D.C., 1947. Mrs. Anderson had acquired the song orally in Georgia. Library of Congress AFS record 8934 A2.

LITTLE SPARROW
(*Come All You Young and Handsome Ladies*)

Come all you young and handsome ladies,
Be careful how you court young men,
They're like a star on the bright May morning,
They first appear and then they're gone.

They tell to you some pleading story,
They vow to you their love is true,
Straight 'way they go and court some other,
And that is the love they have for you.

If I had a-knowed before I courted
Love would have gone so hard with me,
I'd 'a' put my heart in a golden locket
And locked it up with a silver key.

The soundest apple soon will rotten,
The warmest love will soon grow cold,
Young men's advise is so uncertain,
I pray, young girls, don't be too bold.

He took my heart as if it blossomed
And crushed it through his little white hand,
Dear Lord, look down on me a sinner
If ever I trust another man.

If I had wings of some small sparrow,
If I had wings to fly so high,
I'd fly away to my false true lover,
And while he talked I'd sit and cry.

But as it is I am no sparrow,
Nor have I no wings to fly,
So I'll sit down all broken-hearted
And try to pass my troubles by.

"Little Sparrow" was collected by the Federal Music Project, Works Progress Administration (WPA). Boyd County, Kentucky, ca. 1937. Jean Thomas, Supervisor for Boyd County, Ms., with music, in the Archive of Folk Song, Library of Congress.

THE WEEPING WILLOW

Some say my love has proved unfaithful,
That he has broken every vow;
That he has learned to love another lady,
And my heart is broken now.

Bury me beneath the willow,
Beneath the weeping willow tree,
So he may know where I am sleeping,
Perhaps some day he will weep for me.

Many hours we have spent together,
But we have spent them all in vain;
But now it breaks my heart, dear darling,
To think we never meet again.

Go tell my love that I am dying,
And my feeble eyes be closed.
Tell him to come and see me buried
Beneath the weeping willow tree.

To-morrow was our wedding day.
O God, O God, O where is he?
He's gone to seek another lady
That he loves more dear than me.

Take a message to the lady,
The one that stole my love from me;
Tell her to come and see me buried
Beneath the weeping willow tree.

Bury me beneath the willow,
Beneath the weeping willow tree,
So he may know where I am sleeping,
Perhaps some day he will weep for me.

"The Weeping Willow" was collected by Harvey H. Fuson from Evie Owens. In Fuson, *Ballads of the Kentucky Highlands*, London, 1931, p. 126. Without music.

THE LOVER PROVED FALSE

As I walked out one May morning,
When the small birds sang so sweet,
I leaned myself against an old oak tree
To see two lovers meet.
To see two lovers meet, my dear,
And to hear what they would say.
That I might learn a little of their mind,
Before I went away.

"Come in, come, my own true love,
And sit awhile by me,
For it's been three quarters of a year or more
Since together we have been."
"Oh, I can't come in and I won't sit down
For I've not one moment of time,
And your hand it is engaged to another fair maid
And your heart is none of mine.

"Now when your heart was mine, my love,
And your head upon my breast
You could make me believe by the stories you told
That the sun it rose in the west.
Oh, I never will believe a young man again,
Let his eyes be black or brown,
Excepting he was up on yonder gallows tree
And my faith could bring him down."

"The Lover Proved False" is from Carrie B. Grover, *A Heritage of Songs* (privately printed, Gould Academy, Bethel, Maine, n.d.), p. 27.

SALLY'S GARDEN

As down thru Sally's garden one evening as I chanced to stray,
I met my true love, Sandy, just at the closing of the day.
They bade me take love easy just as the leaves fall from the tree,
But I being young and foolish, to wed with him I did agree.

Now my parents they are angry, and they swear my love they will undo
For keeping of his company although his heart to me was true.
But unless they do confine me or banish my true love forever more,
I'll wed my true love, Sandy, at home or on some foreign shore.

Now wasn't I a foolish girl to ever wed with any man?
But it was my love and my good nature that has brought me here in the way
    I am.
But if you were a rake, love, or even were a rover, too,
I'd sooner wed with Sandy than with any man I ever knew.

Oh, I wish I was in Dublin City with my true love along with me,
With money to support us and to keep us in good company,
With money to support us and a flowing bowl on every side.
Come drink, my boys, you're welcome, for I am young and the world is
    wide.

THE WAGONER'S LAD

I'm a poor little girl;　　　　He courted me daily
My fortune's been bad;　　　By night and by day;
I've a long time been courting　But now he is loaded
A wagoner lad.　　　　　And going away.

"Sally's Garden" is from Carrie B. Grover, *A Heritage of Songs* (privately printed, Gould Academy, Bethel, Maine, n.d.), p. 12.

"The Wagoner's Lad" was collected by Mellinger E. Henry from Cleophas L. Franklin, Crossnore, Avery County, North Carolina, 1929. In Henry, *Folksongs from the Southern Highlands*, New York, 1938, p. 279. Without music.

So hard is the fortune
Of poor womankind;
They are always controlled
And always confined.

Controlled by their parents
Till they are made wives;
Then slaves for their husbands
The rest of their lives.

"Your wagon ain't greasy;
Your bill it ain't paid;
Come, sit you down by me,
For I know you can stay."

"My wagon is greased;
My bill it is paid;
So fare you well, Polly,
No longer to stay."

He mounted his horses
With his whip in his hand:
"So fare you well, Polly,
No longer to stand."

So early that morning
As he did arrive
He crossed over the mountain
With tears in his eyes,

To think he must leave her
And see her no more;
He left his girl weeping
On the New River shore.

"I can love a light love;
I can love long;
I can love an old sweetheart
Till a new one comes on.

"I love them and kiss them
And think it proves kind;
Then turn my back upon them
And alter my mind.

"I build my love a castle
On yon mountain high,
Where the wild geese will hear her
As they pass by.

"Where the wild geese will hear
Her cries and her moans,
Sweet instruments of music
And the firing of guns."

OLD SMOKY

On top of old Smoky
All covered with snow
I lost my true lover
By courting too slow.

Courting is a pleasure,
Parting is grief,
But hard-hearted parents
Are worse than a thief.

"Old Smoky" was recorded by Duncan Emrich from the singing of I. G. Greer of Thomasville, North Carolina, at Washington, D.C., 1945. Library of Congress record LP14.

LOVE

"Your parents are against me,
And mine are against you,
But, Nancy, I love you
Whatever they do.

"I'm going now to leave you,
To tell you goodbye,
And leave you a-weeping
On Smoky so high."

"It's raining, it's hailing,
The moon gives no light,
Your horse can't see to travel
This dark, lonesome night.

"Go put up your horse now
And feed him some hay,
Come sit down beside me
As long as you'll stay."

"My horse he is hungry,
But he won't eat your hay,
Your daddy's so durn stingy
I'll feed on the way.

"Old Smoky, old Smoky,
Keep watch o'er my love,
She's as true as your mountains
And as pure as the dove."

THE CUCKOO

The cuckoo is a bonny bird,
She sings as she flies,
She brings us glad tidings,
She tells us no lies,
She sips the sweet flowers,
To make her voice clear,
And she always sing "Cuck-oo"
When summer is near.

Our meetings are pleasure,
Our partings are grief,
But a false-hearted young man
Is worse than a thief,
For a thief can but rob you
And take all you have,
But a false-hearted young man
Will bring you to the grave.

The grave it will rot you
And bring you to dust.
A false-hearted young man
No maiden can trust.
They will kiss you and court you,
Fair maids, to deceive,
And there's not one in twenty
That you can believe.

Oh, I can love little
Or I can love long,
I can love a new sweetheart
When the old one is gone.
I can tell them I love them
To give their hearts ease,
And when their back's to me,
I will love whom I please.

"The Cuckoo" was recorded by Sidney Robertson Cowell from the singing of Mrs. Carrie Grover of Gorham, Maine, at Teaneck, New Jersey, 1941. Library of Congress AFS record 4691 A2. Text with music also in Carrie B. Grover, *A Heritage of Songs* (privately printed, Gould Academy, Bethel, Maine, n.d.), p. 40.

MY LOVE, SHE PASSED ME BY

I rode to church last Sunday;
My love, she passed me by;
I saw her mind was changing
By movement of her eye.

Oh, have you forgot last Sunday
When you give me your lily-white hand
And said if ever you was married,
I sure would be the man?

But now you have broke your promise;
Go home with who you please.
While my poor heart are aching,
You are lying at your ease.

I wish I was in some seaport,
Or in some seaport town;
I set my foot on seaboard
And sail this ocean round.

Some says I love you;
I know that to be true;
And some says we will marry,
But that's more than I can do.

For my people is against it
And yours are the same;
And my name is on your book, love,
Please rub out my name.

For a false-hearted young man
Is worse than a thief;
For a thief will only rob you and take what you have,
But a false-hearted young man will bring you to your grave.

"My Love, She Passed Me By" was collected by Mellinger E. Henry from the singing of Mrs. Samuel Harmon of Cade's Cove, Tennessee, August, 1929. See Mellinger E. Henry, "Ballads and Folk-Songs from the Southern Highlands," *JAF*, 45 (1932):103–105.

LOVE

The grave will only molder you
And turn you to dust;
There's not a boy in a thousand
That a young girl can trust.

I'M GOING TO GEORGIA

I once loved a young man as dear as my life,
And ofttimes I told him I'd make him his wife.
I've fulfilled my promise, I made him his wife
And see what I've come to by being his wife.

   I'm going to Georgia,
   I'm going to roam,
   And if ever I get there,
   I'll make it my home.

My cheeks were once red, as red as a rose,
But now they are as pale as the lilies that grow;
My children all hungry and crying for bread;
My husband, a drunkard, Lord, I wish I were dead!

Come, all young ladies, take warning by me:
Never plant your affections on a green, young tree;
For the leaves will wither and the buds they will die;
Some young man might fool you as one has fooled I.

They'll hug you, they'll kiss you, they'll tell you more lies
Than the cross-ties on the railroad or the stars in the skies;
They'll tell you they love you like stars in the West
But along comes corn whiskey; they love it the best.

Go, build me a cabin on the mountain so high
Where the wild birds and turtledove can hear my sad cry.

"I'm Going to Georgia" was collected by Mellinger E. Henry from Mary E. King, Catlin-
burg, Sevier County, Tennessee, 1929. In Henry, *Folksongs from the Southern Highlands*,
New York, 1938, p. 278. Without music.

FAREWELL, SWEET MARY

Miss Sallie D. Jones of Hillsboro, Pocahontas County, West Virginia, wrote in 1917: "The words of 'Farewell, Sweet Mary' were learned from a youth who was enamored of a girl whose name was Mary, who lived in a farm house just over the hill from his home. She would have none of his advances, however, and he used to go to the top of the hill, and in a rich, mellow voice make the welkin ring with the words of this song. This was in Pendleton County, about forty-seven years ago."

> Your parents don't like me,
>   And well do I know,
> They say I'm not worthy,
>   To knock at your door.
>
>   Farewell, sweet Mary,
>   I bid you adieu,
>   I am ruined forever,
>   By the loving of you.

> I'll build me a castle,
>   On the mountain so high,
> Where the wild geese may see me,
>   As they do pass by.
>
> I'll eat when I'm hungry,
>   And drink when I'm dry;
> I'll think of sweet Mary,
>   And sit down and cry.

> Farewell, sweet Mary,
>   I bid you adieu,
> I am ruined forever,
>   By the loving of you.

"Farewell, Sweet Mary" was communicated to John Harrington Cox by Miss Sallie D. Jones. In Cox, *Folksongs of the South* (Harvard) Cambridge, 1925 (Dover reprint, New York, 1967), p. 433. The words of the lyric are recognizably borrowed from "The Wagoner's Lad," "Old Smoky," "Jack of Diamonds," "Down in the Valley," and appear in other love lyrics as well. A nice mélange.

SO I LET HER GO

I once knew a lass and I've oft heard her tell
She ne'er knew a lad that she loved half so well.
I thought I would take her and make her my wife,
And I would live happy for the rest of my life,
    But I found it not so,
    So I let her go.
I don't care a fig for her, so I let her go.

I went for to meet her one fair summer's night,
And all the way long I was filled with delight,
And all the way long I was filled with her charms
Till I found she was locked in another man's arms.
    And I found it was so,
    So I let her go.
I don't care a fig for her, so now let her go.

They will promise to twenty, they will promise to one,
They will promise to thirty and be constant to none.
They will court you awhile and still have in their mind
To go with some other and leave you behind.
    And I found it was so,
    So I let her go.
I don't care a fig for her, so now let her go.

There are as good fish as e'er caught in the sea,
And I will have one or, by Jove, I'll go free.
I will drink the King's health, all my sorrows to drown,
For I am determined to sail the world around,
    I intend to do so,
    So I let her go.
I don't care a fig for her, so now let her go.

"So I Let Her Go" was recorded by Sidney Robertson Cowell from the singing of Mrs. Carrie Grover of Gorham, Maine, at Teaneck, New Jersey, 1941. Library of Congress AFS record 4697 A2. Text with music also in Carrie B. Grover, *A Heritage of Songs* (privately printed, Gould Academy, Bethel, Maine, n.d.), pp. 61–62.

GOODBYE, LITTLE BONNY BLUE EYES

Goodbye, little bonny blue eyes,
Goodbye, little bonny blue eyes,
I'll see you again, but the Lord knows when,
Goodbye, little bonny blue eyes.

It's my little bonny blue eyes,
It's my little bonny blue eyes,
Six weeks today she left this town,
It's my little darling, you've gone.

Then lay your hand in mine,
Then lay your hand in mine,
If you love me like I love you,
Then lay your hand in mine.

Ninety days in jail's too long,
Ninety days in jail's too long,
Ninety days in jail's too long to stay
From my little bonny blue eyes.

Oh, darling, I'm cross about you,
Oh, darling, I'm cross about you,
I'm cross about you for the way
 you do,
Oh, darling, I'm cross about you.

Then lay your hand in mine,
Then lay your hand in mine,
If you love me like I love you,
Then lay your hand in mine.

I'm a-going to leave you now,
I'm a-going to leave you now,
I'm a-going away, too long to stay
From my little bonny blue eyes.

I'm going to the Georgia line,
I'm going to the Georgia line,
The prettiest girl I ever did see
Has gone to the Georgia line.

Then lay your hand in mine,
Then lay your hand in mine,
If you love me like I love you,
Then lay your hand in mine.

I'm going to leave this town,
I'm going to leave this town,
To see you again but the Lord knows when,
I'm a-going to leave this town.

"Goodbye, Little Bonny Blue Eyes" was recorded by Duncan Emrich from the singing of Bascom Lamar Lunsford of South Turkey Creek, North Carolina, at Washington, D.C., 1949. Library of Congress AFS record 9478 A3.

NEW JAIL

Oh, meet me tonight in the moonlight,
Please meet me in the moonlight alone,
Oh, I have a sad story to tell you,
Must be told in the moonlight alone.

    I wish I had someone to love me,
    Someone to call me their own,
    I wish I had someone to live with,
    For I'm tired of living alone

I'm a-going to my new jail tomorrow,
The place where I've never been before,
With those cold prison bars all around me
And my head on a pillow of stone.

Oh, if I had a ship on the ocean,
All filled with silver and gold,
Before my true love should suffer
I would have that ship anchored and sold.

I'm a-going to my new jail tomorrow,
Going there to pay on my fine,
I'm a-leaving of my country
And my darling girl behind.

I'm a-going to my new jail tomorrow,
The place you never can rest,
And if you see my darling
Tell her I love her the best.

Oh, if I had wings like an angel,
Had wings and I could fly,
I would fly to the arms of my darling
And there I'd be willing to die.

    I wish I had someone to love me,
    Somebody to call me their own,

"New Jail" is from Dorothy Scarborough, *A Song Catcher in Southern Mountains*, Columbia University Press, 1937, pp. 347 and 449.

Somebody to stay with me always
And never to leave me alone.

MY HOME'S ACROSS THE SMOKY MOUNTAINS

My home's across the Smoky Mountains,
My home's across the Smoky Mountains,
My home's across the Smoky Mountains,
And I'll never get to see you any more.

I'm leaving on a Monday morning,
I'm leaving on a Monday morning,
I'm leaving on a Monday morning,
And I'll never get to see you any more.

Goodbye, little sugar darling,
Goodbye, little sugar darling,
Goodbye, little sugar darling,
For I'll never get to see you any more.

Rock my baby, feed it candy,
Rock my baby, feed it candy,
Rock my baby, feed it candy,
For I'll never get to see you any more.

My home's across the Smoky Mountains,
My home's across the Smoky Mountains,
My home's across the Smoky Mountains,
And I'll never get to see you any more.

"My Home's Across the Smoky Mountains" was recorded by Sidney Robertson Cowell from the singing of Bascom Lamar Lunsford of South Turkey Creek, North Carolina, at Leicester, North Carolina, 1936. Library of Congress AFS record 3155 B2.

THE STORMY SCENES OF WINTER

The stormy scenes of winter incline to frost and snow.
Dark clouds around us gather and stormy winds do blow.
The girl that I have chosen to be my only dear,
Her scornful heart is frozen and safe locked up, I fear.

I went one night to see my love; she proved most scornfully.
I asked her if she'd marry, she would not answer me.
"The night it is far spent and it is near to the break of day.
Come, love, I want an answer, come tell to me, I pray."

"I tell you, sir, quite plainly, I choose a single life,
I never thought it suiting that I should be your wife.
I have another more suiting and it's you I'll lay one side,
Come take this for an answer and for yourself provide."

The little birds sing sweetly all in the summer time,
And I, too, would sing sweetly if Flora was but mine.
Some people talk of pleasure, but there's no joy for me.
Farewell to this world of pleasure since fortune frowned on me.

I'll steer my course to Flanders, I'll lead a single life.
Among the bold commanders my gun shall be my wife,
And when I do get money to some tavern I will go,
And I'll drink a health to Flora, although she answers no.

"The Stormy Scenes of Winter" was recorded by Sidney Robertson Cowell from the singing of Mrs. Carrie Grover of Gorham, Maine, at Teaneck, New Jersey, 1941. Library of Congress AFS record 4690 B1. Text with music also in Carrie B. Grover, *A Heritage of Songs* (privately printed, Gould Academy, Bethel, Maine, n.d.), p. 152. Laws, H12.

The Rejected Lover
or The Lonesome Scenes of Winter

The lonesome scenes of winter incline to frost and snow,
Dark clouds they hover 'round me, the stormy winds do blow.

The little birds sing sweetly around on every vine,
My heart would go a-courting if Mary would be mine.

Last night I went to see her, she appeared most scornfully,
I asked her if she'd marry, she wouldn't consent to me.

The night was fast advancing about the break of day,
"I'm waiting for an answer, kind Miss, what do you say?"

"Oh, now as I will tell you, I choose a single life,
I never thought it suited for me to be your wife.

"Now take this for your answer and for yourself provide,
I've found another suitor and you I lay aside."

"As now as you are for changing the old one for the new,
I'll mount the briny ocean with sorrow adieu.

"I'll seek some other fair maiden where love may have its fill,
This world is wide and lonely, if one won't another will."

"The Rejected Lover" was recorded by John A. Lomax and Laurence Powell from the singing of Mrs. Emma Dusenbury, Mena, Arkansas, 1936. Library of Congress AFS record 866 B2. Laws, H12.

Love's Tragedies and Misfortunes

"I'll bury myself in this wide, deep sea
For the blue waves to roll over me."

She plunged her fair body in the wide deep sea
For the blue waves to roll over her pretty blue eyes.

POLLY VAUGHN
(Molly Bawn)

"Come all ye jolly fellows, who delight in a gun,
Beware of late fowling at the setting of the sun,
For I was out fowling, it was just before dark,
And I shot my own true love, I wounded her heart.

"The evening being a late one, when the shower came on,
She crept up under a thorn bush the shower to shun.
With an apron pinned around her, I took her for a swan;
And now to my sorrow, I killed my Polly Vaughn."

He threw down his rifle, to the house he did run,
Saying, "Father, oh, father! Lord, what have I done!
I've killed a dear female, was the joy of my life,
And if she had-a lived, oh, I'd have made her my wife."

Up stepped his old father, with his hair all so gray,
Saying, "Jimmy, oh Jimmy, pray don't run away,
But stay in your own country, till your trial comes on,
And I think you'll be cleared by the laws of our land.

"Polly Vaughn" was recorded by Sidney Robertson Cowell and Laurence Powell from the singing of Mrs. Emma Dusenbury, Mena, Arkansas, 1936. Library of Congress record AFS 3234 B2. Laws, 036.

The day of his trial, to her uncle she appeared,
Saying, "Uncle, oh uncle, Jimmy Reynolds is cleared.
With a apron pinned around me, he took me for a swan,
And now to his sorrow, he killed his Polly Vaughn."

You girls of Carolina need not to be glad,
Polly Vaughn is the fairest, although she is dead.
These girls were all seated, all out in a row,
Polly Vaughn is the fairest in a mountain of snow.

THE SHEFFIELD 'PRENTICE

I was brought up in Sheffield, all of a high degree,
My parents doted on me, they had no child but me;
They rolled me in the riches all of a costly ware,
They bound me as a 'prentice and sent me off afar.

I had not been in Holland months more than two or three,
Until my youngest mistress grew very fond of me;
She told me of gold and silver that she had in her hand,
If I'd consent to marry her, she would be at my command.

Says I, "You honored lady, I cannot wed you both;
I've lately made a promise, I'm bound to fill my oath,
To wed with none but Molly, that charming chambermaid.
Excuse me now, dear mistress, my heart you have betrayed."

One morning, one morning, all in the month of May,
The flowers in the garden was blooming fresh and gay;
A gold ring off her finger, as she was passing by,
She dropped it in my pocket, and for it I must die.

She swore that I had robbed her, and straightway I was brought
Before that grave old justice to answer to my fault.
Six months or more in prison now I was forced to lie,
Before that grave old justice I was condemned to die.

Come all you honored ladies of low and high degree,
Don't glory in my downfall, but straightway pity me.

"The Sheffield 'Prentice" was collected by Laurence Powell from Mrs. Emma Dusenbury,
Mena, Arkansas, 1936. Laws, 039.

Farewell to the vain world, I'll bid it all adieu,
Farewell to charming Molly, I die for loving you.

CAROLINE OF EDINBORO' TOWN

Come all young men and maidens, come listen to my rhyme,
'Tis of a fair young damsel who's scarcely in her prime;
She beats the blushing roses, admired by all around,
'Tis comely young Caroline of Edinboro' Town.

Young Henry being a Highland lad a-courting to her came,
And when her parents came to know they did not like the same;
Young Henry being offended he unto her did say,
"Come rise you up, my dearest Caroline, and with me run away.

"We'll go up to London, love, and there we'll wed with speed,
And then my dearest Caroline shall have happiness indeed."
Being enticed by young Henry, she put on her other gown,
And away went young Caroline of Edinboro' Town.

Over the hills and lofty mountains together they did go,
Till the time they arrived in London far from her happy home;
They had not been in London, not more than half a year,
Till hard-hearted Henry he proved to her severe.

Says Henry, "I'll go to sea, your friends did on me frown,
So beat your way without delay to Edinboro' Town."
Oppressed with grief without relief, this maiden she did go
Unto the woods to eat such fruit as on the bushes grow.

Beneath a lofty, spreading oak, this maiden sat down to cry
A-watching of that gallant fleet as it went passing by;
She gave three shrieks for Henry and plunged her bidy [body] down
And away floated Caroline of Edinboro' Town.

A note, like lies [likewise] her bonnet, she left upon the shore,
And in the note a lock of hair with the words, "I am no more.

"Caroline of Edinboro' Town" was recorded by Vance Randolph from the singing of Charles Ingenthron of Thornton, California, at Walnut Shade, Missouri, 1941. Library of Congress record LP14. Laws, P27.

It's fast asleep, I'm in the deep, the fishes watching round,
'Tis comely young Caroline of Edinboro' Town."

THE BUTCHER BOY

In Jersey City where I did dwell,
Lived a butcher's boy that I loved full well,
He courted me my heart away,
And now with me he will not stay.

There is another in this here town
Where he goes right in and he sits right down,
He takes a pretty girl upon his knee,
And he tells to her what he won't tell me.

Oh, yes, oh, yes, I'll tell you why,
It's because she has more gold than I,
But her gold will melt and her silver fly,
And she'll see the day she's as poor as I.

Oh me, oh my, how can this be,
Shall I love a boy that don't love me?
Oh, no, oh, no, that'll never be
Till apples grow on the hickory tree.

I went upstairs to make my bed,
And nothing to my mother said,
But she clumb up, she follered me,
Says, "Daughter dear, what's a-ailing thee?"

And when her father he came home,
Says, "Daughter dear, where has she gone?"
He went upstairs and the door he broke,
And found her a-hanging by a rope.

He took his knife and cut her down,
And in her bosom these words he found:

"The Butcher Boy" was recorded by Vance Randolph from the singing of Mrs. Lillian Short, Galena, Missouri, 1941. Library of Congress AFS record 5262 B2. Laws, P24.

"Oh, what a foolish maid am I
To hang myself for the butcher's boy.

"Oh, dig my grave both wide and deep,
Place a marble stone at my head and feet,
And on my bosom a snow-white dove
To show the world that I died for love."

A RICH IRISH LADY
(*Sally*)

There was a rich lady, from London she came,
A lady of beauty and Sally by name;
A young man he courted her for a number of years,
And to this young lady he expressed all his cares.

Her riches being great and her honor being high,
As towards this young man she scarcely cast an eye;
Her riches being greater than a king could possess,
Her form and her beauty above all the rest.

"Oh, Sally, oh, Sally, oh, Sally," said he,
"I am sorry that your love and mine can't agree,
I am sorry that your love and mine can't agree,
For I'm wounded in love and I am in misery."

"I really don't hate you nor no other man,
But to say that I love you is more than I can;
I really don't hate you nor no other source,
But I never will marry you unless I am forced."

It was about sixteen weeks went past and was gone
When this young man heared of Sally's downfall;
She sent for this young man, she was sick and about to die,
She was wounded in love and she knew not for why.

"Oh, am I the doctor that you sent for me here,
Or am I the young man who onced loved you dear?"

"A Rich Irish Lady" was recorded by John A. Lomax and Laurence Powell from the singing
of Mrs. Emma Dusenbury, Mena, Arkansas, 1936. Library of Congress AFS record 867.
Laws, P9.

"Oh, you are the young man that can kill or can cure,
And without your assistance I'll die I am sure."

"Oh, Sally, oh, Sally, oh, Sally," said he,
"Don't you remember how you once slighted me?
You slighted me, Sally, you slighted me with scorn,
And now I will reward you for things past and gone."

"For things past and gone, love, forget and forgive
And grant me some longer time here for to live."
"Oh, no I won't Sally while e'er you draw breath
But I'll dance on your grave when you're cold in the earth."

And off of her fingers gold diamond rings she pulled three,
Saying, "Take these and wear them while you're dancing o'er me.
Oh, take these and wear them while you're dancing o'er me,
Ten thousand times over your Sally you'll see."

The Fair Damsel from London
(*The Brown Girl — Pretty Sarah*)

There was a young doctor, from London he came,
He courted a damsel called Sarah by name,
Her wealth it was more than the king could possess;
Her beauty it was more than her wealth at the best.

"O Sarah, O Sarah, O Sarah," said he,
"I am truly sorry that we can't agree,
But if your heart don't turn unto love,
I fear that your beauty my ruin will prove."

"O no, I don't hate you, and no other man,
But to say that I like you is more than I can,
So now you may stop with all your discourse,
For I never 'low to have you unless I am forced."

After twenty-eight weeks had done gone and passed
The beautiful damsel she fell sick at last.

"The Fair Damsel from London" was collected by Cecil Sharp from the singing of Mrs.
Moore, Raburn County, Georgia, 1909. In Sharp, *English Folksongs from the Southern*
Appalachians (Oxford) New York, 1966, I, 298. Without music. Laws, P9.

She sent for the young man she once did deny,
For to come and see her before she did die.

"Am I the young man that you sent for here?
Or am I the young man that you loved so dear?"
"You're the only young doctor can kill or can cure,
And without your assistance I'm ruined, I'm sure."

"O Sarah, O Sarah, O Sarah," said he,
"Don't you remember you once slighted me?
You slighted, deviled me, you slighted me with scorn,
And now I'll reward you for things past and gone."

"Forget and forgive, O lover," said she,
"And grant me some longer a time for to live."
"O no, I won't, Sarah, enduring your breath,
But I'll dance on your grave when you lay in cold death."

Gold rings off her finger ends she pulled three,
Saying: "Take these and wear them when you dance on me.
Ten thousand times over my folly I see."

Now pretty Sarah is dead, as we all may suppose.
To some other rich lady willed all her fine clothes.
At last she made her bed in the wet and cold clay;
Her red, rosy cheeks is moulderin' away.

THE REJECTED LOVER

I once knew a little girl, a charming beauty bright,
And to make her my wife was my own heart's delight,
Oh, was my own heart's delight.

I took her by the hand and I led her to the door,
And I held her in my arms while I asked her once more,
Oh, while I asked her once more.

"The Rejected Lover" was collected by Asher E. Treat from Mrs. M. G. Jacobs and Pearl Jacobs Borusky near Bryant, Wisconsin, and reported by him in *JAF*, 52 (1939):1–51. Laws, P10.

LOVE

She looked up in my eyes with scorn and disdain,
And the answer that she gave me was, "You can't come again."

I stayed away six weeks, which caused her much pain,
Then she wrote me a letter, saying, "Do come again."

I answered her letter for to let her know,
That young men ofttimes venture, where they ought not to go.

Come all you young men and warning take by me:
Never place your affections on a green growing tree.

For the leaves they will wither and the roots they will decay,
And the beauty of a fair girl will soon fade away.
Oh, will soon fade away.

FALSE NANCY

Come all you jolly-hearted sailors,
Who on the foaming oceans roam;
For seven long years I courted Nancy,
Thinking one day to make her my own.

A chain of gold I gave unto her,
And a costly wedding ring likewise;
The chain of gold she fond accepted,
But the wedding ring she did despise.

The chain of gold she wore about her,
She wore it about her neck in view,
Saying, "Be you gone, you young tarry sailor,
For I can have a better man than you."

I went unto her tender mother,
Thinking she might stay my friend;
But she proved more cruel than my jewel,
And for an officer did send.

"False Nancy" was collected from Mrs. Annie V. Marston, West Gouldsboro, Maine, n.d., but ca. 1904. Reported, with music, in *Bulletin of the Folksong Society of the Northeast*, 1 (1930):7. Laws, P12.

She swore that I had wronged her daughter,
And punished for it I should be;
For forty days on bread and water,
That cruel woman confined me.

In a short time after, that maid got married
To one of the blackguards of the town;
He did not in the least regard her,
Which served to pull her proud spirits down.

As I was walking the streets one morning,
I chanced to meet her all on the way;
She, poor soul, in a low condition,
And I myself in a thriving way.

I turned my head around to view her,
And these are the words to her did say:
"Oh, many a bright and sunshiny morning
Turns to a dark and dismal day."

Now all you loyal-hearted lovers,
Turn not your first true love away,
For many a dark and cloudy morning
Turns to a bright and sunshiny day.

EARLY IN THE SPRING

Early, early in the spring
I was pressed on board to serve my king;
And leaving my dearest dear behind,
Who often told me her heart was mine.

When I had her in my arms,
I thought I had ten thousand charms,
Ten thousand promises and kisses sweet,
Saying, "We'll get married when next we meet."

"Early in the Spring" was collected by Adria Kiser from the singing of her mother, Mrs. Ida E. Kiser, Jahile, Virginia, n.d. but ca. 1930. In Mellinger E. Henry, *Folksongs from the Southern Highlands*, New York, 1938, pp. 233–234. Without music. The adaptation of this to the cowboy song, *The Trail to Mexico*, is apparent.

All the time I sailed the sea,
I could not get one moment's ease,
For writing letters to my dearest dear,
And not one word from her could I hear.

At last I sailed to Saintler's town;
I walked the streets both up and down,
Inquiring for my dearest dear,
And not one word from her could I hear.

At last I sailed to her father's hall,
And for my true love I did call:
"Your true love is married; she's a rich man's wife;
She was married to one who is better for her life."

I walked straight up, her hand did take,
Saying, "All false promises and vows will break;
You've proved false, and I've proved true;
For ever and ever I'll bid you adieu."

"If you have wrote letters to this town,
I did not receive a single one;
It is my father's fault, and you'll find;
Oh, don't blame this poor heart of mine."

"I'll curse all gold and silver too
And all the girls that won't prove true,
That will marry a man for his riches' sake
And leave their true lover's heart to break."

"Don't go back on board again;
Oh, don't go back to serve the king;
There are plenty young girls more fairer than I;
Oh, don't go back where the bullets fly."

"Yes, I'll go back on board again;
Yes I'll go back to serve my king;
I will sail the sea and the mountain high;
On the waters I'll ride till the day I die.

"And when I'm ready for my grave,
My body will be found in the ocean wave;
I want to be buried beneath yonder green tree:
And remember, love, I died for thee."

The Trail to Mexico

I made up my mind for to change my way,
To leave my crowd that was so gay,
To leave my native home awhile
And to travel west for manys a mile.

It was early in the month of May
I started for Texas, so far away,
I left my darling girl behind,
She said her heart was only mine.

It was when I embraced her in my arms,
I thought she had a thousand charms,
Her caresses so soft, her kisses so sweet,
Saying, "We'll get married next time we meet."

It was in the year of eighty-three
That A. J. Stinson he hired me,
Saying, "Young fellow, how'd you like to go
And trail my herd into Mexico?"

Oh, it was early in that year
We started south with all them steers;
I'll tell you, boys, it was a lonesome go
As the trail herd rolled into Mexico.

When we arrived in Mexico,
I wrote my girl who had loved me so;
I wrote a letter to my dear,
But no return word did I hear.

Oh, curse your gold and your silver, too;
Oh, curse a girl who won't be true;

"The Trail to Mexico" was collected by Duncan Emrich from Powder River Jack Lee, Denver, Colorado, 1941. Reported, with music, in *Folklore on the American Land*, Boston, 1972, pp. 516–517. Laws, B13.

I'm going back to the Rio Grande
And get me out with a cowboy band.

Lord pity a girl who won't be true,
For a false-hearted love I never knew;
I'm a-going back where the bullets fly
And stay on the cow trail until I die.

THE GIRL I LEFT BEHIND ME
(*My Parents Raised Me Tenderly*)

My parents raised me tenderly,
They had no child but me,
My mind it was on rambling,
With them I could not agree.

There was a wealthy farmer
Who lived neighbors close by,
He had a lovely daughter
On her I cast my eye.

She was so tall and slender,
The fairest of the fair,
I'm sure there is no other
With her I could compare.

I asked her if it made any difference
If I passed over the plains,
She says, "It makes no difference,
But you come back again."

My whip I will turn over
My team I will resign,
I willed my horse and buggy
To the girl I left behind.

I rambled through old Ioway,
Till Utah I was bound,

"The Girl I Left Behind Me" was recorded by Artus M. Moser from the singing of Pleaz Mobley of Manchester, Kentucky, at Harrogate, Tennessee, 1943. Library of Congress record LP12. Laws, P18.

I rambled, rambled and I rambled,
Till I'd rambled this wide world 'round.

At last a letter came to me
'Twas to give me to understand
That the girl I'd left in Ioway
Had married another man.

I turned right around and 'round and 'round,
Not knowin' what to do,
I read it over and over
Until I found it true.

(*Spoken*) Now this is the moral.

If you ever court a pretty fair girl
Just marry her when you can,
For as sure as you go rambling,
She'll marry another man.

SINFUL TO FLIRT
(*Willie Down by the Pond*)

They say 'tis sinful to flirt,
They say my heart's made of stone,
They tell me to speak to him kindly,
And go leave the poor boy alone.

They say he is only a boy,
I'm sure he's much older than I,
If they would leave us alone, sir,
I'm sure much happier we'd be.

I remember one night when he said
He loved me far better than life,
He called me his darling and pet,
And asked me to be his wife.

"Oh, Willie," I said with a smile,
"I'm sure I will have to say no."
He held my hand for a while,
Then said, "Goodbye, I must go.

"Oh, darling, how can this be so,
Or is your heart harder than stone?"
He took a white rose from my hair
And then left me standing alone.

"Sinful to Flirt" was collected by the Federal Music Project, Works Progress Administration (WPA), Boyd County, Kentucky, ca. 1937. Jean Thomas, Supervisor for Boyd County. Ms., with music, in the Archive of Folk Song, Library of Congress. Laws, G19.

Next morning poor Willie was found
In the pond down by the old mill.
He was drowned in the clear blessèd waters
That flowed from the streams in the hills.

His blue eyes were forever closed
And wet was his curly gold hair,
And pressed to his lips they found a white rose,
The white rose he took from my hair.

Oh Willie, dear Willie, come back,
I'll always be faithful and true,
Oh, Willie, my darling, come back to me,
I'll always be faithful to you.

THE LOVER'S LAMENT FOR HER SAILOR

As I was walking down by the seashore
I spied a fair damsel lamenting and mourn.

Crying, "Oh, my love is gone, he's the one I adore,
And he's gone where I'll never see him any more."

She was dressed like a damsel, she looked like a queen,
She was the prettiest maiden that ever I'd seen.

I asked her if she'd marry myself.
The answer she gave me was "My lover's on sea.

"I never will marry, nor be any man's wife.
I'd rather live single the rest of my life.

"A woman may prove true and do all she can,
But there is nothing in this wide world so false as a man.

"I'll bury myself in this wide, deep sea
For the blue waves to roll over me."

She plunged her fair body in the wide, deep sea
For the blue waves to roll over her pretty blue eyes.

"The Lover's Lament for Her Sailor" was reported to H. M. Belden in 1906 by Supt. W. J. Weese of Bowling Green, Pike County, Missouri, who wrote: "This ballad was sung to my mother over forty years ago by a girl playmate of hers, who came from Illinois to Gentry County, Missouri, about that time." In Belden, *Ballads and Songs Collected by the Missouri Folk-Lore Society*, Columbia (reprint edition, 1966), p. 167. Without music.

THE SAILOR AND HIS BRIDE

The moon had risen on the eastern hill,
The stars they shone in twilight still,
While the sailor boy and his lovely bride
Were walking by the ocean side.

"The Sailor and His Bride" was communicated to John Harrington Cox by Mrs. Elizabeth Tapp Peck, Morgantown, Monongalia County, 1916, who obtained it from her mother, who had, in turn, learned it from her mother, Mrs. Elizabeth Wade Mack. In Cox, *Folksongs of the South* (Harvard) Cambridge, 1925, and Dover reprint, New York, 1967, p. 364. Without music.

LOVE

Le lu, la lo, le lu, la lo,
Le lu, la lo, la lo, la le, la lo
While the sailor boy and his lovely bride
Were walking by the ocean side.

"It was scarce three months since we were wed,
And O how quick the moments fled;
That we should part at the dawning of the day,
And the proud ship bear my love away.

"Long months passed away and he came no more,
To his weeping bride on the distant shore;
The ship sank down at the howling of the storm,
And the sea closed over my lover's form.

"I wish I was a-sleeping too,
Beneath the ocean's blue,
With my soul in heaven and my body in the sea,
And the proud waves rolling over me."

Le lu, la lo, le lu, la lo,
Le lu, la lo, la lo, la le, la lo,
"With my soul in heaven and my body in the sea,
And the proud waves rolling over me."

MY DARLING'S ON THE DEEP BLUE SEA

My mamma is dead and she's buried,
My papa's forsaken me,
And I have no one for to love me,
But the sailor on the deep blue sea.

He promised to write me a letter,
He promised to write to me,
But I haven't heard from my darling
Who's sailing on the deep blue sea.

"My Darling's on the Deep Blue Sea" was recorded by Vance Randolph from the singing of Mrs. Gladys McCarthy, Farmington, Arkansas, 1941. Library of Congress AFS record 5352 A3.

It was last Sunday evening,
Just about the hour of three,
When my darling started for to leave me
To sail on the deep blue sea.

He promised to write me a letter,
He promised to write to me,
But I haven't heard from my darling
Who's sailing on the deep blue sea.

"Oh, captain, oh, captain, can't you tell me,
Can't you tell me where he may be?"
"Oh, yes, my little fair maiden,
He is drowned in the deep blue sea."

"Oh, goodbye, dear friends and relations,
This is the last you'll see of me,
For I'm going to end my troubles
By drowning in the deep blue sea."

WILLIAM WAS A ROYAL LOVER

William was a royal lover,
But disobeyed the King's command;
His jewel was of humble station,
But to him was most noble-grand.

"The King's command must be respected.
The foreign service best," said he,
"And keep him under observation,
Not from his jewel to know or see."

He pled for grace but was rejected:
All royal rights he would forfeit.
But stolid was his royal master
As upon his throne he proudly sat.

"William Was a Royal Lover" was recorded by Alan and Elizabeth Lomax from the singing of Capt. Pearl R. Nye, Akron, Ohio, 1937. Library of Congress AFS record 1605 A2.

Poor William he was pressed in service,
Not from his jewel did he hear;
But to his promise he was faithful,
And the thought of her was always dear.

In course of time, the King recalled him.
William's thought was his promised bride.
Not knowing she was dead and buried,
With thoughts of her he was occupied.

When he arrived, to her home he hastened;
The truth he learned, he wept, he cried;
The sunshine of his life had vanished;
Soon, soon he sickened and then died.

THE SILVERY TIDE

There was a fair young creature who lived by the seaside.
For beauty, form and feature she was called the village pride.
There was a young sea captain who Mary's heart did gain,
And so true was she to Henry whilst on the raging main.

All in this young man's absence a nobleman there came
A-courting pretty Mary, but she refused the same,
Saying, "Your vows are vain while on the main, I love but one," she cried.
"So, far begone, I love but one; he's on the silvery tide."

Then mad to desperation this nobleman did say,
"To prove a separation her life I'll take away.
I'll watch her late and early until alone," he cried,
"And I'll send her body floating all on the silvery tide."

Said Mary, in a trembling voice, "My vows I ne'er can break.
My Henry I love dearly and I'll die for his sweet sake."
With a handkerchief he bound her hands, he flung her o'er the side,
And a-shrieking she went floating all on the silvery tide.

"The Silvery Tide" is from Carrie B. Grover, *A Heritage of Songs* (privately printed, Gould Academy, Bethel, Maine, n.d.), pp. 9–10.

In the course of three days after, young Henry returned from sea
Expecting to be happy and to fix his wedding day.
"I'm afraid your true love's murdered," her aged father cried,
"Or has proved her own destruction all on the silvery tide."

Young Henry threw his body down and, weary, could not rest;
The thoughts of drownèd Mary disturbed his aching breast.
He dreamed that he was walking down by the ocean wide
And his own true love saw floating all on the silvery tide.

Young Henry arose, put on his clothes, and at midnight gloom went he
To wander the sand banks over down by the roaring sea.
At daybreak in the morning poor Mary's corpse he espied
As she to and fro was floating all on the silvery tide.

He knew it was his Mary by his own ring on her hand.
He unbound the silken handkerchief, which put him to a stand;
The name of this base murderer in full thereon he espied
Who had drowned pretty Mary all on the silvery tide.

This nobleman was taken and the gallows was his doom
For drowning pretty Mary who scarce was in her bloom.
Young Henry looked dejected, and he wandered till he died
And his last words were, "Poor Mary died on the silvery tide."

THE LOWLANDS OF HOLLAND

This song has been traced as far back at least as 1776 in the manuscripts of David Herd deposited in the British Museum, and interesting local variants of it have been found as far west as Missouri where the final line reads "To the lowlands of Missouri we'll fight for liberty." Mrs. Grover's version from Maine is closer to the British tradition than others found in this country.

Last Easter I was married, that night I went to bed,
There came a bold sea captain who stood at my bed head,

"The Lowlands of Holland" was recorded by Alan Lomax from the singing of Mrs. Carrie Grover of Gorham, Maine, at Washington, D.C., 1941. Library of Congress record LP21. Also in Carrie B. Grover, *A Heritage of Songs* (privately printed, Gould Academy, Bethel, Maine, n.d.), p. 50.

Saying, "Rise, arise, you married man, and come along with me
To the low, low lands of Holland to face your enemy."

She clasped her arms about me, imploring me to stay,
Up speaks this bold sea captain, saying, "Arise and come away!
Arise, arise, you married man, and come along with me
To the low, low lands of Holland to face your enemy."

"Oh, daughter dear, oh, daughter dear, why do you thus lament?
There are men enough in our town to make your heart content."
"There are men enough in our town, but there is not one for me,
For I never had but one true love, and he has gone from me.

"No shoes shall come upon my feet, nor comb come in my hair,
No fire bright or candlelight shine in my chamber more,
And never will I married be until the day I die,
Since cruel seas and angry winds parted my love and me."

YOUNG CHARLOTTIE
or The Frozen Girl

"Young Charlottie" or "The Frozen Girl" is, according to Belden, "perhaps the most widely known and best loved of native American folksongs." Many may disagree with this statement, but the variants of the song which have been located in places as widely separated as Nova Scotia and California, Texas and Michigan do attest to its continuing popularity. Belden points out also that it is "surprising to find it traditionally known in Georgia and Mississippi, where sleighs, let alone freezing to death on a sleigh-ride, must be unknown."

Unlike the majority of ballads and folksongs, the authorship of "Young Charlottie" has been traced to Seba Smith, the Maine-born New York journalist, who published it in *The Rovers* (vol. II, no. 15, p. 225) in December, 1843. This does not make it any the less a folksong, for it has been transmitted by oral tradition and is authorless to its singers and even to most collectors, who have found many variants of tune and text. Com-

"Young Charlottie" was recorded by Duncan Emrich from the singing of I. G. Greer of Thomasville, North Carolina, with dulcimer by Mrs. Greer, at Washington, D.C., 1945. Library of Congress record LP14. Laws, G17.

pare, for example, the variant collected by Carl Sandburg for his *American Songbag* with the one sung here by I. G. Greer.

Young Charlottie lived by the mountain side in a wild and lonely spot,
Not a dwelling house in five miles around except her father's cot;
On many a pleasant winter night young folk would gather there,
Her father kept a social house and she was young and fair.

It was New Year's eve, the sun was low, joy beamed in her bright blue eyes,
As to the window she would go to watch the sleighs pass by;
It was New Year's eve, the sun was down, joy beamed in her bright blue eyes,
She watched until young Charlie's sleigh came swiftly dashing by.

In a village fifteen miles away there's a merry ball tonight,
The air is dreadful, chilly cold but her heart was warm and bright;
"Oh, daughter, dear," the mother said, "this blanket 'round you fold,
'Tis a dreadful night to go abroad, you'll catch your deathly cold."

"Oh, no, oh, no," the daughter said, and she laughed like a gypsy queen,
"To ride in a sleigh all muffled up I never can be seen."
Her cloak and bonnet soon were on, they stepped into the sleigh,
And around the mountain side they went for many miles away.

"Such a night," said Charles, "I never knew, these lines I scarce can hold."
And Charlottie said in a very feeble voice, "I'm growing very cold."
He cracked his whip, he urged his steed much faster than before,
Saying, "It's five long dreadful miles to go and it's o'er ice and snow."

"How fast," said Charles, "the frosty ice keeps gathering on my brow,"
And Charlottie said in a very feeble voice, "I'm growing warmer now."

He drove up to the ballroom door, stepped out and reached his hand,
He asked her once, he asked her twice, he asked her three times o'er,
"Why sit you there like a monument that has no power to move?"
He took her hand in his — Oh, God! — and it was deathly cold.

Young Charles knelt down by her side, the bitter tears did flow,
"My own, my true intended bride, I never more shall know."
He twined his arms about her neck, the bitter tears did flow,
And his thoughts turned back to the place where she said, "I'm growing warmer now."

LOVE

SPRINGFIELD MOUNTAIN

(The original ballad as preserved in the Merrick family)

On Springfield Mountains there did dwell
A likeley youth was known full well
Lieutenant Merrick onley son
A likeley youth near twenty-one.

One friday morning he did go
in to the medow and did mow
A round or two then he did feal
A pisen serpent at his heal.

When he received his deadly wond
he dropt hi sythe apon the ground
And strate for home was his intent
Calling aloude still as he went,

tho all around his voys wase hered
but none of his friends to him apierd
they thought it was some workman calld
And there poor Timothy alone must fall.

So soon his Carfull father went
To seak his son with discontent
and there hes fond onley son he found
ded as a stone apon the ground.

And there he lay down sopose to rest
Withe both his hands Acrost his brest
his mouth and eyes Closed fast
And there poor man he slept his last.

"Springfield Mountain" is from Irma Thompson Ireland, "Springfield Mountain," *Old-Time New England, The Bulletin of the Society for the Preservation of New England Antiquities*, 32 (July 1941):1–8. Wilbraham, Massachusetts, was once known as Springfield Mountain, and there, on August 7, 1761 "Timothy Mirrick, the son of Thomas and Mary Mirrick, was bit by a ratel snake and died within two or three ours, being 22 years, two months, and three days old and very near the point of marridge." The ballad is presumed to have been written by the young woman to whom the unfortunate young man was engaged to be married. Laws, G16.

his father vieude his track with greate concern
Where he had run across the corn
Uneven tracks where he did go
did apear to stagger two and frow.

The seventh of August sixty-one
this fatull axadint was done
Let this a warning be to all
to be prepared when God does call.

The Broken Token, or Love Returned in Disguise

He took his hands all out of his pockets,
And rings and diamonds two or three,
He took out a ring that was broken between them,
She saw it and fell down at his feet.

THE BROKEN TOKEN

"This is 'The Broken Token' or 'A Pretty Fair Maid All in the Garden' as
I learned it from my mother, Mrs. Jane Gentry."

A pretty fair maid all in the garden,
A gay young soldier came riding by,
He stepped up to this honored lady,
Saying, "Oh, kind miss, don't you fancy me?"

"You are not a man of noble honor,
You're not the man that I took you to be,
You are not a man of noble honor,
Or you wouldn't impose upon a poor girl like me.

"I have a true love in the army,
He has been gone these seven years long;
And seven more years I'll wait upon him —
No man on earth shall enjoy me."

"Perhaps he's in some watercourse drownded,
Perhaps he's on some battlefield slain,
Perhaps he's stolen some fair girl and married,
If that's the case, you'll never see him again."

"The Broken Token" was recorded by Duncan Emrich from the singing of Mrs. Maud Long
of Hot Springs, North Carolina, at Washington, D.C., 1947. Library of Congress record
LP21. Laws, N42.

"Perhaps he's in some watercourse drownded,
Perhaps he's on some battlefield slain,
Perhaps he's stolen some fair girl and married —
I'll love the girl that married him."

He took his hands all out of his pockets,
And rings and diamonds two or three,
He took out a ring that was broken between them,
She saw it and fell down at his feet.

He picked her up, he did embrace her
And kisses gave her two or three,
Saying, "I am your poor single soldier,
I have just returned for to marry thee."

THE BANKS OF CLAUDY

As I walked out one evening, all in the month of May,
Down by the flowery garden, where Betsey she did stray,
I overheard this damsel in sorrow to complain,
About her absent lover, who plowed the raging main.

I stepped up to this fair maid; I put her in surprise;
She owned she did not know me, me being in disguise:
"My only dearest darling, my soul and heart's delight,
How far have you to wander this dark and stormy night?"

"Is this the banks of Claudy, or would you please to show?
Pity a maid distracted, for I am forced to go
In search of a young man, and Johnny is his name,
And on the banks of Claudy I'm told he does remain."

"This is the banks of Claudy, the banks on which you stand;
But do not believe in Johnny, for he's a false young man.
Do not believe in Johnny, for he'll not meet you here,
But stay with me till morning, no danger need you fear."

"The Banks of Claudy" was collected by John Harrington Cox from Anna Copley, Shoals, Wayne County, West Virginia, 1915, who had learned it as a child from Julia Stephenson Luther. In Cox, *Folksongs of the South* (Harvard) Cambridge, 1925, and Dover reprint, New York, 1967, p. 321. Without music. Laws, N40.

"Oh, if Johnny was here to-night, he'd keep me from all harm;
But he's in the field of battle, all in his uniform;
He's in the field of battle, his foes he defies;
Like some bright king of honor, he's gone the war to try."

"It's been six weeks and better, since Johnny left the shore;
He's sailing the wild ocean, where foaming billows roar;
He's sailing the wide ocean for honor and great gain;
The ship's been lost, so I've been told, along the coast of Spain."

When she heard this sad news, she fell into despair,
A-wringing of her hands and a-tearing of her hair;
Saying, "Since he's gone and left me, no other will I take,
But in some lonesome valley I'll wander for his sake."

When he saw her love was loyal, he could no longer stand,
But sprang into her arms, saying, "Betsey, I'm your man!
I am that faithful young man, the cause of all your pain,
And since we've met on Claudy's banks, we ne'er shall part again."

JOHNNY GERMANY

'Twas of a brisk young sailor, as I have heard it said;
He met a pretty fair damsel, her countenance looked sad;
He asked her the reason what made her look so down;
So modestly she answered, without one smile or frown:

" 'T is for the loss of my true love, since from me he has gone.
And I have no love token, that ever he'll return."
"Perhaps I saw your true love when I was last at sea;
And I'll relate it over, if this you'll answer me:

"He belonged to the *Rainbow*, and was under Captain Lowe,
By the name of Johnny Germany. Is this the name or no?"
"He belonged to the *Rainbow*, and was under Captain Lowe,
By the name of Johnny Germany." "He's been dead five months or more."

"Johnny Germany" was collected by Anna Copley, Shoals, Wayne County, West Virginia, 1915, from Luther Burwell, who learned it as a child from his mother. In John Harrington Cox, *Folksongs of the South* (Harvard) Cambridge, 1925, and Dover reprint, New York, 1967, p. 328. Without music. Laws, N43.

She turned her back unto him and not one word did say;
She turned her back unto him, and straight she went away;
She went unto her chamber, and there she wept and cried,
And sorely she lamented and wished that she might die.

He dressed himself in scarlet and back to her he came,
With a jovial resolution to comfort her again:
"Cheer up, cheer up, pretty Polly, and leave your tears behind;
Cheer up, cheer up, pretty Polly, and comfort you shall find."

"My loving Johnny Germany, what made you serve me so?"
"O hold your tongue, pretty Polly! I'll serve you so no more.
I only did it for to try you, to see how true you were.

"You are truer than the turtledove; you are redder than the rose;
You are like some blooming blossom; your love and beauty flows."
Polly lived an honest life, all bad company she's shunned;
Polly's lived in Johnny's favor, till at length his heart she's won.

"Farewell unto the *Rainbow*, since Polly's won my heart!
And we will now be married before we do part.
Farewell unto the *Rainbow*, since Polly's won my heart!
We will live together till death us part."

THE MANTLE SO GREEN
(*Lovelye Nancy*)

As I was a-roving one morning in spring
To view the sweet flowers and the meadows so green,
I met a fair damsel, she appeared like the queen,
With her costly fine robes and her mantle so green.

Says I, "My pretty fair maid, if you'll go with me,
I'll join you in wedlock and married we'll be,
I'll dress you in scarlet, as you appear like the queen,
With your costly fine robes and your mantle so green."

"The Mantle So Green" was recorded by Vance Randolph from the singing of Charles
Ingenthron, Walnut Shade, Missouri, 1941. Library of Congress AFS record 5248 B1.
Laws, N38.

"Oh, no, kind sir, you must be refused,
For I'll wed with no man, you must be refused.
These green hills I've wandered for to shun all men's views,
For the lad that I love lies in Fenn Waterloo."

"Now since you are not married, pray tell me your love's name,
For I've been in many a battle and I might have known the name."
"Draw near to my garments and there you'll behold
His name and his surname in letters of gold."

On reaching her garments there I did behold
His name and his surname in letters of gold:
Young William O'Reilly it appeared in my views.
"He was my chief comrade at Fenn Waterloo.

"We fought so victorious, the bullets did fly.
On the plains of Nor Regent your true love doth lie;
We fought for three days until the fourth afternoon,
He received his death summons on the eighteenth of June.

"As he lay a-dying I heard his last cries:
'Draw near, lovelye Nancy, concerning I die.'
Now peace is provided, and the truth I'll declare,
Here is your love's token on the ring that I wear."

She stood in amazement and paler she grew,
She flew from my arms with a heart full of woe,
Saying, "These green hills I've wandered for the lad that I love!"
"Return, lovelye Nancy, your grief I'll remove.

"Lovelye Nancy, lovelye Nancy, 'twas I won your heart
In your father's green gardens where last we did part,
Where I held you in my arms beneath the shade trees,
With your costly fine robes and your mantle so green."

This couple was married, so I've heard people say,
There were noble entertainments on their wedding day.
"Now peace is provided and the wars are all o'er,
You're welcome, lovelye Nancy, to my arms once more."

FAIR PHOEBE AND HER DARK-EYED SAILOR

I'll tell you of a come-lye young lady fair,
Who was walking out for to take the air;
She met a sailor upon the way,
So I paid attention,
So I paid attention, to hear what they might say.

"Fair maid," said he, "why roam you alone?
For the night is coming, and the day's far gone; —"
She said, while tears from her eyes did flow,
"For my dark-eyed sailor,
For my dark-eyed sailor, so manly true and bold."

Cries William, "Drive him from off your mind!
As true a sailor as him, you'll find;
Love turns aside, and cold does grow,
Like a winter's morning,
Like a winter's morning when the hills are clad with snow."

These words did Phoebe's fond heart inflame;
She cries, "On me you shall play no game!"
She drew her dagger, and then did cry,
"For my dark-eyed sailor,
For my dark-eyed sailor, a maid I'll live and die.

"It's seven long years since he left this land;
A diamond ring he took from off my hand;
He broke the token; left half with me,
And the other's rolling,
And the other's rolling at the bottom of the sea.

"His coal black eyes and his curly hair,
His flattering tongue did my heart ensnare;
Genteel he was, and no rake like you,
To advise a maiden,
To advise a maiden to slight the jacket blue.

"Fair Phoebe and Her Dark-Eyed Sailor" was recorded by Phillips Barry from the singing of Mrs. Guy R. Hathaway, Mattawamkeag, Maine, 1932, as learned when a child from her aunt. Reported, with two sets of music, by Barry in *Bulletin of the Folksong Society of the Northeast*, Cambridge, Mass., 6 (1933):8–10. Barry feels that "Fair Phoebe" cannot be earlier than the 1830's. Laws, N35.

THE BROKEN TOKEN, OR LOVE RETURNED IN DISGUISE

"A tarry sailor I'll ne'er disdain,
But always I will treat the same;
To drink your health, here's a piece of coin,
For my dark-eyed sailor,
For my dark-eyed sailor still claims this heart of mine."

When William did this ring unfold,
She seemed distracted midst joy and woe.
"You're welcome, William, I've lands and gold,
For my dark-eyed sailor,
For my dark-eyed sailor, so manly true and bold."

In a cottage down by the riverside,
In unity and love, they now abide;
So, girls, be true while your lover's away,
For a cloudy morning,
For a cloudy morning oft brings a pleasant day.

THE NIGHTINGALES OF SPRING

Down by the ocean side where ships were sailing,
I saw a maid on shore weeping and wailing.
I said unto her, "Sweet, what is it that grieves thee?"
And the answer that she gave, "None can believe me.

" 'Tis seven long years since I and my love last parted,
He left me here on shore, I'm broken-hearted.
He promised to return if life was lent him,
The reason that I mourn, fear death prevent him."

"Your love and I we fought 'neath Earl's banner,
We fought old England's side, justice and honor.
Being a warrior bold of courage valiant,
He scorned to be controlled by his assailant.

"Awhile before he died, being quite heartbroken,
He turned to me and said, 'Bear me this token
To her who is my love, there's none that's fairer,
And tell her to be kind and wed the bearer.' "

"The Nightingales of Spring" was recorded by Sidney Robertson Cowell from the singing of Warde H. Ford, Central Valley, California, 1938. Library of Congress AFS record 4198 A1. Laws, N29.

LOVE

She wrung her hands and cried like one distracted,
She knew not what she said nor how she acted.
She tore away from me all in her anger,
She said, "You've come too late, I'll wed no stranger."

She wrung her hands and cried, being quite amazèd,
I handed her a ring on which she gazed,
"It is my love's," said she, "won't you come nearer?"
And the answer that I gave, "Be pleased, my dear."

When I saw that she'd prove true, my love grew stronger,
I tore off my disguise, 'twould stay no longer.
"To her, my love," said I, "love is no slander,
You are my dear old girl and I'm Philander."

Then hand in hand we walked, long live together,
Then hand in hand we talked, like maids of pleasure.
We both sat down and sang, she sang the clearer,
Of the nightingales of spring — welcome, my dear!

WILLIAM HALL

True love is sweet and true love is pleasant
To a young man's view;
For once I was parted, broken-hearted —
Oh, dear me, what shall I do?

As soon as his parents came to know this,
That he loved this young lady so,
They sent him away across the ocean
That he might see her face no more.

He sailed the ocean over and over
Until he came to his own country shore,
Saying, "If Molly is alive and I can find her,
I'll make her my lawful bride."

"William Hall" is from the manuscript ballad-book of James Ashby of Holt County, Missouri, secured by Miss Welty in 1906. Belden notes that the shift from first person to third person and back again in the narrative is a frequent phenomenon in folk-singing. In Belden, *Ballads and Songs Collected by the Missouri Folk-Lore Society*, Columbia (reprint edition, 1966), p. 156. Without music. Laws, N30.

As I was walking, as I was talking,
As I was walking up the street
Cold drops of rain fell just as it happened
My true love I chanced to meet.

I stepped up to her side so boldly,
Saying, "Pretty miss, do you fancy me?"
"No, I have placed my affections on a brisk young farmer
Who has lately gone to sea."

"Describe him, describe him unto me."

"He was tall, he was neat, he was pretty, he was handsome,
Pretty blue eyes with them all;
He wore jet-black hair and he wore it curled,
And his name was William Hall."

"Oh yes, oh yes, I knew him quite well
And his name was William Hall;
And I saw a French cannon-ball go through him
And in death's cold arms he did fall."

The screams, the screams that she did hallo!
She screamed until she was forced to fall;
And it was all for the sake of her own true lover,
And his name was William Hall.

"Cheer up, cheer up, my pretty little damsel,
Cheer up, cheer up unto me;
Since I have been the cause of all this trouble,
Here is the ring you gave to me."

This couple joined hands together
And to church did straightway go;
And this young couple they got married
Whether their parents was willing or no.

               — *Copyed the 17 Mar. 1875*

WILLIAM AND MARY

As William and Mary stood by the seaside
Their last farewell for to take,
A-sighing and saying, "If you never return
Alas, my poor heart it will break."
"Fear nothing, dear maid," young William he said
As he pressed the fair maid to his side,
"For me do not mourn for when I return
I will make little Mary my bride."

When six years had passed and no news, at last
As she stood by her own cottage door,
A beggar came by with a patch on his eye,
He was lame and did pity implore.
"If your charity you'll bestow upon me,
I will tell you your fortune," he cried,
"If the lad whom you mourn will ever return
To make little Mary his bride."

"Oh then," said she, "if you will tell me,
It is all that I have I will give,
If what you tell me you tell me true.
Oh say does my William live?"
"He lives and," says he, "in great poverty,
All shipwrecked and worn beside.
He'll return no more, because he is poor,
To make little Mary his bride."

"Heaven knows," she cries, "all the joy that I feel,
While yet his misfortune I mourn.
He is welcome to me in his great poverty
With his blue jacket tattered and torn,
For I love him so dear, so true and sincere,
And no other, I swear it, beside.
For if in riches he rolled or was covered in gold
He would make little Mary his bride."

"William and Mary" is from Carrie B. Grover, *A Heritage of Songs* (privately printed, Gould Academy, Bethel, Maine, n.d.), pp. 136–137. Laws, N28.

Then the beggar threw by the patch from his eye,
His old clothes and crutches beside,
In a suit of new clothes and his cheek like the rose,
It was William stood by Mary's side.
"Forgive me, dear maid," young William he said,
"It was but your true love that I tried."
So to church away without further delay,
And he made little Mary his bride.

THE BLIND BEGGAR

In "English and Scottish Ballads," edited by Francis James Childs [sic], I found what must have been the original of this song. It is called "The Blind Beggar of Bednal Green" and is known to be a very old song. Pepys speaks of it in his diary under date of June 25, 1663. He writes that he went with Sir William and Lady Batten and Sir J. Minns to Sir W. Rider's at Bednal Green to dinner, and adds, "A fine place. This very house was built by the blind beggar of Bednal Green, so much talked of and sung in ballads." . . . Father sang a verse or two which neither my sister nor I can remember. Father is the only person that we ever heard sing it.

— CARRIE GROVER

'Tis of a blind beggar who a long time was blind.
He had a fair daughter most comely and kind.
She was comely and handsome in ev'ry degree,
And the name she was known by was Bonny Betsy.

It was early one morning young Betsy arose,
She went to her father and asked for some clothes.
She went to her father with tears in her eyes,
Saying, "I am a-going my fortune to try."

The first to court Betsy was a sailor so bold,
He came to court Betsy her favor to gain.
Saying, "My ships that sail over I will give unto thee,
If you'll grant me your favor, my bonny Betsy."

"The Blind Beggar" was recorded by Alan Lomax from the singing of Mrs. Carrie Grover of Gorham, Maine, at Washington, D.C., 1941. Library of Congress AFS record 4461 B1. Text with music also in Carrie B. Grover, *A Heritage of Songs* (privately printed, Gould Academy, Bethel, Maine, n.d.), pp. 87–88. Laws, N27.

The next to court Betsy was a squire so bold,
He came to court Betsy her favor to gain,
Saying, "My lands and rich livings I will give unto thee,
If you'll grant me your favor, my bonny Betsy."

The next to court Betsy was a nobleman so grand,
He came to court Betsy her favor to gain,
Saying, "My lands and my castles I will give unto thee,
If you'll tell me your father, my bonny Betsy."

"My father's a blind beggar, the truth for to tell,
He is led by a dog with a cup and a bell,
And daily he sits and he asks charity,
Yet he is the father of bonny Betsy."

"Oh then," says the sailor, "it's you I don't crave."
"Oh then," says the squire, "it's you I won't have."
"Oh then," says the nobleman, "let beggars agree;
You are welcome to my arms, my bonny Betsy."

Her father, being standing right there in the door,
"Oh don't slight my daughter because she is poor.
She's not dressed in her silk or her gay apparel,
But I will drop guineas with you for my girl."

He dropped a bright guinea right down on the floor,
He dropped till he had dropped full five thousand score.
Oh, then says the nobleman, "That's the last of my store."
And then the blind beggar dropped five thousand more.

The Female Warrior,
or True Love in the Wars

"My waist is not too slender, love,
  My fingers not too small;
  I'm sure I would not tremble
  To face the cannonball
  Where the guns are loudly rattling
  And the blazing bullets fly
  And the silver trumpets sounding
  To drownd the deadly cry."

JACK MONROE
(Jackie's Gone A-Sailing)

Jackie's gone a-sailing with trouble on his mind,
To leave his native country and his darling dear behind,
Sing ree and sing row and so fare you well, my dear.

"I'll cut my hair, I'll paint my skin, men's apparel I'll put on,
And I'll sail with you, Sweet William, and go on sea with you."
Sing ree and sing row and so fare you well, my dear.

"Your cheeks are red and rosy, your fingers neat and small,
Your waist too slim and slender to face the cannonball."

"My cheeks are red and rosy, my fingers neat and small,
But it never makes me tremble to face the cannonball."

She dressed herself in men's array, and apparel she put on,
And to the field of battle she marched her men along.

The battle being ended, she rode the circle round,
And among the dead and dying, her darling dear she found.

"Jack Monroe" was recorded by Duncan Emrich from the singing of Mrs. Maud Long of Hot Springs, North Carolina, at Washington, D.C., 1947. Library of Congress record LP21. Laws, N7.

LOVE

She picked him up all in her arms, she carried him down to town,
And sent for a London doctor to heal his bleeding wounds.

This couple they got married, so well they did agree;
This couple they got married, and why not you and me?

LISBON

It was on one Monday morning
All in the month of May,
Our ship she slipped her cable
As we were bound for sea.
The wind blew from the southwest;
To Lisbon we were bound.
The hills and the vales were
    garnished
With pretty fair maids all round.

There was a young man among the
    rest
All in the bloom of years
Who went to see his Polly
With bitter sighs and tears;
Who went to see his Polly
To let her understand
That he was going to leave her
To view some foreign land.

"Don't say so, dear William,
Those words have gained my heart;
Come, let us go and marry
Before that we do part;
For I can love no other,
No other one but thee;
So stay at home, dear William,
Be kind and marry me."

"If I were to stay at home, love,
Some other would take my place;
It would be a disappointment,
Besides a sad disgrace.
Our captain has commanded us
And I for one will go;
And for my very life, love,
I dare not answer no."

"My yellow hair then I'll cut off,
Men's clothing I'll put on,
I'll go 'long with you, William,
I'll be your waiting-man,
I'll fear no storm or battle,
Let them be e'er so great,

"Lisbon" was written down for Miss Lowry in 1904 by L. W. Lee, formerly of Howard
County, Missouri, as "one of the ballads that we California miners used to sing with a vim
in the '50s." (I consider the "we" to be somewhat suspect. However . . .) In Belden,
Ballads and Songs Collected by the Missouri Folk-Lore Society, Columbia (reprint edition,
1966), p. 178. Without music. Laws, N8.

THE FEMALE WARRIOR, OR TRUE LOVE IN THE WARS

Like true and faithful servant
Upon you I will wait."

"Your waist it is too slender, love,
Your fingers are too small;
I'm afraid you would not answer
If I should on you call
Where the cannon loudly rattle
And the blazing bullets fly
And the silver trumpets sounding
To drownd the deadly cry."

"My waist is not too slender, love,
My fingers not too small;
I'm sure I would not tremble
To face the cannonball
Where the guns are loudly rattling
And the blazing bullets fly
And the silver trumpets sounding
To drownd the deadly cry."

"Supposing I were to meet with
some fair maid
And she were pleased with me;
If I should meet with some fair maid
What would my Polly say?"
"What would I say, dear William,
Why, I should love her too,
And stand aside like a sailor
While she might talk with you."

"Now don't say so, dear Polly;
Those words have gained my heart.
Come, let us go and marry
Before that we do part."
This couple then got married
And are sailing round the main;
May great success attend them
Till they return again.

THE TRUE LOVERS BOLD

Ye true lovers bold, come listen unto me;
A story I'm going to unfold;
Young Flora was a damsel both virtuous and kind,
And young James was a "*galliant*" sailor bold,
And young James was a "*galliant*" sailor bold.

"It's adieu to lovely Flora," one morning he did say,
"I am forced, I am called to go away
Unto some foreign shore, where the cannons loud do roar,
In battle when the stormy winds do blow."

"The True Lovers Bold" was recorded by Phillips Barry from the singing of Mrs. Guy R. Hathaway, Mattawamkeag, Maine, 1932, reported by Barry in *Bulletin of the Folksong Society of the Northeast*, Cambridge, Mass., 8 (1934): 8–9.

Like a maiden in despair, she tore her yellow hair,
Saying, "Along with you I will go
Unto some foreign shore, where it's loud the cannons roar,
In battle when the stormy winds do blow."

"Oh, no, my lovely Flora, I am sure you must be mad,
To venture your sweet life upon the deep;
Instead of going aloft, upon your pillow soft
Contented at home you might be."

"Oh, you need not persuade, for I am not afraid;
Alone with you I'll go
Unto some foreign shore, where it's loud the cannons roar
In battle when the stormy winds do blow."

Six years lovely Flora she sailed o'er the sea,
Respected by all her ship's crew;
And it never yet was said that young Flora was a maid,
In her trousers and jacket so blue.

On occasion she would fight from morning until night,
Hard-to to the battle she would go;
She would stand by her gun, do her duty like a man,
In battle when the stormy winds do blow.

At length they were discharged, and they both were enlarged;
Straightway unto the captain he did go,
Saying, "Here behold a maid that never was afraid,
In battle when the stormy winds do blow."

Now the captain he did stare when those words he did hear,
He looked on her with surprise;
And he shouted with delight as he gazed on her so bright,
And the tears fell in torrents from his eyes.

"Ye true lovers bold, here is fifty pounds in gold,
To see you get married I will go;
And you can in joy be blest, upon your pillow rest,
Stay at home when the stormy winds do blow."

THE WARS OF SANTA FE

There was a wealthy merchant
In London still did dwell,
He had a daughter Polly,
The truth to you I'll tell.
I'll sing tittery umpty i-ray,
I'll sing tittery ump-ti-e.

Oh, Polly she had sweethearts
Who courted day and night,
And upon Jack the farmer
She placed her heart's delight.
I'll sing tittery umpty i-ray,
I'll sing tittery ump-ti-e.

The old man flew into a passion,
Straightway he did go,
He went unto an officer
For to prove Jack's overthrow.

Saying, "Here is ten bright guineas
Which I will give to thee,
If you'll force young Jack the
    farmer
To the wars in Santa Fe."

Now, Jack he's gone a-sailing
With a sore and troubled mind,
He left his native country
And his darling girl behind.

Oh, Polly went first unto a tailor
And dressed in men's array,
And then unto a company
For to carry her away.

The captain said to her,
"Your fingers are quite slender,
Your waist it is but small,
Your cheeks is mighty rosy red
For to face the cannonball."

"I know my fingers are quite
    slender,
My waist it is but small,
But I don't think I'll tremble
For to face the cannonball."

They landed then in Mexico
So beautiful and gay;
Unto a field of battle
They quickly marched away.

Where cannon loudlye roared
And officers did command,
By the side of her true-love
It was her luck to stand.

Where cannons loudlye roared
And bullets swiftly fly,
A ball from a Spaniard's gun
Cut her true-love down to lie.

She picked him up
And she carried him to a town,
And then unto a doctor
Soon to dress up his wounds.

"The Wars of Santa Fe" was recorded by Sidney Robertson Cowell from the singing of
Ben Rice, Springfield, Missouri, 1936. Library of Congress AFS record 3207 B1.

This couple they got married
And returned home again,
They went unto her father's house
And hollered mighty things.

Saying, "Come on, you brave old
     fellow,
Come go along with me,
And we'll follow Jack the farmer
To the wars in Santa Fe."

"Oh, no, my brave young fellow,
That never can be,
I have a daughter Polly
In the wars in Santa Fe."

Then said her good old mother,
While standing in her place,
"The features of this young man
Resembles Polly's face."

"I am your daughter Polly,
I crossed those rugged plains,
I married young Jack the farmer
And I brought him home again."

CAROLINE AND HER YOUNG SAILOR BOLD

'Twas of a nobleman's daughter,
So lovely and handsome a girl,
Her father possessed of large fortune,
Full twenty-five thousand in gold.

He had one only daughter,
Caroline was her name, I am told,
And out of her drawing room window,
She admired a young sailor bold.

Her cheeks were as red as two apples,
Her eyes were as black as jet,
Caroline she watched his departure,
Went out and with him she met.

Saying, "I am a nobleman's daughter,
Possessed of large fortune and gold,

"Caroline and Her Young Sailor Bold" was collected by Dr. Robert M. Lewis, New Haven, Connecticut, from the singing of Mr. Henry Bunker, Cranberry Isles, Maine, 1926. Reported, with music, by Mary W. Smyth in *Bulletin of the Folksong Society of the Northeast*, Cambridge, Mass., 2 (1931):9–10. Laws, N17.

I'll forsake both my father and mother
To wed with a young sailor bold."

He said, "Oh, my dear honored young lady,
Be commanded your parents to mind,
For sailors they are poor dependents,
When their true loves are left far behind."

"There's nothing can ever persuade me
One moment to alter my mind,
I'll ship and go with my true lover,
He never shall leave me behind."

She dressed like a gallant young sailor,
Forsaking both father and gold,
Five years and a half on the ocean,
She plowed with her young sailor bold.

Five times with her love she was shipwrecked,
But to him she always proved true,
Her duty she done like a sailor,
Went aloft in her jacket so blue.

Her father long wept and lamented,
That his daughter he ne'er should behold,
Till at last she arrived safe in England,
Caroline and her young sailor bold.

Straightway to her father she wandered,
In her trousers and jacket so blue,
Her father immediately fainted,
When first she appeared to his view.

Saying, "Father, dear, forgive me,
Forever deprive me of gold;
Grant one more request, I'm contented
To wed with a young sailor bold."

They were married, and Caroline's fortune
Was twenty-five thousand in gold,
And now they live peaceful and happy,
Caroline and her young sailor bold.

THE JOLLY PLOWBOY

As Jack, the jolly plowboy, was plowing of his land,
With his horses beneath a green shade,
He whistled and he sang as his plough it went along,
Till at length he chanced to meet a pretty maid, pretty maid.
Till at length he chanced to meet a pretty maid.

Oh he whistled and he sang as his plow it went along.
She's a lady of higher degree,
And if her parents come to know she's courted on the plain
They will send her bonnie laddie to the sea, to the sea,
They will send her bonnie laddie to the sea.

Now it happened to be so, when her parents came to know
That she was being courted on the plain,
A press-gang of soldiers did hurry him away.
They have sent him to the war to be slain, to be slain,
They have sent him to the war to be slain.

Now she's dressed herself up in a young man's array
With her pockets well lined with gold
And she marched up the street so nimbly and so neat
That she looked just like a jolly sailor bold, sailor bold,
That she looked just like a jolly sailor bold.

Oh the first place she went was to the admiral of the fleet.
Oh have you seen my jolly ploughboy?
He is sailing o'er the deep, he has gone to join the fleet.
They have sent him to the war to be slain, to be slain,
They have sent him to the war to be slain.

She has pulled out her purse of five hundred pounds,
Of five hundred pounds, aye, and more.
All this she freely paid for her jolly ploughboy
And she rolled him in her arms to the shore, to the shore,
And she rolled him in her arms to the shore.

"The Jolly Plowboy" is from Carrie B. Grover, *A Heritage of Songs* (privately printed, Gould Academy, Bethel, Maine, n.d.), pp. 13–14.

THE FEMALE WARRIOR, OR TRUE LOVE IN THE WARS

Oh happy were true lovers when they did meet,
All their sorrows and troubles are o'er.
They whistle and they sing, cause the valleys for to ring
Since she found the bonnie laddie she adores, she adores,
Since she found the bonnie laddie she adores.

Love's Tricks

"Come strip you quite naked,
Your mother will not know;
Come strip you quite naked,
And let the candle go.

"And let the candle go, my dear,
Without a fear or doubt,
And we'll have a little pleasure
When you blow the candle out."

KITTY MOREY

Come all you girls and all you boys,
And listen to my story,
I'll tell the plan I fell upon
To steal Miss Kitty Morey.

    I titty-atty-ing I-ay I-ay,
    I titty-atty-ing I-o.

I went down to Miss Kitty's house
Just like a jolly fellow,
I told her that the plums and grapes
Were a-getting ripe and mellow.

    I titty-atty-ing I-ay I-ay,
    I titty-atty-ing I-o.

I told her that I suited her
And that I did not flatter,
I told her that my sister Sal
Knew nothing about the matter.

I did not have to ask her twice,
She put on her best bonnet;
My heart was beating mighty fast
As across the fields we ran it.

"And now we're here and all alone,
And no one knows the matter,
It's you must die or else comply,
For I've no time to flatter."

She seemed quite pleased, my
    hand she squeezed,
"There's but one thing I fear, sir.
It's that my pa may come this way,
And he would find us here, sir.

"But if you'll climb the highest tree
That rises in this bower,
And if my father keeps away,
We'll spend a happy hour."

And there she stood beneath the tree
Until I had ascended,
"It's get down as you got up,
For now your fun is ended.

"Kitty Morey" was recorded by the University of Wisconsin Recording Project under the direction of Leland Coon from the singing of Winifred Bundy, Madison, Wisconsin, 1946. Library of Congress AFS record 8364 B. Laws, N24.

"You look just like an owl," she said.
"Your company I shun, sir.
Go eat your plums and suck your
    thumbs,
For I'm a-going to run, sir."

So Katie heeled it o'er the plain
And left me there distracted;
I ripped and swore, my shirt I tore
To think how I had acted.

And three months later from that
    day,
Fair Kate and I were married;
And three months only after that,
A lusty son she carried.

It's time to hush this foolish song,
It's time to quit all rhyming;
For every time this baby squalls,
By George, I feel like climbing.

I titty-atty-ing I-ay I-ay,
I titty-atty-ing I-o.

ON THE BANKS OF SALEE

One evening a young lady fair, her estate rode out to see,
When a roguish knight stepped out and said, "Fair maid, you will ride with
    me."
So it's you and I together, love, how happy we will be,
And we'll both sport together on the banks of Salee.

She looked at him and then about, and said, "Let me lead the way,
For I know these parts quite well, and it's many hours till day."
So it's you and I together, love, how happy we will be,
And we'll both sport together on the banks of Salee.

She was sly just like a fox, she went 'round and 'round and so
When she saw her plans would work, she was cautious, very slow.

She rode on a dapple gray, and he on a dapple brown,
They rode in the chilly greenwoods three hours before it came dawn.

So often he was very rude, and on him then she would frown,
At last she said, "At father's house, there is a bed of down."

At last they reached her father's house, and she rode in through the gate,
And said, "Now I am safe at home. You go before it's too late."

"Oh, curse all women," then said he, "they will always man deceive,
And he is ever fool enough their stories to believe."

"On the Banks of Salee" was recorded by Alan and Elizabeth Lomax from the singing of
Capt. Pearl R. Nye, Akron, Ohio, 1937. Library of Congress AFS record 1606 A.

LOVE

She pulled out a little penknife, and stuck it in the ground,
"I wish this was in any man's heart who would ride for a bed of down."
So it's you and I together, love, how happy we will be,
But we'll not sport together on the banks of Salee.

"You're like the little white rooster, that runs among the hens;
He flaps his wings but dare not crow, you're just like one of them."
So it's you and I together, love, how happy we will be,
But we'll not sport together on the banks of Salee.

KATE AND THE COWHIDE

A lady lived in Lancaster,
Tra-la-liddle-te-i-de-O,
A gamester came a-courting her,
Tra-la-liddle-te-i-ide-O;
He courted her for many a day,
But still this lady answered "Nay."

Sing tiddy, sing taddy,
Sing trum little laddie,
Sing tra-la-liddle-te-i-de-O.

At length he gained her full consent,
And straightway courting another he went,
He left poor Kate quite in despair,
Went courting a lawyer's daughter fair.

"Kate and the Cowhide" was collected, with music, from Mrs. Maude Simpson, Detroit, n.d., but ca. 1930, who had the song from the singing of her grandfather, Mr. Seth Evilsizer (age eighty-two), Alger, Michigan. He had learned the song when he was a boy seven or eight years old from an aunt, Mrs. Chatman, who lived near Zanesville, Ohio. She, in turn, had learned it from an English neighbor who claimed that she personally "knew" the principals in the story, although scholars have traced the genealogy of the ballad to a broadside dated 1689–1690. The informant declared that the ballad was based upon an incident which happened near Zanesville, Ohio.

In Conesville, Schoharie County, New York, a prose version of the ballad is told, and the old home of Kate is pointed out. There her grandchildren are said now to live. (These "facts" from folk transmission are quite as reliable as the statement from a Tennessee woman that Barbara Allen had actually lived "over the ridge" in an adjacent valley, and that the death of William and Barbara had taken place there not too long ago.) In Emelyn Elizabeth Gardner and Geraldine Jencks Chickering, *Ballads and Songs of Southern Michigan* (University of Michigan Press) Ann Arbor, 1939, p. 387. The preceding note, except for the comment on Barbara Allen, is drawn from the Gardner-Chickering book. Laws, N22.

Kate never told to friend nor foe,
Nor did she let her parents know,
But she went unto a tannery,
And with the tanner she did agree.

She received of him an old cowhide,
And she wrapped herself on the inside,
Then she went unto a lonely dell,
For she knew he'd come that way quite well.

At length along that way he came,
And now says Kate, "We'll have some fun."
Then after him she did pursue,
He cried, "Oh, dear, what shall I do?"

With hairy hide, horns on her head,
Which full three feet around her spread;
But when he saw that long black tail,
He tried to run, but his feet they failed.

She seized him fast all by the coat,
And she said to him in a doleful note,
"You've left poor Kate quite in despair,
Went courting the lawyer's daughter fair."

"Oh, master devil, save me now,
And I'll prove true to my former vows,"
"Then see that you do," Kate did reply,
While smiling under the old cowhide.

He went straight home and went to bed,
The thoughts of Kate were in his head,
And early next morning he did arise,
To go and make poor Kate his bride.

Kate never told to friend or foe,
Nor did she let her parents know,
Till three long years they'd married been,
And then she told the joke to him.

JACK THE JOLLY TAR

As Jack walked out of London city,
No one on Jack, oh, to take pity,
As Jack walked out of London city,
No one on Jack, oh, to take pity,
Jack thought he heard the people say
That in the streets he'd have to lay.
A whang dang diddle-de-dang, fol-lo-day.

There was a squire who lived quite handy,
He courted the lawyer's daughter, Nancy;
He courted her both night and day
And agreed with her one night to lay.
A whang dang diddle-de-dang, fol-lo-day.

"I'll tie a string around my finger
And hang it out of the chamber window,
You come up and pull the string
And I'll come down and let you in."

She tied a string around her finger
And hung it out of her chamber window;
Jack came up and pulled the string,
And she came down and let him in.

She slipped the string from off her finger,
But it dangled from her chamber window;
The squire came up and pulled the string;
The string was pulled but he couldn't get in.

To give the squire a friendly warning,
She arose at daylight the next morning;
There she saw Jack in a striped shirt,
His face and hands all covered with dirt.

"Jack the Jolly Tar" was contributed by Mrs. Susie Carr Young, Brewer, Maine, from the singing of her uncle, Mr. Fred W. Fowler, Hampden, Maine, n.d. The stanza in brackets contributed from a variant by Mr. George H. Spurling of Southwest Harbor, Maine. Reported, with music, by Phillips Barry in *Bulletin of the Folksong Society of the Northeast*, Cambridge, Mass., 3 (1931): 10–11. Laws, K40.

"How come you here, you saucy fellow?
You've broke my household and robbed me of my treasure."
"I came up and pulled the string,
And you came down and let me in."
A whang dang diddle-de-dang, fol-lo-day.

["Since it is so, it is no matter,
We'll join our hearts and hands together."
She loved the tarry sailor well,
And told the squire to go to hell.]

BLOW THE CANDLE OUT
(*The Jolly Boatsman*)

Come all ye jolly boatsman boys
That go to see your dear;
The moon is shining bright,
And the stars a-twinkling clear.

I dropped at my love's window
To ease her of her pain;
So quickly she rose and let me in,
And went to bed again.

"Come strip you quite naked,
Your mother will not know;
Come strip you quite naked,
And let the candle go.

"And let the candle go, my dear,
Without a fear or doubt,
And we'll have a little pleasure,
When you blow the candle out.

"Your father and your mother
In yonder's room both lie,
Abracing of each other,
And why not you and I?

"And why not you and I, my dear,
Without a fear or doubt?
We'll have a little pleasure,
When we blow the candle out."

Nine months and better,
Nine months being past,
This beautiful damsel
Brought forth a child at last.

Brought forth a child at last, my
     dear,
Without a fear or doubt,
And she damned the very hour
That she blowed the candle out.

"Blow the Candle Out" was collected by Josiah H. Combs from Mrs. Martha Smith, Knott County, Kentucky, n.d., ca. 1924. Without music. In Combs, *Folksongs of the Southern United States*, Publications of the American Folklore Society (The University of Texas Press) Austin, 1967, pp. 140–141. Laws, P17.

Come all ye young ladies,
Wherever ye may be:
Do not trust a young man
One inch above your knee.

An inch above your knee, my dear,
Without a fear or doubt —
They are seeking out a way
For to blow the candle out.

THE GOLDEN GLOVE
(*The Dog and Gun*)

A lofty young squire from Portsmouth he came,
And courted a nobleman's daughter so fair.
The day was appointed a wedding to be,
The farmer was chosen to give her away.

Instead of getting married the lady went to bed,
The thoughts of the farmer run so in her head,
And how for to gain him it was her intent,
With her dog and her gun to meet him she went.

Hat, coat and trousers this lady put on,
And then she went a-hunting with her dog and her gun;
Oft times she fired but nothing she did kill,
At length the young farmer came into the field.

"Why weren't you at the wedding?" the lady inquired,
"To wait upon the squire and give him his bride?"
"Oh, no," said the farmer, "if the truth I must tell,
I can't give her up for I love her too well."

This pleased the lady to see him so bold,
She pulled out a glove that was flowered in gold;
She said that she found it, just as she came along
As she was a-hunting with her dog and her gun.

The lady went home with her heart full of love,
She put forth the news that she had lost a glove;

"The Golden Glove" was recorded by Jean Thomas and Dorothy Scarborough from the singing of Jilson Setters, Rowan County, Kentucky, ca. 1935. In Dorothy Scarborough, *A Song Catcher in Southern Mountains* (Columbia University Press) New York, 1937, p. 229.

LOVE

"The man that will find it and bring it unto me,
Oh, the man that will find it, his bride I will be."

This pleased the farmer to hear of the news;
He went unto the lady without more delay,
Saying, "Honorable lady, I have found your glove,
If you will be so kind as to grant me your love."

"It's already granted," the lady replied,
"I love the sweet breath of the farmer," she cried.
"I will be mistress of my dairy, go milking of my cow,
While my brisk and jolly farmer goes whistling to his plow."

After they were married, she told him of the fun,
How she hunted up the farmer with her dog and her gun:
"And now I have got him so fastly in my snare,
I will love him forever, I vow and declare."

Oh, I Wish I Were
Single Again

I have always heard of these old men
Until I got one at last.
I wish grim death had seized him
Before I seen his face.

I wish grim death had seized him
And tuk him at a call
So I may have a-married some younger man
To roll me from the wall.

I WISH I WAS SINGLE

When I was single
Marriage I did crave,
Now I am married
And it's trouble to my grave.
Lord, I wish I was a single girl
  again.

Dishes to wash
And the spring to go to,
I've no one to help me,
Lord, I have it all to do.
Lord, I wish I was a single girl
  again.

When I was single
I had plenty to eat,
Now I am married
It's old turnips without the meat.
Lord, I wish I was a single girl
  again.

When I was single
I went dressed so fine,
Now I am married
I wear rags all the time.
Lord, I wish I was a single girl
  again.

Three little children
A-lyin' in the bed,
All of them so hungry
They can't raise up their head.
Lord, I wish I was a single girl
  again.

I took in some washing
Made a dollar or two,
My husband went and stole it
Now I don't know what to do.
Lord, I wish I was a single girl
  again.

"I Wish I Was Single" was collected by Anne and Frank Warner from the singing of Frank Proffitt, Watauga County, North Carolina, 1939. From the Warner Collection, with permission.

LOVE

Oh, I Wish I Were Single Again

When I was a single girl, I went dressed very fine,
Now I am married and have a drunken man to mind.
Oh, I wish I were a single girl again.

When I was a single girl I done as I pleased;
Now I am a married girl with a drunken man to please.
Oh, I wish I were a single girl again.

He goes down to town and stays all day
Drinking and gambling and wasting time away.
Oh, I wish I were a single girl again.

And when he comes home it's a curse and a damn,
Wishing I were dead and he had another dram.
Oh, I wish I were a single girl again.

Spring to go to, and cows to milk and feed,
And the four little children a-crying after me.
Oh, I wish I were a single girl again.

I ONCE LOVED A YOUNG MAN

I once loved a young man as dear as my life,
He often did promise to make me his wife.

He fulfilled his promise, he made me his wife,
But see what I've come to by being his wife.

Oh, here's my dear children all crying for bread,
My husband's off drinking, and I wish I was dead.

I'm going to Georgia, Georgia to roam,
I'm going to Georgia to make it my home.

"Oh, I Wish I Were Single Again" was collected by Harvey H. Fuson from Lizzie Dills. In Fuson, *Ballads of the Kentucky Highlands*, London, 1931, p. 118. Without music.

"I Once Loved a Young Man" was recorded by Herbert Halpert from the singing of Mrs. Kate Peters, Norton, Virginia, 1939. Library of Congress AFS record 2777 A2.

I'll build me a log cabin on the mountain so high,
Where the wild beasts and snowbirds will hear my sad cry.

They'll know I'm a poor girl, a long ways from home,
The road's rough to travel, and nowheres to go.

Come all my young ladies, take warning from me,
That you'll never get struck on a green growing tree.

The leaves they will wither, the roots they will die,
The young man will fool you, for one has fooled I.

They'll hug you, they'll kiss you, and tell you more lies
Than the cross-ties on the railroad and the stars in the sky.

TRIFLING WOMEN

O Lord, I been a-working
Like a dog all day
Just to make another dollar
For you to throw away.

You spend all my money
And go dressed so fine,
While I wear old clothes
And don't have a dime.

You won't bake my biscuits,
You won't cook my beans,
You want to stand by the log road
So you can be seen.

I'd be better off
Just to go on away
And let you do what you want to
All the livelong day.

I'd rather be a-hanging
On a old grapevine
Than to know I have to spend my days
With you all the time.

"Trifling Women" was collected by Anne and Frank Warner from the singing of Frank Proffitt, Watauga County, North Carolina, 1951. From the Warner Collection, with permission.

MARRIED AND SINGLE LIFE

Come, all young men, taking warning by me:
Never be so fast as I've been.
I married me a wife;
She makes me tired of my life —
Makes me strive and do all that I can, can, can;
Makes me strive and do all that I can.

I lived all my days
By the hating of her ways;
And I'm sure I'll not marry any more, more, more;
And I'm sure I'll not marry any more.

When I come home at night,
I never speak a word she can hear.
So fatal is my doom
I go marching to my room
With cold joints all trembling with fear, fear, fear;
With cold joints all trembling with fear.

She dresses me in rags and the worst of old rags;
She dresses like a lady so fine —
Goes sweeping through town
By day and by night,
Where them rowdy boys do drink wine, wine, wine;
Where them rowdy boys do drink wine.

Oh, come, welcome death;
Come take away her breath
And give me back my freedom once more, more, more;
And give me back my freedom once more.

"Married and Single Life" was collected by Mellinger E. Henry from Mr. Cleophas L. Franklin, Crossnore, Avery County, North Carolina, 1929, and reported, without music, in Henry, "Ballads and Folk-Songs from the Southern Highlands," *JAF*, 45(1932):121–122.

I WISH I WERE SINGLE AGAIN

Oh, when I was single, oh then, oh then!
  Oh, when I was single, oh then!
Oh, when I was single my pockets did jingle,
  And I wish I were single again.

I married me a wife, oh, then, oh then!
  I married me a wife, oh then!
I married me a wife, and she led me a life,
  And I wish I were single again.

My wife she took fever, oh then, oh then!
  My wife took fever, oh then!
My wife took fever, and the fever wouldn't leave her,
  And I wish I were single again.

My wife she died, oh then, oh then!
  My wife she died, oh then!
My wife she died, and I laughed till I cried,
  To think I was single again.

I went for a shroud, oh then, oh then!
  I went for a shroud, oh then!
I went for a shroud, and I laughed right out loud,
  So glad I was single again.

I went for a coffin, oh then, oh then!
  I went for a coffin, oh then!
I went for a coffin, and nearly died laughing,
  So glad I was single again.

I went to her grave, oh then, oh then!
  I went to her grave, oh then!
I went to her grave, but I couldn't behave, —

"I Wish I Were Single Again" was collected by Miss Annie Ray Kiefer (now Mrs. H. W. Taylor) from Gable Lewis, Frio County, Texas, and reported in L. W. Payne, Jr., "Songs and Ballads — Grave and Gay," *Texas and Southwestern Lore, PTFS*, 6 (1927):232. Textual inclusions recorded by Duncan Emrich from the singing of I. G. Greer of Thomasville, North Carolina, 1945, Library of Congress AFS record 8770 A1; and by Herbert Halpert from the singing of Mrs. Esco Kilgore, Hamiltontown, Virginia, 1939, Library of Congress AFS record 2834 B1.

LOVE

It was peep, peep this a-way,
And peep, peep that a-way —

I was so happy I was single again.

I married me another, oh then, oh then!
   I married me another, oh then!
I married me another, the devil's stepmother,
   And I wish I were single again.

She beat me, she banged, oh then, oh then!
   She beat me and banged me, oh then!
She beat me, she banged me, she swore she would hang me,
   And I wish I were single again.

She went for the rope, oh then, oh then!
   She went for the rope, oh then!
She went for the rope my neck for to choke,
   And I wish I were single again.

I killed my wife, oh then, oh then!
   I killed my wife, oh then!
I killed my wife with a Barlow knife,
   And then I was single again.

Oh, boys, take warning by me, by me!
   Oh, boys, take warning by me!
The first one is bad, but the second is worse,
   Whenever you cannot agree.

WHEN I WAS A YOUNG MAID

When I was a young maid, young maid,
When I was a young maid, then, oh then,
It was ha-ha this-a-way, ha-ha that-a-way,
   This-a-way, that-a-way, then.

"When I Was a Young Maid" was collected by Katherine Harbison from Miss Dove Harris, Danville, Kentucky, 1939, and reported, with music, *SFQ*, 2 (1938):151.

Men came a-courting, courting,
Men came a-courting, then, oh then,
It was ha-ha this-a-way, ha-ha that-a-way,
 This-a-way, that-a-way, then.

Pretty soon I married, married,
Pretty soon I married, then, oh then,
It was "Yes, my dear" this-a-way, "No, my dear" that-a-way,
 This-a-way, that-a-way, then.

Then we quarreled, quarreled,
Then we quarreled, then, oh then,
It was "Shut your mouth" this-a-way, "Keep it shut" that-a-way,
 This-a-way, that-a-way, then.

Then we made up, made up,
Then we made up, then, oh then,
It was (*kissing noise*) this-a-way, (*kissing noise*) that-a-way,
 This-a-way, that-a-way, then.

Then he took sick, took sick,
Then he took sick, then, oh then,
It was "Send for the doctor" this-a-way, "Send for the doctor" that-a-way,
 This-a-way, that-a-way, then.

Then he died, died,
Then he died, then, oh then,
It was boo-hoo this-a-way, boo-hoo that-a-way,
 This-a-way, that-a-way, then.

Then to the funeral, funeral,
Then to the funeral, then, oh then,
It was boo-hoo this-a-way, boo-hoo that-a-way,
 This-a-way, that-a-way, then.

Coming from the funeral, funeral,
Coming from the funeral, then, oh then,
It was look around this-a-way, look around that-a-way,
 Catch him who you can!

BACHELOR BOLD AND YOUNG

When I was a bachelor bold and young,
I courted me a girl with a clattering tongue;
She promised me she'd marry, but she didn't say when,
The kisses I gave her were a hundred and ten,
The kisses I gave her were a hundred and ten.

Monday morning I married my wife,
I thought to live a happier life;
We sang and we danced and merry did we play,
We sang and we danced till the break of day,
We sang and we danced till the break of day.

Tuesday morning I carried her home,
I thought to myself I had a wife of my own;
She wrinkled up her face and began to scold,
I never was scolded so in my lifetime before.

Wednesday morning I went to the wood,
I thought to my soul she wouldn't prove good;
I got me a hickory, it was about green,
I thought it was the keenest switch I ever had seen.

Thursday morning I whipped her well,
I have no doubt I sent her soul to hell;
But if I have, I never shall repent
The times of whipping her that I have spent.

Friday morning, break of day,
She thought I was going to kill her, scolding away.
Rufus, Rufus, the little devil came,
Carried her away in a shower of rain.

Saturday morning, breakfast time,
I have no wife to bother my mind.
So my week's work is now at an end,
My brandy bottle's my best friend,
My brandy bottle's my best friend.

"Bachelor Bold and Young" was recorded by Herbert Halpert from the singing of Mrs. Ada Mooney, Oxford, Mississippi, 1939. Library of Congress AFS record 3017 A1.

WHEN YOUNG LADIES GET MARRIED

When young ladies get married all pleasure is done,
Adieu to all comfort and trouble comes on.
Their husbands to scold them and their children to squall
Makes many fair faces grow withered and old.
And it's hard times, girls, oh, girls,
And it's hard times, girls.

When young men go courting they dress up so fine,
To court the girls, that's all their design.
But when they get there, they'll flatter and lie,
And keep the girls up till they're ready to die.
And it's hard times, girls, oh, girls,
And it's hard times, girls.

The girls will get sleepy and to themselves say,
"Oh, boys, oh, boys, I wish you'd go away."
But they laugh them to scorn;
Before they'll go home, they'll sleep in the barn.
And it's hard times, girls, oh, girls,
And it's hard times, girls.

Next morning so early, they will arise,
Brush off the straws and rub up their eyes;
And away home they will ride
Like all false lovers, puffed up with pride.
And it's hard times, boys, oh, boys,
And it's hard times, boys.

When they get home, they'll stagger and reel,
"God bless those girls, how sleepy I feel.
I'll not go a-courting, I'll not marry at all
For happy is a man that keeps bachelor's hall."
And it's hard times, boys, oh, boys,
And it's hard times, boys.

"When Young Ladies Get Married" was recorded by Laurence Powell and Sidney Robertson Cowell from the singing of Mrs. Emma Dusenbury, Mena, Arkansas, 1936. Library of Congress AFS record 3230 A2.

LOVE

A bachelor's life, I'm sure it is the best,
Be drunk or be sober, go home to take your rest;
No wife to control you, no children to squall,
So happy is the man that keeps bachelor's hall.
And it's hard times, boys, oh, boys,
And it's hard times, boys.

SONG BALLET
(*I Was Sixteen Years of Age*)

I was sixteen years of age,
A damsel in my prime,
I dearly thought of a married life
And it just at that time.

I fell in love with a gloomy youth
And marry was my plan;
Was not very long till married I was
To my good-looking man.

We just been married just two weeks;
One Sunday afternoon
Sun went down and night got dark
And away went honeymoon.

My man stepped out to take a little walk,
And follow was my plan.
Was not very long till a lady I seen
With my good looking man.

I listened to their takes* of love
To each other they did tell.
Said I to myself: When you come home,
I'll tan your hide right well."

* Talks? Tales?

"Song Ballet" was collected by Mellinger E. Henry from Miss Rachel Tucker, Varnell, Georgia, 1930. (Miss Tucker is the granddaughter of Mr. and Mrs. Samuel Harmon, formerly of Cade's Cove, Tennessee.) Reported without music, by Henry in "Ballads and Folk-Songs from the Southern Highlands," *JAF*, 45 (1932):122–123.

Clock on the mantle was striking one;
My darling he come in:
"Oh, my darling Willie dear,
Wherever have you been?"

"I been to church," said he;
"And that's a lie," said I,
"And nagging is your plan,"
I whaled away with the rolling pin
At my good-looking man.

I knocked him down and broke his back
And ribs and tore his clothes,
And picked up the packing stick
And laid that across his nose.

His face was as black as the chimney sweep's;
All down the streets he run;
There was not a lady fell in love
With my good-looking man.

Come, all you gentlemen and ladies too,
Of a low and high degree,
When you meet a nagging man,
Pitch into him like me.

A RICH OLD MISER

A rich old miser courted me,
His age it was threescore and three,
And mine it was scarce seventeen,
I wish his face I ne'er had seen.

    Leddy and the day, day good day, ma'am,
    Leddy and the day, day good day.

"A Rich Old Miser" was collected, with music, from Mrs. Allan McClellan, near Bad Axe, Michigan, 1935. In Emelyn Elizabeth Gardner and Geraldine Jencks Chickering, *Ballads and Songs of Southern Michigan* (University of Michigan Press) Ann Arbor, 1939, p. 422.

LOVE

If e'er with him I do go out
All for to see a friend or foe,
If anyone saluted me,
It would increase his jealousy.

'Twas one night as he came home,
Like Harry he did rage and foam;
He beat me and he banged me, too,
Till my two sides were black and blue.

Early next morning I do declare
Such bitter knocks I could not bear,
As he lay sleeping on his bed,
I broke my ladle right over his head.

So all young women who has got men
And know not how to conquer them,
I will tell you how I do,
It is with my ladle, and so may you.

Leddy and the day, day good day, ma'am,
Leddy and the day, day good day.

I HAVE ALWAYS HEARD OF THESE OLD MEN

I have always heard of these old men
Until I got one at last.
I wish grim death had seized him
Before I seen his face.

I wish grim death had seized him
And tuk him at a call
So I may have a-married some younger man
To roll me from the wall.

"I Have Always Heard of These Old Men" was collected by Mellinger E. Henry from the singing of Mrs. Mary Tucker, Varnell, Georgia, 1930. Mrs. Tucker is the daughter of Mr. and Mrs. Samuel Harmon of Cade's Cove, Tennessee. See Mellinger E. Henry, "Ballads and Folk-Songs from the Southern Highlands," *JAF*, 45 (1932):124–125.

"Hold your tongue, pretty Polly,
For I am going to town:
I will buy you a beaver bonnet,
Likewise a Holland gown.

"I will buy you a beaver bonnet
A Holland gown likewise;
Also a little black boy
To follow your riding cheer."*

"What care I for your black boy?
Your riding cheer likewise?
I rather married some younger man
With sparkles in his eyes."

I rather wedded some younger man —
Lay on a bed of hay —
As to wedded myself to this old man,
For he is always in the way.

He never in good order;
He never in good tune;
And when he gets away from home —
Not able to return.

This old man he will come boggling in
Just like he had no life.
A young man he come scampering home
Saying, "Kiss me, my dear wife."

* Chair.

Humorous Songs of Love, Courtship, and Marriage

"Oh, supposing I would lay you down, my little maiden
   fair?"
"Oh, then you'd let me up again, oh, kind sir," she
   answered me.
   A-rolling in the dew makes the milkmaid so fair.

"Oh, supposing I would get you a little one, my little
   maiden fair?"
"It's then you'd be the daddy of it, oh, kind sir," she
   answered me.
   A-rolling in the dew makes the milkmaid so fair.

SOLDIER, WON'T YOU MARRY ME?

"O soldier, O soldier, won't you marry me now,
To the beat of the fife and the drum?"
"O how can I marry such a pretty little miss
When I have no shoes to put on?"

Now she ran and she ran to the shoe store
As fast as she could run.
She brought back the very, very best,
And the soldier put it on.

"Soldier, O soldier, won't you marry me now,
To the beat of the fife and the drum?"
"How can I marry such a pretty little miss
When I have no suit to put on?"

O she ran and she ran to the clothing store
As fast as she could run.

"Soldier, Won't You Marry Me?" was recorded by Charles Todd and Robert Sonkin from
the singing of Russ Pike, with guitar accompaniment, at Visalia, California, 1941. Library
of Congress record LP2.

She brought back the very, very best,
And the soldier put it on.

"O soldier, O soldier, won't you marry me now,
To the beat of the fife and the drum?"
"How can I marry such a pretty little miss
When I have no hat to put on?"

Well, she ran and she ran to the hat store
As fast as she could run.
She brought back the very, very best,
And the soldier put it on.

"Soldier, O soldier, won't you marry me now,
To the beat of the fife and the drum?"
"O how can I marry such a pretty little miss
When I have a wife at home?"

BILLY GRIMES

"Tomorrow morn I'll be sixteen, and Billy Grimes the rover*
Has popped the question to me, Ma, and wants me to be his lover.
Tomorrow morn, he says, my Ma, he's coming bright and early
To take a pleasant walk with me across the fields of barley."

"You cannot go, my daughter dear, there is no use of talking,
You cannot go across the fields with Billy Grimes a-walking;
To think of his presumption now, the dirty ugly rover,*
I wonder where your pride has gone to think of such a lover."

"Old Grimes is dead, you know, my ma, and Billy is so lonely,
Besides to say, too [since] Grimes is dead that Billy is the only,
So he'll compare to all that's left and that to say is nearly
A good ten thousand dollars' worth and about six hundred yearly."

"I did not hear you, daughter dear, your last remarks quite clearly,
But Billy is a clever lad and no doubt loves you dearly;

* Drover.

"Billy Grimes" was recorded by Duncan Emrich from the singing of I. G. Greer of Thomasville, North Carolina, at Washington, D.C., 1946. Library of Congress record LP14.

Be ready then tomorrow morn and get up bright and early
To take a pleasant walk with him across the fields of barley."

I'LL BE FOURTEEN NEXT SUNDAY

One morning, one morning, one morning in Spring,
I heard a fair damsel, a lady did sing,
As she sat under her canopy,
"Pray God, I'll get married next Sunday;"
As she sat under her canopy,
"Pray God, I'll get married next Sunday."

"Fourteen years old is too young for to marry,
A girl of that age is very apt to be sorry,
Sing, seven long years that I'll have you to tarry . . ."
"Be fourteen years old next Sunday."
"Sing, seven long years that I'll have you to tarry . . ."
"Be fourteen years old next Sunday."

"My mantle and my shawl is up in my desk,
My true love will be here before I'll get dressed;
My mind is to marrying, I mean to fulfill,
Pray God, I'll get married next Sunday.
My mind is to marrying, I mean to fulfill,
Pray God, I'll get married next Sunday."

ROLLY TRUDUM

As I went out a-walking to breathe the pleasant air,
Rolly-trudum, trudum, trudum-rolly-day,
As I went out a-walking to breathe the pleasant air,

"I'll Be Fourteen Next Sunday" was recorded by Sidney Robertson Cowell from the singing of J. W. Russell, Marion, Virginia, 1936. Library of Congress AFS record 3159 A1.

"Rolly Trudum" was recorded by Vance Randolph from the singing of Mrs. May K. McCord at Springfield, Missouri, 1941. Library of Congress record LP12.

I saw a lady talking to her daughter fair,
Rolly-trudum, trudum, trudum-rolly-day,

"Now hush up, dear daughter, stop your rapid tongue,"
Rolly-trudum, trudum, trudum-rolly-day,
"Now hush up, dear daughter, stop your rapid tongue,
You're talking about marrying and you know you are too young,"
Rolly-trudum, trudum, trudum-rolly-day.

"Oh, hush up, dear Mother, you know I'm a lady grown,"
Rolly-trudum, trudum, trudum-rolly-day,
"Oh, hush up, dear Mother, you know I'm a lady grown,
I've lived seventeen years and I've lived it all alone,"
Rolly-trudum, trudum, trudum-rolly-day.

"Oh, if you was to marry, who would be your man?"
Rolly-trudum, trudum, trudum-rolly-day,
"Oh, if you was to marry, who would be your man?"
"I love a handsome farmer and his name is — Sam,"
Rolly-trudum, trudum, trudum-rolly-day.

"There's doctors and lawyers and men that follow the plow,"
Rolly-trudum, trudum, trudum-rolly-day.
"There's doctors and lawyers and men that follow the plow,
And I'm going to marry for the fidget's on me now,"
Rolly-trudum, trudum, trudum-rolly-day.

"Oh, they've gone for the parson the license for to fetch,"
Rolly-trudum, trudum, trudum-rolly-day,
"They've gone for the parson the license for to fetch,
And I'm going to marry before the sun sets,"
Rolly-trudum, trudum, trudum-rolly-day.

(*Spoken*) Now the mother, she sings a verse.

"Oh, now my daughter's married and well for to do,"
Rolly-trudum, trudum, trudum-rolly-day,
"Now my daughter's married and well for to do,
So hop along, my jolly boys, I think I'll marry, too,"
Rolly-trudum, trudum, trudum-rolly-day.

I LOVE SOMEBODY
(*I Love Little Willie*)

I love somebody, I do, my Ma,
I love somebody, cha ha, ha ha,
I love somebody, but don't you tell Pa,
For I can't help it, you know, my Ma.

He wears a white hat, he does, my Ma,
He wears a white hat, cha ha, ha ha,
He wears a white hat, but don't you tell Pa,
For I can't help it, you know, my Ma.

He's coming to see me, he is, my Ma,
He's coming to see me, cha ha, ha ha,
He's coming to see me, but don't you tell Pa,
For I can't help it, you know, my Ma.

We're going to get married, we are, my Ma,
We're going to get married, cha ha, ha ha,
We're going to get married, but don't you tell Pa,
For I can't help it, you know, my Ma.

Next Thursday night, it is, my Ma,
Next Thursday night, cha ha, ha ha,
Next Thursday night, but don't you tell Pa,
For I can't help it, you know, my Ma.

Oh, now we're married, we are, my Ma,
Oh, now we're married, cha ha, ha ha,
Oh, now we're married, and you may tell Pa,
For I don't care, you know, my Ma.

"I Love Somebody" was recorded by John A. Lomax and Laurence Powell from the singing of Mrs. Emma Dusenbury, Mena, Arkansas, 1936. Library of Congress AFS record 848 B3.

COMMON BILL

Well, I'm in love with a feller, a feller you have seen,
He's neither white nor yellow but he's altogether green;
His name is not so charming, it's only Common Bill,
He urges me to wed to him but I hardly think I will.

Poor Bill, poor silly Bill,
He urges me to wed to him, but I hardly think I will.

He whispers of devotion, devotion pure and deep,
But it sounds so mighty silly that I almost fell asleep;
Now he thinks it would be pleasant for to journey down the hill,
Go hand in hand together, but I hardly think I will.

Poor Bill, poor silly Bill,
He urges me to wed to him, but I hardly think I will.

He came last night to see me and made so long a stay
I began to think the lunkhead would never go away,
And first I learned to hate him and I know I'll hate him still,
He urges me to wed to him but I hardly think I will.

Poor Bill, poor silly Bill,
He urges me to wed to him, but I hardly think I will.

I'm sure I would not choose him if it were in my power,
But he said if I refused him he could not live an hour;
Now you know the Bible teaches that it's very wrong to kill,
So I've thought the matter over and think I'll marry Bill.

"Common Bill" was recorded by Duncan Emrich from the singing of I. G. Greer of Thomasville, North Carolina, with dulcimer accompaniment by Mrs. Greer, at Washington, D.C., 1946. Library of Congress record LP14.

MY GRANDMOTHER GREEN

My grandmother lived on yonder green,
As fine an old lady as ever was seen,
But she always cautioned me with care
Of all the young men to beware.
Tee-eye-tee-oe, tee-yumpy-tumpy-toe,
Of all the young men to beware.

The first come a-courting was little Johnny Green,
As fine a young fellow as ever was seen,
But the words of my grandmother rung in my head
Till I could not hear one word he said.
Tee-eye-tee-oe, tee-yumpy-tumpy-toe,
Till I could not hear one word he said.

Thinks I to myself, there's some mistake
About all this noise these old folks make,
For if grandma herself had a-been so afraid
Why, then she, too, would have been an old maid!
Tee-eye-tee-oe, tee-yumpy-tumpy-toe.
Then she, too, would have been an old maid!

BUFFALO BOY

"Oh, when we going to marry, to marry, to marry,
When we going to marry, dear old buffalo boy?"

"I guess we'll marry in a week, in a week, in a week,
I guess we'll marry in a week, that is if the weather is good."

"Oh, what you going come to the wedding in, the wedding in, the wedding in,
What you going come to the wedding in, dear old buffalo boy?"

"My Grandmother Green" was recorded by Duncan Emrich from the singing of Mrs. Maud Long of Hot Springs, North Carolina, at Washington, D.C., 1947. Library of Congress AFS record 9154 A4.

"Buffalo Boy" was recorded by Duncan Emrich from the singing of Sam Hinton of La Jolla, California, at Washington, D.C., 1947. Library of Congress record LP21.

"I guess I'll come in my ox-cart, my ox-cart, my ox-cart,
I guess I'll come in my ox-cart, that is if the weather is good."

"Oh, why don't you come in your buggy, in your buggy, in your buggy,
Oh, why don't you come in your buggy, dear old buffalo boy?"

"My ox won't work in a buggy, in a buggy, in a buggy,
My ox won't work in a buggy, not even if the weather is good."

"Well, who you going to bring to the wedding, to the wedding, to the
    wedding,
Who you going to bring to the wedding, dear old buffalo boy,"

"I guess I'll bring my children, my children, my children,
I guess I'll bring my children, that is if the weather is good."

"Oh, I didn't know you had no children, no children, no children,
I didn't know you had no children, dear old buffalo boy."

"Why, sure, I've got five children, five children, five children,
Sure I've got five children, maybe six if the weather is good."

"Oh, there ain't a-going to be no wedding, no wedding, no wedding,
There ain't a-going to be no wedding, not even if the weather is good."

NO, SIR, NO

Yonder stands a pretty fair maiden
With her hands as white as snow,
I'll go court her for her beauty,
Till she answers yes or no,
Yes or no, yes or no,
Till she answers yes or no.

"Madam, I have come a-courting,
It's your favor I do deign.
If you'll kindly answers pay me,
Then perhaps I'll come again."
"Huh-uh, no, no, sir, no,"
And she always answered no.

"Madam, I have gold and silver,
Madam, I have a house and land,
Madam, I have a ship on the ocean,
It may be at your command."
"Huh-uh, no, no, sir, no,"
And she always answered no.

"No, Sir, No" was recorded by Alan and Elizabeth Lomax from the singing of Mrs. Lucy Garrison, Providence, Laurel County, Kentucky, 1937. Library of Congress AFS record 1504 A1.

LOVE

"I don't want any of your gold and
  silver,
I don't want your house and land,
I don't want your ship on the ocean,
All I want is a handsome man.
Huh-uh, no, no, sir, no."
And she always answered no.

"Oh, my darling, how I love you,
It breaks my heart you treat me so.
Guess I'll go and marry above you;
Kiss me once before I go."
"Huh-uh, no, no, sir, no,"
And she always answered no.

"Tell me once and tell me truly,
Tell me why you scorn me so,
Tell me why, when asked a
  question
You will always answer no.
Huh-uh, no, no, sir, no,
Why you always answer no?"

"My father was an English sailor,
And before he went to sea
He told me I must answer no
To everything you said to me.
Huh-uh, no, no, sir, no,
I must always answer no."

"If while walking in the garden,
Plucking flowers all wet with dew,
Tell me would you be offended
If I walked and talked with you?"
"Huh-uh, no, no, sir, no,"
And she answered, "No, sir, no."

"If while walking in the garden
I should ask you to be mine,
If I tell you that I love you,
Would you then my heart decline?"
"Huh-uh, no, no, sir, no,"
And she answered, "No, sir, no."

BILLY BOY

"Oh, where have you been, Billy boy, Billy boy?
Oh, where have you been, charming Billy?"
"I've been to seek a wife,
She's the joy of my life,
She's a young thing, and cannot leave her mother."

"Did she bid you come in, Billy boy, Billy boy?
Did she bid you come in, charming Billy?"
"Yes, she bid me come in
With a dimple in her chin,
She's a young thing, and cannot leave her mother."

"Billy Boy" was recorded by Vance Randolph from the singing of Louise McDowell, Galena,
Missouri, 1941. Library of Congress AFS record 5237 B1.

"Did she set for you a chair, Billy boy, Billy boy?
Did she set for you a chair, charming Billy?"
"Yes, she set for me a chair
With ringlets in her hair,
She's a young thing, and cannot leave her mother."

"Can she make a cherry pie, Billy boy, Billy boy?"
Can she make a cherry pie, charming Billy?"
"Yes, she can make a cherry pie
Quick as a cat can wink its eye,
She's a young thing, and cannot leave her mother."

"How old is she, Billy boy, Billy boy?
How old is she, charming Billy?"
Past six, past seven,
Past twenty and eleven,
She's a young thing, and cannot leave her mother."

AS I WALKED OUT ONE MORNING

As I walked out one morning, just as day was dawning,
There I spied a pretty fair miss, looked like the sun a-rising.

   Sing a hoo-raw-ray, sing a hoo-raw-rye,
   Sing a hoo-raw-rattle-rink-a-dandy.

"Where are you going, my pretty fair miss? Where are you going, my
     honey?"
She answered me most modestly, "I'm on an errand for my old mammy."

"May I walk with you, my pretty fair miss? May I walk with you, my
     honey?"
She answered me most modestly, "I will walk with anybody."

"How old are you, my pretty fair miss? How old are you, my honey?"
She answered me most modestly, "I'll be sixteen next Easter Sunday."

"As I Walked Out One Morning" was recorded by Sidney Robertson Cowell from the
singing of David Rice, Springfield, Missouri, 1936. Library of Congress AFS record
3211 A1.

LOVE

It wasn't but a very few days till this young man went a-courting;
He hadn't said but a very few words till the old lady overheard him.

She shoved her broom all in the fire to make a light to find him;
This young man jumped up and cocked his heels, and bade his legs defend
   him.

"It's fare you well, my own true love! It's fare you well, my honey!"
"When will you be back again to be chased by my old mammy?"

"It's fare you well, my own true love. It's fare you well, my honey!
I'll have my girl I love the best, in spite of her darned old mammy."

THE MILKMAID

"Oh, where are you going, my little maiden fair,
With your red, rosy cheeks and your coal-black hair?"
"Oh, I'm a-going a-milking, oh, kind sir," she answered me.
A-rolling in the dew makes the milkmaid so fair.

"Supposing I would go along, my little maiden fair,
With your red, rosy cheeks and your coal-black hair?"
"It's then that you'd come back again, oh, kind sir," she answered me.
A-rolling in the dew makes the milkmaid so fair.

"Oh, supposing I would lay you down, my little maiden fair?"
"Oh, then you'd let me up again, oh, kind sir," she answered me.

"Oh, supposing I would get you a little one, my little maiden fair?"
"It's then you'd be the daddy of it, oh, kind sir," she answered me.

"Oh, what would you lap it in, my little maiden fair?"
"I'd lap it in my petticoats, oh, kind sir," she answered me.

"Oh, what would you rock it in, my little maiden fair?"
"My uncle he's a cradle maker, oh, kind sir," she answered me.

"Oh, supposing I would run away, my little maiden fair,
With your red, rosy cheeks and your coal-black hair?"
"It's then that you'd come back again, oh, kind sir," she answered me.
A-rolling in the dew makes the milkmaid so fair.

"The Milkmaid" was collected by Herbert Halpert from the singing of Allen Clevenger near
Magnolia, New Jersey, 1937. Reported in *JAF*, 52 (1939):58.

MADAME, I HAVE COME A-COURTING

"Madame, I have come a-courting, hum a day, hum a day,
Madame, I have come a-courting, hum a day."
"Well, if that be your desire,
You can sit and court the fire."
Fal tum a link tum, a tu rye day.

"Madame, I have houses and lands, hum a day, hum a day,
Madame, I have houses and lands, hum a day."
"What do I care for your houses and lands?
All I want is a handsome man."
Fal tum a link, tum, a tu rye day.

"Madame, I've got rings and money, hum a day, hum a day,
Madame, I've got rings and money, hum a day."
"What do I care for your rings and money!
I've got a lad that calls me honey."
Fal tum a link tum, a tu rye day.

"Madame, I'll go home to Mother, hum a day, hum a day,
Madame, I'll go home to Mother, hum a day."
"What do I care for you or your mother,
She's a greenhorn, you're another."
Fal tum a link tum, a tu rye day.

OLD GRAY BEARD A-SHAKING

My mammy she told me to open the door,
Hmp-mm, but I won't have him;
I opened the door and he fell on the floor
With his old gray beard a-shaking.

"Madame, I Have Come A-Courting" was recorded by Sidney Robertson Cowell from the singing of George Vinton Graham, San Jose, California, 1938. Library of Congress AFS record 3815 A3 and 4.

"Old Gray Beard A-Shaking" was recorded by John A. Lomax and Laurence Powell from the singing of Mrs. Emma Dusenbury, Mena, Arkansas, 1936. Library of Congress AFS record 847 B3.

My mammy she told me to set him a chair,
Hmp-mm, but I won't have him;
I set him a chair and he looked like a steer,
With his old gray beard a-shaking.

My mammy she told me to set him a stool,
Hmp-mm, but I won't have him;
I set him a stool and he looked like a fool
With his old gray beard a-shaking.

My mammy she told me to give him a piece of pie,
Hmp-mm, but I won't have him;
I give him a piece of pie and he eat like he'd die
With his old gray beard a-shaking.

My mammy she told me to saddle his horse,
Hmp-mm, but I won't have him;
I saddled his horse and I bid him be off,
With his old gray beard a-shaking.

My mammy she told me to put him in the road,
Hmp-mm, but I won't have him;
I put him in the road and he jumped like a toad
With his old gray beard a-shaking.

My mammy she told me to bid him farewell,
Hmp-mm, but I won't have him;
I bid him farewell and I wished him in hell
With his old gray beard a-shaking.

THE GRAY MARE
(*Young Johnny the Miller*)

Young Johnny the miller he courted of late
The farmer's fair daughter called beautiful Kate,
And whose wealthy portion was five thousand pounds,
With ribbons and tassels and furbelow gowns,
With ribbons and tassels and rich diamond rings,
And sumptious apparel,
And sumptious apparel and many fine things.

"The Gray Mare" was recorded by Sidney Robertson Cowell from the singing of George Vinton Graham, San Jose, California, 1938. Library of Congress AFS record 3816 B2. Imperfect text amended from *JAF*, 12 (1899):251. Laws, P8.

A day was appointed, the wedding foretold,
With many fine presents of silver and gold;
When unto her father young Johnny he said,
"I cannot marry this beautiful maid,
Although she is beautiful, charming and fair,
Without the addition,
Without the addition of Tib, the gray mare."

The farmer made answer to young Johnny with speed,
"I thought you had courted my daughter indeed,
And not the gray mare; but since it is thus,
My money once more I'll return to my purse.
And as for my daughter, I vow and declare,
I'll keep both my daughter,
I'll keep both my daughter and Tib, the gray mare."

The money was then vanished out of his life,
And so was Miss Katie, his dear and delight;
And he like a blockhead was kicked out of doors
And forbade by her father to come any more.
It was then that young Johnny began his locks for to tear,
Saying, "I wish I had never,
I wish I had never stood out for the mare."

About a year after or a little above,
He chanced to meet with Miss Katie, his love.
And he said, "My charming creature, oh, don't you know me?"
"If I mistake not, sir, I have seen you," said she,
"Or one of your likeness, with your long yellow hair,
You once came a-courting,
You once came a-courting my father's gray mare."

"It was not the gray mare a-courting I came,
But you, my sweet Kate, sweet Katie by name.
Little did I think your father would doubt
Of giving with Katie the gray mare to boot
For the sake of such a fine dutiful son;
It is, oh, that I'm sorry,
It is, oh, that I'm sorry for what I have done."

"Your sorrow," says Kate, "I value it not;
There's young men enough in this world to be got.
And I think that a girl would be at the last prayer
Who would marry a man that once courted a mare.
And as for a mare, its price is not great,
So fare you well, Johnny,
So fare you well, Johnny, go mourn for your Kate."

OLD WOMAN

"Old woman, old woman, are you fond of carding?
Old woman, old woman, are you fond of carding?"
"Speak a little louder, sir, I'm rather hard of hearing.
Speak a little louder, sir, I'm rather hard of hearing."

"Old woman, old woman are you fond of smoking?
Old woman, old woman are you fond of smoking?"
"Speak a little louder, sir, I'm rather hard of hearing.
Speak a little louder, sir, I'm rather hard of hearing."

"Old woman, old woman, won't you let me court you?"
Old woman, old woman, won't you let me court you?"
"Speak a little louder, sir, I've just begun to hear you.
Speak a little louder, sir, I've just begun to hear you."

"Old woman, old woman, don't you want to marry?
Old woman, old woman, don't you want to marry?"
"Laws a mercy on my soul, I think at last I hear you.
Laws a mercy on my soul, I think at last I hear you."

THE BACHELOR'S COMPLAINT

Once I heard an old bachelor say
When his hair was turning gray,
"I wonder what the matter can be
That all the pretty girls so dislike me!"

"Old Woman" is from "Folk Songs," Bulletin 3 of the WPA Recreation Project in Kentucky, Music Series, n.d., ca. 1940.

"The Bachelor's Complaint" is from Phillips Barry, "Some Aspects of Folksong," *JAF*, 25 (1912):281.

"I tried the rich and I've tried the poor
And many a time I've been kicked out of door.
I've tried silver and I've tried gold,
And many a lie in my life I have told.

"Three good horses I rode them to death,
I rode them as long as they had breath.
Three good saddles rode bare to the tree,
Trying to find the girl that would marry me."

He wept and he mourned and he wailed and he cried,
And in this condition, this bachelor died.
And if he lies here, I fear he'll come to life,
And still be a-trying to get him a wife.

Come all ye pretty fair maids, come gather around,
And put this old bachelor under the ground.
For if he lies here, I fear he'll come to life,
And still be a-trying to get him a wife.

THE WIDOW'S OLD BROOM

I was out in the country one beautiful night,
And spied a fair maiden, my heart's delight,
She was handsome and true, warm-hearted and fair,
A widow's lone daughter, a widow's lone heir.

And when we reached home, the old lady in bed,
And hearing us a-talking she raised her head,
"Who's there?" cried she. I told her my name,
"A-courting your daughter on purpose I came."

"My daughter, my daughter, my daughter," cried she,
"Do you think that my daughter can go before me?
And isn't it strange that a girl so young
Can have all the sweethearts and I can have none?"

"The Widow's Old Broom" was recorded by Vance Randolph from the singing of Charles Ingenthron, Walnut Shade, Missouri, 1941. Library of Congress record LP12.

LOVE

"I know you're a widow whose pockets are large,
I know you're a widow who has a great charge."
"A widow!" cried she, "You scorn my name!"
She up with a broomstick and at me she came.

I flew to the door to escape in the night,
The doors and the windows were all fast quite tight;
The first thing I knew was a rap on the head
That sent me a-reeling in under the bed.

And when I came out the old lady was there,
She hit me another on the head with a chair.
"Oh, murder!" cried I, and flew to the door,
And then the old woman she hit me once more.

She hit me, she kicked me, and at last I got clear,
I mounted my horse and home I did steer;
And when I reached home all bloody and sore,
There never was a fellow skinned up so before.

Young men, young men, be warned by me,
A widow's lone daughter never go to see;
As sure as you do, you'll meet your doom
And carry the marks of the widow's old broom.

ALL NIGHT LONG FOOLING ME

Fooled me once and you fooled me bad,
Bet you'll wish you never had.

    All night long fooling, fooling,
    All night long fooling me.
    Better quit your fooling, fooling, fooling,
    Better quit your fooling, fooling me.

Fooled me last night and the night before,
Bet your life you'll fool me no more.

"All Night Long Fooling Me" was recorded by Herbert Halpert from the singing of Austin
Harmon, Maryville, Tennessee, 1939. Library of Congress AFS record 2918 B3.

All night long fooling, fooling,
All night long fooling me.
All night long fooling, fooling,
All night long fooling me.

Fooled me once and you fooled me twice,
And you fooled me out of my darling wife.

All night long fooling, fooling,
All night long fooling me.
Better quit fooling, fooling, fooling,
Better quit fooling, fooling me.

I DON'T LET THE GIRLS WORRY MY MIND

Little fish swim in the river, big fish swim in the sea,
But there ain't no use of the girls worrying me.
Never was arrested, never paid a fine,
'Cause I don't let the girls worry my mind.

You take this and you take that, and I'll take all I can get,
Standing out in the rain, but I don't ever get wet.
I don't want your whiskey and I don't want your wine,
'Cause I don't let the girls worry my mind.

Monkeys sit in the mountains, monkeys climb the trees,
There ain't no use the girls worrying me.
Never was arrested, never paid a fine,
'Cause I don't let the girls worry my mind.

Bachelor's life is single, the bachelor's life is free,
So what's the use the girls worrying me.
Women spend your money down to the last go 'round,
So you better not let the girls worry your mind.

You take this and you take that, and I'll take all I can get,
Standing out in the rain, but I don't ever get wet.
I don't want your whiskey and I don't want your wine,
'Cause I don't let the girls worry my mind.

"I Don't Let the Girls Worry My Mind" was recorded by John A. Lomax from the singing of H. J. Beeker, Boone, North Carolina, 1936. Library of Congress AFS record 844 A2.

THERE'S MORE PRETTY GIRLS THAN ONE

"Ladies and gentlemen, you see this here contraption that fits snugly around my neck, fastened by a wire and two screws here on the side . . . was made of . . . made it up myself out of a few articles I picked up. First, an auctioneer's horn cost me the big sum of a nickel. And next you see a bathtub stopper that cost me a dime. And then you come on down here . . . in the end of this contraption is a cap off a thermometer bottle. Probably pick 'em up in the junk pile anywhere. Well this is a . . . one of my own contraptions. And now I'll play you a little song . . . 'There's More Pretty Girls than One.' "

There's more pretty girls than one,
There's more pretty girls than one,
For every town I've rambled around,
There's more pretty girls than one.

My mamma told me last night,
She gave me good advice:
"Better stop your rambling around, pretty boy,
And marry you a loving wife."

Look down that lonesome road,
Look down that lonesome road,
Hang down your little head and cry —
For thinking of those pretty little girls
And hoping I never will die.

Look down that lonesome road,
Before you travel on,
I'm leaving you this lonesome song
To sang when I am gone.

There's more pretty girls than one,
There's more pretty girls than one,
For every town I've rambled around
There's more pretty girls than one.

"There's More Pretty Girls than One" was recorded by Charles Todd and Robert Sonkin from the singing (with described instrumental accompaniment) of Wayne Dinwiddie at Visalia, California, 1941. Library of Congress record LP21.

SOLDIER BOY FOR ME

I would not marry a blacksmith,
He smuts his nose and chin;
I'd rather marry a soldier boy
That marches through the wind.

> Soldier boy, soldier boy,
> Soldier boy for me;
> If ever I get married,
> A soldier's wife I'll be.

I would not marry a doctor,
He's always killing the sick;
I'd rather marry a soldier boy
That marches double quick.

I would not marry a farmer,
He's always selling grain;
I'd rather marry a soldier boy
That marches through the rain.

> Soldier boy, soldier boy,
> Soldier boy for me;
> If ever I get married,
> A soldier's wife I'll be.

A Railroader for Me

"Here's an old-timer that I learned from my grandmammy way down in southern Missouri, and this old song I think was written right after the Civil War when they first invented the first steam engines."

A railroader, a railroader,
A railroader for me;
If ever I marry in this wide world,
A railroader's bride I'll be.

Now I would not marry a
    blacksmith,
He's always in the black,
I'd rather marry an engineer
That throws the throttle back.

A railroader, a railroader,
A railroader for me;
If ever I marry in this wide world,
A railroader's bride I'll be.

I would not marry a farmer,
He's always in the dirt,
I'd rather marry an engineer
That wears a stripèd shirt.

"Soldier Boy for Me" was collected by Cecil J. Sharp from the singing of Mr. Bridges, St. Peter's Mission, Franklin County, Virginia, 1918. Text with music in Sharp, *English Folk Songs from the Southern Appalachians* (Oxford) New York, 1932. II, 381.

"A Railroader for Me" was recorded by Charles Todd and Robert Sonkin from the singing of Russ Pike at Visalia, California, 1941. Library of Congress record LP20.

> A railroader, a railroader,
> A railroader for me;
> If ever I marry in this wide world,
> A railroader's bride I'll be.

Chewing Chawing Gum

Mamma sent me to the spring, she told me not to stay;
I fell in love with a pretty little boy, and I stayed there all day.

> Chawing chewing gum, chewing chawing gum,
> Chawing chewing gum, chewing chawing gum.

Oh, first he gave me peaches, then he gave me pears,
Then he gave me fifty cents and kissed me on the stairs.

> Chawing chewing gum, chewing chawing gum,
> Chawing chewing gum, chewing chawing gum.

I gave him back his peaches, I gave him back his pears,
I gave him back his fifty cents and kicked him down the stairs.

Oh, I would not marry a preacher, I'll tell you the reason why,
Every time he opens his mouth he tells a great big lie.

Oh, I would not marry a doctor, I'll tell you the reason why,
He rides all over the country and makes the people die.

Oh, I would not marry a lawyer, I'll tell you the reason why,
Every time he has a case he swears a lot of lies.

Oh, I'll tell you I'd marry a farmer, this is the reason why,
Because he has so much to eat and makes the pumpkin pie.

Mamma don't allow me to whistle, Papa don't allow me to sing,
Mamma won't allow me to marry, but I'll marry just the same.

> Chawing chewing gum, chewing chawing gum,
> Chawing chewing gum, chewing chawing gum.

"Chewing Chawing Gum" was recorded by Herbert Halpert from the singing of Mary Addington, Norton, Virginia, 1939. Library of Congress AFS record 2776 B3, with stanzas collected also by Halpert at Norton, Virginia, from Mrs. Mary Glenn Jesse and Mrs. Esco Kilgore, Library of Congress AFS records 2775 B1 and 2776 B2.

I'll Not Marry at All

I'm determined to be an old maid,
Take my stool, and sit in the shade;
I'll not marry at all, at all,
I'll not marry at all.

I'll not marry a man that's old,
For he will prove a terrible scold.
I'll not marry at all, at all,
I'll not marry at all.

I'll not marry a man that's young,
For he'll deceive with flattering tongue.
I'll not marry at all, at all,
I'll not marry at all.

I'll not marry a man that's rich,
For he'll get drunk and fall in a ditch.
I'll not marry at all, at all,
I'll not marry at all.

I'll not marry a man that's poor,
For he'll go begging from door to door.
I'll not marry at all, at all,
I'll not marry at all.

Old Maid's Song

I wouldn't marry a bachelor;
I'll tell you the reason why:
His nose is always dripping;
His chin is never dry.

I wouldn't marry a lawyer;
I'll tell you the reason why:
He is always in the courthouse
A-making people lie.

"I'll Not Marry at All" was collected by Katherine Harbison from the singing of Miss Dove Harris, Danville, Kentucky, and reported in her article "In the Great Meadow and Lone Prairie," *SFQ*, 2 (1938):153. With music.

"Old Maid's Song" was collected by Mellinger E. Henry from Miss Pauline Franklin, Crossnore, Avery County, North Carolina, 1931. In Henry, *Folksongs from the Southern Highlands*, New York, 1938, p. 309. Without music.

I wouldn't marry a preacher;
I'll tell you the reason why:
He is always in the pulpit
A-making people cry.

I wouldn't marry an old maid;
I'll tell you the reason why:
Her neck is so long and strangly
I'm afraid she will never die.

FATHER GRUMBLE

There was an old man who lived in the wood
As you can plainly see,
Who said he could do more work in one day
Than his wife could do in three.

"If this be true," the old woman said,
"Why, this you must allow:
You must do my work for one day
While I go drive the plow.

"And you must feed [milk] the Tiny cow
For fear she will go dry,
And you must feed the little pigs
That are within the sty.

"And you must watch the speckled hen
Lest she should lay astray,
And you must wind the reel of yarn
That I spun yesterday."

The old woman took the staff in her hand
And went to drive the plow,
The old man took the pail in his hand
And went to milk the cow.

But Tiny hitched and Tiny flitched,
And Tiny cocked her nose,
And Tiny gave the old man such a kick
That the blood ran down to his hose.

"Father Grumble" was recorded by Artus M. Moser from the singing of Jean Ritchie of Viper, Kentucky, at Renfro Valley, Kentucky, 1946. Library of Congress record LP14.

It's "Hey, my good cow!" and "Ho, my good cow!"
And, "Now, my good cow, stand still!
If ever I milk this cow again,
'Twill be against my will."

But Tiny hitched and Tiny flitched,
And Tiny cocked her nose,
And Tiny gave the old man such a kick
That the blood ran down to his hose.

And when he had milked the Tiny cow
For fear she would go dry,
Why then he fed the little pigs
That are within the sty.

And then he watched the speckled hen
Lest she should lay astray,
But he forgot the reel of yarn
His wife spun yesterday.

He swore by all the stars in the sky
And all the leaves on the tree
His wife could do more work in one day
Than he could do in three.

He swore by all the leaves on the tree
And all the stars in heaven
That his wife could do more work in one day
Than he could do in seven.

THE BEST OLD FELLOW IN THE WORLD

"Oh, where are you going, my kind old husband,
Oh, where are you going?" she called him her dear,
"Oh, where are you going, my kind old husband,
The best old fellow in the world?"

(*Spoken*) "Going down to the saloon, where I always go."

"The Best Old Fellow in the World" was recorded by Vance Randolph from the singing of
Charles Ingenthron, Walnut Shade, Missouri, 1941. Library of Congress AFS record 5251.

"Oh, what are you going there for, my kind old husband,
Oh, what are you going there for?" she called him her dear,
"Oh, what you going there for, my kind old husband,
The best old fellow in the world?"

(*Spoken*) "To get drunk, like I always do."

"Won't you wait till after supper, my kind old husband,
Won't you wait till after supper?" she called him her dear,
"Won't you wait till after supper, my kind old husband,
The best old fellow in the world?"

(*Spoken*) "Well, hurry up and get supper."

"Oh, what'll you have for supper, my kind old husband,
Oh, what'll you have for supper?" she called him her dear,
"Oh, what'll you have for supper, my kind old husband,
The best old fellow in the world?"

(*Spoken*) "A peck of eggs, like you always have."

"How'll you have 'em cooked, my kind old husband,
How'll you have 'em cooked?" she called him her dear,
"How'll you have 'em cooked, my kind old husband,
The best old fellow in the world?"

(*Spoken*) "Just fry 'em in water, like you always do."

"Ain't you afraid they'll kill you, my kind old husband,
Ain't you afraid they'll kill you?" she called him her dear,
Ain't you afraid they'll kill you, my kind old husband,
The best old fellow in the world?"

(*Spoken*) "Well, just let me die, like you always do."

"Then I'd have to bury you, my kind old husband,
Then I'd have to bury you," she called him her dear,
"Then I'd have to bury you, my kind old husband,
The best old fellow in the world."

(*Spoken*) "Well, just bury me, like you always do."

"Oh, where shall I bury you, my kind old husband,
Oh, where shall I bury you?" she called him her dear,
"Oh, where shall I bury you, my kind old husband,
The best old fellow in the world?"

(*Spoken*) "Just bury me in the chimney corner, like you always do."

LOVE

"The dog would scratch you out, my kind old husband,
The dog would scratch you out," she called him her dear,
"The dog would scratch you out, my kind old husband,
The best old fellow in the world."

(*Spoken*) "Then just let me go, like you always do."

"Then I'd cry my eyes out, my kind old husband,
Then I'd cry my eyes out," she called him her dear,
"Then I'd cry my eyes out, my kind old husband,
The best old fellow in the world."

THE OLD LADY OF LONDON

There lived a fat old lady, in London she did dwell,
She loved her old man dearly, but another one twice as well.
Saying, "Carry me away,
Oh, carry me away."

She went to the doctor to see if she could find
Some kind of medicine to run her old man blind.
Saying, "Carry me away,
Oh, carry me away."

Oh, she found the medicine, she made him take it all,
He says, "My darling, loving wife, I can't see you at all."

He says, "My darling, loving wife, if I could see the way,
I'd go down to the seashore, and jump in and drown."

She says, "My darling husband, it's there you'll go astray,
I'll go along beside you and show you the way."

They walked side and side together, till they come to the distant shore,
He says, "My darling, loving wife, you'll have to shove me o'er."

She stepped back a step or two to run and shove him in,
And he stepped out to one side — and foremost she went in!

"The Old Lady of London" was recorded by Charles Todd and Robert Sonkin from the singing of Bill Jackson, FSA Camp, Arvin, California, 1941, Library of Congress AFS record 5112 A1. Laws, Q2.

When she saw her sad mistake, she began to scream and squall;
He says, "My darling, loving wife, I can't see you at all."

Then he being chicken-hearted, and fearing she might swim,
He grabbed him up a ten-foot pole and shoved her further in.
Saying, "Carry me away,
Oh, carry me away."

JOHNNY SANDS

There was a man named Johnny Sands, who married Betty Hague,
And though she brought him gold and land, she proved a terrible plague,
For oh, she was a scolding wife, full of caprice and whim,
She made poor Johnny tired of life, and she was tired of him, of him,
And she was tired of him.

Says he, "I think I'll drown myself in the river there below."
Says she, "Pray do, you silly oaf, I wished it long ago."
Said he, "Upon the brink I'll stand, do you run down the hill
And push me in with all your might." Says she, "My love, I will, I will,"
Says she, "My love, I will."

"For fear that I should courage lack and try to save my life,
Pray tie my hands behind my back." "I will," replied his wife.
She tied him fast as you may think and when securely done,
"Now stand," she said, "upon the brink, while I prepare to run, to run,
While I prepare to run."

So down the hill his loving bride now ran with all her force
To push him in. He stepped aside and she fell in, of course.
Now splashing, dashing like a fish, "Oh, save me, Johnny Sands!"
"I can't, my dear, though much I wish, for you have tied my hands, my hands,
For you have tied my hands."

"Johnny Sands" was recorded by Rae Korson and Duncan Emrich from the singing of Sam Hinton of La Jolla, California, at Washington, D.C., 1947. Library of Congress AFS record 8930 A3. Laws, Q3.

DEVILISH MARY

When I was young and in my prime,
I thought I never could marry,
I fell in love with a pretty little girl,
Tune of "She Got Married."

Rinktum-dinktum-tarry,
Prettiest little girl in all this world.
Her name was Devilish Mary.

She washed my clothes in live soap suds,
She peeled my back with switches,
She let me know right up to date
She's gonna wear my britches.

Rinktum-dinktum-tarry,
Prettiest little girl in all this world,
Her name was Devilish Mary.

We'd just been married about two weeks,
We thought we'd better be parted,
She bundled her up a little bundle of clothes
And down the road she started.

Rinktum-dinktum-tarry,
Prettiest little girl in all this world,
Her name was Devilish Mary.

If ever I marry the second time,
It'll be for love nor [not] riches,
I'll marry one about two feet high,
So she can't wear my britches.

Rinktum-dinktum-tarry,
Prettiest little girl in all this world,
Her name was Devilish Mary.

"Devilish Mary" was recorded by Artus M. Moser from the singing of Paul Rogers of Paint Lick, Kentucky, at Renfro Valley, Kentucky, 1946. Library of Congress record LP14. Laws, Q4.

THE CLEVER SKIPPER

There was a clever skipper, in Akron he did dwell,
Who had a lovely woman, and a tailor she loved well.
Did you ever hear the story? Then listen what I say.

She was walking up South Howard Street,
Who but the tailor did she chance for to meet.
Tum a rally tolly dolly, tum a rolly tolly day.

They wined, dined and danced, it was late by the clock,
When up stepped the captain and loudly he did knock.
Tum a rally tolly dolly, tum a rolly tolly day.

They were surprised, the tailor said so quietly,
"Now, now, my lovely woman, and now where shall I creep?"

"In yonders cupboard my husband has a chest,
Yes, in that cupboard a cover you may hide."

They hurried, she packed him up, coat, boots and hat,
She packed him up with the balance of his clothes.

So she ran downstairs and opened the door,
There stood the skipper with a couple other more.

She kindly saluted him, gave to him a kiss,
Says she, "My loving husband, what do you mean by this?"

"I didn't come to rob or break you of your rest,
I'm going on south and came for my chest."

These two canallers jolly, jolly, brave and strong,
They picked up the chest and wagged it along.

They hadn't got more than the middle of the town,
Till the weight of the tailor made the sweat trickle down.

They set the chest down to take a moment's rest;
Says one to the other, "What the devil's in the chest?"

"The Clever Skipper" was recorded by Alan and Elizabeth Lomax from the singing of
Capt. Pearl R. Nye, Akron, Ohio, 1937. Library of Congress AFS record 1603 A. Laws, Q8.

Neither of the two the chest could undo,
Till up stepped the skipper with the balance of the crew.

He unlocked the chest in the presence of them all,
And there lay the tailor like a hog in a stall.

"Now I have got you, I'll take you on sea,
Not leave you here making trouble for me."
Tum a rally tolly dolly, tum a rolly tolly day.

They took him on board, for Portsmouth they did steer,
And this is the last of the tailor we do hear.
Tum a rally tolly dolly, tum a rolly tolly day.

WILL THE WEAVER

"Oh, Mammy, Mammy, now I'm married,
And if I marry where must I tarry?
The womenkind they do declare
The britches they intend to wear."

"Oh, son, oh, son, you can't live with her,
You go home bid her adieu,
You go home bid her adieu,
And let me hear no more of you."

As he went home his neighbors met him,
And this they told him for to fret him,
"You can't guess to save your life
Who I saw hugging up your wife.

"I saw your wife and Will the weaver
A-standing in your door together,
A-standing in your parlor door,
And where they went I saw no more."

He went home all in a wonder,
A-knocking at the door like thunder;

"Will the Weaver" was recorded by Herbert Halpert from the singing of Samuel Harmon, Maryville, Tennessee, 1939. Library of Congress AFS record 2806 A1. Laws, Q9.

"Who is this?" the weaver cried.
"It is my husband, you must hide."

Up on the chimney pole Will he ventured
Before she let her husband enter.
He come in, made this reply,
"I want some grog, for I am dry."

Then while grog it was a-making,
Every hole and corner searching,
He peeked up on the chimney pole
And there he saw some living soul.

'Ha, ha, old boy, now I've found you,
I'll neither shoot you, hang, nor drown you.'
This was thought but wasn't spoke —
'I'll rout you out of here with smoke.'

So he built up a rousing fire
Just to please his heart's desire.
His wife cried out in a free good will,
"Oh, stop your smoke or a man you'll kill."

He reached up and off he took him
And like an old raccoon he shook him.
He went home all in disguise
With black smoke in his face and eyes.

"Oh, wife, oh, wife, I've got a trimming
For meddling with my neighbor's women."
She picked up a stick, she spanged his head,
And what was black she turned it red.

Miscellaneous Songs of Love

Down in the lion's den he boldly entered,
Lions being both wild and fierce;
He marched around and in among them,
Safetly returned her fan again.

MY NEW GARDEN FIELD

Come all you pretty fair maids, I pray you attend
Unto these few lines that I briefly have penned
Concerning lovely Nancy. She's my pride and heart's delight,
For she is my whole day's study and my dream in the night.

On the second day of August, the date of that year,
Down in Cupid's garden where I first met my dear,
You would have thought she was some goddess, or yet some fair young queen
That had come as a torture to torment my mind.

"Oh, I am no goddess," this fair one did say,
"But a-plucking these flowers so bright and so gay,
But a-plucking these flowers that nature doth yield,
For I take great delight in my new garden field."

I says, "My pretty, fair maid, may I make so bold
As your lily-white hand, love, one moment to hold?
It would give me more pleasure than this whole world in store.
Come, grant me this favor and I'll ask for no more."

She turns and says, "Young man, I fear you're in jest,
If I thought you were in earnest, I would think myself blest,

"My New Garden Field" is from Carrie B. Grover, *A Heritage of Songs* (privately printed,
Gould Academy, Bethel, Maine, n.d.), pp. 10–11.

But my father is a-coming," this fair maid did say,
"So fare you well, young man, for I must away."

Now she's gone and she's left me in deep bonds of love.
Kind Cupid, assist me, or some angel above.
King Cupid, assist me and lend me more art,
For she's guilty of murder, and she has won my heart.

Oh, she turns and says, "Young man, I pity your case.
I will leave you no longer to sigh in distress.
My love, I will go along with you to some foreign part,
For you are the first young man that e'er won my heart.

"On Sunday we will go to church and married we'll be
And we'll live together in sweet unity.
So here is my hand, love, I vow to be true,
And to all other young men I now bid adieu."

THE LITTLE DRUMMER

He came to his love's window at the dead of the night,
He called her his jewel, his own heart's delight.
"Now since you've shot the arrow you're the one who can cure,
And if you won't have me I'll die at your door.
And it's oh, my hard fortune."

"Begone, little drummer," this fair one did say,
"Would I be so mean as to marry with thee?
My father's a squire of a high degree
And I am his daughter and heiress to be,
And it's oh, my hard fortune!"

He turned to the door and he bade her farewell,
Saying, "You'll send my soul wandering to heaven or hell;
On the point of my bayonet I will end all this strife

"The Little Drummer" was recorded by Alan Lomax from the singing of Mrs. Carrie Grover of Gorham, Maine, at Washington, D.C., 1941. Library of Congress AFS record 4459 B1. Text with music also in Carrie B. Grover, *A Heritage of Songs* (privately printed, Gould Academy, Bethel, Maine, n.d.), pp. 83–84.

And cut the sweet innocent thread of my life.
And it's oh, my hard fortune!"

"Come back, little drummer," this fair one did say,
"Come back, little drummer, and marry with me.
Turn back, little drummer, marry me if you will,
For I think it a pity your blood for to spill,
And it's oh, my hard fortune!

"Come saddle a steed and to Plymouth we'll go,
Where we will be married in spite of our foes,
And when we are married and all things are done,
What more can they say than we followed the drum?
And it's oh, my hard fortune."

Now when her old father this news came to hear
It's straightway to Plymouth he quickly did steer,
He took them both home and to them he did give
Five thousand a year as long as they lived,
And it's oh, my good fortune.

THERE SHE STANDS A LOVELY CREATURE

When mother was a little girl, she knew an old lady who was so helplessly crippled by rheumatism that she had completely lost the use of her limbs. Each morning some member of her family would place her in her big rocker and there she would sit all day, rocking and singing old songs and hymns. She sat with her right elbow in the padded arm of her chair, ceaselessly rubbing her thumb back and forth across the first joint of her first finger, as these were the only fingers she could move. Mother said that from hearing this old lady singing them she learned: "The Quaker's Wooing," "There She Stands A Lovely Creature," and "Remember the Poor."

— CARRIE GROVER

There she stands a lovely creature.
Who she is I do not know.
I will court her for her beauty,
She can only answer, "No."

"Madam, I have gold and silver,
Madam, I have houses and land,
Madam, I have ships on the ocean,
All will be at your command."

"There She Stands a Lovely Creature" was recorded by Sidney Robertson Cowell from the singing of Mrs. Carrie Grover of Gorham, Maine, at Teaneck, New Jersey, 1941. Library of Congress AFS record 4695 A2. Text with music also in Carrie B. Grover, *A Heritage of Songs* (privately printed, Gould Academy, Bethel, Maine, n.d.), p. 18.

"What care I for gold and silver?
What care I for houses and land?
What care I for ships on the ocean?
All I want is a handsome man."

"Handsome man is out of the
   question,
Handsome man you can not find,
Handsome man is out of the
   question,
Can not be at your command.

"Madam, do not stand on beauty;
Youth and beauty fade away
Like a rose that blooms in the morning
And in evening dies away."

THE NIGHTINGALE

One morning, one morning, one morning in May
I spied a fair couple a-making their way,
One was a lady so bright and so fair,
And the other was a soldier, a gay cavalier.

"Oh, where are you going, my pretty fair maid?
Oh, where are you going, sweet lady?" he said.
"I'm going," said she, "to the banks of the stream,
To see the waters gliding, hear the nightingales sing."

They had not been there but an hour or two
Till out of his satchel a fiddle he drew.
He played her a love-song caused the valleys to ring,
"Hark, hark!" says the lady, "Hear the nightingales sing!"

"Oh, now," says the soldier, " 'tis time to give o'er."
"Oh, no," says the lady, "just play one tune more;
For I'd rather hear the fiddle, or one tug on the string,
Than to see the waters gliding, hear the nightingales sing.

"Oh, now," says the lady, "it's won't you marry me?"
"Oh, no," says the soldier, "that never can be!

"The Nightingale" is from Mrs. Eva Warner Case, Harrison County, Missouri, 1916, in
H. M. Belden, *Ballads and Songs Collected by the Missouri Folk-Lore Society*, Columbia
(reprint edition, 1966), p. 242. Laws, P14.

I've a wife in Low Flanders, with children twice three;
And two and the army's too many for me!

"I'll go home to Flanders and stay there one year,
In place of pure water I'll drink wine and beer.
And if ever I return, 'twill be in the spring
When the waters are gliding and the nightingales sing."

Come all ye fair damsels, take warning from me,
Never place your affections on a green willow tree;
For the leaves they will wither like flowers in the spring
When the waters are a-gliding and the nightingales sing.

Come all ye fair damsels, take warning from me,
Never place your affections on a soldier so free.
For he'll love you and leave you without any ring
To rock your young baby, hear the nightingales sing!

WILLIE LEONARD
or The Lake of Cold Finn

A correspondent who was born in County Kerry wrote Mrs. [Fannie H.] Eckstorm that she heard "Young Willie or the Lake of Cool Finn" sung in her childhood. "The tale of the legend (the old people said it was a true tale) is, a mermaid fell in love with young Willie. There is one time in the year when the mermaids have power over mortals. She had it that day when she waked young Willie up and had him come to the lake. The first time he swam round, he was too strong for her and he swam to an island. . . . His comrade didn't want him to go in again:

Young Willie rested and said "I'll go —"
The waves they were rough and the wind it did blow;
"Willie, dear Willie, don't you go in;
There is deep and false water in the lake of Cool Finn."

The second time he swam around, she pulled him down. His body was never found, and it was a dummy body they had in the casket. So the tale goes."
— PHILLIPS BARRY

"Willie Leonard" was contributed to the Folksong Society of the Northeast by Mr. Thomas E. Nelson, Union Mills, New Brunswick, 1929. Reported, with music and extensive notes, by Phillips Barry in *Bulletin of the Folksong Society of the Northeast*, Cambridge, Mass., 8 (1934):9–12. Laws, Q33.

The ballad contains folk motifs of great antiquity: the sirens, mermaids, the supernatural woman who seeks the love of a mortal man. Barry reports it as being collected from New York, Maine, New Brunswick, and Vermont. From the North in all instances.

> It was early Monday morning Willie Leonard arose,
> And straight to his comrade, young Leonard did go;
> Saying, "Arise, loyal comrade, and let nobody know,
> It's a fine summer morning, and a-bathing we will go."
>
> They walked and they talked till they came to a lane,
> And the first one they met was a keeper of game;
> Saying, "Go back, Willie Leonard, do not venture in,
> For there's deep and false water in the Lake of Cold Finn."
>
> Willie stripped off his clothes and he swam the lake around,
> He swam to an island, but not to dry ground;
> "Go back, loyal comrade, do not venture in,
> For there's deep and false water in the Lake of Cold Finn!"
>
> It was early next morning Willie's sister arose,
> And straight to the bedchamber of her mother she goes;
> "Oh, Mother, dear Mother, I had a strange dream,
> I dreamed I saw Willie in a cold watery stream!"
>
> It was early next morning Willie's mother was there,
> A-wringing of her hands and a-tearing of her hair;
> "Oh, murder, oh, murder, — was there nobody nigh,
> That would venture their life for my own darling boy?"
>
> It was early next morning Willie's uncle was there,
> And he swam around the lake like a man in despair;
> "Was he surely drowned, or did he fall in?
> For there's deep and false water in the Lake of Cold Finn!"
>
> The day of Willie's funeral will be a grand sight,
> There will be four and twenty young men all dressed up in white;
> They will follow his remains till it's laid in the clay,
> They will [bid] young Willie adieu, and they will all march away.
>
> For to see Willie's mother, it would grieve your heart sore,
> And to see Willie's sweetheart, it would grieve your heart more,

> For every fine morning he would her salute,
> With his pinks and red roses and fine garden fruit.

THE LADY OF CARLISLE

This incident, recounted as a fact by Brantôme in his memoirs (1666), was used also by Schiller for his poem "Der Handschuh" and by Robert Browning for "The Glove." In all three, however, the brave knight despises the frivolous lady who has thrust him into needless danger. "The Lady of Carlisle" derives from an eighteenth-century broadside entitled, *The Distressed Lady, or a Trial of True Love. In Five Parts.* The five parts last for fifty-five stanzas. The folk have pared the stanzas to a tight unit and the lover, rather than rejecting the lady, gladly accepts the prize that he has won. The peculiar ship, *Kong Kong Kar*, is derived from the name of one of the suitors, Colonel Carr, in the original ballad. The development is clearly shown.

Original English version:

> *One brought a captain's commission,*
> *Under the brave Colonel Carr,*
> *The other was a first lieutenant*
> *In the* Tyger *man-of-war.*

Kentucky version (1911):

> *One he has a bold lieutenant*
> *A man of honor and of high degree;*
> *The other was a brave sea-captain,*
> *Belonging to a ship called* Karnel Call.

> Down in Carlisle there lived a lady,
> Being most beautiful and gay;

"The Lady of Carlisle" was recorded by Alan Lomax from the singing of Basil May, Salyersville, Kentucky, 1937. Library of Congress album record 1A, issued for the Friends of Music in the Library of Congress.

She was determined to live a lady,
No man on earth could her betray,

Unless it was a man of honor,
Man of honor and high degree;
Then up rose two loving soldiers,
This fair lady for to see.

One being a brave lieutenant,
Brave lieutenant and a man of war,
The other being a brave sea-captain,
Captain on the ship that was *Kong Kong Kar*.

Up spoke this fair young lady,
Saying, "I can't be but one man's bride;
You two come back tomorrow morning
And on this case we will decide."

She ordered her a span of horses,
Span of horses at her command,
Down the road these three did travel
Till they come to a lion's den.

There she stopped and there she halted,
These two soldiers stood gazing around,
And in the space of a half an hour
This young lady lies speechless on the ground.

And when she did recover,
Threw her fan down in the lion's den,
Saying, "Which of you to gain a lady
Will return my fan again?"

Then up stepped this brave lieutenant,
Raised his voice both loud and clear,
"I know I am a true lover of women
But I will not give my life for love."

Then up stepped this brave sea-captain,
Raised his voice both loud and high,
"I know I am a dear lover of women,
I will return her fan or die."

LOVE

Down in the lion's den he boldly entered,
Lions being both wild and fierce;
He marched around and in among them,
Safetly returned her fan again.

And when she saw her true lover coming,
Seeing no harm had been done to him,
She threw herself against his bosom,
Saying, "Here is the prize that you have won."

ALL IN THE DOWNS
(*Susan and William*)

All in the downs the fleet lay moored, their streamers waving in the wind,
When black-eyed Susan came on board, "Oh, where shall I my true love find?
Tell me, ye jovial sailors, tell me true,
Doth my sweet William, doth my sweet William sail among your crew?"

Her William, high upon the yards, rocked by the billows to and fro,
Soon as her well-known voice he heard, he sighed and cast his eyes below.
The cord flies swiftly through his glowing hand,
As quick as lightning, as quick as lightning on the deck he stands.

"Oh, Susan, Susan, lovely dear, my vow shall ever true remain;
Let me kiss off that briny tear, we only part to meet again.
Thy image dear I carry in my heart,
And thou art with me, and thou art with me wheresoe'er thou art.

"Believe not what the landsmen say, that vex with doubts thy constant mind:
'The sailor when away,' they say, 'in every port a sweetheart finds.'
Oh, yes, believe them when they tell thee so,
For thou art with me, for thou art with me wheresoe'er I go."

"All in the Downs" was recorded by Alan Lomax from the singing of Mrs. Marianna Schaupp, Washington, D.C., 1941. Library of Congress AFS record 6081 B1. Laws, O28.

THE LITTLE MOHEA

As I went out walking for pleasure one day,
In sweet recreation to while time away,
As I sat amusing myself on the grass,
Oh, who should come near me but a fair Indian lass.

She sat down beside me, took hold of my hand,
Said, "You look like a stranger and in a strange land;
But if you will follow, you're welcome to come
And dwell in a cottage that I call my own."

The sun was fast sinking far o'er the blue sea
When I wandered alone with my pretty Mohea.
Together we wandered, together we rove,
Till we came to the cot in the cocoanut grove.

Then this kind expression she made unto me,
"If you will consent, sir, to stay here with me
And go no more roving upon the salt sea,
I'll teach you the language of the little Mohea."

"Oh, no, my fair maiden, that never can be,
For I have a true love in my own country,
And I'll never forsake her, for I know she won't me,
And her heart is as true as the little Mohea."

'Twas early one morning, a morning in May,
That to this fair maiden these words I did say,
"I'm going to leave, so-farewell, my dear;
My ship's sails are spreading and home we must steer."

The last time I saw her she stood on the strand
And as my boat passed her she waved me her hand,

"The Little Mohea" appears in H. M. Belden, *Ballads and Songs Collected by the Missouri Folk-Lore Society*, Columbia (reprint edition, 1966), pp. 143-145. "Communicated to Miss Hamilton in 1912 by Shirley Hunt of the Kirksville Teachers College, as sung by her mother, who was reared in Scotland County." Without music. Laws, H8.

LOVE

Saying, "When you get home to the girl that you love,
Think of little Mohea in the cocoanut grove."

And then when I landed on my own native shore,
With friends and relations around me once more,
I gazed all about me — no one could I see
That was fit to compare with my pretty Mohea.

And the girl that I trusted proved untrue to me,
So I'll turn my course backward, far o'er the deep sea;
I'll turn my course backward, from this land I'll flee,
I'll go spend my days with my pretty Mohea.

ON THE LAKES OF PONCHARTRAIN

Through swamps and alligators I wend my weary way,
O'er railroad tracks and crossings my weary feet did stray,
Until the shades of evening some higher ground did gain,
'Twas there I met the Creole girl on the lakes of Ponchartrain.

"Good evening, pretty fair maiden, my money does me no good,
If it was not for the alligators, I'd sleep out in the wood."
"Oh, welcome, welcome, stranger, although our house is plain,
We never turn a stranger out on the lakes of Ponchartrain."

She took me to her father's house and treated me quite well.
Her hair which hung in ringlets upon her shoulders fell;
I tried to paint her beauty but, alas, it was in vain,
So charming was this Creole girl on the lakes of Ponchartrain.

I asked her if she'd marry me, she said it never could be,
She said she had a lover and he was far at sea.
She said she had a lover and true she would remain,
Until he returned to gain his bride on the lakes of Ponchartrain.

"Adieu, adieu, fair maiden, I never shall see you more,
I never shall forget your kindness or the cottage by the shore,

"On the Lakes of Ponchartrain" was recorded from the singing of Mrs. Frances Perry, Black River Falls, Wisconsin, 1946, by the University of Wisconsin Recording Project under the direction of Leland Coon. Library of Congress AFS record 8410 A2. Laws, H9.

And at each social gathering a dripping bowl I'll drain,
I'll drink to the health of the Creole girl on the lakes of Ponchartrain."

PRETTY POLLY OF TOPSHAM

This is a delightfully "personal" song from some two hundred years ago. It has a basis in fact. Barry reports that "Priest Ellis," the "young minister," can be no one but Rev. Jonathan Ellis, minister of Topsham First Parish, installed September 16, 1789, and afterward one of the members of the original Board of Overseers of Bowdoin College. In 1790, he married Mary, daughter of Robert Fulton of Topsham, Maine.

> Come all you fair gallants, fair gallants attend,
> A story, a story to you I will tell;
> 'Tis of a young sea captain, wherein he took delight,
> And he courted a lady whose beauty was bright.
>
> He had not courted her past twelve months, no more,
> When his own business called him from the shore;
> He went unto his Polly all for to take his leave,
> Saying: "Polly, pretty Polly, I pray thee, don't grieve.
>
> "For I'm going to cross the ocean,
> Where the foaming billows roar, and the seas are in motion;
> And if unto America I never do return,
> Here I leave you, pretty Polly, in Topsham to mourn."
>
> Past months two or three he had not been away,
> When a young minister came there for to stay;
> In viewing of her features, she looked so brisk and bold,
> He made love unto her, as I have been told.
>
> Saying, "Polly, pretty Polly, if you can fancy me,
> I will make you as happy as happy can be;

"Pretty Polly of Topsham" was contributed to the Folksong Society of the Northeast by Mrs. Susie Carr Young, Brewer, Maine, as sung by her mother, Mrs. Mary Diana (Fowler) Carr, and her grandmother, Mrs. Mary (Soper) Carr, n.d. Reported, with music, by Phillips Barry in *Bulletin of the Folksong Society of the Northeast*, Cambridge, Mass., 2 (1931): 16–17.

But if to any other young man 'tis you are engaged,
I pray you prove true to the vows you have made."

" 'Tis I am engaged, and the truth I will tell,
'Tis I am engaged, but I don't like so well;
He will be at home, and it is by-and-by,
And then you will see how quick him I'll deny."

This young man came home at last, as I have been told.
He brought home fine riches and fine stores of gold;
He brought home fine ribbons and fine silks so gay,
To adorn pretty Polly on her wedding day.

Saying, "Polly, pretty Polly, since I have been to sea,
Have you seen any other you love better than me?"
Then she turned herself around with a high and haughty air,
Saying, "Priest Ellis I love better, I suppose you don't care!"

Saying, "Polly, pretty Polly, since I must free my mind,
I think you are the falsest of all womankind;
Since I have been so constant, and you have proved untrue,
Farewell, pretty Polly, I bid you adieu.

" 'Tis I will go a-rambling, go rambling for rest,
In hopes to relieve my poor tortured breast;
'Tis I will go a-rambling, like some dove around the shore,
And I never will go near my false Polly any more."

SO I LET HER GO

I once knew a lass and I loved her to tell:
She ne'er knew a lad that she loved half so well!
I thought I would take her and make her my wife
And I would live happy all the rest of my life.
    But I found it not so, so I let her go;
    I don't care a fig for her, so now let her go.

"So I Let Her Go" was recorded by Sidney Robertson Cowell from the singing of Mrs. Carrie Grover of Gorham, Maine, at Teaneck, New Jersey, 1941. Library of Congress AFS record 4697 A2.

I went for to meet her one fair summer's night,
And all the way 'long I was filled with delight.
And all the way 'long I was filled with her charms
Till I found she was locked in another man's arms.
    And I found it was so, so I let her go;
    I don't care a fig for her, so now let her go.

They'll promise to twenty, they'll promise to one,
They'll promise to thirty and be constant to none;
They'll court you awhile and still have in their mind
To go with some other and leave you behind.
    And I found it was so, so I let her go;
    I don't care a fig for her, so now let her go.

There are as good fish as e'er caught in the sea,
And I will have one or, by Jove, I'll go free.
I will drink the King's health all my sorrows to drown,
For I am determined to sail the world 'round.
    I intend to do so, so I let her go;
    I don't care a fig for her, so now let her go.

CHILD BALLADS

Once he kissed her lily-white hands,
Twice he kissed her cheeks,
Three times he kissed her cold corpy lips,
And he fell in her arms asleep.

Professor Francis James Child of Harvard published in the period 1882–1898 his monumental collection of *The English and Scottish Popular Ballads* (Boston) in ten volumes, bound into five. The Child canon contains 305 of the earliest (with an exception or two) of the English-Scottish ballads, most of them with many variants of text and story. The bulk of them were collected in England and Scotland, chiefly from print but some from oral tradition. It was assumed that this particular ballad tradition had not greatly extended — even with Scottish-English settlers — to America, and little effort was made at the time to poke around here hunting for them. Child did send circulars to the public schools on the eastern seaboard requesting inquiry, collecting, and reporting of ballads, but the meager response was discouraging, and he gave up the effort, concluding that of the ballads known, he had better copies from old print or manuscript than were to be collected orally in his time. (The field-collecting technique of going to the source rather than to the "schools" had not been developed in the United States in Child's time.) There is an appendix of about fifty tunes and also a bibliographical list of the whereabouts of tunes, the latter compiled by one of Child's Scottish informants, but otherwise the volumes were published without music.

Not until 1907 did collectors seriously approach ballad collecting in America. Among the first was Olive Dame Campbell (the "Dame" is a given name and not a British honorific) of Georgia, wife of John C. Campbell of the Russell Sage Foundation. She collected during the years 1907–1910 and corresponded with Cecil J. Sharp, who was working the English field. When Sharp visited the United States, Mrs. Campbell persuaded him to collaborate in the field collecting of ballads (as well as other folksongs), and, beginning in Georgia, they traveled and collected chiefly in the Southern Appalachians. Their collection appeared in an original edition of *English Folksongs from the Southern Appalachians, Comprising 122 Songs and Ballads and 323 Tunes*, G. P. Putnam's Sons, 1917. It is out of print. But in 1932 there appeared a work of the same title (which has since been reprinted by Oxford, and which is still in print), edited by Maud Karpeles, containing 274 songs and ballads, with 968 tunes. In this Sharp collection there are better than fifty of the Child ballads with numerous variants. The tradition was proven to be not dead.

Other collectors soon appeared: Phillips Barry, Arthur Kyle Davis, Helen Hartness Flanders, Vance Randolph, John Harrington Cox, H. M. Belden, Josiah Combs, Alan Lomax. So that by now it can quite reasonably be said that the collection of the great English-Scottish ballads (as defined by Child in his canon) in America has been completed. Variants will be found, to be sure, and they should be happily sought out, but if no more were to surface, the work has been done. The great body of material is here in books, articles, archives, private collections across the land — in virtually every state.

Which brings us, appropriately, in point of time in this matter of these ballads to the two great American works on the subject, both indispensable and invaluable: Bertrand Harris Bronson's *The Traditional Tunes of the Child Ballads*, Princeton University Press, 4 volumes, 1958–1972, and Tristram P. Coffin's *The British Traditional Ballad in North America*, Philadelphia, The American Folklore Society, revised edition, 1963. Both are slightly mistitled: Bronson's spine title does not indicate that he gives full textual variants throughout with the tunes, and Coffin's does not point up that he is concerned throughout with the Child ballads only and their story variants. However, open the volumes, and there you are: the two most thorough and scholarly approaches to the American tradition of the British ballads of the Child canon.

Any serious student of the subject, any teacher of these ballads, anyone wishing a full awareness of the changes rung on story and song in the passage of the ballads throughout our land must know these two works. (Coffin's is at the moment regrettably out of print, but will probably be reissued by the AFS in the not distant future; Bronson's four volumes are expensive, but any college or institutional library aspiring to any completeness in the field must have them.) A student, for example, wishing to work on any one of the ballads intensively — for a Ph.D., perhaps — needs both Coffin and the single volume of Bronson containing that particular ballad. From them, as the-end-of-a-beginning, he can then move with reasonable sureness outwards to other collections, other variants. But he must start with these two. I have, therefore, in this section containing selected American variants of Child ballads, given the Child ballad number, the Coffin page number where he studies the story variants and cites published sources, and the Bronson volume and page number, where he begins the full textual and musical consideration of any one ballad named.

I think you will like the ballads: many of them are archaic, and their beauty lies in that; many are soft-spoken; a very goodly number have tears and weepings; some have love; many are death and graves and drownings; some are infanticide and fratricide and terror-murder; others are supernatural with revenants, ghosts, the returned dead; some are remnants of actual history, a great ballad of battle reduced by time to a lovely lyric; a goodly number have symbolism carrying on beyond the strict words; and all have preserved for us the long, long and great tradition of the English and Scotch into this country — Kentucky, Tennessee, Georgia, Virginia, Maine, Missouri — and you would not have it otherwise. It is really incredible (think for a moment) that these ballads from fifteenth-, sixteenth-, seventeenth-, and eighteenth-century England should have survived (words and music) in the memory and on the lips of the generations of Americans who have lived in the back hills, the coves, the valleys, and the sea lands of the Colonies and early states. No one told them to preserve them. They clung to them as they clung to their language and their ancestors. Without books. From memory. Grandmother, great-grandmother. Read the text, in that way. Listen to them on Library of Congress recordings. Be proud that you have them, and humble before the humble people who have given them to you.

I have given slight headnotes where they seem necessary. Where not, I have not.

THE DEVIL'S NINE QUESTIONS

"Oh, you must answer my questions nine,
Sing ninety-nine and ninety,
Or you're not God's, you're one of mine,
And you are the weaver's bonny."

"What is whiter than the milk?
Sing ninety-nine and ninety,
And what is softer than the silk?
And you are the weaver's bonny."

"Snow is whiter than the milk,
Sing ninety-nine and ninety,
And down is softer than the silk,
And I am the weaver's bonny."

"O what is higher than a tree?
Sing ninety-nine and ninety,
And what is deeper than the sea?
And you are the weaver's bonny."

"Heaven's higher than a tree,
Sing ninety-nine and ninety,
And Hell is deeper than the sea,
And I am the weaver's bonny."

"What is louder than a horn?
Sing ninety-nine and ninety,
And what is sharper than a thorn?
And you are the weaver's bonny."

"Thunder's louder than a horn,
Sing ninety-nine and ninety,
And death is sharper than a thorn,
And I am the weaver's bonny."

"What's more innocent than a
      lamb,
Sing ninety-nine and ninety,
And what is meaner than woman-
      kind?
And you are the weaver's bonny."

"A babe's more innocent than a
      lamb,
Sing ninety-nine and ninety,
And the devil is meaner than
      womankind,
And I am the weaver's bonny."

"O you have answered my questions nine,
Sing ninety-nine and ninety,
And you are God's, you're none of mine.
And you are the weaver's bonny."

"The Devil's Nine Questions" was recorded by Alan Lomax and Elizabeth Lomax from the singing of Mrs. Texas Gladden, Salem, Virginia, 1941. Library of Congress record LP1. Child ballad no. 1. Coffin, 22. Bronson, I, 3.

THE ELFIN KNIGHT

"Go tell him to clear me one acre of ground,
Setherwood, sale, rosemary and thyme,
Betwixt the sea and the sea-land side,
And then he'll be a true lover of mine.

"Tell him to plough it all up with an old leather plough,
Setherwood, sale, rosemary and thyme,
And hoe it all over with a pea-fowl's feather,
And then he'll be a true lover of mine.

"Go tell him to plant it all over with one grain of corn,
And reap it all down with an old ram's horn.

"Go tell him to shock it in yonder sea,
And return it back to me all dry."

"Go tell her to make me a cambric shirt,
Without any needle or needle's work.

"Go tell her to wash it in yonders well,
Setherwood, sale, rosemary and thyme,
Where rain nor water never fell,
And then she'll be a true lover of mine.

"Go tell her to hang it on yonders thorn,
Setherwood, sale, rosemary and thyme,
Where man nor thorn was never seen born,
And then she'll be a true lover of mine.

"The Elfin Knight" was collected by Cecil J. Sharp from the singing of Mrs. Cis Jones, Manchester, Kentucky, 1917. In Sharp, *English Folk Songs from the Southern Appalachians*, (Oxford) New York, 1932. I, 25. With music. Child ballad no. 2. Coffin, 23. Bronson, I, 9.

THE FALSE KNIGHT UPON THE ROAD

As in "The Devil's Nine Questions," the basic idea underlying the ballad is that the Devil can carry off the person questioned if he can nonplus him. The child here answers the Devil's questions directly and turns back upon the Devil the wishes which the latter makes until the child places him finally in Hell again. The boy presumably goes on safely to his school. Recovered texts of the ballad in the United States are scarce.

"Where are you going?" said the knight in the road.
"I'm going to my school," said the child as he stood.
He stood and he stood, he well thought on, he stood,
"I'm going to my school," said the child as he stood.

"Oh, what do you study there?" said the knight in the road.
"We learn the word of God," said the child as he stood.
He stood and he stood, he well thought on, he stood,
"We learn the word of God," said the child as he stood.

"Oh, what are you eating there?" said the knight in the road.
"I'm eating bread and cheese," said the child as he stood.

"Oh, won't you give me some?" said the knight in the road.
"No, nare a bite nor crumb," said the child as he stood.

"I wish you were in the sea," said the knight in the road.
"A good boat under me," said the child as he stood.

"I wish you were in the sand," said the knight in the road.
"A good staff in my hand," said the child as he stood.

"I wish you were in a well," said the knight in the road.
"And you that deep in Hell," said the child as he stood.

"The False Knight upon the Road" was recorded by Duncan Emrich from the singing of Mrs. Maud Long of Hot Springs, North Carolina, at Washington, D.C., 1947. Library of Congress record LP21. Child ballad no. 3. Coffin, 24. Bronson, I, 34.

LADY ISABEL AND THE ELF KNIGHT
(*Pretty Polly*)

He followed me up and he followed me down,
    He followed me all the day;
I had not the power to speak one word,
    Or a tongue to answer nay.

"Go bring me some of your father's gold
    And some of your mother's fee,
And I will take you to fair Scotland,
    And there I'll marry thee."

She brought him some of her father's gold
    And some of her mother's fee;
She took him to her father's barn,
    Where the horses stood thirty and three.

"Mount on, mount on that brownie, brownie bay,
    And I on the dapple gray,
And we'll ride away through the lonesome woods
    Three long hours before it is day."

She mounted on the brownie, brownie bay,
    And he on the dapple gray,
And they rode away through the lonesome woods
    Till they came to the deep blue sea.

"Dismount, dismount from your brownie, brownie bay,
    And I off the dapple gray —
Six pretty fair maids I have drowned here
    And the seventh one you shall be."

"Lady Isabel and the Elf Knight" is from Burwell Luther, Wayne County, West Virginia, December, 1915, who had the song "from his mother about fifty years ago." And she in turn had learned it from her mother, who was Highland Scotch. See John Harrington Cox, *Folk-Songs of the South* (Harvard) Cambridge, 1925 (Dover reprint, 1967), pp. 8–9. The stanza in brackets (between 14 and 15) rounds out the ballad and is from Mrs. Elizabeth Tapp Peck, Morgantown, collected in 1916. Without music. Child ballad no. 4. Coffin, 25. Bronson, I, 39.

"O hold your tongue, you villain!" she said,
    "O hold your tongue!" said she —
"You promised to take me to bonny Scotland
    And there to marry me."

"Take off, take off those fine clothing,
    Take off, take off," said he,
"For they are too costly and too fine
    To be rotted in the sea."

"O turn your body round and about
    To view the leaves on the tree;
'Tis a pity such a villain as you
    A naked woman should see."

He turned his body round and about
    To view the leaves on the tree;
She clasped him tight in her arms so white
    And plunged him into the sea.

"Lie there, lie there, you villain," she said,
    "Lie there instead of me!
Six pretty fair maids you have drownèd here,
    And the seventh one has drownèd thee."

She jumped upon her brownie, brownie bay
    And led the dappled gray,
And she returned home to her father's house,
    Two long hours before it was day.

"O where have you been, my pretty Collin,
    So long before it is day?"
"I have been to drown that false-hearted man,
    That strove to drown poor me.

"O hold your tongue, my pretty polly,
    Don't tell no tales on me,
And your cage shall be made of glittering gold,
    Instead of the greenwood tree."

[Then up spoke the old man himself
    From the bedchamber where he lay,
Saying, "What is the matter with my pretty parrot,
    That she's chattering so long before day?"]

"The old cat came to my cage door,
    Intending to weary* me,
And I had to call on pretty Collin,
    To drive the old cat away."

"Well turned, well turned, my pretty little bird,
    Well turned, well turned!" said she;
"And your nest shall be made of leaves of gold,
    Instead of the green willow tree."

EARL BRAND
(*Sweet William*)

In America this ballad is generally known as "Sweet William" or "The Seven Brothers," while in Scotland it was known as "Earl Brand" or "The Douglas Tragedy." Sir Walter Scott felt that the story had its source in some actual event:

The ballad of "The Douglas Tragedy" is one of the few to which popular tradition has ascribed complete locality. The farm of Blackhouse, in Selkirkshire, is said to have been the scene of this melancholy event. There are the remains of a very ancient tower, adjacent to the farmhouse, in a wild and solitary glen, upon a torrent named Douglas burn, which joins the Yarrow after passing a craggy rock called the Douglas craig. . . . From this ancient tower Lady Margaret is said to have been carried by her lover. Seven large stones, erected upon the neighboring heights of Blackhouse, are shown, as marking the spot where the seven brethren were slain; and the Douglas burn is averred to have been the stream at which the lovers stopped to drink [not recounted in the present variant]; so minute is tradition in ascertaining the scene of a tragical tale, which, considering the rude state of former times, had probably foundation in some real event.

Sweet William rode up to the old man's gate
And boldly he did say,
"The youngest daughter she must stay at home,
But the oldest I'll take away."

* For *worry*.

"Earl Brand" was recorded by Duncan Emrich from the singing of I. G. Greer of Thomasville, North Carolina, with dulcimer by Mrs. I. G. Greer, at Washington, D.C., 1948. Library of Congress record LP12. Child ballad no. 7. Coffin, 29. Bronson, I, 106.

"Come in, come in, all seven of my sons,
And guard your sister 'round,
For never shall it be said that the Stuart's* son
Has taken my daughter out of town."

"I thank you, sir, and it's very kind,
I'm none of the Stuart's son,
My father was a 'reginers team,
My mother a Quaker's queen."

So he got on his snow-white steed,
And she on the dapple grey,
He swung his bugle horn around his neck
And they went riding away.

They hadn't gone more'n a mile out of town
Till he looked back again,
And he saw her father and seven of her brothers
Come trippling over the plain.

"Light down, light down, Fair Ellen," said he,
"And hold my steed by the reins,
Till I fight your father and seven of your brothers
Come trippling over the plain."

He stood right there and he stood right still,
Not a word did she return,
Till she saw her father and seven of her brothers
A-rolling in their own hearts' blood.

"Slack your hand, slack your hand, Sweet William," said she,
"Your wounds are very sore,
The blood runs free from every vein,
A father I can have no more."

So he got on his snow-white steed,
And she on the dapple grey,
He sung his bugle horn around his neck
And they went bleeding away.

Soon they rode up to his mother's gate,
And tingling on the ring,
"Oh, mother, oh, mother, asleep or awake,
Arise and let me in.

* Steward's.

"Oh, mother, oh, mother, bind my head,
My wounds are very sore,
The blood runs free from every vein,
For me you will bind them no more."

About two hours before it was day,
The fowls began to crow,
Sweet William died from the wounds that he received,
Fair Ellen died for sorrow.

THE TWO SISTERS

There was an old woman lived on the seashore,
   Bow and balance to me.
There was an old woman lived on the seashore,
Her number of daughters one, two, three, four,
   And I'll be true to my love if my love'll be true to me.

There was a young man came by to see them,
   Bow and balance to me.
There was a young man came by to see them,
And the oldest one got struck on him,
   And I'll be true to my love if my love'll be true to me.

He bought the youngest a beaver hat,
And the oldest one got mad at that.

"Oh, sister, oh, sister, let's walk the seashore,
And see the ships as they sail o'er."

While these two sisters were walking the shore,
The oldest pushed the youngest o'er.

"Oh, sister, oh, sister, please lend me your hand,
And you may have Willie and all of his land."

"I never, I never will lend you my hand,
But I'll have Willie and all of his land."

"The Two Sisters" was recorded by Herbert Halpert from the singing of Horton Barker at Chilhowie, Virginia, 1939. Library of Congress record LP7. Child ballad no. 10. Coffin, 32. Bronson, I, 106.

Sometime she sank and sometime she swam,
Until she came to the old mill dam.

The miller he got his fishing hook,
And fished the maiden out of the brook.

"Oh, miller, oh, miller, here's five gold rings,
To push the maiden in again."

The miller received those five gold rings,
   Bow and balance to me.
The miller received those five gold rings,
And pushed the maiden in again.
   And I'll be true to my love if my love'll be true to me.

The miller was hung at his own mill gate,
   Bow and balance to me.
The miller was hung at his own mill gate,
For drowning little sister Kate.
   And I'll be true to my love if my love'll be true to me.

THE CRUEL BROTHER

There's three fair maids went to play at ball,
   I-o the lily gay,
There's three landlords come court them all,
   And the rose smells so sweet I know.

The first landlord was dressed in blue.
He asked his maid if she would be his true.

The next landlord was dressed in green.
He asked his maid if she'd be his queen.

The next landlord was dressed in white.
He asked his maid if she'd be his wife.

"The Cruel Brother" was collected by Cecil J. Sharp from the singing of Mrs. Julie Williams, Hot Springs, North Carolina, 1917. In Sharp, *English Folksongs from the Southern Appalachians* (Oxford) New York, 1932, I, 36. Child ballad no. 11. Coffin, 36. Bronson, I, 185.

"It's you may ask my old father dear,
And you may ask my mother, too."

"It's I have asked your old father dear,
And I have asked your mother, too.

"Your sister Anne I've asked her not,
Your brother John I had forgot."

Her old father dear was to lead her to the yard,
Her mother, too, was to lead her to the step.

Her brother John was to help her up.
As he /holp/ her up he stabbed her deep.

"Go ride me out on that green hill,
And lay me down and let me bleed.

"Go haul me up on that green hill,
And lay me down till I make my will."

"It's what will you will to your old father dear?"
"This house and land that I have here."

"It's what will you will to your mother, too?"
"This bloody clothing that I have to wear.

"Go tell her to take them to yonders stream,
For my heart's blood is in every seam."

"It's what will you will to your sister Anne?"
"My new gold ring and my silver fan."

"It's what will you will to your brother John's wife?"
"In grief and sorrow the balance of her life."

"It's what will you will to your brother John's son?"
"It's God for to bless and make him a man."

"It's what will you will to your brother John?"
"A rope and a gallows for to hang him on."

LORD RANDAL

"O where have you been, Lord Randal my son?
O where have you been, my only son?"
"I've been a-courting, mother, O make my bed soon,
For I'm sick at the heart and fain would lie down."

"What did you have for your supper, Lord Randal my son?
What did you have for your supper, my only son?"
"A cup of cold poison, mother, O make my bed soon,
For I'm sick at the heart and fain would lie down."

"What would you leave your father, Lord Randal my son?
What would you leave your father, my only son?"
"My wagon and oxen, mother, O make my bed soon,
For I'm sick at the heart and fain would lie down."

"What would you leave your mother, Lord Randal my son?
What would you leave your mother, my only son?"
"My coach and six horses, mother, O make my bed soon,
For I'm sick at the heart and fain would lie down."

"What would you leave your sweetheart, Lord Randal my son?
What would you leave your sweetheart, my only son?"
"Ten thousand weights of brimstone to burn her bones brown,
For she was the cause of my lying down."

EDWARD

"Oh, what's that stain on your shirt sleeve?
Son, please come tell me."
"It is the blood of my little yellow dog
That followed after me."

"Lord Randal" was collected by Cecil J. Sharp from the singing of Miss Florence McKinney, Habersham County, Georgia, 1910. In Sharp, *English Folksongs from the Southern Appalachians* (Oxford) New York, 1932, I, 41. Child ballad no. 12. Coffin, 36. Bronson, I, 191.

"Edward" was recorded by Vance Randolph from the singing of Charles Ingenthron (of Thornton, California) at Walnut Shade, Missouri. Library of Congress record LP12. Child ballad no. 13. Coffin, 39. Bronson, I, 236.

"It is too pale for your little yellow dog,
Son, please come tell me."
"It is the blood of my little yellow horse
That I rode to town today."

"It is too pale for your little yellow horse,
Son, please come tell me."
"It is the blood of my own brother dear
That rode by the side of me."

"Oh, what did you fall out about?
Son, please come tell me."
"We fell out about a sprout
That might have made a tree."

"Oh, what will you do when your father comes home?
Son, please come tell me."
"I'll step on board of yondo (yonder) ship
And sail across the sea."

"Oh, what will you do with Katie dear?
Son, please come tell me."
"I'll take her on board of yondo ship
To bear me company."

"Oh, when will you come back, my dear?
Son, please come tell me."
"When the sun rises never to set,
And you know that'll never be."

BABYLON
or *The Bonnie Banks o' Fordie*

There were three maids lived in a barn; —
    Heckey hi si bernio —
When up there rose a wicked man,
On the bonny banks of Bernio.

"Babylon" was collected by Helen Hartness Flanders from the singing of Mrs. Marjorie L. Porter, Plattsburg, New York, n.d., ca. 1933. Mrs. Porter believed the song was brought from Basin Harbor, Vermont, to Bessboro (now Westport), New York, by her mother's grandmother, Margaret Winans. Reported, with music, by Phillips Barry in *Bulletin of the Folksong Society of the Northeast*, Cambridge, Mass., 7 (1934):6. Child ballad no. 14. Coffin, 40. Bronson, I, 248.

He took the eldest by the hand,
He whirled her round and made her stand.

"Heckry, lass, will you be young Robey's wife?
Or rather would you die by my penknife?"

"Never will I be young Robey's wife;
Rather would I die by your penknife."

So he took her life and laid it by
To keep the greensward compan-eye.

He took the next one by the hand,
He whirled her round and made her stand.

"Heckry, lass, will you be young Robey's wife?
Or rather would you die by my penknife?"

"Never will I be young Robey's wife,
Rather would I die by your penknife."

So he took her life and laid it by,
To keep the greensward compan-eye.

He took the youngest by the hand,
He whirled her round and made her stand.

"Heckry, lass, will you be young Robey's wife?
Or rather would you die by my penknife?"

"Never will I be young Robey's wife,
Neither will I die by your penknife."

So she took his life and laid it by,
To keep her sisters compan-eye.

HIND HORN
(In Scotland Town)

In Scotland town where I was borned
A lady gave to me a ring.

"Hind Horn" was recorded by Carl Fleischauer and Dwight Diller from the singing of Maggie Hammons Parker, Marlinton, West Virginia, 1970. Library of Congress record LP65. Child ballad no. 17. Coffin, 41. Bronson, I, 254.

"Now if this ring proves bright and fair
You know that I have proved true, my dear.

"And if this ring proves old and worn
You knew that your true love is with some other one."

So he went on board and away sailed he,
He sailed and he sailed to some foreign country.

He looked at his ring and his ring was worn,
He knew that his true love was with some other one.

So he went on board and back sailed he,
He sailed and he sailed to his own country.

One morning as I was riding along
I met with a poor old beggar man.

"Old man, old man, old man, I pray,
What news have you got for me today?"

"Sad news, sad news to you I'll say,
For tomorrow is your true love's wedding day."

"So you can take my riding seat,
The beggar's rig I will put on."

"The riding seat ain't fit for me."
Nor the beggar's rig ain't fit for thee."

Oh whether it be right or whether it be wrong,
The beggar's rig he did put on.

So he begged from the rich, he begged from the poor,
He begged from the high to the lowest of 'em all.

Then he went on in an old man's 'ray
Till he came to the steps of yonders gay.

When the bride came trippling down the stairs,
Rings on her finger and gold in her hair,

And a glass of wine d'all in her hand
To gave to the poor old beggar man.

He taked her glass and drinked the wine
And in that glass he placed a ring.

"Oh where did you get it from sea or land,
Or did you steal it from a drownded man's hand?"

"Oh neither did I get it from sea or land,
Or neither did I steal it from a drownded man's hand.

"You gave it to me on our courting day,
Now I'll give it back to you on your wedding day."

Off of her finger the ring she pulled,
And off of her hair the gold did fall.

And between the kitchen and the hall
The beggar's rig he did let fall.

His gold a-showing out more fair than 'em all,
He was the fairest of the young men was in that hall.

"I'll follow my true love wherever he may go,
If I have to beg my food from door to door."

SIR LIONEL

Abram Bailey he'd three sons,
Blow your horn, Center.
And he is to the wildwood gone
Just like a jovial hunter.

As he marched down the greenwood side,
Blown your horn, Center.
A pretty girl there he spied
As he was a jovial hunter.

"There is a wild boar all in these woods,"
Blow your horn, Center.
"He slew the lord and his forty men,"
As you are the jovial hunter.

"Sir Lionel" was recorded by Herbert Halpert from the singing of Samuel Harmon near Marysville, Tennessee, 1939. Library of Congress record LP57. Child ballad no. 18. Coffin, 42. Bronson, I, 265.

"How can I this wild boar see?"
Blow your horn, Center.
"Wind up your horn and he'll come to you,
As you are the jovial hunter."

He wound his horn unto his mouth,
Blow your horn, Center.
He blew East, North, West, and South
As he was a jovial hunter.

The wild boar heared him unto his den,
Blow your horn, Center.
He made the oak and ash down far to bend
As he was a jovial hunter.

They fit three hours by the day,
Blow your horn, Center.
And at length he this wild boar slay
As he was a jovial hunter.

As he marched by the mouth of the wild boar's den,
Blow your horn, Center.
He saw the bones of five hundred men
As he was a jovial hunter.

He meets the old witch-wife on the bridge,
Blow your horn, Center.
"Begone, you rogue, you've killed my pig,
As you are the jovial hunter."

"They is three things I crave of thee,"
Blow your horn, Center.
"Your hawk, your hound, and your gay ladie
As you are the jovial hunter."

"These three things you'll not have of me,"
Blow your horn, Center.
"Neither hawk, nor hound, nor gay ladie,"
As you are the jovial hunter.

He split the old witch-wife to the chin,
Blow your horn, Center.
And on his way he went agin,
Just like a jovial hunter.

263

THE CRUEL MOTHER
(*Down by the Greenwood Side*)

There was a lady lived in York,
   Ha liley and loney;
She fell in love with her father's clerk,
   Down by the greenwood side.

She loved him up and she loved him down,
She loved him till she filled her arms.

She placed her foot against an oak,
First it bent and then it broke.

Then she placed her foot against a thorn,
There those two little babes were born.

She pulled a knife both keen and sharp
And thrust those two little babes to the heart.

She buried those two little babes under a marble stone,
Thinking this would never be known.

One day, sitting in her father's hall,
She spied those two little babes playing ball.

"O babes, O babes, if you are mine,
I'll dress you up in silks so fine."

"O mother, when we were thine,
You never dressed us up in coarse nor fine.

"Now we are up in heaven to dwell,
And you are doomed to hell."

"The Cruel Mother" was collected by Mrs. Hilary G. Richardson, Clarksburg, West Virginia, 1916, from Mrs. Rachel Fogg, who had learned it from her mother, and she from her mother. Reported by Mrs. Richardson in *JAF*, 32 (1919):503, and in John Harrington Cox, *Folksongs of the South* (Harvard) Cambridge, 1925 (Dover reprint, 1967), p. 29. Child ballad no. 20. Coffin, 44. Bronson, I, 276.

THE THREE RAVENS

There were three crows sat on a tree,
And they were black as crows could be.

Said one crow unto his mate,
"What shall we do for grub to eat?"

"I see a horse on yonders plain
Whose body's been but lately slain.

"We'll perch ourselves on his breast bone
And pick his eyes out one by one."

THE BROOMFIELD HILL

I'll lay you five hundred pounds,
Five hundred pounds to ten,
That a maid can't go to the green-broomfield
And come back a maid again.

Then up spoke a sweet young girl,
Her age was not sixteen:
"A maid I'll go to the green-broomfield,
And a maid I'll come back again."

And when she went to the green-broomfield,
Where her lover was sound asleep,

"The Three Ravens" was communicated by T. C. Wright, Miller County, Missouri, in 1916 — from his father's singing — to H. M. Belden. In H. M. Belden, *Ballads and Folksongs Collected by the Missouri Folk-Lore Society*, Columbia (reprint edition, 1966), pp. 31–33. Child ballad no. 26. Coffin, 46. Bronson, I, 308.

"The Broomfield Hill" was collected by Josiah H. Combs from Carey Woofter, Gilmer County, West Virginia, 1924. Without music. In Combs, *Folksongs of the Southern United States*, Publications of the American Folklore Society (The University of Texas Press) Austin, 1967, pp. 113–114. Child ballad no. 43. Coffin, 51. Bronson, I, 336.

With a gay goshork* and a green laurel twig,
And a green broom under his feet,

She pulled a bunch of the green-broom
And smelled of it so sweet;
She scattered a handful over his head,
And another around his feet.

And when she had done what she wagered to do,
She turned herself about,
She hid herself behind a clump of green-broom
To hear what her lover should say.

And when he awoke from out his sleep
A fearsome man was he;
He looked to the east and he looked to the west,
And he wept for his sweetheart to see.

"And where were you, my gay goshork
(That once I loved so dear),
That you wakened me not out of my sleep
When my sweetheart was so near?

"If my hork had wakened me while I slept,
Of her I would have had my will,
Or the buzzards that fly high over the sky
Of her flesh should have had their fill.

"Come saddle me my milk-white steed,
Come saddle me my brown;
Come saddle me the speediest horse
That ever rode through town."

You need not saddle your milk-white steed,
You need not saddle your brown,
For a doe never ran through the street so fast
As the maid ran through the town.

---

* Goshork: goshawk.

THE BISHOP OF CANTERBURY
(*King John and the Bishop*)

A story, a story, a story anon
I'll tell unto thee concerning King John,
He had a great mind for to make himself merry
So he called for the Bishop of Canterbury,
Lolli-doll-lay, Lolli-doll-luddy-tri-ol-de-dum-day.

"Good morning, good morning," the old King did say,
"I've called you to ask you questions three,
And if you don't answer them all right,
Your head shall be taken from your body quite."
Lolli-doll-lay, Lolli-doll-luddy-tri-ol-de-dum-day.

"My first question is, and that without doubt,
How long I'll be traveling this whole world about,
And the next question is when I sit in state
With my gold crown upon my pate
And all the nobility join in great mirth,
You must tell to one penny just what I am worth.

"And the last question is and when I do wink,
You must tell to me presently what I do think."

As the old bishop was returning home
He met this young shepherd and him all alone.
"Good morning, good morning," the young man did say,
"What news do you bring from the old King today?"

"O very bad news," the old bishop did say,
"The King has asked me questions three,
And if I don't answer them all right
My head shall be taken from my body quite."

"The Bishop of Canterbury" was recorded by Sidney Robertson Cowell from the singing of Warde H. Ford at Central Valley, California, 1938. Library of Congress record LP57. Child ballad no. 45. Coffin, 52. Bronson, I, 354.

"Well, I'm sorry a man of such learning as thee
Can't go back and answer the king's questions three,
But if you will lend me a suit of apparel
I'll go to King John and settle the quarrel."

"A suit of apparel I freely will give
And ten thousand pounds as sure as you live."
And now the young shepherd has gone to King John
To settle the quarrel that he had begun.

"Good morning, good morning," the young shepherd did say,
"I've called to answer your questions three.
Your first question is and that without doubt
How long you'll be traveling this whole world about:
If you start with the sun and you travel the same
In twenty-four hours you'll come back again.

"The next question is when you sit in state
With your gold crown upon your pate
And all the nobility join in great mirth,
I'm to tell to one penny just what you are worth.

"For thirty gold pieces our dear Lord was sold
By those old Jews so brazen and bold,
And for twenty-nine pieces I think you'll just do,
For I'm sure he was one piece better than you.

"The last question is and when you do wink
I'm to tell to you presently what you do think,
And that I will do if 'twill make your heart merry,
You think I'm the Bishop of Canterbury.

"And that I am not, as is very well known,
I am his young shepherd and him all alone."

"Go tell the old bishop, go tell him for me
That his young shepherd has outwitted me."
Lolli-doll-lay, Lolli-doll-luddy-tri-ol-de-dum-day.

CAPTAIN WEDDERBURN'S COURTSHIP
(*Bold Robbington*)

As I walked out one evening down by the Strawberry Lane,
It was there I saw Bold Robbington, the keeper of the game.
"It is true I love that handsome maid, and if it was not for the law,
I would take that fair maid round the waist and roll her from the wall."

"Oh, hold your tongue, you silly man, and do not me perplex,
Before that you can lie with me, you must answer questions six;
Six questions you must answer me, and I will put them all,
Then you and I in one bed shall lie, and you lie next to the wall.

"Oh, what is rounder than a ring? What is higher than a tree?
What is worse than a woman's tongue? What is deeper than the sea?
What bird flies far the broad sea across? And where does the first dew fall?
Then you and I in one bed shall lie, and you lie next to the wall."

"This world is rounder than a ring; Heaven is higher than a tree;
The devil is worse than a woman's tongue; Hell is deeper than the sea;
The gull flies far the wide sea across, and there the first dew falls,
So you and I in one bed shall lie, and you lie next to the wall."

"Oh, hold your tongue, you silly man, and do not bother me,
Before that you can lie with me, you must answer questions three;
Three questions you must answer me, and I will put them all
Then you and I in one bed shall lie, and you lie next to the wall.

"You must get for me a winter fruit that in September grew,
You must get for me a silk mantle that never web went through,
A sparrow's thorn, a priest unborn, that shall make us one and all,
Then you and I in one bed shall lie, and you lie next to the wall."

"My father has a winter fruit that in September grew,
My mother has a silk mantle that never web went through;
A sparrow's thorn is easily found, there is one on every claw,
Belshazzar was a priest unborn, so you lie next to the wall."

"Captain Wedderburn's Courtship." As collected from Mrs. Annie V. Marston, West Gouldsboro, Maine, and reported in Phillips Barry, Fannie Hardy Eckstorm, and Mary Winslow Smyth, *British Ballads from Maine* (Yale) New Haven, 1929, p. 93. Without music. Child ballad no. 46. Coffin, 53. Bronson, I, 362.

"Oh, for my breakfast you must get a cherry without a stone,
And for my dinner you must get a chicken without a bone,
And for my supper you must get a bird without a gall,
Then you and I in one bed shall lie, and you lie next to the wall."

"Oh, when the cherry is in the bloom, I am sure it has no stone,
And when the chicken is in the egg, I am sure it has no bone;
The dove it is a gentle bird, and it flies without a gall,
So you and I in one bed shall lie, and you lie next to the wall."

She found her Willie so manfully did Mary's heart enthrall,
He took this young girl by the waist, but — she didn't lie next to the wall.

THE TWO BROTHERS

"Oh, brother, oh, brother, can you play ball
    Or roll a marble stone?"
"No, brother, no brother, I can't play ball
    Nor roll a marble stone."*

He took his tomahawk from him
    And hacked him across the breast.
"Say, now, brother, I reckon you can't play ball
    Nor roll a marble stone."

"Oh, take my hunting shirt from me
    And tear it from gore to gore,
And wrap it around my bleeding breast
    That it might bleed no more."

He took his hunting shirt from him
    And tore it from gore to gore,
And wrapped it around his bleeding breast,
    But it still bled the more.

* The last two lines of each stanza are repeated.

"The Two Brothers" was recorded by Alan Lomax from the singing of Mrs. Texas Gladden at Salem, Virginia, 1941. Library of Congress record LP7. Child ballad no. 49. Coffin, 55. Bronson, I, 384.

"Oh, brother, when you go home to-night,
    My mother will ask for me.
You must tell her I'm gone with some little schoolboys,
    To-morrow night I'll be at home.

"My dear little sister will ask for me.
    The truth to her you must tell.
You must tell her I'm dead and in grave laid
    And buried at Jesseltown.

"Oh, take me up, oh, on your back,
    And carry me to Jesseltown,
And dig a hole and lay me in
    That I might sleep so sound."

He took him up, oh, on his back
    And carried him to Jesseltown,
And dug a hole and laid him in
    That he might sleep so sound.

He laid his Bible under his head,
    His tomahawk at his feet,
His bow and arrow across his breast
    That he might sleep so sweet.

LIZIE WAN

Fair Lucy was sitting in her own cabin door,
Making her laments alone;
Who should come by but her own mother dear,
Saying, "What makes Fair Lucy mourn?"

"I have a cause for to grieve," she said,
"And a reason for to mourn;
For the babe that lies in the cradle asleep,
Dear mother, it is his own."

"Lizie Wan" was recorded by Helen Hartness Flanders from the singing of Mrs. Alice (Slayton) Sicily, North Calais, Vermont, 1933, who recalls that her parents used to sing it together. Reported, with music, by Phillips Barry in *Bulletin of the Folksong Society of the Northeast*, Cambridge, Mass., 7 (1934):6–8. Child ballad no. 51. Coffin, 57. Bronson, I, 403.

Fair Lucy was sitting in her own cabin door,
Making her laments alone;
Who should come by but her own brother dear,
Saying, "What makes Fair Lucy mourn?"

"I have a cause for to grieve," she said,
"And a reason for to mourn;
For the babe that lies in the cradle asleep,
Dear brother, it is your own."

He took her by the lily-white hand
And he led her into the woods;
What he did there, I never can declare,
But he spilt Fair Lucy's blood.

"O, what is that upon your frock,
My son, come tell to me."
"It is one drop of Fair Lucy's blood,
And that you plainly can see."

"What will your father say to you,
When he returns to me?"
"I shall step my foot on board a ship,
And my face he never shall see."

"What will you do with your three little babes,
My son, come tell to me?"
"I shall leave them here at my father's command,
For to keep him companee."

"What will you do with your pretty little wife,
My son, come tell to me?"
"She shall step her foot on board a ship,
And sail the ocean with me."

"What will you do with your houses and lands,
My son, come tell to me?"
"I shall leave them here at my father's command,
For to set my children free."

"When will you return again,
My son, come tell to me?"
"When the sun and the moon set on yonders green hill,
And I'm sure that never can be."

THE KING'S DOCHTER LADY JEAN
(*Queen Jane*)

Queen Jane sat at her window one day
A-sewing a silken seam;
She looked out at the merry green woods
And saw the green nut tree,
And saw the green nut tree.

She dropped her thimble at her heel
And her needle at her toe,
And away she ran to the merry green woods
To gather nuts and so,
To gather nuts and so.

She scarce had reached the merry green woods,
Scarce had pulled nuts two or three,
When a proud forester came striding by,
Saying, "Fair maid, let those be."
Saying, "Fair maid, let those be.

"Why do you pull the nuts," he said,
"And why do you break the tree?
And why do you come to this merry green woods
Without the leave of me,
Without the leave of me?"

"Oh, I will pull the nuts," she said,
"And I will break the tree,
And I will come to this merry green woods;
I'll ask no leave of thee,
I'll ask no leave of thee."

"The King's Dochter Lady Jean" was recorded by Sandy Paton from the singing of Sara Cleveland, Brant Lake, New York, 1965. On Folk Legacy Record No. FSA-33 (A2). This is the unique collection of this Child ballad in America. Child ballad no. 52. Bronson I, 407, and the addenda to IV, 464–465.

He took her by the middle so small
And he gently laid her down,
And when he took what he longed for,
He raised her from the ground,
He raised her from the ground.

"Oh, woe to you, proud forester,
And an ill death may yours be.
Since I'm the King's youngest daughter," she cried,
"You will pay for wronging me,
You will pay for wronging me."

"If you're the King's youngest daughter," he said,
"Then I'm his eldest son;
And woe unto this unhappy hour
And the wrong that I have done,
And the wrong that I have done.

"The very first time I came from sea,
O Jane, you were unborn;
And I wish my gallant ship had sunk
And I'd been left forlorn,
And I'd been left forlorn.

"The very next time I came from sea
You were on your nurse's knee;
And the very next time I came from sea
You were in this woods with me,
You were in this woods with me.

"I wish I ne'er had seen your face,
Or that you had ne'er seen mine;
That we ne'er had met in this merry green woods
And this wrong could be undone,
And this wrong could be undone."

"I wish to God my babe was born
And on its nurse's knee,
And, as for me, I was dead and gone
And the green grass growing over me,
And the green grass growing over me."

LORD BATEMAN

Unlike most of the English ballads — with death, murder, unrequited love — "Lord Bateman" tells a story of adventure and ends happily for Lord Bateman and the Turkish lady. The story of the ballad is very close to a legend told about Gilbert Becket, the father of St. Thomas, but the ballad itself does not derive from the legend, having come into existence independently. Pleaz Mobley's interpretation is an unusually fine one.

> Lord Bateman was a noble lord,
> He held himself of high degree,
> He would not rest nor be contented
> Until he'd voyaged across the sea.

> He sailed east and he sailed westward,
> Until he reached the Turkish shore,
> And there they took him and put him in prison,
> He never expected his freedom any more.

"Lord Bateman" was recorded by Artus M. Moser from the singing, with guitar, of Pleaz Mobley of Manchester, Kentucky, at Harrogate, Tennessee, 1943. Library of Congress record LP12. Child ballad no. 53. Coffin, 58. Bronson, I, 409.

Now the Turk he had one only daughter,
As fair a maiden as eyes did see,
She stole the keys to her father's prison,
Saying, "Lord Bateman I'll set free."

"Have you got house, have you got land, sir,
Do you hold yourself of high degree,
What would you give the Turkish lady
If out of prison I'll set you free?"

"Well, I've got house and I've got land, love,
Half of Northumberland belongs to me,
I'll give it all to the Turkish lady
If out of prison you'll set me free."

She took him to her father's harbor
And gave to him a ship of fame,
"Farewell, farewell to thee, Lord Bateman,
I fear I'll never see you again."

For seven long years she kept that vow true.*
Then seven more, 'bout thirty-three,
Then she gathered all her gay, fine clothing.
Saying, "Lord Bateman I'll go see."

She sailed east and she sailed westward
Until she reached the English shore,
And when she came to Lord Bateman's castle,
She alighted down before the door.

"Is this Lord Bateman's fine castle,
And is his lordship here within?"
"Oh, yes, oh yes," cried the proud young porter,
"He's just taken his young bride in."

"What news, what news, my proud young porter,
What news, what news do you bring to me?"
"Oh, there's the fairest of all young ladies
That ever my two eyes ever did see.

---

* In a stanza omitted by Mobley, the Turkish lady and Lord Bateman had pledged their love to each other in toasts of strong wine.

"She says for you to send a slice of cake, sir,
And draw a glass of the strongest wine,
And not forget the proud young lady
That did release you when confined."

Lord Bateman rose from where he was sitting,
His face did look as white as snow,
Saying, "If this is the Turkish lady,
I'm bound with her love to go."

And then he spoke to the young bride's mother,
"She's none the better nor worse for me,
She came to me on a horse and saddle,
I'll send her back in chariots three.

"She came to me on a horse and saddle,
I'll send her back in a chariot free,
And I'll go marry the Turkish lady
That crossed the roaring sea for me."

DIVES AND LAZARUS

There was a man in olden times,
The scriptures do inform us,
Whose pomp and grandeur and whose crimes
Was great and very numerous.
Poor begging Lazarus at his gate,
To help himself unable.
He was begging humbly for the crumbs
That fell from his rich table.
But not a crumb would he bestow,
Or pity his condition,
The dogs took pity and licked his sores,
More ready to defend him.

"Dives and Lazarus" was recorded by Alan Lomax from the singing of Aunt Molly Jackson of Clay County, Kentucky, at New York City, 1939. Library of Congress record LP57. Child ballad no. 56. Coffin, 61. Bronson, II, 17.

Poor Lazarus died at the rich man's gate,
To Heaven he ascended,
He rested in the bosom of Abraham,
Where all his troubles ended.
The rich man died, was buried, too,
But oh, his awful station:
With Heaven and Hell both placed in view,
He waked up in damnation.
Saying, "I pray thee, father Abraham,
Send Lazarus with cold water,
For I'm tormented in these flames
With a tormenting torture."

"Rich Dives, poor Lazarus cannot come to you,
There is a gulf between us;
Now you must burn on in those flames
As though you had not seen us."
"I have five brothers in yonders world,
Send Lazarus back to tell them
Their wicked brother screams in hell,
With no one to defend him."
"If Lazarus went to yonders world,
Your brothers would not believe him;
They would answer him with cruel words,
And say he had deceived them.

"Forever you must burn in hell,
And forever be tormented,
And your other five brothers will end in hell
If they have not repented."

SIR PATRICK SPENS
(*Sir Patrick Spence*)

The king he sits in Dumferling town,
A-drinking his blood red wine,
"Sir Patrick Spence is the best sailor
That ever sailed the brine."

The king still sits in Dumferling town,
And a-sipping his red, red wine,
"Now where can I get a good sailor
To man this ship o' mine?"

Oh, up then said a yellow-haired lad
Just by the king's left knee,
"Sir Patrick Spence is the best skipper
That ever sailed the sea."

Oh, up then spoke an old, old knight
Right nigh the king's right knee,
"Sir, you are the very, very best sailor
That ever sailed the sea."

The king he wrote a good letter
And a-sealed it with his hand;
And when Sir Patrick Spence got it
He was strolling on the sand.

Sir Patrick read the orders from the king
That made him laugh at first,
But as he read another sad line,
Sir Patrick feared the worst.

He took his ship to far Norway,
A-sailing o'er the sea,
To get a lovely maiden fair
And to fetch her back, said he.

"Sir Patrick Spens" was collected by Edwin C. Kirkland from the singing of Clara J. McCauley, Knoxville, Tennessee, and reported in *SFQ*, 1 (December, 1937): 1–2. Child ballad no. 58. Coffin, 62. Bronson, II, 29.

They sailed and sailed for many a day
Upon the wild, wild sea,
But our good sailor Sir Patrick Spence
Was drowned in the deep.

So the king sits on in Dumferling town,
A-drinking his blood red wine,
"Oh, where can I get a good sailor
To sail this ship of mine?"

YOUNG HUNTING
(*Loving Henry*)

"Get down, get down, lovin' Henry," she cried,
    "And stay all night with me.
Your bed I'll make of the finest silks,
    And all rich vanity."

"Well I can't bed down, no I won't get down
    And stay all night with thee.
There's a little girl in the Arkansas land
    That has long been waiting for me."

As he stooped down to kiss her rosy red cheeks
    A knife she held in her hand,
She plunged it in his snow-white breast,
    She plunged it cold and deep.

She took him by his lily-white hands
    And her sister by the feet,
And they threw him in the dark, dark well,
    Where the water's so cold and deep.

"Lie there, lie there, lovin' Henry," she cried,
    "Till the meat drops from the bone,
And that little girl in the Arkansas land
    Thinks you're long time comin' home."

"Young Hunting" was collected by George W. Boswell from the singing of Paul Brooks Lacy at Stacy Forks, Morgan County, Kentucky, November, 1964. *Kentucky Folklore Record*, 18 (1972):13–14. With music. Child ballad no. 68. Coffin, 66. Bronson, II, 60.

As she turned around to go back home
  A bird in the treetop sang,
And every note seemed to stick her heart,
  "Don't you cry, little birdie, don't sing.

"Fly down, fly down, little birdie," she cried.
  "And sit upon my knee.
Fly down, fly down, little birdie," she cried,
  "And sing your song to me."

"Well I can't fly down, no I won't fly down
  And sit upon your knee;
For the way you just murdered your own sweetheart
  I'm sure you'd murder me."

"If I had a bow of silvery steel,
  An arrow, and a string,
I'd aim right up at your little heart,
  And you'd not sit there and sing."

"If you had a bow of silvery steel,
  An arrow, and a string,
I'd fly away to some tall tree
  And there I'd sit and sing."

LORD THOMAS AND FAIR ANNET
(*The Brown Girl*)

Lord Thomas he was a gay gentleman, the lord of many a dell;
Fair Ellender was a fair young lady, Lord Thomas he loved her well,
Lord Thomas he loved her well.

"Oh, mother, oh, father, come riddle to me, I ask you both as one,
Oh, must I marry fair Ellender or bring the brown girl home,
Or bring the brown girl home?"

"The brown girl she has houses and land, fair Ellender she has none,
Oh, son, we advise you as a great blessing to bring the brown girl home,
To bring the brown girl home."

"Lord Thomas and Fair Annet" was collected by Vance Randolph from the singing of Mrs. May Kennedy McCord, Springfield, Missouri, 1941. Library of Congress record AFS 5298 A. Child ballad no. 73. Coffin, 68. Bronson, II, 88.

He dressed himself in scarlet robes, his waiters all dressed in green,
And every town that he rode through, they took him to be some king,
They took him to be some king.

He rode till he come to fair Ellender's door, he tingled at the ring,
And none so ready as she herself to rise and bid him come in,
To rise and bid him come in.

"What news, what news, Lord Thomas?" she cried, "What news do you
    bring to me?"
"I've come to bid you to my wedding, the brown girl my bride to be.
The brown girl my bride to be."

"Sad news, sad news, Lord Thomas," she cried, "sad news do you bring to
    me,
For I had hoped to be your bride, and you bridegroom to me,
And you bridegroom to me."

"Oh, mother, oh, father, come riddle to me, I ask you both as one,
Oh, must I go to Lord Thomas's wedding, or tarry with you at home,
Or tarry with you at home?"

"Oh, many there be who be your friends, and many there be your foes,
And we would advise you as a great blessing, to tarry with us at home,
To tarry with us at home."

"Oh, many there be who be my friends, and many there be my foes,
But I will risk my fortune and life, and to Lord Thomas's wedding I'll go,
And to Lord Thomas's wedding I'll go."

She dressed herself in satin white, her ladies all dressed in green,
And every town that they rode through they took her to be some queen,
They took her to be some queen.

She rode till she come to Lord Thomas's hall, she tingled at the ring,
And none so ready as he himself to rise and bid her come in,
To rise and bid her come in.

He took her by the lily-white hand, he led her down the hall,
And seated her at the banquet head among the ladies all,
Among the ladies all.

"Is this your bride, Lord Thomas?" she cried. "She is the most wonderful
    brown,
When you could have married the fairest lady that ever the sun shone on,
That ever the sun shone on."

"Throw none of your slurs, fair Ellen," he cried, "throw none of your slurs at me,
For I love the tip of your finger more than the brown girl's whole body,
Than the brown girl's whole body."

The brown girl had a little penknife, with blades both keen and sharp,
Between the short ribs and the long, she pierced fair Ellender's heart,
She pierced fair Ellender's heart.

"Oh, what is the matter, fair Ellen?" he cried, "What makes you look so pale?
You used to have as rosy cheeks as any one in our dale,
As any one in our dale."

"Oh, are you blind, Lord Thomas?" she cried, "or maybe you cannot see
That I can feel my own heart's blood come trickeling to my knees,
Come trickeling to my knees."

He took the brown girl by the hand, he led her down the hall,
And with his sword cut off her head, and kicked it against the wall,
And kicked it against the wall.

He pointed the handle to the sun, the blade unto his breast,
Saying, "Here's the death of two fond lovers, God send our souls to rest,
God send our souls to rest.

"Go bury me 'neath yonder green tree, go dig my grave wide and deep,
And place fair Ellender in my arms, and the brown girl at my feet,
And the brown girl at my feet."

(*Lord Thomas and Fair Ellender*)

"Lord Thomas, Lord Thomas, take my advice.
    Go bring the brown girl home,
For she has land and a house of her own;
    Fair Ellender she has none."

He called it to his waiting maids,
    By one, by two, by three.
"Go bridle, go saddle my milky white steed;
    Fair Ellender I must see."

"Lord Thomas and Fair Ellender" was recorded by Herbert Halpert from the singing of Horton Barker at Chilhowie, Virginia, 1939. Library of Congress record LP7. Child ballad no. 73. Coffin, 68. Bronson, II, 88.

He rode and he rode till he came to her gate.
    So loudly he tingled the rein.*
And none was so ready as fair Ellender herself
    As she rose to let him in.

"I've come to ask you to my wedding today."
    "Bad news, Lord Thomas," says she,
"For I your bride I thought I would be.
    Bad news, Lord Thomas," says she.

She called it to her father and mother
    To make them both as one.
"Shall I go to Lord Thomas's wedding
    Or tarry at home alone?"

She dressed herself so fine in silk,
    Her very maids in green;
And every city that she rode through,
    They took her to be some queen.

She rode and she rode till she came to his gate.
    So loudly she tingled the rein.
And none was so ready as Lord Thomas himself
    As he rose to let her in.

He took her by the lily-white hand;
    He led her through the hall;
He sot her down at the head of the table
    Among the quality all.

"Lord Thomas," says she, "is this your bride?
    I'm sure she looks very brown.
You might have married as fair a young lady
    As ever the sun shone on."

The brown girl had a penknife in her hand,
    It keen and very sharp.
Between the long ribs and the short,
    She pierced Fair Ellender to the heart.

* Ring.

He took the brown girl by the hand;
    He led her through the hall;
And with his sword he cut her head off,
    And kicked it against the wall.

He placed the handle against the ground,
    The point against his breast,
Saying, "Here's the death of three true lovers,
    God send their souls to rest.

"I want my grave dug long and wide,
    And dig it very deep.
I want Fair Ellender in my arms,
    The brown girl at my feet."

FAIR MARGARET AND SWEET WILLIAM
(*Little Marg'et*)

Little Marg'et sitting in her high hall door,
A-combing back her long yellow hair,
Saw sweet William and his new-made bride
A-riding up the road so near.

She throwed down her ivory comb,
She throwed back her long yellow hair,
Said, "I'll go out and bid 'em farewell
And never more go there."

'Twas all lately in the night
When they were fast asleep,
Little Marg'et appeared all dressed in white
Standing at their bed feet.

"How do you like that snow-white pillow?
How do you like your sheet?
How do you like that fair young lady
That lies in your arms asleep?"

"Fair Margaret and Sweet William" was recorded by Artus M. Moser from the singing of Bascom Lamar Lunsford of South Turkey Creek, North Carolina, at Swannanoa, North Carolina, 1946. Library of Congress AFS record 7964 B. Child ballad no. 74. Coffin, 70. Bronson, II, 155.

"Oh, well do I like my snow-white pillow,
Oh, well do I like my sheet,
Much better do I like that fair young lady
That stands at my bed feet."

He called on serving men to go
And saddle the dapple roan,
He went to her father's house and knocked
And he knocked at the door alone.

"Is little Marg'et in the house
Or is she in the hall?"
"Little Marg'et's in her coal-black coffin
With her face turned to the wall."

"Unfold, unfold them snow-white robes,
Be they ever so fine,
And let me kiss them cold corpy lips
For I know they'll never kiss mine."

Once he kissed her lily-white hands,
Twice he kissed her cheeks,
Three times he kissed her cold corpy lips,
And he fell in her arms asleep.

LORD LOVEL

Lord Lovel he stood at his castle gate,
A-combing his milk-white steed,
When along came Lady Nancy Bell
A-wishing her lover good speed, speed, speed,
A-wishing her lover good speed.

"Oh, where are you going, Lord Lovel?" she said,
"Oh, where are you going?" said she.
"I'm going, my dear Lady Nancy Bell,
Strange countries for to see, see, see,
Strange countries for to see."

"Lord Lovel" was collected by C. H. Williams from his brother, George Williams of Bollinger County, Missouri, 1907. Reported in H. M. Belden, *Ballads and Songs Collected by the Missouri Folk-Lore Society*, Columbia (reprint edition, 1966), p. 53. Without music. Child ballad no. 75. Coffin, 72. Bronson, II, 189.

"Oh, when will you be back?" she says,
"Oh, when will you be back?" says she.
"In a year or two, or three at the most,
"I'll return to your fair body, body, body,
I'll return to your fair body."

He had not been gone but a year and a day
Strange countries for to see,
When languishing thoughts came into his head
Lady Nancy Bell he would see, see, see,
Lady Nancy Bell he would see.

He rode, he rode upon his white steed
Till he came to London town;
And there he heard St. Varnie's bell
And the people all mourning 'round, 'round, 'round,
And the people all mourning 'round.

"Is anybody dead?" Lord Lovel he said;
"Is anybody dead?" says he.
"A lord's daughter dead," a lady replied,
"And some call her Lady Nancy, Nancy, Nancy,
And some call her Lady Nancy."

He ordered the grave to be opened forthwith
And the shroud to be folded down,
And there he kissed her clay-cold lips
Till the tears came trickling down, down, down,
Till the tears came trickling down.

Lady Nancy she died as it might be today,
Lord Lovel he died tomorrow.
And out of her bosom there grew a red rose
And out of Lord Lovel's a briar, briar, briar,
And out of Lord Lovel's a briar.

They grew and they grew till they reached the church top,
And there they couldn't grow any higher;
And there they entwined in a true lover knot,
Which true lovers always admire, admire, admire,
Which true lovers always admire.

THE LASS OF ROCH ROYAL
(*Sweet Annie of Roch Royal*)

"O who will shoe my little feet,
And who will glove my hands?
And who will tie my waist so neat,
With the new-made London
 bands?

"O who will comb my yellow hair
With the bright new silver comb?
O who will be daddy to my boy
Till my lover George comes
 home?"

Her father shoed her little feet,
Her mother gloved her hands;
Her sister tied on her waist so neat
The new-made London bands.

Her cousin combed her yellow hair
With the new-made silver comb;
But heaven knew the daddy of her
 boy
Till her lover George came home.

Her father gave her a new ship,
And led her to the sand;
She took her boy up in her arms
And sailed away from the land.

On the sea she sailed and sailed,
For over a month and more,
Till she landed her new ship
Near to her lover's door.

Long she stood at her lover's door,
And long pulled at the string,
Till up got his false mother,
Saying, "Who pulls at the string?"

"O it is Annie of Roch Royal,
Your own, come over the sea
With your own dear son in her
 arms;
So open the door to me."

"Be off! be off! you bold woman,
You come not here for good;
You're only a strumpet, or a bold
 witch,
Or else a mermaid from the sea."

"I'm not a witch nor a strumpet
 bold,
Nor a mermaid from the sea;
But I am Annie of Roch Royal;
So open the door to me.

"So open the door now, dear
 George,
And open it with speed,
Or your young son here in my arms
With the cold will soon be dead."

"If you be Annie of Roch Royal,
Though I know you may not be,
What pledge can you give that I
Have ever kept you company?"

"The Lass of Roch Royal" was collected by Josiah H. Combs from Carey Woofter, Gilmer County, West Virginia, 1924. Combs, *Folksongs of the Southern United States*, Publications of the American Folklore Society (The University of Texas Press) Austin, 1967, pp. 118–121. Without music. Child ballad no. 76. Coffin, 73. Bronson, II, 218.

"O don't you mind, dear George,"
   she said,
When we were a-drinking wine,
How we gave the rings from our
   fingers,
And how the best was mine?

"Though yours was good enough
   for me,
It was not so good as mine;
Yours was made of bright red gold,
While mine had a diamond fine.

"So open the door, now, dear
   George,
And open it with speed,
Or your young son here in my arms
With the cold will soon be dead."

"Away, away, you bold woman,
Take from my door your shame;
For I have gotten another true-love,
And you may hasten home."

"And if you have gotten another
   true-love,
After all the oaths that you swore,
O here is farewell, false George,
For you will never see me more."

Slow-ly, slow-ly went she back
As the day began to dawn;
She set her foot on the new ship,
And bitterly did she mourn.

George started up all in his sleep,
And quick to his mother he said:
"O I dreamed a dream tonight,
   mother,
That made my heart so sad.

"I dreamed that Annie of Roch
   Royal
(The flower of all her kin)
Was standing mourning at my
   door,
But none would let her in."

"O a bold woman stood there at the
   door
With a child all in her arms;
But I wouldn't let her come in the
   house,
For fear she would work you a
   charm."

Quick-ly, quick-ly got he up,
And fast he ran to the sand,
And there he saw his dear Annie
A-sailing from the land.

"And hey, Annie, and hee, Annie,
O Annie, listen to me!"
But the louder he cried, "Annie!"
The louder roared the sea.

The wind blew high, the sea grew
   rough,
The ship was broken in two,
And soon he saw his sweet Annie
Come floating over the waves.

He saw his young son in her arms,
Both tossed about by the tide;
He pulled his hair, and he ran fast,
And he plunged in the sea so wild.

He caught her by the yellow hair
And drew her out on the sand;
But cold and stiff were her snowy
   limbs
Before he reached the land.

O he has mourned over sweet Annie
Till the sun was going down;
Then with a sigh his heart did
       burst,
And his soul to heaven has flown.

THE UNQUIET GRAVE

Oh, I never had but one true love,
In the green woods he was slain,
I'd do as much for my true love
As any girl would do.

I set and weeped all over his grave
Twelve months and one day;
It's when twelve months and one day was up,
Oh, this young man he arose.
Saying, "Why do you weep all over my grave,
For I cannot find no relief?"

"One kiss, one kiss from your clay, clay-cold lips,
One kiss is all that I crave,
One kiss, one kiss from your clay, clay-cold lips,
And then return to your grave."

"If I was to give you one kiss,
Oh, your days would not be long,
It's for my lips they're clay, clay-cold,
And my breath smells earthlye strong."

"The Unquiet Grave" was collected by Herbert Halpert from Allen Clevenger (aged eighty-two) near Magnolia, New Jersey, 1937. Reported by Halpert, with music, in *JAF*, 52 (1939):53. Child ballad no. 78. Coffin, 77. Bronson II, 234.

THE WIFE OF USHER'S WELL
(*The Three Babes*)

There was a lady of beauty rare,
   And children she had three.
She sent them away to the North Countree
   For to learn their grammaree.

They hadn't been gone so very long,
   Scarcely three months and a day,
When there came a sickness all over the land
   And swept them all away.

And when she came this for to know,
   She wrung her hands full sore,
Saying, "Alas, alas, my three little babes,
   I never shall see any more.

"Ain't there a king in heaven," she cried,
   "Who used to wear a crown?
I pray the Lord will me reward
   And send my three babes down."

It was a-come near Christmas time,
   The nights was long and cold,
When her three little babes come a-runnin' down
   To their dear mammy's home.

She fixed them a bed in the backmost room,
   All covered with clean white sheets,
And o'er the top a golden one
   That they might soundly sleep.

"Take it off, take it off," said the oldest one,
   "Take it off, we say again.
A woe, a woe to this wicked world,
   So long since pride began."

"The Wife of Usher's Well" was recorded by Fletcher Collins from the singing of I. G. Greer of Thomasville, North Carolina, 1941. Library of Congress record LP7. Child ballad no. 79. Coffin, 77. Bronson, II, 246.

She spread a table for them there,
    All covered with cakes and wine,
And said, "Come, eat, my three little babes,
    Come, eat, and drink of mine."

"We do not want your cakes, mammy,
    We do not want your wine,
For in the morning by the break of day
    With the Savior we must dine."

LITTLE MUSGRAVE AND LADY BARNARD
(*Little Matthy Groves*)

Oh a high holiday, on a high holiday,
The very first day of the year,
Little Matthy Groves to church did go
God's holy word to hear, hear,
God's holy word to hear.

The first that come in was a gay lady,
And the next that came in was a girl,
And the next that came in was Lord Arnold's wife,
The fairest of them all, all,
The fairest of them all.

She stepped right up unto this one
And she made him this reply,
Saying, "You must go home with me tonight,
All night with me for to lie."

"I cannot go with you tonight,
I cannot for my life;
For I know by the rings that are on your fingers
You are Lord Arnold's wife."

"And if I am Lord Arnold's wife,
I know that Lord Arnold's gone away.
He's gone away to Old England
To see King Hen-e-ry."

"Little Musgrave and Lady Barnard" was collected from Mrs. Eva Warner Case, Harrison County, Missouri, 1916. In H. M. Belden, *Ballads and Songs Collected by the Missouri Folk-Lore Society*, Columbia, 1940 (reprint edition, 1966), p. 58. With music. Child ballad no. 81. Coffin, 79. Bronson, II, 267.

A little footpage was standing by,
And he took to his feet and run.
He run till he came to the waterside,
And he bent on his breast and swum.

"What news, what news, my little footpage,
What news have you for me?
Are my castle walls all tor-en down,
Or are my castles three?"

"Your castle walls are not tor-en down
Nor are your castles three,
But little Matthy Groves is in your house
In bed with your gay lady!"

He took his merry men by the hand
And placed them all in a row,
And he bade them not one word for to speak
And not one horn for to blow.

There was one man among them all
Who owed little Matthy some good will,
And he put his bugle horn to his mouth
And he blew both loud and shrill.

"Hark, hark! hark! hark!" said little Matthy Groves,
"I hear the bugle blow,
And every note it seems to say
'Arise, arise and go!' "

"Lie down, lie down, little Matthy Groves,
And keep my back from the cold,
It is my father's shepherd boys
A-blowing up the sheep from the fold."

From that they fell to hugging and kissing,
And from that they fell to sleep,
And next morning when they woke at the break of day,
Lord Arnold stood at their feet.

"And it's how do you like my fine featherbed,
And it's how do you like my sheets?
And it's how do you like my gay lady
That lies in your arms and sleeps?"

"Very well do I like your fine featherbed,
Very well do I like your sheets,
But much better do I like your gay lady
That lies in my arms and sleeps."

"Now get you up, little Matthy Groves,
And all your clothes put on,
For it never shall be said in Old England
That I slew a naked man."

"I will get up," said little Matthy Groves,
"And fight you for my life,
Though you've two bright swords hanging by your side
And me not a pocket knife."

"If I've two bright swords by my side,
They cost me deep in purse,
And you shall have the better of the two
And I will keep the worse."

The very first lick that little Matthy struck
He wounded Lord Arnold sore,
But the very first lick that Lord Arnold struck,
Little Matthy struck no more.

He took his lady by the hand,
And he downed her on his knee,
Saying, "Which do you like the best, my dear,
Little Matthy Groves or me?"

"Very well do I like your rosy cheeks,
Very well do I like your dimpled chin,
But better do I like little Matthy Groves
Than you and all your kin."

He took his lady by the hand
And led her o'er the plain,
He took the broadsword from his side
And he split her head in twain.

"Hark, hark, hark, doth the nightingale sing,
And the sparrows they do cry;
Today I've killed two true lovers,
And tomorrow I must die!"

BONNY BARBARA ALLAN
(*Barbara Allen*)

Oh, in the merry month of May,
When all things were a-blooming,
Sweet William came from the Western States,
And courted Barbara Allen.

But he took sick, and very sick,
And he sent for Barbara Allen,
And all she said when she got there,
"Young man, you are a-dying."

"Oh yes, I'm sick, and I'm very sick,
And I think that death's upon me;
But one sweet kiss from Barbara's lips
Will save me from my dying."

"But don't you remember the other day
You were down in town a-drinking?
You drank your health to the ladies all round,
And slighted Barbara Allen."

"Oh yes, I remember the other day
I was down in town a-drinking;
I drank my health to the ladies all 'round,
But my love to Barbara Allen."

He turned his face to the wall;
She turned her back upon him;
The very last word she heard him say,
"Hard-hearted Barbara Allen."

As she passed on through London Town,
She heard some bells a-ringing,
And every bell, it seemed to say,
"Hard-hearted Barbara Allen."

"Bonny Barbara Allan" was collected by Harvey H. Fuson from Leon Denny Moses. In Fuson, *Ballads of the Kentucky Highlands*, London, 1931, p. 47. Without music. Child ballad no. 84. Coffin, 82. Bronson, II, 322.

She then passed on to the country road,
And heard some birds a-singing;
And every bird it seemed to say,
"Hard-hearted Barbara Allen."

She hadn't got more than a mile from town
When she saw his corpse a-coming;
"O bring him here, and ease him down,
And let me look upon him.

"Oh, take him away! Oh, take him away!
For I am sick and dying!
His death-cold features say to me,
'Hard-hearted Barbara Allen.'

"O father, O father, go dig my grave,
And dig it long and narrow;
Sweet William died for me to-day;
I'll die for him to-morrow."

They buried them both in the old graveyard,
All side and side each other.
A red, red rose grew out of his grave,
And a green briar out of hers.

They grew and grew so very high
That they could grow no higher;
They lapped, they tied in a true-love-knot —
The rose ran 'round the briar.

LADY ALICE
(*George Collins*)

I

George Collins came home last Saturday night,
He was taken down sick an' died;

Version 1 of "Lady Alice" was recorded by Duncan Emrich from the singing of Bascom
Lamar Lunsford of South Turkey Creek, North Carolina, at Washington, D.C., 1949. Library
of Congress AFS record 9474 B3. Child ballad no. 85. Coffin, 86. Bronson, II, 392.

His true love was in the next room door,
Sewing her silk so fine.

When she heard George Collins was dead,
She laid her silks aside,
She got down on her bended knees,
She wept, she mourned, she cried.

"Oh, Mary, oh, Mary, get up from there,
Why do you weep an' mourn?
For there are other young men around,
To see you weep and mourn."

"Mother, oh, Mother, I know there are
Other young men aroun'.
I'll follow George Collins by night and by day,
I'll follow him to his grave.

"Lay off, lay off that coffin lid,
Unfold those sheets so white,
So I may kiss those cold pale lips,
For I'm sure they'll never kiss mine.

"God pity the dove that mourns for her love,
And flies from pine to pine,
And may you be as true to your love
As I have been to mine."

II

George Collins drove home one cold winter night,
    George Collins drove home so fine;
George Collins drove home one cold winter night,
    And taken sick and died.

Miss Mary was a-sitting in yonders room,
    Sewing her silks so fine,
When she heard poor George was dead,
    She laid her silks aside.

Version II of "Lady Alice" was collected by Dorothy Scarborough from the singing of Paul Osborne, Hoot Owl Hollow, Drill, Virginia, ca. 1932. Reported, with music, in Scarborough, *A Song Catcher in Southern Mountains*, New York, 1937. Child ballad no. 85. Coffin, 86. Bronson, II, 392.

She followed him up, she followed him down,
    She following him to his grave,
And down on low on bended knees
    She weeped, and she moaned, and she prayed.

Sit down the coffin, screw off the lid,
    Lay back the linen so fine,
For I want to kiss his pale cold lips
    For I'm sure he'll never kiss mine.

Oh, daughter, oh, daughter, what makes you weep?
    There are more boys than one.
Oh, Mother, George has won my heart
    And now he's dead and gone.

See that lonesome dove a-flying,
    Flying from pine to pine;
Weeping for its own true love
    Just like I weep for mine.

III

George Collins come home last Friday night,
And there he take sick and died;
And when Mrs. Collins heard George was dead,
She wrung her hands and cried.

Mary in the hallway, sewing her silk,
She's sewing her silk so fine,
And when she heard that George were dead,
She threw her sewing aside.

She followed him up, she followed him down,
She followed him to his grave,
And there all on her bended knee
She wept, she mourned, she prayed.

"Hush, up, dear daughter, don't take it so hard,
There's more pretty boys than George."
"There's more pretty boys all standing around,
But none so dear as George."

Version III of "Lady Alice" was collected by Cecil J. Sharp from the singing of Mrs. Dora Shelton, Allanstand, North Carolina, 1916. In Sharp, *English Folksongs from the Southern Appalachians* (Oxford) New York, 1932, I, 196. Child ballad no. 85. Coffin, 86. Bronson, II, 392.

Look away, look away, that lonesome dove
That sails from pine to pine;
It's mourning for its own true love
Just like I mourn for mine.

Set down the coffin, lift up the lid,
And give me a comb so fine,
And let me comb his cold, wavy hair,
For I know he'll never comb mine.

Set down the coffin, lift up the lid,
Lay back the sheetings so fine,
And let me kiss his cold, sweet lips,
For I know he'll never kiss mine.

IV

She says the coffin to be opened,
An' then the shroud to be folded down,
An' then she kissed them clay-cold lips
Until the tears come a-runnin' down.

"Set him down, set him down," Lady Alice she cried,
"Set him down on the grass so green,
An' before the sun goes down in the West
My corpse'll be a-layin' by his'n."

George Collins rode out the very next night,
He rode out all alone,
An' the first thing he saw when he got there
Was fair Eleanor washin' a white marble stone,

Oh don't you see that turtle-dove
A-flyin' from pine to pine?
He's a-mournin' for his own true love,
So why not me, why not me for mine?

Version IV of "Lady Alice" was collected by Vance Randolph from the singing of Miss Lisbeth Hayes, Fayetteville, Arkansas, 1920. Reported, with music, in Randolph, *Ozark Folksongs*, Columbia, Missouri, 1946, I, 139. Child ballad no. 85. Coffin, 86. Bronson, II, 392.

PRINCE ROBERT
(*Harry Saunders*)

And it's forty miles to Nicut Hill,
The nearest way you may go;
But Harry Saunders has taken a wife
That he dares not to bring home.

His mother called to her hired girl,
"Sally, draw me a cup of tea,
For I see my son Harry is coming
To eat a meal with me."

His mother lifted the cup of tea
And touched her lips to the drink;
But never a drop of the poison cup
Of drinking did she think.

Harry took that cup of tea
And put it to his mouth;
He opened his bright red lips,
And the poison went quickly down.

His wife set at Nicut Hill
Waiting for Harry to come;
She called to her own sister dear,
"Has my husband now come home?"

She went up to her room
And put on a riding-skirt;
She went out to the stable old
And saddled her roan steed.

But when she came to Harry's home
The guests were in the hall;
The hearse was standing by the yard,
And the friends were mourning all.

"Prince Robert" was collected by Josiah H. Combs from F. C. Gainer, Tanner, Gilmer County, West Virginia, 1924. Without music. In Josiah H. Combs, *Folksongs of the Southern United States*, Publications of the American Folklore Society (The University of Texas Press) Austin, 1967, pp. 121–123. Child ballad no. 87. Coffin, 88. Not reported by Bronson, since it has not been collected with music.

"I've come for none of his gold," she cried,
"Nor for none of his lands so wide;
But his watch and his chain they ought to go
To his own sweet bride."

"You will get none of his gold," his mother said,
"Nor none of his lands so wide;
His watch and his chain I threw in the well,
From his own sweet bride to hide."

And then she kissed his cold white cheeks,
And then she kissed his chin,
And then she kissed his bright red lips,
Where there was no breath come in.

And then she fell upon the floor,
Her head beside the bier;
Her heart did break, it was so sore,
But she shed not any tear.

LAMKIN
(*Bolakins*)

Bolakins was a very fine mason
    As ever laid stone.
He built a fine castle
    And the pay he got none.

"Where is the gentleman?
    Is he at home?"
"He's gone down to Marion
    For to visit his son."

"Where is the lady?
    Is she at home?"
"She's upstairs sleeping,"
    Said the foster to him.

"How will we get her down
    Such a dark night as this?"
"We'll stick her little baby
    Full of needles and pins."
They stuck her little baby
    Full of needles and pins.

"Lamkin" was recorded by Herbert Halpert from the singing of Mrs. Lena Bare Turbyfill at Elk Park, North Carolina, 1939. Library of Congress record LP7.

Through folk transmission, words have become changed: "foster" should read "false nurse"; "many marigolds" should be "as much red gold"; and "the stake of stand-by" be "the stake a-standing by." Child ballad no. 93. Coffin, 89. Bronson, II, 428.

The foster she rocked,
    And Bolakins he sung,
While blood and tears
    From the cradle did run.

Down come our lady,
    Not thinking any harm.
Old Bolakins,
    He took her in his arms.

"Bolakins, Bolakins,
    Spare my life one day.
I'll give you many marigolds
    As my horse can carry away.

"Bolakins, Bolakins,
    Spare my life one hour.
I'll give you daughter Bessie,
    My own blooming flower."

"You better keep your daughter
    Bessie
    For to run through the flood,
And scour a silver basin
    For to catch your heart's blood."

Daughter Bessie climbed up
    In the window so high,
And saw her father
    Come riding hard by.

"Oh, father, oh, father,
    Can you blame me?
Old Bolakins
    Has killed your lady.

"Oh, father, oh, father,
    Can you blame me?
Old Bolakins
    Has killed your baby."

They hung old Bolakins
    To the sea-gallows tree
And tied the foster
    To the stake of stand-by.

THE MAID FREED FROM THE GALLOWS
("*Hangman, Slack on the Line*")

"Hangman, hangman, slack on the line,
    Slack on the line a little while.
I think I see my father coming
    With money to pay my fine.

"Oh, father, father, did you bring me money,
    Money to pay my fine?
Or did you come here to see me die
    On this hangman's line?"

"The Maid Freed from the Gallows" was collected by Dorothy Scarborough from the singing of Edwin Swain, 1925, who learned the ballad from Florida Negroes. In Scarborough, *On the Trail of Negro Folksongs*, Cambridge, Mass.: Harvard University Press, 1925, p. 39. With music. Child ballad no. 95. Coffin, 91. Bronson, II, 448.

"No, I didn't bring you any money,
   Money to pay your fine,
But I just came here to see you die
   Upon this hangman's line."

"Hangman, hangman, slack on the line,
   Slack on the line a little while.
I think I see my mother coming
   With money to pay my fine.

"Oh, mother, mother, did you bring me any money,
   Money to pay my fine?
Or did you just come here to see me die
   Upon this hangman's line?"

"No, I didn't bring you any money,
   Money to pay your fine,
But I just came here to see you die
   Upon this hangman's line."

"Hangman, hangman, slack on the line,
   Slack on the line a little while;
For I think I see my brother coming
   With money to pay my fine.

"Oh, brother, brother, did you bring me any money,
   Money to pay my fine?
Or did you just come here to see me die
   Upon this hangman's line?"

"No, I didn't bring you any money,
   Money to pay your fine,
But I just came here to see you die
   Upon this hangman's line."

"Hangman, hangman, slack on the line,
   Slack on the line a little while;
For I think I see my sister coming
   With money to pay my fine.

"Oh, sister, sister, did you bring me any money,
   Money to pay my fine?
Or did you just come here to see me die
   Upon this hangman's line?"

"No, I didn't bring you any money,
  Money to pay your fine,
But I just came here to see you die
  Upon this hangman's line."

"Hangman, hangman, slack on the line,
  Slack on the line a little while,
I think I see my truelove coming
  With money to pay my fine.

"Oh, True Love, True Love, did you bring me any money,
  Money to pay my fine?
Or did you just come here to see me die
  Upon this hangman's line?"

"True Love, I got gold and silver,
  Money to pay your fine.
How could I bear to see you die
  Upon this hangman's line?"

The Sycamore Tree

"Oh, hangman, hangman, slacken your rope
And wait a little while;
I think I see my father coming,
A-riding from many a mile.

"Oh, have you come with silver and gold
And money to buy me free,
Or have you come to see me hung
Upon the sycamore tree?"

"No gold nor silver have I here,
Nor money to buy you free;
But I have come to see you hang
Upon the sycamore tree."

[Thus with "mother," "brother," "sister," until the lover appears, who is similarly addressed, but who replies:]

"The Sycamore Tree" was collected by Alton C. Morris from the singing of Mrs. Ruth Simmons, Jacksonville, Florida, 1950. In Morris, *Folksongs of Florida* (University of Florida Press) Gainesville, 1950, p. 297. With music. Child ballad no. 95. Coffin, 91. Bronson, II, 448.

"Yes, gold and silver have I here,
And money to buy you free;
But I've not come to see you hang
Nor hung you shall not be."

WILLIE OF WINSBURY

Fair Mary sat at her father's castle gate,
A-watching the ships coming in;
Her father he came and sat by her side,
For he saw she looked pale and thin —
For he saw she looked pale and thin.

"Are you sick? Are you sick, dear Mary?" he said,
"Are you sick? Are you sick?" quoth he,
"Or are you in love with a jolly sailor lad,
Who sails the distant seas?"

"I am not sick, dear father," she says,
"I am not sick," quoth she,
"But I'm in love with a jolly sailor lad,
John Barbour is his name."

"Is it so? Is it so, dear Mary?" he said,
"Is it so? Is it so?" quoth he,
"If you're in love with a jolly sailor lad,
Then hangèd he shall be!"

Then the old man he called up his merry, merry men,
By one, by two, by three,
John Barbour had been the very last man,
But now the first was he.

"Willie of Winsbury" was recorded on dictaphone and transcribed by Helen Hartness Flanders and Elizabeth Flanders from the singing of Miss Mary Louise Harvey, Woodstock, Vermont, n.d. "Miss Harvey learned this ballad from her mother, Mrs. Rebecca Greenough, who came to Vermont in 1853, soon after her marriage: she learned it from her grandmother, Mrs. Rebecca Hoyt (born ca. 1780), who lived near Concord, New Hampshire." Reported in the *Bulletin of the Folksong Society of the Northeast*, Cambridge, Mass., 9 (1935):6. With music. Child ballad no. 100. Coffin, 96. Bronson, II 495.

"Will you marry my daughter?" the old man said,
"Will you marry my daughter?" quoth he,
"Will you sing and play and dance with her,
And be heir to my houses and lands?"

"Yes, I'll marry your daughter," the young man said,
"I'll marry your daughter," quoth he,
"I'll sing and play and dance with her,
But a fig for your houses and lands!"

"Although John Barbour is my name,
I'm the Duke of Cumberland,
And for every pound that you give her,
I'll give her ten thousand pounds."

THE BAILIFF'S DAUGHTER OF ISLINGTON
(*The Bailer's Daughter of Ireland Town*)

Oh, there was a youth and a noble youth,
The squire's only son,
He fell in love with the bailer's daughter,
It's of fair Ireland town.

But it's when his parents came to know
The venshuns of their son,
They sent him down to fair London town,
Apprentice there to learn.

For him to mind his books and study law
And leave his dear behind;
"Oh, she I adore if I never see her more,
And still runs in my mind."

It's when the youth of fair Ireland town
Came out for to sport and play,
Oh, the bailer's daughter was amongst the rest,
So shyly stole away.

"The Bailiff's Daughter of Islington" was collected by Herbert Halpert from the singing of Allen Clevenger (age eighty-two) near Magnolia, New Jersey, 1937, and reported, with music, in "Some Ballads and Folk Songs from New Jersey," *JAF*, 52 (1939):54. Child ballad no. 105. Coffin, 96. Bronson, II, 495.

She dressed herself in men's array,
The roads being dusty and dry,
And it's who should she meet but her own true love
As he came riding by.

She boldly stepped up to him,
Took hold of the bridle rein,
"One penny, one penny, one penny," cries she,
"To relieve this trouble of mine."

"Where are you from, my brave young youth,
What city, country, or town?"
"It's I am from fair Ireland town
Where I bore a-many a frown."

"If you are from fair Ireland town,
Fair Ireland town," cries he,
"What news, what news from the bailer's daughter,
Pray tell it unto me?"

"The bailer's daughter she is dead,
And her green grave lies low,
The bailer's daughter she is dead,
Being dead some months ago."

Then it's "Take from me my milk-white steed,
My saddle and my bow,
I will go to some furrin' count-er-ey,
Where no one does me know."

"No you need not give your milk-white steed,
Your saddle nor your bow,
Nor you need not go to some furrin' count-er-ey,
Where it's no one does you know.

"For the bailer's daughter she's not dead
But standing by your side."
Then he lit so light from his milk-white steed,
And he kissed her over and again,
Saying, "Here I meet with my own true love
I never expect to see again."

THE KNIGHT AND THE SHEPHERD'S DAUGHTER

A shepherd's daughter watching sheep —
Knight William riding by;
"O — what will I give that pretty fair maid,
One night with me to lie!"

    Ri fol diddle O day.

He took her by the slender waist,
And laid her on the green;
He took her by the lily-white hand,
And lifted her up again.

    Ri fol diddle O day.

He mounted on his milk-white steed,
And swiftly he did ride;
She, being young and nimble-foot,
She followed him side by side.

And when she came to the King's castle,
She knocked so loud did ring;
O who was so ready as the King himself,
To rise and let her in.

"What news, what news, my pretty fair maid,
What news have you brought to me?
Has any of my goods been stole this night,
Or any of my castles won?"

["None of your goods has been stole this night,
Nor any of your castles won,]
But I've been robbed of my body,
Which grieves me worse than all."

"The Knight and the Shepherd's Daughter" was recorded by Phillips Barry (on dicta-phone) from the singing of Mrs. Eva A. Cooley (aged eighty), Exeter, Maine, formerly of Smithfield, Maine, n.d. Reported by Barry in *Bulletin of the Folksong Society of the Northeast*, Cambridge, Mass., 9 (1935):7. With music. Child ballad no. 110. Coffin, 99. Bronson, II, 535.

"If he be a married man,
Hangèd he shall be;
But if he be a single man,
His body I'll give to thee."

The King called up his merry men all,
By one, by two, by three;
Knight William used to be the first —
The last of all came he.

Knight William brought five hundred pounds,
And laid it on the aisle;
Says he, "Take this, you wanton girl,
And go maintain your child!"

"I don't want your gold," she said,
"Nor I don't want your fee;
But I will have your fair body,
Which the King has given to me!"

After the wedding it was o'er,
And all was through and done;
She proved to be the King's daughter,
And he but a blacksmith's son.

    Ri fol diddle O day.

ROBIN HOOD AND LITTLE JOHN

When Robin Hood was about eighteen years old,
He chancèd to meet Little John,
A jolly brisk blade, just fit for his trade,
For he was a sturdy young man.

"Robin Hood and Little John" was collected by Edwin C. Kirkland and Mary Neal Kirkland from the singing of Mrs. Marianna Schaupp, Knoxville, Tennessee, and reported in *SFQ*, 2 (1938):72. Sung also by Mrs. Schaupp for the Library of Congress, AFS record 6081 A. "Mrs. Schaupp learned it from her father, Marion Taylor Cummings, who had it from his mother, Frances Hayden Cummings, once of Kentucky. It has been in the family at least 80 years." Child ballad no. 125. Coffin, 102. Bronson, III, 26. Note the interval rhyme in the third of each stanza.

Although he was Little, his limbs they were large,
His stature was seven feet high,
Wherever he came, he soon quickened his name,
And he presently caused them to fly.

One day these two met on a long narrow bridge,
And neither of them would give way,
When Robin stepped up to the stranger and said,
"I'll show you brave Nottingham play."

"You speak like a coward," the stranger he said,
"As there with your longbow you stand.
I vow and protest you may shoot at my breast
While I have but a staff in my hand."

"The name of a coward," said Robin, "I scorn,
And so my longbow I lay by;
And then for your sake a staff I will take,
The faith of your manhood to try."

Then Robin he stepped out into a grove,
And pulled up a staff of green oak,
And this being done straight back he did come
And thus to the stranger he spoke.

"Behold thou my staff, it is lusty and tough,
On this long narrow bridge let us play;
Then he who falls in, the other shall win
The battle, and then we'll away."

Then Robin hit the stranger a crack on the crown
Which caused the blood to appear,
And thus so enraged they more closely engaged
And they laid on the blows most severe.

The stranger hit Robin a crack on the crown,
Which was a most terrible stroke;
The very next blow laid Robin below
And tumbled him into the brook.

"Oh where are you now?" the stranger he cried.
With a hearty laugh in reply,
"Oh, faith, in the flood," called bold Robin Hood,
"And floating away with the tide."

Then Robin he waded all out of the deep
And he pulled himself up by a thorn;
Then just at the last he blew a loud blast
So merrily on his bugle horn.

The hills they did echo, the vales they did ring,
Which caused his gay men to appear,
All dressed in green, most fair to be seen;
Straight up to the master they steer.

"What aileth thee, Master?" quoth William Stutely,
"You seem to be wet to the skin."
"No matter," said he, "this fellow you see
In fighting hath tumbled me in."

"We'll pluck out his eyes, and duck him likewise."
Then seized they the stranger right there.
"Nay, let him go free," quoth bold Robin Hood,
"For he's a brave fellow. Forbear!

"Cheer up, jolly blade, and don't be afraid
Of all these gay men that you see.
There are fourscore and nine, and if you will be mine
You shall wear of my own livery."

A brace of fat deer was quickly brought in,
Good ale and strong liquor likewise;
The feast was so good, all in the greenwood,
Where this jolly babe was baptized.

THE BOLD PEDLAR AND ROBIN HOOD
(*Robin Hood and the Pedlar*)

'Tis of a pedlar, a pedlar trim,
A pedlar trim he seemed to be,
He strapped his pack all on his back,
And he went linking o'er the lea.

"The Bold Pedlar and Robin Hood" was recorded by Alan Lomax from the singing of Mrs. Carrie Grover of Gorham, Maine, at Washington, D.C., 1941. Library of Congress AFS record 4454 A1. Child ballad no. 132. Coffin, 104. Bronson, III, 40.

He met two men, two troublesome men,
Two troublesome men they seemed to be,
And one of them was bold Robin Hood
And the other Little John so free.

"What have you there?" cried bold Robin Hood,
"What have you there, pray tell to me?"
"I have six robes of the gay green silk
And silken bowstrings two or three."

"If you have six robes of the gay green silk
And silken bowstrings two or three,
Then, by my faith," cried bold Robin Hood,
"The half of them belong to me."

The pedlar he took off his pack,
He hung it low down by his knee,
Saying, "The man who beats me three feet from that,
The pack and all it shall go free."

Bold Robin Hood drew his nut-brown sword,
The pedlar he drew out his brand,
They fought until they both did sweat.
"Oh, pedlar, pedlar, stay your hand!"

"Oh, fight him, master," cried Little John,
"Oh, fight him, master, and do not flee."
"Now, by my faith," cried the pedlar trim,
" 'Tis not to either he or thee!"

"What is your name?" cried bold Robin Hood,
"What is your name, pray tell to me?"
"No, not one word," cried the pedlar trim,
"Till both your names you tell to me."

"The one of us is bold Robin Hood,
The other Little John so free."
"Oh, now I have it at my good will
"Whether I'll tell my name to thee.

"I am Gamble Gold of the gay greenwood,
Far, far beyond the raging sea.
I killed a man on my father's land
And was forced to leave my own counteree."

"If you're Gamble Gold of the gay greenwood,
  Far, far beyond the raging sea,
Then you and I are sister's sons,
  What nearer cousins can we be?"

They sheathed their swords with friendly words
  And so like brothers did agree,
Then unto an alehouse in the town
  Where they cracked bottles merrily.

SIR HUGH, OR, THE JEW'S DAUGHTER
(Little Harry Hughes and the Duke's Daughter)

It was on a May, on a midsummer's day,
  When it rained, it did rain small;
And little Harry Hughes and his playfellows all
  When out to play the ball.

He knocked it up, and he knocked it down,
  He knocked it o'er and o'er;
The very first kick little Harry gave the ball,
  He broke the duke's windows all.

She came down, the youngest duke's daughter,
  She was dressed in green;
"Come back, come back, my pretty little boy,
  And play the ball again."

"I won't come back, and I daren't come back,
  Without my playfellows all;
And if my mother she should come in,
  She'd make it the bloody ball."*

* She'd make my blood to fall.

"Sir Hugh" was collected by William Wells Newell (prior to 1883) in New York City from the singing of a child "living in one of the cabins near Central Park. . . . The mother of the family had herself been born in New York, of Irish parentage, but had learned from her own mother and handed down to her children such legends of the past as the ballad we cite." In W. W. Newell, *Games and Songs of American Children*, 2nd ed., New York, 1903 (Dover reprint, 1963), pp. 75–78. With music. Child ballad no. 155. Coffin, 107. Bronson, III, 72.

She took an apple out of her pocket,
　And rolled it along the plain;
Little Harry Hughes picked up the apple,
　And sorely rued the day.

She takes him by the lily-white hand,
　And leads him from hall to hall,
Until she came to a little dark room,
　That none could hear him call.

She sat herself on a golden chair,
　Him on another close by;
And there's where she pulled out her little penknife
　That was both sharp and fine.

Little Harry Hughes had to pray for his soul,
　For his days were at an end;
She stuck her penknife in little Harry's heart,
　And first the blood came very thick, and then came very thin.

She rolled him in a quire of tin,
　That was in so many a fold;
She rolled him from that to a little draw-well
　That was fifty fathoms deep.

"Lie there, lie there, little Harry," she cried,
　"And God forbid you to swim,
If you be a disgrace to me,
　Or to any of my friends."

The day passed by, and the night came on,
　And every scholar was home,
And every mother had her own child,
　But poor Harry's mother had none.

She walked up and down the street,
　With a little sally-rod in her hand;
And God directed her to the little draw-well,
　That was fifty fathoms deep.

"If you be there, little Harry," she said,
　"And God forbid you to be,
Speak one word to your own dear mother,
　That is looking all over for thee."

"This I am, dear mother," he cried,
  "And lying in great pain,
With a little penknife lying close to my heart,
  And the duke's daughter she has me slain.

"Give my blessing to my schoolfellows all,
  And tell them to be at the church,
And make my grave both large and deep,
  And my coffin of hazel and green birch.

"Put my Bible at my head,
  My busker* at my feet,
My little prayerbook at my right side,
  And sound will be my sleep."

SIR ANDREW BARTON
(*Andrew Batann*)

This ballad goes back in point of historic time to the days of Henry VIII when his captains, Sir Thomas and Sir Edward Howard, captured the Scottish pirate and marauder, Sir Andrew Barton.

I

There once were three brothers from merry Scotland,
From merry Scotland were they,
They cast a lot to see which of them
Would go robbing all o'er the salt sea.

The lot it fell to Andrew Batann,
The youngest one of the three,
That he should go robbing all o'er the salt sea
To maintain his three brothers and he.

* In other versions it is "Testament."

Version 1 of "Sir Andrew Barton" was recorded by Sidney Robertson Cowell from the singing of Warde H. Ford at Central Valley, California, 1938. Library of Congress record LP58. A possible amalgamation of Child ballads nos. 167 and 250 ("Sir Andrew Barton" and "Henry Martyn"), but see Bronson. Child ballad no. 167. Coffin, 112. Bronson, III, 133.

He had not sailed but one summer's eve
When a light it did appear,
It sailed far off and it sailed far on
And at last it came sailing so near.

"Who art, who art," cried Andrew Batann,
"Who art that sail so nigh?"
"We are the rich merchants from old Eng-l-and,
And I pray you will let us pass by."

"O no, O no," cried Andrew Batann,
"O no, that never can be,
Your ship and your cargo I'll take them away
And your merry men drown in the sea."

When the news reached old Eng-l-and
What Andrew Batann had done
Their ship and their cargo he'd taken away
And all of their merry men drowned.

"Build me a boat," cried Captain Charles Stuart,
"And build it strong and secure,
And if I don't capture Andrew Batann
My life I'll no longer endure."

He had not sailed but one summer's eve
When a light it did appear,
It sailed far off and it sailed far on
And at last it came sailing so near.

"Who art, who art," cried Captain Charles Stuart,
"Who art that sails so nigh?"
"We're the jolly Scots robbers from merry Scotland
And I pray you will let us pass by."

"O no, O no," cried Captain Charles Stuart,
"O no, that never can be.
Your ship and your cargo I'll take it away
And your merry men drown in the sea."

"What ho, what ho," cried Andrew Batann,
"I value you not one pin,
For while you show me fine brass without,
I'll show you good steel within."

Then broadside to broadside these ships they stood;
And like thunder their cannon did roar;
They had not fought but two hours or so
Till Captain Charles Stuart gave o'er.

"Go home, go home," cried Andrew Batann,
"And tell your king for me,
While he remains king upon the dry land
I'll remain king of the sea."

II

While in the majority of American texts, the pirate triumphs to the discomfiture of the king, the last three stanzas of some texts read otherwise:

"Peel on! peel on!" said Andy Bardan,
And loud the cannon did roar;
And Captain Charles Stewart took Andy Bardan,
He took him to fair England's shore.

"What now, what now?" said Andy Bardan,
"What now my fate it will be!"
The gallows is ready for Andy Bardan,
The bold robber around the salt sea.

"Go dig my grave both wide and deep,
And dig it close to the sea;
And tell my brothers as they pass by
I've done robbing around the salt sea."

Version II of "Sir Andrew Barton" was communicated by Miss Lucy Laws of Christian College, Columbia, Missouri, to H. M. Belden in 1911, as learned by her in her childhood in Mercer County, Kentucky, from Charlie Sims: "He was a pensioner of the Civil War. . . . He came to Mercer County in the late sixties." In H. M. Belden, *Ballads and Songs Collected by the Missouri Folk-Lore Society*, Columbia (reprint edition, 1966), pp. 88–89.

THE DEATH OF QUEEN JANE

Jane Seymour, wife of King Henry the Eighth, was in grievous labor, begging for surgery to save her unborn child. Henry refused sanction to operate and to sacrifice the mother for the child, but when it became apparent that surgery was necessary, the operation was performed and the child saved. Jane, however, died. According to historical records, her death took place twelve days after the birth of Prince Edward on October 12, 1537. The ballad is of rare occurrence in the United States.

I

Queen Jane was in labor
Six weeks and some more;
The women grew wearied,
And the midwife gave o'er.

"O women, kind women,
I take you to be,
Just pierce my right side open
And save my baby."

"O no," said the women,
"That never could be;
I'll send for King Henry
In the time of your need."

King Henry was sent for
On horseback and speed;
King Henry he reached her
In the hour of her need.

King Henry he come
And he bent o'er the bed:
"What's the matter with my
   flower
Makes her eyes look so red?"

"O Henry, kind Henry,
Pray listen to me,
And pierce my right side open
And save my baby."

"O no," said King Henry,
"That never could be,
I would lose my sweet flower
To save my baby."

Queen Jane she turned over
And fell in a swound,
And her side was pierced open
And the baby was found.

The baby were christened
All on the next day;
But its mother's poor body
Lay cold as the clay.

So black was the mourning,
So yellow was the bed,
So costly was the white robe
Queen Jane was wrapped in.

Version 1 of "The Death of Queen Jane" was collected by Cecil J. Sharp from the singing of Mrs. Kate Thomas, St. Helen's, Lee County, Kentucky, 1917. In Sharp, *English Folksongs from the Southern Appalachians* (Oxford) New York, 1932, I, 230. With music. Child ballad no. 170. Coffin, 170. Bronson, III, 144.

Six men wore their robes,
Four carrying her along;
King Henry followed after
With his black mourning on.

King Henry he wept
Till his hands was wrung sore.
The flower of England
Will flourish no more.

And the baby were christened
All on the next day,
And its mother's poor body
Lying mouldering away.

II

Well, Jane was in labor for three days or more,
She grieved and she grieved and she grieved her heart sore,
She sent for her mother, her mother came o'er.
Said, "The Red Rose of England shall flourish no more."

Well, Jane was in labor for three days or four,
She grieved and she grieved and she grieved her heart sore,
She sent for her father, her father came o'er,
Said, "The Red Rose of England shall flourish no more."

Well, Jane was in labor for four days or more,
She grieved and she grieved and she grieved her heart sore,
She sent for Prince Henry, Prince Henry came o'er,
Said, "The Red Rose of England shall flourish no more."

MARY HAMILTON
(*The Four Marys*)

Word has come from the kitchen
And word has come to me
That Mary Hamilton drowned her babe
And throwed him into the sea.

Version II of "The Death of Queen Jane" was recorded by Artus M. Moser from the singing of Bascom Lamar Lunsford of South Turkey Creek at Swannanoa, North Carolina, 1946. Library of Congress record LP21. Child ballad no. 170. Coffin, 113. Bronson, III, 144.

"Mary Hamilton" was recorded by Alan Lomax from the singing of Mrs. Texas Gladden at Salem, Virginia, 1941. Library of Congress record LP7. Child ballad no. 173. Coffin, 114. Bronson, III, 150.

Down came the old Queen,
   Gold tassels around her head.
"Oh, Mary Hamilton, where's your babe
   That was sleeping in your bed?

"Oh, Mary, put on your robe so black
   And yet your robe so brown,
That you might go with me this day
   To view fair Edinburgh town."

She didn't put on her robe so black,
   Nor yet her robe so brown,
But she put on her snow-white robe
   To view fair Edinburgh town.

As she passed through the Cannogate [Canongate],
   The Cannogate passed she,
The ladies looked over their casements and
   They wept for this lady.

As she went up the Parliament steps,
   A loud, loud laugh laughed she.
As she came down the Parliament steps,
   She was condemned to dee.

"Oh, bring to me some red, red wine,
   The reddest that can be,
That I might drink to the jolly bold sailors
   That brought me over the sea.

"Oh, tie a napkin o'er my eyes,
   And ne'er let me see to dee,
And ne'er let on to my father and mother
   I died 'way over the sea.

"Last night I washed the old Queen's feet
   And carried her to her bed,
And all the reward I received for this —
   The gallows hard to tread.

"Last night there were four Marys,
   To-night there'll be but three.
There was Mary Beaton and Mary Seton
   And Mary Carmichael and me."

ARCHIE O CAWFIELD
(*Bold Dickie*)

As I walked out one morning in May,
Just before the break of day,
I heard two brothers making their moan,
And I listened a while to what they did say,
    I heard two brothers making their moan,
    And I listened a while to what they did say.

"We have a brother in prison," said they,
"Oh in prison lieth he!
If we had but ten men just like ourselves,
The prisoner we would soon set free!"
    "If we had but ten men just like ourselves,
    The prisoner we would soon set free."

"Oh, no, no, no!" Bold Dickie said he,
"Oh, no, no, that never can be!
For forty men is full little enough
And I for to ride in their company.

"Ten to hold the horses in,
Ten to guard the city about,
And ten for to stand at the prison door,
And ten to fetch poor Archer out."

They mounted their horses, and so rode they,
Who but they so merrily!
They rode till they came to a broad river's side,
And there they alighted so manfully.

They mounted their horses, and so swam they,
Who but they so manfully;
They swam till they came to the other side,
And there they alighted so drippingly.

"Archie O Cawfield" was written from memory by J. M. Watson of Clark's Island, Massachusetts, and communicated to *JAF*, 8 (1895):256, by Miss Mary P. Frye. With music. The same informant contributed the ballad to Francis James Child's collection (published 1889) with very slight textual variations from that gathered by Miss Frye. Child ballad no. 188. Coffin, 117. Bronson, III, 175.

They mounted their horses, and so rode they,
Who but they so gallantly;
They rode till they came to that prison door,
And there they alighted so manfully.

"Poor Archer, poor Archer!" Bold Dickie says he,
"Oh, look you not so mournfully!
For I've forty men in my company,
And I have come to set you free."

"Oh no, no, no!" poor Archer says he,
"Oh no, no, that never can be,
For I have forty pounds of good Spanish iron
Betwixt my ankle and my knee."

Bold Dickie broke lock, Bold Dickie broke key,
Bold Dickie broke everything he could see;
He took poor Archer under one arm,
And carried him out so manfully.

They mounted their horses, and so rode they,
Who but they so merrily!
They rode till they came to that broad river's side
And there they alighted so manfully.

"Bold Dickie, Bold Dickie," poor Archer says he,
"Take my love home to my wife and children three;
For my horse grows lame, he cannot swim,
And here I see that I must dee."

They shifted their horses, and so swam they,
Who but they so daringly;
They swam till they came to the other side,
And there they alighted so shiveringly.

"Bold Dickie, Bold Dickie!" poor Archer says he,
"Look you yonder there and see;
For the high sheriff he is a-coming,
With an hundred men in his company."

"Bold Dickie, Bold Dickie!" High Sheriff says he,
"You're the damndest rascal that ever I see;
Go bring me back the iron you've stole,
And I will set the prisoner free."

"Oh, no, no, no!" Bold Dickie says he,
"Oh, no, no, that never can be!
For the iron will do to shoe the horses, —
The blacksmith rides in our company."

"Bold Dickie, Bold Dickie!" High Sheriff says he,
"You're the damndest rascal that ever I see!"
"I thank you for nothing," Bold Dickie says he,
"And you're a damned fool for following me!"

THE GYPSY DAVY

It was late last night when my lord come home,
Inquirin' 'bout his lady.
'N' the only answer he received:
"She's gone with the Gypsy Davy,
Gone with the Gypsy Dave."

"Go saddle for me my buckskin horse
And a hundred-dollar saddle,
Point out to me their wagon tracks,
And after them I'll travel,
After them I'll ride."

Well, he had not rode till the midnight moon
Till he saw the campfire gleamin',
And he heard the gypsy's big guitar,
And the voice of the lady singin'
The song of the Gypsy Dave.

"Well, have you forsaken your house and home?
Have you forsaken your baby?
Have you forsaken your husband dear
To go with the Gypsy Davy,
And sing with the Gypsy Dave?"

"The Gypsy Davy" was recorded by Alan Lomax from the singing of Woody Guthrie of Okemah, Oklahoma, at Washington, D.C. 1940. Library of Congress record LP1. Child ballad no. 200. Coffin, 119. Bronson, III, 198.

"Yes, I've forsaken my house and home
To go with the Gypsy Davy,
And I'll forsake my husband dear
But not my blue-eyed baby,
Not my blue-eyed babe."

She laughed to leave her husband dear,
And her butlers and her ladies,
But the tears come a-trickelin' down her cheeks
When she thought about her blue-eyed baby,
And thought of her blue-eyed babe.

"Take off, take off your buckskin boots,
Made of Spanish leather,
And give to me your lily-white hand,
'N' we'll go back home together,
Go back home again.

"Take off, take off your buckskin gloves,
Made of Spanish leather,
And give to me your lily-white hand,
'N' we'll go back home together,
Go back home again."

"No, I won't take off my buckskin gloves,
Made of Spanish leather;
I'll go my way from day to day,
And sing with the Gypsy Davy,
'N' sing with the Gypsy Dave."

LORD DERWENTWATER
(*The King's Love-Letter*)

Bronson summarizes, with opening comment, the history of this rare fragment in the notes to LC record LP58:

This is an extraordinary survival indeed! What's the Jacobite Rising of 1715 to Florida, or Lord Derwentwater to Mrs. Griffin that she should lament for

"Lord Derwentwater" was recorded by John A. Lomax from the singing of Mrs. G. A. Griffin at Newberry, Florida, 1937. Library of Congress record LP58. Child ballad no. 208. Coffin, 124. Bronson, III, 264.

him? The narrative behind this disordered and confusing text is as follows: Derwentwater, a Scottish Earl who rose to support his companion in France, James Stewart, the Old Pretender, against the House of Hanover and George I, was captured at the battle of Preston (November 14, 1715), was attainted and brought to the block, February 24, 1716. His youth — he was only 27 — and his open bearing excited popular sympathy for his fate. The ballad describes the summons to London for trial and the Earl's premonitions of doom. In earlier versions, he leaves houses and land to his eldest son, ten thousand pounds to his second son, and a third of his estate to his lady, who is in child-bed when he departs. Probably "It's two and two" is a corruption of "to you and to you." On the way his horse stumbles, and his nose begins to bleed — two bad omens. The "jolly old man" who commands his life is properly the "headsman with a broad axe."

Professor Alton Morris, who discovered Mrs. Griffin's large repertoire of folksong and brought it to the attention of the Library of Congress, reported her singing of this in *JAF*, 47 (1934) 95–96, and also in his *Folksongs of Florida* (University of Florida Press) Gainesville, 1950, 308–310.

The king he wrote a love-letter
And he sealed it all with gold
And he sent it to the Duke of Melanto
To read it if he could.

The first few lines that he did read
It caused him for to smile,
But the next few lines that he did read
The tears from his eyes did flow.

He called up his oldest one
To bridle and saddle my steed,
"For I've got to go to Lunnon Town
Although I have no need."

It's make your will, you Duke of Melanto,
It's make your will all around.
"It's two and two to my two oldest sons,
It's two, it's two all around,
For all of my steeds and the rest of my property
We'll retain to her lady's side."

Before he rode up in the edge of town
He met a jolly old man,
"Your life, your life, you Duke of Melanto,
Your life I will command."

He stooped over the window
There the flowers swelled so gay,
Till his nose gushed out and bleed;
"Come all you lords, you pretty lords, ye,
Be kind to my baby,
Come all you lords, you pretty lords, ye,
Be kind to my baby,
For all my steeds and the rest of my property
We'll retain to her lady's side."

GEORDIE
(*Georgie*)

"Come sad-dle me my fast-est steed,
Come bri-dle up my po-ny,
And I'll ride a-way to the King's high court
To plead for the life of Georgie."

The lady has great stores of gold,
Of jewels she has many,
All this would she give to the royal king
To save the life of Georgie.

As the king rode over London Bridge
So early in the morning,
He met this lady on her way,
Inquiring for her Georgie.

"Oh where are you going, my pretty fair maid,
So early in the morning?"

Version 1 of "Geordie" was recorded by Alan Lomax from the singing of Mrs. Carrie Grover of Gorham, Maine, at Washington, D.C., 1941. Library of Congress AFS record 4458 A3. Text with music also in Carrie B. Grover, *A Heritage of Songs* (privately printed, Gould Academy, Bethel, Maine, n.d.), pp. 82–83. Child ballad no. 209. Coffin, 124. Bronson, III, 268.

She says, "I am going to the king's high court
For to plead for the life of Georgie."

The king looked over his left shoulder
So early in the morning,
"I'm afraid you're too late, my pretty fair maid,
For he is condemned already."

"Oh who has he murdered, or what has he done?
Oh has he robbed anybody?"
"He has stole three pearls from the royal king
And has sold them in a hurry."

"Oh, he shall be hung with a chain of gold
(Such chains there are not many),
For he was born of the royal blood
And was loved by a noble lady.

"He shall be buried in marble stones
(Such stones there are not many),
And he shall be covered all with the same,
Saying, 'Here lies the body of Georgie.' "

Georgie Wedlock

"Oh, Georgie Wedlock is my name
And many a man doth know me,
And many a bad deed have I done,
But this will overthrow me.

"Is there a postman in this town
That will ride for me to Stalden,
That will ride for me to Stalden town,
With a letter to a lady?"

"Go saddle me up my milk-white steed,
Go saddle him trim and neatly,

Version II of "Geordie" was recorded by John A. Lomax and Laurence Powell from the singing of Mrs. Emma Dusenbury, Mena, Arkansas, 1936. Library of Congress AFS record 873 A2. Child ballad no. 209. Coffin, 124. Bronson, III, 268.

I'll ride for you to Stalden town,
With a letter to a lady."

The sun went down as he got there,
And supper it was ready,
And this young lady, she was there,
And she was brief and merry.

She took the letter in her hand
And broke it open most speedily,
She had not read but a line or two,
Till she saw the case of Georgie.

"Is there a postman in this town,
That will ride with me to Stalden,
That will ride with me to Stalden town,
To plead the case of Georgie?"

"Go saddle me up my milk-white steed,
Go saddle him trim and neatly,
I'll ride with you to Stalden town,
To plead the case of Georgie."

The cart drove up as they got there,
And the rope it was made ready
And the king looked over his right shoulder,
And he saw a trim neat lady.

She ran her hand into her pocket
Saying, "Gents, oh, I have plenty,
And I'll lay you down ten thousand pounds,
If you'll spare the life of Georgie."

"If you lay me down ten thousand pounds,
I'll spare the life of Georgie,
You need not weep nor sigh any more
For I'll spare the life of Georgie."

Now Georgie is a free man in this town
By one he does love dearly,
Now Georgie's a free man in this town,
By the loving of a lady.

BONNIE GEORGE CAMPBELL
(*Bonnie James Campbell*)

High up on highland and low upon Tay
Bonnie George Campbell rode out on a day.
Saddled and bridled and gallant rode he,
Home came his good horse but never came he.

Out came his old mother, a-weeping full sore,
And out came his bonnie bride tearing her hair.
Saddled and bridled and booted rode he,
A plume in his helmet, a sword at his knee.

My meadow lies green and my corn is unshorn,
My barn is to build and my babe is unborn.
Empty home came his saddle, all bloody to see
And home came his good horse, but never came he.

THE RANTIN LADDIE

Oft have I played at cards and dice,
Because they were so enticing;
But this is a sad and sorrowful day
To see my apron rising.

My father he does but slight me,
And my mother she does but scorn me,
And all my friends they do make light of me,
And all the servants they do sneer at me.

"Bonnie George Campbell" was collected by the Federal Music Project, Works Progress Administration (WPA), Boyd County, Kentucky, ca. 1937. Jean Thomas, Supervisor for Boyd County. Ms., with music, in the Archive of Folk Song, Library of Congress. Child ballad no. 210. Coffin, 126. Bronson, III, 290.

"The Rantin Laddie" was collected by Josiah H. Combs from Mrs. Nora Edman, Big Springs, Calhoun County, West Virginia. Without music. In Josiah H. Combs, *Folksongs of the Southern United States*, Publications of the American Folklore Society (The University of Texas Press) Austin, 1967, pp. 127–128. Child ballad no. 240. Coffin, 240. Bronson, III, 423.

Oft have I played at cards and dice,
For the love of my laddie;
But now I must sit at my father's fireboard,
And rock my bastard baby.

But had I one of my father's servants,
For he has so many,
That will go to the eastern shore
With a letter to the rantin laddie.

"Here is one of your father's servants,
For he has so many,
That will go to the eastern shore
With a letter to the rantin laddie."

"When you get there to the house,
To the eastern shore so bonnie,
With your hat in your hand, bow down to the ground,
Before the company of the rantin laddie."

When he got there to the house,
To the eastern shore so bonnie,
With his hat in his hand he bowed down to the ground,
Before the company of the rantin laddie.

When he looked the letter over
So loud he burst out laughing;
But before he read it to the end,
The tears they were down dropping.

"O who is this, O who is that,
Who has been so ill to my Maggie?
O who is this dares be so bold,
So cruel to treat my lassie?"

"Her father he will not know her,
And her mother she does but scorn her;
And all her friends they do make light of her,
And all the servants they do sneer at her."

"Four and twenty milk-white steeds,
Go quick and make them ready;

As many gay lads to ride on them,
To go and bring home my Maggie.

"Four and twenty bright-brown steeds,
Go quick and make them ready;
As many bold men to ride on them,
To go and bring home my Maggie."

Ye lassies all, where'er ye be,
And ye lie with an east-shore laddie,
Ye'll happy be and ye'll happy be,
For they are frank and free.

JAMES HARRIS
(*The Daemon Lover*)

As "The Daemon Lover" in Sir Walter Scott's *Minstrelsy*, the seducer turns supernatural on the voyage, and strikes the topmast with his hand and the foremast with his knee, breaking the gallant ship to pieces. As Bronson points out in his note to LC record LP58, the ballad now tells a story that is in no need of explanation, having its counterparts in every day's newspapers. It has been widely collected in America in variants going back to seventeenth-century broadside tradition in England. The seduction, the abandonment of the child, the remorse, and the death of the protagonists and the ship go to make up a tale — with unearthly overtones — that has quite naturally survived in folk transmission.

The House-Carpenter

"Well met, well met, you old true-love!
Well met, well met!" said he.
"I've just returned from the seashore sea,
From the land where the grass grows green.

"Well, I could have married a king's daughter there,
And she would have married me;

"The House-Carpenter" was recorded by Alan and Elizabeth Lomax from the singing of Mrs. Texas Gladden, Salem, Virginia, 1941. Library of Congress record LP1. Child ballad no. 243. Coffin, 243. Bronson, III, 429.

But I refused the golden crown
All for the sake of thee.

"If you'll forsake your house-carpenter,
And come and go with me,
I'll take you where the grass grows green,
To the lands on the banks of the sea."

She went 'n' picked up her sweet little babe
And kissed it one, two, three,
Saying, "Stay at home with your papa dear,
And keep him good company."

She went and dressed in her very best,
As everyone could see.
She glistened and glittered and proudly she walked
The streets on the banks of the sea.

They hadn't been sailing but about three weeks —
I'm sure it was not four —
Till this young lady began to weep,
And her weeping never ceased any more.

"Are you mourning for your house-carpenter?
Are you mourning for your store?"
"No, I'm mourning for my sweet little babe
That I never will see any more."

They hadn't been sailing but about four weeks —
I'm sure it was not more —
Till the ship sprang a leak from the bottom of the sea,
And it sank to rise no more.

Well Met, Well Met, My Old True Love

"Well met, well met, my old true love,
Well met, well met," said he,
"I have just returned from the salt, salt sea,

"Well Met, Well Met, My Old True Love" was recorded by Robert F. Draves from the singing of Mrs. Pearl Jacobs Borusky at Antigo, Wisconsin, 1940. Stanzas in brackets interpolated from the singing of the same ballad by Clay Walters at Salyersville, Kentucky, 1937. Both versions of the ballad on Library of Congress record LP58. Child ballad no. 243. Coffin, 137. Bronson, III, 429.

And it's all for the sake of thee,
And it's all for the sake of thee.

"I once could have married a king's daughter fair
And she could have married me
But I refused that rich crown of gold
And it's all for the sake of thee,
And it's all for the sake of thee."

"If you could have married a king's daughter fair,
I'm sure you are much to blame,
For I am married to a house-carpenter
And I think he's a fine young man,
And I think he's a fine young man."

"If you'll forsake your house-carpenter
And go along with me,
I will take you where the grass grows green
On the banks of the sweet Willie,
On the banks of the sweet Willie."

"If I forsake my house-carpenter
And go along with thee,
What have you got for my support
And to keep me from slavery?
And to keep me from slavery?"

"I have six ships upon the sea
And the seventh one at land,
And if you come and go with me
They shall be at your command,
They shall be at your command."

She took her babe into her arms
And gave it kisses three
Saying, "Stay at home, my pretty little babe
To keep your father company,
To keep your father company."

She dressed herself in rich array
To exceed all others in the town,
And as she walked the streets around

She shone like a glittering crown,
She shone like a glittering crown.

They had not been on board more than two weeks—
I'm sure it was not three—
Until one day she began to weep,
And she wept most bitterly,
And she wept most bitterly.

"O are you weeping for your houses or your land
Or are you weeping for your store
Or are you weeping for your house-carpenter
You never shall see anymore,
That you never shall see anymore?"

"I'm not weeping for my houses or my land
Nor I'm not weeping for my store,
But I am weeping for my pretty little babe
I never shall see anymore,
I never shall see anymore."

["What hills, what hills, my own true love,
That look so white like snow?"
"It's the hills of Heaven, my own true love,
Where all righteous people go."

"What hills, what hills, my own true love,
That look so dark and low?"
"It's the hills of Hell, my own true love,
Where you and I must go."]

They had not been on board more than three weeks
It was not four, I am sure,
Until at length the ship sprung a leak
And she sunk to arise no more,
And she sunk to arise no more.

"A curse, a curse to all seamen,
And a curse to a sailor's wife,
For they have robbed me of my house-carpenter
And have taken away my life,
And have taken away my life."

THE SUFFOLK MIRACLE
(*Lady, Lady, Lady Fair*)

Lady, lady, lady fair,
Many suitors had she there;
There was a man of low degree,
And among them all she fancied he.

Also her father came to know,
And forty miles he made her go;
And there to stay four months and a day,
Till her true love was laid in the clay.

One night she was standing dressing of her head,
She heard a low and a mournful sound;
Saying, "Loose them bands that's so tight bound,
And ride behind your heart's design."

He knew her father guild and* well,
Likewise her mother, all safe too;
Saying, "Dress you up so neat and fine,
And ride behind your heart's design."

As they rode on, she kissed his lips,
They was as cold as cold as clay,
Saying, "When we get there a good fire we'll have,"
Not knowing he was from the grave.

They rode on till they came to Garland's gate,
And there he complained his head did ache;
A handkerchief she pulled out,
And with the same she bound it up.

Saying, "We hain't got but a few more miles to go,
Till I land you in your father's door;
Go in, go in, go safe to bed,
And I will see your horses fed."

* Garland?

"The Suffolk Miracle" was recorded by John A. Lomax and Laurence Powell from the singing of Mrs. Emma Dusenbury at Mena, Arkansas, 1936. Library of Congress AFS record 873 B1. Child ballad no. 272. Coffin, 142. Bronson, IV, 84.

They rode up and knocked at the door;
Her father's surprised who's at the door.
"It is your daughter, didn't you send for her?"
And mentioned such a messenger.

Her father sprung up all out of the bed,
To think his daughter had rode with the dead;
He wrung his hands, he wept full sore;
Her mother dear, she wept much more.

Next morning so early to the grave they went,
To give this damsel some content;
The handkerchief was around his head,
And he had been four months dead.

Now it's a warning to old folks,
That won't let young ones have their will:
The first they'll love, they'll never forget,
They'll still stand to it, they'll love them yet.

There Were an Old and Wealthy Man

There were an old and wealthy man,
He had a daughter great and grand,
She were neat, handsome, and tall,
She had a handsome face withal.

There were many a guy there came this way
This handsome lady for to see.
At length there were a widow's son,
'Twas found he were her chosen one.

It was when the old folks came this to know
They sent her two thousand miles from home
Which broke this young man's tender heart*
To think that he and his love must part.

* The young man's heart is *literally* broken, and he dies for love.

"There Were an Old and Wealthy Man" was recorded by Maud Karpeles and Sidney Robertson Cowell from the singing of Mr. Dol Small at Nellysford, Virginia, 1950. Library of Congress record LP58. Child ballad no. 272. Coffin, 142. Bronson, IV, 84.

It was on the cold and stormy night
He started for his heart's delight;
He rode till he came to the place he knew,
Says he, "My love, I've come for you.

"It's your father's request, your mother's heed,
I've come for you all in great speed,
And in two weeks or a little mo'
I'll set you safe at your father's do'."

They rode till they came to the old man's gate,
He did complain his head did ache;
With a handkerchief that she had out,
With it she bound his head about.

They rode till they came to the old man's stile,
Says he, "My love, let's tarry awhile."
"Alight, alight, alight," says she,
"And I will put your steeds away."

She knocked upon her father's do',
The sight of her lover she saw no mo'.
"It's welcome home, my child," says he,
"What trusty friend has come for thee?"

"It's the one I love, I love so well,
I love him better than tongue can tell."
It made the hair stand on the old man's head
To think that he'd been twelve months dead.

Then princes grand and judges, too,
Summons'd for to witness this grave's undo:
It's though he had been twelve months dead
Her handkerchief were around his head.

Now this is warning to young and old
Who love their children better than gold,
If you love them, give them their way
For fear their love may lead astray.

OUR GOODMAN

Tellers of tales of all countries have loved the stories of the simple husband outwitted by his cleverer wife. The stories have their source in the folk tales of the Middle Ages and their flowering in Boccaccio, Rabelais, and Chaucer. "Our Goodman" goes back to England of the seventeenth century, but its basic roots are earlier.

The first night when I came home
As drunk as I could be
I found a horse in the stable
Where my horse ought to be.

"Oh come here, my little wifie,
And explain this thing to me,
How come a horse in the stable
Where my horse ought to be?"

"You blind fool, you crazy fool,
Can't you never see,
It's nothing but a milk cow,
You're crazy to me."

"I've traveled this world over,
Ten thousand miles or more,
But a saddle upon a milk cow,
I never did see it before."

The second night when I came
   home,
As drunk as I could be,
I found a coat a-hanging on the
   rack
Where my coat ought to be.

"Oh come here, my little wifie,
And explain this thing to me,
How come a coat a-hanging on the
   rack
Where my coat ought to be?"

"You blind fool, you crazy fool,
Can't you never see,
It's nothing but a bed quilt,
You're crazy to me."

"I've traveled this world over,
Ten thousand miles or more,
But a pocket upon a bed quilt,
I never did see it before."

The third night when I came in
As drunk as I could be,
I found a head a-laying on the
   pillow
Where my head ought to be.

"Oh come here, my little wifie,
And explain this thing to me,
How come a head a-laying on the
   pillow
Where my head ought to be?"

"Our Goodman" was recorded by Artus M. Moser from the singing, with guitar, of Orrin Rice at Harrogate, Tennessee, 1943. Pfc. Orrin Rice was, during World War II, a member of the 325th Glider Infantry Regiment of the 82nd Airborne Division. He died of wounds received in action during the Normandy invasion, on June 11, 1944. Library of Congress record LP12. Child ballad no. 274. Coffin, 143. Bronson, IV, 95.

"You blind, crazy fool,
Can't you never see,
It's nothing but a cabbage head,
You're crazy to me."

"I've traveled this world over,
Ten thousand miles or more,
But a moustache on a cabbage
    head,
Well, I never did see it before."

GET UP AND BAR THE DOOR

The wind it blew from east to west,
And it blew all over the floor;
Said old John Jones to Jane, his wife,
"Get up and shut the door."

"My hands are in the sausage meat,
So I cannot get them free;
And if you do not shut the door yourself,
It never will be shut by me."

Then they agreed between the two
And gave their hands on it,
That whoever spoke a word the first
Was to rise and shut the door.

There were two travelers journeying late,
A-journeying across the hill,
And they came to old John Jones's
By the light from the open door.

"Does this house to a rich man belong?
Or does it belong to a poor?"
But never a word would the stubborn two say
On account of shutting the door.

The travelers said good-evening to them,
And then they said good-day;
But never a word would the stubborn two say
On account of shutting the door.

"Get Up and Bar the Door" was collected by Mr. Carey Woofter, Glenville, Gilmer County, 1924, from the recitation of Mrs. Sarah Clevenger of Briar Lick Run, near Perkins, Gilmer County, West Virginia. She learned it from her grandmother, Mrs. Rebecca Clevenger, who came from Loudon County, Virginia, seventy-eight years prior to that. In John Harrington Cox, *Folk-Songs of the South* (Harvard) Cambridge, 1925 (Dover reprint, 1967), pp. 516–517. Child ballad no. 275. Coffin, 145. Bronson, IV, 130.

And so they drank of the liquor strong,
And so they drank of the ale:
"For since we have got a house of our own,
I'm sure we can take of our fill."

And then they ate of the sausage meat
And sopped their bread in the fat;
And at every bite old Jane she thought,
"May the devil slip down with that."

Then says the one to the other,
"Here, man, take out my knife,
And while you shave the old man's chin,
I will be kissing the wife."

"You have eat my meat and drinked my ale,
And would you make of my old wife a whore?"
"John Jones, you have spoken the first word,
Now get up and shut the door."

THE WIFE WRAPT IN WETHER'S SKIN

Sweet William he married him a wife,
  Jennifer June and the rosymaree,
To be the sweet comfort of his life,
  As the dew flies over the green vallee.

It's she couldn't into the kitchen go,
  Jennifer June and the rosymaree,
For fear of soiling her white-heeled shoes,
  As the dew flies over the green vallee.

It's she couldn't wash and it's she wouldn't bake
For fear of soiling her white apron-tape.

It's she couldn't card and it's she wouldn't spin
For fear of soiling her delicate skin.

"The Wife Wrapt in Wether's Skin" was contributed to the Missouri Folk-Lore Society in 1916 by Mrs. Case of Harrison County, as remembered from her childhood. H. M. Belden, *Ballads and Songs Collected by the Missouri Folk-Lore Society*, Columbia (reprint edition, 1966), pp. 92–94. With music. Child ballad no. 277. Coffin, 146. Bronson, IV, 143.

Sweet William came whistling in from the plow,
Says, "Oh my dear wife, is my dinner ready now?"

She called him a dirty, paltry whelp:
"If you want any dinner, go get it yourself."

Sweet William went out unto the sheepfold
And out a fat wether he did pull.

Upon his knees he did kneel down
And soon from it did strip the skin.

He laid the skin on his wife's back,
And he made his stick go whickety whack.

"I'll tell my father and all my kin
How you this quarrel did begin."

"You may tell your father and all your kin
How I have thrashed my fat wether's skin."

Sweet William came whistling in from the plow,
Says, "Oh my dear wife, is my dinner ready now?"

She drew her table and spread her board,
    Jennifer June and the rosymaree,
And 'twas "Oh, my dear husband" with every word,
    As the dew flies over the green vallee.

And now they live free from all care and strife,
    Jennifer June and the rosymaree,
And now she makes William a very good wife,
    As the dew flies over the green vallee.

THE FARMER'S CURST WIFE

There was an old man at the foot of the hill,
If he ain't moved away he's livin' there still.
Sing heigh! diddle-eye, diddle-eye, fie!
Diddle-eye, diddle-eye, day!

"The Farmer's Curst Wife" was recorded by Herbert Halpert from the singing of Horton Barker, Chilhowie, Virginia, 1939. Library of Congress record LP1. Child ballad no. 278. Coffin 148. Bronson, IV, 174.

He hitched up his horse and he went out to plow,
But how to get around he didn't know how.
Sing heigh! diddle-eye, diddle-eye, fie!
Diddle-eye, diddle-eye, day!

The Devil came to his house one day,
Says, "One of your family I'm a-gonna take away."

[*The Devil selects the farmer's scolding wife:*]

"Take her on, take her on, with the joy of my heart;
I hope by gollies you'll never part!"

The Devil put her in a sack,
And the old man says, "Don't you bring her back."

When the Devil got her to the forks of the road,
He says, "Old lady, you're a terrible load."

When the Devil got her to the gates of Hell,
He says, "Punch up the fire, we want to scorch her well,"

In come a little devil a-draggin' a chain;
She upped with the hatchet, and split out his brains.

Another little devil went climbin' the wall,
An' says, "Take her back, Daddy, she's a-murderin' us all."

The old man was a-peepin' out of the crack,
And saw the old Devil come a-waggin' her back.

She found the old man sick in the bed,
And upped with the butterstick and paddled his head.

The old woman went whistlin' over the hill.
"The Devil wouldn't have me, so I wonder who will?"

This is what a woman can do:
She can outdo the Devil and her old man, too.

There's one advantage women have over men:
They can go to Hell and come back again.
Sing heigh! diddle-eye, diddle-eye, fie!
Diddle-eye, diddle-eye, day!

THE CRAFTY FARMER
(*The Oxford Merchant*)

In the abridged edition of this work, Child admitted this ballad to the canon with a single introductory sentence: "This very ordinary ballad has enjoyed great popularity, and is given for that reason and as a specimen of its class." Bronson, in his headnote to the Library of Congress recording, happily adds: "There must be some special appeal in a ballad which 'has enjoyed great popularity' for more than a century; and perhaps in this case it is a sort of simple childlike happiness, the quality of a story in which all turns out surprisingly well, against odds not too alarming but sufficient to elicit an anxious concern in the listener. . . . It is impossible to hear it without feeling better."

In Oxford there lived a merchant by trade,
He had for his servants a man and a maid,
A true Hampshire lad he had for his man
All for to do his business, his name it was John.
    Laddy tell I day, tell I do, laddy laddy tell I day.

One morning quite early he called upon John,
And Johnny heard his master and quickly did run.
"Oh take this cow and drive her to the fair
For she's in good order and her I can spare."
    Laddy tell I day, tell I do, laddy laddy tell I day.

So Johnny took the cow and away he did go,
He drove her to the fair, as far as I do know.
Before the day was over he sold her to a man,
Who paid him the chink, which was six pounds ten.

They went to a tavern for to get a drink,
'Twas there the tradesman laid down the chink.
Johnny turned to the lady and unto her did say,
"Oh, what shall I do with my money, I pray?"

"The Crafty Farmer" was recorded by Sidney Robertson Cowell from the singing of Warde H. Ford at Central Valley, California, December, 1938. Library of Congress record LP58. Child ballad no. 283. Coffin, 151. Bronson, IV, 282. Bronson includes this as Child 283 on LP58, but Coffin qualifies this in his discussion, claiming the tale not to be the true "Crafty Farmer" but the more widely known "Yorkshire Bite" or, as here, "Hampshire Bite."

"Sew it up in your coat lining," the lady did say,
"For fear you will be robbed along the highway."
The highwayman sat behind him a-drinking up his wine,
And said he to himself, "That money's all mine."

Then Johnny took his leave and away he did go,
The highwayman followed after him, as far as I do know.
He overtook the lad upon the highway,
"You're well overtaken, young man," said he.

"Oh jump on behind me, oh jump on and ride."
"How far are you going?" Little Johnny replied,
"About twelve miles, as far as I do know";
And Johnny jumped a-horseback and away he did go.

They rode along together till they came to a dark lane,
There the highwayman spoke up very plain:
"Deliver up your money without fear or strife,
Or in this lonesome valley you'll lose your pleasant life."

So Johnny, seeing there was no time for dispute,
Came down from the horse without fear or doubt;
From his coat lining he pulled the money out
And in the tall grass he strewed it well about.

The highwayman suddenly got down, got down from his horse,
And little did he think it was for his loss,
For while he was picking the money that was thrown
Little Johnny jumped his horseback and away he did go.

The highwayman followed after him and bid him for to stay,
But Johnny never minded him and still rode away,
And home to his master thus he did bring
Horse, saddle, and bridle and many a fine thing.

The servant maid, seeing Little Johnny's return,
She went and told his master, as near as I can learn,
The master came out and he looked very cross
And said, "Have you turned my cow into a hoss?"

"Oh no, dearest Master, your cow I have sold,
But be robbed on the highway by a highwayman bold,
And while he was picking the money in his purse
All for to make amends I came off with his horse."

The saddlebags were opened, and there, as I've been told
Ten thousand pounds and silver and gold,
A brace of loaded pistols. "Oh, Master, I vow,
I think for a boy I have well sold your cow."
    Laddy tell I day, tell I do, laddy laddy tell I day.

"Oh yes, for a boy you have done quite rare;
Two-thirds of this money you shall have for your share,
And as for the villain with whom you had to fight,
I think you've played him a true Hampshire bite."
    Laddy tell I day, tell I do, laddy laddy tell I day.

THE SWEET TRINITY
(*The Golden Vanity or The Golden Willow Tree*)

There was a little ship in South Amerikee,
    Crying, O the land that lies so low.
There was a little ship in South Amerikee,
She went by the name of the Golden Willow Tree,
    As she sailed in the lowland lonesome low,
    As she sailed in the lowland so low.

We hadn't been a-sailing more than two weeks or three,
    Crying, O the land that lies so low.
We hadn't been a-sailing more than two weeks or three
Till we came in sight of the British Roverie,
    As she sailed in the lowland lonesome low,
    As she sailed in the lowland so low.*

---

* The following stanza has been omitted by the singer at this point:

> Up stepped the Captain, says, "What we going to do?"
>   Crying, O the lonesome land so low.
> Up stepped the Captain, says, "What we going to do?
> If we overtake them, they'll cut us in two,
>   And they'll sink us in the lowland lonesome low,
>   They'll sink us in the lowland so low."

"The Sweet Trinity" was recorded by Alan and Elizabeth Lomax from the singing, with banjo, of Justus Begley at Hazard, Kentucky, 1937. Library of Congress record LP7. Child ballad no. 286. Coffin, 153. Bronson, IV, 312.

Up stepped a little carpenter boy,
    Crying, O the lonesome land so low.
Up stepped a little carpenter boy,
Says, "What will you give me for the ship that I'll destroy?
    And I'll sink 'em in the lowland lonesome low,
    And I'll sink 'em in the lowland so low."

"I'll give you gold or I'll give thee" —
    Crying, O the lonesome land so low —
"I'll give you gold or I'll give thee
The fairest of my daughters as she sails upon the sea,
    If you'll sink 'em in the lowland lonesome low,
    If you'll sink 'em in the land that lies so low."

Then he turned upon his back and away swam he,
    Crying, O the lonesome land so low.
He turned upon his back and away swum he.
He swum till he came to the British Roverie,
    As she sailed in the lowland lonesome low,
    As she sailed in the lowland so low.

He had a little instrument fitted for his use,
    Crying, O the lonesome land so low.
He had a little instrument fitted for his use.
He bored nine holes and he bored them all at once,
    And he sank her in the lowland lonesome low,
    And he sank her in the lowland so low.

Well, he turned upon his breast and back swum he,
    Crying, O the lonesome land so low.
He turned upon his breast and back swum he.
He swum till he came to the Golden Willow Tree,
    As she sailed in the lowland lonesome low,
    As she sailed in the lowland so low.

"Captain, O Captain, come take me on board" —
    Crying, O the lonesome land so low —
"O Captain, O Captain, come take me on board,
And do unto me as good as your word,
    For I sank 'em in the lowland lonesome low,
    I sank her in the lowland so low."

"Oh, no, I won't take you on board" —
    Crying, O the lonesome land so low —
"Oh, no, I won't take you on board,
Nor do unto you as good as my word,
    Though you sank 'em in the lowland lonesome low,
    Though you sank 'em in the lowland so low."

"If it wasn't for the love that I have for your men" —
    Crying, O the land that lies so low —
"If it wasn't for the love that I have for your men,
I'd do unto you as I done unto them.
    I'd sink you in the lowland lonesome low,
    I'd sink you in the lowland so low."

He turned upon his head and down swum he,
    Crying, O the lonesome land so low,
He turned upon his head and down swum he,
He swum till he came to the bottom of the sea,
    Sank himself in the lowland lonesome low,
    Sank himself in the lowland so low.

THE MERMAID

Most texts have Friday rather than Saturday as the night for setting sail, Friday traditionally being a day of ill omen for starting on any voyage. The sight of a mermaid also meant disaster to seamen, and the entrenched mediaeval superstition is not unrelated to the fear Odysseus and his men had of the Sirens.

Version 1 of "The Mermaid" was contributed to the Missouri Folk-Lore Society in 1911 by Agnes Shibley of the Kirksville State Teachers College, who learned it from her mother. H. M. Belden, *Ballads and Songs Collected by the Missouri Folk-Lore Society*, Columbia (reprint edition, 1966), pp. 101–102. Without music. Child ballad no. 289. Coffin, 153. Bronson, IV, 312.

I

One Saturday night as we set sail,
Not being far from shore,
'Twas then that I spied a pretty fair maid
With a glass and a comb in her hand, her hand,
With a glass and a comb in her hand.
  The stormy wind did blow,
  And the raging sea did roll,
  And we poor sailors came leaping to the top
  While the landsmen lay down below, below, below,
  While the landsmen lay down below.

Then up came a boy of our gallant ship
And a noble-spoken boy was he,
Saying, "I've a mother in distant York town
This night is a-weeping for me."

Then up came a lad of our gallant ship
And a beautiful lad was he,
Saying, "I've a sweetheart in distant York town
This night is a-looking for me."

Then up came the clerk of our gallant ship
And a noble-spoken man was he,
Saying, "I've a wife in distant York town
This night a widow will be."

Then up came the captain of our gallant ship —
There is no braver man than he —
Saying, "For the want of a yawl-boat we'll be drowned
And we'll sink to the bottom of the sea."

Then three times round our gallant ship turned,
Three times round turned she;
Three times round our gallant ship turned,
Then she sank to the bottom of the sea.

II

Mrs. Dusenbury in Arkansas had no Maine-knowledge of the sea or "land-lubbers," so consequently introduced a "landlord" sleeping down below.

Version II of "The Mermaid" was recorded by Sidney Robertson Cowell and Laurence Powell from the singing of Mrs. Emma Dusenbury, Mena, Arkansas, 1936. Library of Congress record LP58. Child ballad no. 289. Coffin, 153. Bronson, IV, 132.

(Folk etymology: within the limits of her understanding.) When asked by collector Powell what the landlord was doing, Mrs. Dusenbury replied: "Sleepin', I reckon." "Mask" for "mast" is easy enough. It must be remembered that Mrs. Dusenbury was totally blind and that all her songs came to her through their beauty of tune and text. She gave 125 great traditional songs to the Library of Congress. Recorded songs. The slip to "mask" from "mast" (which she had never seen) must be excused by you.

As I sailed out one Friday night
I was not fur from land,
When I spied a pretty girl a-combing up her hair
With a comb and a glass in her hand.

And the sea is a-roar, roar, roar,
And the stormy winds may blow,
While us poor sailor boys are climbing up the mask,
And the landlord a-lying down below.

Up stepped the captain of our gallant ship,
A well spoken captain was he,
Saying "We're all lost for the want of a boat,
And will sink to the bottom of the sea."

Up stepped the mate of our gallant ship,
A well spoken mate was he,
Saying "We're all lost for the want of a boat,
And will sink to the bottom of the sea.

"I have a wife and children three,
This night they're looking for me,
They may look, they may wait till the cold water rise,
They may look to the bottom of the sea.

"I have a mother and sisters three,
This night they're waiting for me,
They may look, they may wait till the cold water rise,
They may look to the bottom of the sea."

TROOPER AND MAID

I

There was a man a-coming from the south, it being dark and gloomy,
She knew the soldier by his horse, because she loved him dearly.
Dearly, oh, dearly.
She knew the soldier by his horse, because she loved him dearly.

She caught him by the bridle rein, she led him to the stable.
"Here's oats and corn for the soldier's horse, come feed him at your leisure."
Dearly, oh, dearly.
"Here's oats and corn for the soldier's horse, come feed him at your leisure."

She took him by the lily-white hand, she led him to the table,
"Here's cakes and beer for you, my dear, come eat and drink with pleasure."

She tripped upstairs to make his bed, she made it soft and easy,
Then she came tripping down the steps, saying, "At last, my dear, it's
   ready."

He pulled off his lily-white robe, he laid it on the table,
A sword and pistol by its side, saying, "At last, my dear, I'm able."

He had been in bed not more than two hours, when he heard the war drum
   beating;
He 'rose, he 'rose and put on his clothes, saying, "Alas, my dear, I leave
   you."

"Oh, when are you a-coming back? And when will we get married?"
"When gray goose quills turn to silver pins, oh then, my dear, we'll marry."
Dearly, oh, dearly.
"When gray goose quills turn to silver pins, oh then, my dear, we'll marry."

Version 1 of "Trooper and Maid" is from Arthur Kyle Davis, *Traditional Ballads of Virginia*
(Harvard) Cambridge, 1929, p. 544. With music. Child ballad no. 299. Coffin, 161. Bronson, IV, 424.

II

"Feed your horse we're able,
Here's oats and corn for you, young man,
To feed your horse we're able."

She took him by his lily-white hand,
And led him to the table.
"Here's cakes and wines for you, young man,
Eat and drink we're able."

She pulled off her lily-white gown
And laid it on the table.
The soldier off with his uniform
And into bed with the lady.

They hadn't been laying in bed but one hour
When he heard the trumpet sound.
She cried out with a thrilling cry:
"O Lord, O Lord, I'm ruined."

Version II of "Trooper and Maid" was collected by Cecil J. Sharp from the singing of Mrs. Tom Rice, Big Laurel, North Carolina, 1916. In Sharp, *English Folksongs from the Southern Appalachians* (Oxford) New York, 1932, I, 305. Child ballad no. 299. Coffin, 161. Bronson, IV, 424.

HYMNS, RELIGIOUS PIECES, CAROLS

Selections from The Sacred Harp
and The Social Harp

Hymns and Religious Pieces

Carols and Christmas Pieces

Selections from
The Original Sacred Harp
and The Social Harp

What wondrous love is this! Oh, my soul! Oh, my soul!
What wondrous love is this! Oh, my soul! Oh, my soul!
   What wondrous love is this
   That caused the Lord of bliss
To bear the dreadful curse for my soul, for my soul,
To bear the dreadful curse for my soul.

All the selections which follow from *The Original Sacred Harp* were recorded by George Pullen Jackson and Alan Lomax at the thirty-seventh annual session of the Alabama Sacred Harp Singing Convention at Birmingham, Alabama, August, 1942, and all appear on Library of Congress record LP11. I have not, therefore, repetitively noted this in the footnote following each selection. All page references are to the 1971 Denson revision of *The Original Sacred Harp*, cited in the bibliography. *The Original Sacred Harp* was first published in 1844.

All page references to *The Social Harp* are to the facsimile reprint of the 1855 edition — the first — as edited by John F. Garst (University of Georgia) and Daniel W. Patterson (University of North Carolina), and printed by the University of Georgia Press, 1973, cited in the bibliography.

The majority of titles for the selections from the *Sacred Harp* and *Social Harp* refer to the tunes and music compositions and were given to them by the composers, either commemorating the place of composition or otherwise honoring it. The titles generally do not refer to the texts. They make a dignified, unique, and colorful list. Mear, Windham, Northfield . . .

WINDHAM

Broad is the road that leads to death
    And thousands walk together there;
But wisdom shows a narrow path
    With here and there a trav'ler.

"Deny thyself, and take thy cross"
    Is the Redeemer's great command;
Nature must call her gold but dross,
    If she would gain this heav'nly land.

MEAR

Will God forever cast us off,
    His wrath forever smoke
Against the people of His love,
    His little chosen flock?

Think of the tribes so dearly bought
    With the Redeemer's blood,
Nor let Thy Zion be forgot,
    Where once Thy glory stood.

WONDROUS LOVE

What wondrous love is this! Oh, my soul! Oh, my soul!
What wondrous love is this! Oh, my soul!
    What wondrous love is this,
    That caused the Lord of bliss
To bear the dreadful curse for my soul, for my soul,
To bear the dreadful curse for my soul.

"Windham" was led by "Uncle Dock" Owen of Sand Mountain, Marshall County, Alabama. Words by Isaac Watts (1674–1748). *Original Sacred Harp*, p. 38.

"Mear" was led by Paine Denson of Birmingham, Alabama. Words by Jesse Mercer (Georgia, 1769–1841). *Original Sacred Harp*, p. 49.

"Wondrous Love" was led by Lee Wells of Jasper, Alabama. Author unknown. *Original Sacred Harp*, p. 159. For the stanzaic pattern, see "Captain Kidd" and "Sam Hall."

When I was sinking down, sinking down, sinking down,
When I was sinking down, sinking down,
　When I was sinking down
　Beneath God's righteous frown,
Christ laid aside His crown for my soul, for my soul,
Christ laid aside His crown for my soul.

And when from death I'm free, I'll sing on, I'll sing on,
And when from death I'm free, I'll sing on,
　And when from death I'm free,
　I'll sing and joyful be,
And through eternity I'll sing on, I'll sing on,
And through eternity I'll sing on.

LOVER OF THE LORD

Lovers of pleasure more than God,
　For you He suffered pain;
For you the Savior spilt His Blood,
　And shall He bleed in vain?

Oh, you must be a lover of the Lord,
Oh, you must be a lover of the Lord,
Oh, you must be a lover of the Lord,
Or you can't go to heaven when you die.
Or you can't go to heaven when you die.

"Lover of the Lord" was led by Lonnie P. Odem of St. Joseph, Tennessee. George Pullen Jackson notes that "R. H. Reeves made this song for the 1869 edition of *The Sacred Harp* out of a gospel hymn then popular . . . of which he used the infectious chorus without change." *Original Sacred Harp*, p. 124.

MONTGOMERY

Early, my God, without delay,
    I haste to seek Thy face;
My thirsty spirit faints away
    Without Thy cheering grace.
So pilgrims on the scorching sand
    Beneath a burning sky
Long for a cooling stream at hand,
    And they must drink or die.

NORTHFIELD

How long, dear Savior, O how long
    Shall this bright hour delay?
Fly swift around, ye wheels of time,
    And bring the promised day.

MOUNT ZION

The hill of Zion yields
    A thousand sacred sweets,
Before we reach the heav'nly fields,
    Or walk the golden streets.
Then let your songs abound,
    And every tear be dry;
We're marching through Immanuel's ground,
    To fairer worlds on high.

"Montgomery" as led by Mrs. Delilah Denson Posey of Birmingham, Alabama. Words by Isaac Watts. *Original Sacred Harp*, p. 189.

"Northfield" as led by Paine Denson of Birmingham, Alabama. Words by Isaac Watts. *Original Sacred Harp*, p. 155.

"Mount Zion" as led by Mrs. Maud Moncrief of Birmingham, Alabama. Author unknown. *Original Sacred Harp*, p. 220.

MILFORD

If angels sung a Savior's birth,
    On that auspicious morn,
We well may imitate their mirth,
    Now He again is born.

STRATFIELD

Through every age, eternal God,
    Thou art our rest, our safe abode;
High was Thy throne ere Heav'n was made
    Or earth Thy humble footstool laid.

BALLSTOWN

Great God, attend while Zion sings
The joy that from Thy presence springs;
To spend one day with Thee on earth
Exceeds a thousand days of mirth.

"Milford" as led by Mrs. M. L. Mann of Opelika, Alabama. Words attributed to John Stephenson (Ireland, 1772–1833). *Original Sacred Harp*, p. 273.

"Stratfield" as led by John M. Dye of Birmingham, Alabama. Words by Isaac Watts. *Original Sacred Harp*, p. 142.

"Ballstown" as led by Ernestine Tipton of Birmingham, Alabama. Words by Isaac Watts. *Original Sacred Harp*, p. 217.

EDOM

With songs and honors sounding loud,
    Address the Lord on high;
Over the heav'ns He spreads His clouds,
    And waters veil the sky.
He sends His show'rs of blessings down
    To cheer the plains below;
He makes the grass the mountains crown
    And corn in valleys grow.

FILLMORE

Great God, let all my tuneful pow'rs
    Awake, and sing Thy mighty name;
Thy hand revolves my circling hours,
    Thy hand from whence my being came.
Thus will I sing till nature cease,
    Till sense and language are no more;
And after death Thy boundless grace
    Through everlasting years adore.

"Edom" as led by Mrs. Delilah Denson Posey of Birmingham, Alabama. Words by Isaac Watts. *Original Sacred Harp*, p. 200.

"Fillmore" as led by Ernestine Tipton of Birmingham, Alabama. Words by Ottiwell Heginbothom (England, 1744–1768). *Original Sacred Harp*, p. 434.

SARDIS

Come on, my fellow pilgrims, come
And let us all be hast'ning home.
We soon shall land on yon blest
    shore,
Where pain and sorrow are no
   more;
There we our Jesus shall adore,
   Forever blest.

No period then our joys shall know,
Secure from ev'ry mortal foe;
No sickness there, no want nor pain
Shall e'er disturb our rest again,
When with Immanuel we reign,
   Forever blest.

MISSION

Young people, all attention give,
   While I address you in God's name;
You who in sin and folly live,
   Come, hear the counsel of a friend.
I've sought for bliss in glitt'ring toys
   And ranged the luring scenes of vice;
But never knew substantial joys,
   Until I heard my Savior's voice.

"Sardis" as led by "Uncle Dock" Owen of Sand Mountain, Marshall County, Alabama. Words possibly by Miss Sarah Lancaster of Georgia for the 1869 edition of *The Sacred Harp. Original Sacred Harp*, p. 460.

"Mission" as led by A. Marcus Cagle of Atlanta, Georgia. Author unknown. *Original Sacred Harp*, p. 204.

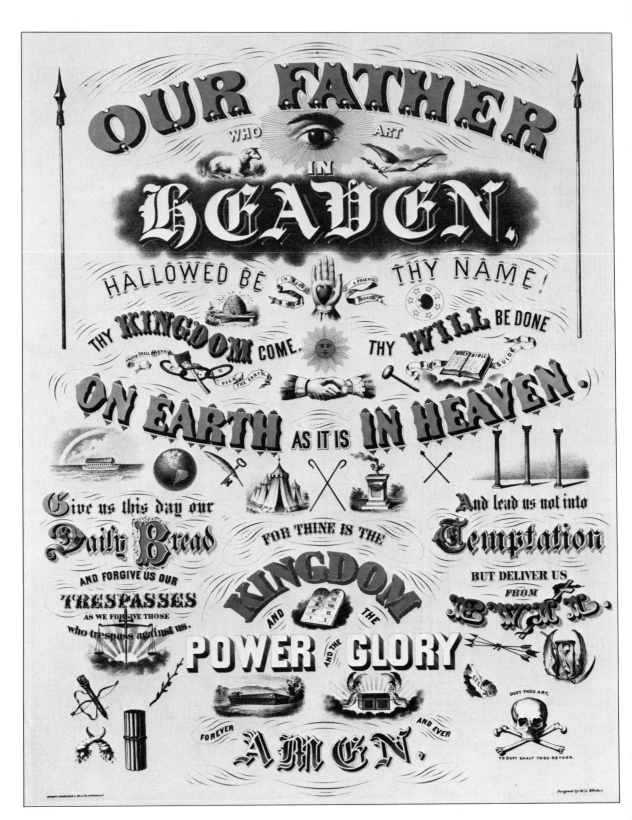

VAIN WORLD ADIEU

When for eternal worlds we steer,
And seas are calm and skies are clear,
And faith in lively exercise,
And distant hills of Canaan rise,
The soul for joy then claps her wings,
And loud her hallelujah sings,
Vain world, adieu;
And loud her Hallelujah sings,
Vain world, adieu,
Vain world, adieu.

HEAVENLY VISION

I beheld, and lo a great multitude, which no man could number:
Thousands of thousands, and ten times thousands,
Thousands of thousands, and ten times thousands,
Stood before the Lamb, and they had palms in their hands, and they cease
   not day nor night, saying,
Holy, holy, holy, holy, holy, Lord God Almighty,
Which was, and is, and is to come,
Which was, and is, and is to come,
And I heard a mighty angel flying through the midst of Heav'n, crying with
   a loud voice,
Woe, woe, woe, woe
Be unto the earth by reasons of the trumpet which is yet to sound.
And when the last trumpet sounded, the great men and nobles, rich men
   and poor, bond and free, gathered themselves together, and cried to the
   rocks and mountains to fall upon them and hide them from the face of
   Him that sitteth on the throne;
For the great day of the Lord is come, and who shall be able to stand?
For the great day of the Lord is come, and who shall be able to stand?
And who shall be able to stand?

"Vain World Adieu" as led by A. Marcus Cagle of Atlanta, Georgia. Author unknown. *Original Sacred Harp*. p. 329.

"Heavenly Vision" as led by Paine Denson of Birmingham, Alabama. Words by William Billings (Massachusetts, 1746–1800), the text based on Revelation, 5–7. *Original Sacred Harp*, p. 250.

DAVID'S LAMENTATION

David the king was grieved and moved,
He went to his chamber, his chamber, and wept;
And as he went he wept, and said,
O my son! O my son!
Would to God I had died,
Would to God I had died,
Would to God I had died,
For thee, O Absalom, my son, my son!
O my son! O my son!

SHERBURNE

While shepherds watched their flocks by night,
    All seated on the ground,
The angel of the Lord came down,
    And glory shone around.

SHOUTING SONG

Jesus, grant us all a blessing,
Shouting, singing, send it down;

    Shout, oh, glory! sing glory, hallelujah!
    I'm going where pleasure never dies.

"David's Lamentation" as led by Howard Denson of Tuscaloosa, Alabama. Words by William Billings. Text is based on II Samuel 18:33. *Original Sacred Harp*, p. 268.

"Sherburne" as led by R. M. Hornsby of Clay County, Alabama. Words by Nahum Tate (England, 1652–1715; of Tate and Brady, noted psalm book authors), first published 1698. The words were later sung to folk-carol tunes for Christmas. *Original Sacred Harp*, p. 186.

"Shouting Song." Author unknown. *The Social Harp*, 1855, p. 110.

Lord above, may we go praying,
And rejoicing in thy love.

Shout, oh, glory! sing glory, hallelujah!
I'm going where pleasure never dies.

SHOUT FOR JOY

I'm glad that I am born to die;
From grief and woe my soul shall fly;

O, shout for joy, give God the glory,
I expect to join the army by and by.

Sweet angels beckon me away,
To sing God's praise in endless day.

O, shout for joy, give God the glory,
I expect to join the army by and by.

THE TRAVELER

I'm trav'ling to my grave,
I'm trav'ling to my grave,
I'm trav'ling to my grave,
To lay this body down.

My fathers died a-shouting,
Rejoicing in the Lord;
The last word I heard them say,
Was about Jerusalem, the saints' delightful home.

"Shout for Joy." Author unknown. *The Social Harp*, 1855, p. 104.

"The Traveler." Author unknown. *The Social Harp*, 1855, p. 37.

THE BRANCH CANNOT BEAR FRUIT, EXCEPT IT ABIDE IN THE VINE

EVENING SHADE

The day is past and gone,
The evening shades appear;
O may we all remember well,
The night of death is near.

We lay our garments by,
Upon our beds to rest;
So death will soon disrobe us all
Of what we here possess.

Lord, keep us safe this night,
Secure from all our fears;
May angels guard us while we
    sleep,
Till morning light appears.

And when we early rise,
And view th'unwearied sun,
May we set out to win the prize,
And after glory run.

"Evening Shade." Words by John Leland (Massachusetts, 1754–1851). *The Social Harp*, 1855, p. 169.

And when our days are past,
And we from time remove,
O may we in Thy bosom rest,
The bosom of Thy love.

LIVERPOOL

Young people all, attention give,
And hear what I shall say;
I wish your souls with Christ to
    live,
In everlasting day.

Remember you are hast'ning on
To death's dark, gloomy shade;
Your joys on earth will soon be
    gone,
Your flesh in dust be laid.

PLENARY

Hark! from the tombs a doleful sound,
Mine ears attend the cry;
Ye living men, come, view the ground
Where you must shortly lie.
Where you must shortly lie,
Where you must shortly lie,
Ye living men, come, view the ground
Where you must shortly lie.

NINETY-FIFTH

When I can read my title clear,
To mansions in the skies,
I'll bid farewell to ev'ry fear,
I'll bid farewell to ev'ry fear,
And wipe my weeping eyes.

Should earth against my soul
    engage,
And fiery darts be hurled,
Then I can smile at Satan's rage,
Then I can smile at Satan's rage,
And face a frowning world.

"Liverpool." Author unknown. *The Social Harp*, 1855, p. 76.

"Plenary." Author unknown. *The Social Harp*, 1855, p. 123. The first four lines are a common epitaph on tombstones in old graveyards in England and New England.

"Ninety-Fifth." Words by Isaac Watts. *The Social Harp*, 1855, p. 24.

There I shall bathe my weary soul
In seas of heav'nly rest,
And not a wave of trouble roll,
And not a wave of trouble roll
Across my peaceful breast.

THE PROMISED LAND

On Jordan's stormy banks I stand,
And cast a wishful eye
To Canaan's fair and happy land,
Where my possessions lie.
I am bound for the promised land,
I'm bound for the promised land,
Oh, who will come and go with me?
I am bound for the promised land.

ECSTASY

Oh, when shall I see Jesus,
And reign with him above?
And from the flowing fountain,
Drink everlasting love.

When shall I be delivered
From this vain world of sin?
And with my blessed Jesus,
Drink endless pleasures in.

Oh! had I wings I would fly away and be at rest,
And I'd praise God in his bright abode.

"The Promised Land." Words of first four lines by Samuel Stennett (England, d. 1795). *The Social Harp*, 1855, p. 114.

"Ecstasy." Words by John Leland (Massachusetts, 1754–1841). *The Social Harp*, 1855, p. 112.

DEEP SPRING

As on the cross, the Saviour hung,
And wept, and bled, and died,
He pour'd salvation on a wretch
That languished at his side.

His crimes, with inward grief and shame,
The penitent confessed,
And turned his dying eyes to Christ,
And thus his pray'r address'd:

"Jesus, thou Son and heir of heaven!
Thou spotless lamb of God!
I see thee bathed in sweat and tears,
And welt'ring in thy blood.

"Yet quickly from these scenes of woe,
In triumph thou shalt rise,
Burst through the gloomy shades of death,
And shine above the skies."

GREENWICH

Lord, what a thoughtless wretch was I,
To mourn, and murmur, and repine,
To see the wicked placed on high,
In pride and robes of honour shine.

But, oh, their end, their dreadful end;
Thy sanctuary taught me so,
On slip'ry rocks I see them stand,
And fiery billows roll below.

"Deep Spring." Author unknown. *The Social Harp*, 1855, p. 249.

"Greenwich." Author unknown. *The Social Harp*, 1855, p. 173.

THE LONESOME DOVE

Ye weary, heavy laden souls,
Who are oppressed sore,
Ye trav'lers through the wilderness
To Canaan's peaceful shore.

Thro' chilling winds and beating rains,
The waters deep and cold,
And enemies surrounding you,
Take courage and be bold.

Tho' storms and hurricanes arise,
The desert all around,
And fiery serpents oft appear
Through the enchanted ground.

Dark nights, and clouds, and gloomy fear —
And dragons often roar —
But while the gospel trump we hear,
We'll press for Canaan's shore.

"The Lonesome Dove." Author unknown. *The Social Harp*, 1855, p. 97.

Hymns
and Religious Pieces

Oh, when I'm in trouble,
Down on my knees,
When I was in trouble,
Lord, remember me,
Oh, when I'm in trouble,
Lord, remember me,
Lord, do, Lord, remember me.

THE MOULDERING VINE
THE DYING FATHER'S FAREWELL
MR. DAVIS'S EXPERIENCE
MRS. SAUNDER'S EXPERIENCE

Emma Backus reported in her *Journal of American Folklore* article, cited with each of these songs, that "the songs have been taken by me from the lips of elderly reciters, who have given them as current and popular in Central North Carolina in the days of their youth, about the first quarter of the 19th century." They are an extraordinary group to have survived in oral tradition. In a note to "Mrs. Saunder's Experience," the collector says that she had "heard before of the two marks of Satan, one in the head and one in the hand [with], I believe, this shape ✝ ." "Mrs. Saunder's Experience" was collected "from a lady, eighty-five years old, who, when a girl, learned them [it?] from her grandfather. The song, therefore, was sung in Central North Carolina before 1750." Mrs. Backus uses "them" rather than "it," although the following sentence refers to a single song. It is probable that the last two "Experience" songs are from the same unnamed informant. The texts are given with music.

THE MOULDERING VINE

Hark, ye sighing sons of sorrow,
Learn from me your certain doom,
Learn from me your fate tomorrow,
Dead, perhaps laid in your tomb;
See all nature fading, dying,
Silent all things seem to pine,
Life from vegetation flying,
Brings to mind the mouldering vine.

See in yonder forest standing,
Lofty cedars, how they nod,
Scenes of nature, how surprising,
Read in nature nature's God;
While the annual frosts are cropping
Leaves and tendrils from the trees,
So our friends are early dropping,
We are like to one of these.

Hollow winds about me roaring,
Noisy waters 'round me rise,
Whilst I sit my fate deploring,
Tears fast streaming from my eyes;
What to me is Autumn's treasure,
Since I know no earthly joy,
Long I've lost all youthful pleasure,
Time must youth and wealth destroy.

"The Mouldering Vine" was collected by Emma M. Backus and reported in "Early Songs from North Carolina," *JAF*, 14 (1901):287.

THE DYING FATHER'S FAREWELL

The time is swiftly rolling on,
When I must faint and die,
My body to the dust return,
And there forgotten lie.
Let persecution rage around,
And Antichrist appear,
My silent dust beneath the ground,
There's no disturbance there.

My little children near my heart,
And nature seems to bind,
It grieves me sorely to depart,
And leave you all behind.
O Lord, a father to them be,
And keep them from all harm,
That they may love and worship thee,
And dwell upon thy charms.

My loving wife, my bosom friend,
The object of my love,
The time's been sweet I've spent with you,
My sweet and harmless dove.
For I can never come to thee,
Let this not grieve your heart,
For you will shortly come to me,
Where we shall never part.

"The Dying Father's Farewell." Backus, "Early Songs from North Carolina," *JAF*, 14 (1901):288–289. Closely related to "The Dying Minister" in *The Original Sacred Harp* (1844), 1971 revision, p. 83.

MR. DAVIS'S EXPERIENCE

Come all ye young people and all my relations,
Come, listen awhile, and to you I will tell,
How my bowels did move with desire for salvation,
While enwrapt in the gales and breezes from hell.
I was not yet sixteen when Jesus first called me,
To think of my soul and the state I was in,
I saw myself standing a distance from Jesus.
Between me and him was a mountain of sin.

The devil perceived that I was convincèd,
He strove to persuade me that I was too young,
That I would get weary before my ascension,
And wish that I had not so early begun.
Sometimes he'd persuade me that Jesus was partial,
When he was a-setting of poor sinners free,
That I was forsaken and quite reprobated,
And there was no mercy at all for poor me.

And now I've found favor in Jesus, my Savior,
And all his commandments I'm bound to obey,
I trust he will keep me from all Satan's power,
Till he shall think proper to call me away.
So farewell, all kinfolks, if I can't persuade you
To leave off your follies and go with a friend,
I'll follow my Savior in whom I've found favor,
My days to his glory I'm bound for to spend.

"Mr. Davis's Experience." Backus, "Early Songs from North Carolina," *JAF*, 14 (1901): 289–290.

MRS. SAUNDER'S EXPERIENCE

With faith I trust in Christ the Lord,
Who did my mind console;
I'll tell you, my Gospel friend,
The travail of my soul.
The early part of life I trod
In vanity and mirth,
Quite thoughtless of the living God,
The author of my birth.

At length I thought I was not right,
My wrong could plainly see,
Then I assumed a serious turn,
Became a Pharisee.
I'd oft repeat a formal prayer,
But only with my tongue,
And thank the Lord, I'm not so vile,
As such or such a one.

In ignorance I wandered on,
On works alone I stood,
And wished that all that saw my walk
Might think that I was good.
Predestination sounded hard,
So did Election, too,
I thought if I would do my part,
The rest the Lord would do.

The Baptists did this doctrine teach,
But it appear'd so vain,
I thought such men should never preach
These principles again.
As I disliked those sentiments,
I seldom went to hear,
And when I did, felt anger rise,
Instead of godly fear.

"Mrs. Saunder's Experience." Backus, "Early Songs from North Carolina," *JAF*, 14 (1901): 290–292.

I prayed that God would give me faith,
And help me to believe.
Some gloomy days of sorrow pass'd,
But still found no relief.
This Baptist man again I went to hear,
His theme free grace and love,
He mentioned those the Lord had seal'd,
And took to him above.

He likewise said that Satan hath
A mark to put upon
The forehead or the hand of those
That he claims for his own.
Marked in the forehead they are bold,
And care not what they do,
They have no fear of God above,
Neither of man below.

The others when with Christians are,
The mark will try to hide,
But when they meet the forehead mark,
Their hand will open wide.
This was a blow severe indeed,
And I condemned did stand,
And told a friend when I came out,
The mark was in my hand.

All earthly thoughts did vanish now
From my distracted mind,
I read the Scriptures, tried to pray,
No comfort could I find.
Each judgment in the holy writ
Appeared to point at me,
And no sweet promise could I find
To reach my misery.

Amidst this torture, fear of hell
Was not much on my mind,
But God seemed angry, frowned on me,
No comfort could I find.
In reading of the word of truth,

The Lord this promise gave,
Though he cause grief, in mercy still,
He will compassion have.

I felt a gleam of hope arise,
But yet I could not see
How a just God could mercy have
On such a wretch as me.
Still did I hope and try to pray,
My soul was in a strait,
This was the word that came to me,
Although it tarry, wait.

My soul was filled, my eyes o'errun,
With wonder, love, and praise;
I thought that joy and peace would crown
The remnant of my days.
Election, too, how sweet the word!
For had I not been one
Gave to the Savior ere he died,
I should have been undone.

Call in thy sons and daughters, Lord,
And may I live to see
My dear relations keep thy word,
And meekly follow thee.
Oh, let thy righteous will be done,
May I submissive be,
And trust in God whose grace alone
Can set a captive free.

MY BURIED FRIENDS

My buried friends can I forget or must the grave eternal sever?
I know them now as I did then and in my heart they live forever.
They loved me once with love sincere and never did their love deceive me,
But often in my conflicts here they'd rally quick 'round to relieve me.

"My Buried Friends" was recorded by Sidney Robertson Cowell from the singing of Charles Spencer, Crandon, Wisconsin, 1937. Library of Congress AFS record 3294 A1.

I fain would weep but what of tears? No tears of mine can recall them,
Nor would I wish that rolling cares, no cares like mine, should e'er befall
    them.
They rest in realms of light and love, they dwell upon the Mount of Glory.
They bask in beams of bliss above and shout to tell their happy story.

I heard them bid the world adieu, I saw them on the rolling billows,
Their far off home appeared in view while yet they tread the dying pillow.
I heard the parting pilgrim tell, while passing Jordan's stormy river,
"Adieu to earth, for all is well, now all is well with me forever."

Oh, how I long to join their wings and range their fields of blooming
    flowers;
Come, holy watcher, come and bring a mourner to your blissful bowers.
I'd feed with rapture on my way, nor would I pause at Jordan's River,
With songs I sent her in love's day and live with my loved friends forever.

YOUNG PEOPLE WHO DELIGHT IN SIN

Young people who delight in sin,
I'll tell you what has lately been:
A lady who was young and fair,
She died in sin and deep despair.

She would go to frolics, dance and play,
In spite of all her friends would say;
Saying, "I'll turn to God when I am old,
And He will then receive my soul."

One Friday she was taken ill,
Her stubborn heart began to yield,
Crying, "Alas, my days are spent,
Too late, my God, now to repent!"

She called her mother to her bed,
Her eyes were rolling in her head,
"When I am dead, remember well
Your wicked daughter screams in hell.

"Young People Who Delight in Sin" was recorded by Sidney Robertson Cowell from the singing of S. F. Russell, Marion, Virginia, 1936. Library of Congress AFS record 3158 B1.

"My earthly father, fare you well,
My soul is lost and doomed to hell.
The flaming wrath begins to roll,
I am a lost and ruined soul."

She gnawed her tongue before she died,
She wrung her hands and screamed and cried,
Saying, "Must I burn forever more
Until thousand thousand years are o'er?"

Her sparkling eyes then rolled around,
While death did bring her to the ground.
The coffin, grave and winding-sheet
Did hold her lifeless frame complete.

"Young people who have this heard,
Take warning at my dying word,
That you may escape those hellish pains
Though I am doomed to endless flames."

THE ANGEL OF DEATH

There's a man going 'round taking names,
There's a man going 'round taking names,
He took my mother's name and he filled my heart with pain,
There's a man going 'round taking names.

There's a man going 'round taking names,
There's a man going 'round taking names,
He took my father's name and he filled my heart with pain,
There's a man going 'round taking names.

There's a man going 'round taking names,
There's a man going 'round taking names,
He took my sister's name and he filled my heart with pain,
There's a man going 'round taking names.

"The Angel of Death" was collected by Vance Randolph from Enos Calkins, Little Rock, Arkansas, 1921, and sung for the Library of Congress by Vance Randolph, AFS record 5242 B1. Calkins had learned the song in the 1890's from a man named Wilks, at Verona, Missouri.

There's a man going 'round taking names,
There's a man going 'round taking names,
He took my brother's name and he filled my heart with pain,
There's a man going 'round taking names.

There's a man going 'round taking names,
There's a man going 'round taking names,
He took my sweetheart's name and he filled my heart with pain,
There's a man going 'round taking names.

A POOR WAYFARING STRANGER

I am a poor wayfaring stranger
While traveling through this world of woe,
Yet there's no sickness, toil or danger
In that bright world to which I go.
I'm going there to see my father,
I'm going there no more to roam,
I'm only going over Jordan,
I'm only going home.

I know dark clouds will gather around me,
I know my way is rough and steep,
Yet beauteous fields lie just before me,
Where God's redeemed their virgils keep.
I'm going there to see my mother,
She said she'd meet me when I come,
I'm only going over Jordan,
I'm only going over home.

I'll soon be freed from every trial,
My body asleep in the old churchyard,
I'll drop the cross of self-denial,
And enter on my great reward.

"A Poor Wayfaring Stranger" was collected by the Federal Music Project, Works Progress Administration (WPA), Floyd County, Kentucky, ca. 1937. Edith F. James, Supervisor for Floyd County. Ms., with music, in the Archive of Folk Song, Library of Congress. See also *The Original Sacred Harp* (1844), 1971 revision, p. 457.

I'm going there to see my classmates,
Who have gone before me, one by one,
I'm only going over Jordan,
I'm only going over home.

I want to wear a crown of glory
When I get home to that good land,
I want to shout salvation's glory
In concert with that blood-washed band.
I'm going there to see my Savior,
To sing his praise forevermore,
I'm only going over Jordan.
I'm only going over home.

ZION'S SONS AND DAUGHTERS

See the fountain opened wide
That from our sinning frees us,
Flowing from the wounded side
Of our Immanuel Jesus.

Ho, everyone that thirsts,
Come ye to the waters;
Freely drink and quench your thirst
With Zion's sons and daughters.

Dying sinners, come and try,
The waters will relieve you;
Without money come and buy,
For Christ will freely give you.

He who drinks shall never die,
These waters fail him never;
Sinners, come and now apply,
And drink and live for ever.

Weeping Mary, full of grief,
Came begging for these waters;
Jesus gave her full relief
With Zion's sons and daughters.

See the woman at the well,
Conversing with the Savior;
Soon she found that He could tell
The whole of her behavior.

When she asked and she obtained
A drink, her heart was flaming;
Thus the gift divine she obtained,
And ran to town proclaiming.

The thief had only time to think
And tell his dreadful story;
Jesus gave him leave to drink,
He drank and fled to glory.

"Zion's Sons and Daughters" was collected by Harvey H. Fuson from Mrs. Louisa Moses. In Fuson, *Ballads of the Kentucky Highlands*, London, 1931, p. 214. Without music.

DEATH-BED SONG

While sorrows encompass me round,
And endless distresses I see,
Astonished I cry, "Can a mortal be found
That's surrounded with troubles like me!"

Few hours of peace I enjoy,
And these are succeeded by pain;
If a moment of praising my God I employ,
I have hours and days to complain.

Oh, when shall my sorrow subside?
Oh, when shall my sufferings cease?
Oh, when to the bosom of Christ be conveyed,
To the mansions of glory and peace?

May I be prepared for that day,
When Jesus shall bid me remove,
And filled with His power go shouting away
To the arms of my heavenly love.

My spirit to glory conveyed,
My body laid low in the ground,
I wish not a tear at my grave to be shed,
But let all join in praising around.

No sorrow be vented that day,
When Jesus has called me home;
But singing and praising let each brother say,
"He has gone from the evil to come."

If souls there immortal can know,
Or visit their brethren beneath,
Perhaps I may join you while singing you go,
After laying my corpse in the earth.

"Death-Bed Song" was collected by Harvey H. Fuson from Mrs. Louisa Moses. In Fuson, *Ballads of the Kentucky Highlands*, London, 1931, p. 217. Without music.

Immersed in the ocean of love,
I then like an angel shall sing,
Till Christ shall descend with a shout from above,
And make all creation to ring.

Our slumbering bodies obey,
And swifter than thoughts shall arise;
And changed in a moment go shouting away
To mansions of love in the skies.

WHEN I SURVEY THE WONDROUS CROSS

When I survey the wondrous cross
On which the Prince of Glory died,
My richest gain I count but loss,
And pour contempt on all my pride.

Forbid it, Lord, that I should boast
Save in the cross of Christ my God.
All vain things that charm me most
I sacrifice them to his flood.

See from his head, his hands, his feet,
Sorrow and love flowed mingling down.
Did e'er such love and sorrow meet
Or thorns compose so rich a crown?

His dying crimson like a robe
Spreads o'er his body on the tree.
When I am dead to all the globe,
And all the globe is dead to me,

Were the whole realm of nature mine,
That were a present far too small.
Love so amazing, so divine,
Demands my soul, my life, my all.

"When I Survey the Wondrous Cross" was collected by the Federal Music Project, Works Progress Administration (WPA), Floyd County, Kentucky, ca. 1937. Edith F. James, Supervisor for Floyd County. Ms., with music, in the Archive of Folk Song, Library of Congress. Words by Isaac Watts. See *The Original Sacred Harp*, p. 447.

THE SONS OF LEVI

Come all ye Knights, ye Knights of Molites,
Come learn to do as I have done;
You might have seen an armour brighter
Within the New Jerusalem.

    We are the true-born sons of Levi,
    We are the true-born sons of God;
    We're the root and branch of David,
    The glorious bright and morning star.

Moses planted Aaron's rod,
In one night the rod did bud;
Moses smote the Egyptian waters,
And that very night they turned to blood.

When Joshua and I crossed over Jordan,
When Joshua and I crossed over home,
The seven trumps and the ram's horn sounded,
Sounded loud before the throne.

    We are the true-born sons of Levi,
    We are the true-born sons of God;
    We're the root and branch of David,
    The glorious bright and morning star.

HIDE THOU ME

When this troubled life is over, hide Thou me;
When this troubled life is over, hide Thou me;
When this troubled life is over, let Thy bosom be my pillow;
Hide Thou me, Rock of Ages, safe in Thee.

"The Sons of Levi" was collected by Harvey H. Fuson from C. M. Moses. In Fuson, *Ballads of the Kentucky Highlands*, London, 1931, p. 203. Without music.

"Hide Thou Me" was collected by Harvey H. Fuson from Mrs. Louisa Moses. In Fuson, *Ballads of the Kentucky Highlands*, London, 1931, p. 204. Without music.

We're climbing up Jacob's ladder, hide Thou me;
We're climbing up Jacob's ladder, hide Thou me;
We're climbing up Jacob's ladder, every rung gets higher and higher;
Hide Thou me, Rock of Ages, safe in Thee.

We are working for our Master, hide Thou me;
We are working for our Master, hide Thou me;
We are working for our Master, He will lead us to green pasture;
Hide Thou me, Rock of Ages, safe in Thee.

When this world is all on fire, hide Thou me;
When this world is all on fire, hide Thou me;
When this world is all on fire, let Thy bosom be my pillow;
Hide Thou me, Rock of Ages, safe in Thee.

ATTEND, YOUNG FRIENDS, WHILE I RELATE

Attend, young friends, while I relate
The danger you are in,
The devils that around you wait
While subject unto sin.

Although you flourish like the rose
While in its branches green,
Your sparkling eyes in death must close,
No more will they be seen.

In silent shades you must lie down,
Long in your grave to dwell,
Your friends will then stand weeping 'round
And bid a long farewell.

How small this world will then appear
At that tremendous hour,
When you Jehovah's voice shall hear
And feel his mighty Power.

"Attend, Young Friends, While I Relate" was collected by the Federal Music Project, Works Progress Administration (WPA), Floyd County, Kentucky, ca. 1937. Edith F. James, Supervisor for Floyd County. Ms., with music, in the Archive of Folk Song, Library of Congress.

In vain you'll mourn your days are past:
Alas, those days are gone.
Your golden hours are spent at last
And never will return.

O! Come this moment and begin,
While life's sweet moments last:
Turn to the Lord, forsake all sin,
And he'll forgive the past.

O, THAT I HAD SOME SECRET PLACE

O, that I had some secret place
Where I might hide from sorrow,
Where I might see my Savior's face;
And thus be saved from terror.
O, had I wings like Noah's dove,
I'd leave this world and Satan;
I'd fly to heaven on wings of love,
Where Jesus stands inviting.

I have my bitter and my sweet,
While through this world I travel;
I sometimes shout and sometimes weep,
Which makes my foes to marvel,
Yet, let them think and think again,
I feel I'm bound for heaven.
I hope I shall with Jesus reign,
And therefore I will serve him.

"O, That I Had Some Secret Place" was collected by the Federal Music Project, Works Progress Administration (WPA), Floyd County, Kentucky, ca. 1937. Edith F. James, Supervisor for Floyd County. Ms., with music, in the Archive of Folk Song, Library of Congress.

'TIS SWEET TO REST IN LIVELY HOPE

Jesus, thou art the sinner's friend,
As such I look to thee.
Now in the bowels of Thy love,
O Lord, remember me.

Remember Thy pure word of grace,
Remember Calvary,
Remember all Thy dying groans,
And then remember me.

'Tis sweet to rest in lively hope
That when my change shall come,
Angels will hover 'round my bed
And waft my spirit home.

Thou wondrous advocate with God,
I yield myself to Thee.
While Thou art sitting on thy
   throne,
O Lord, remember me.

RUFUS MITCHELL'S CONFESSION

Come all you men and maidens,
And hearken unto me,
I will tell you my condition
And what it used to be.

I used to be a sinner
That wandered from the Lord,
I neither heard his counsel
Nor read His Holy word.

My name is Rufus Mitchell
The truth to you I'll tell,
I used to drink and gamble
And picked my banjo well.

I kept my evil habits
And served as Satan's slave,
Although my conscience told me
I had a soul to save.

In spite of all my conscience
I'd tell what was not true,
I would sing a joyful ditty
And picked my banjo, too.

Wars between these parties,
The gray coats and the blue,
I volunteered for freedom,
I picked my banjo, too.

" 'Tis Sweet to Rest in Lively Hope" was collected by the Federal Music Project, Works Progress Administration (WPA), Floyd County, Kentucky, ca. 1937. Edith F. James, Supervisor of Floyd County. Ms., with music, in the Archive of Folk Song, Library of Congress.

"Rufus Mitchell's Confession" is from "Kentucky Folksongs" (Library of Congress ms.), Federal Music Project, Works Progress Administration (WPA), n.d.

In scouting I was skillful,
In battle I was brave,
Thought nothing about life and
    death
But to liberate the slave.

Then fever came upon me
And brought me near the grave,
And many Christians told me
I had a soul to save.

I came into this country
To see what I could do,
I kept my evil habits
And picked the banjo, too.

I went to hear the Gospel
To see if His word were true.
I laughed and mocked the preacher
And picked my banjo, too.

And when he called for sinners
The tears streamed in my eyes,
I bowed before the altar,
I laid my banjo by.

LITTLE BESSIE

Hug me closer, closer, Mother,
Put your arms around me tight,
For I'm cold and tired, dear Mother,
And I feel so strange tonight.
Something hurts me here, dear Mother,
Like a stone upon my breast,
And I wonder, wonder, Mother,
Why it is I cannot rest.

All the day while you were working
As I lay upon my bed,
I was trying to be patient
And to think of what you said,
How the King, blessed Jesus,
Loves his lambs to watch and keep —
Oh, I wish He would come and take me
In His arms that I might sleep.

"Little Bessie" was collected by the Federal Music Project, Works Progress Administration (WPA), Floyd County, Kentucky, ca. 1937. Edith F. James, Supervisor for Floyd County. Ms., with music, in the Archive of Folk Song, Library of Congress.

Just before the lamps were lighted,
Just before dear Mother came,
While the room was very quiet
I heard some one call my name.
All at once a window opened
On a field of lambs and sheep,
Some were at the brooks a-drinking,
Some were lying fast asleep.

In a moment I was looking
On a world so bright and fair
Which was filled with little children,
And they seemed so happy there.
They were singing, oh, so sweetly,
Sweetest songs I ever heard,
They were singing sweeter, Mother,
Than our little yellow bird.

But I did not see the Savior
Though I strained my eyes to see,
And I wonder if He saw me
Would he speak to such as me.
All at once a window opened,
One so bright upon me smiled,
And I knew it must be Jesus
When He said, "Come here, my child.

"Come up here, my little Bessie,
Come up here and live with me,
Where little children never suffer
Through the long eternity."
Then I thought of all you told me
Of that bright and happy land,
I was going when you called me,
When you came and kissed my hand.

HANDWRITING ON THE WALL

Luke and John,	My fathers,
It is the handwriting on the wall.	It's the handwriting on the wall.
Luke and John,	My fathers,
It is the handwriting on the wall	It's the handwriting on the wall.

I want somebody read it and tell me what it says,
It's the handwriting on the wall.

Lord, have mercy!	My sisters,
It's the handwriting on the wall.	It's the handwriting on the wall.
Lord, have mercy!	My sisters,
It's the handwriting on the wall.	It's the handwriting on the wall.

I want somebody read it and tell me what it says,
It's the handwriting on the wall.

YOU'RE GOING TO REAP JUST WHAT YOU SOW

You're going to reap just what you sow,
You're going to reap just what you sow,
Sow it in the morning and a-reap it in the evening,
You're going to reap just what you sow.

"Handwriting on the Wall" was recorded by John A. Lomax and Ruby Pickens Tartt from the singing of Dock and Henry Reed and Vera Hall, Livingston, Alabama, 1937. Library of Congress record LP3.

"You're Going to Reap Just What You Sow" was recorded by Charles Seeger from the singing of Rebecca and Penelope Tarwater, Washington, D.C., 1936. Library of Congress AFS record 2089 A2 and B1.

LITTLE BLACK TRAIN

There's a little black train a-coming,
Better get your business right.
There's a little black train a-coming,
And it may be here tonight.

The old man said to his servants,
"I have no future fear.
I'll build my barn a little larger,
I'll last for many a year."

But God said to that man,
"Thou fool, it is tonight
Thy soul will be required at their hands,
And who will bear thy fright?"

There's a little black train a-coming,
Better get your business right,
There's a little black train a-coming,
And it may be here tonight.

THE MAN OF CALVARY
(Easter Day Service)

After the Reverend Sin-Killer Griffin, prison chaplain at Darrington State Farm, Sandy Point, Texas, had heard a replay of the recording of his Calvary sermon, he said to John A. Lomax: "Mr. Lomax, for a long time I've been hearing that I'm a good preacher. Now I know it."

"Little Black Train" was collected by the Federal Music Project, Works Progress Administration (WPA) Floyd County, Kentucky, ca. 1937. Edith F. James, Supervisor for Floyd County. Ms., with music, in the Archive of Folk Song, Library of Congress.

"The Man of Calvary" was recorded by John A. Lomax from a sermon by Sin-Killer Griffin, Negro prison chaplain, at Darrington State Farm, Sandy Point, Texas, 1934. Library of Congress record LP10.

This is an incredibly beautiful and rhythmic wedding of poetry and music, drama and oratory.

For a longer version see John A. Lomax and Alan Lomax (Ruth Crawford Seeger, music editor), *Our Singing Country*, New York, 1941.

. . . Roman soldiers come riding in full speed on their horses and splunged
   Him in the side.
We seen blood and water came out.
Oh-h, Godamighty placed it in the minds of the people
Why, the water is for baptism
And the blood is for cleansin'.
I don't care how mean you've been,
Godamighty's blood'll cleanse you from all sin.
I seen, my dear friends,
How the times moved on.
Great God looked down,
He began to look at the temple —
Jesus said to tear down the temple
And in three days I'll rise up again in all sight.
They didn't know what He was talkin' about.
Jesus was talkin' about His templed body.
I seen while He was hanging,
The mounting began to tremble on which Jesus was hanging on.
The blood was dropping on the mounting,
Holy blood, dropping on the mounting,
My dear friends, corrupting the mounting.
I seen about that time while the blood was drop-ping down,
One — drop — after — another,
I seen the sun that Jesus made in creation;
The sun rose, my dear friends,
And it recognized Jesus hanging on the cross.
Just as soon as the sun recognized its Maker,
Why it clothed itself in sack cloth-ing and went down,
Oh-h, went down in mournin'.
"Look at my Maker dying on the cross."
And when the sun went down,
We seen the moon, that was his Maker, too,
Oh-h, he made the moo-oon,
My dear friends, yes, both time and seasons.

We seen, my dear friends,
When the moon recognized Jesus dying on the cross,
I seen the moon, yes, took with a judgment hemorrhage and bled away.
Good God, looked down.
Oh-h the dyin' thief on the cross
Saw the moon goin' down in blood.
   I see, my dear friends,
About that time they looked at that,
And when the moon went down, it done bled away.
I seen the little stars, great God, that was there;
They remembered Jesus when He struck on the anvil of time.
And the little stars began to show their beautiful ray of light,
And the stars recognized their Maker dying on the cross;
Each little star leaped out of its silver orbit,
Come to make the funeral torches of a dark and unbenointed world.
It got so dark until the men who was puttin' Jesus to death,
They said they could feel the darkness in their fingers.
Great Godamighty, they were close to one another.
And it was so dark they could feel one another,
They could hear one another talk, but they couldn't see each other.
I heard one of the centurions say,
"Sholy, sholy, this must be the Son of God."
'Bout that time, we seen, my dear friends,
The prophet Isaiah said the dead in the grave would hear His voice and
   come forward.
They saw the dead gettin' up out of the grave.
On the east side of Jerusalem,
Gettin' up out of the grave,
Walking about,
Going down in town.
Oh-h, 'way over on Nebo's mounting!
We seen the great lawgiver
Got up out of his grave and began to walk about, my dear friends,
Walking because Jesus said it was finished.
We notice, my dear friends,
Here about that time, I shouldn't wonder, my dear friends,
The church will save you when you get into trouble.
I heard the church so many times singing when you get overwhelmed into
   trouble.

I heard the church said:
How can I die while Jesus lives?
How can I die while Jesus lives?

DO, LORD, REMEMBER ME

Oh, when I'm in trouble,
  Down on my knees,
When I was in trouble,
  Lord, remember me,
Oh, when I'm in trouble,
  Lord remember me,
Lord, do, Lord, remember me.

  Oh, do, Lord, do, Lord, Lord, remember me,
  Do, Lord, do, Lord, oh, Lord, remember me.
  Hallelujah!
  Do, Lord, do, Lord, oh, Lord, remember me.
  Oh, do, Lord, remember me.

Oh, when I am dyin',
  Lord, remember me,
Oh, when I am dyin',
  Lord, remember me,
Oh, when I am dyin',
  Lord, remember me,
Oh, do, Lord, remember me.

Oh, I'm gonna take a little journey,
  Lord, remember me.
I'm gonna take a little journey,
  Lord, remember me.
Oh, I'm gonna take a little journey,
  Lord, remember me,
Oh, do Lord, remember me.

"Do, Lord, Remember Me" was recorded by John A. Lomax and Harold Spivacke from the singing, with banjo accompaniment, of Jimmie Strothers (blind) and Joe Lee at State Farm, Virginia, 1936. Library of Congress record LP10.

DIG MY GRAVE

Go and dig my grave both long and narrow,
Make my coffin neat and strong.

Dig my grave both long and narrow,
Make my coffin neat and strong.

Two, two to my head, good Lord,
Two, two to my feet,
Now but two, two to carry me, Lord, when I die.

Now my soul's gonna shine like a star,
    My soul's gonna shine like a star,
My Lord, my soul's gonna shine like a star;
Lord, I'm bound to heaven when I die.

I'M A SOLDIER IN THE ARMY OF THE LORD

Army of the Lord,
In the army, in the army,
Just a soldier, just a soldier,
In the army of the Lord.
Just a soldier,
In the army,
Just a soldier,
In the army of the Lord,
Just a soldier,
In the army.

I'm gonna keep on the top
In the army of the Lord,
I'm gonna keep on the top
In the army.
I'm gonna keep on the top
In the army of the Lord.
I'm gonna keep on the top
In the army.
I'm gonna keep on the top
In the army of the Lord.
I'm gonna keep on the top
In the army.

"Dig My Grave" was recorded by Alan Lomax and Mary Elizabeth Barnicle from the singing of David Pryor and Henry Lundy, Nassau, the Bahamas, 1935. Library of Congress record LP5.

"I'm a Soldier in the Army of the Lord" was recorded by Alan Lomax, Lewis Jones, and John W. Work from the singing of the congregation of Silent Grove Baptist Church, with trombone and guitar accompaniment, at Clarksdale, Mississippi, 1942, for a study jointly sponsored by the Library of Congress and Fisk University of Nashville, Tennessee. Library of Congress record LP59.

In the army, army of the Lord,
In the army,
Just a soldier,
Just a soldier,
In the army of the Lord,
Just a soldier,
In the army.

AIN'T NO GRAVE CAN HOLD MY BODY DOWN

Ain't no grave can hold my body down.
Ain't no grave can hold my body down, my body down.
When the first trumpet sound,
I'll be gettin' up, walkin' round.
Ain't no grave can hold my body down.
Ain't no grave can hold my body down.
Ain't no grave can hold my body down, my body down.
Now when that first trumpet sound,
I'll be gettin' up, walkin' round.
Ain't no grave can hold my body down.
When I heard of a beautiful city,
The street was paved with gold.
Then I had not been to Heaven.
Oh, Lord, I've been told.
Then I found this throne of grace.
It's gonna 'point my soul a place.
Ain't no grave can hold my body down.
Ain't no grave can hold my body down.
Ain't no grave can hold my body down.
When that first trumpet sound,
I'll be gettin' up, walkin' round.
Ain't no grave can hold my body down.
When Jesus was hangin' on the cross,
It made poor Mary moan.
He looked down on His disciples

"Ain't No Grave Can Hold My Body Down" was recorded by Alan Lomax and Lewis Jones from the singing of Bozie Sturdivant at Silent Grove Baptist Church, Clarksdale, Mississippi, 1942. Library of Congress record LP10.

"They've taken my mother home."
Ain't that a pity and dark shame,
How they crucified the Name!
Ain't no grave can hold my body down.
Ain't no grave can hold my body down.
Ain't no grave can hold my body down.
When the first trumpet sound,
I'll be gettin' up, walkin' round.
Ain't no grave can hold my body down.

THIS TRAIN DON'T CARRY NO GAMBLERS

This train don't carry no gamblers, this train, this train,
This train don't carry no gamblers, this train, this train,
This train don't carry no gamblers, no hard sports or midnight ramblers,
This train don't carry no gamblers, this train, this train.

This train don't carry no loafers, this train, this train,
This train don't carry no loafers, this train, this train,
This train don't carry no loafers, no smart skippers or cigarette smokers,
This train don't carry no loafers, this train, this train.

This train is bound for glory, this train, this train,
This train is bound for glory, this train, this train,
This train is bound for glory, there to shout and sing a story,
This train is bound for glory, this train, this train.

THE BLOOD-STRAINED BANDERS

If you want to go to heaven,
Over on the other shore,
Keep out of the way of the blood-strained banders.*
O good Shepherd, feedin' my sheep.

* Bandits?

"This Train Don't Carry No Gamblers" was recorded by Charles Seeger from the singing of Penelope and Rebecca Tarwater, Washington, D.C., 1936. Library of Congress AFS record 2087 A2.

"The Blood-Strained Banders" was recorded by John A. Lomax from the singing of Jimmie Strothers, with four-string banjo accompaniment, State Farm, Virginia, 1936. Library of Congress record LP3.

Some for Paul, some for Silas,
Some for to make-uh my heart rejoice.
Don't you hear lambs a-crying?
O good Shepherd, feedin' my sheep.

If you want to go to heaven,
Just over on the other shore,
Keep out of the way of the gunshot devils.
O good Shepherd, feedin' my sheep.

Some for Paul, some for Silas,
Some for to make-uh my heart rejoice.
Don't you hear lambs a-crying?
O good Shepherd, feedin' my sheep.

If you wants to go to heaven,
Just over on the other shore,
Keep out of the way of the long-tongue liars.
O good Shepherd, feedin' my sheep.

Some for Paul, some for Silas,
Some for to make-uh my heart rejoice.
Don't you hear lambs a-crying?
O good Shepherd, feedin' my sheep.

OH! DEATH

What is this that I can see,
Cold icy hands taking hold of me,
For Death has come, you all can
see.
Hell gate is open wide for me.

Oh! Death, Oh! Death,
Can't you spare me
Over for another year!

I'll lock your jaws till you can't
talk,
I'll bind your legs till you can't
walk,
I'll close your eyes so you can't see
I'll bring you unto me.

Oh! Death, Oh! Death,
Can't you spare me
Over for another year!

"Oh! Death" was collected by the Federal Music Project, Works Progress Administration
(WPA), Floyd County, Kentucky, ca. 1937. Edith F. James, Supervisor for Floyd County.
Ms., with music, in the Archive of Folk Song, Library of Congress.

DARK WAS THE NIGHT

The sweat like drops of blood run down,
In agony He prayed,
In agony He prayed.

I heard my blessed Savior say,
"Come unto me and rest,
Come unto me and rest."

He bid me come to Him and rest,
My head upon His breast,
My head upon His breast.

"Dark was the Night" was collected by Frank C. Brown from the singing of Miss Jennie Belvin, Durham, North Carolina, ca. 1921. From *The Frank C. Brown Collection of North Carolina Folklore* (Duke University Press) Durham, 1952, III, 585.

Carols and Christmas Pieces

Joseph were a young man, a young man were he,
And he courted Virgin Mary, the Queen of Galilee,
And he courted Virgin Mary, the Queen of Galilee.

THE CHERRY-TREE CAROL

The source of the Cherry-Tree Carol is found in the Pseudo-Matthew gospel, which is briefly summarized by Professor Child:

On the third day of the flight into Egypt, Mary, feeling the heat to be oppressive, tells Joseph that she will rest for a while under the palm-tree. Joseph helps her light from her beast, and Mary, looking up from under the tree and seeing it full of fruit, asks for some. Joseph somewhat testily expresses his surprise that she should think of such a thing, considering the height of the tree: he is much more concerned to get a supply of water. Then Jesus, sitting on his mother's lap, bids the palm to bow down and refresh his mother with its fruit. The palm instantly bends its top to Mary's feet.

In folk passage, the palm becomes the cherry tree, and the Child speaks from Mary's womb or the Lord speaks down from Heaven.

I

When Joseph was an old man,
  An old man was he,
He married Virgin Mary,
  The Queen of Galilee.

As Joseph and Mary
  Were walking one day:
"Here are apples, here are cherries
  Enough to behold."

Version 1 of "The Cherry-Tree Carol" was collected by Josephine McGill and printed in *JAF*, 29 (1916):293–294: "This beautiful carol was found by the present writer in the mountain region of Kentucky near Hindman, Knott County." Child ballad no. 54. Coffin, 60. Bronson, II, 3.

Then Mary spoke to Joseph
  So meek and so mild:
"Joseph, gather me some cherries,
  For I am with child."

Then Joseph flew in anger,
  In anger flew he:
"Let the father of the baby
  Gather cherries for thee."

Then Jesus spoke a few words,
  A few words spoke he:
"Let my mother have some cherries;
  Bow low down, cherry-tree."

The cherry-tree bowed low down,
  Bowed low down to the ground,
And Mary gathered cherries
  While Joseph stood around.

Then Joseph took Mary
  All on his right knee:
"O, what have I done?
  Lord have mercy on me!"

Then Joseph took Mary all,
  All on his left knee:
"O, tell me, little baby,
  When thy birthday will be."

"On the sixth day of January
  My birthday will be,
When the stars in the elements
  Shall tremble with glee."

II

Joseph were a young man, a young man were he,
And he courted Virgin Mary, the Queen of Galilee,
And he courted Virgin Mary, the Queen of Galilee.

Mary and Joseph were a-walking one day,
"Here is apples and cherries a-plenty to behold,
Here is apples and cherries a-plenty to behold."

Mary spoke to Joseph so meek and so mild,
"Joseph, gather me some cherries, for I am with child,
Joseph, gather me some cherries, for I am with child."

Joseph flew in anger, in anger he flew,
Saying, "Let the father of your baby gather cherries for you,"
Saying, "Let the father of your baby gather cherries for you."

The Lord spoke down from Heaven, these words he did say,

Version II of "The Cherry-Tree Carol" was recorded by Artus M. Moser from the singing of Mrs. Maud Long at Hot Springs, North Carolina, 1946. Library of Congress record LP14.

"Bow you low down, you cherry tree, while Mary gathers some,
Bow you low down, you cherry tree, while Mary gathers some."

The cherry tree bowed down, it was low on the ground,
And Mary gathered cherries while Joseph stood around,
And Mary gathered cherries while Joseph stood around.

Then Joseph took Mary all on his right knee,
"Pray tell me, little baby, when your birthday shall be,
Pray tell me, little baby, when your birthday shall be."

"On the fifth day of January my birthday shall be
When the stars and the elements shall tremble with fear,
When the stars and the elements shall tremble with fear."

Then Joseph took Mary all on his left knee,
Saying, "Lord, have mercy upon me, for what have I done?"
Saying, "Lord, have mercy upon me, for what have I done?"

III

Joseph and Mary walked one day
All in an orchard good.
The trees were full of cherries
As red as any blood.

Mary spoke to Joseph,
Her words were soft and kind:
"Pick me one cherry, husband,
For they do fill my mind."

Then Joseph answered Mary,
His words was most unkind:
"Let your lover pick your cherries;
I care not what's on your mind."

And then the little baby spoke
Unto the cherry bough:
"Bend down your branch to my mother
And give her cherries now."

Then all the cherry tree bowed down
Unto sweet Mary's hand,
And she cried out, "See, Joseph,
I have cherries at my command."

Old Joseph was ashamed
That he had done Mary wrong,
And told her to be cherry*
And not to feel cast down.

* For "cheery." Did the child who sang this song confuse the two words?

Version III of "The Cherry-Tree Carol." H. M. Belden and Arthur Palmer Hudson (eds.), in *The Frank C. Brown Collection of North Carolina Folklore*, II, 61. "Mrs. Dennis H. Sutton secured this from the singing of a little girl in the Miller's Gap school, Madison County. It was near Christmas time, and Mrs. Sutton started to teach the children 'O Little Town of Bethlehem'; whereupon one of them said 'I know a tune about Bethlehem' and proceeded to sing the following."

And all the stones in Bethlehem,
In the streets and in the wall,
Cried out in praise of Mary,
And loud they cried to all.

IV

Joseph was an old man,
An old man was he,
When he married Mary,
The Queen of Galilee.

And they heard while walking
Angel voices sing,
"Lo, this night shall be born
Our Lord and Heavenly King.

Joseph and Mary walked
Through a garden gay,
Where the cherries grew
Upon every tree.

"He neither shall be born
In a house nor a hall,
Nor in Paradise,
But within a stall."

THE TWELVE DAYS OF CHRISTMAS

The Council of Tours in 567 proclaimed a festive season of twelve days linking Christmas on December 25 with the Feast of the Epiphany (or Old Christmas) on January 6. The song dates back to at least the thirteenth century. It is essentially a "forfeit game" song. As each day was cumulatively sung out by a leader, it was repeated by each individual in the group playing the game. When any one individual missed the cumulative totals as the song progressed, he or she was obliged to pay some agreed-upon forfeit.

I

The first day of Christmas my true love sent to me
A parteridge upon a pear tree.

Version IV of "The Cherry-Tree Carol." Mellinger E. Henry, "Still More Ballads and Folksongs from the Southern Highlands," *JAF*, 45 (1932):13. Obtained from Miss Mary Wheeler, Paducah, Kentucky, January, 1931.

"The Twelve Days of Christmas" was contributed by Pamela McArthur Cole to *JAF*, 13 (1900): 229–230: "This rhyme, once in use as a carol, has been very popular in New England where it circulated in numerous variants. This version was obtained from Miss Nichols, Salem, Mass., about 1800." In many sections of New England, the spelling would not be "parteridge," but, rather "paatridge," with a longish and very flat *a*.

A few variants, giving only the final and cumulative last stanza follow.

The second day of Christmas my true love sent to me
Two turtle doves and a parteridge upon a pear tree.

The third day of Christmas my true love sent to me
Three French hens, two turtle doves, and a parteridge upon a pear tree.

The fourth day of Christmas my true love sent to me
Four colly birds, three French hens, two turtle doves, and a parteridge upon
    a pear tree.

The fifth day of Christmas my true love sent to me
Five gold rings, four colly birds, three French hens, two turtle doves, and a
    parteridge upon a pear tree.

The sixth day of Christmas my true love sent to me
Six geese a-laying, five gold rings, four colly birds, three French hens, two
    turtle doves, and a parteridge upon a pear tree.

The seventh day of Christmas my true love sent to me
Seven squabs a-swimming, six geese a-laying, five gold rings, four colly
    birds, three French hens, two turtle doves, and a parteridge upon a pear
    tree.

The eighth day of Christmas my true love sent to me
Eight hounds a-running, seven squabs a-swimming, six geese a-laying, five
    gold rings, four colly birds, three French hens, two turtle doves, and a
    parteridge upon a pear tree.

The ninth day of Christmas my true love sent to me
Nine bears a-beating, eight hounds a-running, seven squabs a-swimming,
    six geese a-laying, five gold rings, four colly birds, three French hens, two
    turtle doves, and a parteridge upon a pear tree.

The tenth day of Christmas my true love sent to me
Ten cocks a-crowing, nine bears a-beating, eight hounds a-running, seven
    squabs a-swimming, six geese a-laying, five gold rings, four colly birds,
    three French hens, two turtle doves, and a parteridge upon a pear tree.

The eleventh day of Christmas my true love sent to me
Eleven lords a-leaping, ten cocks a-crowing, nine bears a-beating, eight
    hounds a-running, seven squabs a-swimming, six geese a-laying, five gold
    rings, four colly birds, three French hens, two turtle doves, and a parte-
    ridge upon a pear tree.

HOLIDAY

PRESENTS

Entered according to act of congress in the year 1871 by Kimmel & Voigt in the office of the librarian at Washington D.C.

The twelfth day of Christmas my true love sent to me
Twelve ladies a-dancing, eleven lords a-leaping, ten cocks a-crowing, nine
bears a-beating, eight hounds a-running, seven squabs a-swimming, six
geese a-laying, five gold rings, four colly birds, three French hens, two
turtle doves, and a parteridge upon a pear tree.

II

The twelfth day of Christmas my true-love sent to me twelve bulls a-roaring,
eleven lords a-leaping, ten hounds a-hunting, nine hares a-running, eight
maids a-dancing, seven swans a-swimming, six geese a-laying, five gold
rings, four colored birds, three French hens, two turtle doves, a partridge
on a pear-tree.

III

The twelfth day of Christmas my love sent to me twelve lords a-leaping,
eleven maids a-milking, ten cows and calves, nine oxen lowing, eight
hares a-running, seven swans a-swimming, six geese a-laying, five gold
rings, four collie birds, three French hens, two turtle doves, and a
partridge in a pear tree.

IV

The twelfth day of Christmas my true love sent to me twelve bells a-ringing,
eleven lords a-leading, ten ladies dancing, nine lambs a-bleating, eight
[forgotten by the singer], seven swans a-swimming, six geese a-laying,
five gold rings, four colly birds, three turtle doves, two French hens, and
some part of a juniper tree.

Version II of "The Twelve Days of Christmas" was recorded by Alton C. Morris from the singing of Mrs. Susie Morrison at Gainesville, Florida, April, 1937. Library of Congress AFS record 989 A1.

Version III of "The Twelve Days of Christmas" was contributed by Mrs. L. L. McDowell to *TFSB*, 11 (1946): 2–3: "My grandfather used to say this for me when I was very small. . . ."

Version IV of "The Twelve Days of Christmas" was collected by George Lyman Kittredge, December 30, 1877, from Mrs. Sarah G. Lewis of Barnstable, Mass. (born in Boston, 1799). Mrs. Lewis learned the song when a young girl from her grandmother, Mrs. Sarah Gorham. See G. L. Kittredge, "Ballads and Songs," *JAF*, 30 (1917): 365–367.

V

On the twelfth day of Christmas my true love sent to me twelve knights
a-riding, eleven hounds a-howling, ten bells a-beating, nine lords a-leaping, eight ladies dancing, seven swans a-swimming, six geese a-laying,
five gold rings, four American hens, three collie birds, two turtle-doves,
and a partridge upon a fair tree.

VI

The twelfth day of Christmas my love she sent to me twelve bulls a-beller-
ing, eleven lords a-limping, ten ladies dancing, nine wolves a-howling,
eight deers a-running, seven swans a-swimming, six geese a-laying, five
gold rings, four collie birds, three French hens, two turtle doves, and a
partridge upon a pear tree.

VII

The twelfth day of Christmas my true love sent to me
Twelve lords a-reaping,
Eleven golden pippins,
Ten fiddlers playing,
Nine ladies dancing,
Eight hounds a-running,
Seven swans a-swimming,
Six geese a-flying,
Five gold rings,
Four college birds,
Three French hens,
Two turtle doves, and a part of a juniper tree.

Version V of "The Twelve Days of Christmas" was collected ca. 1912 from "Mrs. Uriah
Holt, Andover, Mass., 95 years old," and reported in the Kittredge article cited above.
Mrs. Holt is having no nonsense with any *French* hens!

Version VI of "The Twelve Days of Christmas" was communicated to the Missouri Folk-
Lore Society in 1904 by W. S. Johnson as sung by an acquaintance of his, Mrs. M———,
in Tuscumbia, Miller County, Missouri. In H. M. Belden, *Ballads and Songs Collected by
the Missouri Folk-Lore Society*, Columbia (reprint, 1966), pp. 512–513.

Version VII of "The Twelve Days of Christmas" is from a little collection of twelve songs,
"Family Songs, compiled by Rosa S. Allen. As sung by the Allens at the Homestead, Castle
Hill, Medfield, Massachusetts, 1899." Cited by Phillips Barry in "Some Traditional Songs,"
JAF, 18 (1905):56–59.

UPON A CHRISTMAS MORNING

The tune for this is, of course, from the traditional English children's game, "Here we go 'round the mulberry bush." Elizabeth Poston (*The Second Penguin Book of Christmas Carols*, 1970, p. 29) reports that its "earliest version is in Forbes' *Cantus* (Aberdeen, 1666), while an American version is in Marcus Lafayette Swan's *The New Harp of Columbia*, 1867." Our two versions are from oral tradition, as indicated.

I

Two little ships were sailing by,
Were sailing by, were sailing by,
Two little ships were sailing by,
Upon a Christmas morning.

Guess who was in one of them,
One of them, one of them,
Guess who was in one of them
Upon a Christmas morning.

The blessed Virgin and her son,
And her son, and her son,
The blessed Virgin and her son
Upon a Christmas morning.

Guess who was in the other of
them,
Other of them, other of them,
Guess who was in the other of them
Upon a Christmas morning.

George Washington and his son,
And his son, and his son,
George Washington and his son
Upon a Christmas morning.

I wash my face in a golden vase,
A golden vase, a golden vase,
I wash my face in a golden vase
Upon a Christmas morning.

I wipe my face on a lily-white towel,
A lily-white towel, a lily-white
towel,
I wipe my face on a lily-white towel
Upon a Christmas morning.

I comb my hair with an ivory comb,
An ivory comb, an ivory comb,
I comb my hair with an ivory comb
Upon a Christmas morning.

Version 1 of "Upon a Christmas Morning." W. W. Newell, "Old English Songs in American Versions," *JAF*, 5 (1892):326, who says that it was sung "a few years ago by Catholic children in the streets of New York." I have taken the liberty of reordering the stanzas. The last three come first in Newell's account.

II

As I sat on a sunny bank,
As I sat on a sunny bank,
As I sat on a sunny bank,
On Christmas Day in the morning.

I saw three ships come sailing by,
I saw three ships come sailing by,
I saw three ships come sailing by,
On Christmas Day in the morning.

And who do you think was in those three ships,
And who do you think was in those three ships,
And who do you think was in those three ships,
But Joseph and his fair lady.

Then he did whistle and she did
    sing,
Then he did whistle and she did
    sing,
Then he did whistle and she did
    sing,
On Christmas Day in the morning.

And all the angels in heaven did
    sing,
And all the angels in heaven did
    sing,
And all the angels in heaven did
    sing,
On Christmas Day in the morning.

And all the bells on earth did ring,
And all the bells on earth did ring,
And all the bells on earth did ring,
On Christmas Day in the morning.

For joy that Christ is born our
    King,
For joy that Christ is born our
    King,
For joy that Christ is born our
    King,
On Christmas Day in the morning.

MARY AND THE BABY, SWEET LAMB

Oh, Mary and the Baby, sweet Lamb,
Oh, Mary and the Baby, sweet Lamb,
Oh, Mary and the Baby, sweet Lamb,
Oh, Mary and the Baby, sweet Lamb.

Version II of "Upon a Christmas Morning" is from the University of Virginia Manuscript Collection of Folk Music. Collected by Winston Wilkinson from Arthur Morris, Charlottesville, Virginia, 1936.

"Mary and the Baby, Sweet Lamb" was recorded by John A. Lomax from the singing of Ella Mitchell and Velma Wright at Lubbock, Texas, January 1937. Library of Congress AFS record 913 B2.

It's a holy Baby, sweet Lamb,
It's a holy Baby, sweet Lamb,
It's a holy Baby, sweet Lamb,
Oh, Mary and the Baby, sweet Lamb.

I love that Baby, sweet Lamb,
I love that Baby, sweet Lamb,
I love that Baby, sweet Lamb,
Oh, Mary and the Baby, sweet Lamb.

Oh, Mary and the Baby, sweet Lamb
Oh, Mary and the Baby, sweet Lamb
Oh, Mary and the Baby, sweet Lamb
Oh, Mary and the Baby, sweet Lamb.

It's a God-sent Baby, sweet Lamb,
It's a God-sent Baby, sweet Lamb,
It's a God-sent Baby, sweet Lamb,
Oh, Mary and the Baby, sweet Lamb.

Oh, Mary and the Baby, sweet Lamb,
Oh, Mary and the Baby, sweet Lamb,
Oh, Mary and the Baby, sweet Lamb,
Oh, Mary and the Baby, sweet Lamb.

THE LITTLE CRADLE ROCKS TONIGHT IN GLORY

The first line of the last stanza has been incorrectly transcribed by Elizabeth
Poston (*The Second Penguin Book of Christmas Carols*), who would seem
to have had it from Ruth Crawford Seeger (*The Book of Christmas Carols*,
New York, 1953). The "he" is Gullah for "his," and *not* "the," as both have
it. "Don't you hear the foot on the treetop" is weak as over against "Don't
you hear His foot on the treetop." The song is clearly Gullah Negro.

The little cradle rocks tonight in glory,
In glory, in glory,

"The Little Cradle Rocks Tonight in Glory." Emma M. Backus, "Christmas Carols from
Georgia," *JAF*, 12 (1899):272. Rather than perpetuating the presumed "negro" spelling
("De leetle cradle rocks tonight in glory. . . ." and "Don' yo' hear he foot on de tree-
top. . . .," I have "corrected" the spelling to give the poem its place in this collection.

The little cradle rocks tonight in glory,
The Christ child born in glory.

Peace on earth, Mary rock the cradle,
Mary rock the cradle, Mary rock the cradle,
Peace on earth, Mary rock the cradle,
The Christ child born of glory.

The Christ child passing, singing softly,
Singing softly, singing softly,
The Christ child passing, singing softly,
The Christ child born in glory.

Don't you hear His foot on the treetop,
Foot on the treetop, foot on the treetop,
Don't you hear His foot on the treetop,
Soft like the south wind blow?

JESUS BORNED IN BETHLEA

Jesus borned in Bethlea, Jesus borned in Bethlea,
Jesus borned in Bethlea, and in the manger lay.
And in the manger lay, and in the manger lay,
Jesus borned in Bethlea, and in the manger lay.

THE JOYS OF MARY

The very first joy that Mary had
It was the joy of one
To see her own son Jesus
To suck her breast bone.

    To suck her breast bone, good man,
    And blessed shall he be

"Jesus Borned in Bethlea" was recorded by Sidney Robertson Cowell from the singing of S. F. Russell, Marion, Virginia, 1936. Library of Congress AFS record 3160 A1.

Edith Cutting, "The Joys of Mary," *NYFQ* (1947):323–324. Secured from relatives. The last stanza was lacking and is supplied from tradition.

> Through Father, Son, and Holy Ghost
> And Christ Eternity.*

The very next joy that Mary had
It was the joy of two
To see her own son Jesus
To make the lame to go.

> To make the lame to go, good man,
> And blessed shall he be
> Through Father, Son, and Holy Ghost
> And Christ Eternity.

The very next joy that Mary had
It was the joy of three
To see her own son Jesus
To make the blind to see.

The very next joy that Mary had
It was the joy of four
To see her own son Jesus
To open the prison door.

The very next joy that Mary had
It was the joy of five
To see her own son Jesus
To bring the dead alive.

The very next joy that Mary had
It was the joy of six
To see her own son Jesus
To bear the crucifix.

The very next joy that Mary had
It was the joy of seven
To see her own son Jesus
To open wide the gates of Heaven.

The very next joy that Mary had
It was the joy of eight
To see her own son Jesus
To make the crooked straight.

* This should probably read "eternally."

The very next joy that Mary had
It was the joy of nine
To see her own son Jesus
Turn water into wine.

The very next joy that Mary had
It was the joy of ten
To see her own son Jesus
To feed ten thousand men.

The very next joy that Mary had
It was the joy of eleven
To see her own son Jesus
Ascending up to Heaven.

Ascending up to Heaven, good man,
And blessed shall he be
Through Father, Son, and Holy Ghost
And Christ Eternity.

[The very next joy that Mary had
It was the joy of twelve
To see her own son Jesus
Shut close the gates of hell.
Shut close the gates of hell, good man,
And blessed shall he be
Through Father, Son, and Holy Ghost
And Christ Eternity.]

CAROL OF THE NUMBERS

I'll sing you a one-O
Green grow the rushes-O
What is your one-O?
Green grow the rushes-O

"Carol of the Numbers" was recorded by Duncan Emrich from the singing of Eugenia and Charles Anderson of Ruxton, Maryland, at Washington, D.C., 1947. Library of Congress AFS record 8934 B3.

For one is one and stands alone
And ever more shall be-O.

I'll sing you a two-O
   Green grow the rushes-O
What is your two-O
   Green grow the rushes-O
Two, two, the lily-white boys
Clothed all in green-O,
For one is one and stands alone
And ever more shall be-O.

I'll sing you three-O
   Green grow the rushes-O
What is your three-O?
   Green grow the rushes-O
Three, three, the rivals,
Two, two, the lily-white boys
Clothed all in green-O,
For one is one and stands alone
And ever more shall be-O.

Four for the Gospel makers

Five for the cymbals at your door

Six for the six proud walkers

Seven for the seven stars in the sky

Eight for the April rainers

Nine for the nine bright shiners

Ten for the Ten Commandments

Eleven for the 'leven that went to heaven

Twelve for the twelve Apostles

I'll sing you twelve-O
   Green grow the rushes-O
What is your twelve-O?
   Green grow the rushes-O
Twelve for the twelve Apostles

Eleven for the 'leven that went to heaven
Ten for the Ten Commandments
Nine for the nine bright shiners
Eight for the April rainers
Seven for the seven stars in the sky
Six for the six proud walkers
Five for the cymbals at your door
Four for the Gospel makers
Three, three, the rivals
Two, two, the lily-white boys
Clothed all in green-O,
For one is one and stands alone
And ever more shall be-O.

WARS
AND OTHER
DISASTERS

The Wars and Historical Pieces

The Assassination of Presidents

Disasters

The Wars
and Historical Pieces

Come all you loyal Unionists, wherever you may be,
I hope you'll pay attention and listen unto me,
For well you know the blood and woe, the misery and toil
It took to down Secession on Virginia's bloody soil!

MONTCALM AND WOLFE

One of the decisive battles of the world was fought at Quebec in 1759
where the destiny of the North American continent was at stake. The
British under the command of General James Wolfe drew up their forces
on the Plains of Abraham, where the battle with the French under General
Louis Montcalm was waged. There are deep undertones of personal sentiment in the ballad, for Wolfe and Montcalm had been close friends. Also,
Wolfe was a young man of thirty-two, recently betrothed in England,
where he was never to return.

> Bad news has come to town, bad news is carried,
> Some says my love is dead, some says he's married.
> As I was a-pondering on this, I took to weeping,
> They stole my love away whilst I was sleeping.
>
> "Love, here's a ring of gold, long years I've kept it,
> Madame, it's for your sake, will you accept it?
> When you the posy read, pray think on the giver,
> Madame, remember me, for I'm undone forever."
>
> Then away went this brave youth, and embarked on the ocean,
> To free Americay was his intention;
> He landed in Quebec with all his party,
> The city to attack, being brave and hearty.

"Montcalm and Wolfe" was collected by Anne and Frank Warner from the singing of
"Yankee" John Galusha, Minerva, New York, 1939. Sung by Frank Warner in his
Disc Album "Hudson Valley Songs."

He drew his army up in lines so pretty
On the Plains of Abraham, back of the city,
At a distance from the town where the French would meet him
In double numbers who resolved to beat him.

Montcalm and this brave youth together walked,
Between two armies they like brothers talked,
Till each one took his post and did retire,
It was then these numerous hosts commenced their fire.

Little did he think death was so near him,
Oh, little did he think death was so near him,
When shot down from his horse was this our hero,
We'll long lament his loss in tears of sorrow.

He raisèd up his head where the cannon did rattle,
And to his aide he said, "How goes the battle?"
His aide-de-camp replied, "It's ended in our favor."
Then says this brave youth, "I quit this earth with pleasure."

THE DYING SERGEANT

There can be little question that this song was a contemporary piece probably written, as the text makes clear, on or about December 17, 1776. Mrs. Betsey Gray, who came to Vermont by ox team in 1793, used to sing "The Dying Sergeant" and it has come down traditionally in her family from that time.

Come all you heroes, where'er you be,
That walk by land or sail by sea,
Come hear the words of a dying man
And surely you'll remember them.

In '76, that fatal year,
As by our signal doth appear,
Our fleet set sail for America,
'Twas on the fourteenth day of May.

"The Dying Sergeant" was collected by Helen Hartness Flanders from the singing of Mrs. Ellen Nye Lawrence, Montpelier, Vermont, 1931. In Helen Hartness Flanders, *The New Green Mountain Songster* (Yale) New Haven, 1939, p. 118. With music.

'Twas a dark and dismal time
Our fleet set sail for the northern line,
Where drums did beat and the trumpet sound
And into Boston we are bound.

And when to Boston we did come
We thought the noise of the British drum
Would drive the rebels from that place
And fill their hearts with sore distress.

But to our woeful, sad surprise,
We saw them like grasshoppers rise,
To fight like heroes much in rage,
Which sorely frightened General Gage.

Like lions roaring for their prey,
They fear no danger, no, not they;
True British blood runs in their veins
While them with courage it sustains.

We sailed to York, as you've been told,
With the loss of many a Briton bold,
And there we many a traitor found,
False to the land where he belonged.

They told us 'twas a garden place
And that our armies might with ease
Burn down their towns, lay waste their lands,
In spite of all their boasting bands.

A garden place it was indeed,
And in it grew many a bitter weed,
Which did pull down our brightest hopes
And sorely wounded our British troops.

'Tis now December, the seventeenth day.
Since we set sail for America,
Full fifteen thousand have been slain —
Bold British heroes on the plain.

Now I've received my mortal wound.
Adieu unto old English ground.
My wife and children they'll mourn for me
While I lie in cold America.

Fight on, fight on, American boy,
But ne'er heed bold Britain's thundering noise.
Maintain your rights, years after year.
God's on your side, you need not fear.

The glory of Great Britain's soil
Is now eclipsed for a while,
But it shall shine bright in meridian year
Although our king is most severe.

His crown shall fade most certainly,
A reward for all his cruelty;
America shall her rights maintain
While proud, cold England sinks with shame.

THE STATELY SOUTHERNER

With the outbreak of war, John Paul Jones, a Scotch sailor who had settled
in Virginia, offered his services to the Continental Congress. His knowledge
of English waters made him invaluable, and in 1778 he was sent to cruise
among the British Isles with the eighteen-gun *Ranger*. He cruised in the
Irish Channel, set fire to shipping in harbors, captured merchantmen, and
defeated the twenty-gun sloop *Drake*. The sailing feat recounted in this
ballad is also dramatically told by James Fenimore Cooper in *The Pilot*.
How the *Ranger* became the *Stately Southerner* of this song can be ac-
counted for only through oral tradition.

It was the *Stately Southerner*, that carried the Stripes and Stars,
The whistling wind from west-nor'west blew through her pitch-pine spars,
With her starboard tacks aboard, my boys, she hung up to the gale,
'Twas an autumn night, we raised the light on the Old Head of Kinsale.

It was a clear and cloudless night; the wind blew steady and strong,
As gaily over the sparkling deep our good ship bowled along.
With the fiery foam beneath her bows the white waves she did spread,
And bending alow her bosom in snow, she buried her lee cathead.

"The Stately Southerner" is from Joanna C. Colcord, *Songs of American Sailormen*,
New York, 1938, p. 126. With music. Laws, A3.

There was no talk of short'ning sail by him who walked the poop,
And 'neath the press of her ponderous jib the boom bent like a hoop;
And the groaning waterways told the strain that held her stout main-tack,
But he only laughed as he gazed beaft at the white and glist'ning track.

The mid-tide meets in the channel waves that flow from shore to shore,
And the mist hung heavy along the land from Featherstone to Dunmore,
And that sterling light on Tuskar Rock, where the old bell tolls each hour,
And the beacon light that shone so bright was quenched on Waterford
tower.

What looms upon our starboard bow, what hangs upon the breeze?
'Tis time our good ship hauled her wind abreast the old Saltees,
For by her ponderous press of sail and by her stunted spars
We saw that our morning visitor was a British man-o'-war.

Up spake our noble Captain then as a shot ahead of us passed:
"Haul snug your flowing courses! Lay your topsails to the mast!"
Those Englishmen gave three loud hurrahs from the deck of their covered
ark,
And we answered back by a solid broadside from the deck of our patriot
bark.

"Out booms! Out booms!" our skipper cried: "Out booms and give her
sheet!"
For the swiftest keel that ever was launched in all of the British fleet
Came pondering down upon us with the white foam at her bow;
"Out booms! Out booms! and give her sheet! spare not your canvas now!"

But a swifter keel was 'neath our feet, nor did our seaboys dread
When the Star-Spangled Banner was hoisted, to the mizzen peak was
spread;
And amid a thundering shower of shot with stunsails hoisting away,
Down the North Channel Paul Jones did steer just at the break of day.

PAUL JONES'S VICTORY

On September 23, 1779, Paul Jones encountered a fleet of forty ships off
Flamborough Head. They were merchantmen bound for England under the

"Paul Jones's Victory" is from D. P. Horton, *Naval Songs*, New York, 1889, II, 126.
With music. Laws, A4.

convoy of the forty-four-gun *Serapis*, Captain Richard Pearson, and the twenty-gun *Countess of Scarborough*. Jones ordered his ships to form in battle line, but only the *Pallas* obeyed, attacking the *Countess of Scarborough*. Jones's forty-two-gun *Bonhomme Richard* engaged the *Serapis* single-handed. Jones, with his ship on fire and near to sinking, was asked to surrender. He replied with the classic, "I have just begun to fight!" and finally forced Pearson to strike his colors. During the encounter the French ally, the *Alliance*, unaccountably poured several broadsides into the *Richard*, killing many of the crew. For his defense of the convoy, Captain Pearson was knighted by the king. When Paul Jones heard of this, he remarked, "Should I fall in with him again, I'll make a lord of him."

An American frigate, a frigate of fame,
With guns mounting forty, the *Richard* by name,
Sailed to cruise in the channels of old England,
With a valiant commander, Paul Jones was his name.

    Hurrah! Hurrah! Our country forever, Hurrah!

We had not cruised long before he espies
A large forty-four and a twenty likewise,
Well manned with bold seamen, well laid in with stores,
In consort to drive us from old England's shores.

About twelve at noon Pearson came alongside,
With a loud speaking trumpet, "Whence came you?" he cried.

"Return me an answer, I hailed you before,
Or if you do not, a broadside I'll pour."

Paul Jones then said to his men every one,
"Let every true seaman stand firm to his gun!
We'll receive a broadside from this bold Englishman,
And like true Yankee sailors, return it again."

The contest was bloody, both decks ran with gore,
And the sea seemed to blaze, while the cannon did roar,
"Fight on, my brave boys," then Paul Jones he cried,
"And soon we will humble this bold Englishman's pride.

"Stand firm to your quarters, your duty don't shun,
The first one that shrinks, through the body I'll run,
Though their force is superior, yet they shall know
What true, brave American seamen can do."

The battle rolled on, till bold Pearson cried,
"Have you yet struck your colors? then come alongside!"
But so far from thinking that the battle was won,
Brave Paul Jones replied, "I've not yet begun!"

We fought them eight glasses, eight glasses so hot,
Till seventy bold seamen lay dead on the spot;
And ninety brave seamen lay stretched in their gore,
While the pieces of cannon most fiercely did roar.

Our gunner in great fright to Captain Jones came,
"We gain water quite fast and our side's in a flame."
Then Paul Jones said in the height of his pride,
"If we cannot do better, boys, sink alongside!"

The *Alliance* bore down and the *Richard* did rake,
Which caused the bold hearts of our seamen to ache;
Our shot flew so hot that they could not stand us long,
And the undaunted Union-of-Britain came down.

To us they did strike and their colors hauled down;
The fame of Paul Jones to the world shall be known,
His fame shall rank with the gallant and brave,
Who fought like a hero our freedom to save.

Now all valiant seamen where'er you may be,

Who hear of this combat that's fought on the sea,
May you also do like them, when called to do the same,
And your names be enrolled on the pages of fame.

Your country will boast of her sons that are brave,
And to you she will look from all dangers to save,
She'll call you dear sons, in her annals you'll shine,
And the brows of the brave shall green laurels entwine.

So now, my brave boys, have we taken a prize,
A large forty-four and a twenty likewise!
Then God bless the mother whose doom is to weep
The loss of her sons in the ocean so deep.

Hurrah! Hurrah! Our country forever, Hurrah!

YANKEE DOODLE

Father and I went down to camp
Along with Captain Goodwin,
And there we saw the men and boys
As thick as hasty pudding.

  Yankee Doodle, keep it up,
  Yankee Doodle dandy!
  Mind the music and the steps,
  And with the girls be handy!

There was Captain Washington
Upon a slapping stallion,
Giving orders to his men,
I guess there was a million.

And there they had a swamping gun
As big as a log of maple,
On a deuced little cart,
A load for father's cattle.

And every time they fired it off,
It took a horn of powder;
It made a noise like father's gun,
Only a nation louder.

And there I saw a little keg,
Its heads were made of leather —
They knocked upon it with little sticks
To call the folks together.

The troopers, too, would gallop up
And fire right in our faces,
It scared me almost half to death
To see them run such races.

But I can't tell you half I saw,
They kept up such a smother,
So I took off my hat, made a bow,
And scampered home to mother.

  Yankee Doodle, keep it up,
  Yankee Doodle dandy!
  Mind the music and the steps,
  And with the girls be handy!

"Yankee Doodle" is traditional and is from childhood memory in Framingham, Massachusetts.

And among the hundreds of other stanzas:

Yankee Doodle went to town
A-riding on a pony,
He stuck a feather in his hat
And called it macaroni!

Yankee Doodle went to town,
He bought a bag of peaches,
He rode so fast a-coming back,
He smashed them all to pieces!

Yankee Doodle, find a girl,
Yankee Doodle dandy,
Take her to the fair today
And buy a box of candy!

MAJOR ANDRÉ
(*Arnold's Treason*)

Benedict Arnold, who felt that he had been unjustly treated by Congress, determined to revenge himself by betraying the fortress of West Point, commanding the Hudson, to the British. Major John André was sent by the British commander in New York City to confer with the traitor. As André was returning to New York from his mission, he was stopped and searched by three militiamen, among them John Paulding. He was found to be a spy, and was tried and executed at Tappan, New York, on October 2, 1780. As the last stanza indicates, public sympathy strongly favored Major André and ran high against Arnold, who made his escape to the British lines.

Come all you gallant heroes, I'd have you lend an ear,
I'll sing you a small ditty that will your spirits cheer,
Concerning a young gentleman whose age were twenty-two,
And he fought for North Americay with a heart both just and true.

The English they did taken him and kept him close confined,
They put him into prison and kept him for some time;
By his being bold and valiant, resolved not there to stay,
He set himself at liberty and so he come away.

"Major André" is from the *New American Songster*, 1817, and cited with a parallel orally collected text by Herbert Halpert in "Ballads and Folksongs from New Jersey," *JAF*, 52 (1939):62. With music for the partial collected text.

The Unfortunate DEATH of MAJOR ANDRE

(Adjutant General to the English Army) at Head Quarters in New York, Oct.ʳ 2. 1780, who was found within the American Lines in the character of a Spy.

Hamilton delin.   Goldar sculp.

'Twas of the scouting party which rode from Tarrytown,
A-meeting this young officer, a man of high renown.
"I think by your experience, sir, you are the British force,
I'll trust to you to tell to me the dangers are all o'er."

Then up steps John Paulding, which was this young man's name,
"Come tell to me your business, sir, and when from hence you came,
Or I'll have you welled searched, sir, before you do pass by."
By strict examination found him to be a spy.

When he found his projects would soon be brought to light,
He asked for ink and paper, and liberty to write.
A line to traitor Arnold to let him know his fate.
He begged on his desistance, alas it was too late.

When traitor Arnold read those lines it put him in a fright,
He called for men and bargey, and sailed for New York straight;
And now he goes a-'cruiting and fighting for a King.
He left poor Major André on the gallows for to swing.

On the day of execution he looked both meek and mild,
He looked on his spectators and gave a pleasant smile,
Which filled each mind with horror and caused each heart to bleed.
Every man wished André clear, and Arnold in his stead.

COLUMBIA

Thus down a lone valley with cedars o'erspread,
From the noise of the town I pensively stray'd,
The bloom from the face of fair heaven retired,
The wind ceased to murmur, the thunders expired.
Perfumes as of Eden flow'd sweetly along,
And a voice as of angels enchantlingly sung:
"Columbia, Columbia, to glory arise,
The queen of the world and the child of the skies."

"Columbia" was collected by Emma M. Backus and reported in her "Early Songs from North Carolina," *JAF*, 14(1901):293–294. See the headnote to "The Mouldering Vine," where she says that the "songs have been taken by me from the lips of elderly reciters, who have given them as current and popular in Central North Carolina in the days of their youth, about the first quarter of the nineteenth century." See a close variant with six stanzas in *The Social Harp*, 1855, p. 63.

To conquest and slaughter let Europe aspire,
Whelm nations in blood or wrap cities in fire,
Thy heroes the rights of mankind shall defend,
And triumph pursue them and glory attend.
A world in thy realm; for a world be thy laws,
Enlarged as thy empire and just as thy cause,
On freedom's broad basis that empire shall rise,
Extend with the main and dissolve with the skies.

Fair science her gate to thy sons shall unbar,
And the east see thy morn hide the beams of her star,
New bards and new sages unrivaled shall soar,
To frame unextinguished when time is no more.
To the last refuge of virtue design'd,
Shall fly from all nations the best of mankind,
There grateful to Heaven with transport shall bring,
Their incense more fragrant than odors of spring.

Thy fleets to all nations thy power shall display,
The nations admire and the oceans obey,
Each shore to thy glory its tribute unfold,
And the east and the south yield their spices and gold.
As the dayspring unbounded thy splendors shall flow.
And earth's little kingdom before thee shall bow,
While the ensigns of union in triumph unfurl'd
Hush anarchy's sway, and give peace to the world.

JOLLY SOLDIER

I once was a seaman stout and bold,
Ofttimes I've ploughed the ocean;
I've ploughed it all o'er and o'er again,
For honor and promotion.

Aboard a man-of-war and merchantman,
Many be the battles that I've been in;
It was all for the honor of George Washington,
And I'll still be the jolly, jolly soldier.

"Jolly Soldier." *The Social Harp*, 1855, p. 194.

432

MOUNT VERNON

What solemn sound the ear invades,
What wraps the land in sorrow's shade?
From heaven the awful mandate flies,
The Father of his country dies.

Where shall our country turn its eye,
What help remains beneath the sky?
Our friend, protector, strength, and trust,
Lies low and mould'ring in the dust.

YE PARLIAMENT OF ENGLAND

Ye Parliament of England, ye Lords and Commons, too,
Consider well what you're about, what you're about to do,
For you're to war with Yankees, and I'm sure you'll rue the day
You roused the Sons of Liberty in North Americay!

You first confined our commerce, and said our ships shan't trade,
You next impressed our seamen and used them as your slaves;
You then insulted Rodgers, while ploughing o'er the main,
And had we not declared war, you'd have done it o'er again.

You thought our frigates were but few and Yankees could not fight,
Until brave *Hull* your *Guerrière* took, and banished her from your sight.
The *Wasp* then took your *Frolic*, we'll nothing say to that,
The *Poictiers* being of the line, of course she took her back.

The next, your *Macedonian*, no finer ship could swim,
Decatur took her giltwork off, and then he sent her in.
The *Java* by a Yankee ship was sunk, you all must know;
The *Peacock* fine, in all her plume, by Lawrence down did go.

"Mount Vernon." *The Social Harp*, 1855, p. 172.

"Ye Parliament of England" is from Joanna C. Colcord, *Songs of American Sailormen*, New York, 1938, p. 128. With music. A patriotic review of naval engagements during the War of 1812.

Then, next you sent your *Boxer* to box us all about,
But we had an *Enterprising* brig that boxed your *Boxer* out;
She boxed her up to Portland, and moored her off the town,
To show the sons of liberty the *Boxer* of renown.

The next upon Lake Erie, where Perry had some fun,
You own he beat your naval force, and caused them for to run;
This was to you a sore defeat, the like ne'er known before:
Your British squadron beat complete, some took, some run ashore.

There's Rodgers, in the *President*, will burn, sink, and destroy;
The *Congress*, on the Brazil coast, your commerce will annoy;
The *Essex*, in the South Seas, will put out all your lights,
The flag she waves at her masthead — "Free Trade and Sailors' Rights!"

THE CONSTITUTION *AND THE* GUERRIÈRE

During the war of 1812, Captain Isaac Hull put out in the *Constitution* from Boston harbor and met the British frigate *Guerrière* off Halifax on August 19. In a battle lasting only twenty-five minutes the forty-four-gun *Constitution* reduced the thirty-eight-gun *Guerrière* to a complete wreck. The ship was totally dismasted and her hull so riddled that she was not thought worth towing into port, and was blown up. On the *Guerrière* 79 of the crew were killed or wounded, while the American losses amounted to seven killed and seven wounded.

It ofttimes has been told, that the British seamen bold
Could flog the tars of France so neat and handy, oh!
But they never found their match, till the Yankees did them catch,
Oh, the Yankee boys for fighting are the dandy, oh!

The *Guerrière*, a frigate bold, on the foaming ocean rolled,
Commanded by proud Dacres the grandee, oh,
With as choice a British crew, as a rammer ever drew,
Could flog the Frenchmen two to one so handy, oh!

"The *Constitution* and the *Guerrière*" is from D. P. Horton, *Naval Songs*, New York, 1889, II, 100. With music. Laws, A6.

When this frigate hove in view, says proud Dacres to his crew,
"Come clear ship for action and be handy, oh!
"To weather gauge, boys, get her," and to make his men fight better,
Gave them to drink, gunpowder mixed with brandy, oh!

Then Dacres loudly cries, "Make this Yankee ship your prize,
You can in thirty minutes, neat and handy, oh!
Twenty-five's enough, I'm sure, and if you'll do it in a score,
I'll treat you to a double share of brandy, oh!"

The British shot flew hot which the Yankees answered not,
Till they got within the distance they called handy, oh!
"Now," says Hull unto his crew, "Boys, let's see what we can do,
If we take this boasting Briton we're the dandy, oh!"

The first broadside we poured carried her mainmast by the board,
Which made this lofty frigate look abandoned, oh!
Then Dacres shook his head and to his officers said.
"Lord! I didn't think those Yankees were so handy, oh!"

Our second told so well that their fore and mizzen fell,
Which dous'd the Royal ensign neat and handy, oh!
"By George!" says he, "we're done," and they fired a lee gun,
While the Yankees struck up Yankee Doodle Dandy, oh!

Then Dacres came on board to deliver up his sword,
Tho' loth was he to part with it, it was so handy, oh!
"Oh! keep your sword," says Hull, "For it only makes you dull,
Cheer up, and let us have a little brandy, oh!"

Now, fill your glasses full and we'll drink to Captain Hull,
And so merrily we'll push about the brandy, oh!
John Bull may toast his fill, but let the world say what they will,
The Yankee boys for fighting are the dandy, oh!

THE BANKS OF CHAMPLAIN

'Twas autumn and 'round me the leaves were descending,
And lonely the woodpecker tapped on a tree,
While thousands their freedom and rights were defending,
The din of their arms sounded dismal to me.
For Sandy, my love, was engaged in the action,
Without him I value this world not a fraction,
His death would have ended my life in distraction
As lonely I strayed on the banks of Champlain.

As I paused to listen to the cannon's loud thunder,
My elbow I leaned on a rock by the shore,
The sound nearly parted my heart-strings asunder,
For I thought I should see my dear Sandy no more.
The cannon had ceased but the drums they were beating,
The foes of our country far northward retreating,
The neighboring damsels each other were greeting
With songs of delight by the banks of Champlain.

Our army triumphant, our squadron victorious!
With laurels unfaded our Spartans returned!
My eyes never looked on a scene half so glorious,
My heart with such rapture before never burned.
For Sandy, my love, was that moment appearing,
A vision to every countenance cheering
Was rendered to me more doubly endearing
By the feat he performed on the banks of Champlain.

"The Banks of Champlain" was recorded by Alan Lomax from the singing of Mrs. Marianna Schaupp, Washington, D.C., 1941. Library of Congress AFS record 6079 A1. This song came to Mrs. Schaupp through her grandfather, Joseph Cummings, who fought with Hull at Detroit in 1813.

JAMES BIRD

This ballad recounts with accuracy James Bird's enlistment, service, and death on charges of desertion following Perry's battle on Lake Erie on September 10, 1813. Bird's letter to his parents referred to in the song was dated November 9, 1814. The ballad, written later in the same year by Charles Miner, was published in his own paper, *The Gleaner*, at Wilkes-Barre, Pennsylvania.

Sons of freedom, listen to me, and ye daughters, too, give ear,
You a sad and mournful story as was ever told shall hear.

Hull, you know, his troops surrendered, and defenseless left the west,
Then our forces quick assembled, the invader to resist.

Among the troops that marched to Erie were the Kingston volunteers,
Captain Thomas, their commander, to protect our west frontiers.

Tender were the scenes of parting, mothers wrung their hands and cried,
Maidens wept their swains in secret, fathers strove their hearts to hide.

But there's one among the number, tall and graceful is his mien,
Firm his step, his look undaunted, scarce a nobler youth is seen.

One sweet kiss he snatched from Mary, craved his mother's prayer once
    more,
Pressed his father's hand, and left them for Lake Erie's distant shore.

Soon they came where noble Perry had assembled all his fleet,
There the gallant Bird enlisted, hoping soon the foe to meet.

Where is Bird? The battle rages. Is he in the strife or no?
Now the cannons roar tremendous, dare he meet the hostile foe?

Aye, behold him, see him, Perry! In the self-same ship they fight.
Though his messmates fall around him, nothing can his soul affright.

Ah, behold, a ball has struck him! See the crimson current flow!
"Leave the deck!" exclaimed brave Perry. "No," cried Bird, "I will not go!"

"James Bird" was collected for the Missouri Folk-Lore Society by Miss Williams, in 1904 as sung by her aunt. Reported, without music, in H. M. Belden, *Ballads and Songs Collected by the Missouri Folk-Lore Society*, Columbia (reprint edition, 1966), pp. 296–297. Laws, A5.

"Here on deck I took my station, ne'er will Bird his colors fly.
I'll stand by you, gallant captain, till we conquer or we die."

Still they fought, though faint and bleeding, till the Stars and Stripes arose,
Victory having crowned our efforts, all triumphant o'er our foes.

And did Bird receive a pension? Was he to his friends restored?
No, he never to his bosom clasped the maid his heart adored.

Soon there came most dismal tidings from Lake Erie's distant shore.
Better, better had Bird perished 'mid the battle's awful roar!

"Read this letter, brothers, sisters; 'tis the last you'll hear from me.
I must suffer for deserting from the brig *Niagara*."

"Dearest parents," said the letter, "this will bring sad news to you.
Do not mourn your first belovèd, though this brings his last adieu."

Lo, he fought so brave at Erie, freely bled and nobly dared!
Let his courage plead for mercy, let his precious life be spared!

See, he kneels upon his coffin. Sure his death can do no good!
Spare him! Hark! Oh, now they've shot him! See, his bosom streams with
   blood!

Farewell, Bird! Farewell forever! Home and friends he'll see no more.
But his mangled corpse lies buried on Lake Erie's distant shore.

THE BATTLE OF NEW ORLEANS

On January 8, 1815, the British forces under General Edward Packenham
attacked the hastily entrenched forces of General Andrew Jackson in an
attempt to capture New Orleans. "The Battle of New Orleans" is a contemporary, realistic piece describing the engagement. Original manuscript
spelling has been retained.

   'Twas on the eighth of January, just at the dawn of day.
      We spied those British officers all dress'd in bat'l array;

"The Battle of New Orleans" was collected by Paul G. Brewster from Martin G. Fowler,
Petersburg, Indiana, 1935. Fowler's grandfather had taken part in the battle and had sung
this song to his children and grandchildren. Reported by Brewster in *SFQ*, 1 (1937):25.
Laws, A7.

Old Jackson then gave orders, "Each man to keep his post,
  And form a line from right to left, and let no time be lost."

With rockets and with bombshells, like comets we let fly;
  Like lions they advanced us, the fate of war to try.
Large streems of firey vengence upon them we let pour
  While meny a brave Commander lay withering in his gore.

Thrice they marched up to the charge, and thrice they gave the ground;
  We fought them full three hours, then bugle horns did sound.
Great heaps of human pyramids lay strewn before our eyes;
  We blew the horns and rang the bells to drown their dying cries.

Come all you British noblemen, and listen unto me;
  Our Frontiersmen has proved to you America is free.
But tell your Royal Master when you return back home
  That out of thirty thousand men but few of you returned.

THE MAID OF MONTEREY

On September 20, 1846, Monterey was invested by American troops under General Zachary Taylor and was surrendered three days later. This song is a kind tribute to the compassion of an "enemy."

The moon was shining brightly upon the battle plain,
The gentle breeze fanned lightly the features of the slain;
Our guns had hushed their thundering, our drums in silence lay,
Then came the *señorita*, the Maid of Monterey.

She cast a look of anguish on dying and on dead,
Her lap she made a pillow for those who groaned and bled,
And when our bugles sounded, just at the break of day,
All blessed the *señorita*, the Maid of Monterey.

She gave the thirsty water, she dressed the bleeding wound,
Her gentle prayer she uttered for those who groaned around,
And when the dying soldier one brief prayer did pray,
He blessed the *señorita*, the Maid of Monterey.

Although she loved her nation, and prayed that it might live,
Yet for the dying foeman she had a tear to give,
Then cheers to that bright beauty, who drove death's pangs away,
The meek-eyed *señorita*, the Maid of Monterey.

THE CUMBERLAND'S *CREW*

The Confederate ironclad *Virginia*, formerly the steam frigate *Merrimac*, engaged the wooden Union sloop *Cumberland* and the frigate *Congress* near

"The Maid of Monterey" was collected by J. Frank Dobie from Mrs. Hal B. Armstrong, Austin, Texas, and reported by Dobie in "More Ballads and Songs of the Frontier Folk," *Foller de Drinkin Gou'd, PTFS*, 8 (1928):163. With music from two other informants.

"The *Cumberland*'s Crew" was collected by Anne and Frank Warner from the singing of Lena Bourne (Grammy) Fish, East Jaffrey, New Hampshire, 1941. From the Warner Collection, with permission. A good variant is on Library of Congress record LP29, sung by Capt. Pearl R. Nye at Akron, Ohio, 1937, and transcribed with music in *Folklore on the American Land* (Little, Brown), 1972. Laws, A18.

Newport News on March 8, 1862. Under merciless raking fire from the *Virginia* and with absolutely no hope of anything but destruction, Lieutenant Morris of the *Cumberland* was asked to surrender. He replied, "Never! We will sink with our colors flying!"

The Cumberland*'s Crew*

O, comrades, come gather and join in my ditty,
It's of a terrible battle which happened of late.
Let each Union tar drop a sad tear of pity
While he thinks on the once gallant *Cumberland*'s fate.
Oh the ninth day of March told a terrible story
And many a brave tar to this world bade adieu;
Our flag it was wrapped in a mantle of glory
By the heroic deeds of the *Cumberland*'s crew.

On that ill-fated day, about ten in the morning,
The sky it was cloudless and bright shone the sun,
When the drum of the *Cumberland* sounded a warning
Which told every seaman to stand by his gun.
Then an iron-clad frigate down on us came bearing,
And high in the air the Rebel flag flew,
The pennant of treason she proudly was wearing
Determined to conquer the *Cumberland*'s crew.

Up steps our bold captain with stern resolution
Says, "Boys, at this monster we'll never be dismayed,
We swore to maintain our beloved Constitution,
To die for our country we are not afraid.
We'd fight for the Union, for our cause it is glorious,
To the Stars and Stripes we will ever prove true,
We'll sink at our quarters or conquer victorious!"
He was answered by cheers of the *Cumberland*'s crew!

Our gallant ship opened, her guns roared like thunder,
Her broadsides like hail on the Rebels did pour.
The people gazed awestruck with terror and wonder
When the shots struck her side and then glanced o'er.

But the pride of our Navy ne'er could be daunted
Though dead and wounded on the decks were strewn;
The flag of our Union it boldly was planted
Sustained by the blood of the *Cumberland*'s crew.

When the traitors found cannon could not avail them
While fighting our heroes, with God on their side,
The power of Secession had no power to quell them
Though blood from the scuppers crimsoned the tide.
She struck her amidships, her planks she did sever,
With sharp iron prow pierced our noble ship through,
But still as she sank in the dark rolling river,
"We'll die at our guns!" cried the *Cumberland*'s crew.

Oh, slowly they sank in Virginia's waters,
Their voices on earth will never be heard more,
They will be wept for by Columbia's sons and daughters,
May their blood be avenged on Virginia's shore.
In that blood-stained grave they are silently lying,
And their souls have forever to this world bid adieu,
Yet the Star-Spangled Banner above them is flying —
It was nailed to the mast by the *Cumberland*'s crew.

O Columbia, the birthright of freedom's communion,
Our flag never floated so proudly before
For the spirit of those who died for the Union
Above its broad folds does exultingly soar.
And wherever in battle our sailors assemble,
God bless our dear banner, the Red, White and Blue.
Beneath its bright stars we'll cause tyrants to tremble
Or die at our guns like the *Cumberland*'s crew.

The Cumberland *and the* Merrimac

Come all my jolly seamen, likewise the landsmen, too,
It is a dreadful story I will unfold to you.

"The *Cumberland* and the *Merrimac*" was collected by Anne and Frank Warner from the singing of "Yankee" John Galusha, Minerva, New York, 1941. From the Warner Collection, with permission. Laws, A26.

It's all about the *Cumberland*, the ship so true and brave,
And it's many's the loyal seamen that met a watery grave.

It was early in the morning, just at the break of day,
When our good ship the *Cumberland* lay anchored in the bay,
When the man from on the look-out down to the rest did say,
"There is something like a house-top, to the larboard she does lay."

Then our captain took his telescope and he gazed far o'er the blue.
Turning 'round he said as follows to his brave and loyal crew:
"That thing you see over yonder just like a turtle's back
Is that cursed Rebel steamer they call the *Merrimac!*"

Then our decks were cleared for action, each gun was pointed true,
But still that Rebel steamer came steaming o'er the blue.
And on she kept a-coming till no distance did us part,
When she sent a ball a-humming that stilled the beat of many's the heart.

In vain we poured our broadsides into her ribs of steel,
But still no breach was in her, no damage did she feel.
Up stepped the Rebel commander, in a voice of thunder spoke:
"Pull down your flying colors or I'll sink your Yankee boat!"

Then our captain's eyes did glisten, his face grew pale with rage,
And in a voice of thunder to the Rebel commander said:
"My crew is brave and loyal and by me they will stand
And before I'll strike my colors you can sink me and be damned!"

Then this ironclad she left us a hundred yards or more;
The screeching and screaming of her balls our wooden sides she tore.
She struck us right amidships, her ram went crashing through,
And the waters they came pouring in on the brave and loyal crew.

"It's you, my loyal comrades, may seek your lives to save,
But I'll not leave the *Cumberland* while she does ride the wave."
They swore that they would not leave her and manned the guns afresh,
And broadside after broadside poured till the waters reached their breast.

And as they down went sinking, down in the briny deep
The Stars and Stripes still floated from the maintop's highest peak!

Maggie Mac

'Twas on a Monday morning, just at the break of day,
I spied a lofty steamship to an anchor in the Bay,
When a man from our masthead, our topmast so high,
"There's something up to windward like a housetop I espy."

    And we'll hoist up our flag and long may it wave
    Over the Union so noble and so brave,
    We'll hoist up our flag and long may it wave
    Over the station as she slumbers in the grave.

Our captain took up his telescope, he spied all o'er the blue,
"Come, all you jolly comrades, and I will tell you true,
That object you see yonder just like a turtle's back,
It is the rebel monster, they call it *Maggie Mac*."

Our decks were cleared for action, our guns were pointed true,
But yet the rebel monster came steaming o'er the blue;
On she kept coming, when fifty yards apart
She sent a ball whistling which was the beat of many's the heart.

We gave to her a broadside and to her ribs of steel,
No damage did we do to her and no danger did she feel,
And then the noble captain in a thundering voice he spoke.
"Haul down your flying colors or I'll sink your Yankee boat!"

Our captain on the quarter-deck his face grew pale with rage,
And turning to the rebels in a thundering voice he said,
"My men is true and loyal, and under me will stand,
Before I pull my colors down you can sink me and be hanged!"

"*Maggie Mac*" is from Helen Creighton, *Songs and Ballads from Nova Scotia*, Toronto, 1932, J. M. Dent & Sons (Canada), Limited (Dover reprint, 1966), p. 282. With music. Laws, A26.

VIRGINIA'S BLOODY SOIL

Come all you loyal Unionists, wherever you may be,
I hope you'll pay attention and listen unto me.
For well you know the blood and woe, the misery and toil
It took to down Secession on Virginia's bloody soil!

When our good old flag, the Stars and Stripes, from Sumter's
    walls was hurled,
And high o'erhead on the forrardest walls the Rebels their flag unfurled,
It aroused each loyal Northern man and caused his blood to boil
For to see that flag — Secession's rag — float o'er Virginia's soil.

Then from o'er hills and mountaintops there came that wild alarm:
Rise up, ye gallant sons of North! Our country calls to arms!
Come from the plains o'er hill and dale, ye hardy sons of toil,
For our flag is trampled in the dust on Virginia's bloody soil!

And thousands left their native homes, some never to return,
And many's the wife and family dear were left behind to mourn,
There was one* who went among them who from danger would ne'er recoil,
Now his bones lie bleaching on the fields of Virginia's bloody soil.

When on the field of battle, he never was afraid,
Where cannons loud would rattle, he stood there undismayed.
When bullets rained around him, he stood there with a smile,
Saying, "We'll conquer, boys, or leave our bones on Virginia's bloody soil."

In the great fight of the Wilderness where's many the brave men fell,
Our Captain led his comrades on through rebel shot and shell;
The wounded 'round they strewed the ground, the dead lay heaped in piles,
The comrades weltered in their blood on Virginia's bloody soil.

* Captain Dennis Barnes of Minerva, New York.

"Virginia's Bloody Soil" was collected by Anne and Frank Warner from the singing of "Yankee" John Galusha, Minerva, New York, 1940. The song was written by James McCoy of Minerva. Both McCoy and Galusha are now, of course, dead. It is a very nice "local" song out of the Civil War. Frank Warner sang this for the Library of Congress, 1947, AFS record 8935 A2. Used with permission.

The Rebels fought like fury, or tigers drove to bay,
They knew full well if the truth they'd tell, they could not win the day;
It was hand to hand they fought 'em, the struggle was fierce and wild
Till a bullet pierced our Captain's brain, on Virginia's bloody soil.

And now our hero's sleeping with thousands of the brave,
No marble slab does mark the place that shows where he was laid.
He died to save our Union, he's free from care and toil,
Thank God the Stars and Stripes still wave above Virginia's soil.

THE BATTLE OF BULL RUN*

This day will be remembered by America's noble sons,
If it hadn't 'a' been for Irishmen, what would our Union done?
'Twas hand to hand we fought 'em, all in the broiling sun;
Stripped to the pants, we did advance at the Battle of Bull Run!

THE RED, WHITE AND RED

On the banks of the Potomac there's an army so grand,
Its objects are subjects of Dixie's fair land;
They say that they've split our great Union in two,
And altered the colors of the Red, White and Blue.

Hurray, hurrah, we're a nation to dread,
We'll stand by our colors, the Red, White and Red!

'Twas a nice little fight on the tenth of last June,
Old Bethel Magruger licked old Picayune.

* Fragment.

"The Battle of Bull Run" was collected by Anne and Frank Warner from the singing of "Yankee" John Galusha, Minerva, New York, 1940. Sung by Frank Warner for the Library of Congress, 1947, AFS record 8935 B2, and used with permission. This fragmentary text was all that John Galusha was able to recall of another of the Civil War ballads heard by him during the campaigns.

"The Red, White and Red" was collected by Anne and Frank Warner from the singing of "Yankee" John Galusha, Minerva, New York, 1940. Sung by Frank Warner for the Library of Congress, 1947, AFS record 8935 A7. Used with permission.

It commenced in the morning and fought till they fled,
And victory waved over the Red, White and Red!

On the banks of the Potomac the Yankees we met
And we gave them such a licking they'll never forget;
They started for Richmond and thought they'd get through,
But we made them skedaddle with their Red, White and Blue.

They never will subdue us, that you will see,
While there's Davis, Bragg, Beauregard, Johnson and Lee,
Magruger and Stonewall and others ahead.
We'll all die defending the Red, White and Red!

Hurray, hurrah, we're a nation to dread,
We'll all die defending the Red, White and Red!

THE BATTLE OF SHILOH

This war ballad would seem to stem from the original British "The Heights of Alma" (Laws, J19), where the first stanza may be compared with the one here. The Alma River, in the Crimea, was the scene of a bloody battle between the Russians and British, both sides losing thousands. At Shiloh the battle was a virtual draw, but the South in the long run lost through the constant weakening of its forces. The dead and wounded in the battle numbered 20,000.

Ye loyal Britons, I pray draw near
Unto the news I have brought you to hear;
I'm sure it will make your hearts to cheer,
For the vict'ry is gained at Alma.

Shiloh:

Come all you Southerners, now draw near,
Unto my story approach you here,
Each loyal Southerner's heart to cheer
With the victory gained at Shiloh.

"The Battle of Shiloh" was collected by Cecil Sharp from the singing of Philander Fitzgerald, Nash, Virginia, 1918. In Sharp, *English Folksongs from the Southern Appalachians* (Oxford) New York, 1932, **II**, 172. With music.

O it was on April the sixteenth day,
In spite of a long and muddy way,
We landed safe at Corinth Bay
All on our route to Shiloh.

That night we lay on the cold ground,
No tents nor shelters could we find;
And in the rain we almost drowned
All on our way to Shiloh.

Next morning a burning sun did rise
Beneath the eastern cloudless sky,
And General Beauregard replied:
"Prepare to march to Shiloh."

And when our Shiloh hove in view,
It would the bravest hearts subdue
To see the Yankee melody crew
That held the works at Shiloh.

For they were strongly fortified
With batteries on the river-side.
Our generals viewed the plains and cried:
"We'll get hot work at Shiloh."

And when those batteries strove to gain,
The balls fell around us thick as rain,
And many a hero there was slain,
Upon the plains of Shiloh.

The Thirty-third and the Zouaves,
They charged the batteries and gave three cheers,
And General Beauregard rang the airs
With Southern steel at Shiloh.

Their guns and knapsacks they threw down,
They ran like hares before the hounds.
The Yankee Dutch could not withstand
The Southern charge at Shiloh.

Now many a pretty maid did mourn
A lover who'll no more return;
The cruel war has from her torn;
His body lies at Shiloh.

THE DRUMMER BOY OF SHILOH

On Shiloh's dark and bloody ground
The dead and wounded lay around.
Amid these were a drummer boy
Who beat the drum that day.

A wounded soldier helt him up;
This drum was by his side;
He clasped his hands and raised his eyes,
And prayed before he died.

"Look down upon the battlefield
As Thou art a Heavenly Friend;
Have mercy on our simple souls."
The soldiers cried, "Amen."

They gathered 'round the little group;
Each soldier knelt and cried:
"Oh, listen to the drummer boy,
Who prayed before he died."

They fold the winding sheet;
I've pound a key unto his grave.
How many loved the drummer boy
Who prayed before he died!

How many homes are desolate!
How many hearts are sore!
How many loved the drummer boy
Who prayed before he died!

"The Drummer Boy of Shiloh" was collected by Mellinger E. Henry from Mrs. William Franklin, Crossnore, Avery County, North Carolina, 1930. In Henry, *Folksongs from the Southern Highlands*, New York, 1938, p. 366. Without music. Laws, A15.

THE BATTLE OF ANTIETAM CREEK

'Twas on the field of Antietam where many's the soldier fell,
Is where occurred the story which now to you I'll tell;
The dead lay all around me, we all together lay,
For we had had a fearful fight upon the field that day.

And as I lay there musing upon the damp cold ground,
My knapsack for a pillow, my blankets wrapped around,
And as I lay there musing, I heard a bitter cry,
It was, "Lord Jesus, save me, and take me home to die!

"I was the eldest brother, just three years ago
I left my home and kindred for the State of Ohio;
Not finding any other work to which I might apply,
I bound myself apprentice, my fortune for to try.

"I did not like my master, he did not use me well,
So I fixed a resolution not long with him to dwell,
And with this resolution from him I ran away,
I started then for New Orleans and cursed be the day.

" 'Twas there I was conscripted and sent into the field,
Not having any other hope but I must die or yield,
And so with many another boy I marched away that night
And this has been the tenth time that I have been in fights.

"I thought the boy who shot me had a familiar face,
But in the battle's fury 'twas difficult to trace;
I thought it was my brother Jay, if him I could but see,
I'd kiss him and forgive him and lay me down and die."

I quickly ran unto him and heard his story o'er,
It was my long-lost brother who lay weltering in his gore;
As I spoke of our loved ones left behind and soothed his fevered brow,
He whispered, "My dear brother, I can die happy now."

"The Battle of Antietam Creek" was recorded by Sidney Robertson Cowell from the singing of Warde H. Ford at Central Valley, California, 1939. Library of Congress record AFS 4213 A.

Then quickly as a slumbering babe his fluttering eyelids closed,
I saw him sink with shortening breath to death's long last repose;
And with many a tear and sad farewell, I scooped a narrow grave,
And there he sleeps beneath the sod by Antietam's rippling wave.

GOIN' 'CROSS THE MOUNTAIN

Goin' 'cross the mountain
O, fare thee well,
Goin' 'cross the mountain
You can hear my banjo tell.

Got my rations on my back,
My powder it is dry,
Goin' 'cross the mountain,
Chrissy, don't you cry.

Going 'cross the mountain
To jine the boys in Blue,
When it's all well and done
Then I'll come back to you.

Going 'cross the mountain
If I have to crawl,
To give Jeff's men a little taste
Of my rifle ball.

'Way 'fore it's good daylight
If nothing happens to me,
I'll be way down
In old Tennessee.

I 'spect you'll miss me when I'm
    gone,
But I'm going through;
When this fighting's over
Then I'll come back to you.

Goin' 'cross the mountain
O, fare thee well,
Goin' 'cross the mountain
You can hear my banjo tell.

DAN ELLIS'S BOYS

They aint no use a-telling, boy, what's for you to do,
Since you are starting out to fight for the Blue.

"Goin' 'cross the Mountain" was collected by Anne and Frank Warner from the singing of Frank Proffitt of Watauga County, North Carolina, 1959. From the Warner Collection, with permission.

"Dan Ellis's Boys" was collected by Anne and Frank Warner from the singing of Frank Proffitt of Watauga County, North Carolina, 1960. From the Warner Collection, with permission.

You'll have to do the best you can and watch out night and day
Them sneaking, lowdown Home Guards that's wearing of the Gray.

We gathered more than a hundred
  strong
In a place called Piney Flats,
More than half the sorry lot
Had squirrel tails on their hats.

Dan Ellis swore, by God, he said,
"You won't need any guns:
When Jeff's men see you comin'
By God, you'll see 'em run!"

FARE YOU WELL, MY DARLING

Oh, fare you well, my darling,
Oh, fare you well, my dear,
Don't grieve for my long absence
While I am a volunteer.

Since it's been my misfortune
A soldier for to be,
Content yourself, my darling,
And don't grieve after me.

I am going to Pensacola
To tarry for a while
Away from my darling,
Yes, about five hundred mile.

When the cannon loudly roar
And the bullets swiftly fly,
The drums and fifes are a-beating
To drown their deadly cry.

Oh, see how she wrings her lily-white hands,
How mournfully she doth cry:
"You'll go and join the army
And in the war you'll die.

"You'll be placed in the center,
It's there to be slain.
It will burst my heart asunder
If I never see you again.

"You have now joined the army
And enlisted for the war.
I hope the Lord will spare you
And bring you home again.

"When the cannon roar like
  thunder
And the bullets are flying around,
I hope they all will miss you
And leave you safe and sound.

"Then you can mount your battery
And turn the wheels around
And shout out our victory
All over the Southern land.

"Fare You Well, My Darling" was "One of the songs secured for Miss Hamilton in 1909 by Edna Letsom of the West Plains High School from Jas. L. McAnally of the 10th Iowa." In H. M. Belden, *Ballads and Songs Collected by the Missouri Folk-Lore Society*, Columbia (reprint edition, 1966), p. 380. Without music.

"I will stay at home contented
And true* a single life
And long to see the time to come
To be a soldier's wife."

WHEN THIS CRUEL WAR IS OVER

Dearest love, do you remember,
When we last did meet,
How you told me that you loved me,
Kneeling at my feet?
Oh, how proud you stood before me
In your suit of blue,
When you vowed to me and country
Ever to be true!

Weeping sad and lonely,
Hopes and tears are vain.
When this cruel war is over,
Praying that we meet again.

When the summer breeze is sighing
Mournfully along,
Or when autumn leaves are falling,
Sadly breathes the song.
Oft in dreams I see thee lying
On the battle plain,
Sorely wounded, even dying,
Calling, but in vain.

If amid the din of battle
Nobly you should fall,
Away from those who love you,
None to hear you call,

* Miswritten, presumably, for "lead."

"When This Cruel War Is Over" is ". . . From the copy of it made by James Ashby of Holt County, Missouri, in his MS ballad-book, secured in 1906 by Miss Welty. Ashby may have copied it from print, or may simply have known it from hearing it sung." In H. M. Belden, *Ballads and Songs Collected by the Missouri Folk-Lore Society*, Columbia (reprint edition, 1966), p. 381.

Who would whisper sounds of comfort,
Who would soothe your pain?
Oh, the many cruel fancies
Ever in my brain!

But your country calls you, darling.
Angels cheer your way;
While our nation's sons are fighting
We can only pray.
Nobly strike for God and liberty;
Let all nations see
How we love the starry banner,
The emblem of the free!

BROTHER GREEN

O come to me, my brother Green, for I am shot and bleeding;
Now I must die, no more to see my loving wife and children.
The Southern foe has laid me low, on this cold ground to suffer;
Stay, brother, stay, and put me away, and write my wife a letter.

I know that she has prayed for me, I know her prayers are answered;
She prayed that I might be prepared, if I should fall in battle.
Tell her that I am prepared, and hope we'll meet in heaven;
For I believe in Jesus Christ, my sins are all forgiven.

My dear wife, you must not grieve, to kiss my little children;
For they will call for me in vain, when I am gone to heaven.
Dear Mary, you must treat them well, and train them up for heaven;
Teach them to love the Lord, and they will be forgiven.

My little babes, I love them both; if I could once more see them,
I'd bid them both a long farewell, until we meet in heaven.
But here I am in Tennessee, and they are in Ohio,
And now I am too far away to hear their silvery voices.

"Brother Green" was contributed to John Harrington Cox by John B. Adkins, Branchland,
Lincoln County, West Virginia, 1916. In Cox, *Folksongs of the South*, New York (Dover
reprint edition, 1967), p. 273. Without music.

Sister Nancy, you must not grieve o'er the loss of your dear brother;
I am going home to Jesus Christ, to meet my blessed mother.
I am dying, brother Green! O I do die so easy!
I know that death has lost its sting, because I love my Jesus.

Dear father, you have suffered long, and prayed for my salvation;
Now I must leave you all at last, so fare-you-well, temptation.
Two brothers yet I can't forget are fighting for the Union;
For this, dear wife, I've lost my life, to put down this rebellion.

THE LAST FIERCE CHARGE
(*The Message That Never Was Sent*)

It was just before the last fierce charge, two soldiers drew a-rein,
With a solemn look and a shake of hands, that they never might meet again.
They had travelled together through a-many a mile, they had travelled for
    many a mile,
But always before they had met with the foe with a calm and a hopeful
    smile,
But always before they had met with the foe with a calm and a hopeful
    smile.

One had blue eyes and curly hair, nineteen but a month ago,
He had red on his cheeks and down on his lips; he was only a boy, you know.
The other was tall, dark, stern and proud, whose fate in this world looked
    dim;
He had a fair face on his breast, 'twas the only joy to him,
He had a fair face on his breast, 'twas the only joy to him.

They looked into each other's face with an awful, ghastly gloom,
And the first to speak was the tall stern man, saying, "Charlie, my hour has
    come.
We will ride together up the hill, but you will ride back alone.
Oh, promise a little trouble to take for me when I'm dead and gone.

"I have a fair face on my breast, I will wear it into the fight;
Her eyes are blue as a diamond shoe, her smile's like the morning light.

"The Last Fierce Charge" was recorded by Austin E. Fife from the singing of Ephraim
Ellertson, Provo, Utah, 1946. Library of Congress AFS record 8706 A1. Laws, A17.

Write to her, Charlie, when I die; send back this fair, fond face.
And tell her, Charlie, where I lie and where is my resting place."

"I will do your bidding, comrade mine, should I ride back alone.
Should you ride back and I should not, Lake Erie is my home;
Should you ride back and I should not, you will do the same for me,
For I've a mother, comrade mine, — write to her tenderly."

Just then the order came for to charge; for an instant hand touched hand.
They answered "Yea!" and away they sped, that brave, devoted band.
They rode together up the hill 'midst rebel shot and shell,
They cheered each other on their way while many a comrade fell.

Before they reached that awful height, oh, the height that they could not
    gain,
The few that were left of the brave young band rode slowly back again.
But among the dead that were left behind was the boy with the curly hair;
And the tall, stern man with the haughty brow lay dead beside him there.

Now who will write to that blue-eyed girl the words that her lover had said,
And who will write to that mother kind, and tell her her boy is dead?
Oh, when she hears of the dreadful news, it will cause her grief and pain,
Until she crosses the river of death and stands by her boy again.

THE CRIPPLE FOR LIFE
or THE POOR VOLUNTEER

"Oh, now I've come back to you, Mother, wearied, and wasted and worn,
With my locks matted over my forehead, and clothes all blood-stained and
    torn.
No wonder you shrank when you saw me, as if I had struck you a blow,
I'm not looking much like that young fellow you parted with three years
    ago.

"For he was stalwart and handsome, eager and fierce for the strife,
But this one is wasted and weary, wounded, a cripple for life.
But, Mother, God knows for the Union I'd fight till the very last breath,
But just twenty-one and a cripple, for me it had better been death.

"The Cripple for Life" was recorded by Austin E. Fife from the singing of Andrew Sproul,
Washington, Utah, 1947. Library of Congress AFS record 8641 A and B.

"Now, Mother, don't weep, it is cruel to utter one word of regret;
It was all that I had and I gave it; my right arm is left to me yet.
With that and my pension, dear Mother, 'twill keep the grim wolf from our
    door,
And if you're contented and happy, God help me to ask for no more.

"Not for you, darling Mother, not only, but one there was when I left
Whose eyes were brighter than heaven, and lips like the ripe cherry's cleft;
'Twas Maggie, my darling, God bless her; I meant to have made her my
    wife.
She promised, but how can I ask her to wed with a cripple for life?

"Hark, hark! who is that I hear sobbing, just now in a chamber close by?
'Tis Maggie, my dear and my darling. Come kiss me and bid me goodbye.
But, oh, what is that you are saying? My loss only makes me more dear?
God bless you, dear Maggie, you've given new life to a poor volunteer."

ONE-AND-TWENTY

My father was a farmer gay,
And I longed for one-and-twenty.
With beef and corn in plenty,
I hoed, I mowed, I held the plow,

My birthday came, my father urged,
But strongly I resisted.
My sister wept, my mother prayed,
But off I went and enlisted.

They marched me on through wet and dry,
Through tombs so loudly moaning,
The dreadful sounds did fill my ears,
And I wished that I was mowing.

I lost my leg, the foe came on,
They had me in their clutches,
I starved in prison until peace came,
And hobbled home on crutches.

"One-and-Twenty" was communicated to Emelyn Elizabeth Gardner and Geraldine Jencks
Chickering in 1916 by Miss Florence Myers of Ypsilanti, Michigan, who had previously
learned the song from a lumberjack. In Gardner and Chickering, *Ballads and Songs of
Southern Michigan* (University of Michigan Press) Ann Arbor, 1939, p. 241. With music.

The Assassination
of Presidents

Zolgotz, mean man,
He shot McKinley with his handkerchief on his hand,
In Buffalo, in Buffalo.

BOOTH KILLED LINCOLN

The title of this ballad is "Booth," or "Booth Killed Lincoln." It's an old fiddle tune, and there are a few variants of the song. I heard my father hum it and sing a few of the stanzas when I was just a boy about six or ten years old.

— BASCOM LAMAR LUNSFORD

Wilkes Booth came to Washington, an actor great was he,
He played at Ford's Theater, and Lincoln went to see;
It was early in April, not many weeks ago,
The people of this fair city all gathered at the show.

The war it is all over, the people happy now,
And Abraham Lincoln arose to make his bow;
The people cheer him wildly, arising to their feet,
And Lincoln waving of his hand, he calmly takes his seat.

And while he sees the play go on, his thoughts are running deep,
His darling wife, close by his side, has fallen fast asleep;
From the box there hangs a flag, it is not the Stars and Bars,
The flag that holds within its folds bright gleaming Stripes and Stars.

J. Wilkes Booth he moves down the aisle, he had measured once before,
He passes Lincoln's bodyguard a-nodding at the door;

"Booth Killed Lincoln" was recorded by Duncan Emrich from the singing of Bascom Lamar Lunsford of South Turkey Creek, North Carolina, at Washington, D.C., 1949. Library of Congress record LP29.

He holds a dagger in his right hand, a pistol in his left,
He shoots poor Lincoln in the temple, and sends his soul to rest.

The wife awakes from slumber, and screams in her rage,
Booth jumps over the railing, and lands him on the stage;
He'll rue the day, he'll rue the hour, as God him life shall give,
When Booth stood in the center stage, crying, "Tyrants shall not live!"

The people all excited then, cried everyone, "A hand!"
Cried all the people near, "For God's sake, save that man!"
Then Booth ran back with boot and spur across the backstage floor,
He mounts that trusty claybank mare, all saddled at the door.

J. Wilkes Booth, in his last play, all dressed in broadcloth deep,
He gallops down the alleyway, I hear those horses' feet;
Poor Lincoln then was heard to say, and all has gone to rest,
"Of all the actors in this town, I loved Wilkes Booth the best."

CHARLES GUITEAU

On July 2, 1881, President James A. Garfield was fatally shot in the Baltimore and Potomac Railway depot in Washington, D.C., by Charles Guiteau, a disappointed office seeker. Guiteau was convicted of assassination and hanged in the jail in Washington on June 30, 1882.

I

Come all ye gentle Christians, wherever you may be,
And likewise pay attention to these few words from me.
For the murder of James A. Garfield I am condemned to die.
Upon the twentieth day of June, upon the scaffold high.

My name it is Charles Guiteau, it's a name I'll never deny,
I left my aged parents, in sorrow they must die,
Oh, little did they think while in my youthful bloom,
That I'd be led to a scaffold high to meet a fatal doom.

Version 1 of "Charles Guiteau" was recorded by Vance Randolph from the singing of Dr. George Hastings, Fayetteville, Arkansas, 1941. Library of Congress AFS record 5362 B2. Laws, E11.

It was down by the railroad I tried to make my escape,
But Providence was against me, it proved to be too late;
So they took me to the jailhouse all in my youthful bloom,
But I'll be led to a scaffold high to meet a fatal doom.

I tried to prove insane, but it proved to be no use,
For the people were against me, to escape there was no clue;
So Judge Cox read the sentence and the clerk he took it down,
And I'll be led to a scaffold high to meet a fatal doom.

My sister came to see me, to bid me a last goodbye,
She threw both arms around my neck and wept most bitterly.
She said, "My darling brother, today you must surely die
For the murder of James A. Garfield upon a scaffold high."

My name it is Charles Guiteau, it's a name I'll never deny,
I left my aged parents, in sorrow they must die.
Oh, little did they think while in my youthful bloom,
That I'd be led to a scaffold high to meet a fatal doom.

II

Come all ye Christian people, wherever you may be,
Likewise pay attention to these few lines from me;
On the thirtieth day of June, when I am condemned to die,
For the murder of James A. Garfield upon a scaffold high."

My name is Charles Guiteau, my name I'll never deny,
To leave my aged parents in sorrow for to die,
But little did I think when in my youthful bloom
That I'd be carried to the scaffold to meet my fatal doom.

My sister came to see me, to bid me a last farewell,
She threw her arms around me, and bitterly did dwell;
She said, "Brother darling, [for this] you surely must die
For the murder of James A. Garfield, upon the scaffold high."

They carried me to the depot, I thought I'd make my escape,
But Providence was against me, and I found I was too late;

Version II of "Charles Guiteau" was recorded by Duncan Emrich from the singing of Bascom Lamar Lunsford of South Turkey Creek, North Carolina, at Washington, D.C., 1949. Library of Congress record LP29. Laws, E11.

They took me to a prison, all in my youthful bloom,
They carried me to the scaffold to meet my fatal doom.

Now, well, I'm on the scaffold, I bid you all adieu,
The hangman is a-waiting for a quarter of an hour or two;
The black cap's o'er my forehead, I never more can see,
But when I'm dead and buried, you'll all remember me.

My name is Charles Guiteau, my name I'll never deny,
For the killing of James A. Garfield, for that I'm doomed to die.

ZOLGOTZ

President William McKinley was assassinated by Leon Czolgosz, who shot him twice with a pistol hidden in a handkerchief on September 6, 1901, at the Pan American Exposition in Buffalo, New York. The President died September 14. Czolgosz was convicted and was electrocuted October 29, 1901, in the Auburn State Prison.

The title of this song is "Zolgotz." It's another assassination song. There are some variants to the song; sometimes it's called the "White House Blues." I heard Willard Randall sing it about 19 and 23.

— BASCOM LAMAR LUNSFORD

Zolgotz, mean man,
He shot McKinley with his handkerchief on his hand,
In Buffalo, in Buffalo.

Zolgotz, you done him wrong,
You shot McKinley when he was walking along,
In Buffalo, in Buffalo.

The pistol fires, then McKinley falls,
And the doctor says, "McKinley, cain't find the ball,"
In Buffalo, in Buffalo.

"Zolgotz" was recorded by Duncan Emrich from the singing of Bascom Lamar Lunsford of South Turkey Creek, North Carolina, at Washington, D.C., 1949. Library of Congress record LP29.

They sent for the doctor, the doctor come,
He come in a trot, and he come in a run,
To Buffalo, to Buffalo.

He saddled his horse, and he swung on his mane,
And he trotted the horse till he outrun the train
To Buffalo, to Buffalo.

Forty-four boxes all trimmed in braid,
The sixteen-wheel driver, boys, they couldn't make the grade
To Buffalo, to Buffalo.

Forty-four boxes trimmed in lace,
Take him back to the baggage, boys, where we can't see his face,
In Buffalo, in Buffalo.

Mrs. McKinley took a trip, and she took it out west,
Where she couldn't hear the people talk about McKinley's death,
In Buffalo, in Buffalo.

The engine whistled down the line,
Blowing every station, McKinley was a-dying,
In Buffalo, in Buffalo.

Seventeen coaches all trimmed in black
Took McKinley to the graveyard, but never brought him back,
To Buffalo, to Buffalo.

Seventeen coaches all trimmed in black
Took Roosevelt to the White House, but never brought him back,
To Buffalo, to Buffalo.

[*Spoken*] "That was Theodore Roosevelt . . ."

Disasters and Tragedies

Galveston with a sea-wall   Wasn't that a mighty storm!
   To keep the water down,   Oh, wasn't that a mighty storm with water!
But the high tide from the ocean   Wasn't that a mighty storm
   Washed water over the town.   That blew the people away!

THE MIRAMICHI FIRE

Quoting from the Bangor (Maine) *Daily Commercial* for July 29, 1870:
"*The Merimachi Fire as Told in Verse.* The following is an account of the
famous Merimachi fire which occurred (October 7) in 1825, written in
verse by Thos. M. Jordan. The poem was found printed on a separate sheet
of paper now yellowed by age, by John N. Merrill of this city, while searching an old trunk in a house at Olamon recently. The poem, it is said, gives
a good description of that terrible calamity." It is not necessary to go
beyond the poem to sense the terror of that conflagration. For those who
may wish greater detail, however, the best known history of the fire is in
Robert Cooney, *A Compendious History of the Northern Part of the
Province of New Brunswick, and of the District of Gaspé, in Lower Canada,*
Halifax, 1832, pp. 65–73. As the ballad states, within a period of eight
hours, an area of one hundred miles by forty-two miles . . . with more
than two hundred dead. . . . Not to speak of the fish and the wild
beasts . . .

     This is the truth what I now tell you,
     For mine eyes in part did see,

"The Miramichi Fire" was reported by Phillips Barry in *Bulletin of the Folksong Society
of the Northeast*, Cambridge, Mass., 11 (1936):21–23. Without music, but Barry gives the
music for two variants recorded by him on dictaphone records in 1934, attesting to the
traditional currency of the ballad in Maine. Laws, G24.

What did happen to the people
On the banks of Miramichi.*

The seventh evening of October,
Eighteen hundred twenty-five,
Two hundred people fell by fire,
It scourged those that did survive.

Some said it was because the peoples' sins
Did rise like mountains high,
Which did ascend up to Jehovah,
He would not see and justify.

In order to destroy their lumber,
And the country distress,
He sent the fire in a whirlwind
From the howling wilderness.

'Twas on the nor'west first discovered,
Twenty-two men there did die;
When it had swept o'er the meadows,
To Newcastle it did fly.

When the people were a-sleeping,
Fire seized upon the town,
Though fine and handsome was the village,
It soon tumbled to the ground.

It burnt three vessels that were building,
And two more at anchor lay;
Many that did see the fire
Thought it was the Judgement Day.

Twelve more men were burnt by fire
In the compass of that town,
Twenty-five more on the water,
In a scow upset and drown.

A family below Newcastle
Were destroyed among the rest,
Father, mother and three children,
One an infant at the breast.

* Pronounced "MirramiSHEE."

Thirteen families were residing
Just out back of Gretna Green;
All of them were burnt by fire,
Only one alive was seen.

Then it passed to Black River,
Where it did burn sixty more;
So it forced its way with fury,
Till it reached the briny shore.

Forty-two miles by one hundred
This great fire did extend,
All was done within eight hours,
Not exceeding over ten.

As I have spoken of things collective,
Now I intend to personate
And speak of some of my acquaintance,
With whom I was an intimate.

A lady was drove to the water,
Where she stood both wet and cold,
Notwithstanding her late illness,
Had a babe but three days old.

Six young men, both smart and active,
Were to work on the nor'west,
When they saw the fire coming,
To escape it tried their best.

About two miles from where their camp stood,
There we found each one of them,
But to paint their sad appearance,
I cannot with tongue or pen.

To see these fine, these blooming young men,
All lay dead upon the ground,
And their brothers standing mourning,
Spread a dismal scene around.

Then we dug a grave and buried
Those whom did the fire burn,
Then each of us that was a-living,
To our dwelling did return.

I heard the sighs, the cries and groaning,
Saw the falling of the tears;
By me this will not be forgotten,
Should I live a hundred years.

Sisters weeping for their brother,
Father crying for his son,
And with bitter heartfelt sorrow,
Said the mother, "I'm undone."

It killed the wild beasts of the forest,
In the river all the fish,
Such another horrid fire,
See again I do not wish.

THE BROOKLYN THEATER FIRE

On December 5, 1876, some three hundred persons died in a tragic fire at the Brooklyn Theater during a performance of *The Two Orphans*.

One evening bright stars they were shining,
And the moon it shone clear on our land,
Our city in peace and in quiet,
The hour of midnight was at hand.
But hark! do you hear the cry "Fire"?
How dismal the bells they do sound.
The Brooklyn Theater is burning,
It's fast burning down to the ground.

We never can forget those *Two Orphans*,
Bad luck seemed to stand in their wake;
It seems they were brought to our city,
The lives of our dear friends to take.

The doors they were open at seven,
The curtains were rolled up at eight;

"The Brooklyn Theater Fire" was recorded from the singing of Lester A. Coffee, Harvard, Illinois, 1946, by the University of Wisconsin Recording Project under the direction of Leland Coon. Library of Congress AFS record 8421 B2. Laws, G27.

And those that had seats they were happy;
Outsiders were mad they were late.
The play it went on very smoothly,
Till sparks from the curtain did fly;
It was then men, women and children,
"Oh, God, save our lives!" they did cry.

Next morning among the black ruins —
Oh, God, what a sight met our eyes!
The dead they were lying in all shape,
And some could not be recognized.
Mothers were weeping and crying
For sons who were out on that night,
Oh, God, may their souls rest in heaven,
All those who were innocent and bright.

What means this large gathering of people,
Upon such a cold winter day?
What means this long line of hearses,
Decked out in their mournful array?
It's away to the cemetery of Greenwood,
Where the winds through the cold winter blow,
It is there where the funeral is going,
The dead and unknown for to lie.

We never can forget those *Two Orphans*,
Bad luck seemed to stand in their wake;
It seems they were brought to our city,
The lives of our dear friends to take.

THE MILWAUKEE FIRE

Before dawn on January 10, 1883, Milwaukee suffered one of its worst disasters: seventy-one lives were known to be lost in the burning of the hotel,

"The Milwaukee Fire" was recorded by Robert F. Draves and Helene Stratman-Thomas from the singing of Robert Walker at Crandon, Wisconsin, 1941. Library of Congress record LP55. Laws, G15.

the Newhall House, but since the hotel register was lost in the fire, no exact check of the number missing could be made. The hotel, at the corner of Broadway and Michigan, was opened on August 26, 1857. It was a brick structure, six stories high, with 300 rooms. Built at a cost of $155,000, it was considered the finest and largest hotel in the West. Previous fires had occurred in 1863 and 1880. The inquest determined that the Newhall House was set on fire by a person or persons unknown, but also that the owners were guilty of culpable negligence in not having provided more outside escapes in case of fire.

In 1884 the ballad "The Milwaukee Fire; or The Burning of the Newhall House," with words and music by J. W. Kelley, was published by S. Brainard's Sons. Mr. Walker, who sang the present version for the Library of Congress, had no knowledge of the published ballad. He learned it in the Wisconsin lumber camps.

In 1946 a recording was made of "The Milwaukee Fire" sung by Mrs. Ella Mittelstaedt Fischer of Mayville, who, as a girl of twelve, was an eyewitness to the fire. Even after sixty-three years, her recollection of the horror was so vivid that she could not sing the song without being overcome by emotion.

For further reference see the notes to Library of Congress record LP55, from which this information comes.

'Twas the gray of early morning when the dreadful cry of "Fire!"
Rang out upon that cold and piercing air.
Just that little word alone was all it did require
For to send dismay and panic ev'rywhere.

The firemen worked like demons as to all was in their pow'r,
To save a life or try to soothe a pain.
It'd made the strongest heartsick, for within less than half an hour,
All was hushed, and further efforts were in vain.

When the dreadful 'larm was sounded through that oft-condemned hotel,
They rushed in mad confusion ev'ry way.
The smoke was suffocating, and blinding them as well;
The fire king could not be held at bay.

From ev'ry window, men and women wildly would beseech
For help, in tones of anguish and despair.
What could have been their feelings, when the ladder would not reach,
And death clasped around them ev'rywhere?

WARS AND OTHER DISASTERS

Up in the highest window stood a servant girl alone,
And the crowd beneath all stood with bated breath.
They turned away their faces with many the stifled groan
When she jumped to meet perhaps as hard a death.

In one window you could see a man, his wife stood by his side;
They tell us that this man was a millionaire.
To save him from this dreadful fire, they left no means untried;
Gold nor treasure had no value there.

A boy stood in the window, and his mother down below,
And when she saw the flames approaching wild,
With upraised hands to pray for him, she knelt down in the snow,
And the stoutest heart could not restrain a tear.

She madly rushed toward the fire, and she wildly tore her hair,
Saying "Take me, O God, but spare my pride, my joy."
She saw the flames surround him, and then in darkest fear,
Said, "O God, have mercy on my only boy."

They tell us now that this hotel had been on fire before,
And not considered safe for sev'ral years,
But still the men that owned it let it run on as before,
But they are not to blame, it now appears.

Incend'arism this time, has been the cause, they say,
But who the fiend is they cannot tell,
But Milwaukee will not rest neither by night or day,
Till the matter is investigated well.

But that will be no benefit to those that passed away,
In this, Milwaukee's greatest fun'ral pyre,
And peace be to their ashes, the best that we can say,
For the victims of this great and dreadful fire.

THE SHERMAN CYCLONE

The Sherman tornado occurred on May 15, 1896.

Come, friends, if you will listen, a story I will tell,
'Tis of a great tornado you all remember well,
It struck the town of Sherman on the fifteenth day of May,
And a portion of our city was completely swept away.

We saw the storm approaching, the clouds grew deathly black,
And through our little city it left an awful track.
The people fled in terror their lives were swept away,
Now beneath the sod they're sleeping till the final Judgement Day.

WASN'T THAT A MIGHTY STORM?

Five thousand people were killed in a hurricane and flood at Galveston, Texas, September 8, 1900. According to Mr. James G. Timmins in the Houston *Daily Post* of September 10, water was "three feet deep in the rotunda of the Tremont Hotel and six feet deep in Market Street."

Galveston with a seawall
   To keep the water down,
But the high tide from the ocean
   Washed water over the town.

Wasn't that a mighty storm!
   Oh, wasn't that a mighty storm with water!
Wasn't that a mighty storm
   That blew the people away!

"The Sherman Cyclone" was recorded by John A. Lomax from the singing of Mrs. Hallie May Preece, Austin, Texas, 1937. Library of Congress AFS record 926 A2. Laws, G31. The author was a blind entertainer, Mrs. Mattie Carter East, who sang at picnics and religious meetings and sold broadsides of her song at ten cents. A more extended version is to be found in William A. Owens, *Texas Folk Songs*, PTFS 23 (1950).

"Wasn't That a Mighty Storm?" was recorded by John A. Lomax from the singing of Sin-Killer Griffin and congregation at Darrington State Farm, Sandy Point, Texas, 1934. Library of Congress record LP10.

Their trumpets give them warning,
  "You'd better leave this place."
They never thought of leaving
  Till death looked them in the face.

The trains they were loaded
  With people leaving town.
The tracks give away from the ocean.
  The trains they went on down.

Death like a cruel master,
  As the wind began to blow,
Rode out on a train of horses.
  Said, "Death, let me go."

Now, Death, in 1900 —
  That was fifteen years ago —
You throwed a stone at my mother.
  With you she had to go.

Now, Death, your hands is icy,
  You've got them on my knees.
You done carried away my mother,
  Now come back after me.

The trees fell on the island,
  The houses give away.
Some people strived and drownded,
  Some died 'most every way.

The lightning played [?]
  The thunder began to roar,
The wind it began blowing,
  The rain began to fall.

The sea it began rolling,
  The ships could not land
I heard the captain crying,
  "Please save a drownding man."

    Wasn't that a mighty storm!
      Oh, wasn't that a mighty storm with water!
    Wasn't that a mighty storm
      That blew the people away!

THE SANTA BARBARA EARTHQUAKE

The Santa Barbara earthquake occurred on June 29, 1925. Thirteen persons were killed and the damage estimated at $10,000,000. Experts felt that the earthquake was not particularly severe and would have caused slight damage except for careless construction methods used in many Santa Barbara buildings.

Way out in California
Upon a hill so tall,
Was the town of Santa Barbara
That they thought would never fall.

But on one fatal morning,
The sun rose in the sky,
The people all were praying,
"Oh, Lord, please hear our cry."

"The Santa Barbara Earthquake" was recorded by Charles Todd and Robert Sonkin from the singing of Vester Whitworth, FSA camp, Arvin, California, 1940. Library of Congress record AFS 4098 B1.

When daylight found the people
With sad and aching heart,
They were searching for their
　families
That the earthquake tore apart.

But some of them were sleeping
Beneath the fallen stone,
Their lips were closed forever,
Never more to cry and mourn.

It's just another warning
From God up in the sky,
To tell all you good people
That he still remains on high.

We do not know the moment
When he shall call us home,
But we should all be ready
Before our time has come.

THE WEST PALM BEACH STORM

On the sixteenth day of September, nineteen twenty-eight,
God start to ride in a hurry, he rode till very late.

　In the storm, oh, in the storm
　Lord, somebody got drownded in the storm.

He rode out on the ocean, sent the lightning through his reel,
Stepped on the land of West Palm Beach and the wicked heart did weep.

Out in Okeechobee, families rushed out at the door,
And somebody's poor old mother hasn't been seen any more.

Some mothers looked at their children, and they begin to cry,
"Christ Lord, have mercy, for we all must die."

I'll tell you wicked people what you had better do,
Go down and get the Holy Ghost and you'll live the life through.

All around Okeechobee all scattered on the ground,
The last account of the dead they had was twenty-two hundred found.

Some people are yet missing and haven't been found, they say,
But this we know, they will all come forth in the resurrection day.

When Gabriel sounds the trumpet and the dead begin to rise,
I'll meet the saints and chosen up in the heavenly skies.

"The West Palm Beach Storm" was recorded by Alton Morris from the singing of Viola
Jenkins, Gainesville, Florida, 1937. Library of Congress AFS record 977 A.

THE TUPELO DESTRUCTION

Two hundred and sixteen persons were killed by a tornado at Tupelo, Mississippi, April 5, 1936. The Meridian *Star* of April 8 called the tornado "the most disastrous storm in the history of Mississippi." The United Press in the same paper estimated that tornadoes had killed nearly 500 people in six southern states in ten days. There is a heavy sense of religious judgment in the version given here.

> In Tupelo, Mississippi,
> A very sinful town,
> The people were as wicked
> As anywhere else was found.
> They would drink, cheat and rob,
> And they would not obey God,
> So he sent out a warning through the land.

> God just sent out a warning through the land,
> God just sent out a warning through the land,
> The white and the black, the rich and the poor,
> All alike they had to go,
> For God sent out a warning through the land.

> It was late one Sunday evening,
> Just about nine o'clock,
> When the cyclone struck in Tupelo,
> And the town began to rock.
> There was wind, hail and fire,
> For God surely was passing by,
> And he sent out a warning through the land.

> I heard women screaming,
> I heard children groan,
> I heard men a-crying,
> "Oh, Lord, I am left alone."
> Oh! It all sounded so hard,
> But the folks just wouldn't hear God,
> So he sent out a warning through the land.

"The Tupelo Destruction" was recorded by Herbert Halpert from the singing of Lulu Morris and congregation, Tupelo, Mississippi, 1939. Library of Congress AFS record 2958 A and B.

Some bodies were torn into pieces,
Some that had to drown;
Some were burned into ashes
And some could not be found.
It was an awful sight,
For God surely did work that night,
He just sent out a warning through the land.

    God just sent out a warning through the land,
    God just sent out a warning through the land,
    The white and the black, the rich and the poor,
    All alike they had to go,
    For God sent out a warning through the land.

Some were floating on the water,
Some were sailing through the air,
People, you may not believe it,
But there is a God somewhere.
He can wound, he can heal,
And he can do just as he feels,
And he sent out a warning through this land.

There was no respect of person,
Nothing of the kind,
The cattle on a thousand hills,
God said, "All are mine,"
So when the cyclone struck that night,
It killed many, black and white,
God just sent out a warning through the land.

Now, people, heed that warning,
And quit your sinful way,
Though God spared you over,
He is coming again some day.
You may be rich or you may be poor,
But when God calls then you must go,
For he sent out a warning through the land.

    God just sent out a warning through the land,
    God just sent out a warning through the land,
    The white and the black, the rich and the poor,
    All alike they had to go,
    For God sent out a warning through the land.

THE CABIN CREEK FLOOD

A sad and mournful history
On which I now will speak,
Concerning that awful storm
That flooded Cabin Creek.

Five long hours the rain did fall,
The thunder loudly rolled,
The sadness of the awful day
The grief I can't unfold.

The miners hurried to their homes
And found them swept away,
Many hearts were weeping then,
And many knelt to pray.

Poor hungry souls on mountain tops,
The children cry for bread,
Uncle Sam sent out his force
The hungry soon were fed.

"The Cabin Creek Flood" was collected by the Federal Music Project, Works Progress Administration (WPA), Boyd County, Kentucky, ca. 1937. Jean Thomas, Supervisor for Boyd County. Ms., with music, in the Archive of Folk Song, Library of Congress.

SONGS OF OCCUPATIONS, SEA, FOREST, MINES

Sea Shanties

Forecastle Songs

Lumbering

The '49ers

The Hardrock Men

Coal

Sea Shanties

We sailed away from Liverpool, bound for the Gulf of Mexico.
'Way, haul away, haul away my Rosy,
'Way, haul away, haul away my Johnny-O.

We sailed into Galveston and loaded up with cotton-o.
'Way, haul away, haul away my Rosy,
'Way, haul away, haul away my Johnny-O.

I n *Folklore on the American Land* I considered the use of shanties as work songs and included the following which are not repeated here: "A-Roving, or The Amsterdam Maid"; "Shenandoah"; "Rio Grande"; "Rolling Home"; "Homeward Bound, or Goodbye, Fare You Well"; "The Dead Horse"; "Blow, Boys, Blow"; "Roll, *Alabama*, Roll!"; "Hanging Johnny"; "Paddy Doyle"; "Haul the Bowline"; "The Drunken Sailor." Those shanties and those given here are — with one or two exceptions — all available on Library of Congress records LP26 and LP27.

PADDY, GET BACK

"Paddy, Get Back" is a capstan shanty of rather infrequent appearance. Apart from the interesting picture it gives of a certain aspect of sea life (the lying shipping-master and the rough mates), it is most valuable, since within the shanty itself recognition is given to the importance of the shanties in promoting unison work. Richard Maitland, an old sailor, now dead, was recorded by Alan Lomax.

(*Spoken*) "It's called, 'Paddy, Get Back' . . ."

"Paddy, Get Back" was recorded by Alan Lomax from the singing of Richard Maitland at Sailors' Snug Harbor, Staten Island, New York, 1939. Library of Congress record LP26.

I was broke and out of a job in the city of London,
I went down the Shadwell docks to get a ship.

> Paddy, get back, take in the slack,
> Heave away your capstan, heave a pawl, heave a pawl!
> 'Bout ship and stations there be handy,
> Rise, tacks and sheets and mainsail, haul!

(*Spoken*) ("This is a capstan shanty now . . .")

There was a Yankee ship a-laying in the basin,
Oh, they told me she was going to New York.

If I ever lay my hands on that shipping master,
Oh, I'll murder him if it's the last thing that I do.

When the pilot left the ship way down the channel,
Oh, the captain told us we were going around Cape Horn.

The mate and second mate belonged to Boston,
And the captain hailed from Bangor down in Maine.

The three of them were rough and tumble fighters,
When not fighting amongst themselves, they turned on us.

Oh, they called us out one night to reef the topsails,
Now with belaying pins a-flying around the deck.

Oh, and we came on deck and went to set the topsails,
Not a man among the bunch could sing a song.

We had tinkers, we had tailors and firemen, also cooks,
And they couldn't sing a shanty unless they had the books.

Oh, wasn't that a bunch of hoodlums
For to take a ship around Cape Horn!

MAITLAND: "Now this song . . . I forgot to explain it in the first place
. . . it commences . . . The solo is sung by the shantyman sitting on
the capstan head, where he always does sing . . . sit in case of singing
shanties. The shantyman sits there and does nothing, while the crew,
walking around the capstan, are singing. The chorus begins at:

> Paddy, get back, take in the slack,
> Heave away the capstan, heave a pawl, heave a pawl,

'Bout ship and stations there be handy,
Rise, tacks and sheets and mainsail, haul!

LOMAX: "And show us where the pull . . . where the . . . comes. . . ."

MAITLAND: "That's what I'm telling them now. This 'Paddy, get back' is the chorus . . ."

LOMAX: "And that's where they pull?"

MAITLAND: "There's no pull in a capstan shanty! They're walking around the capstan with the bars!"

ROLL THE COTTON DOWN

Oh, away down South where I was born,
Oh, roll the cotton down,
Away down South where I was born,
Oh, roll the cotton down.

A dollar a day is the white man's pay,
Oh, roll the cotton down,
Oh, a dollar a day is the white man's pay,
Oh, roll the cotton down.

I thought I heard our old man say,
Oh, roll the cotton down,
I thought I heard our old man say,
Oh, roll the cotton down.

We're homeward bound to Mobile Bay,
Oh, roll the cotton down,
We're homeward bound to Mobile Bay,
Oh, roll the cotton down.

Oh, hoist away that yard and sing,
Oh, roll the cotton down,

"Roll the Cotton Down" was recorded by Sidney Robertson Cowell from the singing of Captain Leighton Robinson, as shantyman, and Alex Barr, Arthur Brodeur, and Leighton McKenzie at Belvedere, California, 1939. Library of Congress record LP27.

Oh, hoist away that yard and sing,
Oh, roll the cotton down.

(*Spoken*) "That's enough."

A LONG TIME AGO

Now this is a song that's very popular in the vessels bound across with cotton from Mobile, New Orleans, Savannah, Charleston, any place where they load cotton, and it's usually sang with a gusto when they do sing it.

— RICHARD MAITLAND

Way down South where I was born,
Way ay ay yah,
I've picked the cotton and hoed the corn,
Oh a long time ago.

In the good old State of Alabam',
Way ay ay yah,
So I've packed my bag, and I'm going away,
Oh a long time ago.

When I was young and in my prime,
Oh, I served my time in the Black Ball Line.

I'm going away to Mobile Bay,
Where they screw the cotton by the day.

Five dollars a day is a white man's pay,
And a dollar and a half is a black man's pay.

When the ship is loaded, I'm going to sea,
Way ay ay yah,
For a sailor's life is the life for me,
Oh a long time ago.

"A Long Time Ago" was recorded by Alan Lomax from the singing of Richard Maitland at Sailors' Snug Harbor, Staten Island, New York, 1939. Library of Congress record LP27.

WHISKY JOHNNY

This halyard shanty was a favorite, and frequently sung with an eye to the skipper, with the hope that he would pass out a ration of grog.

Oh, whisky here, and whisky there,
Whisky Johnny,
Oh, whisky here, and whisky there,
Oh, whisky for my Johnny.

Oh, I'll drink whisky when I can,
Whisky Johnny,
Oh, I'll drink whisky while I can,
Oh, whisky for my Johnny.

Oh, whisky gave me a broken nose.

And whisky made me pawn my
   clothes.

Oh, if whisky were a river, and I
   were a duck.

I'd swim around till I got right
   drunk.

Oh, whisky landed me in jail.

Oh, whisky in an old tin pail,
Whisky Johnny,
Oh, whisky in an old tin pail,
Oh, whisky for my Johnny.

SO HANDY, ME BOYS, SO HANDY

This halyard shanty tells no story, but simply urges the men on to the immediate work in hand. What Maitland has to say about "doubling up" on the pull when the mate is out of humor applies not only to this shanty but to other halyard shanties as well.

Now handy high and handy low,
Handy, me boys, so handy,

"Whisky Johnny" was recorded by Sidney Robertson Cowell from the singing of Captain Leighton Robinson, as shantyman, and Alex Barr, Arthur Brodeur, and Leighton McKenzie at Belvedere, California, 1939. Library of Congress record LP27.

"So Handy, Me Boys, So Handy" was recorded by Alan Lomax from the singing of Richard Maitland at Sailors' Snug Harbor, Staten Island, New York, 1939. Library of Congress record LP27.

Oh, it's handy high and away we'll go,
Handy, me boys, so handy.

Hoist her up from down below,
Handy, me boys, so handy,
We'll hoist her up through frost and snow,
Handy, me boys, so handy.

We'll hoist her up from down below,
We'll hoist her up and show her clew.

One more pull and that will do,
Oh, we'll sing a song that'll make her go.

Now it's growl you may, but go you must,
If you growl too much, your head they'll bust.

Now one more pull and then belay,
And another long pull and we'll call it a day.

Now handy high and handy low,
Oh, one more pull and we'll send her alow.

We'll hoist her up and show her clew,
Handy, me boys, so handy,
And we'll make her go through frost and snow,
Handy, me boys, so handy.

LOMAX (*Spoken*): "What kind of a shanty is that?"

MAITLAND: "Well, that's a pulling shanty. You see where they . . . *han*dy, me boys . . . Is that thing going? . . . That's a hoisting shanty, it goes . . . you can either take a single long pull except when the mate is out of humor, and he sings out to 'double up, double up,' then you take a pull at '*han*dy, me boys, *han*dy.' "

LOMAX: "Was that a very popular shanty?"

MAITLAND: "Yes, sure it's very popular!"

BLOW THE MAN DOWN

This halyard shanty came into being ca. 1818 with the establishment of the great Black Ball Line of packets sailing between New York and Liverpool, although the line itself is not mentioned in this version. The word "blow" as used in the chorus meant to "knock" or "strike." The packet sailors called the rough second and third mates "blowers and strikers," the terms being synonymous.

We will pull, we will haul, hearty, healthy, and gay,
Heave away, away, blow the man down,
Like husky strong seamen to earn able pay,
Oh, give us some time to blow the man down.

We will pull, the commands of our skipper obey,
Heave away, away, blow the man down,
We will haul till we hear the command to belay,
Oh, give us some time to blow the man down.

We'll expend all the energy we can afford,
We'll joyfully heave the dead horse overboard.

We will heave with all might, we will heave with all main,
We will heave till the mainbrace needs splicing again.

We will heave when we're sickened by roughness of sea,
We will heave when recovering from a big spree.

We will heave when the salt horse and hog becomes rank,
We will heave for good treatment — our officers think.

To heave is what seamen should know how to do,
And sometimes a vessel is forced to heave, too [heave-to].

We'll heave heaving lines to a tender ashore,
Leave heaving of cargo to strong stevedore.

We will heave everywhere on the world's surface round,
We will heave the most joyfully when homeward bound.

"Blow the Man Down" was recorded by Helen Stratman-Thomas and Aubrey Snyder on a joint field-collecting project for the University of Wisconsin and the Library of Congress from the singing of Noble B. Brown, Woodman, Wisconsin, 1946. Library of Congress record LP27.

Blow the man down, bullies, blow the man down,
Heave away, away, blow the man down,
We'll heave the most joyfully when homeward bound,
Oh, give us some time to blow the man down.

HAUL AWAY, MY ROSY

Talk about your harbor girls around the corner, Sally.
'Way, haul away, haul away, my Rosy,
'Way, haul away, haul away, my Johnny-O.

But they couldn't come to tea with the girls from Booble Alley.
'Way, haul away, haul away, my Rosy,
'Way, haul away, haul away, my Johnny-O.

I once loved a French girl, but she was fat and crazy.

With her "Parlez-vous, oui, oui, français" she nearly drove me crazy.

King Louis was the king of France before the Revolution.

"Haul Away, My Rosy" was recorded by Alan Lomax from the singing of John M. ("Sailor Dad") Hunt of Marion, Virginia, at Washington, D.C., 1941. Library of Congress record LP2.

But the people cut his head off, then he lost his constitution.

We sailed away from Liverpool, bound for the Gulf of Mexico.

We sailed into Galveston and loaded up with cotton-o.
'Way, haul away, haul away, my Rosy,
'Way, haul away, haul away, my Johnny-O.

We loaded cargo there, my boys, then we took it light and easy.
'Way, haul away, haul away, my Rosy,
'Way, haul away, haul away, my Johnny-O.

SALLY BROWN

I shipped on board of a Liverpool liner,
'Way, hey, roll and go.
And we'll go all night and we'll go till mornin',
I spend my money along with Sally Brown.

Sally Brown is a nice young lady.
'Way, hey, roll and go.
And we'll go all night and we'll go till mornin',
I spend my money along with Sally Brown.

She's tall and dark but not too shady.
'Way, hey, roll and go.
And we'll go all night and we'll go till mornin',
I spend my money along with Sally Brown.

Her mother don't like a tarry sailor.
'Way, hey, roll and go.
And we'll go all night and we'll go till mornin',
I spend my money along with Sally Brown.

She wants her to marry a one-legged captain.
'Way, hey, roll and go.
And we'll go all night and we'll go till mornin',
I spend my money along with Sally Brown.

"Sally Brown" was recorded by Alan Lomax from the singing of John M. ("Sailor Dad") Hunt of Marion, Virginia, at Washington, D.C., 1941. Library of Congress record LP2.

REUBEN RANZO

Unverified tradition has it that Reuben Ranzo was a Boston tailor who was shanghaied aboard a whaling vessel and subjected, as the song states, to the hardships and indignities of life at sea on a long voyage. Other variants of the halyard shanty are kinder to poor Reuben: the daughter of the skipper intercedes for him, he becomes a good sailor, and marries her.

Poor old Reuben Ranzo,
Ranzo, boy, Ranzo,
Poor old Reuben Ranzo,
Ranzo, boy, Ranzo.

He shipped aboard a whaler,
Ranzo, boy, Ranzo,
But Ranzo was no sailor,
Ranzo, boy, Ranzo.

He could not do his duty,
For neither love nor beauty.

He could not find his sea legs,
Used clumsy, awkward land pegs.

He could not coil a line right,
Did not know end from rope's
    bight.

Could not splice the main brace,
He was a seasick soft case.

He could not box the compass,
The skipper raised a rumpus.

The old man was a bully,
At sea was wild and woolly.

Abused poor Reuben plenty,
He scourged him five-and-twenty.

He lashed him to the mainmast,
The poor seafaring outcast.

Poor Reuben cried and pleaded,
But he was left unheeded.

Some vessels are hard cases,
Keep sailors in strict places.

Do not not show any mercy,
For Reuben, James, nor Percy.

The ocean is exacting,
Is often cruel acting.

A sailor never whimpers,
Ranzo, boy, Ranzo,
Though shanghaied by shore crimpers,
Ranzo, boy, Ranzo.

(*Spoken*) "I learned that aboard a sailing ship on a voyage from San Francisco to Falmouth, England."

"Reuben Ranzo" was recorded by Helen Stratman-Thomas and Aubrey Snyder on a joint field-collecting project for the University of Wisconsin and the Library of Congress, from the singing of Noble B. Brown, Woodman, Wisconsin, 1946. Library of Congress record LP26.

Forecastle Songs of the Sea and Sailors and Wrecks and Disasters at Sea

'Tis of a sad and dismal story that happened off the fatal rock,
When the *New Columbia* in all her glory, how she received that fatal shock.

THE SAILORS' ALPHABET

A   is the aftermost part of the ship,
B   is the bowsprit on the bow of the ship,
C   is the capstan the sailors goes round,
D   is the davits where the jolly boat hangs down.
E   is the ensign red, white and blue,
F   is the forecastle that holds the ship's crew.
G   is the gangway where the mate takes his stand,
H   is the halliards that never could strand.
I   is the iron that binds the ship round,
J   is the jibboom on the bowsprit is found.
K   is the kilson that leads fore and aft,
L   is the larboard where the backstays hold fast.
M   is the mainmast through the deck rove,
N   is the nasty old cook and his stove.
O   is the orders for us to beware,
P   is the pumps that cause the sailors to swear.
Q   is the quadrant that guides the ship round,
R   is the rigging that never can break.
S   is the starboard side of our ship,

"The Sailors' Alphabet" was collected from Mr. Fred Phippen of Islesford, Maine, 1925, and reported in Fannie Hardy Eckstorm and Mary Winslow Smyth, *Minstrelsy of Maine*, New York, 1927, p. 233 (Gryphon Books reprint, Ann Arbor, Michigan, 1971).

T   is the topmast that never can split.
U   is the ugly old Captain so blunt,
V   is the victuals as salt as old junk.
W   is for water that is salt as brine,
XYZ will bring it in a rhyme.

WHEN JONES'S ALE WAS NEW

This forecastle song was sung either at sea or, more happily, when ashore with a mug of beer and a good crew around a tavern table. Originally a traditional shore song, it had no stanza relating to the sailor, but this oversight was taken care of as soon as it moved to sea. The great collector of sea shanties and songs, William Main Doerflinger, cites a specific instance of its transfer from shore to sea as occurring in 1892, but indicates that it also may have been earlier. In 1941, this song was sung by "Sailor Dad" for President Franklin Delano Roosevelt at an entertainment at the White House.

There was six jovial tradesmen, they all sat down to drinking,
For they were jolly good fellows, and enjoyed their drinking, too.
They sat themselves down to be merry, for everyone was gay and jolly,
"You're welcome as the hills," says Molly.
When Jones's ale was new, my boys, when Jones's ale was new;
When the landlord's daughter she came in, and we kissed those rosy cheeks
    again,
We all sat down and then we'd sing,
When Jones's ale was new, my boys, when Jones's ale was new.

"When Jones's Ale Was New" was recorded by John A. Lomax from the singing of John M. ("Sailor Dad") Hunt of Marion, Virginia, at Washington, D.C., 1941. Library of Congress record LP27.

Now the first to come in was a soldier, with his knapsack over his shoulder,
For none could be more bolder, and his long broadsword he drew;
He swore every man should spend a pound, and they should treat all hands
    around,
And he jolly well drank their healths all 'round,
When Jones's ale was new, my boys, when Jones's ale was new;

Now the next to come in was a sailor, with his marlinspike and his sheaver,
For none could be more clever among this jovial crew;
He called the landlord into the place, and said it was time to splice the main
    brace,
And if he didn't he'd wreck the place,
When Jones's ale was new, my boys, when Jones's ale was new.

Now the next to come in was a tinker, and he was a jolly bedrinker,
And he was a jolly bedrinker among this jovial crew;
He mended pots, he mended kettles, his tinker's tools were made of good
    metals,
Good lord, how his hammer and nails would rattle,
When Jones's ale was new, my boys, when Jones's ale was new.

The next to come in was a rolling man, who ground the farmer's wheat at the
    old mill dam,
Who could drink more beer than Joe McCann, who was one of the jovial
    crew;
He would whistle and sing the whole day long, and always singing a merry
    old song,
And at night he'd join this jovial throng,
When Jones's ale was new, my boys, when Jones's ale was new.

Now the last to come in was a ragman, with his ragbag over his shoulder,
And none could be more bolder among this jovial crew;
They called for pots, they called for glasses, they all got drunk like old jack-
    asses,
And they burnt the old ragman's bag to ashes,
When Jones's ale was new, my boys, when Jones's ale was new;
Then the landlord's daughter she came in, and we kissed those rosy cheeks
    again,
We all sat down and then we'd sing
When Jones's ale was new, my boys, when Jones's ale was new.

CAPTAIN BUNKER

J. Ross Browne's *Etchings of a Whaling Cruise* is a wonderfully readable
and important book covering the early days of American sailing and whaling.
It preceded *Moby-Dick* by several years, just as Browne's book on the Com-

"Captain Bunker" is from J. Ross Browne, *Etchings of a Whaling Cruise*, New York, 1846,
pp. 47–48.

stock Lode and Nevada preceded Mark Twain's *Roughing It*, and his book on Mediterranean travels was ahead of Twain's *Innocents Abroad*. Browne is an important and neglected literary figure, with a fantastic career as traveler and observer. He was, to boot, a consummate artist, and his illustrations catch his times with humor and spirit. In *The Whaling Cruise* (1846), he gives three stanzas and a chorus for "Captain Bunker," introducing the scene (and giving us first-hand a picture of folksong in its habitat at sea):

After supper we had a social smoke. The musician of the ship was then called upon for a song. Seating himself comfortably on the fore-hatches, he cleared his throat, and gave us to understand, by way of a prelude, that he was a very indifferent singer. "He used to know some bang-up songs, but somehow he had forgotten them all." This, of course, only served to whet our curiosity, and draw forth renewed calls for a song. "Tom was a first-rate singer. Everybody knew Tom could sing. It was no use to deny it; Tom *must* sing!" Pressed on all sides, Tom stuck his pipe in the galley, and scratched his head to rub up the musical organs. He then assured us that he knew a great many songs. "Come, Tom," cried a chorus of voices, "give us 'Captain Bunker.' "

"Well, if I must, I must; here goes for 'Captain Bunker.' "

Tom then gave us the following whaling ditty. As it is a good specimen of sea-spun poetry, I give it without alteration.

> Our Captain stood upon the deck, a spyglass in his hand,
> A viewing of those gallant whales that blowed at every strand.
> Get your tubs in your boats, my boys, and by your braces stand,
> And we'll have one of those gallant whales, hand, boys, over hand!
>
> > So be cheery, my lads! let your hearts never fail
> > While the bold harpooneer is a-striking of the whale!
>
> "Overhaul, overhaul! your davit-tackles fall,
> Till you *land* your boats in the sea, one and all!"
> Our waist-boat got down, and of *course* she got the start:
> *"Lay me on, Captain Bunker, I'm hell for a long dart!"*
>
> Our first mate he struck, and the whale he went down;
> The captain he stood by, all ready for to bend on;
> Which caused the whale to vomic, and the blood for to spout;
> In less than ten minutes, he rolled both fins out!
>
> > So be cheery, my lads! let your hearts never fail
> > While the bold harpooneer is a-striking of the whale!

BLOW, YE WINDS

'Tis advertised in Boston, New York and Buffalo,
Five hundred Americans a-whaling for to go. Singing —

    Blow, ye winds of morning, and blow, ye winds, high-o!
    Clear away your running gear, and blow, ye winds, high-o!

They send you to New Bedford, that famous whaling port,
And give you to some land-sharks to board and fit you out.

They send you to a boarding-house, there for a time to dwell;
The thieves they there are thicker than the other side of hell!

They tell you of the clipper ships a-going in and out,
And say you'll take five hundred sperm before you're six months out.

It's now we're out to sea, my boys, the wind comes on to blow;
One half the watch is sick on deck, the other half below.

But as for the provisions, we don't get half enough;
A little piece of stinking beef and a blamed small bag of duff.

Now comes that damned old compass, it will grieve your heart full sore,
For theirs is two-and-thirty points and we have forty-four.

Next comes the running rigging, which you're all supposed to know;
'Tis "Lay aloft, you son-of-a-gun, or overboard you go!"

The cooper's at the vise-bench, a-making iron poles,
And the mate's upon the main hatch a-cursing all our souls.

The Skipper's on the quarter-deck a-squinting at the sails,
When up aloft the lookout sights a school of whales.

"Now clear away the boats, my boys, and after him we'll travel,
But if you get too near his fluke, he'll kick you to the devil!"

Now we have got him turned up, we tow him alongside;
We over with our blubber-hooks and rob him of his hide.

"Blow, Ye Winds" is from Joanna C. Colcord, *Songs of American Sailormen*, New York, 1938, pp. 191–192. With music.

Now the boat-steerer overside the tackle overhauls,
The Skipper's in the main-chains, so loudly he does bawl!

Next comes the stowing down, my boys, 'twill take both night and day,
And you'll all have fifty cents apiece on the hundred and ninetieth lay.

Now we are bound into Tonbas, that blasted whaling port,
And if you run away, my boys, you surely will get caught.

Now we are bound into Tuckoona, full more in their power,
Where the skippers can buy the Consul up for half a barrel of flour.

But now that our old ship is full and we don't give a damn,
We'll bend on all our stu'nsails and sail for Yankee land.

When we get home, our ship made fast, and we get through our sailing,
A winding glass around we'll pass and damn this blubber whaling! Singing —

Blow, ye winds of morning, and blow, ye winds, high-o!
Clear away your running gear, and blow, ye winds, high-o!

THE GREENLAND WHALE FISHERY

One thousand eight hundred and twenty-four
And March the twenty-third,
We hoisted the colors of our masthead
And for Greenland bore our way, brave boys,
And for Greenland bore our way.

Our Captain being on the mast so high
With a spyglass in his hand,
"Here's a whale, here's a whale, here's a wild fish," he cried,
"And she blows at every spang, brave boys,
And she blows at every spang."

"The Greenland Whale Fishery" was collected by a Miss Hamilton in 1910 from Fred
Wilkinson of the West Plains High School, Missouri, who found it in an "old MS collection
made by his grandmother, Eliza Robbins, of Brownington, Vermont." In H. M. Belden,
Ballads and Songs Collected by the Missouri Folk-Lore Society (University of Missouri
Press) Columbia (reprint edition, 1966), pp. 104–105. Without music. Music with one
stanza recorded by Alan Lomax from the singing of Mrs. Carrie Grover of Gorham, Maine,
at Washington, D.C., 1941. Library of Congress AFS record 4463 A1. Laws, K21.

Our boatswain being on the quarterdeck
And a merry good man was he:
"Overhaul, overhaul, let your jibsheet fall,
And launch your boat on the sea, brave boys,
And launch your boat on the sea."

Our boat being launched and the men all in,
And she flourishes with her tail;
Capsized our boat and lost five men —
Nor did we catch that whale, brave boys,
Nor did we catch that whale.

The news unto the captain went,
"We have lost your 'prentice boy;"
And hearing of this dreadful news
He down with the colors all, brave boys,
He down with the colors all.

In losing of this wild fish
It grieved his heart full some,
But in losing of the five jolly tars
It grieved him ten times more, brave boys,
It grieved him ten times more.

Oh, Greenland is a barren place,
Neither light nor day to be seen;
The ice and the snow, and the wild fish do play,
And the daylight seldom seen, brave boys,
And the daylight seldom seen.

Now a-weigh your anchors now, brave boys,
For the winter star I see.
It is time for to leave such a cold country
And for England bore away, brave boys,
And for England bore away.

THE TEMPEST

Mrs. Carrie Grover wrote:

I can remember hearing my father sing this song ever since I can remember, and something in the way he sang it always gripped me and made me feel the tragedy of it even before I was old enough to understand the meaning of it all. My sister says it always made her feel the same way. He would sit gazing into space, or out of the window, with a far away expression in his eyes. I have often wondered if while singing this song he was not reliving a terrific storm at sea, the worst he ever experienced.

He was sailing as Able Seaman on board a sailing vessel, and as he was an extra good helmsman the captain asked him if he could take a second trick at the wheel, for the man who was to take his place at the helm had been taken sick and had to go below. If I remember, a trick at the wheel meant standing at the helm and steering the vessel for four hours, when another man would take it for four hours. So for eight consecutive hours my father steered the vessel with the lightning dancing up and down the spokes of the wheel as he held it, on the railings around the deck and on the waves in front of him. He said the lightning was blue. When he was relieved, he went below and threw himself face down, and to use his own words he was stone blind for a fortnight.

My mother said that for years after they were married he would throw himself face down on a bed or couch during an electrical storm because of the severe pain in his eyes, and ever since I can remember his eyes would pain and the flesh seem to puff up around them every time there was a thunder storm.

> Cease rude Boreas blust'ring railers
> List ye landsmen all to me.
> Messmates, hear a brother sailor
> Sing the dangers of the sea.
>
> From bounding billows first in motion,
> Where the distant whirlwinds rise,
> Unto the tempestuous troubled ocean,
> Where the seas contend with skies.

"The Tempest" is from Carrie B. Grover, *A Heritage of Songs* (privately printed, Gould Academy, Bethel, Maine, n.d.), pp. 122–124.

Now don't you hear the bos'n calling,
"By topsail sheets and halyards stand.
Down topgallants quick be hauling,
Down your staysails, hand, boys, hand.

"Now she freshes, set the braces,
The lee topsail sheets let go,
Luff, boys, luff. Don't make wry faces,
Up your topsails nimbly cleu."

Now you all on down beds sporting,
Safely locked in beauty's arms,
Fresh enjoyments, wanton courting,
Free from all but love's alarms,

Whilst 'round us roars the tempest louder.
Think what fear our mind enthralls.
Harder yet it still blows harder;
Hark! once more the bos'n calls.

"Your topsails' yards point to the wind, boys,
See all's clear to reef each course.
Let the foresheet go. Don't mind, boys,
Though the weather should be worse."

Oh don't you hear the thunder's roaring
Peal on peal contending clash?
Whilst on our heads fierce rain falls pouring
And in our eyes blue lightnings flash.

Whilst all around us one dark water;
All above us one dark sky.
Different deaths at once surround us.
Hark! What means that dreadful cry?

"The foremast's gone!" cried every tongue out,
Whilst on the lee twelve feet 'bove deck
A leak beneath the chest tree's sprung out,
Call all hands to clear the wreck.

"Quick, the lanyard's cut to pieces.
Come, my hearties stout and bold,
Plumb the well; the leak increases;
Four feet water in the hold!

"Whilst o'er the ship the waves are beating,
We, our wives and children mourn.
Alas! from hence there's no retreating
Alas! to them there's no return.

"Still the leak is gaining on us,
Both chain pumps are choked below,
Heaven have mercy here upon us,
Only this can help us now.

"O'er the lee beam is the land, boys,
Let the guns o'erboard be thrown,
To the pumps call every hand, boys,
See, our mizzenmast is gone.

"The leak we've found, it can not pour fast,
We've lightened her a foot or more.
Up and rig a jury foremast,
She rights! she rights! Boys, we're off shore!"

THE LIGHTNING FLASH

When I was young and in my prime, my age twenty-two,
I fell in love with a pretty girl; the truth I'll tell to you.
I courted her for seven years, till her father came to know,
He says: "I'll have you cross the seas, where the stormy winds do blow."

On the fourteenth day of September last, Queen's Harbor we sailed away;
Bound down to Gibraltar in a sweet and a pleasant gale,
The wind blew fair, our course we steered, our ship before the wind,
But still my heart was filled with love for the girl I left behind.

When we got to our distant port, we stopped a short time there,
Our orders run to Milliger* the weather being fair;
The very next day we sailed away, all with a cloud of sail,
When the storms arise, eclipsed the sun; they blew a tremendous gale.

The wind it riz to a hurricane, it blew a tremendous gale, —
And the captain says, "My brave boys, go reef the main topsail!"
No sooner when his order was given, up aloft we lay,
Like hearty tars to lay those yards, his orders to obey.

When we got to the main topsail, a horrid flash came on, —
Oh, God! How I remember the last eclipse of the sun!
The thunder rolled tremendously, and the lightning around us flash,
The heavy sea rolled over us, and sand on deck did dash.

* "Malaga."

"The Lightning Flash" was recorded by Mary W. Smyth from the singing of Mr. John P. A. Nesbitt of St. Stephen, New Brunswick, n.d. Reported, with music, by Phillips Barry, in *Bulletin of the Folksong Society of the Northeast*, Cambridge, Mass., 3 (1931):14–15. Laws, K6.

Early next morning wasn't we a sight to view!
Our captain was washed overboard and three men of the crew;
The thunder rolled tremendously, and by that veil of light,
I and three of those sailors, by that lightning we lost our sight.

But thanks be unto kind Providence that carried us back on shore,
Back to dear old Ireland, to the girl whom I adore;
To me she did prove loyalty, — constant and kind to me,
We join our hands in wedlock bands, but her face I ne'er can see!

THE LOSS OF THE DUE DISPATCH

Carrie Grover writes:

This story is supposd to have been written by a member of the crew. My father and oldest brother told the story as they heard it from one of the survivors, a man by the name of Shaw. His wife, who was also one of the survivors, could not bear to hear it mentioned, but would burst into tears and leave the room if the subject was mentioned.

Mr. Shaw said that as the survivors huddled together on the rock they held each other's hands so that if one fell asleep he could be held back from sliding off the rock. Every time the tide rose it would break over the rock, often taking at least one of their number. Some of them became crazed and jumped into the water and drowned.

This song was so sad that I never learned much of it except the tune, though I have heard my father sing it many times. When I tried to find the words I could find no one of my family who knew the song, but a son of my father's oldest sister still remembered it and sent the words to me from Nova Scotia. So, thanks to my cousin Frank Spinney, who is over ninety years old, I got the words of the song that seems to have been forgotten by so many.

You landsmen and you seamen bold,
With hearts both stout and strong,
I pray you pay attention
To a melancholy song.
When you hear my dreadful story
I am sure you will make known.

"The Loss of the *Due Dispatch*" is from Carrie B. Grover, *A Heritage of Songs* (privately printed, Gould Academy, Bethel, Maine, n.d.), pp. 125–127.

I was born in the town of Patrick York,
In the county of Tyrone.

My name it is John Williams,
A man just in my prime,
For to deceive young women
I always was inclined.
It was four unlawful children
Were laid unto my charge,
I was forced to leave my country
And then set out at large.

It was on the ship called *Due Dispatch*,
We made our way straight down,
It was with peace and quietness
Our good ship did resound.
It was in the dead time of the night
Our ship she struck a rock,
Our passengers on deck did fly
And there received the shock.

Our captain's name was Lanchester,
A small boat he did fling
And two of our cabin passengers
Into the boat did spring.
The first and second roll she gave
The boat it hove up keel,
And these two young men they both were lost,
These young men's name was Steele.

And then, to our amazement,
Our ship she split in twain
And many of our passengers
Went floating on the main.
The rest of us climbed on the rock,
Where we clung with fear and dread,
And there we clung for five long days
Without support of bread.

Our sufferings can ne'er be told
As on that rock we stood,
With water to our middle

As the tide did flow and ebb.
The weeds that grew upon the rock
We ate instead of bread,
We killed and ate the captain's dog,
Likewise we drank his blood.

We talked of eating human flesh
That lay upon the rock
And many of our passengers
With hunger down did drop.
But God is always merciful
And relief He sent straightway,
Our empty boat did chance to drift
To the island of Cap Ray.

It was there a fisherman did dwell,
Our boat he espied and caught,
Which made him think there was a wreck,
Right well he knew the spot.
So as the sea quit raging
A boat he then put out,
He came unto the very spot,
To him we did call out.

He took us to the island
Where his lonely hut did stand;
This island was inhabited
By one lone fisherman.
A little bread and water
Was all he could afford,
Five more days in starvation
I am going to record.

And then by chance a ship there came,
Commanded by Captain Grant,
He took us all to Halifax,
God's blessing on him rest.
'Twas in the poorhouse of that place
We received the best of care,
To God alone our praise we give
Who safely brought us there.

FIFTEEN SHIPS ON GEORGES BANKS

The Fisherman's Memorial and Record Book, published in Gloucester in 1873, gives an account of this great gale of February 24, 1862, when thirteen vessels with their entire crews were lost and two other vessels were lost after the crews had been taken off.

Many of the best skippers of the town were lost in the gale, as several of them were on board some of the vessels lost, having taken this trip because their own vessels were not quite ready to start. There were lost in this gale one hundred and twenty men and fifteen vessels, leaving seventy widows and one hundred and forty fatherless children.

— Note from Eckstorm and Smyth

Come all ye bold undaunted ones who brave the winter's frost,
And ye who sail on Georges Banks, where thousands have been lost.

Come all ye grieving mothers, come wives and sweethearts, too,
Likewise ye loving sisters, who bade them last adieu.

It was in the month of February, in eighteen sixty-two,
The vessels sailed from Gloucester, with each a hardy crew.

The course they steered was east south east, Cape Ann passed out of sight;
They anchored on the Banks next day with everything all right.

But on the twenty-fourth at night the gale began to blow,
The sea rolled up like mountains, the ships rocked to and fro.

The thoughts of home and loving ones did grieve their hearts full sore,
Unwelcome news to many — they would see their homes no more.

No tongue could e'er describe that sea, the sky was filled with snow,
When fifteen sail did founder there and down to bottom go.

"Fifteen Ships on Georges Banks" was collected by Fannie Hardy Eckstorm and Mary Winslow Smyth from Mrs. Seth S. Thornton, of Southwest Harbor, Maine, 1926, as reported to her by "M. C. Gilley, of Southwest Harbor, who heard it sung in his youth by sailors and fishermen." In Eckstorm and Smyth, *Minstrelsy of Maine*, Boston and New York, 1927, p. 283. Without music. Laws, D3.

One hundred and seventy nine brave men so lately left our land,
Now sleep beneath on Georges Banks, that rough and shifting sand.

One hundred and seventy children these men have left at home,
And eighty-two sad widows the loss of husband mourn.

I pray that they'll be reconciled and not give way to grief,
For there's a widow's God above, and he will give relief.

There are soldiers in the army and in the navy, too,
Who knew and loved the lost ones and will sympathize with you.

We'll bid adieu to Georges Banks, dry up those tearful eyes,
For if we part upon this shore, we'll meet beyond the skies.

THE TITANIC

The White Star luxury liner *Titanic*, on its maiden voyage from Liverpool, sank on the night of April 14, 1912, following a collision with an iceberg in the North Atlantic. One thousand five hundred and thirteen people lost their lives.

It was on one Monday morning just about one o'clock
When the great *Titanic* began to reel and rock.
People began to scream and cry,
Saying, "Oh, Lord, I'm going to die!"
It was sad when that great ship went down.

Don't you know it was sad when that great ship went down,
It was sad when that great ship went down,
Husbands and wives, little children lost their lives,
It was sad when that great ship went down.

People aboard the ship was a long way from home,
With friends standing around didn't know their time had come;
But death came riding by, sixteen hundred had to die,
It was sad when that great ship went down.

"The *Titanic*" was recorded by John A. Lomax from the singing of Walter Caldwell, Ashland, Kentucky, 1937. Library of Congress AFS record 1023 A1. Laws, D24.

When Paul he was a sailor, his men all standing around,
God sitting in his Kingdom, not a man should be drowned;
Sixteen hundred and threescore
All got landed on that shore,
It was sad when that great ship went down.

    Don't you know it was sad when that great ship went down,
    It was sad when that great ship went down,
    Husbands and wives, little children lost their lives,
    It was sad when that great ship went down.

Great *Titanic*

    Out on the ocean, great wide ocean,
    Great *Titanic* out on the ocean, sinking down.

In the year of nineteen hundred and twelve
They built that great ship and built her well,
Great *Titanic* out on the ocean, sinking down.

She left the harbor with a rapid speed,
Carrying everything the people need,
Great *Titanic* out on the ocean, sinking down.

Well, the band was a-playing and the people was gay,
They didn't know that death was a-coming their way.

Captain persuaded the people to think
The great *Titanic* was too safe to sink.

The water rushed in with a mighty roar,
And the captain knew she'd soon be on the ocean floor.

Captain's orders was to gather around,
Get them lifeboats and let them down.

The captain's orders were scattered fast,
"Save the women and the children, let the men go last!"

"Great *Titanic*" was recorded by John A. Lomax from the singing of Frank Woodward, Sally Howard, and Floretta and Hattie Jones, Mobile, Alabama, 1937. Library of Congress AFS record 991 A1. And also by Lomax from the singing of Washington (Lightning) and group of convicts at Darrington State Farm, Sandy Point, Texas, 1933. Library of Congress AFS record 188. Text composite of both.

When the lifeboats landed, the women turned around,
Crying, "Look across the ocean where my husband drowns."
Great *Titanic* out on the ocean, sinking down.

Out on the ocean, great wide ocean,
Great *Titanic* out on the ocean, sinking down.

THE LOSS OF THE NEW COLUMBIA

Because of its wealth of detail, there would seem to be no doubt that this recounts an actual sea disaster off the New England or Newfoundland coast. Mrs. Grover learned this song from her father, who himself sailed from Maine ports in the last century.

'Tis of a sad and dismal story that happened off the fatal rock,
When the *New Columbia* in all her glory, how she received that fatal shock.

We sailed from England in December, from Liverpool the eighteenth day,
And many hardships we endured while coming to Americay.

Two passengers from Pence came with us, two brothers were from Birmingham,
They took the leave of all their people to settle in New Eng-e-land.

We anchored in four fathoms water, thinking all of our lives to save,
But 'twas all in vain for shortly after — poor souls, they met a watery grave.

Our ship she dragged away her anchor and on a rock she split in two,
And out of eighty brave young seamen, they all were lost excepting two.

Our captain, he being long afflicted, sick in his cabin said to his mate,
"Bring me on deck, that's my desire, where I may meet my unhappy fate."

He looked all 'round with eyes surrender, he took the leave of all his crew,
He gave his papers unto a servant, who chanced to be one of the two.

What was most shocking early next morning was to see the shores all lined
along
With the bodies of these shipwrecked sailors, to the *New Columbia* did
belong.

"The Loss of the *New Columbia*" was recorded by Alan Lomax from the singing of Mrs. Carrie Grover of Gorham, Maine, at Washington, D.C., 1941. Library of Congress record LP21.

Their flesh was mangled all to pieces, grinding upon the rocks on shore,
'Twould melt the hardest heart to pity to see them lying in their gore.

They were all taken and decently buried, most melancholy to relate,
To see so many brave young seamen all meet with such an unhappy fate.

May God protect all absent seamen, while plowing o'er the distant main,
And keep them clear from rocks and dangers, and safe return them home
  again.

May God protect all absent seamen, the mother and the fatherless,
And send his blessing on these poor people who have lost their sons in such
  distress.

THE FLYING CLOUD

My name is Edward Hollander, as you may understand,
I was born in the city of Watertown, in the far and eastern land.
I being young and in my prime, and beauty on me smiled,
My parents doted all on me, I being the only child.

My father bound me to a trade, it was in Trenton town;
He bound me to a cooper there by the name of William Brown.
I served my master faithfully for eighteen months or more,
Then I shipped on board of the *Ocean Queen* bent for Belfrazer* shore.

And when I struck Belfrazer shore I met with Captain Moore,
The commander of the *Flying Cloud* belonging to Baltimore.
He cordially invited me a slavery voyage to go
To the burning shore of Affaric, where the sugarcane does grow.

The *Flying Cloud* was a clipper built, four hundred tons or more;
She could easily sail around any ship that sailed from Baltimore.
Her sails were as white as the driven snow and on them not one speck;
She had thirty-two brass guns, my boys, she carried upon her deck.

* This is Valparaiso in other variants.

"The *Flying Cloud*" was collected by Miss Colquitt Newell from A. F. Nelson of Madison,
Wisconsin, 1913. Nelson had learned it some twenty years before from neighboring farm
boys in Dane County, Michigan. In H. M. Belden, *Ballads and Songs Collected by the
Missouri Folk-Lore Society* (University of Missouri Press) Columbia (reprint edition,
1966), p. 128. Laws, K28.

TO BE SOLD, on board the

Ship *Bance-Island*, on tuesday the 6th of *May* next, at *Ashley-Ferry*; a choice cargo of about 250 fine healthy

NEGROES,

just arrived from the Windward & Rice Coast. ——The utmost care has already been taken, and shall be continued, to keep them free from the least danger of being infected with the SMALL-POX, no boat having been on board, and all other communication with people from *Charles-Town* prevented.

Austin, Laurens, & Appleby.

N. B. Full one Half of the above Negroes have had the SMALL-POX in their own Country.

And in a short time after we had struck the African shore,
Eighteen hundred of those poor souls on board with us we bore.
We made them walk out on our planks as we stored them down below;
Scarce eighteen inches to the man was all that she would go.

The very next day we set to sea with our cargo of slaves.
It would have been better them poor souls had they been in their graves.
For the plagued fever came on board and swept one half away;
We drew their bodies up on deck and hove them in the sea.

And in a short time after we struck the Cubian shores,
We sold them to the planters there to be slaves for ever more,
To hoe in the rice and coffee fields beneath the burning sun,
To worry out a wretched life till their career was done.

Our money soon being spent and gone, we set to sea again,
When Captain Moore came out on deck and spoke to all his men:
"There is gold and silver to be had if you'll with me remain;
We will hoist aloft our pirate flag and scour the Spanish Main."

We all agreed but five young men, who told us them to land.
Two of them were Boston boys and two from the New Foundland,
And one was a young Irish lad belonging to Trymoor.
I would to God I would have joined those men and went with them on shore.

We robbed and plundered many a ship while on the Spanish Main,
We caused many a mother's heart an orphan to remain;
We made them walk out on our planks and take a watery grave,
For the saying of our captain was, "A dead man tells no tales."

We were often chased by many a ship, both frigate and liner, too.
It was all in vain across the main as at our stern they flew;
It was all across the Spanish Main with their cannons thundering loud,
They could not catch the *Ocean Queen*, they dreaded the *Flying Cloud*.

It was all in vain of them catching us, till the *Dreadnaught* came in view,
She fired a shot across our deck, a signal to heave to.
We gave to her no answer, but sailed before the wind,
When a chance shot struck our mizzenmast; it was then we fell behind.

We cleared our deck for action then, as she hove along our side,
And first across our quarterdeck there flowed a crimson tide.
We fought till Captain Moore was killed and eighty of his men;
Then a bombshell set our ship on fire — we had to surrender then.

They took us down to Rulawarp* bound down in iron chains
For the robbing and plundering of ships at sea while on the Spanish Main.
It was whiskey and bad company that made a wreck of me;
So, boys, beware of my sad plight and curse all piracy.

Now I will bid adieu to the shady grove and the girl that I love dear,
Her voice like music soft and sweet I never more shall hear;
I never shall kiss those ruby lips or stroke the lily-white hand,
But die a sad and scornful death down in this foreign land.

THE WILD BARBAREE

This song is based upon the Child ballad (285) of "*The George Aloe* and
the *Sweepstake*" which describes an early encounter between the French
and English. The early ballad seems to have been revived when the piratical
forays along the Algerian coast brought special meaning to "the coast of
Barbary" in the late eighteenth century. The *Prince of Wales* was built in
England in 1794. The transmission to this country of a sea song was not
unusual, but in this instance may have been stimulated by the fact that
Stephen Decatur in 1815 decisively defeated Algerian pirates on the "coast
of the wild Barbaree." The song was traditionally popular in the American
navy, and several texts have been recovered from Maine, where it was known
to Mrs. Grover's father.

> Two lofty ships of Eng-e-land set sail,
> Blow high, blow low, and so sailed we,
> And one was *Prince of Luther* and the other *Prince of Wales*,
> Cruising down round the coast of the wild Barbaree.
>
> "Look ahead, look astern, look to wind'ard and to lee,"
> Blow high, blow low, and so sailed we,
> "There's a lofty ship astern and for us she does make way,"
> Cruising down round the coast of the wild Barbaree.

* This is usually Newgate.

"The Wild Barbaree" was recorded by Alan Lomax from the singing of Mrs. Carrie Grover
of Gorham, Maine, at Washington, D.C., 1941. Based on Child ballad No. 285, "The
George Aloe and the *Sweepstake*." Library of Congress record LP21. Laws, K33.

"Oh, hail her, oh, hail her," our gallant captain cries,
Blow high, blow low, and so sailed we,
"Are you man-o'war or a privateer?" said he.
Cruising down round the coast of the wild Barbaree.

"I am neither man-o'war or a privateer," said he,
Blow high, blow low, and so sailed we,
"But I am a saucy pirate a-seeking for my fee."
Cruising down round the coast of the wild Barbaree.

Then for broadside for broadside these two ships did go,
Blow high, blow low, and so sailed we,
Till at length the *Prince of Luther* shot the pirate's mast away.
Cruising down round the coast of the wild Barbaree.

Then for quarter, for quarter the pirate captain cried,
Blow high, blow low, and so sailed we,
But the quarter that we gave them was to sink them in the sea,
Cruising down round the coast of the wild Barbaree.

Oh, we fought them for better than three hours as you see,
Blow high, blow low, and so sailed we,
But their ship it was their coffin and their grave it was the sea,
Cruising down round the coast of the wild Barbaree.

THE WIND SOU'WEST

You gentlemen of England far and near
Who live at ease far from all care,
It's little do you think and little do you know
What we poor seamen undergo,
With the wind sou'west and a dismal sky,
And the ruffling seas rolled mountains high.

On the second day of April, 'twas on that day
Our captain called us all away.
He took us from our native shore
While the wind sou'west and loud did roar
With the wind sou'west and a dismal sky
And the ruffling seas rolled mountains high.

On the fifth day of April, 'twas on that day,
When we spied land on the loward lay.
We saw three ships to the bottom go
While we, poor souls, tossed to and fro,
With the wind sou'west and a dismal sky,
While the ruffling seas rolled mountains high.

On the sixth day of April, 'twas on that day,
When our captain and foremast washed away.
Our mast being gone, the ship sprang a leak,
And we thought we should sink in the watery deep,

"The Wind Sou'west" is from Carrie B. Grover, *A Heritage of Songs* (privately printed, Gould Academy, Bethel, Maine, n.d.), pp. 131 and 133. Laws, K2.

With the wind sou'west and a dismal sky,
And the ruffling seas rolled mountains high.

The second mate and eighteen more
Got into the longboat and rowed for shore,
But what must it have been for their poor wives
A-losing their husbands' precious lives
With the wind sou'west and a dismal sky,
While the ruffling seas rolled mountains high?

On the seventh day of April, 'twas on that day
When we arrived in Plymouth Bay,
What a dismal tale had we for to tell
Of how we acted in that gale,
With the wind sou'west and a dismal sky,
And the ruffling seas rolled mountains high.

THE BAY OF BISCAY

You gentlemen of England who live at home at ease,
It's little do you think or know the dangers of the seas;
When we receive our orders, we are obliged to go
'Cross the main to proud Spain, let the wind blow high or low.

On the second day of August from Spithead we set sail,
With *Ramsay* in our company, blessed with a pleasant gale.
We sailed along together to the Bay of Biscay-o,
Where dreadful storms came on and the wind began to blow.

Then *Ramsay* in our company she could no longer stay,
It was by stress of weather from us she bore away;
She put into Gibraltar where she told the people so,
That she feared we were all lost in the Bay of Biscay-o.

But as Heaven provided, it was not quite so bad,
Though first we lost our mainmast and with it went our flag;

"The Bay of Biscay" was recorded by Alan Lomax from the singing of Mrs. Carrie Grover of Gorham, Maine, at Washington, D.C., 1941. Library of Congress AFS record 4464 B. Laws, K3.

And then we lost our mizzenmast, six of our guns also,
And of men we lost ten in the Bay of Biscay-o.

Our captain on the quarterdeck, it killed him outright,
Gold rings upon his fingers were burst asunder quite;
Gold rings upon his fingers, it bursted them in two,
There he lay till next day when we overboard him threw.

But as yet we had not perceived this melancholy stroke,
For in the side of our good ship there was a great hole broke,
Which caused our gun room with water for to flow.
There we rolled and tolled in the Bay of Biscay-o.

The storm it being over, we rigged a jury-mast,
We put in to Gibraltar where we came to at last;
We put in to Gibraltar where we lay at the New Mole,
And the people they came flocking in, our state for to behold.

They said we were the terriblest sight that ever they did know,
We ne'er repined, but drank wine till we drownded all our woe;
We ne'er repined, but drank wine till we drownded all our woe,
Here's a long, fare you well to the Bay of Biscay-o.

THE ISLE OF MAN SHORE
(*The Desolate Widow*)

On the Isle of Man shore, I carelessly wandered
One Saturday's evening when calm was the air;
I espied a fair maid with a child in her arms,
[I] inclined to the rocks, her grief to declare.

With sorrowful accents, I heard her complaining,
Saying: "Willie, dear Willie, come back unto me";
Then again she exclaimed, "Oh, no more shall I see him,
My own dearest Willie lies under the sea."

From the Quays of Den Darken, a steam packet sailed away;
Bound unto Liverpool, last Wednesday set sail;
The weather being fair as the land disappeared,
Our hearts they were merry, both gentle and gay.

But the night coming down, both darksome and dreary,
The wind had increased to a terrible storm;
"Look out for the lighthouse!" the captain he called out.
"I fear that this night we shall all suffer harm."

The seas rolled like mountains, no shelter to fly to,
The ship by the billows was tossed to and fro;
Two men were swept over into the main foaming ocean,
While women and children were crying below.

Some fell on their knees, Heaven's mercy imploring,
And some lay insensible, or sunk in despair;
The seas loudly roaring, the sailors all swearing,
And when that they heard us, they mocked at our prayer.

But my Willie stood by me, to cheer and protect me,
While my helpless infant I pressed to my breast,

"The Isle of Man Shore" was contributed by Mrs. Annie V. Marston, West Gouldsboro, Maine, n.d. Reported, with music, by Phillips Barry in *Bulletin of the Folksong Society of the Northeast*, Cambridge, Mass., 1 (1930):8–9. Laws, K7.

517

We shouted for aid, but no help came near us,
So now, tender Christians, think of our distress.

Two boats were launched out in the main foaming ocean,
In one of them was my infant and I,
But before they reached the shore, they were all overwhelmed,
And soon in the deep, forty bodies did lie.

But my Willie being brave, to the ship he returned again,
And I was safely landed on the Isle of Man shore;
But to save his old father, his own life he ventured,
Now, alas! I am doomed to behold him no more.

And now I am left a poor discontent widow,
Scare one year in wedlock as you plainly see;
To beg for my bread among hard-hearted strangers, —
May Heaven smile down on my infant and me.

JOHNNY GALLAGHER

Mothers of sailors, I hope you will draw nigh
For to hear of the sad news, it will cause you to cry,
Of the noble Johnny Gallagher who sailed to and fro,
He was lost on Lake Michigan where the stormy winds blow.

"Oh, Johnny, my dear son, in the dead of the night
I awoke from a dream which gave me a fright;
And to Traverse City I beseech you not to go,
For you'll never cross Lake Michigan where the stormy winds blow."

"Oh, Mother, dear Mother, those your dreams are not true,
I will shortly return and prove it to you;
For the Lord will protect me wherever I go
And I'll cross o'er Lake Michigan where the stormy winds blow.

"Oh, Nancy, lovely Nancy, don't stop me, my dear,
I will shortly return, so come dry up your tears.

"Johnny Gallagher" was recorded by Alan Lomax from the singing of J. W. Green, Beaver Island, Michigan, 1938. Library of Congress AFS record 2273 A. Laws, D17.

And home in our cottage the full bumpers will flow,
When I cross o'er Lake Michigan where the stormy winds blow."

It was in October of seventy-three,
We left Beaver Harbor and we had a calm sea,
And to Traverse City our destination to go,
For to cross o'er Lake Michigan where the stormy winds blow.

We left Traverse City at nine the next day
And down to Elk Rapids we then bore away;
We put in our stores and to sea we did go
For to cross o'er Lake Michigan where the stormy winds blow.

At nine that same night a light we espied,
That is the first island we are drawing nigh;
We carried all sails, the lookout he did go,
We were crossing Lake Michigan where the stormy winds blow.

Oh, Johnny got up and he spoke to his crew,
He says, "My brave boys, now be steady and true,
Stand by your fore halliards, let your main halliards go,
There's a squall on Lake Michigan where the stormy winds blow."

The lookout is running before the storm gale,
Our rudder unshipped and o'erboard went her sails,
And the billows came foaming like mountains of snow:
"We will never cross Lake Michigan where the stormy winds blow."

"Oh," said brother Johnny, with heart full sore,
"For to think that we'll never return to the shore!
God help our poor parents, how their tears down will flow,
For we'll sleep in Lake Michigan where the stormy winds blow."

THE GIRLS AROUND CAPE HORN

The famed ship *California*, a ship of high renown,
She lay in Boston harbor, 'long-side of thet pretty town,
A-waiting for our orders to sail far from home,
And our orders came for Rio, boys, and then around Cape Horn.

"The Girls around Cape Horn" is from Joanna C. Colcord, *Songs of American Sailormen*,
New York, 1938, p. 178. With music.

When we arrived in Rio we lay there quite a while,
A-fixing up our rigging and bending our new sails.
From ship to ship they cheered us as we did sail along,
And they wished us pleasant weather while rounding of Cape Horn.

While rounding of Cape Horn, my boys, fair nights and pleasant days.
Next place we dropped our anchor was in Valparaiso Bay,
Where those Spanish girls they did roll down, I solemnly do swear
They far excell those Yankee girls with their dark and wavy hair.

They love a Yankee sailor when he goes on a spree;
He'll dance and sing and make things ring, and his money he will spend free,
And when his money it is all gone, on him they won't impose;
They far excell those Liverpool girls who will pawn and steal his clothes.

Here's health to Valparaiso along the Chile main,
Likewise to those Peruvian girls, they treated me so fine,
If ever I live to get paid off, I'll sit and drink till morn,
A health to the dashing Spanish girls I met around Cape Horn.

THE GREEN BED

Young Johnny sails the sea, young Johnny sails the shore,
Young Johnny sailed to London, where he had been before.
"You are welcome home, young Johnny, you are welcome home from sea,
For last night daughter Polly lay dreaming of thee.

"What luck, what luck, young Johnny? What luck have you had at sea?"
"I have had very poor luck," young Johnny said to me.
"Call down your daughter Polly, and sit her on my knee,
We'll drown all melancholy and married we will be."

"My daughter Polly's absent, she can't be seen today;
And if she was at home, she would not let you stay.
And if she was at home, she'd turn you out of doors,
For, young Johnny, she is rich, and you are very poor."

"The Green Bed" was recorded by Sidney Robertson Cowell from the singing of George Vinton Graham, San Jose, California, 1938. Library of Congress AFS record 3816 B1. Some textual interpolations from H. M. Belden, *Ballads and Songs Collected by the Missouri Folk-Lore Society* (University of Missouri Press) Columbia (reprint edition, 1966), pp. 160–162. Laws, K36.

Young Johnny looked around, he looked upon them all,
And then he began his reckonings for to call.
"It's forty shillings of the old and thirty of the new . . ."
Double handfuls of gold and silver out young Johnny drew.

Down came her daughter Polly, all with a smiling face,
She threw her arms around him, so sweetly did embrace.
Saying, "You're welcome home, young Johnny, you're welcome home from
     sea,
For the green bed is empty, and you shall lie there with me."

"Before I'd lie there, I'd lie within the street,
For when I had no money, my lodging I might seek;
But now I have got money, I will make the taverns whirl
With a bottle of good brandy, and on my knee a girl!"

A TRIP TO THE GRAND BANKS

The author of this song, which gives a fine picture of the fisherman's life off
the Banks, was Amos Hanson of Orland, Maine. No date for its composition
is given by Barry, but he reported in 1932 receiving a fragment of another
song by Hanson from Hanson's daughter, Mrs. Hallie Hanson Soper, who
said that her father composed it "when he was a very young man." So the
song would go back well into the last century.

   The *snapeyes* in the song are small codfish, so called because they bite at
fish eyes used for bait. *Hagduls* or *hagdens* are jaegers or skua gulls that
rob smaller species of their catch, and *Careys* are stormy petrels, or "Mother
Carey's chickens."

   Early in the spring when the snow is all gone,
   The Penobscot boys are anxious their money for to earn;
   They will fit out a fisherman, one hundred tons or nigh,
   For the Grand Banks of Newfoundland their luck for to try.

   Sailing down the river, the weather being fine,
   Our homes and our friends we leave far behind;
   We pass by Sable Island, as we've oft done before,
   Where the waves dash tremendous on a storm beaten shore.

"A Trip to the Grand Banks" was collected by Mrs. Susie C. Young from Mrs. Phila
Roberts Howard, South Penobscot, Maine, 1932. Reported, with music, by Phillips Barry in
Bulletin of the Folksong Society of the Northeast, Cambridge, Mass., 4 (1932):16.

Now the vessel is our quarters, the ocean is our home,
And islands, capes and headlands we leave far astern;
We run to the eastward for three or four days,
Then round to and "sound" upon the western edge.

Then we run for the shoals and we run for the rocks,
Where the hagduls and Careys, they surround us in flocks;
We let go our best anchor, where the seas run so high,
On the Grand Banks of Newfoundland the snapeyes for to try.

Early in the morn at the dawn of the day,
We jump into our dories, and we saw, saw away;
The snapeyes steal our bait, and we rip and we rave,
If ever we get home again, we'll give up the trade.

In this way we pass the summer, through dread and through fear,
In fog mulls and gales of wind, and big ships passing near;
They sometimes run the schooners down, and sink them in the deep,
The thoughts of such scenery is horrid to repeat.

Now the salt is all wet but one half a pen,
The colors we will show, and the mainsail we bend,
Wash her down and scrub the decks, — the dories we will stow,
Then heave up the anchor! To the westward we go!

THE SCHOONER FRED DUNBAR

Written by Amos Hanson of Orland, Maine, "The Schooner *Fred Dunbar*" has, according to Barry, long been a favorite song about Penobscot Bay. The song describes scenes from the daily life of Penobscot fishermen, together with naming real persons (including the author, "Amos H.," in the fifth stanza) involved in the events. The word "cowboy" in the second stanza supports the New England origin of the now thoroughly acclimated Southwestern cattle-country term.

"The Schooner *Fred Dunbar*" was recorded by Phillips Barry from the singing of Mrs. Emery Howard and her son, Mr. Julian Howard, North Bluehill, Maine, 1932. Words by Amos Hanson of Orland, Maine, n.d., but ca. 1850–1860 (?). Reported, with music (with notes as above), by Barry in *Bulletin of the Folksong Society of the Northeast*, Cambridge, Mass., 5 (1933):15–16. Laws, D14.

Bagaduce, the starting-point, is Castine, Maine; Green's Landing is on Isle au Haut, in Penobscot Bay. The course of the *Fred Dunbar* went via the coast of Nova Scotia and the Gut of Canso to Port Mulgrave, then along the west coast of Cape Breton Island to Cape Mabou (Mardeau) and to Margaree Island, then across the Gulf of St. Lawrence to Chaleur Bay, bordering the counties of Restigouche and Gloucester, New Brunswick.

You darling girls of Bagaduce, who live along the shore,
'Tis little do you think or know what sailors do endure;
Or if you did, you would treat them with more respect than before, —
You never would go with a landloper while sailors are on shore.

O, those Penobscot cowboys will tell you girls fine tales,
Of the hardships they endure while they are in the cornfields;
They will feed their hens and punch their pigs and make their mothers roar,
While we, like jovial-hearted boys, go to the Bay Chaleur.

You darling girls of Bagaduce, perhaps you'd like to know
The names of all our sailors before we start to go;
Their names and dispositions I'll endeavor to explain,
Before we set our canvas to plough the raging main.

The first was Hiram Wardwell who runs the *Rory O'More;*
The next was Captain Perkins who roams the golden shore;
They're very much respected by all both fore and aft,
Two better men cannot be found on an Androscoggin raft.

There was little Herman, Leroy and Bill, and Oliver Quinn and Steel,
And Amos H., the author, who an entry sheep did steal;
The next was little Owen, who loves the girls so well,
The last was young Horatio, — we called him the *Admiral.*

On board of the schooner *Fred Dunbar*, well found in fishing gear,
We crowded on our canvas, for Green's Landing we did steer;
When we arrived at anchor, the sun was very low,
'Twas there we shipped young Stinson, and Captain Mood' Thurlow.

When we arrived at Port McGrave, we hauled in for our salt;
We took our little fiddle to have a little waltz;
There was twelve of us when we started, our songs through the woods did roar;
When we arrived, I was surprised, I could not count but four.

The first day of September, broad off Cape Mardeau,
We struck a squall from our south-south-east which broke our boom in two;
So galliantly she weathered it and it was fine to see,
She walked to the windward with mainsail down, bound out to Margaree.

The last day of September will be remembered well,
And how poor sailors fared that night, no tongue can ever tell;
The wind blew high, the seas grew rough, and in torrents fell the rain,
I never saw such a night before, and hope I shan't again.

You darling girls of Bagaduce, the time is drawing nigh,
When soon you'll see the Stars and Stripes from the *Fred*'s main topmast fly;
Get ready, galliant lasses, put on your other gowns,
For soon you'll see the *Fred Dunbar* come sailing up to town.

O now this voyage is ended, and we've arrived on shore,
With our pockets full of greenbacks we have earned to the Bay Chaleur;
So merrily we'll dance and sing, as we have done before,
And when our money is all gone, we'll plough the bay some more.

THE DREADNOUGHT

There's a saucy, wild packet and a packet of fame,
She belongs to New York and the *Dreadnought*'s her name,
She is bound to the westward where the strong winds do blow,
Bound away in the *Dreadnought*, to the westward we go.

The time of her sailing is now drawing nigh,
Farewell, pretty May, I must bid you goodbye;
Farewell to old England and all there we hold dear,
Bound away in the *Dreadnought*, to the westward we'll steer.

Oh, the *Dreadnought* is hauling out of a Waterloo Dock,
When the boys and the girls on the pier heads do flock;
They will give us three cheers while their tears freely flow,
Saying, "God bless the *Dreadnought* wheresoe'er she may go."

"The *Dreadnought*" is from S. B. Luce, *Naval Songs*, New York (2nd ed.), 1902, p. 67.
Laws, D13.

Oh, the *Dreadnought* is waiting in the Mersey so free,
Waiting for the *Independence* to tow her to sea,
For to round that black rock where the Mersey does flow,
Bound away in the *Dreadnought*, to the westward we'll go.

Oh, the *Dreadnought*'s a-bowling down the wild Irish sea,
Where the passengers are merry, with hearts full of glee,
While the sailors like lions walk the decks to and fro,
Bound away in the *Dreadnought*, to the westward we'll go.

Oh, the *Dreadnought*'s a-sailing the Atlantic so wide,
Where the dark, heavy seas roll along her black sides,
With the sails neatly spread and the red cross to show,
Bound away in the *Dreadnought*, to the westward we'll go.

Oh, the *Dreadnought*'s becalmed on the banks of Newfoundland,
Where the water's so green and the bottom is sand,
Where the fish of the ocean swim around to and fro,
Bound away in the *Dreadnought*, to the westward we'll go.

Oh, the *Dreadnought*'s arrived in America once more,
We'll go ashore, shipmates, on the land we adore,
See our wives and our sweethearts — be merry and free,
Drink a health to the *Dreadnought*, wheresoe'er she may be.

Here's a health to the *Dreadnought*, and to all her brave crew,
Here's a health to her Captain and officers, too,
Talk about your flash packets, *Swallow Tail* and *Black Ball*,
But the *Dreadnought*'s the clipper to beat one and all.

THE DOM PEDRO

It's of a flash packet, a packet of fame,
She belongs to New York and *Dom Pedro*'s her name,
She is rammed up and jammed up, on deck and below,
We are bound to Shanghai in the *Dom Pe-de-ro*.

"The *Dom Pedro*" was recorded by Alan Lomax from the singing of Capt. Richard Maitland, Sailors' Snug Harbor, Staten Island, New York, 1939. Library of Congress AFS records 2530 B and 2531 A. Laws, D12.

Singing merry, merry, merry are we,
No mortal on earth is like sailors at sea,
Singing hi derry, ho derry, hi derry down,
Give a sailor his grog and then nothing goes wrong.

The pilot came down and these words he did say,
"Get ready, my boys, for we're sailing today."
We cast off her lines and we gave her the slip,
And down Boston Harbor at a pretty good clip.

It's now that we're sailing down off Cape Cod,
Where many a hardy flash packet has trod,
The wind it breezed up and the sea it did boil,
And just at eight bells we took in the main royal.

It's now that we're sailing down under the Line,
We'd caught our rain water and had plenty of time,
We filled all our casks, as you plainly can see,
And we're heading this ship far away for Shanghai.

It's now that we've arrived in the ports of Shanghai,
We're a-mending our sails and we're straightening her up.
We'll get three days' leave before loading again,
And buy all the presents we can find in the town.

Now that we're loaded and ready for sea,
The mate says, "We're going to Boston again."
When we get there, oh, how jolly we'll be,
We'll be twenty bold sailors all the way from Shanghai.

THE FAIR MAID BY THE SHORE

Mrs. Carrie Grover says:

This song was sung by the wife of my oldest brother, who learned it from an old man who lived in her grandmother's family when she was a child. He came from Ireland and was, I believe, an old soldier. He was a veteran of the

"The Fair Maid by the Shore" was recorded by Alan Lomax from the singing of Carrie Grover of Gorham, Maine, at Washington, D.C., 1941. Library of Congress AFS record 4453 A1. Text with music also in Carrie B. Grover, *A Heritage of Songs* (privately printed, Gould Academy, Bethel, Maine, n.d.), pp. 154–155. Laws, K27.

battle of Waterloo and gave my brother the remains of what had been the knife, fork and spoon, hinged together so they would need the least possible space, that he used at the battle of Waterloo. The knife was gone, but the fork and spoon are still intact and are now in the possession of my younger daughter, Ethel Mills.

There was a fair maiden who lived on the shore,
And she was sore oppressed, Oh,
And none could she find for to comfort her mind
As she roamed all alone by the shore, shore,
As she roamed all alone by the shore.

There was a sea captain who followed the sea,
Let the wind blow high or blow low, Oh,
"I will die, I will die, oh," the captain did cry,
"If I don't get that maid from the shore, shore,
If I don't get that maid from the shore."

The captain had silver, the captain had gold,
The captain had costly wearing,
All this would he give to his jolly ship's crew
For to bring him that maid from the shore, shore,
For to bring him that maid from the shore.

Slowly, slowly she came on board,
The captain he gave her a cheer, Oh,
He seated her down in the cabin below,
Saying, "Adieu to all sorrow and care, care."
Saying, "Adieu to all sorrow and care."

She seated herself in the stern of the ship
Where the waves rolled high and rolled low, Oh,
And she sang so sweet, so genteel and complete
That the seamen she sang all to sleep, sleep,
That the seamen she sang all to sleep.

She partook of his silver, she partook of his gold,
She partook of his costly wearing,
She took his broadsword for to make her an oar
To paddle her back to the shore, shore,
For to paddle her back to the shore.

527

"Your men must be crazy, your men must be mad,
Your men must be deep in despair, Oh.
I've deluded them all as well as yourself,
I'm again a fair maid on the shore, shore,
I'm again a fair maid on the shore."

THE BANKS OF DEE

The moon had climbed the highest hill
That rises o'er the source of Dee,
And from its eastern summit shed
Her silver light on towers three.

Sweet Mary there had laid her head
To muse on Sandy far at sea,
When soft a passing spirit said,
"Sweet Mary, weep no more for me."

Then Mary raised her lovely head
To see what spirit there might be,
And saw poor Sandy shivering stand,
With pallid cheek and hollow een.

"Oh, Mary dear, cold is the clay
That lies beneath the stormy sea;
Far, far from thee I sleep in death,
So, Mary, weep no more for me.

"Oh, Mary dear, thyself prepare
To follow me unto that shore,
Where we shall know no future care,
And grief and sorrow know no more."

The black cock crew, the spirit fled,
No more of Sandy could she see,
But soft his passing spirit said,
"Sweet Mary, weep no more for me."

"The Banks of Dee" was recorded by Alan Lomax from the singing of Mrs. Marianna Schaupp, Washington, D.C., 1941. Library of Congress AFS record 6082 A1. Laws, K20.

THE ROCKY ISLAND

A sailor's trade is a weary life,
It robs fair maids of their heart's delight;
It causes them for to weep and to mourn,
A-waiting for their sailor boy to return.

Dark is the color of my sweetheart's hair,
His cheeks are red as the roses fair,
He's the fairest one among them all,
I'll have my sailor boy or I'll have none at all.

"Father, father, come build me a boat
That over the ocean I may float,
And every ship that I pass by,
Oh, there I'll inquire for my sweet sailor boy.

"Captain, captain, come tell me true,
Is my sweet William among your crew?
Come tell me quick and give me joy,
That I may find my sweet sailor boy."

"No, fair maiden, he is not here,
We lost him many a mile from here,
A rocky island as we passed by —
Oh, there we lost your sweet sailor boy."

She wrang her hands and she tore her hair,
As if a lady in despair;
She rowed her boat against a rock,
For this fair lady's heart was broke.

"Give me a chair and sit me down,
A pen and ink, and I'll write a song,
At the end of every word I'll drop a tear,
At the end of every line I'll cry 'Oh, my dear!'

"Dig my grave both long and deep,
Place a marble stone at my head and feet,
Upon my breast a turtledove
To let the wide world know I died for love."

"The Rocky Island" was recorded by Austin E. Fife from the singing of Mrs. Mary Hafen Leavitt, St. George, Utah, 1947. Library of Congress AFS record 8648 B1. Laws, K12.

Lumbering

Come all you sons of freedom and listen to my theme,
Come all you roving lumberjacks that run the Saginaw stream.
We'll cross the Tittabawassee where the mighty waters flow,
And we'll roam the wild woods over and once more a-lumbering go.

And once more a-lumbering go.
We will roam the wild woods over
And once more a-lumbering go.

THE LUMBERMAN'S ALPHABET

A   is for axes, you very well know, and
B   is for boys that use them so;
C   is for chopping, which they do begin, and
D   is the danger they oft times get in.

So merry, so merry, so merry are we,
No mortals on earth more contented could be,
With a Hi! Dera! Ho! Dera! Down!
At the woodsman's shanty there's nothing goes wrong.

E   is for echo that through the woods rang, and
F   is for foreman, the head of the gang;
G   is the grindstone that swiftly goes 'round, and
H   is for the handle so smooth and so round.

I   is for iron, with which they do mark pine, and
J   is for jolly boys, all in a line.
K   is for the keen-edge our axes we keep, and
L   is for the lice to keep us from sleep.

"The Lumberman's Alphabet" was reported by Mrs. Ella M. Patterson, Hampden Highlands, Maine, and included in Fannie Hardy Eckstorm and Mary Winslow Smyth, *Minstrelsy of Maine*, New York, 1927, p. 30. Without music. A close variant is on Library of Congress record LP56, recorded by Alan Lomax from the singing of Gus Schaffer at Greenland, Michigan, 1938.

M is for the moss that we chink into our camps,
N is for the needle with which we mend our pants,
O is for owls that hoot by night, and
P is for the pines that always fall right.

Q is for quarreling, which we don't have 'round, and
R is for river, which we drive our logs down;
S is for sled, so stout and so strong, and
T is for the team to draw it along.

U is for use, which we put our teams to, and
V is the valley which we draw our sleds through, and
W is for woods that we leave in the spring
And now I have sung all that I'm going to sing.

So merry, so merry, so merry are we,
No mortals on earth more contented could be,
With a Hi! Dera! Ho! Dera! Down!
At the woodsman's shanty there's nothing goes wrong.

ONCE MORE A-LUMBERING GO

Come all you sons of freedom and listen to my theme,
Come all you roving lumberjacks that run the Saginaw stream.
We'll cross the Tittabawassee where the mighty waters flow,
And we'll roam the wild woods over and once more a-lumbering go.

And once more a-lumbering go.
We will roam the wild woods over
And once more a-lumbering go.

When the white frost hits the valley, and the snow conceals the woods,
The lumberjack has enough to do to find his family food.
No time he has for pleasure or to hunt the buck and doe;
He will roam the wild woods over and once more a-lumbering go.

With our crosscut saws and axes we will make the woods resound,
And many a tall and stately tree will come crashing to the ground.
With cant hooks on our shoulders to our boot tops deep in snow,
We will roam the wild woods over and once more a-lumbering go.

"Once More A-Lumbering Go" was recorded by Alan Lomax from the singing of Carl
Lathrop at St. Louis, Michigan, 1938. Library of Congress record LP56.

You may talk about your farms, your houses and fine places,
But pity not the shanty boys while dashing on their sleigh;
For around the good campfire at night we'll sing while wild winds blow,
And we'll roam the wild woods over and once more a-lumbering go.

Then when navigation opens and the water runs so free,
We'll drive our logs to Saginaw, once more our girls to see,
They will all be there to welcome us and our hearts in rapture flow;
We will stay with them through summer then once more a-lumbering go.

    And once more a-lumbering go.
    We will stay with them through summer,
    Then once more a-lumbering go.

When our youthful days are ended and our stories are growing old,
We'll take to us each man a wife and settle on the farm.
We'll have enough to eat and drink, contented we will go;
We will tell our wives of our hard times, and no more a-lumbering go.

    And no more a-lumbering go.
    We will tell our wives of our hard times
    And no more a-lumbering go.

THE FARMER AND THE SHANTY BOY
(*Trenton Town*)

As I strolled out one evening just as the sun went down,
So carelessly I wandered till I came to Trenton town.
I heard two maids conversing as I slowly passed them by.
One said she loved a farmer's son, and the other a shanty boy.

The one that loved the farmer's son, these words I heard her say:
The reason that she loved him, at home with her he'd stay,
He would stay at home all winter long, to the woods he would not go,
And when the spring would come in his fields, then he would plough and
    sow.

"The Farmer and the Shanty Boy" was collected by Miss Colquitt Newell from A. F. Nelson, Madison, Wisconsin, 1912. In H. M. Belden, *Ballads and Songs Collected by the Missouri Folk-Lore Society* (University of Missouri Press) Columbia (reprint edition, 1966), p. 443.

"All for to plough and sow his fields," the other one did say,
"If his crops should prove a failure, his debts he could not pay.
If his crops should prove a failure, grain markets being low,
The sheriff then would sell his grain to pay the debts he'd owe."

"As for the sheriff selling grain, that does not me alarm,
For there's no use in being in debt when you're on a good farm.
You raise your grain all on your farm, don't work through storm and rain,
While your shanty boy works hard each day his family to maintain."

"Oh, how I love my shanty boy who goes off in the fall!
He is both stout and healthy and fit to stand a squall.
With pleasure I'll receive him, in the spring when he comes down,
For his money with me he'll share quite free, while your mossback he has
    none."

"Oh, how you praise your shanty boy who goes off in the fall!
He's ordered out before daylight to stand the storms and squalls,
While happy and contented my farmer's son will stay
And tell to me some tales of love while raging storms go by."

"Oh, I could not listen to the silly stuff your mossback has to say,
For some of them are green enough the cows might eat for hay;
How easy it is to tell them when they come into town,
For the little kids run after them, saying, 'Mossy, how are you now?'"

"Oh, what I have said of your shanty boy I pray you'll me excuse,
And from this silly mossback I hope I may get free.
If ever I get free from him, with a shanty boy I'll go,
And leave him brokenhearted, his field to plough and sow."

Now here's good luck to the shanty boys that make the wild woods ring,
For they cut the pine in the wintertime and drive it in the spring.

THE ROVING SHANTY BOY

I am a roving shanty boy, love to sing and dance,
I wonder what my girl would say if she could see my pants:
Fourteen patches on each knee, sixteen on my stern,
Wear them whilst out in the woods, homeward they return.

"The Roving Shanty Boy" was recorded by Alan Lomax from the singing of John Norman,
Munising, Michigan, 1938. Library of Congress AFS record 2355 A.

> Still I'm a jovial fellow,
> Will spend my money free,
> Take a drink most any time,
> Lager beer with me.

You ought to see my Liza, she thinks a pile of me,
You ought to see her throw herself when I get on a spree;
Trots off like some quarter horse, sailing round the horn,
With her head and tail up like a steer rushing through the corn.

> Still I'm a jovial fellow,
> Will spend my money free,
> Take a drink most any time,
> Whiskey clear with me.

With my patched-up pants and river boots, mud clear to the knee,
Lice on me like cherry pits, wrastling with the fleas,
Still I'm a jovial fellow, will spend my money free,
Take a drink most any time — whiskey clear with me.

THE SHANTY BOYS AND THE PINE

This and the following two songs recount in considerable detail aspects of the daily life of the lumberman in the Wisconsin and Michigan woods. A Wisconsin origin for "The Shanty Boys and the Pine" is claimed.

Emery DeNoyer, singer of this first song, was blinded when a young boy but, gifted with a fine voice, he became an entertainer and, with his father, visited lumber camps on Sundays to sing to the lumbermen and, in turn, to learn from them added songs for his repertoire.

Come all you jolly fellows, come listen to my song;
It's all about the pinery boys, and how they get along,
They're the jolliest lot of fellows, so merrily and fine;
They will spend their pleasant winter months in cutting down the pine.

Some will leave their friends and homes, and others they do love dear,
And into the lonesome pinewoods their pathway they do steer,
Into the lonesome pinewoods all winter to remain,
A-waiting for the springtime to return again.

"The Shanty Boys and the Pine" was recorded by Robert F. Draves from the singing of Emery DeNoyer at Rhinelander, Wisconsin, 1941. Library of Congress record LP55.

Springtime comes, oh glad will be its day;
Some return to home and friends, while others go astray.
The sawyers and the choppers, they lay their timber low,
While swampers and the teamsters, they haul it to and fro.

Next comes the loaders, before the break of day;
"Load up your sleighs five thousand feet, to the river haste away!"
Noontime rolls around, our foreman loudly screams,
"Lay down your tools, me boys, and we'll haste to pork and beans."

We arrive at the shanty; the splashing then begins,
The banging of the water pails, the rattling of the tins.
In the middle of the splashing, our cook for dinner does cry;
We all arise and go, for we hate to lose our pie.

Dinner being over, we into our shanty go;
We all fill up our pipes and smoke till ev'rything looks blue.
"It's time for the woods, me boys," our foreman, he does say;
We all gather up our hats and caps, to the woods we haste away.

We all go out with a welcome heart and a well contented mind,
For the winter winds blow cold, among the waving pines.
The ringing of saws and axes, until the sun goes down.
"Lay down your tools, me boys, for the shanties we are bound."

We arrive at the shanty with cold and wet feet;
Take off our overboots and packs, at supper we must eat.
Supper being ready, we all arise and go,
For it ain't the style of a lumberjack to lose his hash, you know.

At three o'clock in the morning out bold cook loudly shouts,
"Roll out, roll out, you teamsters, it's time that you were out."

The teamsters, they get up in a fright, and manful wail,
"Where's my boots, oh where's my packs, my rubbers have gone astray."
The other men, they then get up, their packs they cannot find;
And they lay it to the teamsters, and they curse them till they're blind.

Springtime comes, oh glad will be its day.
"Lay down your tools, me boys, and we'll haste to break away."
The floating ice is over, and business now destroyed.
Three hundred able-bodied men are wanted on the Pelican drive.

JOHNNY CARROLL'S CAMP

Dr. E. C. Beck reports that "Bill McBride had one of those remarkable memories found now and then among folksingers. His large repertoire amazed such veteran collectors and authorities as John and Alan Lomax and Stith Thompson. Bill had been a chopper, swamper, teamster, top-loader, and riverhog for some of the biggest outfits of the Great Lakes pinewoods. On a log he was as agile as a cat. . . ." Michigan's Chippewa River is one of the streams feeding the Saginaw, source of some of the world's best white pine.

One evening in November I happened for to stray
To Johnny Carroll's lumbering camp on the banks of the Chippewa;
With him I tried to grub and chop and level down the roads,
To make ready for our wintry snow through which our logs are towed.

With grub hoes, pries, and axes we loosened the roots and stumps
And we filled up all the hollows as we leveled down the lumps.
Now to be a perfect woodsman and to learn the lumbering trade,
You must spend a certain length of time a-toiling on the grade.

Now, choppers, grind your axes, and sawyers, file your saws,
And teamsters, mend your harnesses, for these are lumbering laws.
The blacksmith and the tinker, they mend our tools so neat;
We dare not fear the work, brave boys, our tools they're all complete.

Our cooks they are good-natured, we get the best of board;
We get the best variety our country can afford:
Potatoes, apples, turnips, beans, and syrup, so pure and sweet.
Although we have no appetite we cannot help but eat.

There's bread and biscuits, pie and cookies, all seasoned to our taste;
And our cooks be very careful there is nothing goes to waste.
Our sleeping camp is well arranged with bunks long, wide and deep;
And as night upon us reaches, boys, we quickly go to sleep.

"Johnny Carroll's Camp" was recorded by Alan Lomax from the singing of Bill McBride at Mt. Pleasant, Michigan, 1938. Library of Congress record LP56.

The chore boy in the morning gets up and starts the fires,
And keeps our camp so neat and clean we cannot but admire.
You'd ought to see us working as the weather is mild and fair;
With chains, cant hooks, peaveys, how we work the stately pine.

From daylight until dark, brave boys, we toil day after day
A-working in the pinewoods on the banks of the Chippewa.

When winter 'tis all over and our lumbering 'tis all done,
We'll go out on the river, boys, and there we'll have some fun.
We'll start our logs a-floating and we'll drive them down the stream.
And before we'll face for home, brave boys, we'll sing the lumbering theme.

TURNER'S CAMP ON THE CHIPPEWA

Come all you jolly shanty boys that work the shanty and go,
Come listen to my story, and I will tell to you
Our trials and our hardships we undergo each day
While working up in Turner's camp along the Chippewa.

I started up from Saginaw to go up the Chippewa.
I landed in a place called Clare about eleven o'clock that day.
The place, it being so stumpy, I thought I was next to Hell;
So I jumped on board of old Sax's stage and came to Isabelle.

While laying around in Isabelle I thought I'd go to work
Away up in the lumber camp where there was no time to shirk.
I started after dinnertime to take a little tramp;
I fetched up just at suppertime to Charlie Turner's camp.

At three o'clock next morning the cook his horn did blow
For to call the boys unto their hash and for the woods to go.
At first they put me sawing, but they found that would not pay,
So when the boys from Quebec left we went to load the sleigh.

In loading up those darned old sleighs, of course I being so green,
The piling up of those top logs I never before had seen.
The driver, being in a hurry for to get upon his route,
Would kick the log and roll the log and shove the log about.

"Turner's Camp on the Chippewa" was recorded by Alan Lomax from the singing of Bill
McBride at Mt. Pleasant, Michigan, 1938. Library of Congress record LP56. Laws, C23.

When the last load was on the sleigh to the river we would go,
To sing the songs of many things that happened years ago.
Some would sing of "Johnnie Troy," the other "The Cumberland Crew,"
But of all the songs that I loved best was "Bold Jack Donohue."

'Twas on the sixteenth day of May when bright the sun did shine.
Our camps had got all busted up and our men had got their time.
Our teams had got all through hauling in; the birds began to sing.
They commenced to break their rollways and I knew it must be Spring.

STIRLING'S HOTEL

There's old Molly Hogan who cooks from a book,
She's the chief chambermaid and the past-e-ry cook,
The pies that she bakes us, good God, how they smell!
A dog wouldn't eat them at Stirling's Hotel.

There's old Jack McKissick who cuts wood for his board:
But fishes instead, wouldn't work if he could.
The fish that he catches, good God, how they smell!
A dog wouldn't eat them at Stirling's Hotel.

And old Ed Starkes who works in the saloon,
The drinks that he gives, you could hold in a spoon.
For these little drinks he charges like hell,
And he gets all the money 'round Stirling's Hotel.

All our beds they are crummy with bugs and with lice,
And holes in the walls seem to vomit the mice;
And the breeze from the pantry has an old rotten smell,
It revives all the boarders at Stirling's Hotel.

"Stirling's Hotel" was recorded by Sidney Robertson Cowell from the singing of Pat Ford, Central Valley, California, 1938. Library of Congress AFS record 4207 A1. Pat Ford heard this in 1905 on the banks of the Wolf River in Jennings, Wisconsin, and states that it was written by river drivers.

JACK HAGGERTY

I'm a heartbroken raftsman, from Greenville I came,
My virtue's departure, alas, I defame.
But the strong darts of Cupid have caused me much grief,
My heart breaks within me, I can ne'er find relief.

I can tell you my troubles without much delay,
How my sweet little Lucy my heart stole away.
She was a blacksmith's daughter all by the Flat River side,
And I always intended for to make her my bride.

My occupation, I am a raftsman where the white waters roll,
My name 'tis engraved on the rocks and sand shoals.
On shop, bar, and housetop, well, I am very well known,
They call me Jack Haggerty, I'm the pride of the town.

I dressed her in jewels and finest of lace
And the costliest muslin myself I was braced.
I gave her my wages, all for her a keepsake,
I begrudged her of nothing that I had on the earth.

I worked on the river and gained quite a stake,
I was steadfast and steady, and I ne'er played the rake.
I'm a boy that stands happy on the boiling white stream,
My thoughts were of Lucy and she haunted my dreams.

One day on the river a letter I received,
She said from all promises herself she'd relieve.
A marriage with her lover she had a long time delayed,
And the next time he saw her she'd no more be a maid.

On her mother, Jane Tucker, I lay all the blame,
She caused her to leave me and to blacken my name,
And cast out the ringing that God would soon tie,
And left me a wanderer till the day that I die.

"Jack Haggerty" was collected, with music, from Mr. Chauncey Leach, Kalkaska, Michigan, 1934, who had learned the song in Mt. Pleasant, ca. 1895, from Charlie March, who worked on the Muskegon River. In Emelyn Elizabeth Gardner and Geraldine Jencks Chickering, *Ballads and Tunes of Southern Michigan* (University of Michigan Press) Ann Arbor, 1939, p. 267. Laws, C25.

So good-bye to Flat River, for me there's no rest,
I will shoulder my peavey and I will go west.
I will go to Muskegon some comfort to find
And leave my own Lucy and Flat River behind.

Now come all ye young men with hearts stout and true,
Don't depend on the women, you're beat if you do;
And whenever you see one with long chestnut curls,
Just think of Jack Haggerty and the Flat River girl.

THE BANKS OF THE GASPEREAUX

In 1933, Phillips Barry wrote that "no version of this pretty ballad has, to our knowledge, yet been printed. It may be one of the oldest woods songs, going back to the square-timber era, when Maine men worked on Canadian drives. Before 1850, square-timber running 'ceased to be a Maine industry unless upon some waters in the eastern parts tributary to the Saint John River.'" The Gaspereaux, running through the counties of Sunbury, Northumberland and Queens, New Brunswick, is a feeder to the port of St. John.

Come all you jolly lumbermen, I'd have you for to know
The Yankees they'll return no more to drive the Gaspereaux;
You told them all the lies you could; you were their bitter foe;
Bad luck attend those wild galoots who live on Gaspereaux.

You thought to scare those Americans and fill their hearts with fear,
You told them they could not get out their lumber the first year;
But our boss he says, "My brave boys, we'll let those galpins know, —"
And in seven days with his boys so brave, he drove the Gaspereaux.

One of the natives had a daughter, and she was handsome too,
And she was much admired by one of the Yankee crew;
Because she wore a purple dress and a red apron also,
They called her Robin Redbreast on the banks of Gaspereaux.

"The Banks of the Gaspereaux" was recorded by Phillips Barry from the singing of Mrs. Guy R. Hathaway, Mattawamkeag, Maine, 1932, as learned from her father, Mr. F. B. Shedd of Mattawamkeag. Reported by Barry, with music, in *Bulletin of the Folksong Society of the Northeast*, Cambridge, Mass., 5 (1933):13–14. Laws, C26.

The first time that I saw this bird she filled me with surprise,
To see such a charming creature appear before my eyes;
I watched her with amazement to see where she did go;
She flew into my arms on the banks of Gaspereaux.

I says, "My pretty fair one, come go along with me,
And I will show you a short cut across this counteree;
I'll dress you up in rich apparel and to the church we'll go,
And we'll leave these dismal scenes behind on the banks of Gaspereaux."

"O no, O no," this fair maid says, "I cannot leave my home, —
My sisters, they'd lament for me, and papa he would moan;
But you go and ask my papa, and to the church we'll go,
And I'll be your kind companion on the banks of Gaspereaux."

The next was to the old man and that without delay,
"I wish to wed your daughter, — an answer, sir, I pray."
"O yes, O yes," the old man says, "but from me she can't go.
She can be your kind companion on the banks of Gaspereaux."

"O no, O no," the young man says, "this place I cannot bear,
We'll go unto the state of Maine, and we'll be happy there."
"O no, O no," the old man says, "It's from me she can't go,
Why can't you live contented on the banks of Gaspereaux?"

"It's now, my lovely Robin, it's you and I must part!"
And little did they know the grief and woe that lay at his troubled heart;
For her hair hung down in ringlets, while the tears from her eyes did flow,
When she parted with her own true love on the banks of Gaspereaux.

Now these true lovers parted and sorely they complain,
For one lives in Gaspereaux and the other in the state of Maine;
The state we roam all over and we'll ramble to and fro,
And we'll think of lovely Robin on the banks of Gaspereaux.

It's now our lumber's rafted and going to St. John,
And when that we get it there, we'll put it in the pond;
We'll drink our health to Robin, the Stars and Stripes also,
Likewise those kind old people we left in Gaspereaux.

THE LITTLE BROWN BULLS

Not a thing on the river McCluskey did fear
As he pulled the stick o'er the big spotted steer.
They were young, quick and sound, girting eight feet and three.
Said McCluskey, the Scotchman, "They're the laddies for me."

Bull Gordon, the Yankee, of skidding was full,
As he said "Whoa hush," to his little brown bulls —
Short-legged and soggy, girting six feet and nine.
Said McCluskey, the Scotchman, "Too light for our pine."

'Twas three to the thousand our contract did call;
The skidding was good for the timber was tall.
McCluskey he swore that he'd make the day full,
And he'd skid two to one of the little brown bull.

"Oh no" said Bull Gordon, "that you cannot do,
Although we all know you've the pets of the crew,
But mark you, my boy, you will have your hands full
If you skid one more log than my little brown bull."

The day was appointed and soon it draw nigh,
For twenty-five dollars their fortunes to try.
Each eager and anxious that morning were found
As the scalers and judges appeared on the ground

With a whoop and a yell McCluskey to view,
With his big spotted steers, the pets of the crew.
Both chewing their cuds, "Oh boys, keep your jaws full,
For you easily can beat them, the little brown bulls."

Then up stepped Bull Gordon, with pipe in his jaw,
With his little brown bulls with their cuds in their mouths.
And little did we think when we see them come down,
That a hundred and forty they could jerk around.

"The Little Brown Bulls" was recorded by Alan Lomax from the singing of Carl Lathrop at St. Louis, Michigan, 1937. Library of Congress record LP56. Laws, C16.

Then up spoke McCluskey, "Come strip to the skin,
For I'll dig you a hole and I'll tumble you in.
I will learn a damned Yankee to face a bold Scot,
I will cook you a dose and you'll get it red-hot."

Said Gordon to Stebbin, with blood in his eye,
"Today we must conquer McCluskey or die."
Then up spoke old Kennebec, "Oh boy, never fear,
For you never will be beaten by the big spotted steer."

The sun had gone down when the foreman did say,
"Turn out, boys, turn out, you've enough for the day.
We have scaled them and counted them, each man to his team;
And it's well do we know now which one kicks the beam."

After supper was over, McCluskey appeared
With a belt ready made for his big spotted steers.
To form it he'd torn up his best mackinaw;
For he swore he'd conduct it according to law.

Then up spoke the scaler, "Hold on, you, a while,
For your big spotted steers are behind just one mile.
You've skidded one hundred and ten and no more,
And the bulls have you beaten by ten and a score."

The shanty did ring and McCluskey did swear
As he tore out by handsful his long yellow hair.
Says he to Bull Gordon, "My colors I pull;
So here, take the belt for your little brown bulls."

Here's health to Bull Gordon and Kennebec John:
The biggest day's work on the river they've done.
So fill up your glasses, boys, fill them up full;
We will drink to the health of the little brown bull.

THE WILD MUSTARD RIVER

Dr. E. C. Beck says: "There is white water in 'The Wild Mustard River.'"
The boiling power of these mighty streams which, in moments of uncontrolled wrath, tossed logs like giant matchsticks brought frequent tragedy

"The Wild Mustard River" was recorded by Alan Lomax from the singing of Carl Lathrop
of St. Louis, Michigan, 1938. Library of Congress record LP56. Laws, C5.

and death to the lumberman. This song — and those that follow through "Lost Jimmie Whalen" — record such deaths.

There is no certain location for the Wild Mustard River: some old-timers call it the Omuska, others the Old Musky.

Down by the Wild Mustard River,
Down by the old Emry Dam,
We arose from our blankets one morning
To flood from the reservoir dam.

When the waters come rustling and rolling,
Our peaveys and pikes we'd apply,
Not thinking that one of our number
This day had so horribly to die.

On the river there was none any better
On a log than our friend Johnny Styles.
He had worked there more than any other,
But he always was reckless and wild.

But today his luck went against him,
His foot it was caught in the jam;
And you know how that creek runs a-howling
When you flood from the reservoir dam.

But we were all there in a moment,
Just as soon as he gave his first shout;
And you know how that creek runs a-howling —
It rolls in, but it never rolls out.

We worked for an hour and a quarter,
We worked till our time come to spare.
And we had a hole well worked through her
When like lightning she hauled out of there.

We rode her down and pulled up in dead water;
We worked till the sweat down us poured;
We pulled his dead body from in under,
But it looked like poor Johnny no more.

His flesh was all cut up in ringlets
And rolled out as flat as your hand.
We'll hold peace on this earth for his body
While the Lord holds his soul in command.

THE JAM ON GERRY'S ROCKS

Come all you true-born shanty boys, wherever ye may be,
Come set ye on the deacon seat and listen unto me.
I'll sing you the song of Gerry's Rocks and a hero you should know —
The bravest of all shanty boys is our foreman, young Monroe.

It being on one Sunday's morning ere the daylight did appear;
Our logs were piling mountains high, we could not keep them clear.
"Cheer up, cheer up, my every man, revolve your heart of woe.
We'll break the jam on Gerry's Rocks," cries our foreman, young Monroe.

Some of those boys were willing, while others they hid from sight,
For to break a jam on Sunday they did not think it was right,
When six of our Canadian boys did volunteer to go
And break the jam on Gerry's Rocks with her true love, young Monroe.

They had not picked off many logs when Monroe to them did say,
"I must send you back up the drive, my boys, for the jam will soon give
     away."
Alone he freed the key log then, and when the jam did go,
It carried away on the boiling flood our foreman, young Monroe.

When the rest of the boys got back to camp, the sad news came to hear,
In search of his dead body down the river they did steer.
When there they found to their surprise, their sorrow, grief, and woe,
All bruised and mangled on the beach laid the corpse of young Monroe.

They picked him up most tenderly, smoothed down his waving hair.
There was one fair form among them whose cries did rend the air —
The fairest lass of Saginaw let tears of anguish flow,
But her mourns and cries could not awake her true love, young Monroe.

The Mrs. Clark, a widow, lived by the river side;
It was her only daughter, Monroe's intended bride.
The wages of her dearest love the boss to her did pay,
And a gift of gold was sent to her by the shanty boys next day.

"The Jam on Gerry's Rocks" was recorded by Alan Lomax from the singing of Bill
McBride at Mt. Pleasant, Michigan, 1938. Library of Congress record LP56. Laws, C1.

When she received the money, she thanked them tearfully;
But it was not her portion long on earth for to be.
For it was just six weeks or so when she was called to go,
And the shanty boys laid her to rest by her true love, young Monroe.

JIMMY JUDGE

Come all you jolly seamen who plough that restless deep,
Think of those jolly raftsmen who in their graves do sleep;
'Tis of as fine a young man as ever the sun shone on,
It was on the Bonshai River that he was drownded on.

Now Jimmy Judge was the young man's name, as you shall quickly see,
He was his father's only hope and his mother's only joy.
His hair hung down in ringlets, his skin was white as snow,
He was admired by old and young wherever he did go.

It was on the Bonshai River a little below Lock Anne,
Where he got on to break a jam and with it he fell in;
He tried his whole activity his precious life to save,
But it was all in vain, it was all no use, he met a watery grave.

Now early the next morning these raftsmen all turned out
To search the stream on every side to find their comrade dear,
To search the stream on every side where the water swift did glide,
When a fisher boy, as I've been told, his floating corpse espied.

His aged father cried, "Alas, I am undone!"
His aged mother cried, "I've lost my only son!"
The girl who'd loved him dearly in sorrow pined away,
For Jimmy Judge is drownded and we'll never see him more.

Now here's to our Creator whose name we do adore,
For Jimmy Judge is drownded and we'll never see him more.
I hope his soul's in Heaven, and happy may it be,
I hope his soul's in Heaven for now and eternity.

"Jimmy Judge" was recorded by Alan Lomax from the singing of Mrs. Carrie Grover of Gorham, Maine, at Washington, D.C., 1941. Library of Congress AFS record 4456 A2. Last two lines supplied from Phillips Barry, *The Maine Woods Songster* (Harvard) Cambridge, Mass., 1939, p. 56. Laws, C4.

SAMUEL ALLEN

Ye tender-hearted people, I pray you lend an ear,
And when you have my story heard, you can but drop a tear;
Concerning Samuel Allen, a man both strong and brave,
And on a stream called Rocky Brook, he met with a watery grave.

He was both tall and handsome, his age was twenty-one,
And if I do remember right, he was an only son;
His father bade him a fond farewell, as the Gibson train rolled by,
And then walked slowly homeward, — the tears bedimmed his eye.

I'll tell you now of Rocky Brook, that sad and dismal place,
No matter where you work on it, death stares you in the face;
The rocks stand up like mountains high, for miles along the shore,
'Twould fill your heart with misery, to hear the waters roar.

'Twas on one Monday morning, the sun was shining clear,
When Samuel Allen last attempted with neither dread nor fear, —
He went up to the rolling dam, to see what he could do —
In trying to get the boom prepared to sluice the lumber through.

He looked first up and down the stream, a-looking for a jam,
When the water made an awful rush, and tore away the dam;
The boom that he was standing on was quickly torn away;
And soon within the raging tide, his lifeless body lay.

'Twas ten o'clock in the forenoon, he received this fatal blow;
Some people think he lost his life while in the undertow;
He was cut and bruised about the head, his body it was bare —
O, what a sight it must have been to comrades who were there!

They took him to his father's house, 'twould grieve your heart full sore
To see the people mourn for grief around the cottage door;
There was one fair form among them, I will not speak her name,
Who had hoped to be his wedded wife, when home again he came.

"Samuel Allen" was recorded by Phillips Barry from the singing of Mr. Herbert L. Merry, Thorndike, Maine, 1934. Reported, with music, by Barry in *Bulletin of the Folksong Society of the Northeast*, Cambridge, Mass., 9 (1935): 19–21. Laws, C10.

But hope gave way to dark despair when she beheld the form
Of him who promised all through life to shield her from the storm;
And hand in hand no more to roam the hills of Gerick Vale,
Both night and morn, this maid forlorn her saddened fate bewails.

He leaves an aged father, quite well along in years,
Likewise a fair young sweetheart to wait for him in tears; —
He took her by the hand that day when he left his father's door,
But little did he think that he would never see her more.

His body in the churchyard to rest is laid away,
A-waiting for the Savior's call, on that great Judgment Day;
When friend and foe must rise and go at the Archangel's call,
And there abide the Lord beside, the Father of us all.

PETER AMBERLEY

My name is Peter Emily, as you might understand,
I was born on Prince Edward Island, close by the ocean strand.
In eighteen hundred eighty-two, when the flowers was in full bloom,
I left my native country my fortune to persume.

I landed in New Brunswick, in that lumbering countree;
I hired to work in the lumber woods, which proved my destiny;
I hired to work in the lumber woods, where they cut the tall spruce down;
When loading two sleds from the yard I received my deathly wound.

There is danger on the ocean, when the seas roll mountains high,
There is danger on the battlefield, where the angry bullets fly,
There is danger in the lumber woods, where death lies solemn there,
And I have fell a victim to that great and monstrous snare.

Here's a due to my old father, it was him that drove me here,
I think his punishment too hard and his treatment too severe;
It is not right to press a boy, or try to keep him down,
It's apt to drive him from his home when he is far too young.

"Peter Amberley" is from Fannie Hardy Eckstorm and Mary Winslow Smyth, *Minstrelsy of Maine*, Boston and New York, 1927 (reprint, Gryphon Press, Ann Arbor, 1971), pp. 99–102. The first five stanzas were collected by Mr. Sidney Sykes, at John Ross's camps, Lobster Lake, Maine, 1902. The last two stanzas in brackets are from the *Maine Sportsman*, December, 1903. Texts without music. Two sets of music reported by Phillips Barry in *Bulletin of the Folksong Society of the Northeast*, Cambridge, Mass., 2 (1931):13–14. Laws, C27.

Here's a due unto a dearer friend, I mean my mother dear,
Who reared a son who fell as soon as he left her tender care.
Little did my mother know, when she sang sweet lullaby,
What countries I might travel in, or what death I might die.

[Here's adieu to Prince Edward Island
That garden in the seas;
No more I'll roam its flowery banks
To enjoy a summer breeze;
No more I'll watch those gallant ships
As they go sailing by,
With colors flying gaily
Above their canvas high.

[Here's adieu unto my younger friends,
Those Island girls so true,
Long may they live to grace the Isle
Where my first breath I drew.
The world will roll on just the same
As before I passed away;
What signifies the life of man
When his body it is clay?]

ON THE BANKS OF THE LITTLE EAU PLEINE

One evening last June as I rambled, the greenwoods and valleys among,
The mosquito's notes were melodious, and so was the whippoorwill's song.
The frogs in the marshes were croaking, the tree toads were whistling for rain,
And the partridges 'round me was drumming, on the banks of the Little Eau Pleine.

The sun in the west was declining and tinkling the treetops with red,
My weary feet bore me onward, not caring wherever they led.
I happened to see a young schoolma'am, she was mourning in a sorrowful strain,
She was mourning for a jolly young raftsman, on the banks of the Little Eau Pleine.

"On the Banks of the Little Eau Pleine" was recorded by Alan Lomax from the singing of Bill McBride, Mt. Pleasant, Michigan, 1938. Library of Congress AFS record 2263 B2. Laws, C2.

I stepped up beside this young schoolma'am, and thus unto her I did say,
"Why is it you're mourning so sadly when all things are smiling and gay?"
She said, "It's for a young raftsman, for whom I so sadly complain.
He has left me alone here to wander, on the banks of the Little Eau Pleine."

Saying, "Alas, my dear Johnny has left me, I'm afraid I shall see him no
    more.
He is down on the lower Wisconsin, he's a-pulling a fifty-foot oar.
He went off on a trip with Ross Gamble, and has left me in sorrow and pain;
And 'tis over two months since he started from the banks of the Little Eau
    Pleine."

"Will you please tell me what kind of clothing your jolly young raftsman did
    wear?
For I also belong to the river, perhaps I have seen him somewhere.
If to me you will plainly describe him, and tell me your young raftsman's
    name,
Perhaps I can tell you the reason he's not back to the Little Eau Pleine."

"His pants were made out of two meal sacks, with a patch a foot square on
    each knee;
His shirt and his jacket were dyed with the bark from the butternut tree.
He wore a large open-faced ticker, with almost a yard of steel chain,
When he went away with Ross Gamble, from the banks of the Little Eau
    Pleine.

"He wore a red sash round his middle, with an end hanging down by each
    side;
His shoes, number ten, were of cowhide, with heels about four inches wide.
His name it was Honest Johnny Murphy, and on it was neither a stain;
And he was as jolly a raftsman as ever on the Little Eau Pleine.

"He was stout, broad-shouldered and manly, his height about six-foot-one,
His hair it was inclined to be sandy and his whiskers as red as the sun.
His age was somewhere about thirty, he neither was foolish nor vain;
He loved the Wisconsin River, was the reason he left the Eau Pleine."

"If Johnny Murphy's the name of your raftsman, I used to know him quite
    well;
But sad is the tale I must tell you, your Johnny is drowned in the Dell.
They buried him near a scrub Norway, you will never behold him again;
No stone marks the spot where your raftsman sleeps far from the Little Eau
    Pleine."

When the schoolma'am had heard this information, she fainted and fell as if
    dead;
I scooped up my hat full of water, and poured it on the top of her head.
She opened her eyes and looked wildly, like someone was nearly insane,
And I was afraid she would perish on the banks of the Little Eau Pleine.

"My curses attend you, Wisconsin! May your rapids and falls cease to roar;
May every low head and sandbar be as dry as a log schoolhouse-floor!
May the willows upon all your islands lie down like a field of ripe grain,
For taking my jolly young raftsman away from the Little Eau Pleine!

"My curse lies upon you, Ross Gamble, for taking my Johnny away;
I hope that the ague will seize you, and shake you down into the clay!
May your lumber go down to the bottom, and never rise to the surface again!
You had no business a-taking Johnny Murphy away from the Little Eau
    Pleine.

"Now I will desert my vocation, I won't teach district school any more,
But I will go some place where I'll never hear the squeak of the fifty-foot oar.
I'll go to some far foreign country, to England, to France or to Spain,
But I'll never forget Johnny Murphy, on the banks of the Little Eau Pleine."

LOST JIMMIE WHALEN

As slowly and sadly I strayed by the river,
A-watching the sunbeams as evening drew nigh,
As onward I rambled I spied a fair damsel,
She was weeping and wailing with many a sigh.

Sighing for one who is now lying lonely,
Sighing for one whom no mortal can save,
For the dark, rolling waters flow sadly around him,
As onward they roll o'er young Jimmie's grave.

"Jimmie," said she, " won't you come to my arms
And give me sweet kisses as oftimes you've done?"

"Lost Jimmie Whalen" was recorded by Sidney Robertson Cowell from the singing of Bob
Walker, Crandon, Wisconsin, 1937. Library of Congress AFS record 3287 A1. Partial text
supplemented from Phillips Barry, *The Maine Woods Songster* (Harvard), Cambridge,
1939. Laws, C8.

You promised you'd meet me this evening, my darling,
Oh, come, dearest Jimmie, but come from the grave."

Slowly there rose from the depths of the river
A vision of beauty more bright than the sun
While red robes of crimson encircled around him,
Unto this fair maiden he speaking begun.

"Why did you call me from the realms of glory
Back to this cold earth I soon have to leave?
To clasp you once more in my fond loving arms,
To see you once more I have came from my grave.

"Oh, hard were my struggles from the wild, rushing waters,
That encircled around me on every side;
And the last thought I had was of God, darling,
I was hoping one day that you'd sure be my bride."

"Jimmie," she cried, "won't you tarry here with me,
And never, no, never, no more from me part?
Then take me away with you, Jimmie, my darling,
For to sleep with you down in your cold, silent grave."

"Darling," he says, "you are asking a favor
Which no mortal person can grant unto thee,
For Death is the dagger that keeps us asunder,
And wide is the gulf lies between you and me.

"Still, as you wander alone by the waters,
I will ever be near you to guide and to save,
I will ever endeavor to keep you from danger,
I will guide you, my darling, from my silent grave."

"Adiew —" then he said, and he vanished before her,
And straight to the skies he did seem for to go,
Leaving this fair maid alone and distracted,
A-weeping and wailing in sorrow alone.

As she sank down on the ground she was standing,
With the deepest of sorrow, these words she did say,
"My darling," she cried, "Oh, my lost Jimmie Whalen,
I will sigh till I die by the side of your grave!"

CANADA-I-O

I

There was a gallant lady all in her tender youth,
She dearly lov'd a sailor, in truth she lov'd him much,
And for to get to sea with him the way she did not know,
She long'd to see that pretty place called Canada-I-O.

She bargained with a sailor all for a purse of gold,
When straightway he led her down into the hold,
Saying, I'll dress you up in sailor's clothes, the colour shall be blue,
You soon shall see that pretty place called Canada-I-O.

And when her lover heard of this he flew into a rage,
And the whole ship's company was willing to engage,
Saying, I'll tie your hands and feet, my love, and overboard you'll go,
You ne'er shall see that pretty place called Canada-I-O.

Up steps the noble captain, and says that thing shan't be,
For if you drown that fair maid all hangèd you shall be,
I'll dress you up in sailor's clothes, the colour shall be blue,
You soon shall see that pretty place, called Canada-I-O.

She had not been in Canada for the space of half a year,
Before this captain married her, and callèd her his dear,
She does dress in silks and satins and she cuts a gallant show,
She's now the finest lady in Canada-I-O.

Come all you pretty fair maids, wherever you may be,
You must follow your true lovers when they are gone to sea.
And if the mate proves false to you, the captain he'll prove true,
You see the honour I have gained by wearing of the blue.

(England)

"Canada-I-O" is from the *Forget Me Not Songster*, New York, 1847, and later editions. This is an English "sea" song printed in the American songster. Back of it there lies also a most sentimental "Caledonia," which had no popular circulation but which gave dubious birth to "Canada-I-O."

II

Come, all ye jolly lumbermen, and listen to my song,
But do not get discouraged, the length it is not long,
Concerning of some lumbermen, who did agree to go
To spend one pleasant winter up in Canada-I-O.

It happened late one season in the fall of fifty-three,
A preacher of the gospel one morning came to me;
Said he, "My jolly fellow, how would you like to go
To spend one pleasant winter up in Canada-I-O?"

To him I quickly made reply, and unto him did say,
"In going out to Canada depends upon the pay.
If you will pay good wages, my passage to and fro,
I think I'll go along with you to Canada-I-O."

"Yes, we will pay good wages, and will pay your passage out,
Provided you sign papers that you will stay the route;
But if you do get homesick and swear that home you'll go,
We never can your passage pay from Canada-I-O.

"And if you get dissatisfied and do not wish to stay,
We do not wish to bind you, no, not one single day;
You just refund the money we had to pay, you know,
Then you can leave that bonny place called Canada-I-O."

It was by his gift of flattery he enlisted quite a train,
Some twenty-five or thirty, both well and able men;
We had a pleasant journey o'er the road we had to go,
Till we landed at Three Rivers, up in Canada-I-O.

But there our joys were ended, and our sorrows did begin;
Fields, Phillips and Norcross they then came marching in;
They sent us all directions, somewhere I do not know,
Among those jabbering Frenchmen up in Canada-I-O.

This version was collected from Mrs. Annie V. Marston, West Gouldsboro, Maine, n.d., but ca. 1904. Reported, with music, by Fannie Hardy Eckstorm in *Bulletin of the Folksong Society of the Northeast*, Cambridge, Mass., 6 (1933):10–13. Laws, C17a. Ephraim Braley of Judson, Maine, had spent the bitter winter of 1854 lumbering in Canada. He came upon a copy of the *Forget Me Not Songster* and wrote this satiric parody upon that "pretty place called Canada-I-O." It was to move to lumbering country in Pennsylvania, Michigan, Wisconsin, and elsewhere, and finally wind up in Texas as "The Buffalo Skinners."

After we had suffered there some eight or ten long weeks,
We arrived at headquarters, up among the lakes;
We thought we'd find a paradise, at least they told us so,
God grant there may be no worse hell than Canada-I-O.

To describe what we have suffered is past the art of man,
But to give a fair description I will do the best I can;
Our food the dogs would snarl at, our beds were on the snow,
We suffered worse than murderers up in Canada-I-O.

Our hearts were made of iron and our souls were cased with steel,
The hardships of that winter could never make us yield;
Fields, Phillips and Norcross they found their match, I know,
Among the boys that went from Maine to Canada-I-O.

But now our lumbering is over and we are returning home,
To greet our wives and sweethearts and never more to roam,
To greet our friends and neighbors; we'll tell them not to go
To that forsaken, God-damned place called Canada-I-O!

(Maine)

Colley's Run-I-O

Come all you jolly lumbermen, and listen to my song,
I'll tell you all my story, and I won't detain you long,
Concerning some husky lumbermen who once agreed to go
And spend a winter recently on Colley's Run-i-O.

We landed in Lock Haven in the year of 'seventy-three,
A minister of the gospel one evening said to me:
"Are you the party of lumbermen that once agreed to go
And spend a winter pleasantly on Colley's Run-i-O?"

"Oh, yes, we'll go to Colley's Run, to that we will agree,
Provided you pay good wages, our passage to and fro,
Then we'll agree to accompany you to Colley's Run-i-O,
Then we'll agree to accompany you to Colley's Run-i-O."

"Colley's Run-I-O" was recorded by Rae Korson from the singing, with guitar, of L. Parker Temple at Washington, D.C., 1946. Library of Congress record LP28. Laws, C17c.

But now the spring has come again, and the ice-bound streams are free,
We'll float our logs to Williamsport, have friends we'll haste to see;
Our sweethearts they will welcome us, and bid others not to go
To that God-forsaken gehooley of a place called Colley's Run-i-O!

(Pennsylvania)

Michigan I-O

It was early in the season, the fall of 'sixty-three;
The preacher of the gospel, one day he come to me.
He says, "My clever fellow, how would you like to go
For to spend a winter a-lumbering in Michigan I-O?"

Oh, so boy, I stepped up to him, these words to him did say,
"I'm going out there a-lumbering depends upon the pay.
If you will pay good wages, my passage to and fro,
I'll go spend a winter a-lumbering in Michigan I-O."

Oh it's "I will pay good wages, I'll pay your passage out,
Providing you'll sign papers that you will stay the route.
Oh but if you do get homesick and swear it's home you'll go,
I'll not pay your passage over to Michigan I-O."

Oh and by that kind of flattery we enlisted quite a train,
Oh some twenty-five or thirty young able-bodied men.
Oh we had a pleasant voyage on the road we had to go,
Oh they landed us in Saginaw called Michigan I-O.

Oh it's now our joys are ended and our troubles they've begun.
Oh Smith and Williams' agents, how they come rolling in.
Oh they sent us in a country, the road we did not know;
Oh 'twas upon the Rifle River in Michigan I-O.

For to tell the way we suffered, it is beyond the heart of man,
But to give the fair description, I'll do the best I can.
Our grub the dogs they'd laugh at, our beds built on the snow.
Oh God grant there is no bigger Hell than Michigan I-O.
Our grub the dogs they'd laugh at, our beds built on the snow.
Oh God grant there is no bigger Hell than Michigan I-O.

"Michigan I-O" was recorded by Alan Lomax from the singing of Lester Wells at Traverse City, Michigan, 1938. Library of Congress record LP56. Laws, C17b.

Oh it's now the winter is finished and it's homeward we are bound.
It's in this cursed country, no longer we'll be found.
We'll go home to our wives and sweethearts, tell others not to go
To that God-forsaken country-o called Michigan I-O.
We'll go home to our wives and sweethearts, tell others not to go
To that God-forsaken country-o called Michigan I-O.

(Michigan)

The Buffalo Skinners

It happened in Jacksboro in the year of 'seventy-three,
A man by the name of Crego came stepping up to me,
Saying, "How do you do, young fellow, and how would you like to go
And spend one summer pleasantly on the range of the buffalo?"

It's me being out of employment, boys, this to Crego he [I] did say,
"This going out on the buffalo range depends upon the pay;
But if you will pay good wages, give transportation, too,
I think that I will go with you to the range of the buffalo."

The season being over, old Crego he did say,
The crowd had been extravagant, was in debt to him that day.
We coaxed him and we begged him, and still it was no go:
We left old Crego's bones to bleach on the range of the buffalo.

Oh, it's now we've crossed Pease River, boys, and homeward we are bound,
No more in that hell-fired country shall ever we be found,
Go home to our wives and sweethearts, tell others not to go,
For God's forsaken the buffalo range and the damned old buffalo.

(Texas)

"The Buffalo Skinners" was recorded at the Library of Congress, Washington, D.C., from the singing of John A. Lomax of Dallas, Texas, 1941. Library of Congress record LP28. Laws, B10.

A SHANTY MAN'S LIFE

A shanty man's life is a drearisome life,
Though sometimes 'tis free from all care.
'Tis swinging an ax from morning till night
In the midst of the forest so drear.
    'Tis swinging an ax from morning till night
    In the midst of the forest so drear.

We are lying in the shanty; it's bleak and it's cold,
While cold, wintry winds do blow.
The wolves and the owls with their terrible growls
Disturb us from our midnight dreams.
    The wolves and the owls with their terrible growls
    Disturb us from our midnight dreams.

Transported we are from all pretty, fair maids.
There's no whisky seen till it's spring.
There's not a friend near to wipe away a tear
While sorrow a sad mind will bring.
    There's not a friend near to wipe away a tear
    While sorrow a sad mind will bring.

Had we ale, wine, or beer, our spirits to cheer
While here in the woods the long while,
Or a glass of anything while here all alone
To cheer up our long, long exile.
    Or a glass of anything while here all alone
    To cheer up our long, long exile.

About four o'clock our noisy little cook
Cries, "Boys, it is the break of day."
With heavy sighs from slumber we rise
To go with the bright morning star.
    With heavy sighs from slumber we rise
    To go with the bright morning star.

When springtime comes in, double troubles begin,
For the water it is piercing cold.

"A Shanty Man's Life" was collected and reported by E. C. Beck in *Songs of the Michigan Lumberjacks* (University of Michigan Press) Ann Arbor, 1941, pp. 26–27. Beck cites numerous informants, including Nels Plude of Saginaw.

Dripping wet are our clothes and we're almost froze,
And our pike poles we scarcely can hold.
    Dripping wet are our clothes and we're almost froze,
    And our pike poles we scarcely can hold.

You can talk about your farms, but your shanty boy has charms;
They are far superior to all.
They will join each other's hearts until death them all parts
Whether they be great or small.
    They will join each other's hearts until death them all parts
    Whether they be great or small.

So rafting I'll give o'er and anchored safe on shore
Lead a quiet and a sober life;
No more will I roam but contented stay at home
With a smiling and a charming little wife.
    No more will I roam but contented stay at home
    With a smiling and a charming little wife.

(Michigan)

The Cowboy's Life Is a Very Dreary Life

    You can talk about your farms and your Chinaman's charms,
    You talk about your silver and your gold,
    But the cowboy's life is a very dreary life,
    It's a-riding through the heat and the cold.

Early every morning, you'll hear the boss say,
"Get up, boys, it's the breaking of day";
It's now for to rise with your little sleepy eyes,
And the bright dreamy night's passed away.

When springtime comes, double hardships begun,
The rain it's so fresh and so cold,
We almost freeze from the water on our clothes,
And the cattle you can scarcely hold.

Cowboys, take my advice, setting out for to roam,
But you better stay at home with your kind and loving little wife.

(Texas)

"The Cowboy's Life Is a Very Dreary Life" was recorded by John A. Lomax from the singing of Sloan Matthews, Pecos, Texas, 1942. Library of Congress record LP28.

The '49ers

I came from Salem City with my washbowl on my knee,
I'm going to California the gold dust for to see,
It rained all night the day I left, the weather it was dry,
The sun so hot I froze to death, oh, brothers, don't you cry.

> Oh! California! That's the land for me,
> I'm going to Sacramento with my washbowl on my
> knee.

THE CALIFORNIAN

When news of the Gold Rush reached New England, one of the companies sailing from Massachusetts was the Salem and California Mining and Trading Company. The original members of the company purchased the barque *La Grange* and changed the name of their group to the La Grange Company. It was from members of this company that the "Society of California Pioneers of New England" afterwards came into being. The *La Grange* sailed from Phillips Wharf, Salem, on March 17, 1849. The wharf was crowded with hundreds of relatives, friends and observers, and before the vessel pulled out, the members of the company sang "The Californian," the words for which were written by Jesse Hutchinson of the famous New England family troupe. The ship took one hundred and eighty-four days to reach San Francisco.

> We've formed our band and are well manned
> To journey afar to the promised land,
> Where the golden ore is rich in store
> On the banks of the Sacramento shore.
>
> > Then ho! Boys, ho! who to California go,
> > For the mountains cold are covered with gold,
> > Along the banks of the Sacramento.
> > Ho! ho! away we go, digging up gold in Francisco.

"The Californian" is from O. T. Howe, *Argonauts of '49* (Harvard) Cambridge, 1923, p. 79.

Oh, the gold is there, most anywhere,
And they dig it out with an iron bar,
And when it's thick, with a spade and pick,
They've taken out lumps as big as a brick.

Oh, don't you cry or heave a sigh,
We'll come back again by and by,
Don't breathe a fear or shed a tear,
But patiently wait about two year.

We expect our share of the coarsest fare,
And sometimes to sleep in the open air,
Upon the cold ground we shall all sleep sound
Except when the wolves are howling 'round.

As off we roam over the dark sea foam,
We'll never forget our friends at home,
For memories kind will bring to mind
The thoughts of those we leave behind.

In the days of old, the Prophets told
Of the City to come, all framed in gold;
Peradventure they foresaw the day
Now dawning in Californi—a.

THE SAN FRANCISCO COMPANY

The barque *San Francisco* sailed from Beverly, Massachusetts, on August 15, 1849, and arrived in San Francisco Bay after the voyage around the Horn on January 11, 1850, having been at sea one hundred and forty-nine days. The song of "The San Francisco Company" was composed by Captain Isaac W. Baker shortly after the vessel cleared Beverly harbor, to the favorite tune of the '49ers, "Oh, Susannah."

The San Francisco Company, for San Francisco bound,
Our barque is *San Francisco*, too, the same name all around.
A company of jolly boys as ever got together,
All bound for California in spite of wind and weather.

"The San Francisco Company" is from O. T. Howe, *Argonauts of '49* (Harvard) Cambridge, 1923, p. 90.

Oh, California, we'll see you bye and bye
If we've good luck, and if we don't, why, bless you, don't you cry.

We started from Old Beverly 'mid cheers from great and small,
We hope to get back bye and bye when we'll return them all.
The day we left the wind was fair and pleasant was the sky,
The fair sex wept, the boys hurrahed, and we'd no time to cry.

We doubled close 'round Beverly bar, 'twas close upon our lee,
We then hove to and called the roll, and squared away for sea.
We've forty men in Company, a cook and steward, too,
We've twenty pigs, a dog and cat, and what is that to you?

Now here's success you'll surely say, to all you willing souls,
And may you have the joyful chance of filling all your bowls.
But not just yet, but bye and bye, and full of glittering ore,
And then return to where you wish and never want for more.

I CAME FROM SALEM CITY

I came from Salem City, with my washbowl on my knee,
I'm going to California the gold dust for to see.
It rained all night the day I left, the weather it was dry,
The sun so hot I froze to death, oh, brothers, don't you cry.

Oh! California! That's the land for me,
I'm going to Sacramento with my washbowl on my knee.

I jumped aboard the 'Liza ship and travelled on the sea,
And every time I thought of home, I wished it wasn't me.
The vessel reared like any horse, that had of oats a wealth,
It found it couldn't throw me, so, I thought I'd throw myself.

I thought of all the pleasant times we've had together here,
I thought I ought to cry a bit, but couldn't find a tear.
The pilot bread was in my mouth, the gold dust in my eye,
And, though I'm going far away, dear brothers, don't you cry.

I soon shall be in Francisco, and then I'll look around,
And when I see the gold lumps there, I'll pick them off the ground.
I'll scrape the mountains clean, I'll drain the rivers dry,
A pocket full of rocks bring home, so, brothers, don't you cry.

"I Came from Salem City" is from O. T. Howe, *Argonauts of '49* (Harvard) Cambridge, 1923, p. 78. To the tune of "Oh, Susannah."

*THE DYING CALIFORNIAN**

Lie up nearer, brother, nearer, for my limbs are growing cold,
And your presence seemeth dearer when your arms around me fold.
I am dying, surely dying, soon you'll miss me from your berth,
And my form it will be lying 'neath the ocean's briny surf.

Hearken to me, brother, hearken, I have something I would say
Ere this veil my vision darkens and I go from hence away.
I am going, surely going, but my hope in God is strong;
I am willing, brother, knowing that He doeth no thing wrong.

Tell my father when you greet him that in death I prayed for him,
Prayed that I might one day meet him in a world that's free from sin.
Tell my mother, God assist her, now that she is growing old,
That her son would fain have kissed her when his lips grew pale and cold.

Hearken to me, catch each whisper, 'tis my wife I speak of now,
Tell, oh, tell her how I missed her when the fever burned my brow;
Hearken to me, closely listen, don't forget a single word,
That in death my eyes did glisten with the tears her memory stirred.

Tell her now to kiss my children like the kiss I last impressed,
Hold them as at last I held them folded closely to my breast;
Give them early to their Maker, putting all her trust in God,
And He never will forsake her, He has said so in His word.

Oh, my children, heaven bless them, they were all my life to me,
Would I could once more caress them ere I sink beneath the sea;
'Twas for them I crossed the ocean, what my hopes were I'll not tell,
But they've gained an orphan's portion, yet He doeth all things well.

Tell my sister I remember every kindly parting word,
And my heart has been kept tender with the thoughts her memory stirred.
Tell them I never reached the haven, where I sought the precious dust,
But I've gained a port called heaven, where the gold can never rust.

* Understood to be one going to California: i.e., who had committed himself to California.

"The Dying Californian" was recorded by Sidney Robertson Cowell from the singing of George Vinton Graham, San Jose, California, 1938. Library of Congress AFS record 3810 B. The last six lines supplied from H. M. Belden, *Ballads and Songs Collected by the Missouri Folk-Lore Society*, Columbia, 1940 (reprint edition, 1966), pp. 350–351.

Urge upon them to secure an entrance, for they'll find their father there,
Faith in Jesus and repentance will secure for each a share.
Hark, I hear my Saviour calling, 'tis His voice, I know full well,
When I'm gone, oh, don't be weeping, brother, here's my last farewell.

COMING AROUND THE HORN

Now, miners, if you'll listen, I'll tell you quite a tale,
About the voyage around Cape Horn, they call a pleasant sail;
We bought a ship, and had her stowed with houses, tools and grub,
But cursed the day we ever sailed in the poor old rotten tub.

   Oh, I remember well the lies they used to tell,
   Of gold so bright it hurt the sight, and made the miners yell.

We left old New York City, with the weather very thick,
The second day we puked up boots, oh, wasn't we all seasick!
I swallowed pork tied to a string, which made a dreadful shout,
I felt it strike the bottom, but I could not pull it out.

We all were owners in the ship, and soon began to growl,
Because we hadn't ham and eggs, and now and then a fowl;
We told the captain what to do, as him we had to pay,
The captain swore that he was boss, and we should him obey.

We lived like hogs penned up to fat, our vessel was so small,
We had a "duff" but once a month, and twice a day a squall;
A meeting now and then was held, which kicked up quite a stink,
The captain damned us fore and aft, and wished the box would sink.

Off Cape Horn, where we lay becalmed, kind Providence seemed to frown,
We had to stand up night and day, none of us dared sit down;
For some had half a dozen boils, 'twas awful, sure's you're born,
But some would try it on the sly, and got pricked by the Horn.

We stopped at Valparaiso, where the women are so loose,
And all got drunk as usual, got shoved in the calaboose;

"Coming around the Horn" is from *Put's Original California Songster*, 4th ed., San Francisco, 1868, p. 37. Tune: "Dearest Mae" from *Minstrel Songs Old and New*, Boston, 1898, p. 32.

Our ragged, rotten sails were patched, the ship made ready for sea,
But every man, except the cook, was up town on a spree.

We sobered off, set sail again, on short allowance, of course,
With water thick as castor oil, and stinking beef much worse;
We had the scurvy and the itch, and any amount of lice,
The medicine chest went overboard, with bluemass, cards and dice.

We arrived at San Francisco, and all went to the mines,
We left an agent back to sell our goods of various kinds;
A friend wrote up to let us know our agent, Mr. Gates,
Had sold the ship and cargo, sent the money to the States.

JOE BOWERS

"Joe Bowers" ranks with "Sweet Betsey from Pike" and the various parodies upon "Oh, Susannah" as a favorite of the gold rush of '49 which has been widely preserved since in oral tradition. Its origin is uncertain. One account credits authorship to Frank Swift, one of two hundred Argonauts from Pike County [Missouri] who left for the gold fields in '49, and states that the song was written about an actual person, Joe Bowers, who was a member of the company. An account perhaps more to be credited assigns authorship to John Woodward, who played with Johnson's Minstrels in 1849 and the early fifties. According to this account, Joe Bowers is merely a typical figure of the forty-niners, and not a real person. It is possible, of course, that Woodward picked the song up from miners, but much more probable that it was his minstrel-composition.

My name it is Joe Bowers, I have a brother Ike,
I came from old Missouri, yes, all the way from Pike;
I'll tell you why I left there and how I came to roam,
And leave my dear old mother so far away from home.

I used to court a gal there, her name was Sally Black,
I axed her if she'd marry me, she said it was a whack!

"Joe Bowers" was recorded by Vance Randolph from the singing of Charles Ingenthron at Walnut Shade, Missouri, 1941. Library of Congress record LP30. Laws, B14.

But she says to me, "Joe Bowers, before we hitch for life,
You ought to have a little home to take your little wife."

"Oh, Sally, dear Sally, oh, Sally, for your sake,
I'll go to Californy and try to raise a stake."
Says she to me, "Joe Bowers, you are the man to win,
Here's a kiss to bind the bargain," and she hoved a dozen in.

(Vance Randolph is recording Charles Ingenthron, who hesitates, and there is a brief conversation.)

INGENTHRON: "Could you stop it, or . . ."

RANDOLPH: "I've already stopped it . . ."

I.: "Well, that's what I . . ."

R.: "Just take your time . . ."

I.: "Them songs, you know, that I . . . that I'm not used to singing, I hang up on 'em. That's the trouble. I've spoilt two."

R.: "Just take your time, Charley."

When I got in that country, I hadn't nary red,
I had such wolfish feelings I wished myself most dead,
But the thoughts of my dear Sally soon made those feelings git,
And whispering hopes to Bowers — I wish I had them yet.

At length I went to mining, put in my biggest licks,
Went down upon the boulders just like a thousand bricks;
I worked both late and early, in rain and sleet and snow,
I was working for my Sally, 'twas all the same to Joe.

At length I got a letter from my dear brother Ike,
It came from old Missouri, yes, all the way from Pike;
It brought to me the darndest news that ever you did hear,
My heart was almost busted, so pray excuse this tear.

It said that Sal was false to me, her love for me had fled,
Said she'd got married to a butcher, and the butcher's hair was red;
And more than that the letter read, 'twas enough to make me swear,
Said Sally had a baby, and the baby had red hair.

SWEET BETSEY FROM PIKE

Oh, don't you remember sweet Betsey from Pike,
Who crossed the big mountains with her lover Ike,
With two yoke of cattle, a large yellow dog,
A tall shanghai rooster and one spotted hog.

    Singing, goodbye, Pike County, farewell for awhile,
    We'll come back again when we've panned out our pile,
    Singing tooral lal, looral lal, looral lal lay,
    Singing tooral lal, looral lal, looral lal lay.

One evening quite early they camped on the Platte,
'Twas near by the road on a green shady flat,
Where Betsey, sore-footed, lay down to repose,
While with wonder Ike gazed on his Pike County rose.

Their wagon broke down with a terrible crash,
And out on the prairie rolled all kinds of trash;
A few little baby clothes done up with great care —
'Twas rather suspicious, though all on the square.

The shanghai ran off and the cattle all died;
That morning the last piece of bacon was fried;
Poor Ike was discouraged, and Betsey got mad,
The dog drooped his tail and looked wondrously sad.

They stopped at Salt Lake to inquire the way,
When Brigham declared that sweet Betsey should stay;
But Betsey got frightened and ran like a deer,
While Brigham stood pawing the ground like a steer.

They soon reached the desert, where Betsey gave out,
And down in the sand she lay rolling about;
While Ike, half distracted, looked on with surprise,
Saying, "Betsey, get up, you'll get sand in your eyes."

"Sweet Betsey from Pike" is from *Put's Golden Songster*, San Francisco, 1858, p. 50. Tune:
"Villikins and His Dinah." Laws, B9.

Sweet Betsey got up in a great deal of pain,
Declared she'd go back to Pike County again;
But Ike gave a sigh, and they fondly embraced,
And they traveled along with his arm round her waist.

They suddenly stopped on a very high hill,
With wonder looked down upon old Placerville;
Ike sighed when he said, and he cast his eyes down,
"Sweet Betsey, my darling, we've got to Hangtown."

Long Ike and sweet Betsey attended a dance,
Ike wore a pair of his Pike County pants;
Sweet Betsey was covered with ribbons and rings;
Says Ike, "You're an angel, but where are your wings?"

A miner said, "Betsey, will you dance with me?"
"I will that, old hoss, if you don't make too free;
But don't dance me hard, do you want to know why?
Dog on you! I'm chock full of strong alkali!"

This Pike County couple got married, of course,
And Ike became jealous — obtained a divorce;
Sweet Betsey, well satisfied, said with a shout,
"Goodbye, you big lummox, I'm glad you've backed out!"

THE NATIONAL MINER

When gold was first discovered at Coloma, near the mill,
All the world at first endeavored to get here, and they keep a-coming still;
When our war was through with Mexico, and we paid them for the land,
Those who fought at Palo Alto were driven off by nations they had tanned.

Down in the deep ravines, hear that roaring sound,
There the miners are a-digging, digging in the cold, damp ground.

"The National Miner" is from *Put's Original California Songster*, 4th ed., San Francisco, 1868, p. 40. Tune: "Massa's in the Cold, Cold Ground."

When our glorious Yankee nation sent her warships to the coast,
They left the mines for all creation — now, tell me, who is benefited most?
Here we're working like a swarm of bees, scarcely make enough to live,
And two hundred thousand Chinese are taking home the gold we ought to
    have.

Here they make their Queen Victoria laws, in spite of Uncle Sam,
And jump our diggings, say they'll break our jaws — our government they
    say ain't worth a damn.
When I make enough to take me home, I'll leave the mines well satisfied,
I'll give old Johnny Bull my long-tom, to prospect where it never has been
    tried.

    Down in the deep ravines, hear that roaring sound,
    There the miners are a-digging, digging in the cold, damp ground.

WHEN I WENT OFF TO PROSPECT

The few names of mining camps given here are some indication of the many
colorful ones which dotted the hills, valleys, and ravines of the Sierra
Nevada during the Gold Rush days.

I heard of Gold at Sutter's Mill, at Michigan Bluff and Iowa Hill,
But never thought it was rich until I started off to prospect.
At Yankee Jim's I bought a purse, inquired for Iowa Hill, of course,
And travelled on, but what was worse, fetched up in Shirttail Canyon.

    A sicker miner every way had not been seen for many a day;
    The devil it always was to pay, when I went off to prospect.

When I got there, the mining ground was staked and claimed for miles
    around,
And not a bed was to be found, when I went off to prospect.
The town was crowded full of folks, which made me think 'twas not a hoax,
At my expense they cracked their jokes, when I went off to prospect.

"When I Went Off to Prospect" is from *Put's Original California Songster*, 4th ed., San
Francisco, 1868, p. 46. Tune: "King of the Cannibal Islands."

I left my jackass on the road, because he wouldn't carry the load;
I'd sooner pick a big horn toad, when I went off to prospect.
My fancy shirt, with collar so nice, I found was covered with body-lice;
I used unguentum once or twice, but could not kill the grey-backs.

At Deadwood I got on a tight, at Groundhog Glory I had a fight;
They drove me away from Hell's Delight, when I went off to prospect.
From Bogus-Thunder I ran away, at Devil's Basin I wouldn't stay;
My lousy shirt crawled off one day, which left me nearly naked.

Now al! I got for running about was two black eyes and a bloody snout;
And that's the way it did turn out, when I went off to prospect.
And now I'm loafing around dead broke, my pistol and tools are all in soak,
And whiskey bills at me they poke — but I'll make it right in the morning!

LOUSY MINER

It's four long years since I reached this land,
In search of gold among the rocks and sand,
And yet I'm poor when the truth is told,
I'm a lousy miner, I'm a lousy miner in search of shining gold.

I've lived on swine till I grunt and squeal,
No one can tell how my bowels feel,
With slapjacks swimming round in bacon grease.
I'm a lousy miner, I'm a lousy miner, when will my troubles cease?

I was covered with lice coming on the boat,
I threw away my fancy swallow-tailed coat,
And now they crawl up and down my back,
I'm a lousy miner, I'm a lousy miner, a pile is all I lack.

My sweetheart vowed she'd wait for me
Till I returned, but don't you see
She's married now, sure, so I'm told,
Left her lousy miner, left her lousy miner, in search of shining gold.

Oh, land of gold, you did me deceive,
And I intend in thee my bones to leave,

"Lousy Miner" is from *Put's Original California Songster*, 4th ed., San Francisco, 1868, p. 48. Tune: "The Dark-Eyed Sailor."

So farewell, home, now my friends grow cold,
I'm a lousy miner, I'm a lousy miner in search of shining gold.

THE MINER'S LAMENT

When the gold fever raged I was doing very well,
With my friends all around, young and old;
'Twas a long time ago, and I bade them farewell,
And embarked for the land of gold.

Oh, miners, poor miners, hungry and cold!
Though poor, I'll return to my home far away,
So, farewell to the land of gold.

'Twas a hard thing to part from those little ones so gay,
That were playing in the yard round the door,
And my wife sobbed aloud as I started away,
Saying, "Farewell, I'll see you no more!"

Now the little gold locket my wife used to wear
Seems to fade by disease every breath,
Once happy and gay, now the picture of despair,
And those little ones all paler than death.

I dreamed I was at home in the old orchard tread,
With those loved ones so gay, it did seem,
As I reached for the apples that hung o'er my head,
Disappointed I woke from my dream.

Cold, wet and hungry, I've slept on the ground,
When those visions of happiness came,
But sad and disheartened, awoke by the sound
Of the screech-owl that lit on my claim.

I toiled night and day with the hope of gaining wealth,
Through the cold winter's rain with delight,
But, alas! sad misfortune has ruined my health,
So, my fond friends at home, all, goodnight.

"The Miner's Lament" is from *Put's Original California Songster*, 4th ed., San Francisco, 1868, p. 49. Tune: "Lilly Dale."

ROOT HOG OR DIE

The original "Root Hog or Die" appears to have been a minstrel song dealing with the Revolutionary War and the War of 1812, and it appeared in print in *The Dime Song Book* (Boston, 1859). It was popular and parodies upon the original text were numerous. The present California version — via an eastward drift to Missouri — describes the poker, whisky, and calaboose vicissitudes of an emigrant.

Well, I went to California in the year of Seventy-six [sic],
When I landed there, I was in a turrible fix,
Didn't have no money for vittles for to buy,
And the only thing for me was to — Root hog or die.

Well, I went from there down to Berloo,
I met with a feller who said he'd put me through,
'Twas in a game of poker that he gave the cards a sly,
And he took all my money, saying — Root hog or die.

Well, I got mad, and I begin to swear,
Poured down the corn juice till I got on a tear,
Marshal of the city he was standing there near by,
Took me to the calaboose to — Root hog or die.

Well, they took me to court next morning just at ten,
There stood the judge and a dozen other men,
They found me twenty dollars, that I thought was rather high,
But there's no use a-whining, it was — Root hog or die.

Now come, young fellers, and take my advice,
Don't go to shooting poker, go to playing any dice,
For if you do, you'll get too much of rye,
And you land in the calaboose to — Root hog or die.

"Root Hog or Die" was recorded by Vance Randolph from the singing, with guitar, of Jimmy Denoon, Bradleyville, Missouri, 1941. Library of Congress record LP30.

THE GAMBLER

A gambler's life I do admire, Du-da, du-da,
The best of rum they do require, Du-da, du-da, day;
The poker sharps begin to pout, Du-da, du-da,
I played all night and cleaned them out, Du-da, du-da, day.

> I'm bound to play all night, I'm bound to play all day,
> I bet my money on the ace and king, who dare bet on the trey?

Monte's might hard to beat, Du-da, du-da,
They say the dealer's bound to treat, Du-da, du-da, day;
Bar-keeper, give me a glass of porter, Du-da, du-da,
Gin for me, with a glass of water, Du-da, du-da, day.

The king's a layout from the top, Du-da, du-da,
That's where I let my money drop, Du-da, du-da, day;
I like to deal, and I like to buck, Du-da, du-da,
I'm down on noisy chuck-aluck, Du-da, du-da, day.

There's faro sledge, and twenty-one, Du-da, du-da,
For me to beat 'tis only fun, Du-da, du-da, day;
Gamblers, always hold your tongue, Du-da, du-da,
French monte-dealers have all been hung, Du-da, du-da, day.

What will we do these license times? Du-da, du-da,
I'll steal before I'll work the mines, Du-da, du-da, day;
The miners used to bet their dust, Du-da, du-da,
But now they lay it away to rust, Du-da, du-da, day.

I used to wear a ruffled shirt, Du-da, du-da,
But now I'm covered with rags and dirt, Du-da, du-da, day;
A Colt's revolver and a Bowie knife, Du-da, du-da,
I'm bound to gamble all my life, Du-da, du-da, day.

"The Gambler" is from *Put's Original California Songster*, 4th ed., San Francisco, 1868, p. 35. Tune: "Bobtail Mare" or "Camptown Races."

CLEMENTINE

In a cavern in a canyon, excavating for a mine,
Dwelt a miner, forty-niner, and his daughter, Clementine.

   Oh, my darling, oh, my darling, oh, my darling Clementine,
   You are lost and gone forever, dreadful sorry, Clementine.

Light she was and like a fairy, and her shoes were number nine,
Herring boxes without topses, sandals were for Clementine.

Drove her ducklings to the water, every morning just at nine,
Hit her foot against a splinter, fell into the foaming brine.

Ruby lips above the water, blowing bubbles soft and fine,
Alas, for me! I was no swimmer, so I lost my Clementine.

In a churchyard, near the canyon, where the myrtle doth entwine,
There grow roses and other posies fertilized by Clementine.

Then the miner, forty-niner, soon began to droop and pine,
Thought he ought to join his daughter, now he's with his Clementine.

In my dreams she still doth haunt me, robed in garments soaked in brine,
Though in life I used to kiss her, now she's dead, I draw the line.

PROSPECTING DREAM

I dreamed a dream the other night, when everything was still,
I dreamed that I was carrying my long-tom down a hill,
My feet slipped out and I fell down, oh, how I jarred my liver,
I watched my long-tom till I saw it fetch up in the river.

"Clementine" was recorded by Sidney Robertson Cowell from the singing of John McCready, Groveland, California, 1939. Library of Congress AFS record 3348 B1.

"Prospecting Dream" is from *Put's Original California Songster*, 4th ed., San Francisco, 1868, p. 11. Tune: "Oh, Susannah."

Oh, what a miner, what a miner was I,
  All swelled up with the scurvy, so I really thought I'd die.

My matches, flour and Chile beans, lay scattered all around,
I felt so bad I wished to die, as I lay on the ground,
My coffee rolled down by a rock, my pepper I could not find,
'Twas then I thought of Angeline, the girl I left behind.

I took my shovel, pick and pan, to try a piece of ground,
I dreamed I struck the richest lead that ever had been found;
Then I wrote home that I had found a solid lead of gold,
And I'd be home in just a month, but what a lie I told!

I dug, I panned and tommed awhile, till I had but a dollar,
I struck it here, and right down there I could not raise the color;
John Chinaman he bought me out, and pungled down the dust,
Then I had just an ounce in change to start in on a "bust."

I went to town and got drunk, in the morning, to my surprise,
I found that I had got a pair of roaring big black eyes;
And I was strapped, had not a cent, not even pick or shovel,
My hair snarled up, my breeches torn, looked like the very devil.

I then took up a little farm, and got a senorita,
Grey-eyed, hump-backed, and black as tar — her name was Marguerita;
My pigs all died, hens flew away, Joaquin* he stole my mules,
My ranch burnt down, my blankets up, likewise my farming tools.

I left my farm and hired out to be a hardware clerk,
I got kicked out 'cause couldn't write, so again I went to work;
But when they caught me stealing grub, a few went in to boot him,
And others round were singing out, "Hang him, hang him, shoot him!"

---

* Joaquin Murieta, the widely known bandit who terrorized farms during the Gold Rush period. He was finally caught, executed, and his head pickled in a large jar for the edification of outlaws and sightseers.

SWEET JANE

This is one of the few songs recounting a happy and successful return from the California goldfields. The majority of the '49er songs deal with dysentery, chills, fever, poor diggings, jail, homesickness, death. Not this one: it is almost too good to be true.

"Farewell, sweet Jane, for I must go across the flowing sea,
My trunk is now on Johnson's boat with all my company."

She wet her lips with flowing tears, and then I kissed her hand,
"Oh, think of me, sweet Willie dear, when in some foreign land."

"Weep not for me, sweet lovely girl, come dry those lovely eyes,
For I'll return to you again, unless your Willie dies."

For nine long years I labored hard, and digging for my wealth;
I lived on bread and salty lard and never lost my health.

I loaded up my trunk with gold and then I thought of Jane;
And anxious thoughts would homeward rove, while I recrossed the main.

I heard aloud the thunder out of the cannon's mouth,
I'll soon be welcome to the shore of my old sunny South.

And while at last we sailed in sight of our old native town,
And our good captain gave command to take the rigging down,

I saw a crowd of lovely girls come marching to the ship,
I saw sweet Jane with all those curls and I began to skip.

I ran and met her on the wharf, my heart was filled with joy,
We were so full we could not talk — I caught her in my arms.

We marched along the marble walk up to her father's door,
The crowd all looked so nice and clean while standing on the floor.

The parson read the marriage law which binds us both for life,
Now Jane is mine without a doubt, a sweet and lovely wife.

"Sweet Jane" was recorded by Herbert Halpert from the singing of Mrs. Esco Kilgore, Norton, Virginia, 1939. Library of Congress AFS record 2778 A1. Laws, B22.

The Hardrock Men

We're the hardrock men,
And we work underground,
And we don't want sissies
Or foremen around.
We work all day,
And we work all night,
And we live on powder
And DYNAMITE!

OH, GIVE ME THE HILLS

In 1903, R. C. Warner of Denver heard this song sung in Virginia Canyon outside of Idaho Springs, Colorado, by "Springheel" Riley, a blacksmith from Leadville and "the wildest little agitatin' Irishman you ever knew." Warner feels that the tune to which it is sung may have been "the original tune of 'Home on the Range.'" This is probably not the case, however. According to Boswell Reed of Denver, "Home on the Range" was popular in Elbert County, Colorado, in 1885; it was one of his mother's favorite songs and the first one that he, as a child, remembers hearing her sing. The textual relationship, however, is apparent.

Oh, give me the hills
And the ring of the drills,
And the rich silver ore in the ground,
Where seldom is heard
A discouraging word,
And many true friends will be found.

Oh, give me the camp
Where the prospectors tramp,
And business is always alive,
Where dance halls come first
And the faro banks burst
And every saloon is a dive.

"Oh, Give Me the Hills" was collected by Duncan Emrich from the singing of R. C. Warner, Denver, Colorado, and reported with music in the *California Folklore Quarterly*, 1 (1941): 220.

Oh, give me the steed
And the gun that I need,
Shoot game from my own cabin door,
With Glenwood below
Where the one-lungers go,
And we'll camp on the banks of the Grand.*

Oh, give me the wife,
The pride of my life,
She can ride, she can shoot like a man,
She's a fond and true heart
And we never will part,
Together we'll roam through the land.

Oh, give me the hills
And the roaring stamp mills,
And the riches that in the hills lie,
We'll work and we'll play
All the livelong day,
Oh, there let me live till I die.

LAMENT WHILE DESCENDING A SHAFT

This ditty was given to me by Eric Kraemer, Stanford graduate and assayer for the Arizona-Comstock. Kraemer and his wife purchased an old brewery on the Six Mile Canyon — outside Virginia City on the road to Dayton — and in the process of making the place livable struck enough pay dirt in the backyard to cover the original purchase price.

Down in the hole we go, boys,
Down in the hole we go.
The nine hundred level
Is hot as the devil —
I envy the man with the hoe.

* "The Grand": the present Colorado River is still known among oldtimers as the Grand. Its headwaters are in Grand Lake, Colorado.

"Lament while Descending a Shaft" was collected by Duncan Emrich from Eric Kraemer, Virginia City, Nevada, ca. 1937.

MY SWEETIE'S A MULE IN THE MINE

This ditty was sung to me by Tex McKinney, an old miner, at the time filling in between mining jobs as bartender at the Virginia Hotel in Virginia City, Nevada. The hotel has since burned to the ground and Tex has drifted out of the Comstock section. He sang it to me with great relish to the tune of "Blessed Be the Tie That Binds."

> My sweetie's a mule in the mine,
> I drive her without any lines,
> On the rumble I sit,
> Tobacco I spit
> All over my sweetie's behind.

SAYS THE MINER TO THE MUCKER

Given me by "Deacon" Blake in Virginia City, who heard it in the late '80's or early '90's as a song. The point of the ditty is that mucker's wages were fifty cents less per day than those of the miner.

Says the miner to the mucker,   "Save up your money,
"Will you give me a chew?"   Save up your rocks,
Says the mucker to the miner,   And you'll always have a chew,
"I'm damned if I do.   In your old tobacco box."

DYNAMITE SONG

This song was given me by "Red" Parsons at the Windsor Hotel in Denver.

"My Sweetie's a Mule in the Mine" was collected by Duncan Emrich from Tex McKinney, Virginia City, Nevada, ca. 1940.

"Says the Miner to the Mucker" was collected by Duncan Emrich from "Deacon" Blake, Virginia City, Nevada, ca. 1940.

"Dynamite Song" was collected by Duncan Emrich from "Red" Parsons, Denver, Colorado, ca. 1941.

Parsons had broken his back on a tunnel job in Tucumcari and was on his way to the Mayo Clinic. He first heard this while working on the Moffat.

We're the hardrock men	Old Johnny Deen
And we work underground,	Used lots of dynamite;
And we don't want sissies	He crimped all his caps
Or foremen around.	With a single bite.
We work all day,	But he got some new teeth
And we work all night,	From a dentist one day —
And we live on powder	And the first cap he bit
And DYNAMITE!	Blew his whole head away!

> Then slam it with a singlejack,
> And turn it around!
> We're the hardrock men
> And we work underground!
> We work underground in the candle light,
> And we live on powder
> And DYNAMITE!

Then pull out the steel	Oh, sometimes she shoots
From the hole in the rock!	When you don't want her to,
And put in the spoon	And then she won't shoot
And heave out the muck!	Spite of all that you do!
Fill her up with powder	And that's why dynamite
And tamp her down tight,	Is just like a mule —
And break down the face	And the man who says it ain't
With DYNAMITE!	He's a goldarned fool!

> Then slam it with a singlejack
> And turn it around!
> We're the hardrock men
> And we work underground!
> We work underground
> By the candle light,
> And we live on powder
> And DYNAMITE!

COUSIN JACK SONG

Sung for me by Oakley Johns of Grass Valley, California. Israel James claims that the song was written by Charley Tregonning of Grass Valley.

You ask me for a song, folks,
And I'll try to please you all,
Don't blame me if I do not suit
For nature has its call.

But for singing and for mining
They have somehow got the knack,
It's a second nature to that class
Of lads called Cousin Jacks.

You'll find them on the mountain top,
You'll find them on the plain,
You'll find those boys where'er you go
And you'll find their mining claims.

They come from distant Tombstone
And Virginia on the hill,
You ne'er can beat a Cousin Jack
For hammering on the drill.

Amongst you other Irishmen
Do justice if you can,
For there's none that can compete
With the good old Cornishman.

But for singing and for mining
They have somehow got the knack,
It's a second nature to that class
Of lads called Cousin Jacks.

"Cousin Jack Song" was collected by Duncan Emrich from Oakley Johns, Grass Valley, California, 1941. The Cousin Jacks are, of course, Cornishmen, famous for their mining ability.

TRAMP MINER'S SONG

This tramp miners' song is a favorite in all the camps of the West. While the words here localize it in Butte, names of mines, camps, and shift bosses are changed to suit whatever camp the miner may be in. I have heard it in Idaho Springs, on the Mother Lode, in Lovelock, and in an all-night diner west of Salt Lake City.

There were miners from Bisbee,
Timbermen from Butte,
And cowboys from Polson
To muck the rock in the chute.

And I got me a job
On the first day of May,
And five and a quarter
They said was the pay.

And I worked four shifts
And I dragged my time,
The hell with Eddie Kane
And his Big Diamond Mine.

And I went to the Coeur d'Alene
And I rustled the King,
But he said, "For a tramp like you
There isn't a thing."

So I went back to Butte,
And I rustled the Con,
And I rustled the Sweat,
And the winter is over
And I'm rustling yet.

CASEY JONES

One of the great dangers in tunneling and blasting for gold is the possibility of a "missed hole" — where the fuse in a dynamite charge seems to have fizzled out and become dead only to reignite, explode the charge, and trap the miner under tons of earth.

"Tramp Miner's Song" was collected by Duncan Emrich from Joe Tracy, Virginia City, Nevada, 1941, and reported in *California Folklore Quarterly*, 1 (1942):226.

"Casey Jones" was collected by Duncan Emrich from Bill Gilbert, Grass Valley, California, Christmas Day, 1940. Gilbert had first heard the song in 1918 at Chicago Park, near Colfax, California, when he was president of the Western Federation of Miners. The specific reference to the Liberty Bell would indicate a Grass Valley origin for the parody. Reported in the *California Folklore Quarterly*, 1 (1941):220.

Come all you muckers and gather here,
A story I'll tell you of a miner dear,
Casey Jones was the miner's name,
On a Burleigh machine he won his fame.

    Casey Jones was a ten-day miner,
    Casey Jones was a ten-day man,
    Casey Jones took a chance too many,
    And now he's mining in the promised land.

The story I am about to tell
Happened at a mine called the Liberty Bell.
They went into the crosscut and mucked her out,
And Casey said, "We'd better step about."

Casey said, "We'd better dig in
Before that damned old shift boss comes in;
If he finds out we've been taking five,
He'll send us to the office to get our time."

They went into the crosscut, put up the bar,
Placed the machine up on the arm,
Put in a starting drill with its bit toward the ground,
Turned on the air and she began to pound.

Casey said, "If I haven't lied,
There is a missed hole on that right-hand side."
His partner said, "Oh gracious me,
If it ever went off where would we be."

They went into the crosscut to drill some more,
The powder exploded with a hell of a roar;
It scorched poor Casey just as flat as a pan,
And now he's a-mining in the promised land.

Casey said just before he died,
"There's one more machine I would like to have tried."
His partner said, "What can it be?"
"An Ingersoll jackhammer, now don't you see."

    Casey Jones was a ten-day miner,
    Casey Jones was a ten-day man,
    Casey Jones took a chance too many,
    And now he's mining in the promised land.

I'M ONLY A BROKEN-DOWN MINER

This poignant little ditty was sung by Frank Connolly in Virginia City, Nevada, to the tune of "My Bonnie Lies over the Ocean." It is current and popular on the mining "circle" from Butte to Bisbee. It is to be sung through once with normal voice; the second time, the first four words of the last line are roared out and the last two, by contrast, softened pathetically.

> I'm only a broken-down miner,
> You can tell by the looks of my clothes,
> I've spent all my dough on the women,
> How much, Jesus Christ only knows.

THE HARD-WORKING MINER

> To the hard-working miner whose dangers are great,
> So many while mining have met their sad fate,
> While doing their duty as miners all do,
> Shut out from daylight, and their loving ones, too.
>
> Only a miner killed in the ground,
> Only a miner, and one more is gone,
> Killed by an accident, no one can tell,
> His mining is over — poor miner, farewell.
>
> He leaves his dear wife, and his little ones, too,
> To earn them a living as all miners do,
> And while he is working for those that he loved,
> He met a sad fate from a boulder above.

"I'm Only a Broken-Down Miner" was collected by Duncan Emrich from the singing of Frank Connolly in Virginia City, Nevada, 1940, and reported in the *California Folklore Quarterly*, 1 (1941):220.

"The Hard-Working Miner" was collected by Duncan Emrich from the singing of Mrs. Walter Mosch, Central City, Colorado, and Israel James, Grass Valley, California. Combined text, reported with music in the *California Folklore Quarterly*, 1 (1941):220.

Though comrades were near him, so quick was the call,
The message of death, the miner did fall,
Though comrades were near him, no one could say,
Now the poor fellow rests in his grave.

    Only a miner killed in the ground,
    Only a miner, and one more is gone,
    Killed by an accident, no one can tell,
    His mining is over — poor miner, farewell.

ONLY A MINER

Down in the mine, in the dark, dismal drift,
Two miners were working their long midnight shift,
With muscles of steel and a heart of good will,
The music kept time with the hammer and drill.

Unconscious of danger, the mid-hour had fled,
They heard not the crash of the rock overhead,
Till it fell like a bolt to the death-blow of one,
At the feet of his comrade, he sank with a moan.

"Partner, goodbye!" then he sank in the clay,
The candle's dim light on his dim vision lay.
His partner bent o'er him, his life was all gone,
Death ended his shift, and his mercy was done.

Mother, Joe's dead, he was killed in the mine:
This telegram trembles along o'er the line;
The fate she had feared had taken her boy,
Cut down in his manhood her pride and her joy.

    Only a miner killed in the breast,*
    Only a workingman gone to his rest,

---

* The "head" or "face" of the tunnel where the rounds of dynamite were placed for blasting the rock.

"Only a Miner" was collected by Duncan Emrich from the singing of "Doughbelly" and "Dinger" Williams in Georgetown, Colorado, who had heard it sung at Silver Plume, Colorado, by Susie Ingram in the 1890's. Reported with music in the *California Folklore Quarterly*, 1 (1941):220. In the third stanza "mercy" should probably be "mission."

Read on his grave 'neath the whispering pines:
Our Joe, aged just 20, was killed in the mines.

THE MINER BOY

One morning as I rambled,
Through the fields I took my way,
In hopes of seeing my miner boy
And for a while to stay,
In hopes of seeing my miner boy
My love, my life, my joy,
My heart was depressed, I could find no rest
For the thoughts of my miner boy.

Said the mother to the daughter,
"I'll confine you to your room,
You never shall marry a miner boy,
It would certainly be your doom;
For the way they have of living,
And of toiling on through life,
Daughter, dear, now do you hear,
You can't be a miner's wife."

Said the daughter to the mother,
"Why are you so unkind?
I never shall marry no other one,
He's the one that suits my mind,
With his trousers made of corduroy
And jacket of true blue,
I'd rather marry my miner boy
Than live at home with you."

So fill the glasses to the brim,
Let the toast go merrily round,
Drink to the health of the miner boy
That works down in the ground.
When his work is over,
He comes whistling home with joy,

"The Miner Boy" was collected by Duncan Emrich from the singing of Mrs. Walter Mosch, Central City, Colorado, with the variant last stanza from Israel James, Grass Valley, California. Reported with music in the *California Folklore Quarterly*, 1 (1941):220.

> Happy is the girl
> That marries the miner boy.

Israel James knew no more than the last stanza which can, of course, stand alone as a toast:

> Here's health to the jolly miner lad
> Which under the brace goes down,
> To seek for tin and copper
> To make himself a crown,
> His teeth are white as ivory,
> His hair is black as jet,
> Here's to the jolly miner lad
> And all that he gets!

Coal

No pen can write the awful fright
And horror that prevailed
Among those dying victims
In the mines of Avondale.

DOWN IN A COAL MINE

I am a jovial collier lad, as blithe as blithe can be,
And let the times be good or bad, they're all the same to me;
There's little of this world I know and care less for its ways,
And where the dog star never glows, I wear away the days.

Down in a coal mine, underneath the ground,
Where a gleam of sunshine never can be found;
Digging dusky diamonds all the year around,
Away down in a coal mine, underneath the ground.

My hands are horny, hard, and black from working in the vein,
Like the clothes upon my back my speech is rough and plain;
And if I stumble with my tongue I've one excuse to say,
It's not the collier's heart that's bad, it's his head that goes astray.

At every shift, be it soon or late, I haste my bread to earn,
And anxiously my kindred wait and watch for my return:
For death that levels all alike, whate'er their rank may be,
Amid the fire and damp may strike and fling his darts at me.

How little do the great ones care who sit at home secure,
What hidden dangers colliers dare, what hardships they endure;
The very fires their mansions boast, to cheer themselves and wives,
Mayhap were kindled at the cost of jovial colliers' lives.

"Down in a Coal Mine" was recorded by George Korson from the singing of Morgan Jones at Wilkes-Barre, Pennsylvania, 1946. Library of Congress record LP16. Last three stanzas from Korson, *Minstrels of the Mine Patch*, p. 277.

Then cheer up, lads, and make ye much of every joy ye can;
But let your mirth be always such as best becomes a man;
However fortune turns about we'll still be jovial souls,
For what would America be without the lads that look for coals?

THAT LITTLE LUMP OF COAL

A bituminous coal mine was like a city built underground where work was carried on in darkness. What to a confused visitor might look like an inextricable labyrinth actually was a systematically laid-out underground factory, cut out of rock and coal. From the drift mouth (or from the bottom of a slope or shaft, whichever the entrance happened to be) there ran an avenue called a "main entry," wide enough for a railroad track; this was the principal traveling way for the mine workers and for the transportation of coal. Driven off the main and at a right angle to it were headings or branch entries, like cross streets in a city. Off these branch entries were the "rooms," the daily workshops of the miners.

It was a miner's task to win the coal by advancing on the face of the seam until the room had been mined out, when he would move on to another room. The side walls, called "ribs," were also of coal. They were left standing in columns to support the roof until all the rooms had been mined out. Then, one by one, they were retrieved by means of an extraordinarily hazardous operation called "robbing."

— GEORGE KORSON

Oh, to those who know no better,
And the ones that do not care,
I'll take this means of telling you
What a miner has to bear.
When your servant fires the furnace
And the smoke and blazes roll,
Just stop and think who suffered
For that little lump of coal.

Oh, he gets up in the morning,
He's in the land of Nod,

"That Little Lump of Coal" was recorded by George Korson from the singing of William March and Richard Lawson at Kenvir, Kentucky, 1940. Library of Congress record LP60.

And at the family altar
He will kneel and ask his God
For to care for and protect him
From dangers underground,
So he can come back in the evening
To his family safe and sound.

Oh, he eats a hasty breakfast,
Fills up his carbide flask,
Picks up his lamp and bucket
And he's ready for his task.
Says good-bye to wife and baby,
Stops to kiss them at the door;
He doesn't know if he'll see them
In his life any more.

Oh, he's soon below the surface,
Gets his car up in its place.
As he swings his pick and shovel
The sweat pours off his face.
Oh, he's tired, weak and weary —
Two hours have rolled around.
But he's got six more to suffer
Till he gets above the ground.

Oh, he's got to set some timbers,
Then drill a hole or two,
And then he'll roll some dummies;
Then there's something else to do.
So he stays, toils, and labors,
Loads every car he can,
To earn a measure living
And to pay the clothing man.

When he lines up at the office
With the others in a row,
With their statements signed and ready
For their little bit of dough,
And everything he's buying
Is away up in the air,

Do you think what he is asking for
Is anything unfair?

Oh, he only asks for wages
That enable him to share
A part of mortal pleasures,
And that is only fair:
Oh, it's a six-hour day, and Saturday
To stay at home and see
The sun rise in the morning
Like God aimed for us to be.

So brother, when you're knocking
On the man that digs the coal,
Just stop and think he's human
And he's got a heart and soul.
And don't forget the millions
Of tons he loaded out,
When the Kaiser tried to smear on us
His lager beer and kraut.

So you tell your pals and neighbors,
Your servants and your wife,
The plaster of your office room
Cannot crush out your life.
Oh, he's just a dirty miner
A sort of human mole,
That takes those dangerous chances
For this little lump of coal.

THE OLD MINER'S REFRAIN

"The Old Miner's Refrain," one of the oldest anthracite ballads, recalls the former custom of employing old miners to pick slate in the breaker alongside boys. As mechanical slate pickers displaced manual picking, there no longer was any place for old men in the breaker. This ballad reflects the full cycle of

"The Old Miner's Refrain" was recorded by George Korson from the singing of Daniel Walsh at Centralia, Pennsylvania, 1946. Library of Congress record LP16. Stanzas from 3 on are from Korson, *Minstrels of the Mine Patch*, p. 274.

an anthracite miner's career — from the age of eight when he first went into the breaker until he returned to it again a very old man. Summed up are his hopes, dreams, thwarted ambitions and the fear of a dependent old age.

— GEORGE KORSON

I'm getting old and feeble and I cannot work no more,
I have laid my rusty mining tools away;
For forty years and over I have toiled about the mines,
But now I'm getting feeble, old and gray.
I started in the breaker and went back to it again,
But now my work is finished for all time;
The only place that's left me is the almshouse for a home,
Where I'm going to lay this weary head of mine.

Where are the boys that worked with me in the breakers long ago?
Many of them now have gone to rest;
Their cares of life are over and they've left this world of woe;
And their spirits now are roaming with the blest.

In the chutes I graduated instead of going to school —
Remember, friends, my parents they were poor;
When a boy left the cradle it was always made the rule
To try to keep starvation from the door.
At eight years of age to the breaker first I went,
To learn the occupation of a slave;
I was certainly delighted, and on picking slate was bent —
My ambition it was noble, strong and brave.

At eleven years of age I bought myself a lamp —
The boss he sent me down the mine to trap;
I stood in there in water, in powder smoke and damp;
My leisure hours I spent in killing rats.
One day I got promoted to what they called a patcher,
Or a lackey for the man that drives the team:
I carried sprags and spreaders and had to fix the latch —
I was going through my exercise, it seems.

I next became a driver, and thought myself a man;
The boss he raised my pay as I advanced:
In going through the gangway with the mules at my command,
I was prouder than the President of France.

But now my pride is weakened and I am weakened too;
I tremble till I'm scarcely fit to stand:
If I were taught book-learning instead of driving teams,
Today, kind friends, I'd be a richer man.

I next became a miner and laborer combined,
For to earn my daily bread beneath the ground.
I performed the acts of labor which came in a miner's line —
For to get my cars and load them I was bound.
But now I can work no more, my cares of life are run;
I am waiting for the signal at the door;
When the angels they will whisper, "Dear old miner, you must come
And we'll row you to the bright celestial shore."

A COAL MINER'S GOODBYE

Conway created this song while lying flat on his back in a cast waiting for death. Falling slate had broken his back and paralyzed him from the waist down in the Guyan Eagle mine at Amherstdale, West Virginia, in 1938. He was still bed-ridden when he sang for me on May 28, 1940.

— GEORGE KORSON

For years I have been a coal miner,
I worked day by day in the mine;
But no longer am I a coal miner,
I have come to the end of the line.

I toiled 'neath the ground like the others,
Of hard knocks I have had quite a few
Now my prayer as you labor, my brothers,
Is that God will be watching o'er you.

May he throw His great arm round about you,
From harm keep everyone free;
I guess I'll be lonesome without you,
Since it's quitting time forever for me.

"A Coal Miner's Goodbye" was recorded by George Korson from the singing of Archie Conway at Man, West Virginia, 1940. Library of Congress record LP60.

My tools are all rusty, I reckon,
I last saw them stacked up inside,
No longer to me do they beckon,
Since I started that last fatal ride.

Some day I'll be absent forever,
Then be true to your union, I pray,
I'll deposit my transfer in heaven
Where no slate fall will come night or day.

We will have a good local in heaven,
Up there where the password is "Rest,"
Where the business is praising our Father,
And no scabs ever mar or molest.

Our Savior is on the committee,
He is pleading our cases alone,
For ages He's been on committee,
Pleading daily to God on the throne.

The Bible up there is the Journal,
And the members all know it is true;
The contract up there is eternal —
It was written for me and for you.

No strikes ever happen in heaven,
The Boss loves the men, I declare,
The house is in order in heaven —
I hope I shall see you up there.

UNION MAN

This short ditty, sung with good humor by Albert Morgan, is an excellent example of the way the folk reflect in their songs the varied phases of their life. Better than an economist's report, the five stanzas are a satiric comment on rising wages and rising prices. They were composed by the singer and have circulated widely in the lower anthracite region.

— GEORGE KORSON

"Union Man" was recorded by George Korson from the singing of Albert Morgan in the Newkirk Tunnel Mine itself, Tamaqua, Pennsylvania, 1946. Library of Congress record LP16.

I think I sing that little song,
Hope I say it nothing wrong,
Hope my song she bring you cheer
Just like couple of shots of beer.

> Union man! Union man!
> He must have full dinner can!
> AFL, CIO
> Callin' strike, out she go!

We all got contract, she expire:
Mr. Lewis mad like fire;
Miners strikin' too much time,
Uncle Sam take over mines.

We signin' contract, we get raise
After strikin' twenty days.
Butcher comes and ringin' bell
He raises price — what the hell!

I'm drinkin' too much beer last
   night,
To go to work I don't feel right.
In my can some bread and meat,
I'm too dam' sick; I cannot eat.

I fire shot at ten o'clock,
Tumble brushes full of rock,
Timber breakin' o'er my head,
Jeepers cripes, I think I'm dead!

> Union man! Union man!
> He must have full dinner can!
> AFL, CIO
> Callin' strike, out she go!

BLUE MONDAY

I went uptown last Saturday night,
Intending to get one drink,
The boys were all standing in front of the bar
Telling what they could think.
Their entries they were driving,
Rooms and pillars too;
I never saw such a mess of coal
As around that barroom flue.

> But it's always the same blue Monday,
> Blue Monday after pay.
> Your shots are bad and your buddy is mad,
> And the shaft will work all day.

"Blue Monday" was recorded by George Korson from the singing of Michael F. Barry, New Kensington, Pennsylvania, 1940. Library of Congress record LP60.

Now I'll have no more blue Mondays
To make my hair turn gray;
I'll join the White Ribbon and then I'll be givin'
Me wife the whole of me pay.

The track layers and the drivers,
Machine men and loaders too,
They are all sitting around the tables
Telling what they could do.
But if they would only stay at home
Their dollars and dimes to save,
When a strike come on they could sing this song;
"Operator, your work we don't need."

DRILL MAN BLUES

Recording George C. "Curley" Sizemore's mine ballads in his home at Lochgelly, West Virginia, on March 27, 1940, was an unpleasant experience. A rock driller in the mines, Sizemore suffered from silicosis, or "miner's asthma," an occupational disease, a symptom of which is shortness of breath. There were frequent breaks in his singing as he paused for breath. He said new ballads take shape in his mind, but he cannot sing them spontaneously because he would get a mouthful of rock dust if he parted his lips.

— GEORGE KORSON

I used to be a drill man,
Down at Old Parlee;
Drilling through slate and sand rock,
Till it got the best of me.

Rock dust has almost killed me,
It's turned me out in the rain;
For dust has settled on my lungs,
And causes me constant pain.

I can hear my hammer rollin',
As I lay down for my sleep;

"Drill Man Blues" was recorded by George Korson from the singing of George Sizemore at Lochgelly, West Virginia, 1940. Library of Congress record LP60.

For drilling is the job I love,
And this I will repeat.

It's killed two fellow workers,
Here at Old Parlee;
And now I've eaten so much dust, Lord,
That it's killin' me.

I'm thinkin' of poor drill men,
Away down in the mine,
Who from eating dust will end up
With a fate just like mine.

TWO-CENT COAL

"Two-Cent Coal" commemorates a major disaster on the Monongahela River near Pittsburgh in 1876. Morrison recollected that the river was frozen to a depth of fourteen inches, which was deep enough to support the crossing of a team of horses hauling a wagonload of hay. Because of the ice, the river coal mines were idle from Christmas to late February. The miners pooled meager resources to keep alive.

Their plight was worsened by a cut in wages from three cents to two cents a bushel, the equivalent of fifty cents a ton. When the ice broke suddenly, tipples and other mine property were destroyed and swept down the river. The hapless miners interpreted this destruction as God's retribution against the operators for cutting the men's wages.

— GEORGE KORSON

Oh, the bosses' tricks of '76
They met with some success,
Until the hand of God came down
And made them do with less.
They robbed the honest miner lad
And drunk his flowin' bowl,
Through poverty we were compelled
To dig them two-cent coal.

But the river it bein' frozen —
Of course, the poor might starve;
What did those tyrant bosses say?
"It's just what they deserve."
For God who always aids the just,
All things He does control:
He brought the ice and He sent it
    down
And sunk the two-cent coal.

"Two-Cent Coal" was recorded by George Korson from the singing of David Morrison (aged eighty-one) at Finlayville, Pennsylvania, 1940. Library of Congress record LP60.

Their tipples, too, fled from our view,
And down the river went.
They seemed to cry as they passed by:
"You tyrants, now repent!
For while you rob the miner lad,
Remember, you've a soul.
For your soul is sinkin' deeper
Than the ice sunk your two-cent coal."

It's to conclude and finish,
Let us help our fellow man,
And if our brother's in distress
Assist him if you can,
To keep the wolf all from his door,
And shelter him from the cold,
That he never again shall commit the crime
Of diggin' two-cent coal.

THE SHOOFLY

This ballad articulates the thoughts of the miners in the depression of the early '70's. In 1871 the little mine patch of Valley Furnace received a blow from which it never recovered: the mine gave out. Normally the miners might have found jobs at the Shoofly, a nearby colliery. There, however, a bad seam had been struck and men were being laid off. The only alternative to starvation was to gather meager belongings, leave old associations, and trek across the Broad Mountain into the Mahanoy Valley, then being opened to mining.

These troubles preyed on the mind of a little old Irishwoman in Valley Furnace. Her heart was breaking because of the debts she owed in the store and because all her good neighbors were deserting the village. Felix O'Hare, who kept night school for breaker boys at nearby Silver Creek Patch, used to pass the woman's cottage on his way to and from school. The simple mining folk believed that his meager book learning, acquired by dint of much whale oil burned after working hours, equipped him to solve all of life's problems. And so the little old woman would stop him as he went by and pour out her troubles to him. He lent a sympathetic ear and tried to comfort her.

One evening, profoundly moved, he spent half the night trying to put into a ballad some of the things she had told him, and thus created "The Shoofly." Never formally published, the ballad spread by word of mouth and in a short time the whole region was singing it. Only his immediate family knew that O'Hare had composed the ballad and the little Irishwoman herself was not told that its author was her schoolmaster confidant. When she heard it sung, however, and identified herself with the "old lady" in the ballad she gave a curse upon the man who had thus exploited her. Not long afterward, O'Hare was drowned in Silver Creek.

— GEORGE KORSON

"The Shoofly" was recorded by George Korson from the singing of Daniel Welsh at Centralia, Pennsylvania, 1946. Library of Congress record LP16.

As I went a-walking one fine summer's morning,
It was down by the Furnace I chanced for to stroll,
I espied an old lady, I'll swear she was eighty,
At the foot of the dirt banks a-rooting for coal;
And when I drew nigh her she sat on her hunkers
For to fill up her scuttle she just had begun —
And to herself she was singing a ditty,
And these are the words the old lady did sing:

> Crying Ochone! Sure I'm nearly distracted,
> For it's down by the Shoofly they cut a bad vein;
> And since they condemned the old slope at the Furnace,
> Shure all me fine neighbors must leave here again.

" 'Twas only last evenin' that I asked McGinley
To tell me the reason the Furnace gave o'er.
He told me the company had spent eighty thousand,
And finding no prospects they would spend no more.
He said that the Diamond it was rather bony,
Besides too much dirt in the seven-foot vein;
And as for the Mammoth, there's no length of gangway,
Unless they buy land from old Abel and Swayne.

"And as for Michael Rooney, I owe him some money,
Likewise Patrick Kearns, I owe him some more;
And as for old John Eagen, I'll ne'er see his wagon,
But I think of the debt that I owe in the store.
I owe butcher and baker, likewise the shoemaker,
And for plowin' me garden I owe Pat McQuail;
Likewise his old mother, for one thing and another,
And to drive away bother, an odd quart of ale.

"But if God spares me children until the next summer,
Instead of a burden, they will be a gain;
And out of their earnin's I'll save an odd dollar,
And build a snug home at the 'Foot of the Plane.'
Then rolling in riches, in silks and in satin,
I ne'er shall forget the days I was poor,
And likewise the neighbors that stood by my children,
Kept want and starvation away from me door."

THE HARD-WORKING MINER

The hard-working miners
Their dangers are great,
And many while working
Have met their sad fate.
They're doing their duty
As all miners do,
Shut out from the daylight
And darling ones too.

He leaves his companions
And little ones too,
To earn them a living
As all miners do.
And while he was working
For those that he loved,
The boulder that crushed him,
It came from above.

The miner is gone,
We'll see him no more,
God be with the miner
Wherever he goes.
And may he be ready
Thy call to obey,
And looking to Jesus
The only true way.

God be with the miners,
Protect them from harm,
And shield him from danger
With Thy dear strong arm.
Then pity his dear children
Wherever they be,
And take him at last
Up to heaven with Thee.

THE MINER'S DOOM

"The Miner's Doom" is an old Welsh ballad which enjoyed a vogue in the anthracite region, where many miners were Welsh. Thomas Jones of Seek, Schuylkill County, who gave me the text in 1925, had sung the ballad in his old home in South Wales.

— GEORGE KORSON

At five in the morning, as jolly as any,
The miner doth rise to his work for to go,

"The Hard-Working Miner" was recorded by George Korson from the singing of G. C. Cartin at Braeholm, West Virginia, 1940. Library of Congress record LP60.

"The Miner's Doom" was recorded by George Korson from the singing of Daniel Walsh, Centralia, Pennsylvania, 1946. Library of Congress record LP16.

600

He caresses his wife and his children so dearly
And bids them adieu before closing the door;
And goes down the deep shaft at the speed of an arrow,
His heart light and gay without fear or dread,
Has no thoughts of descending to danger and peril —
But his life is depending on one single thread.

His wife is his queen and his home is his palace,
His children his glory, to maintain them he tries,
He'll work like a hero; he faces all danger,
He'll deprive his own self their bare feet to hide.
Now his day's work is o'er, he's homeward returning,
He thinks not how the change in an hour will be,
But he thinks how his wife and his children will greet him —
But his home and his children he'll nevermore see.

Now his wife had been dreaming of her husband so dearly,
She'd seen him in danger — "God help me," she cried;
Too true was the dream of a poor woman's sorrow.
The rope broke ascending; her dear husband died.
Their home that morning was as jovial as any,
But a dark cloud came rolling straight o'er their door —
A widow, three children are left for to mourn him;
The one that they ne'er will see any more.

At the day of his funeral the great crowds had gathered,
He was loved by his friends, by his neighbors, by all,
To the grave went his corpse, by his friends he was followed,
The tears from our eyes like the rain they did fall,
And the widow, lamenting the fate of her husband,
Broken-hearted she died on the dear loved one's tomb,
To the world now is left their three little children
Whose father had met with a coal miner's doom.

JOHN J. CURTIS

When John J. Curtis was blinded in an accident in the Morea mine in May, 1888, he was helpless. Joseph Gallagher of Lansford wrote a ballad for him, and broadsides of it were printed by the Lansford *Record*. Led by a Scranton boy, Curtis roamed all over the region singing or reciting the ballad "John J. Curtis," and selling the broadsides for a livelihood.

— GEORGE KORSON

My name is John J. Curtis,
My age is twenty-eight,
I was born in Schuylkill County
And there I met my fate.
So now with your attention
If you will be so kind,
I will tell you of that fatal day
That I was stricken blind.

It was on a bright May morning,
As the sun peeped o'er the hill,
The little birds sang loud and sweet:
I seem to hear them still;
My heart was filled with purest joy
As to the mines I did stray,
To earn an honest living
In the colliery of Morea.

At eight o'clock I climbed the pitch,
And to my work did go,
I drilled two holes and loaded them —
Touched one and fled below.
It soon went off; I then went back
To the one that did remain,
When by its mouth it too went off
And blew me down again.

"John J. Curtis" was recorded by George Korson from the singing of Andrew Rada at Shenandoah, Pennsylvania, 1946, but previously collected from Rada in 1938 and from Gallagher in 1925. First two stanzas on Library of Congress record LP60 and last three from Korson, *Minstrels of the Mine Patch*, p. 200. Laws, G29.

I lay there in the darkness;
I was buried in the coal,
The blood in streams ran down my cheeks;
Great lumps o'er me did roll.
When I got free, my cap and lamp
Was all that I could find,
And when I struck a match
'Twas then I knew that I was blind.

Now kind folks, do have pity
On whom you chance to find
Wandering through your city,
That in both eyes is blind;
You know not when your day will come
That this same path you'll stray,
So be kind-hearted while you can
To the miner from Morea.

THE DYING MINE BRAKEMAN

I tried tracing the author. His identity eluded me until May 29 when I met Orville J. Jenks in the subdistrict office of the United Mine Workers of America at Welch, West Virginia.

When Jenks had completed singing this ballad, I asked him the usual question:

"Who made it up?"

"I did," he replied unhesitatingly.

This is how Jenks described the origin of his ballad:

"One day in 1915 when I was working as a motorman inside the No. 3 mine of the Republic Coal Company at Corbin (Cabin Creek district), West Virginia, there was a wreck. A motor hauling a trip of cars was coming off the mouth of sixth left, which was pretty steep.

"I was standing still on the main entry just above the mouth of sixth left when the accident happened. The motorman had been sitting on the deck of the motor up in front and the young brakeman was on the stirrup in the rear of the motor when a loaded car next to the motor was wrecked. The boy brake-

"The Dying Mine Brakeman" was recorded by George Korson from the singing of Orville J. Jenks at Welch, West Virginia, 1940. Library of Congress record LP60. Laws, G11.

man leaped in the dark and fell under the trip. Two cars passed over him before the trip could be brought to a stop.

"I found his mangled body under the third car. The accident made a terrible impression on me. The idea for the ballad came to me as I was lifting the boy's body from the bloody mess. All the words did not come at once, but after mulling the idea over in my mind for a week, the ballad was finally finished and I wrote it down on paper. Then I suited a tune to it."

— GEORGE KORSON

See that brave and trembling motorman,
Said his age was twenty-one.
See him stepping from his motor
Crying, "Lord, what have I done?

"Have I killed my brave young coupler,
Is it right that he is dying?
Well, I tried to stop the motor,
But I could not stop in time."

See the car wheels running o'er him,
See them bend his weary head;
See his sister standing o'er him
Crying "Brother, are you dead?"

"Yes, sister, I am dying
Soon I'll reach a better shore,
Soon I'll gain a home in heaven
Where this coupling will be no more.

"Tell my brother in the heading —
These few words I'll send to him;
Never, never venture coupling,
If he does, his life will end.

"Tell my father — he's a weighboss,
All he weighs to weigh it fair,
They will have true scales up yonder
At that meeting in the air.

"Tell my mother I've gone to glory,
Not to grieve for me no more,
Just to meet me over yonder
On that bright and golden shore."

THE AVONDALE MINE DISASTER

"The Avondale Mine Disaster" recounts the anthracite industry's first major tragedy, in which 110 men and boys were lost. In the manner of early collieries, the Avondale was ventilated by means of a furnace built on the bottom level, its flue running up the height of the shaft. This shaft, leading to the breaker above, was the outlet.

The fire started early in the morning of September 6, 1869, when the flue partition caught fire. The flames roared up the shaft and fired the breaker. Men and boys, their only avenue of escape cut off, and the air currents stopped, fought a desperate battle against gases. Rescue work began immediately after the fire was extinguished. A box with a slot top containing a dog attached to a lighted lantern was let down into the shaft to test the air. While the dog survived, the light in the lantern was snuffed out by black damp.

However, the mere fact that the dog had come back alive held out a slender hope to hundreds of anxious people that their loved ones might still be alive. Volunteers went down the shaft, only to return immediately gasping for air. Even after this experience, Thomas W. Williams and David Jones,

> *Two Welshmen brave, without dismay,*
> *And courage without fail,*
> *Went down the shaft, without delay,*
> *In the mines of Avondale.*

When they reached the bottom, they signalled for a pick and shovel, but died before using them. After the gases had been cleared, a crew descended to the bottom, where they found the bodies of the two heroic Welshmen and those of the other victims.

— George Korson

> Good Christians all, both great and small,
>   I pray you lend an ear,
> And listen with attention while
>   The truth I will declare;
> When you hear this lamentation,
>   It will cause you to weep and wail,
> About the suffocation
>   In the mines of Avondale.

"The Avondale Mine Disaster" was recorded by George Korson from the singing of John J. Quinn at Wilkes-Barre, Pennsylvania, 1946. Library of Congress record LP76B. Laws, G6.

On the sixth day of September,
 Eighteen sixty-nine,
Those miners all then got a call
 To go work in the mine;
But little did they think that [day]
 That death would soon prevail
Before they would return again from
 The mines of Avondale.

The women and their children,
 Their hearts were filled with joy,
To see their men go to their work
 Likewise every boy;
But a dismal sight in broad daylight,
 Soon made them turn pale,
When they saw the breaker burning
 O'er the mines of Avondale.

From here and there, and everywhere,
 They gathered in a crowd,
Some tearing of their clothes and hair,
 And crying out aloud —
"Get out our husbands and our sons,
 Death he's going to steal
Their lives away without delay
 In the mines of Avondale."

But all in vain, there was no hope
 One single soul to save,
For there is no second outlet
 From the subterranean cave.
No pen can write the awful fright
 And horror that prevailed,
Among those dying victims,
 In the mines of Avondale.

A consultation then was held,
 'Twas asked who'd volunteer
For to go down this dismal shaft,
 To seek their comrades dear;

Two Welshmen brave, without dismay,
    And courage without fail,
Went down the shaft, without delay,
    In the mines of Avondale.

When at the bottom they arrived,
    And thought to make their way,
One of them died for want of air,
    While the other in great dismay,
He gave the sign to hoist him up,
    To tell the dreadful tale,
That all was lost forever
    In the mines of Avondale.

Every effort then took place
    To send down some fresh air;
The men that next went down again
    They took of them good care;
They traversed through the chambers,
    And this time did not fail
In finding those dead bodies
    In the mines of Avondale.

Sixty-seven was the number
    That in a heap were found,
It seemed that they were bewailing
    Their fate underneath the ground;
They found the father with his son
    Clasped in his arms so pale.
It was a heart-rending scene
    In the mines of Avondale.

Now to conclude, and make an end,
    Their number I'll pen down —
A hundred and ten of brave strong men
    Were smothered underground;
They're in their graves till this last day,
    Their widows may bewail,
And the orphans' cries they rend the skies
    All round through Avondale!

PAYDAY AT COAL CREEK

Payday, payday, O payday,
Payday at Coal Creek tomorrow,
Payday at Coal Creek tomorrow.

Payday, payday, O payday,
Payday don't come at Coal Creek no more,
Payday don't come no more.

Bye-bye, bye-bye, O bye-bye,
Bye-bye, my woman, I'm gone,
Bye-bye, my woman, I'm gone.

You'll miss me, you'll miss me, you'll miss me,
You'll miss me when I'm gone,
You'll miss me when I'm gone.

I'm a poor boy, I'm a poor boy, I'm a poor boy,
I'm a poor boy and a long ways from home,
I'm a poor boy and a long way from home.

He's a rider, O he's a rider, O he's a rider,
O he's a rider, but she'll leave that rail some time,
O he's a rider, but she'll leave that rail some time.

"Payday at Coal Creek" was recorded by Alan and Elizabeth Lomax from the singing, with five-string banjo, of Pete Steele, Hamilton, Ohio, 1938. Library of Congress record LP2. Coal Creek is in Tennessee.

SONGS OF *A* GROWING NATION
Cowboys, Mormons, Outlaws, and Others

Songs of the Mormons

"Westward the Course . . ."

The Cowboy

Work Chants

Railroading

Murders

Outlaws and Bad Men

Hangings

Blues

Miscellaneous Songs

Songs of the Mormons

Hurray! Hurrah! The railroad's begun!
Three cheers for our contractor, his name's Brigham
  Young;
Hurray! Hurrah! We're light-hearted and gay,
Just the right kind of boys to build a railway.

These traditional Mormon songs are secular and historical. They go back in time more a hundred years to the earliest days of settlement and pioneering, and are, for the opening of Utah and the West, unique documents. As items of general Americana alone they are extremely rare, but when we consider that they relate to a single group of people and to the final establishment of a single state, their importance is still further enhanced. The reason for this lies, not alone in their intrinsic worth as historical documents for Utah, but also because songs of this nature, dealing with early pioneering and settlement, are virtually nonexistent in the folk tradition for any other state in the Union. True, there are individual songs dealing with the pioneer days of various states, but a full bodied group such as this from Utah does not appear elsewhere. It should be noted further that these songs are a selection only, and that still other secular and historical songs of Utah are to be found in the collections of the Library of Congress. All these songs were sung by Mormons living in Utah, and all were acquired traditionally in the folk manner, either at first hand from those who first "made" them or as they were handed down orally within a family or community group. The majority are found on Library of Congress record LP30.

THE HANDCART SONG

The first Mormon handcart company left Iowa City on June 9, 1856, while the last handcart company to cross the plains arrived in Salt Lake on September 24, 1860. There was no handcart travel in 1858, but in each of the other four years several companies crossed the plains, with the heaviest travel in 1856 and 1857. The emigrants who used this mode of travel and transportation were chiefly of English and Scandinavian origin, all anxious to reach Utah, but unable to afford wagons and teams for the crossing after contributing to their passage by ship and railroad as far as Iowa City, the terminus of the Rock Island Railroad. In 1855, President Brigham Young had written to the presiding head of the British Mission: "We will send experienced men to that point [Iowa City] with instructions to aid them in every possible way; and let the Saints who intend to immigrate to Utah the coming season understand that they are expected to walk and draw their carts across the plains. Sufficient teams will be furnished to haul the aged, infirm, and those who are unable to walk. A few good cows will be sent along to furnish milk, and some beef cattle for the people to kill along the road. Now, have them gird up their loins and come while the way is open."

The emigrants girded their loins. They had need to: the walk from Iowa City to Salt Lake was 1300 miles.

Typical of the companies which crossed the plains were those under the direction of James G. Willie and Edward Martin. Willie's Company was made up of "500 souls, 120 carts, 5 wagons, 24 oxen, 45 beef cattle"; Martin's Company had "575 souls, 146 carts, 7 wagons, 30 oxen, and 50 beef cattle." The carts themselves were two-wheelers made of sturdy hickory or oak, with shafts running forward from under the body of the cart; a connecting bar of wood across the shafts linked them in front, so that one or two persons walking behind the bar could push on it. Others, walking behind, pushed at the rear of the cart. On each cart were loaded flour, food, bedding, clothing, cooking utensils, and a tent. Small children also rode on them. The crossing of the plains by most of the companies was begun during the first week of June, and the arrival in Salt Lake attained during the

"The Handcart Song" was recorded by Austin E. Fife from the singing of L. M. Hilton at Ogden, Utah, 1946. Library of Congress record LP 30.

last week of September, averaging fourteen weeks for the trip. The majority of the crossings were successful, and the number of deaths — in spite of the obvious hardships — was held to a minimum. Willie's and Martin's Companies, which have been cited, were, however, unfortunate in this respect. Like the ill-fated Donner party, the reason for the disasters which befell them was chiefly that they both started westward late in July, all persons fully aware of the danger lying ahead.

On September 4, Captain Willie's cattle were run off by Indians, and rations had to be reduced at North Bluff Creek, six hundred miles from Iowa City. On September 30, the Company reached Fort Laramie with five hundred miles still to go through mountainous country. On October 12, the rations were cut again: ten ounces for men, nine for women, six for children, and three for infants. On October 19, the last flour was used, and the first snow fell that night; the following morning *undrifted* snow on the level was eighteen inches deep. Word of the plight of this Company and of Martin's, which was suffering in the same way, had gone ahead to Salt Lake, however, through Elder Franklin Richards, returning on horseback from the east. Brigham Young immediately ordered twenty-seven trained scouts, with provisions, to go to the rescue. These men traveled to the east of Fort Bridger before locating the unfortunate Company. For some their arrival was too late: nine persons died that night, and altogether over one-sixth of the Company had perished. The scouts gave what provisions they could to the Company and urged its despairing members forward to Fort Bridger, where Brigham Young had sent fifty wagons to bring them in to Salt Lake. They arrived in Salt Lake City on November 9.

Of Martin's Company, some sentences from the reports of the scouts will suffice:

"When we overtook the Martin Company, we found them strung out for miles. Old men were tugging at loaded carts, women were pulling sick husbands, and children struggling through the deep snow. . . . They camped that night in a place where there was neither wood nor shelter and it was bitter cold. Several deaths occurred that night and others were dying."

For these Companies, there was no "dancing upon the plains." They were rescued, however, with expeditions from Salt Lake City; and had Brigham Young and others in Salt Lake known of their late departure and straitened circumstances, the rescue parties would have reached them earlier. Without the rescue parties, disaster to these Companies would have been complete.

"The Handcart Song" comes down to us from the 1857–1860 period, and, in happier circumstances than those of the Willie and Martin Companies, buoyed the courageous pioneers on their westward trek to the "valley."

[In the preparation of the foregoing note, extensive use has been made of the article "Handcart Pioneers of Utah" in *Heart Throbs of the West*, 1939, I, 71–86, the official publication of the Daughters of Utah Pioneers.]

(*Spoken*) "This song was sung by those who crossed the plains in handcarts, made up on the way, and has been a song that everyone loved to sing in Utah ever since pioneer days. My grandmother sang it to me when I was a baby, and I can't remember when I didn't sing it and know it and love it."

Ye saints who dwell on Europe's shore, prepare yourselves for many more
    [forever more?]
To leave behind your native land, for sure God's judgments are at hand.
For you must cross the raging main before the promised land you gain,
And with the faithful make a start to cross the plains with your handcart.

    For some must push and some must pull, as we go marching up the hill,
    So merrily on our way we go, until we reach the valley-o.

The lands that boast of modern light, we know are all as dark as night,
Where poor men toil and want for bread, where peasant hosts are blindly
    led,
These lands that boast of liberty you ne'er again would wish to see,
When you from Europe make a start to cross the plains with your handcart.

    For some must push and some must pull, as we go marching up the hill,
    So merrily on our way we go, until we reach the valley-o.

As on the road the carts are pulled, 'twould very much surprise the world
To see the old and feeble dame thus lend a hand to pull the same;
And maidens fair will dance and sing, young men may [be more] happy
    than the king,
And children too, will laugh and play, their strength increasing day by day.

But some will say, "It is too bad, the saints upon the foot to pad,
And, more than that, to pull a load as they go marching o'er the road."
But then we say, "It is the plan to gather up the best of men,
And women, too, for none but they will ever travel in this way."

And long before the valley's gained, we will be met upon the plains
With music sweet and friends so dear, and fresh supplies our hearts to
    cheer;
And then with music and with song, how cheerfully we'll march along,
And thank the day we made a start to cross the plains with our handcarts.

When you get there among the rest, obedient be and you'll be blessed,
And in God's chambers be shut in while judgements cleanse the earth from
    sin;
For we do know it will be so, God's servant spoke it long ago,
We say it is high time to start to cross the plains with our handcarts.

    For some must push and some must pull, as we go marching up the hill,
    So merrily on our way we go, until we reach the valley-o.

TITTERY-IRIE-AYE

Like "The Handcart Song," "Tittery-Irie-Aye" comes to us from pioneer
days orally transmitted. Beyond what Mr. Watkins has to say of it — suggesting that it was sung on the handcart journey or, more probably, made
up very shortly after arrival in Salt Lake — there seems to be nothing
known. It contains historical references to the expulsion from Nauvoo and
the halt at Council Bluffs, and describes early houses of folk architecture
and construction at Salt Lake City. In addition, however, the leavening
note of humor "concerning spiritual women that make a hell of a fuss"
should be noted, as should also the irreverent comment on polygamy, in-
dicating that within the Mormon ranks themselves there would soon be a
ready willingness to abandon that institution.

(*Spoken*) "This is Joseph H. Watkins of Brigham City, eighty-five and a
half years old. I'm going to try to sing for you an old pioneer song. It was
sang when the people was coming across the plains. And a good many years
after, we had Brother Ensign, an old pioneer, that came across with the
handcarts, sing this song in the gatherings where the people were gathered.
This song is as follows. . . ."

"Tittery-Irie-Aye" was recorded by Austin E. Fife from the singing of Joseph H. Watkins,
Brigham City, Utah, 1946. Library of Congress record LP30.

Come, all my good people, and listen to my song,
Although it's not so very good, it's not so very long.
    And sing tittery-irie-aye, sing tittery-irie-o.
    And sing tittery-irie-aye, sing tittery-irie-o.

Now concerning this strange people, I'm now a-going to sing,
For the way they have been treated, I think it is a sin.
    And sing tittery-irie-aye, sing tittery-irie-o.

They've been driven from their homes and away from Nauvoo,
For to seek another home in the wilderness anew.

Oh, they stopped among the Indians, but there don't deem to stay,
And they'll soon be a-packing up and jogging on their way.

They made a halt at Council Bluffs, but there don't mean to stay;
Some feed the cattle rushes, and some per-rairie hay.

Oh, of logs we build our houses, of dirt we have for floors,
Of sods we build our chimneys, and shakes we have for doors.

There is another item, to mention it I must,
Concerning spiritual women that make a hell of a fuss.

Some men have got a dozen wives, and others have a score,
And the man that's got but one wife's a-looking out for more.

Now, young men, don't get discouraged, get married if you can,
But take care don't get a woman that belongs to another man.

Now concerning this strange people, I've nothing more to say,
Until we all get settled in some future day.

THE BOYS OF SANPETE COUNTY

To assist Mormon emigrants crossing the plains, wagon trains with provisions were sent out to meet them from Utah at the direction of President Brigham Young. One such group, composed of young men from Sanpete County, trekked eastward in June, 1868, without mishap until they reached

"The Boys of Sanpete County" was recorded by Austin E. Fife from the singing of Alva E. Christiansen, Manti, Utah, 1946. Library of Congress AFS record 8709 A1.

Green River. The waters were swollen and treacherous, and the balky cattle refused to ford. The cattle were then loaded on a ferry, which overturned in midstream, sweeping six men of the party to their deaths. This song was written by surviving members of the group and has come down in oral tradition in Utah.

We, the boys of Sanpete County, in obedience to the cause,
Started out with forty wagons to bring emigrants across.
Without fear or thought of danger, lightly on our way we sped,
Every heart with joy abounding, Captain Seeley at our head.

To accomplish our great mission we were called to fill below,
We left our friends and dear relations o'er the dreary plains to go.
Over hills and by the fountains, through the mud and in the dust,
Slowly climbed the lofty mountains, far above the snow's white crust.

When the sun to us declining, glad we welcome close of day,
By some stream or gushing fountain, to refresh at night we stay.
And we reached the Green River ferry, on her banks all night we stayed,
Morning ferried our wagons, thinking soon to roll away.

Next to drive our cattle over, but we found they would not swim,
Though the boys were in the water many hours to their chins.
Thus we tried from morn till evening, weather most severe and cold,
For the water and the labor brought us low, though we were bold.

And the mighty winds were blowing all the day and night before,
And the gurgling, rushing waters drove our cattle back to shore.
To accomplish our great mission we were called to fill below,
We left our friends and dear relations o'er the dreary plains to go.

As the boys were passing over, water in the boat did pour;
Captain cried, "Boys, we've gone under, we shall die this very hour!"
Down they went and crushed the tackling, 'neath those waters all went down,
And that mighty, rushing current swept them up with objects 'round.

Some to oxen's horns were clinging, till with them life's step was o'er,
Boys and cattle all went under, ne'er again to step on shore.
Some to planks and boards were clinging, down the swelling tide did float;
Some by heaven seemed protected, driven to shore upon the boat.

One had landed on an island, clinging to the willows green,
But to him life was extinguished, he fell backward in the stream.
These six boys from parents taken and from friends whom they did love,
But we soon again shall meet them in that better land above.

ON THE ROAD TO CALIFORNIA
or *The Buffalo Bullfight*

(*Spoken*) "During the rendition of music gathered by Evan Stephens for the semicentennial, he collected these words. And they were sung by a gentleman of Scandinavian birth, who sang in dialect. We became fascinated with his dialect and, as boys will, learned to imitate him. So I have sung this song as we used to sing it together as boys."

> The Mormons, led by Colonel Cooke,
> While passing down St. Pedro's brook,
> Just turning o'er a little rise,
> The grass was up to our mules' eyes.
>
> > On the road to California,
> > On that hard and tedious journey,
> > Far across the Rocky Mountains,
> > Crystal streams and flowing fountains.
>
> Just as our mules begun to pull,
> Out from the grass there jumped a bull;
> As soon as he appeared in sight,
> He raised his head all ready for a fight.
>
> I saw a man as I passed by,
> A bull had hooked him in the thigh;
> And from the thigh the blood did pour,
> Three inches deep it made a gore.
>
> When this bull battle it was o'er
> And sound of musket heard no more,
> We went next day and there found slain
> Four mules, twelve bulls upon the plain.

"On the Road to California" was recorded by Austin E. Fife from the singing of William T. Morris at St. George, Utah, 1947. Library of Congress record LP30.

On the road to California,
On that hard and tedious journey,
Far across the Rocky Mountains,
Crystal streams and flowing fountains.

ST. GEORGE

The first and last stanzas of this humorous, as well as prideful, song come very close to describing accurately the conditions faced by the early Mormon pioneers who settled southern Utah at the direction of Brigham Young. When certain families were notified by the authorities that they had been "elected" to emigrate there from Salt Lake to establish farms and communities, they "shuddered." Men came home from the meetings, and slapped their hats down with a rebellious "I won't do it!" Overnight reflection, however, and a consciousness of their duty led them to ultimate acceptance of the task, and the wagons trekked south out of Salt Lake in the direction of Utah's "Dixie." The first street was nothing more than a strip of barren desert separating two lanes of wagons; women forgot what flowers had looked like; dust, alkali, and heat made life almost unbearable. Yet the pioneers stuck it out, and, for those at least who live there today, St. George is "a place that everyone admires!"

The following song, "Once I Lived in Cottonwood," is in the same "miserable" vein, unredeemed at the time of its singing by any "vines and fruit trees," or virtually anything else to make life bearable.

(*Spoken*) "The song was written by Charlie Walker, an early pioneer in the St. George Valley of Utah, in Washington County. The words and music was written by Mr. Walker, and the song was sung quite consistently by Samuel L. Adams, who was my grandfather."

Oh, what a dreary place this was when first the Mormons found it,
They said no white man here could live, and Indians prowled around it.
They said the land it was no good, and the water was no gooder,
And the bare idea of living here was enough to make men shudder.

Mesquite! Soap-root! Prickly-pears and briars!
St. George ere long will be a place that everyone admires!

"St. George" was recorded by Austin E. Fife from the singing of Rudger McArthur, St. George, Utah, 1947. Library of Congress record LP30.

Now green lucerne in verdant spots redeems our thriving city,
Whilst vines and fruit trees grace our lots with flowers sweet and pretty,
Where once the grass in single blades grew a mile apart in distance,
And it kept the crickets on the hop to pick up their subsistence.

The sun it is so scorching hot, it makes the water sizz, sir,
And the reason that it is so hot is just because it is, sir.
The wind with fury here doth blow, that when we plant or sow, sir,
We place one foot upon the seeds and hold them till they grow, sir.

Mesquite! Soap-root! Prickly-pears and briars!
St. George ere long will be a place that everyone admires!

ONCE I LIVED IN COTTONWOOD

Oh, once I lived in Cottonwood and owned a little farm,
But I was called to Dixie, which gave me much alarm;
To raise some cane and cotton I right away must go,
But the reason why they sent me, I'm sure I do not know.

I hooked old Jim and Molly up, all for to make a start,
To leave my house and garden it almost broke my heart.
We moved along quite slowly and often looked behind,
For the sands and rocks of Dixie kept running through my mind.

At length we reached the Black Ridge, where I broke my wagon down,
I could not find a carpenter, we were twenty miles from town,
So with a clumsy cedar pole I fixed an awkward slide,
My wagon pulled so heavy then that Betsey couldn't ride.

While Betsey was a-walking I told her to take care,
When all upon a sudden she struck a prickly pear,
Then she began to blubber up as loud as she could bawl,
"If I was back in Cottonwood, I wouldn't come at all!"

And when we reached the Sandy, we could not move at all,
For poor old Jim and Molly began to puff and bawl.

"Once I Lived in Cottonwood" was recorded by Austin E. Fife from the singing of Francis Y. Morse, St. George, Utah, 1947. Library of Congress AFS record 8664 B.

I whipped and swore a little, but could not make the route,
For myself, the team and Betsey were all of us give out.

And next we got to Washington, where we stayed a little while
To see if April showers would make the venture smile,
But, oh, I was mistaken and so I went away,
For the red hills of November looked just the same in May.

I feel so sad and lonely, now there's nothing here to cheer
Except prophetic sermons which we very often hear;
They'll hand them out by the dozens and prove them by the Book —
I'd rather have some roasting ears to stay at home and cook.

I feel so weak and hungry now, I think I'm nearly dead,
'Tis seven weeks next Sunday since I have tasted bread;
Old carrot tops and lucerne greens we have enough to eat,
But I'd like to change my diet off for buckwheat cakes and meat.

I brought this old coat with me about two years ago,
And how I'll get another one I'm sure I do not know.
May Providence protect me against the wind and wet,
I think myself and Betsey these times we'll ne'er forget.

My shirt is dyed with wild ox root, with greasewood for to set,
I fear the colors all will fade when once it does get wet;
They said we could raise madder and indigo so blue,
But that turned out a humbug, the story was not true.

The hot winds whirl around me and take away my breath,
I've had the chills and fever till I nearly shook to death.
All earthly tribulations are but a moment here,
And if I do prove faithful a righteous crown shall wear.

My wagon sold for sorghum seed to make a little bread,
And poor old Jim and Molly long, long ago are dead;
There's only me and Betsey left to hoe the cotton tree,
May heaven help that Dixieite wherever he may be!

MARCHING TO UTAH

The pride of the Mormons in their accomplishments and their strength and unity in the face of any and all adversities are clearly reflected in this rousing song.

Who'd ever think that Utah would stir the world so much?
Who'd ever think the Mormons were widely known as such?
I hardly dare to scribble or such a subject touch,
For all are talking of Utah.

Hurrah! Hurrah! We Mormons have a name!
Hurrah! Hurrah! We're on the road to fame!
No matter what they style us, it's all about the same,
For all are talking of Utah.

They say that Utah cannot be numbered as a state;
They wished our lands divided, but left it rather late.
It's hard to tell of Mormons, what next will be their fate,
For all are talking of Utah.

They say they've sent an army to set us Mormons right,
To generate on Utah and show us Christian right,
Release our wives and daughters, and put us men to flight,
For all are talking of Utah.

Whatever may be coming, we cannot well foresee,
For it may be the railroad or some great prodigy;
At least the noted Mormons are watching what's to be,
For all are talking of Utah.

I now will tell you something you never thought of yet,
We bees are nearly filling the hive of Deseret.
If hurt, we'll sting together and gather all we get,
For all are talking of Utah.

Hurrah! Hurrah! We Mormons have a name!
Hurrah! Hurrah! We're on the road to fame!

"Marching to Utah" was recorded by Austin E. Fife from the singing of Rose Thompson, St. George, Utah, 1947. Library of Congress AFS record 8662 A.

No matter what they style us, it's all about the same,
For all are talking of Utah.

ECHO CANYON

"Echo Canyon" and "The Utah Iron Horse," which follows it, are two songs dating from the period of the construction of the last link in the transcontinental railroad. "Echo Canyon" was sung by Mormon men working on the final stretch of the Union Pacific, coming from the west, and "The Utah Iron Horse" was sung by Mormons working on the Central Pacific, coming from the east. This work, undertaken in 1868 through a contract let to Brigham Young by the railroads, resulted in the completion of the final link and the attendant golden-spike-driving ceremonies at Promontory Point on May 10, 1869. The first song, "Echo Canyon," is optimistic and jubilant in tone. It also, within the text, reflects something of the way of life of the men — the "ten hours" daily work, the sober and industrious attitude toward their work, and the anticipation of returning home when the railroad is completed. Within the song also, in the next to last stanza, is specific recognition of the end of one era and the beginning of a new. The railroad marked the final opening of the West.

"This is L. M. Hilton, Ogden, Utah. I'm going to sing 'Echo Canyon,' or 'Hurray! Hurrah! The railroad's begun.' Mormon boys and men, under the direction of Brigham Young, who helped build the railroad into Utah in 1868 and '69 composed this song, and it has been sung in Utah ever since. My grandparents taught it to me when I was a small boy, and I have sung it all my life."

In the Canyon of Echo, there's a railroad begun,
And the Mormons are cutting and grading like fun;
They say they'll stick to it until it's complete,
For friends and relations they're longing to meet.

Hurray! Hurrah! The railroad's begun!
Three cheers for our contractor, his name's Brigham Young;

"Echo Canyon" was recorded by Austin E. Fife from the singing of L. M. Hilton, Ogden, Utah, 1946. Library of Congress record LP30.

> Hurray! Hurrah! We're light-hearted and gay,
> Just the right kind of boys to build a railway.

Now there's Mister Reed, he's a gentleman, too,
He knows very well what we Mormons can do;
He knows in our work we are faithful and true,
And if Mormon boys start it, it's bound to go through.

Our camp is united, we all labor hard,
And if we are faithful, we'll gain our reward;
Our leader is wise and a great leader, too,
And all things he tells us, we're right glad to do.

The boys in our camp are light-hearted and gay,
We work on the railroad ten hours a day;
We're thinking of fine times we'll have in the fall,
When we'll be with our ladies and go to the ball.

We surely must live in a very fast age:
We've traveled by ox team and then took the stage,
But when such conveyance is all done away,
We'll travel in steam cars upon the railway.

The great locomotive next season will come
To gather the saints from their far distant home,
And bring them to Utah in peace here to stay
While the judgments of God sweep the wicked away.

THE UTAH IRON HORSE

"The Utah Iron Horse," unlike "Echo Canyon," strikes a somewhat sceptical note, expressing sentiments not held by Mormons today, but, nevertheless, historically valuable and complementing the mood of "Echo Canyon." By way of background to an understanding of the sceptical mood, it should be remembered that the Mormons had carved their inland empire out of the desert and, at long last, had found a home, after the persecutions which had driven them the width of the country. Even in Utah, the United States army had been sent against them, and this in spite of the Mormon contribution to the war with Mexico. It is small wonder, then, that certain

"The Utah Iron Horse" was recorded by Austin E. Fife from the singing of Joseph H. Watkins, Brigham City, Utah, 1946. Library of Congress record LP30.

of the Mormons had their doubts about the "civilization" that would be brought to them with the completion of the railroad; they still had very vivid memories of that "civilization" — at Nauvoo and elsewhere — which they had left behind.

The last two lines of the second stanza should be understood as coming from the tourists and outlanders who would visit Utah, and whose eyes would be round with ignorant wonder over the outrageous things they had heard and expected to see, rather than looking to the real achievements of the Mormons — irrigation, settlement, industry, unity. In this connection, the Danites were supposedly the alleged "secret police" of Brigham Young, meting out punishment to those who strayed from the fold. Actually, there is historical controversy over this. There was, of course, strict but just discipline within the Mormon ranks — how else account for the handcart companies, the Mormon Battalion, and the settlement of arid southern Utah? Decisions were taken, orders given, and the orders obeyed. This very discipline, however, which created Utah and gave the Mormons their strength, seemed incomprehensible to non-Mormons pushing westward on the frontier, and itself gave rise to unfounded exaggerations of enforced "police action." Also, the lawless non-Mormon elements of the neighboring frontier were quick to seek a scapegoat for their crimes, and found a ready one in the maligned Mormon.

This song first appeared in print in *The Bee-Hive Songster*, published in Utah in 1868, where the text is considerably longer. It was reprinted in the official publication of the Daughters of the Utah Pioneers, *Heart Throbs of the West*, 1943–1944, V, 521. Apart from being longer, the printed text differs in other respects from the song as sung by Mr. Watkins, and it is doubtful that he ever saw it in print. It is to be presumed that he learned it orally as a boy eight years old, in 1869, as he says. The fact that it comes to us directly from that period is in itself remarkable.

"My name is Joseph Hammond Watkins, Brigham City. I learned this song in 1868, or '69, rather. This song was composed by some people from Logan that had a contract on the Central Pacific Railroad in Weber Canyon in 1868. And the other . . . the railroad was coming in from the west, the Union Pacific, and this song was made appropriate for that occasion. This was in 1868, and the two railroads met at Promontory Point in 1869."

The iron horse draweth nigh, with its smoke nostrils high,
Eating fire while he grazes, drinking water while he blazes,

Then the steam forces out, whistles loud — "Clear the route!"
For the iron horse is coming with a train in his wake.

We have isolated been, but soon we shall be seen,
Through this wide mountain region, folks can learn of our religion:
"Count each man many wives, how they're held in their hives,
And see those dreadful Danites, how they lynch many lives."

"Civilized" we shall be, many folks we shall see,
Lords and nobles, quacks and beggars, anyhow we'll see the niggers;
Saints will come, sinners, too, we'll have all that we can do,
For this great Union Railroad it will fetch the Devil through.

"Westward the Course . . ."

How happy am I when I crawl into bed,
With rattlesnakes rattling just under my head,
And the gay little bedbug, so cheerful and bright,
He keeps me a-going two-thirds of the night.

Westward the course was not always one of glory and empire. That was for Greeley and whomever sitting in the overstuffed chairs. More often it was of the rough earth and the blood and the sweat of a hard frontier. These are some of its songs and words, not unrelated to those of the '49ers, the hardrock men, the Mormons, the cowboy, and others. It was a wild and powerful land. It took doing to tame. And the men who tamed did not always — but sometimes — realize that they were doing so. They laughed at themselves and the land, and with themselves: they needed to — to survive.

STARVING TO DEATH ON A GOVERNMENT CLAIM

My name is Frank Taylor, a bachelor I am,
I'm keeping old batch on an elegant plan,
You'll find me out West in the county of Lane
A-starving to death on a Government claim.

Hurrah for Lane County, the land of the free,
The home of the bedbug, grasshopper and flea,

"Starving to Death on a Government Claim" was sung and recorded at Galena, Missouri, 1941, by Vance Randolph who learned it from the singing of Mr. C. C. Bayer of Little Rock, Arkansas, in 1917, who had, in turn, acquired it traditionally from a family named Lampson living near Fayetteville, Arkansas. Library of Congress record LP30.

I'll sing of its praises and boast of its fame
A-starving to death on a Government claim.

My clothes they are ragged, my language is rough,
My bread is case-hardened and solid and tough,
But I have a good time and live at my ease
On common sop-sorghum and old bacon grease.

628

How happy am I when I crawl into bed,
With rattlesnakes rattling just under my head,
And the gay little bedbug, so cheerful and bright,
He keeps me a-going two-thirds of the night.

How happy am I on my Government claim,
I've nothing to lose and I've nothing to gain,
I've nothing to eat and I've nothing to wear,
And nothing from nothing is honest and fair.

Oh, come to Lane County, there's room for you all,
Where the wind never stops and the rains never fall,
Oh, join in the chorus and sing of her fame,
A-starving to death on a Government claim.

Oh, don't be downhearted, you poor hungry men,
We're all just as free as the pigs in the pen,
Just stick to your homestead and fight with your fleas,
And pray to your Maker to send some more breeze.

Now all you poor sinners, I hope you will stay
And chaw on your hardtack till you're toothless and grey,
But as for myself I don't aim to remain
And slave like a dog on no Government claim.

Farewell to Lane County, the pride of the West,
I'm going back East to the girl I love best,
I'll stop in Missouri and get me a wife,
And live on corn dodgers the rest of my life.

SANFORD BARNEY

My name is Sanford Barney, and I came from Little Rock town,
I've traveled this wide world over, I've traveled this wide world 'round,
I've had many ups and downs through life, better days I've saw,
But I never knew what misery was till I came to Arkansas.

"Sanford Barney" was recorded by Fletcher Collins from the singing of I. G. Greer of
Thomasville, North Carolina, with dulcimer by Mrs. Greer, at Greensboro, North Carolina,
1941. Library of Congress record LP7.

'Twas in the year of '82 in the merry month of June,
I landed at Hot Springs one sultry afternoon.
There came a walking skeleton, then gave to me his paw,
Invited me to his hotel, 'twas the best in Arkansas.

I followed my conductor unto his dwelling place,
It was starvation and poverty pictured on his face,
His bread it was corn dodgers, and beef I could not chaw,
He charged me fifty cents a meal in the state of Arkansas.

I started back next morning to catch the early train,
He said, "Young man, you better work for me. I have some land to drain.
I'll give you fifty cents a day, your washing and all chaw.
You'll feel quite like a different man when you leave old Arkansas."

I worked for the gentleman three weeks, Jess Harold was his name,
Six feet, seven inches, in his stocking length, and slim as any crane,
His hair hung down like ringlets beside his slackened jaw,
He was a photygraft of all the gents that 'uz raised in Arkansas.

His bread it was corn dodgers as hard as any rock,
It made my teeth begin to loosen, my knees begin to knock,
I got so thin on sage and sassafras tea I could hide behind a straw,
I'm sure I was quite like a different man when I left old Arkansas.

I started back to Texas a quarter after five;
Nothing was left but skin and bones, half dead and half alive.
I got me a bottle of whisky, my misery for to thaw;
Got drunk as old Abraham Linkern when I left old Arkansas.

Farewell, farewell, Jess Harold, and likewise darling wife,
I know she never will forget me in the last days of her life.
She put her little hand in mine and tried to bite my jaw,
And said, "Mr. Barney, remember me when you leave old Arkansas."

Farewell, farewell, swamp angels, to canebrake and the chills,
Fare thee well to sage and sassafras tea and corn-dodger pills.
If ever I see that land again, I'll give to you my paw,
It will be through a telescope from here to Arkansas.

LITTLE OLD SOD SHANTY

"Little Old Sod Shanty" is an adaptation of W. S. Hays' "Little Old Log Cabin in the Lane," which appeared in 1871 and was widely popular, lending itself to numerous parodies. The most famous of them all is this one, so much so that it has totally supplanted "Little Old Log Cabin." It is not an unfair account of the hardships and way of life of the early settler on the western plains of Nebraska and adjoining states during the period of first settlement.

> I'm looking mighty seedy while holding down my claim,
> My victuals are not always of the best,
> And the mice play shyly round me as I nestle down to rest
> In that little old sod shanty on the claim.
>
> > The hinges are of leather and the windows have no glass,
> > The board roof lets the howling blizzard in,
> > And I hear the hungry coyote as he slinks up through the grass
> > 'Round that little old sod shanty on my claim.
>
> When I left my Eastern home a bachelor oh so gay,
> To wend my way up in this (world to) wealth and fame,
> Whoever thought I'd be so low as to burning twisted hay
> In that little old sod shanty on my claim.
>
> > The hinges are of leather and the windows have no pane,
> > The board roof lets the howling blizzard in,
> > And I hear the hungry coyote as he prowls up through the grass
> > 'Round that little old sod shanty on the claim.
>
> I wish that some kind-hearted girl would pity on me take
> And relieve me from this mess that I am in;
> The angel, how I'd bless her if this her home she'd make
> In that little old sod shanty on my claim.

"Little Old Sod Shanty" was recorded by Vance Randolph from the singing of Jimmy Denoon at Bradleyville, Missouri, 1942. Library of Congress record LP20.

And if kind fate should bless us with now and then a heir,
To cheer our hearts in honest pride and fame,
Oh, then we'd be contented for the toil that we had spent
In that little old sod shanty on my claim.

> Where the hinges are of leather and the windows have no pane,
> The board roof lets the howling blizzard in,
> And I hear the hungry coyote as he slinks up through the grass,
> 'Round that little old sod shanty on the claim.

THE SIOUX INDIANS

I'll sing you a song and it'll be a sad one
Of our trials and our troubles and how they begun;
We left our dear kindred, our friends and our home,
And we crossed the wide districts and mountains to roam.

We crossed the Missouri and joined a large train,
Which carried us over mountains, through valleys and plain;
And often of a evening a-huntin' we'd go
To shoot the fleet antelope and the wild buffalo.

We heard the Sioux Indians all out on the plains,
A-killing poor drivers and burning their trains,
A-killing poor drivers with arrows and bows;
When captured by Indians no mercy they'd show.

We traveled three weeks till we come to the Platte,
A-pitching our tents at the head of the flat;
We spread down our blankets on a green shady ground
Where the mules and the horses were grazing around.

While we're taking our refreshment we hyeard a loud yell:
The 'hoop of Sioux Indians come up from the drill*
We spraing to our rifles with a flash in each eye,
And says our brave leader, "Boys, we'll fight till we die."

* Dell.

"The Sioux Indians" was recorded by John A. and Bess Lomax from the singing of Alex Moore, Austin, Texas, 1940. Library of Congress record LP1. Laws, B11.

They made a bold dash and they come near our train;
The arrows fell around us like showers of rain,
But with our long rifles we fed 'em hot lead
Till a many a brave warrior around us lie dead.

We shot the bold chief at the head of their band;
He died like a warrior with a bow in his hand.
And when they saw the brave chief lie dead in his gore,
They 'hooped and they yelled and we saw them no more.

In our little band there were just twenty-four,
And of the Sioux Indians five hundred or more.
We fought them with courage, we spoke not a word;
The 'hoop of Sioux Indians was all could be heard.

We hooked up our horses, we started our train;
Three more bloody battles, this trip on the plain,
And in our last battle three of the brave boys fell,
And we left them to rest in the green shady drill.*

THE DREARY BLACK HILLS

Kind friends, you must pity my horrible tale,
I'm an object of pity, I'm looking quite stale,
I give up my trade selling Wright's Patent Pills
To go hunting gold in the dreary Black Hills.

 Don't go away, stay at home if you can,
 Stay away from that city, they call it Cheyenne,
 For old Sitting Bull and Comanche Bill
 They'll lift up your hair on the dreary Black Hills.

The roundhouse in Cheyenne is filled every night
With loafers and bummers of most every plight;
On their backs is no clothes, in their pockets no bills,
Each day they keep starting for the dreary Black Hills.

"The Dreary Black Hills" was recorded by John A. Lomax from the singing of Harry Stephens of Denison, Texas, at Dallas, Texas, 1942. Library of Congress record LP28.

I got to Cheyenne, no gold could I find,
I thought of the lunch route I'd left far behind;
Through rain, hail, and snow, froze plumb to the gills,
They call me the orphant of the dreary Black Hills.

Kind friends, to conclude, my advice I'll unfold,
Don't go to the Black Hills a-hunting for gold;
Railroad speculators their pockets you'll fill
By taking a trip to those dreary Black Hills.

Don't go away, stay at home if you can,
Stay away from that city, they call it Cheyenne,
For old Sitting Bull and Comanche Bill
They'll lift up your hair on the dreary Black Hills.

FREIGHTING FROM WILCOX TO GLOBE

Come all you jolly freighters that ever hit the road,
That ever hauled a load of coke from Wilcox to Globe,
That's the way I've made my living for ten long years or more,
Hauling coke for Leverman and Myers, no wonder I am poor.

So, it's home, dearest, home, home you ought to be,
Over on the Gila in the white man's counteree,
Where the poplar and the ash and mesquite will ever be,
Growing green along the river, there's a home for you and me.

Barb wire and bacon is all that they would pay,
You get a check on Leverman to get your grain and hay,
You ask them for five dollars, old Myers'd scratch his pate,
And the clerks in their white collars say, "Get down and pull your freight."

Perhaps you'd like to know, boys, what we have to eat,
A little bit of bread and a dirty piece of meat,
A little bit of coffee, and sugar's on the sly,
So it's go it if you like it, boys — Root hog or die.

"Freighting from Wilcox to Globe" was recorded by Peter Tufts from the singing of John Busby at Chandler, Arizona, 1949, on a joint collecting project for the Library of Congress and the University of Arizona Folklore Committee. Library of Congress record LP30.

The Cowboy

So we buried him there on the prairie, and the coyotes still
    howl o'er his grave,
And his soul is now a-resting from the unkind cut she
    gave;
And many another young cowboy, as he passes by that
    pile of stones,
Recalls some similar woman and thinks of his mouldering
    bones.

As with the "Sea Shanties," the cow country songs which appeared in *Folklore on the American Land* have not — with some few exceptions — been repeated here. "The Old Chisholm Trail" is one of the exceptions: it belongs always in every selection or collection of cattle country verse. It has been sung from every saddle that ever rode the West.

ONE MORNING IN MAY
or The Young Girl Cut Down in Her Prime

"When I was a young girl, I used to seek pleasure,
When I was a young girl, I used to drink ale;
Out of a alehouse and into a jailhouse,
Right out of a barroom and down to my grave.

"Come, Papa, come, Mama, and sit you down by me,
Come sit you down by me and pity my case;
My poor head is aching, my sad heart is breaking,
My body's salivated and I'm bound to die.

"Oh, send for the preacher to come and pray for me,
And send for the doctor to heal up my wounds;

"One Morning in May" was recorded by Alan and Elizabeth Lomax from the singing of
Mrs. Texas Gladden, Salem, Virginia, 1941. Library of Congress record LP1. Laws, Q26–B1.

635

My poor head is aching, my sad heart is breaking,
My body's salivated and Hell is my doom.

"I want three young ladies to bear up my coffin,
I want four young ladies to carry me on;
And each of them carry a bunch of wild roses
To lay on my coffin as I pass along."

One morning, one morning, one morning in May,
I spied this young lady all wrapped in white linen,
All wrapped in white linen and cold as the clay.

St. James Infirmary

I went down to Saint James this morning,
Saw my loving little woman down there,
All covered in her snow-white blanket,
So cold, so sweet, so fair.

She is gone, let her go, God bless her,
She's mine wherever she may be,
She may travel this wide world over,
But she will never find a pal like me.

When I die, good woman, won't you bury me,
On my tombstone put the letters in black,
Say, "There lays that good easy riding daddy,
Good God, won't you please bring him back."

Go get sixteen coal-black horses,
And a brand new rubber-tire hack,
Taking seven pretty women to the graveyard,
Only six of them coming back.

Go get six rolling dice hustlers,
Seven black-headed women to sing a song,

"St. James Infirmary" was collected by the Federal Music Project, Works Progress Administration (WPA), Floyd County, Kentucky, ca. 1937. Edith F. James, Supervisor for Floyd County. Ms., with music, in the Archive of Folk Song, Library of Congress. Laws, B1.

Fill my casket full of moonshine whiskey,
So I can drink as the hearse rolls along.

Going down to the dark blue ocean,
May be shot with a great cannonball,
But when I finish life's story —
A woman was the cause of it all.

The Streets of Laredo

As I walked out in the streets of Laredo,
As I walked out in Laredo one day,
I spied a poor cowboy wrapped up in white linen,
Wrapped in white linen as cold as the clay.

Oh, beat the drums slowly, and play the fife lowly,
Play the dead march as you carry me along,
Take me to the green valley, there lay the sod o'er me,
For I'm a young cowboy, and I know I've done wrong.

Let sixteen gamblers come handle my coffin,
Let sixteen cowboys come sing me a song,
Take me to the graveyard, and lay the sod o'er me,
For I'm a poor cowboy, and I know I've done wrong.

It was once in the saddle I used to go dashing,
It was once in the saddle I used to go gay,
First to the dram house, and then to the card house,
Got shot in the breast, and I'm dying today.

Get six jolly cowboys to carry my coffin,
Get six pretty maidens to bear up my pall,
Put bunches of roses all over my coffin,
Put roses to deaden the sods as they fall.

Oh, bury me beside my knife and my six-shooter,
My spurs on my heel, my rifle by my side,

"The Streets of Laredo" was recorded by John A. Lomax from the singing of Johnny Prude at Fort Davis, Texas, 1942. Library of Congress record L28. Laws, B1.

And over my coffin put a bottle of brandy,
That's the cowboy's drink, and carry me along.

We beat the drums slowly and played the fife lowly,
And bitterly wept as we bore him along,
For we all loved our comrade, so brave, young, and handsome,
We all loved our comrade, although he'd done wrong.

EARLYE, EARLYE, IN THE SPRING

'Twas earlye, earlye in the Spring
I was pressed on board for to serve my King,
But to leave my dearest dear behind
Who ofttimes said her heart was mine.

As she lay smiling in my arms
I thought her worth ten thousand charms,
With her handsome arms and kisses sweet,
Saying, "We'll get married next time we meet."

As I was sailing on the sea
I took an opportunity
To write a letter to my dearest dear,
But nothing from her could I hear.

I went all to her father's house,
Her love and life of him I ask;
He answered me with a quick reply,
"She's married and you I must deny."

I ask of him what did she mean
To let her own fair promise break
And marry to another for the parents' sake.

He answered me all in her name,

"Earlye, Earlye, in the Spring" was recorded by Vance Randolph from the singing of
Charles Ingenthron, Walnut Shade, Missouri, 1941. Library of Congress AFS record 5249
A1. The text is a variant of "The Seaman's Complaint," the British antecedent of "The Trail
to Mexico." See Laws, B13.

"She's married to a richer life,
So you go hunt you another wife."

Oh, cursed be the gold and the silver, too,
And all the pretty fair maids that won't be true,
And let their own fair promise break
And marry to another for the parents' sake.

Now since I've lost my golden crown,
I'll sail this ocean around and around;
I'll sail the sea till the day I die,
And then split the waves where the bullets fly.

"Oh, Willie, Willie, stay on shore,
Don't go to the raging seas any more.
Don't go where the raging seas and the bullets fly,
There's girls in the world that's as good as I."

"I'll go where the fifes and the drums do play,
Where music ceases not night nor day,
For I'd rather be on the raging sea
As to be in a false lover's company."

THE ZEBRA DUN

Well, I was camped out on the draw at the head of Cimarron,
Along came a stranger who wanted to auger* some,
He was an educated fellow, his words just came in herds,
And he astonished the natives with his big, jawbreaking words.

He asked us for some breakfast, he hadn't had a smell,
We opened up the chuck box, and bid him help himself,
He took a plate of beefsteak, some bread, and some beans,
And then began to talk about those fairy queens.

He talked about the weather, ropes, spurs, and other things,
He did not seem to know much 'bout working on the range,

* Argue.

"The Zebra Dun" was recorded by Duncan Emrich from the singing of J. M. Waddell of Kermit, Texas, at Washington, D.C., 1948. Library of Congress record LP28. Laws, B16.

But he just kept on spouting till he made the boys all sick,
And they began to study just how to play a trick.

He was traveling across the country, straight 'cross the 7 D's,
It seemed he'd lost his job down on the Santa Fe's,
He'd had some trouble with his boss, he did not state the cause,
But said he would like to get a fresh, fat saddle horse.

"Yes, we can let you have one, just fresh and fat as you please."
This tickled the boys almost to death, they laughed down in their sleeves,
So Shorty grabbed the lariat, and he caught the Zebra Dun,
And turned him to the stranger, then waited for the fun.

Old Dun he's a rocky outlaw, and being very wild,
He could paw the white out of the moon every jump for over a mile,
Old Dun he stood quite still, and did not seem to know,
The stranger had him saddled when he was a-fixing up to go.

But when that chap mounted, old Dun he quit the earth,
He traveled perpendicular for all he was worth,
Old Dun he pitched and bellered, just like some yearling calf,
The stranger was sitting in his saddle, just a-twirling his mustache.

He thumbed him in the neck, and he spurred him as he whirled
To show us flunky punchers he was the wolf of the world,
Old Dun he picked up his head, and decided to let him ride,
It hurt the old boy's feelings, he'd rather to have died.

He turned him back to the camp, he'd pitched for over a mile,
The stranger being very tired, though he began to smile;
He rode up and dismounted. Said I, "You need not go,
I can give you a lasting job, and bank you up with dough.

"If you can sling the catgut just like you rode old Dun,
Well, you're the man I've been a-looking for just since the year of one."
"Well, I can sling the catgut and do not do it slow,
I catch by both forefeet nine times out of ten for dough.

"And when the herd's stampeding, I'm right there on the spot,
I put them back to milling like stirring in the pot."

But there's one thing for certain, and that you cannot scorn,
All educated fellows are not greenhorns.

RED WHISKEY

"This is Dick Devall, the cowboy singer from Reed, Oklahoma. I'm going to shoot the other barrel!"

Oh, Molly, oh, Molly, I've told you before,
Go make me a pallet, I'll sleep on the floor.

I've rambled, I've trambled, I've rambled around,
I ache for the cow country, for cow country I'm bound.

It's whiskey, red whiskey, red whiskey I cry,
If I don't get m'red whiskey, I surely will die.

It's ride wild horses while rambling around,
I can ride the wildest bronco that's ever been found.

Oh, Molly, oh, Molly, I've told you before,
Go make me a pallet, I'll sleep on the floor.

Yes, I've rambled, I've trambled, I've rambled around,
I can ride the wildest bronco that's ever been found.

If the ocean was whiskey and I was a duck,
I'd go to the bottom for one sweet sup.

But the ocean ain't whiskey and I'm no duck,
So play the Jack of Diamonds and go get drunk.

Oh, Molly, oh, Molly, I've told you before,
Go make me a pallet, I'll sleep on the floor.

It's beefsteak when I'm hungry, red whiskey when I'm dry,
Pretty girls when I'm lonesome and heaven when I die.

"Red Whiskey" was recorded by John A. Lomax from the singing of Dick Devall of Reed, Oklahoma, at Dallas, Texas, 1946. Library of Congress record LP20.

THE OLD CHISHOLM TRAIL

Oh, you come along, boys, you listen to my tale,
Tell you 'bout my troubles on the old Chisholm trail.
I rode up the trail, April twenty-third,
Rode up the trail with the Bar Ten herd.

 Cum a ti yi yippy, yippy I, yippy ay,
 Ti yi yippy yippy I, yippy ay,
 Cum a ti yi yippy yippy ay.

I jumped on my broncho, I raked him down his flank,
Oh, he started into pitching and I landed on the bank.
Well, I leaps to my saddle and I gives a little yell,
Oh, the leaders broke the country and the cattle went to hell.

Oh, I ride with my slicker and I ride all day,
And I packed along a bottle for to pass the time away;
With my feet in the stirrups and my hand on the horn,
I'm the best damned cowboy that ever was born.

We'll round up these cattle, boys, the weather's getting cold,
And the ornery sons of mavericks are getting hard to hold.
We'll trail 'em up to Kansas and we'll bunch 'em on the pens,
And that'll be the last of the old Bar Tens.

She's cloudy in the west and she looks like rain,
And my danged old slicker's in the wagon again;
The gale starts a-blowing and the rain begins to fall;
And it looks, by God, like we're a-going to lose 'em all.

I'm going to hang up my spurs, and my chaps and my saddle,
Never more will I ride around the longhorn cattle.
Says I, "Old boss, will you give me my roll?"
Oh, the boss had me figured ten dollars in the hole.

Oh, I know a girl who's a-going to leave her mother,
All the devils down in hell couldn't stir up such another;

"The Old Chisholm Trail" was collected by Duncan Emrich from Powder River Jack Lee, Denver, Colorado, 1941.

She rides on a pinto and she works on the drag,
With her petticoats a-flopping like a pair of saddle bags!

Oh, I'm out night-herding by the lone Squaw Butte,
When I run my sights on a lone coyote;
He's a-hellin' and a-yellin' — as he drifts by,
I snakes out my lassoo and I loops him on the fly.

No chaps, no slicker, and she pours down rain,
And I swears to my hoss I'll never ride night herd again;
Oh, I'll head back south and I'll marry me a squaw
And live all my life on the sandy Washitaw.

Oh, the shorthorns rattle and the longhorns battle,
Never had such a ride around the locoed cattle;
I'll trade my outfit as soon as I can,
And I won't punch cows for no damned man.

It's along 'fore daylight, they start in to feed,
The steers all a-dragging, with the pointers in the lead;
They head on north where the grass grows green,
And now for the biscuits, and the bacon and the beans.

The herd stampedes, I'm a-riding on a run,
I'm the quickest shooting cowboy that ever drew a gun;
Well we rounded them up and run 'em in the pens,
And that was the last of the old Bar Tens.

We rode into Abilene and hits her on the fly,
Oh, we bedded down the cattle on the hill close by;
A beef in the herd and the boss says kill it,
I shot him in the rump with the handle of the skillet.

Oh, Abilene city is a dang fine town,
We'll licker up and twirl those heifers all around;
Then back once more with my bridle and my hoss,
For old John Chisholm is a damned fine boss.

Old Scandalous John is the trail-herd boss,
And he yells his orders from a raw-boned hoss;
He says, "Cowboys, yore too damned slow!"
We spool our beds and away we go.

I never hankered for to plow or hoe,
And punching steers is all I know;
With my knees in the saddle and a-hanging to the sky,
Herding dogies up in Heaven in the sweet bye and bye.

Cum a ti yi yippy, yippy I, yippy ay,
Ti yi yippy yippy I, yippy ay,
Cum a ti yi yippy yippy ay.

THE TEXAS COWBOY

Oh, I am a Texas cowboy, just off the Texas plains,
My trade is cinching saddles and pulling the bridle reins.
It's I can throw the lasso with the greatest of ease
And mount my bronco pony and ride him where I please.

Ho-loo-loo-loo-loo.

Oh, it's on the rolling prairie, free from toil and strife,
Behind a bunch of longhorns I'll journey all my life.
It's if I had a little stake, boys, it's married I would be,
For the dearest girl in all the world has fell in love with me.

Oh, it's on the rolling prairies, where the dusty billows rise,
Fifty miles from water and the grass a-scorching dry;
The boss is mad and ringy, just as plain as you can see,
I am bound to quit the trail, boys, and an honest farmer be.

Oh, it's when there comes a rain, boys, one of the general kind,
The lake all full of water and the grass a-waving fine,
The boss'll shed his frown, boys, and fall in smiles, you see.
I am bound to quit the homestead, and a roving cowboy be.

Oh, it's when we get them bedded, you'll think it's for the night,
Some horse'll shake a saddle and give the herd a fright;
They'll rise to their feet, and then they'll dash away,
And in less than half a moment's time, you'll hear some cowboy say:

Ho-loo-loo-loo-loo.

"The Texas Cowboy" was contributed by Arbie Moore to *Texas and Southwestern Lore*, PTFS, 6 (1927):196.

Oh, it's when you get them bedded, you'll feel most forlorn,
A cloud in the west a-rising, fire playing on their horns.
The boss'll say, "Stay with 'em, boys, your pay you'll get in gold."
I am bound to follow the F A steers until I am too old.

    Ho-loo-loo-loo-loo.

I RIDE AN OLD PAINT

I ride an old Paint and I lead an old Dan,
I'm going to Montan' for to throw the hoolihan,
They feed in the coolees, they water in the draw,
Tails are all matted, their backs are all raw.

    Ride around, little dogies, ride around them slow,
    The fiery and the snuffy are raring to go.

I've worked in the town and I've worked on the farm,
And all I got to show is just this muscle in my arm;
Got a blister on my foot, got a callus on my hand,
But I'll be a cowpuncher long as I can.

    Ride around, little dogies, ride around them slow,
    The fiery and the snuffy are raring to go.

Old Bill Jones had two daughters and a song,
One daughter went to Denver and the other went wrong,
His wife she died in a poolroom fight,
But still old Bill sings from morning to night.

    Ride around, little dogies, ride around them slow,
    The fiery and the snuffy are raring to go.

When I die, take my saddle from the wall
And lead my old pony out of his stall;
Tie my bones to his saddle, turn our faces toward the west,
We'll ride the prairies that we love the best.

    Ride around, little dogies, ride around them slow,
    The fiery and the snuffy are raring to go.

"I Ride an Old Paint" was recorded by Duncan Emrich from the singing of Sam Hinton of La Jolla, California, at Washington, D.C., 1947. Library of Congress AFS record 8931 A6.

BUCKING BRONCO

My lover's a cowboy, wild broncos he breaks,
He promised to quit it just for my sake;
He ties up one foot and the saddle puts on,
With a leap and a bound he is mounted and gone.
Oh, the first time I met him, 'twas early in spring,
He was riding a bronco, a high-headed thing;
He tipped me a wink, as he gaily did go,
For he wished me to look at his bucking bronco.

The next time I met, 'twas late in the fall,
He was swinging the gals at the Miles City ball;
We chatted and laughed as we danced to and fro,
He promised never to ride on another bronco.
He made me some presents, among them a ring,
The return that I gave me — a far better thing —
'Twas a young maiden's heart, I would have you all know,
And he won it by riding his bucking bronco.

My love has a gun and that gun he can use,
But he's quit his gunfighting as well as his booze;
But sold him his saddle, his spurs and his rope,
And there's no more gunfighting, now that's what I hope.
All you young maidens, where e'er you reside,
Beware of the cowboy who sings the rawhide;
He'll rope you and hog-tie you, he'll leave you and go
In the spring up the trail on his bucking bronco.

I'VE GOT NO USE FOR THE WOMEN

I first heard this song sung, with a variant text but the same sentiment, by

"Bucking Bronco" was collected by Duncan Emrich from Powder River Jack Lee, Denver, Colorado, 1941.

"I've Got No Use for the Women" was recorded by Duncan Emrich from the singing of an eight-year-old child at the Palo Verde Ranch School outside of Mesa, Arizona, in 1928. He had, of course, picked it up orally. What he made of the "woman" business I do not know, but he was well aware of the shooting, the ranger, and the prairie grave. He was of and from the Southwest.

Oh, I've got no use for the women, a true one may never be found,
They'll use a man just for his money, when it's gone they'll turn him down;
And they're all alike at the bottom, selfish and grasping for all,
They'll stick by a man while he's winning, and laugh in his face at his fall.

My pal was an honest young cowboy, honest and upright and true,
But he turned to a hard-shooting gunman on account of a girl named Lou;
He fell in with the evil companions, the kind that are better off dead,
When a *vaquero* insulted her picture, he filled him full of lead.

All through the long night they trailed him, through mesquite and thick
    chaparral,
And I couldn't help think of that woman as I saw him pitch and fall;
If she'd been the pal that she should have, he might have been raising a son
Instead of out there on the prairie to die by the ranger's gun.

Death's sharp sting did not trouble, his chances for life were too slim,
But where they were putting his body meant all the world to him;
He lifted his head on his elbow, the blood from his wounds flowed red.
He looked at his friends grouped around him and these are the words that
    he said:

"Oh, bury me out on the prairie where the coyotes can howl o'er my grave,
Bury me there on the prairie, but from them my bones please save.
Oh, wrap me up in my blanket and lower me deep in the ground,
And cover me over with boulders of granite gray and round."

So we buried him there on the prairie and the coyotes still howl o'er his
    grave,
And his soul is now a-resting from the unkind cut she gave;
And many another young cowboy as he passes by that pile of stones
Recalls some similar woman and thinks of his mouldering bones.

Sam Hinton of La Jolla, California, at Washington, D.C., 1947. Library of Congress AFS record 8932 B5.

Work Chants

Quarter less four,
Half twain,
Quarter twain,
Mark twain.
Quarter less twain,
Nine and a half feet,
Nine feet,
Eight and a half feet.

UNLOADING RAILS

. . . All right now, listen to me right good.
Walk up until you're almost to the car.
Inside men, step back.
Outside, pull up good and strong.
Head high!
Throw it away!
That's all right!
I heard it ring.
Come on back and get another one now. . . .

Walk to the car, steady yourself.
Head high!
Throw it away!
That's just right.
Go back and get another one.
You got the wrong one that time. . . .

Walk humble and don't you stumble,
And don't you hurt nobody.
Walk to the car and steady yourself.
Stand a minute.
Head high!

"Unloading Rails" was recorded by John A. and Ruby T. Lomax from the calling of Henry Truvillion at Wiergate, Texas, 1940. Library of Congress record LP8.

Good-by, rail!
Good iron!
I heard it ring-nnng. . . .
Go back and get another one. . . .

All right, steady.
Stand a minute.
Get your wind a minute.
Head high!
Good-by, old rail!
That's all right, son.
Go back and get another one. . . .

Walk humble and don't you stumble.
Don't let me hurt nobody.
This is the safety-first company.
Steady!
Head-high!
Good-by!
That's all right!
I heard it ring!
Now let's go back and get another one. . . .

TAMPING TIES

Tamp 'em up solid,
All the livelong day.
Tamp 'em up solid,
Then they'll hold that midnight mail.
The captain don't like me.
Won't allow me no show.
Well, work don't hurt me,
Don't care where in the world I go.
Work don't hurt me,
Like the early rise.
Well, work don't hurt me,

"Tamping Ties" was recorded by John A. and Ruby T. Lomax from the calling of Henry
Truvillion at Wiergate, Texas, 1940. Library of Congress record LP8.

But that's the thing that hurts my pride,
That hurts my pride,
That hurts my pride,
That hurts my pride.

LINING TRACK

God told Noah about the rainbow sign,
No more water but a fire next time.
Hey boys, can't you line, hey boys, just a hair,
Hey boys, can't you line, hey boys, just a hair.

All right, we're movin' on up the joint ahead.

Capt'n keep a-hollerin' 'bout the joint ahead,
Ain't said nothin' about the hog and bread.
Hey boys, can't you line, hey boys, just a hair,
Ho boys, line them over, hey boys, just a hair.

Better move it on down to the center head.

Capt'n keep a-hollerin' about the joint ahead,
Ain't said nothin' 'bout the bowl and bread.
Hey boys, can't you line, hey boys, just a hair,
Ho boys, line them over, hey boys, just a hair.

Ol' soul, let's move ahead, children.
All right, is you right? Yes, we're right.

Gone to town, goin' to hurry back,
See Corinna when she ball the jack,
Hey boys, can't you line, hey boys, just a hair.

All right, Capt'n keep a-hollerin' about the joint ahead.
All right, children, will you move?
Move on down, ol' soul,
Is you right, children? Yes we're right.

Goin' to town, gonna hurry back,

"Lining Track" was recorded by Herbert Halpert from the singing of Henry Hankins at Tascumbia, Alabama, 1939. Library of Congress record LP61.

See Corinna when she ball the jack,
Hey boys, can't you line, ho boys, just a hair.

TRACK-LINING SONG

Hey, boys, joint ahead.
I'm gonna tell you something now.
Oh, all I want — my navy beans,
A big fat woman and a wheeler team.
Hi, hi, won't you line 'em?
Hi, hi, won't you line 'em?
Ho, ho, won't you line 'em?
See Eloise go lining track.

If I could, I surely would
Stand on the rock where Moses stood.
Oh, boys, in the morning,
Hi, hi, a'ternoon,
Hi, boys, in the evening,
I'd be standing there all the time.

Oh, boys, want to tell you something now.
Oh, way down yonder in the harvest field,
Angels working at the chariot wheel.
Oh, boys, won't you line 'em,
Oh, boys, won't you line 'em,
Oh, boys, won't you line 'em,
See Eloise go lining track.

Oh, if I'd known my cap'n was blind,
Wouldn't went to work till the clock struck nine.
Ho, boys, he can see.
Hi, hi, he ain't blind.
Hi, hi, got a Waterbury.
He, hi, he can tell time. . . .

"Track-Lining Song" was recorded by John A. and Alan Lomax from the singing of Allen Prothero, State Penitentiary, Nashville, Tennessee, 1933. Library of Congress record LP2.

GO DOWN, OLD HANNAH

James (Iron Head) Baker says that he first sang this song in 1908, on long hot summer days when, about three o'clock in the afternoon, the sun (Old Hannah) seemed to stop and "just hang" in the sky.

Go down, old Hannah,
Won't you rise no more?
Go down, old Hannah,
Won't you rise no more?

That if you work
He'll treat you well,
And if you don't
He'll give you hell.

Lawd, if you rise,
Bring Judgment on.
Lawd, if you rise,
Bring Judgment on.

Oh, go down, old Hannah,
Won't you rise no more?
Won't you go down, old Hannah,
Won't you rise no more?

Oh, did you hear
What the captain said?
Oh, did you hear
What the captain said?

Oh, long-time man,
Hold up your head.
Well, you may get a pardon
And you may drop dead.

Lawdy, nobody feels sorry
For the lifetime man.
Nobody feels sorry
For the lifetime man.

POOR LITTLE JOHNNY

Way down in the bottom,
Where the cotton so rotten,

"Go Down, Old Hannah" was recorded by John A. and Alan Lomax from the singing of James (Iron Head) Baker, Will Crosby, R. D. Allen, and Moses (Clear Rock) Platt, Central State Farm, Sugarland, Texas, 1933. Library of Congress record LP2.

"Poor Little Johnny" was recorded by John A. and Ruby T. Lomax from the singing of Harriet McClintock, Livingston, Alabama, 1940. Library of Congress record LP4.

You won't get your hundred here today,
You won't get your hundred here today.

Poor little Johnny,
He's a poor little fellow,
He won't get his hundred here today,
He won't get his hundred here today.

MISSISSIPPI SOUNDING CALLS

Samuel Clemens (Mark Twain) took his pseudonym from calls such as these.

I

No bottom,
Mark four,
Quarter less four,
Quarter less five,
Half twain,
Quarter twain.

II

Quarter less four,
Half twain,
Quarter twain,
Mark twain,
Quarter less twain,
Nine and a half feet,
Nine feet,
Eight and a half feet.

"Mississippi Sounding Calls" was recorded by Herbert Halpert from the calling of Joe Shores at Greenville, Mississippi, 1939. Library of Congress record LP8.

HEAVING THE LEAD LINE

Now we're stuck there [. . .]
For the lead line drapped off right now.
Well, old deckhand, when you git on top
I'm gonna hear that line [. . .]
Let the old boat draw.
Lord, I'm throwin' lead line on the la'board side.
Quarter less twain,
Don't you change your mind.
Heave it in the water just-a one more time.
Eight feet and a half, Mr. Pilot, will you change your mind.
Run him on a slow bell,
Run him on a slow bell.
Quarter less twain on the sta'board side.
Mr. Pilot, will you change your mind.
Drap it on over on the left-hand side.
Tell me there's a buoy, a buoy right on the bar.
The light is twisted, and you can see just how.
Pull a little over to the la'board side.
Lawd, Lawd.
Quarter less twain,
Quarter less twain,
Quarter less twain,
Quarter less twain,
Lawd, Lawd, now send me quarter less twain.
Throw the lead line a little higher out.
I've gone low down, so mark twain,
Mark twain.
Come ahead, Mr. Pilot, a little bit strong.
I've done got over, and I believe we're gonna
Throw the lead line over —
No bottom here.

"Heaving the Lead Line" was recorded by Herbert Halpert from the calling of Sam Hazel at Greenville, Mississippi, 1939. Library of Congress record LP8.

HAMMER, RING

Won't you ring, old hammer?
    Hammer, ring.
Won't you ring, old hammer?
    Hammer, ring.

Broke the handle on my hammer,
    Hammer, ring.
Broke the handle on my hammer,
    Hammer, ring.

Got to hammerin' in the Bible.

Gonta talk about Norah.

Well, God told Norah.

You is a-goin' in the timber.

You argue some Bible.

Well, Norah got worried.

What you want with the timber?

Won't you build me a ark, sir?

Well, Norah asked God, sir.

How high do you want it?

Build it forty-two cubits.

Every cubit have a window.

Well, it started in to rainin'.

Old Norah got worried.

He called in his children.

Well, Norah told God, sir.

This is a very fine hammer.

Got the same old hammer.

Got to hammerin' in the timber,
    Hammer, ring.
Got to hammerin' in the timber,
    Hammer, ring.

    Won't you ring, old hammer?
        Hammer, ring.
    Won't you ring, old hammer?
        Hammer, ring.

"Hammer, Ring" was recorded by John A. and Alan Lomax from the singing of Jesse Bradley and group at the State Penitentiary, Huntsville, Texas, 1934. Library of Congress record LP8.

Railroading

Oh, I don't like a railroad man,
No, I don't like a railroad man,
A railroad man will kill you when he can,
And he'll drink up your blood like wine.

CALLING TRAINS

The call here begins with New Orleans and ends with Chicago, the route of
the Illinois Central's *Panama Limited:*

All out for Illinois Central.
New Orleans.
Ponchatoula.
Hammond.
Amite, Independence.
Fluker, Kentwood, Osyka, Magnolia, McComb.
Brookhaven, Wesson, Hazlehurst, Crystal Springs.
Terry, Byram, Jackson, Tougaloo, Ridgeland, Gluckstadt, Madison, Can-
ton.
Vaughan, Pickens, Goodman, Durant, Winona, Grenada.
Sardis, Memphis, Dyersburg, Fulton, Cairo, Carbondale.
Centralia, Effingham, Mattoon, Champaign, Kankakee, Chicago.
Train on Track Four.
Aisle Number Two.

"Calling Trains" was recorded by John A. Lomax from the chant of an old traincaller from
New Orleans, Louisiana, at State Penitentiary, Parchman, Mississippi, 1936. Library of
Congress record LP61.

656

JOHN HENRY

Professor Guy B. Johnson, author of *John Henry: Tracking Down a Negro Legend*, Chapel Hill, 1929, wrote: "I prefer to believe that (1) there was a Negro steel driver named John Henry at Big Bend Tunnel, that (2) he competed with a steam drill in a test of the practicability of the device, and that (3) he probably died soon after the contest, perhaps from fever." The Big Bend Tunnel on the Chesapeake and Ohio Railroad, nine miles east of Hinton, West Virginia, was under construction from 1870 to 1872.

— NOTE FROM LAWS.

"John Henry" was collected by John Harrington Cox from Professor Josiah H. Combs, West Virginia University, 1924, who had obtained it in Knott County, Kentucky. In Cox, *Folksongs of the South* (Harvard) Cambridge, 1925 (Dover reprint, 1967), p. 185. Without music. Laws, I1.

When John Henry was a little babe,
    A-holding to his mama's hand,
Says, "If I live till I'm twenty-one,
    I'm going to make a steel-driving man, my babe,
    I'm going to make a steel-driving man."

When John Henry was a little boy,
    A-sitting on his father's knee,
Says, "The Big Bend Tunnel on the C. & O. Road
    Is going to be the death of me, my babe,
    Is going to be the death of me."

John he made a steel-driving man,
    They took him to the tunnel to drive;
He drove so hard he broke his heart,
    He laid down his hammer and he died, my babe,
    He laid down his hammer and he died.

O now John Henry is a steel-driving man,
    He belongs to the steel-driving crew,
And every time his hammer comes down,
    You can see that steel walking through, my babe,
    You can see that steel walking through.

The steam drill standing on the right-hand side,
    John Henry standing on the left;
He says, "I'll beat that steam drill down,
    Or I'll die with my hammer in my breast, my babe,
    Or I'll die with my hammer in my breast."

He placed his drill on the top of the rock,
    The steam drill standing close at hand;
He beat it down one inch and a half
    And laid down his hammer like a man, my babe,
    And laid down his hammer like a man.

Johnny looked up to his boss-man and said,
    "O boss-man, how can it be?
For the rock is so hard and the steel is so tough,
    I can feel my muscles giving way, my babe,
    I can feel my muscles giving way."

Johnny looked down to his turner and said,
    "O turner, how can it be?
The rock is so hard and the steel is so tough
    That everybody's turning after me, my babe,
    That everybody's turning after me."

They took poor Johnny to the steep hillside,
    He looked to his heavens above;
He says, "Take my hammer and wrap it in gold
    And give it to the girl I love, my babe,
    And give it to the girl I love."

They took his hammer and wrapped it in gold
    And gave it to Julia Ann;
And the last word John Henry said to her
    Was, "Julia, do the best you can, my babe,"
    Was, "Julia, do the best you can."

"If I die a railroad man,
    Go bury me under the tie,
So I can hear old Number Four,
    As she goes rolling by, my babe,
    As she goes rolling by.

"If I die a railroad man,
    Go bury me under the sand,
With a pick and shovel at my head and feet,
    And a nine-pound hammer in my hand, my babe,
    And a nine-pound hammer in my hand."

I WISH I WAS A MOLE IN THE GROUND

Oh, Teddy wants a nine-dollar shawl,
Oh, Teddy wants a nine-dollar shawl,
When I come off the hill with a forty-dollar bill,
It's "Baby, where you been so long?"

"I Wish I Was a Mole in the Ground" was recorded by Artus M. Moser from the singing, with banjo, of Bascom Lamar Lunsford at Swannanoa, North Carolina, 1946. Library of Congress record LP21.

Oh, I don't like a railroad man,
No, I don't like a railroad man,
A railroad man will kill you when he can,
And he'll drink up your blood like wine.

Oh, Teddy, let your hair roll down,
Oh, Teddy, let your hair roll down,
Let your hair roll down and your bangs curl around,
Oh, Teddy, let your hair roll down.

I wish I was a lizard in the spring,
Yes, I wish I was a lizard in the spring,
If I was a lizard in the spring, I'd hear my darling sing,
And I wish I was a lizard in the spring.

Oh, I've been in the Bend so long,
Yes, I've been in the Bend so long,
If I was a mole in the ground, I'd root that mountain down,
And I wish I was a mole in the ground.

GEORGE ALLEN

The tragic accident described in this ballad occurred on October 23, 1890, near Hinton, West Virginia.

Along come that F.F.V., the swiftest on the line,
Travelin' o'er that C. & O. road twenty minutes behind the time.
He pulled in at Sunville, his quarters on the line,
Just taking off strict orders from the signal just behind.

When he got to London, his engineer was there,
His name was Georgie Allen with his curly golden hair.
His fireman, Jack Dickson, was standing by his side
Awaiting for his orders and in his cab to ride.

Along come Georgie's mama with a bucket on her arm,
"Be careful, George, my darling son, be careful how you run,
If you run your engine right you'll get there just on time,
Been a many a man who's lost his life by trying to make lost time."

"George Allen" was recorded by Herbert Halpert from the singing, with banjo, of Austin Harmon at Maryville, Tennessee, 1939. Library of Congress record LP61. Laws, G3.

"Oh mother, I know your advice is good and later I'll take heed,
But my ol' engine she's all right — I'm sure that she will speed.
O'er this road I mean to go with a speed unknown to all,
When I blow my whistle at the old stockyard they'd better heed my call."

Oh Georgie said to his fireman Jack, "There's a rock ahead I see,
Oh there's death awaiting to receive both you and me,
All from this engine you must go your darling life to save,
For I want you to be an engineer when I'm sleeping in my grave."

"No," says Jack, "that won't do; with you I'll stay and die."
"No," says George, "that won't do; I'll die for both you and I."
From this engine Jack did go — the river was rolling high,
He waved his hand at Georgie as the runaway train dashed by.

Down the track she darted, against the rocks she crashed,
The engine she turned upside down on Georgie's tender breast.
The doctors hastened to him, says, "George, my son, lie still,
The only hope to seek for your life it would be God's holy will."

His head was lying in the firebox door while the burning flames rolled on,
His face was covered up in blood, his eyes you could not see.
The last words that poor Georgie said was, "Nearer, my God, to thee."

THE WRECK OF THE ROYAL PALM

The Southern Railway wreck of this ballad took place on December 23, 1926, near Rockmart, Georgia.

On a dark and stormy night
The rain was falling fast.
The two black trains on the
  Southern road
With a screaming whistle blast
Were speeding down the line
For home and Christmas Day.
On the Royal Palm and the Ponce
  de Leon
Was laughter bright and gay.

The coming down the curve
At forty miles an hour,
The Royal Palm was making time
Amid the drenching shower.
There came a mighty crash,
The two great engines met,
And in the minds of those who live
It's a scene they can't forget.

It was an awful sight
Amid the pouring rain,
The dead and dying lying there
Beneath that mighty train.
No tongue can ever tell,
No pen can ever write,
No one would know but those who
  saw
The horrors of that night.

On board the new great train
The folks were bright and gay.
When like a flash the Master
  called,
They had no time to pray.
Then in a moment's time
The awful work was done,
And many souls that fatal night
Had made their final run.

There's many a saddened home
Since that sad Christmas Day,
Whose loved ones never shall
  return
To drive the blues away.
They were on the Royal Palm
As she sped across the state,
Without a single warning cry
They went to meet their fate.

We're on the road of life
And like the railroad men,
We each should do our best to
  make
The station if we can.
So let us all take care
To keep our orders straight,
For if we get our orders mixed
It'll surely be too late.

"The Wreck of the Royal Palm" was recorded by Wyatt Insko from the singing, with guitar, of Clarence H. Wyatt at Berea, Kentucky, 1954. Library of Congress record LP61. Laws, dG51.

HENRY K. SAWYER

The *Bangor Daily Whig and Courier*, for June 9, 1848, carried the following news item:

FATAL RAILROAD ACCIDENT

A fatal accident occurred on the Oldtown Railroad yesterday morning, the engine having run off the track about two miles this side of Stillwater. There were four men upon the engine, and one of them, Mr. Henry Sawyer, the superintendent of repairs on the road, was caught by the arm between the pipes and the earth, and held there for some time, the hot water running upon his body, scalding him in an awful manner. When taken out he had his senses perfectly, and gave directions with perfect self-possession, although aware that he could not live but a short time. He was brought to this city and died at noon, aged 35 years. He has left a wife and an adopted child. He has been employed upon the road for twelve years, and has sustained during that time a good reputation as a worthy man and a good citizen.

The engine ran off a steep embankment, and turned upside down into the swamp. Mr. Sawyer stated that he should have escaped had it not been for the house erected upon the engine. No other person was injured, and it has not been ascertained how much the engine is damaged.

Henry K. Sawyer was buried in the Stillwater Cemetery, where his wife, Mary Jane Sawyer, who died less than a year later, on March 8, 1849, is also buried.

> It was one Sunday morning of June the eighth day,
> When Henry K. Sawyer from home went away;
> When Henry K. Sawyer, a man of renown,
> Took a seat on the tender, to ride to Old Town.
>
> 'Twas down near Stillwater they ran off the track,
> The wood on the tender struck him on the back;
> The engine capsized, and sad to relate,
> Which placed this poor man in a horrible state.

"Henry K. Sawyer" was recorded (for dictaphone) by Mr. Orlon Merrill of Charlestown, New Hampshire, 1931, who learned it as a child from his grandfather in Maine. Reported, with music and notes on the collection, by Phillips Barry in *Bulletin of the Folksong Society of the Northeast*, Cambridge, Mass., 9 (1935):17–19. Laws, G5.

The weight of the engine confinèd him down,
While steam and hot water gave him his death wound;
In this situation thirty minutes he lay;
Till at length they released him by digging away.

And when they survived him, brought tears to their eyes,
His shrieks met* the air, his poor groans met the skies;
He cries, "God have mercy, and suffer my life,
And suffer me once more to see my dear wife."

A car was then taken from the rear of the train,
And on this same car, the poor sufferer was lain;
Six men took the car and they ran it for their life,
And he once more did work† and converse with his wife.

They ran it six miles in three-fourths of an hour,
Until they were released by the strength of horsepower,
But when they arrived at the depot they saw
His poor distressed wife standing in agony.

There was many there collected to see his sad face‡
Which pain would have relieved, but it was then too late;
He was taken from the car, carried into a room,
And in a short time the poor man met his doom.

This happened at seven; he expired at noon;
In the morning no one thought of his dying so soon;
He turned to his wife, saying "Jane, I must die,"
With a calm resignation he bade her good-by.

'Twas twelve years or better he had worked on this track;
He never was known once a duty to lack.
Now think on this widow and on her distress,
And make her a present, and God will you bless.

* Rent?
† Talk?
‡ Fate?

I'M GOING TO ROCKY ISLAND

I'm going to Rocky Island, ho, my honey, hey;
Going to Rocky Island, I'm going there to stay.

I see that train a-coming, she's coming around the curve,
She's whistling and blowing, she's straining every nerve.

I'm going to Rocky Island, ho, my honey, hey,
To see my candy darling, where I'm going to stay.

Catch my horse and I'll ride him, ho, my honey, hey,
Catch my horse and I'll ride him, on a long summer day.

Ride him to Rocky Island, ho, my honey, hey,
Ride him to Rocky Island, on a long summer day.

LOST JOHNNY

Oh, I wonder where my lost Johnny's gone,
Oh, I wonder where my lost Johnny's gone,
Oh, I wonder where my lost Johnny's gone,
Oh, he's gone to that new railroad,
He's gone to that new railroad.

Go make me a pallet on the floor,
Go make me a pallet on the floor,
Go make me a pallet on the floor,
Believe I will eat morphine and die,
Believe I will eat morphine and die.

I'll go if I have to ride the rail,
I'll go if I have to ride the rail,
I'll go if I have to ride the rail,
To the road where my Johnny is,
To the road where my Johnny is.

"I'm Going to Rocky Island" is from "Folk Songs from East Kentucky" (mimeographed), collected by the Folk Song Project of the Federal Music Project in Kentucky (WPA), n.d., ca. 1939. Last two stanzas composite from the singing of J. M. Mullins, West Liberty, Kentucky, 1937. Library of Congress AFS record 1565 B.

"Lost Johnny" was collected by Harvey H. Fuson from Mrs. Ethel Edwards. In Fuson, *Ballads of the Kentucky Highlands*, London, 1931, p. 151. Without music.

665

THE ROCK ISLAND LINE

Well, Jesus died to save me in all of my sin,
Well-a, glory to God, we goin' to meet Him again.

I says the Rock Island Line is a mighty good road.
I says the Rock Island Line is the road to ride.
I says the Rock Island Line is a mighty good road.
If you want to ride, you gotta ride it like you're flyin'.
Buy your ticket at the station on the Rock Island Line.

Well, the train left Memphis at half pas' nine.
Well, it made it back to Little Rock at eight forty-nine.

Well, Jesus died to save me in all of my sin.
Well-a, glory to God, we goin' to meet Him again.

I says the Rock Island Line is a mighty good road.
I says the Rock Island Line is the road to ride.
I says the Rock Island Line is a mighty good road.
If you want to ride, you gotta ride it like you're flyin'.
Buy your ticket at the station on the Rock Island Line.

WAY OUT IN IDAHO

Come all you jolly railroad men, and I'll sing you if I can
Of the trials and tribulations of a godless railroad man,
Who started out from Denver his fortunes to make grow
And struck the Oregon Short Line way out in Idaho.

Way out in Idaho, way out in Idaho,
A-working on the narrow-gauge, way out in Idaho.

"The Rock Island Line" was recorded by John A. Lomax from the singing of Kelley Pace, Charlie Porter, L. T. Edwards, Willie Hubbard, Luther Williams, Napoleon Cooper, Albert Pate, and Willie Lee Jones, Cumins State Farm, Gould, Arkansas, 1934. Library of Congress record LP2.

"Way Out in Idaho" was recorded by Alan Lomax from the singing, with guitar, of Blaine Stubblefield of Weiser, Idaho, at Washington, D.C., 1938.

I was roaming around in Denver one luckless rainy day
When Kilpatrick's man-catcher stepped up to me and did say,
"I'll lay you down five dollars as quickly as I can
And you'll hurry up and catch the train, she's starting for Cheyenne."

He laid me down five dollars, like many another man,
And I started for the depot — was happy as a clam.
When I got to Pocatello, my troubles began to grow,
A-wading through the sagebrush in frost and rain and snow.

When I got to American Falls, it was there I met Fat Jack.
They said he kept a hotel in a dirty canvas shack,
Said he, "You are a stranger and perhaps your funds are low,
Well, yonder stands my hotel tent, the best in Idaho."

I followed my conductor into his hotel tent,
And for one square and hearty meal I paid him my last cent.
Jack's a jolly fellow, and you'll always find him so,
A-working on the narrow-gauge way out in Idaho.

They put me to work next morning with a cranky cuss called Bill,
And they give me a ten-pound hammer to strike upon a drill.
They said if I didn't like it I could take my shirt and go,
And they'd keep my blankets for my board way out in Idaho.

Oh it filled my heart with pity as I walked along the track
To see so many old bummers with their turkeys on their backs.
They said the work was heavy and the grub they couldn't go,
Around Kilpatrick's dirty tables way out in Idaho.

But now I'm well and happy, down in the harvest camp,
And I'll — there I will continue till I make a few more stamps.
I'll go down to New Mexico and I'll marry the girl I know,
And I'll buy me a horse and buggy and go back to Idaho.

THE DYING HOBO

"My name's George Lay. I picked up this song along with several others in the hobo jungles of the late '30's when we was trying to scram around over the country and find a dime, which is hard to do and is a lot harder to keep

"The Dying Hobo" was recorded by Mary Celestia Parler from the singing of George Lay at Heber Springs, Arkansas, 1959. Library of Congress record LP61. Laws, H3.

it after you found it. There's a lot of guys along there that — a — the ink still wet on diplomas from their colleges and there's a lot of guys that had never been inside of a school. 'Bout the only entertainment was had were these old songs at night. Now I don't know what the name of this one is — it's just one they used to sing a lot."

Just out of San Francisco one cold December day,
Beneath an eastbound boxcar a dying hobo lay.
His comrade stood beside him, his hat was in his hand,
For he knew that his old buddy was goin' to a distant land.

"Go tell my girl in Frisco no longer will I roam,
I've caught an eastbound boxcar and I'm on my way back home.
I'm goin' to a better land where you don't have to change your socks,
Where beer and foam come trickling down the rocks."

The dying hobo closed his eyes and drew his last breath,
His comrade stole his coat and hat and kept on headin' West.

THE BIG ROCK CANDY MOUNTAINS

One evening as the sun went down
And the jungle fire was burning,
Down the track came a hobo hiking.
And he said, "Boys I'm not turning,
I'm headed for a land that's far away,
Beside the crystal fountains,
So come with me, we'll go and see
The Big Rock Candy Mountains."

In the Big Rock Candy Mountains,
There's a land that's fair and bright,
Where the handouts grow on bushes,
And you sleep out every night.
Where the boxcars all are empty,
And the sun shines every day
On the birds and the bees,
And the cigarette trees,

"The Big Rock Candy Mountains" was recorded by Sam Eskin from the singing of Harry McClintock at San Pedro, California, 1951. Library of Congress record LP61.

And the lemonade springs
Where the bluebird sings
In the Big Rock Candy Mountains.

In the Big Rock Candy Mountains
All the cops have wooden legs,
And the bulldogs all have rubber teeth,
And the hens lay softboiled eggs.
There the farmer's trees are full of fruit,
And the barns are full of hay,
And I'm bound to go
Where there ain't no snow,
And the rain don't fall,
And the wind don't blow
In the Big Rock Candy Mountains.

In the Big Rock Candy Mountains
You never change your socks,
And the little streams of alcohol
Come a-trickling down the rocks.
There ain't no shorthandled shovels,
No axes, spades, or picks,
And I'm bound to stay
Where they sleep all day,
Where they hung the Turk
That invented work
In the Big Rock Candy Mountains.

In the Big Rock Candy Mountains
All the jails are made of tin,
And you can walk right out again
As soon as you are in.
Where the brakemen have to tip their hats,
And the railroad bulls are blind,
There's a lake of stew,
And a gin lake, too,
You can paddle all around 'em
In a big canoe
In the Big Rock Candy Mountains.

Murders

Little attention did I pay,
I beat her more and more,
I beat her till the blood run down,
Her hair was yellow as gold.

JOHNSON-JINKSON

Johnson, he was riding along, as fast as he could ride,
He thought he heard a woman, he heard a woman cry.

Johnson getting off his horse and searching, looked all around,
Until he came to a woman with her hair pinned to the ground.

"Woman, dearest woman, who has brought you here for a span?
Who has brought you here this morning, with your hair pinned to the
　　ground?"

"It were three bold and struggling men, with swords keen in hand,
Who brought me here this morning, with my hair pinned to the ground."

Johnson being a man of his own, and being a man and bold,
He put off his overcoat to hug her from the cold.

Johnson getting on his horse, and the woman getting on behind,
Along this lonesome highway rode, their fortunes for to find.

They were riding all along, as fast as they could ride,
She drew her fingers to her ears, and gave three shivering cries.

"Johnson-Jinkson" was recorded by Charles Todd and Robert Sonkin from the singing of
Troy Cambron at Arvin, California, 1940. Library of Congress AFS record 4138 B1. Laws,
L4. The song goes back to a seventeenth century English broadside, "The Three Worthy
Butchers of the North," who are attacked by ten highwaymen and the woman. How it wound
its way across the centuries to an Okie camp in California is quite wonderful to consider and
demonstrates the tenacity with which the folk cling to at least certain of their songs and
traditions.

Out sprung three bold and struggling men, with swords keen in hand,
Who did commanded Johnson, commanded him to stand.

"I'll stop then," said Johnson, "I'll stand then," said he,
"For I never worried in my life afraid of any of three."

Johnson killing two of them, not watching the woman behind,
While he was after the other one, she stabbed him from behind.

The day was free and a market day, and the people all passing by
Who saw this awful murder, and saw poor Johnson die.

THE OXFORD GIRL
Expert Town

It was in the city of Expert
Once where I used to dwell,
It was in the city of Expert Town
I owned a flouring mill.

I fell in love with a nice young girl,
Dark rolling was her hair [roving was her eye].
I told her that I'd marry her
If me she'd never deny.

I fell in love with another girl,
I loved her just as well,
The Devil put it in my mind
My first true lover to kill.

I called down to her sister's house
At eight o'clock one night,
But little did the poor girl think
I owed her in despite.

"We'll have a walk, we'll have a talk
Down by the meadow field,
We'll also have a private talk
And set our wedding day."

"Expert Town" was recorded by Vance Randolph from the singing, with guitar, of Mrs. Mildred Tuttle at Farmington, Arkansas, 1942. Library of Congress record LP12. Laws, P35.

We walked along, we talked along
Till we came to the levelest ground,
I picked me up a stick of wood
And knocked the poor girl down.

She fell upon her bending knees
Crying, "Lord have mercy on me!
Oh, Willie, oh, Willie, don't murder me now,
For I'm not prepared to die!"

Little attention did I pay,
I beat her more and more,
I beat her till the blood run down,
Her hair was yellow as gold.

I picked her up by the lifeless hair,
I swung her round and around,
I swung her on the water top
That flows through Expert Town.

Her sister swore my life away
Without a bitter doubt
She swore that I was the very same man
That taken her sister out.

They took me on suspicion,
Locked me up in Expert jail,
I had no one to pay off my fine,
No one to go my bail.

And now they're going to hang me
And I'm not prepared to die;
They're going to hang me up in the air
Between the earth and sky.

The Wexford Girl

My tender parents brought me here
Providing for my wealth;

"The Wexford Girl" was collected by Mrs. Mellinger E. Henry from the singing of Mrs.

And in a town of wickedness
He fixed me out a mill.

Here came a wanting lass;
She had a wanting eye;
I promised her I'd marry her,
And with her I did lie.

A very few weeks and afterwards
Here came that lass again:
"I pray you, young John, you'd marry me;
You've got me with a child."

Perplexed was I on every side;
No comfort I could find
But to take my darling's life from her
My wicked heart inclined.

I went to my love's sister's house;
It was getting late at night.
But little did the poor creature think
I owed her any spite.

"Come, take a walk with me, my dear;
We'll pint the wedding day";
I tuk her by her lily-white hand;
I led her through the field.

I drew a stake then out of the fence;
I hit her in the face;
She fell on her bending knee;
For mercy loud did cry:
"I pray, young John, don't murder me,
For I'm not fit to die."

I kept putting on more and more.
She did resign her breath,
And wasn't I a crazy soul
To put my love to death?

I tuk her by the hair of the head;
I drug her through the field;

Samuel Harmon, Bade's Cove, Blount County, Tennessee, in 1930. In Henry, *Folksongs from the Southern Highlands*, New York, 1938, pp. 214–216. Without music. Laws, P35.

673

I drug her to the river bank
And plunged her in the deep.

Right straight home then I run;
My master strangely on me gazed:
"What's the matter, young Johnny?" he says,
"You look as pale as death.

"You look like you've been running
And almost spent for breath.
How came you by, young John," he says,
"These trembling hands enfold?

"How came you, young John," he says,
"Those bloody hands and clothes?"
I answered him immediate lie:
"A-bleeding at the nose."

He stood; he strangely on me gazed,
But no more he said.
I jerked a candle out of his hands
And made my way to bed.

I lay there all that long night;
I had but little rest;
I thought I felt the flames of hell
Strike within my guilty breast.

The very next morning by daylight
Ten guineas I offered any man,
Ten guineas I offered any man,
This damsel they would find.

The very next morning by sunrise,
This damsel she were found,
Floating by her brother's door
In Harry Fairy Town.

Then her sister against me swore;
Good reasons without a doubt;
By coming there after dark,
And calling her out.

"My Lord, my God,
Look down on me
And pray receive my soul."

THE GOSPORT TRAGEDY

My mother used to tell a story about my grandfather's sister, to whom she referred as Aunt Jinnie Hinds, who was singing this song one morning while out in the pasture milking her cow at her home in Windsor. A party of soldiers came along while she was singing and stood listening to her song. When the song was finished, they came forward and the captain gave her a piece of gold to sing them the song again.

— CARRIE GROVER

In Gosport of late a young damsel did dwell.
For wit and for beauty few could her excel.
A young man did court her for to be his dear,
And he by his trade was a ship's carpenter.

He said, "Dearest Mary, if you will agree
And give your consent, dear, for to marry me,
Your love, dear, can cure me of sorrow and care.
Consent then to wed with a ship carpenter."

With blushes as charming as roses in bloom,
She said, "Dearest Willie, to wed I'm too young,
For young men are fickle, I see very plain;
If a young maid is kind, her they quickly disdain."

"My own charming Mary, how can you say so?
Your beauty is the haven to which I would go,
And if I find channel and chance for to steer,
I there will cast anchor and stay with my dear."

It was all in vain that she strove to deny,
For he, by his cunning, soon made her comply,

"The Gosport Tragedy" is from Carrie B. Grover, text with music, *A Heritage of Songs* (privately printed, Gould Academy, Bethel, Maine, n.d.), pp. 43–45. Laws, P36A.

And by his base deception he did her betray
And in sin's hellish path he did lead her astray.

Now when this young damsel with child she did prove,
She soon sent the tidings to her faithless love.
He swore by the heavens that he would prove true,
And said, "I will marry no damsel but you."

At length these sad tidings she came for to hear,
His ship was a-sailing, for sea he must steer,
Which pained this poor damsel and wounded her heart
To think with her true love so soon she must part.

She said, "Dearest Willie, ere you go to sea,
Remember the vows you have made unto me;
If you go and leave me, I ne'er can find rest.
Oh, how can you leave me with sorrow oppressed?"

With tender embraces he to her did say,
"I'll marry my true love ere I go to sea,
And if on the morrow, my love, I can ride down,
The ring I can buy our fond union to crown."

With tender embraces they parted that night
And promised to meet the next morning at light.
William said, "Dearest Mary, you must now go with me
Before we are married, our friends for to see."

He led her o'er hills and through hollows so deep
Till at length this fair damsel began for to weep.
"Oh Willie, I fear you have led me astray
On purpose my innocent life to betray."

He said, "You've guessed right, for no power can you save,
For 'twas only last night I was digging your grave."
When poor, wretched Mary did hear him say so,
The tears from her eyes like a fountain did flow.

Then down on her knees Mary to him did say,
"Oh take not my life lest my soul you betray.
Oh pity my infant, and spare my poor life;
Let me live full of shame if I can't be your wife."

"Oh there is no time thus disputing to stand,"
And, taking his sharp, cruel knife in his hand,
He pierced her fair breast, whence the blood it did flow
And into the grave her fair body did throw.

He covered her body and quick hastened home,
And left nothing but the small birds her fate for to mourn.
He returned to his ship without any delay
And set sail for Plymouth to plow the salt sea.

One night to the captain this fair maid did appear,
And she in her arms held an infant most dear.
"Oh help me, oh help me," she to him did say.
Then to his amazement she vanished away.

The captain then summoned his jovial ship's crew
And said, "My brave fellows, I fear some of you
Have murdered some damsel ere you came away
Whose injured ghost haunts you all on the salt sea."

Then poor, frightened Willie he fell on his knees,
The blood in his veins seemed with horror to freeze.
It's, "Oh, cruel monster, and what have I done?
God help me, I fear my poor soul is undone.

"Oh poor, injured Mary, your forgiveness I crave,
For soon must I follow you down to the grave."
No one but this poor wretch beheld the sad sight,
And raving, distracted, he died the next night.

PRETTY POLLY

I

"Pretty Polly, pretty Polly, come and go with me,
Pretty Polly, pretty Polly, come and go with me,

Version 1 of "Pretty Polly" was recorded by Alan and Elizabeth Lomax from the singing of Pete Steele, Hamilton, Ohio, 1938. Library of Congress record 1B, issued for the Friends of Music in the Library of Congress. Laws, P36B.

Pretty Polly, pretty Polly, come and go with me,
Before we get married, some pleasure to see."

"Pretty Willie, pretty Willie, I fear your way,
Pretty Willie, pretty Willie, I fear your way,
Pretty Willie, pretty Willie, I fear your way,
You're taking my body all out astray."

He led her o'er the hills and the valleys so deep,
He led her o'er the hills and the valleys so deep,
He led her o'er the hills and the valleys so deep,
And at last pretty Polly begin to weep.

She threw her arms around him, she suffered no fear,
She threw her arms around him, she suffered no fear,
She threw her arms around him, she suffered no fear,
"How can you kill a poor girl that loves you so dear?"

He stabbed her to the heart and the blood it did flow,
He stabbed her to the heart and the blood it did flow,
He stabbed her to the heart and the blood it did flow,
And into the grave pretty Polly did go.

He threw some dirt o'er her and turned to go home,
He threw some dirt o'er her and turned to go home,
He threw some dirt o'er her and turned to go home,
Left nothing behind but the birds to mourn.

II

"Pretty Polly, pretty Polly, come go 'long with me,
Pretty Polly, pretty Polly, come go 'long with me,
Before we git married, some pleasure to see."

She got up behind him and away they did go,
She got up behind him and away they did go,
Over the hills to the valley so low.

They went up a little farther and what did they spy?
They went up a little farther and what did they spy?
A new-dug grave and spade lying by.

Version II of "Pretty Polly" was recorded by Alan and Elizabeth Lomax from the singing of
E. C. Ball, Rugby, Virginia, 1941. Library of Congress record LP1. Laws, P36B.

He stobbed her to the heart, her heart blood it did flow,
He stobbed her to the heart, her heart blood it did flow,
And into the grave pretty Polly did go.

He threw somethin' over her and turned to go home,
He threw somethin' over her and turned to go home,
Leaving nothing behind him but the girl left to mourn.

Gentlemen and ladies, I'll bid you farewell,
Gentlemen and ladies, I'll bid you farewell,
For killin' pretty Polly will send my soul to Hell.

FLORELLA,
or The Jealous Lover

Down by the weeping willow
Where the violets are in bloom,
There lies a fair young maiden
All silent in a tomb.

She died not broken-hearted,
No sickness e'er befell,
But all in an instant parted
From the one she loved so well.

'Twas on a summer's evening,
As gently fell the dew,
Down to a lonely cottage
A jealant lover drew.

"Come, love, and let us wander
Out over the meadows gay,
Come, love, and let us ponder
All over our wedding day."

"Oh, Edward, I am weary,
And do not care to roam,
For roaming is so dreary,
I pray you take me home."

Up stepped that jealant lover
And with a silent cry,
"No mortal one shall love you,
In an instant you shall die."

Down, down she sank before him
And humbly begged for life,
But into her snow-white bosom
He plunged the fatal knife.

"Oh, Edward, I forgive you,
Though this is my last breath,
I never did deceive you."
She closed her eyes in death.

Down by the weeping willow
Where the violets are in bloom,
There lies a fair young maiden
All silent in the tomb.

"Florella" was recorded by Vance Randolph from the singing of Callista O'Neill, Day, Missouri, 1941. Library of Congress AFS record 5243B1. Stanza 3 is interpolated from Belden (p. 329) with the reading of *jealant* for *jealous* to agree with Randolph's text. Laws, F1: "Nothing certain is known about the origin of this piece, which is one of the most popular of all white ballads apparently native to this country."

PEARL BRYAN

Pearl Bryan, of Greencastle, Indiana, was murdered by Scott Jackson, the father of her unborn child, and his accomplice, Alonzo Walling. Pearl's headless body was found near Fort Thomas, Kentucky, February 1, 1896. The murderers were executed March 20, 1897. The two young men were medical students, and they had persuaded Pearl Bryan to drive with them to Kentucky, where she was decapitated. Some versions depict the girl's sister as asking the murderers for her head.

A horrible crime was committed,
Soon was brought to light,
For parents to look on their headless
   girl
'Twas a sad and dreadful sight.

The girl who was beheaded
Pearl Bryan was her name,
It was done by medical students
Studying for fame.

This is a horrible tragedy
Its lines are sad to read,
Walling and Scott Jackson
Are the men who did the deed.

Scott Jackson has his sentence,
The deed he did deny,
On the thirtieth day of June
On the scaffold he must die.

He tried to plead innocent,
An appeal to obtain,
His lawyers pleaded to the court,
But found their plea in vain.

Walling's case is not decided
Though soon it will be tried,
The jury will make the verdict
His punishment to decide.

The worst crime ever committed,
So sad we cannot forget,
To all such cruel wretches
Their lives should pay the debt.

The parents have the sympathy
Of all our human race,
How sad it was to find their child
And could not see her face.

It's true it's very sad to die
And pay a debt this way,
"No sympathy for such a wretch,"
You hear the people say.

At last the case is left to God
To guide his wretched soul,
If he does not confess on earth
At the Judgment it will be told.

"Pearl Bryan" was collected by the Federal Music Project, Works Progress Administration (WPA), Boyd County, Kentucky, ca. 1937. Jean Thomas, Supervisor for Boyd County. Ms., with music, in the Archive of Folk Song, Library of Congress. Laws, F2.

Poor troubled parents,
Your grief is hard to bear,
Your child may be in heaven
You should try to meet her there.

We all must take the bitter cup
And be numbered with the dead,
If you meet your child in heaven
You will find the missing head.

Pearl Bryant

'Twas late one winter's evening,
The sorrowful tale was told,
Scott Jackson says to Luns Walling,
"Let's go out for a stroll."

Walling answered softly,
While strolling by his side,
"Let's take the lady fair,
Pearl Bryant, for a ride."

The cab then 'twas ordered
For them to take a stroll,
And if you'll only listen
The half has not been told.

The cab then arriving,
Pearl Bryant sat in tears,
Thinking of the happiness
She'd had in the last few years.

"Oh, what have I done, Scott Jackson,
For you to take my life?
You know that I've always loved you,
And I would have been your wife.

"There's room for your name in the album,
There's room for your love in my breast;
There's room for us both in heaven,
Where true lovers evermore rest."

"Pearl Bryant" was recorded by George W. Hibbitt and William Cabell Greet from the sing-ing of Bascom Lamar Lunsford of South Turkey Creek, North Carolina, at New York City, 1935. Library of Congress AFS record 1824 B. Laws, F2.

Early, early next morning,
The people gathered round,
Says, "Here lies a woman's body,
But her head cannot be found."

The bloodhounds then were ordered,
To tell the tale they said.
"Here lies a woman's body,
But we can't find her head."

In came Pearl Bryant's sister,
A-falling on her knees,
A-pleading with Scott Jackson,
Her sister's head, oh please.

Jackson's just that stubborn,
Not a word then he said.
"When I meet my sister in Heaven,
There'll be no missing head."

In came Luns Walling's mother,
A-pleading for her son,
A-pleading to the jurors
For the first crime he'd ever done.

The jurors made no answer,
But unto their feet they sprung,
Says, "For the crime the boys committed,
The boys must be hung."

'Twas on the thirtieth day of January,
This sorrowful crime was done,
Scott Jackson and Luns Walling,
Pearl Bryant's life they won.

So now, young ladies, take warning,
Before it is too late,
Of the crime the boys committed,
In the old Kentucky State.

THE LILY OF THE WEST

When first I came to Louisville, some pleasure for to find,
I spied a maid from Lexington quite pleasing to my mind,
Her sparkling eyes and saucy cheeks like an arrow pierced my breast,
They called her handsome Florie, the Lily of the West.

Her curly locks of yellow hair in ringlets shone like gold,
They were enough to entice me then, and all men young and old;
She had a ring on every finger, so handsome was she dressed,
They called her handsome Florie, the Lily of the West.

One evening as I walked out, down by yon shady grove,
I spied a man of low degree conversing with my love.
He sung her a song of melody, which so enraged my breast,
He called her handsome Florie, the Lily of the West.

I stepped up to my rival, my dagger in my hand,
I took him by the collar and boldly bid him stand.
I was mad to desperation, I swore I'd pierce his breast,
Saying, "Go! false-hearted Florie, the Lily of the West."

In due time came my trial, I boldlye made my plea;
A flaw in the indictment they said would set me free.
But she turned both judge and jury, so handsome was she dressed,
They smiled on handsome Florie, the Lily of the West.

But now I am convicted, to prison I must go,
For five long years in Frankfort, which fills my heart with woe.
She's robbed me of my liberty, deprived me of my rest,
I never can forgive her, the Lily of the West.

"The Lily of the West" was recorded by Vance Randolph from the singing of Charles Ingenthron, Walnut Shade, Missouri, 1941. Library of Congress AFS record 5245 B1. Ref. Laws, *Native American Balladry*, p. 279.

LULA VIRES

The brutal murder of Lula Vires is recounted with factual accuracy in this ballad. Her murder by John Coyer took place at Elkhorn City, Kentucky, in October, 1917. She was thrown into Big Sandy River and her body was not found until from four to six months later at Hanging Rock, near Ironton, Ohio. At the time of her death, she was unmarried but had a child whose father was supposed to have been Coyer. Coyer was placed in the Floyd County jail but was, inexplicably, later released to join the army. [Note abstracted from Laws, *Native American Balladry*, 1964, p. 65.]

Come all you good people
From all over the world,
And listen to a story
About a poor young girl.

Her name was Lula Vires,
In Auxier she did dwell,
A place in old Kentucky,
A town you all know well.

She loved young John Coyer,
Engaged to be his wife,
He ruined her reputation
And later took her life.

They went to Elkhorn City
Sixty-six miles away,
And registered at a hotel
Until the close of day.

And as the darkness foll
They went out for a stroll,
It was in cold December
The wind was blowing cold.

They went down to the river,
Cold water was running deep;
John said to Lula,
"In the bottom you must sleep."

"Do you really mean it, John?
It surely can't be true.
How could you stand to murder
A poor helpless girl like me."

She threw her arms around him,
"Oh, John, please spare my life,
So that I can go back to mother
If I can not be your wife."

She threw her arms around him,
Before him she did kneel;
Around her waist he tied
A piece of railroad steel.

He threw her in the river,
The bubbles they did rise,
They burst upon the water
With a sad and mournful sight.

"Lula Vires" was collected by the Federal Music Project, Works Progress Administration (WPA), Floyd County, Kentucky, ca. 1937. Edith F. James, Supervisor for Floyd County. Ms., with music, in the Archive of Folk Song, Library of Congress. Laws, F10.

He hastened to the depot
And bounded* a train for home,
And thinking that his crime
Would never more be known.

Poor Lula, she was missing,
Nowhere could she be found,
They searched the world all over
For many miles around.

John Coyer joined the army,
Four months had gone and past,
But in the Ohio River
The body was found at last.

They took her from the river
And took her to the town,
The steel that was tied around her
Weighed even thirty pound.

They held an inquest over her,
The people were in doubt;
They could not recognize her,
They could not find her out.

They sent for a reporter,
His name was Arodent,
He printed it in the paper
And around the world it went.

Her mother was setting in her home
When she read the news,
She quickly left her chair,
Ran to the telephone.

Saying, "I will send a message
Or I will go and see
If it is my daughter,
It surely can not be."

She boarded a train for Ironton
And arrived right at the place,
And described the clothing she
    wore,
When she saw the corpse fell
    fainting to the floor,

Saying, "John Coyer must be
    arrested
And placed in jail,"
And for that awful murder
No one could go his bail.

He was arrested and placed in Floyd
County jail
When soon an army officer came
And took him straight away

He took him off to France,
And he never returned to stand trial
For the awful deed that he had done.

---

* Boarded.

ROSE CONNOLEY

Rose Connoley loved me as dearly as she loved her life,
And many's the time I've told her I'd make her my lawful wife.
But Satan and Satan's temptation have overpowered me,
And caused me to murder that fair young maid they called Rose Connoley.

One night down there by the garden my love and I did meet,
And there we sat discoursing, till at length she fell asleep.
I had a bottle of merkley* wine, and this she did not know;
So there I poisoned my own true love, down there by the river below.

I ran my skeever through her — it was a bloody knife —
And threw her into the river — it was a shocking sight.
I threw her into the river, the worst now you may see,
For my name it is Patsey O'Railly, who murdered Rose Connoley.

My father has often told me that money would set me free,
If ever I murdered that fair young maid they call Rose Connoley,
My father may stand in his cottage door with many a watering eye,
And gaze upon his own dear son, swinging on the gallows high.

POOR ELLEN SMITH

While Peter Degraph states that he has been falsely accused of murdering his sweetheart, he really did — according to the verdict — shoot and kill her near Mount Airy, North Carolina. He was executed for the crime, and while he waited to be taken to the chair he called for a guitar and this song was composed and sung by him. So great was the feeling for and against Degraph that it had to be declared a misdemeanor for the song to be sung in a gathering of any size for the reason that it always fomented

---

* Error for Burgundy?

"Rose Connoley" was collected by John Harrington Cox from Mr. M. F. Morgan, Ravenswood, Jackson County, 1915. "It was popular in the oil fields of Wetzel County (West Virginia) about 1895." In Cox, *Folksongs of the South* (Harvard) Cambridge, 1925 (Dover reprint, 1967), p. 314. Without music. Laws, F6.

"Poor Ellen Smith" was recorded by Herbert Halpert from the singing of Mrs. W. L. Martin, Hillsville, Virginia, 1939. Library of Congress AFS record 2745B. Laws, F11.

a riot. The date of the murder is not given in this note drawn from Laws and from Ethel Park Richardson, *American Mountain Songs*, New York, 1927.

Come, all ye good people, my story to hear,
And what happened to me in June of last year.
It's of poor Ellen Smith and how she was found,
A ball through her heart, lying cold on the ground.

It's true I'm in jail a prisoner now,
But God is here with me and hears every vow.
Before Him I promise the truth to relate
And tell all I know of poor Ellen's sad fate.

The world of my story's no longer a part
But knows I was Ellen's own loving sweetheart,
They knew my intention was to make her my wife,
I loved her too dearly to take her sweet life.

I saw her on Monday before that sad day
They found her poor body and took her away;
That she had been killed had never entered my mind,
Till a ball through her heart they happened to find.

Oh, who was so cruel, so heartless, so base,
As to murder poor Ellen in such a lonesome place?
I saw her that morning so still and so cold,
And heard the wild stories the witnesses told.

I choked back my tears, for the people all said
That Peter Degraph had shot Ellen Smith dead!
My love is in her grave with her hand on her breast
The bloodhound and sheriffs would give me no rest.

They got their Winchesters and hunted me down,
But I was away in old Mount Airy town.
I stayed off a year and I prayed all the time
That the man might be found who committed the crime,

So I could come back and my character save
Ere the flowers had faded on poor Ellen's grave.
So I came back to Winston my trial to stand,
To live or to die as the law might command.

Ellen sleeps calmly in the lonely churchyard,
While I looked through the bars and God knows it's hard!
I know they will hang me, at least if they can,
But I know I will die an innocent man.

My soul will be free when I stand at the bar
Where God tries His cross, and there, like a star,
That shines in the night, with an innocent shine,
Oh, I do appeal to the Justice of Time!

ELLEN FLANNERY

Come all you people from every
   land,
And listen to my tale of woe;
I'll tell you of a terrible crime
Which happened not long ago.

Floyd Frazier is now in prison,
For the murder of the first degree,
He killed an innocent woman,
This world may plainly see.

He killed poor Ellen Flannery
And hid her in the wood,
And then ran to the nearest stream
To wash away the blood.

He crept into his cabin
And lay there all the night,
Believing his crime was hidden
From everybody's sight.

She had five little children
From door to door they ran,
To look for their poor mother,
But, alas, no mother came.

At last they all grew hungry
And they fell asleep,
To wake up in the morning
To cry and to weep.

The night being long and dreary
Until the break of dawn,
Her neighbors all did gather
To see what had been done.

They searched all around her cabin,
Went wandering up and down,
At last Joseph Williams found her,
And she was a dreadful wound.

He found her body lying,
Her soul had taken its flight,
The rocks that were piled upon her,
It was a terrible sight.

They took her to her cabin,
And there not long to stay,
And then into the graveyard
Until the Judgment Day.

"Ellen Flannery" was recorded by Herbert Halpert from the singing of Mrs. Goldie Hamilton, Hamiltontown, Virginia, 1939. Library of Congress AFS record 2782 B1, with stanzas 4 and 6 from the singing of Mrs. Martha Shupe, also of Hamiltontown, Library of Congress AFS record 2781 B. Laws, F19. Laws states that "the history of this ballad has not been traced."

This young man was arrested
And hurried to the jail;
The jury pronounced him guilty,
And would not allow him bail.

He owned that he did kill her
And all that he had done;
I think his case is dangerous,
For he has a risk to run.

They took him down to Pineville,
And there not long to dwell;
The crime he had committed
Will send his soul to hell.

FULLER AND WARREN

In January, 1820, Amasa Fuller killed Palmer Warren at Lawrenceburg, Dearborn County, Indiana. Fuller had courted "a young lady residing with her uncle in Lawrenceburg," but during his absence from town in November, she became engaged to Palmer Warren and was to have married him January tenth, the day of the fatal murder. Returning to Lawrenceburg, Fuller called on Warren, asked him to sign a written statement renouncing the girl and to admit in it that he had told falsehoods about Fuller. Warren refused, and Fuller — armed with two pistols — killed Warren with a single shot over the heart. Fuller was taken and, although the case was appealed to the Indiana supreme court, he was finally hanged. Unconfirmed tradition has it that the song was composed by Moses Whitecotton, a riming justice of the peace in Indiana. Whether there was any basis in fact for the statement that Fuller was already married or that the two doctors held the hanging rope in their hands after it had broken is uncertain. The balladist's detailed reference should perhaps be credited.

Ye sons of Columbia, your attention I do crave
While a sorrowful ditty I will tell
Which has happened here of late down in Indiana state
Of a hero but a few can excel.

Like Samson he courted the choice of the fair
And intended to make her his wife,
When like Delilah fair, she his heart did ensnare
And it cost him his honor and his life.

"Fuller and Warren" was collected by Miss Colquitt Newell from W. T. Street, Farmington, Missouri, 1912. In H. M. Belden, *Ballads and Songs Collected by the Missouri Folk-Lore Society*, Columbia, 1940 (reprint edition, 1966), p. 304. Without music. Laws, F16.

A gold ring he gave her as a token of true love,
And the flower was the image of a dove;
They mutually agreed to be married in speed,
And were promised by the powers above.

But this fickle-minded maid had promised to wed
Young Warren, a liver in the place;
With hearts full of woe and with sad overthrow
It ended in shame and disgrace.

When Fuller came to know he was deprived of his dear,
Which he'd promised by the powers to wed,
With his heart full of woe straight to Warren he did go
And smiling unto Warren he said:

"Oh, Warren, you have injured me to gratify your cause
By reporting that I'd lost a legal wife.
Now acknowledge that you've wronged me, before I break the law,
Or I will deprive you of your life."

Then Warren said to Fuller: "Your request must be denied,
For my heart to your true love is bound.
Oh, Fuller, I can say this is my wedding day
In spite of all your heroes in town."

Then Fuller, in a passion of love and anger bound,
Which at length caused many for to sigh,
With one fatal shot he killed Warren on the spot,
And smiling said, "I'm ready now to die."

Then Fuller was condemned by the honorable court
Of Lawrenceburg in Dearborn for to die,
The ignominious death to hang above the earth
Like Haman on the gallows so high.

When the morning came that brave Fuller was to die,
He smiled and bid the world adieu.
Like an angel he did stand, for he was a handsome man;
On his breast he wore a ribbon of blue.

Ten thousand spectators then smote upon their breasts,
And the guards dropped a tear from their eye,
Saying, "Cursed be she who has caused this misery;
In his stead she had ought for to die."

But the mighty God of love looked in anger from above,
And the rope flew asunder as the sands.
Two doctors for their prey they did murder, we might say,
For they hung him by the main strength of hand.

But his body was buried, and the doctors lost their prey,
And the lady deprived of her groom.
And his spirit it exalted above the starry skies,
While they silently lament their doom.

Of all the ancient history that I can understand,
Which we're bound by the scripture to believe,
Bad women are essentially the downfall of man,
As Adam was beguiled by Eve.

So, young men, beware, be cautious and be wise
Of such women when you're courting for wives.
Look in Genesis, and Judges, and in Samuel, Kings, and Job,
And the truth of the doctrine you'll find.

For marriage is a lottery and few gain the prize
That's both pleasing to the heart and to the eye.
So those who never marry may well be called wise.
So, gentlemen, excuse me; goodbye.

MARY WYATT AND HENRY GREEN

Louis C. Jones thoroughly reports the background of this murder ballad
which, in essence, deals with the murder by poisoning (opium and arsenic)
by Henry Green, the black sheep of a prominent Rensselaer County, New
York family, of his wife of ten days, Mary Wyatt. She was a child in a
family of eighteen, had gone to Lowell, Massachusetts, to work in the mills,
and then joined a company of traveling temperance players, producing in
Massachusetts and New York *The Reformed Drunkard*. Green joined the
company of players, and a quick courtship culminated in marriage on

"Mary Wyatt and Henry Green" was recorded by Helen Hartness Flanders from the singing
of Elmer George, North Montpelier, Vermont, 1935. Reported by Louis C. Jones, with
added notes by Phillips Barry, in *Bulletin of the Folksong Society of the Northeast*, Cambridge, Mass., 12 (1937):14–18. The last three stanzas in brackets from the same article
and reprinted there from Helen Hartness Flanders and George Brown, *Folk-Songs and
Ballads of Vermont* (Stephen Daye Press) Brattleboro, 1931, p. 67. Laws, F14.

February 10, 1845. Green's mother remonstrated with her son for having married beneath him, and a former sweetheart, Alzina Godfrey, may have done or said something shortly after the marriage which made Green regret his act. In any event, the poisoning began, and on the nineteenth Mary Wyatt died after forty-eight hours of pathetic agony. Green left obvious trails of his murderous activity, was arrested, tried, and sentenced to death by Judge Amasa J. Parker. He was hanged on the tenth day of September, 1845.

Come, listen to my tragedy, good people, young and old;
An awful story you shall hear, 'twill make your blood run cold;
Concerning a fair damsel; Mary Wyatt was her name —
She was poisoned by her husband, and he hung for the same.

Mary Wyatt she was beautiful, not of a high degree,
And Henry Green was wealthy, as you may plainly see;
He said, "My dearest Mary, if you'll become my wife,
I will guard you and protect you through all this gloom of life."

"O Henry, I would marry you, I would give my consent,
But before that we'd been married long, I fear you would repent;
Before that we'd been married long, you'd make me a disgrace,
Because I'm not as rich as you, which ofttimes is the case."

"O Mary, dearest Mary, how can you grieve me so?
I'll vow and 'clare by all that's fair, I always will prove true;
But unless you consent to become my wife, you'll surely end my life,
For no longer do I wish to live, unless you are my wife."

Believing what he said was true, she then became his wife,
But little did she think, poor girl, that he would end her life;
O little did she think, poor child, and little did she explain [expect]
That he would end her precious life (he'd just sworn to protect).

They had not been married but a week or two, when she was taken ill,
Great doctors were sent for, to try their powerful skill;
Great doctors were sent for, but none of them could save,
And soon it was proclaimed she must go to her grave.

O when her brothers heard of this, straightway to her did go,
Saying, "Sister dear, you're dying, the doctors tell us so";
Saying, "Sister dear, you're dying, your life is at an end";
Saying, "Haven't you been poisoned by the one you call your friend?"

"I'm on my deathbed lying, I know that I must die,
I know I'm going before my God, and the truth I won't deny;
I know my Henry's poisoned me — dear brothers, for him send,
For I love him now as dearly as when he was my friend."

When Henry heard those tidings, straightway to his wife to see,
Saying, "Mary, my dearest Mary, was you ever deceived in me?"
Three times she called "Dear Henry," then, and sank into a swoon;
He gazed on her indifferently, and in silence left the room.

"Now Henry has deceived me, — how my poor heart is wrung!
But when I'm dead and buried, O don't have poor Henry hung!
I freely have forgiven him —" and she turned upon her side;
"In Heaven meet me, Henery!" and she sweetly smiled and died.

[An inquest on her body held according to our laws,
And soon by them it was proclaimed that arsenic was the cause.
Young Henry Green was sent for, locked up in Troy jail,
There to await his trial; the court would not take bail.

[Young Henry Green was sent for and called upon the stand,
To answer for the blackest deed committed in our land;
He said that he was innocent; her friends he did defy;
He said that he was innocent, although it had been tried.

[Judge Baker read the sentence; he appeared to be unmoved.
Judge Baker read the sentence; he said he must be hung:
He said, "When autumn leaves turn pale and summer days have fled
He, too, must close his youthful life, and slumber with the dead."]

THE ASHLAND TRAGEDY

This song was composed by Elijah Adams in Ashland, Kentucky. The crime which it relates was the murder of two Gibbons children, Fannie and Robert, and a Miss Emma Charcoola, who was staying with them. The

Version 1 of "The Ashland Tragedy" was collected by John Harrington Cox from Mrs. Hannah Bradshaw, Matewan, Mingo County, Kentucky, 1918. In Cox, *Folksongs of the South* (Harvard) Cambridge, 1925 (Dover reprint, 1967), pp. 189–191. Without music. Laws, F25.

perpetrators of the deed were George Ellis, William Neal, and Ellis Craft. George Ellis was hanged by a mob, and the other two, having been tried and convicted, were hanged by the sheriff. The crime took place in the early 1880's, and Craft and Neal were hanged in 1884. The hanging took place at Grayson, Carter County, Kentucky. At the time of the execution "Lige" Adams had a *stack* of printed ballads, stood on a big rock, and sold them as fast as three men could pass them out.

"The people of Mt. Sterling" are brought into the first variant because the prisoners were at one time removed there to protect them from the lynch mob.

I

Dear Father, Mother, Sister, come listen while I tell
All about the Ashland tragedy, of which you know full well.
'Twas in the town of Ashland, all on that deadly night,
A horrible crime was committed, but soon was brought to light.

Three men who did the murder, was Craft, Ellis, and Neal;
They thought the crime they had concealed, but God the same revealed.
George Ellis, one of the weakest, who could not bear the pain,
To J. B. Powell, trembling, revealed the horrid stain.

Ellis Craft, who was the leader, and had an iron heart,
Caused a son and two lovely daughters from their mother's embrace to part.
Poor Neal, he may be innocent, but, from what George Ellis tells,
The crime he has committed will send his soul to hell.

He dragged poor Emma from her bed and threw her on the floor,
Crushed her head with an iron bar, her blood did run in gore.
In my own imagination I can see her little hands
Upheld, crying for mercy, murdered by cruel hands.

Those little white hands so tender, upheld in prayer to him,
Falls useless at her bleeding side, her eyes in death grow dim.
Craft committed the same offence, and murdered the other two;
While their forms were cold in death, Craft says, "What shall we do?"

Then Neal proposed to burn them up, to hide their bloody stain,
While some other three might arrested be, and them not bear the blame.
Then, in tones of thunder, Craft told Ellis to get to camp,
And pour oil on the children, while they stood with bloody hands.

694

Then Craft he lit a match and touched it to their clothes,
The flame loomed up with melting heat, and away the wretches goes.
Then off they went, I have no doubt, as fast as they could go,
And thought no one their bloody crime would ever, ever know.

Then early next morning the town in mourning wept,
To see the children's burning forms, the sight they can't forget:
Such screams and bitter weeping of friends that stood around,
Their heartstrings torn and bleeding, tears falling to the ground.

Poor little Robert Gibbons, a helpless orphan child,
Died in defence of his sister; to her he was loving and mild.
For their three forms are buried, they sleep beneath the sod,
Murdered while defending their ventures, and their souls are at rest with
    God.

At rest in the golden city, where God himself gives light,
Where crystal streams are flowing, in the city where there is no night;
They're with the white-robed angels, whose harps are made of gold,
Whose crowns are set with brilliant stars, forever in the dear Lord's hold.

There is one thing yet I do remember well:
Major Allen with his bloody hounds caused tears and tide to swell;
They hovered round those dreadful fiends that sent death knell through
    town,
Caused other friends from friends to part; for hell such men are bound.

The people of Mt. Sterling, who rate themselves so high,
Ought to be in favor of justice and say that he should die.
I suppose they have forgotten that they have daughters too,
And law and right should be their aim, to protect their children too.

May law and justice be dealt out, and spread from plain to plain,
And in the future day enjoy a moral land again!
Now all dear fathers and mothers, a warning take by this,
Stay at home with your children, and guard against crimes like this.

Remember the advice I give you is from a true and loving heart;
I hope you'll take its earnest heed, from its teachings never part.
Remember the world is wicked, no mortal you can trust;
Trust God, who is all wisdom and doeth all things just.

II

Dear mothers, fathers, sisters, come listen while I tell
All about the Ashland tragedy, of which you know full well.
It was in the town of Ashland, one long and dreadful night,
A horrible crime committed and soon was brought to light.

The men who did the murder was George Ellis, Craft and Neill,
They thought their crime they did conceal, but God the same revealed.
Poor Neill, he may be innocent from what George Ellis says,
The crime that he committed will send his soul to hell.

He drug poor Emmy from her bed, and threw her on the floor,
And crushed her head with an iron bar, her blood did run in gore.
In my own imagination I can see her little white hands
Upheld and crying for mercy, and murdered by cruel hands.

Then Neill committed the same offense and murdered the other two;
Then Craft composed to burn them up to hide their bloody sin,
Lest some of the three might arrested be, and them not bear the blame.
Then off they went, I have no doubt, as fast as they could go,
And thought no one this bloody crime could ever, ever know.

Then early next morning the town in mourning wept,
To see the children's burning forms, a sight you can't forget.
Such screams and bitter weeping from friends who stood around,
With heartstrings torn, and bleeding, tears was falling to the ground.

For little Robert Gibbon, the helpless orphan child,
Died in the defense of his sister, to her was love and mild.
Now these three forms are buried, they sleep beneath the sod,
Murdered by the defense of virtue, their souls at rest with God.

At rest in the Golden City, where God himself gives light,
Where the crystal streams are flowing in the City where there is no night.
They're with the white-robed angels, whose harps are made with gold,
Whose crowns are thick with brilliant stars, forever in the dear Lord's fold.

George Ellis was taken by a mob force, and justly got his doom,
. . . . works of all, could not refuse a tomb.
The children will be angels, take wings and fly away;
While the other three will demons be, confined in Hell to stay.

Version II of "The Ashland Tragedy" was recorded by Herbert Halpert from the singing of
Joe Hubbard, Hamiltontown, Virginia. Library of Congress AFS record 2825 A1. Laws, F25.

THE PEDDLER AND HIS WIFE

According to Fuson, the couple were robbed and murdered on Martin's Fork, of the Cumberland River, Harlan County, Kentucky, about 1905.

> One day the sun was rising high,
> A day in merry June;
> The birds set singing on a tree,
> All Nature seems in tune.
>
> A peddler and his wife were traveling
> Along a lonely way,
> A-sharing each other's toil and care,
> They both were old and gray.
>
> They were laboring, toiling hard,
> A living for to make;
> They did not know, nor did they think,
> They there their lives would take.
>
> Just as the wagon came along,
> Shots rang out upon the air;
> And, while the echo died away,
> Terrible was the experience there.
>
> His wife pitched out upon the ground
> And tossed her dying head;
> The men rushed up to take her gold,
> Poor lady, she was dead.
>
> The horse rushed on the dying man,
> Till kind friends checked his speed.
> Alas, alas, it was too late
> To stop this horrible deed.
>
> Now they are sleeping in their tomb,
> Their souls have gone above,
> Where thieves disturb them now no more,
> For all is peace and love.

"The Peddler and His Wife" was collected by Harvey H. Fuson from Milt Unthank. In Fuson, *Ballads of the Kentucky Highlands*, London, 1931, p. 116. Without music.

THE MURDER OF GOINS

Pretending to help Goins, Boggs leads him to his death at the hands of bandits. Goins was possibly a horse trader who made trips along the Clinch and Powell Rivers in Virginia. The date of the murder is not known.

Come all you young people
That live far and near,
And I'll tell you of some murder
That was done on the nine-mile
    spur.

They surrounded poor Goins,
But Goins got away,
He went to Ely Boggs',
He went there to stay.

Ely Boggs he foreknew him,
His life he did betray,
Saying, "Come and go with me,
And I'll show you an highway."

Quickly they started up the
    nine-mile spur,
Boys, they made no delay,
Till they came to the crossroads,
Where Goins they did slay.

When they got in hearing,
They were lying by the field,
"Your money's what we're after,
And Goins we will kill."

When they got in gunshot,
They bid him for to stand;
"Your money's what we're after,
Your life is in our hands."

"Sweet heaven, sweet heaven,"
How loud he did cry,
"To think of my companion,
And now I have to die."

When the gun did fire,
It caused his horse to run,
The bullet failed to kill him,
George struck him with his gun.

After they had killed him,
With him they would not stay,
They drank up all his whiskey
And then they rode away.

His wife she was sent for,
She made no delay;
She found his grave dug
Along by the way.

Oh, kill a man for riches
Or any such a thing!
I pray the Lord have mercy
Till Judgment kills the same.

"Sweet heaven, sweet heaven,"
We heard her to mourn,
"Here lies his poor body,
Where is his poor soul [gone]?"

"The Murder of Goins" was recorded by Herbert Halpert from the singing of Finley and James Taylor Adams, Dunham, Kentucky, 1939. Library of Congress AFS record 2771 A1. Laws, F22.

NAOMI WISE

Come all you young people, a story I will tell
About a maid they called Naomi Wise;
Her face was fair and handsome, she was loved by everyone,
In Randolph County now her body lies.

They say she had a lover, young Lewis was his name,
Each evening he would have her by his side
She learned to love and trust him, and she believed his words,
He told her she was soon to be his bride.

One summer night he met her and took her for a ride,
She thought that she was going to be wed,
They came to old Deep River and so the story goes,
"You have met your doom," these words the villain said.

She begged him just to spare her, the villain only laughed,
They say that he was heartless to the core,
And in the stream he threw her below the old mill dam
And sweet Naomi's smile was seen no more.

Next day they found her body a-floating down the stream
And all the folks for miles around did cry,
Young Lewis left the country, they fetched him back again,
But they could not prove that he caused her to die.

They say that on his deathbed young Lewis did confess
And said that he had killed Naomi Wise,
And now they know her spirit still lingers round the place
To save the young girls from some villain's lies.

Young people, all take warning, and listen while I say,
You must take care before it is too late,
Don't listen to the story some villain's tongue will tell
Or you are sure to meet Naomi's fate.

"Naomi Wise" was recorded by Vance Randolph from the singing of Mrs. Lillian Short at
Galena, Missouri, 1941. Library of Congress record LP12. Laws, F31.

THE DEATH OF SAMUEL ADAMS

In the state of old Kentucky,
One cold and stormy night,
A horrible crime was committed
And later brought to light.

A man was cruelly murdered,
Samuel Adams was his name.
His body cut to pieces,
They accused Joe Schuster's gang.

He left his home one morning,
Employment to seek,
And told his loving family
He'd just be gone one week.

He went down to Auxier,
One week he went to stay,
But little did he think
It was his fatal day.

Alas, he went to sleep.
That night while he lay on his bed,
They crept into his room
And knocked him on the head.

They cut and maimed his body
Most frightful to behold,
And hid him on the river banks
Down in the sand so cold.

His friends soon grew uneasy
And searched for him in vain,
From Jacks Creek down to Auxier,
But nothing could they gain.

At last the Lord with power,
He showed what He could do,
And sent a swirling flood
To wash him into view.

His body was discovered
And placed beneath the clay,
Where peacefully he may sleep
Until the Judgment Day.

Joe Schuster was arrested,
Also his foreign band
For killing Samuel Adams
And burying him in the sand.

They placed them in the county jail,
There to remain awhile.
In the hands of law and justice,
They all must stand their trial.

Their faces all grew pale
As the jury did file in,
And judge he read the verdict:
A life in the Frankfort pen.

"The Death of Samuel Adams" was collected by the Federal Music Project, Works Progress Administration (WPA), Floyd County, Kentucky, ca. 1937. Edith F. James, Supervisor for Floyd County. Ms., with music, in the Archive of Folk Song, Library of Congress. Laws, dF62.

ELLA SPEED

It was on the twenty-first day of December,
The man was tall and slender,
The man begin to call on Ella Speed,
And the next day she begin to show him around.

Ella had a .45,
So it wouldn't give one never-mind;
Ella's man had a Colt .41,
Never thought it would bring her to the burying ground.

Bring out your rubber-tired hearse, your rubber-tired hack,
Everybody in the hack, bring her mother back;
Ella's mother begin to weep and cry:
"The onliest daughter I had, now she's dead and gone.

"See, see what, see what Ella's man have done,
See what, see what Ella's man have done,
See what, see what, see what Ella's man have done,
Killed my daughter with a smoking .41."

All the people got the news in St. Louis,
All went home and dressed in red,
Went on down to tell Ella's friends,
Said, "Ella Speed is dead and in her grave."

Ella spoke one word before she died
("He killed my darling little child"),
Cried, "When you bury me, won't you bury me in a cave,
So I won't have so long to lay?"

"Ella Speed" was recorded by John A. Lomax from the singing of Tricky Sam, State Penitentiary, Huntsville, Texas, 1934. Library of Congress AFS record 215 B2. Laws, I6.

Outlaws and Bad Men

I was born in Boston, a city you all know well,
Brought up by honest parents, the truth to you I'll tell,
Brought up by honest parents, and reared most tenderly,
Till I became a sporting man at the age of twenty-three.

MULBERRY MOUNTAIN

As I was going over Mulberry Mountain,
I met Captain Evans and his money he was counting;
Oh, first I drew my pistol and then I drew my rapier,
Saying, "Deliver up your money, for I am a bold receiver."

Mush a ring a ding a day,
Right toor a noddy-o,
Right toor a noddy-o,
There's whiskey in the bar.

Oh, when I got my money it was a pretty penny,
I put it in my pocket and I carried it home to Molly;
She swore by her Maker that she never would deceive me,
But the devil's in the women, for they never can be easy.

Next morning when I woke, between six and seven,
Surrounded by strong guards and among them Captain Evans;
She'd unloaded both my pistols and loaded them with water,
And in prison chains they bound me and they carried me to the slaughter.

Now I have two brothers and they are in the army,
One he is in Cork and the other in Killarney;
And if I had them here I'd be jovial, brisk and jolly,
For I'd sooner have them here this night than you, deceiving Molly.

"Mulberry Mountain" was recorded by Alan Lomax from the singing of Mrs. Carrie Grover of Gorham, Maine, at Washington, D.C., 1941. Library of Congress AFS record 4452 A1. Laws, L13A.

DICK TURPIN AND BLACK BESS,
or My Bonnie Black Bess

Dick Turpin, the notorious highwayman, was born in Hempstead in Essex in 1706 and in his youth began a career of crime with brutal robberies of lonely farmhouses, torturing with a gang of robbers the farmers and their families to discover where valuables were hidden. With the hanging of two members of the gang, Turpin joined with Tom King, a highwayman on the Cambridge road. On one of their forays, they stole a horse from a Mr. Major in Epping Forest and were traced through it to the Red Lion in Whitechapel. About to be arrested, Turpin fired at the constable but missed and killed his companion. With bloodhounds on his trail, Turpin escaped to Long Sutton and thence to Yorkshire, where he engaged in horse trading. Shortly thereafter he was committed to York Castle on suspicion of stealing a black mare and foal. He was tried, found guilty and sentenced to death. He ascended the scaffold on April 7, 1739, and met his death with courage at the age of thirty-three. The legend of his ride from London to York in ten hours is considered apocryphal and owes its existence to an exciting account in Harrison Ainsworth's novel *Rookwood*, published in 1834. Ainsworth presumably transferred to Dick Turpin the story of an actual ride made by the highwayman "Swift Nick" in 1676. To establish an alibi following a robbery, "Swift Nick" rode from Gadshill to York, a distance of 190 miles, in fifteen hours.

> When fortune's blind goddess had shied my abode,
> And friends proved unfaithful, I took to the road
> To plunder the wealthy, to relieve my distress,
> And to aid me I bought you, my bonnie black Bess.
>
> How still you would stand when some carriage I'd stopped,
> While I picked up the jewels its inmates had dropped;
> I ne'er robbed a poor man or did I distress
> The widow or orphan, my bonnie black Bess.

"Dick Turpin and Black Bess" was recorded from the singing of William Jacob Morgan, Berlin, Wisconsin, 1946, by the University of Wisconsin Recording Project under the direction of Leland Coon. Library of Congress AFS record 8386 B1. Laws, L9.

When sable's black midnight her mantle had spread
O'er the fair face of nature, how softly you'd tread;
Through fate or good fortune, though an unwelcome guest,
We took millions of fortune, my bonnie black Bess.

When Arden's famed justice did me hotly pursue,
From London to York Town like lightning you flew;
No tollgate could stop you, broad rivers you'd breast,
You took me in ten hours, my bonnie black Bess.

Ill fate now comes o'er me and oppressed is my lot,
The law now pursues me for the man that I shot;
To save me, dear Bessie, you did do your best,
You're worn out and weary, my bonnie black Bess.

Hark, the bloodhounds approacheth but they never can catch
A beast like you, Bessie, so gallant, so brave;
You must die, my dear friend, though it does me oppress;
Lie there, I have shot you, my bonnie black Bess.

In future's bright ages when I'm dead and gone,
My story will be handed from father to son;
Though some they may pity, yet they all must confess
'Twas in kindness I shot you, my bonnie black Bess.

Now I'll climb yonder sapling so stately and tall,
And there I'll await the swift, fatal ball;
I'll die like a man and I'll soon be at rest,
Fare-thee-well now forever, my bonnie black Bess.

THE WILD COLLOINA* BOY

I'll tell you of a wild Colloina boy, Jack Dollard was his name;
He was born in Erin's sunny isle, in a place called Castlemaine.

* Colonial.

"The Wild Colloina Boy" was collected, with music, from Mrs. Lyons, Belding, Michigan, 1934, who learned the song from her son, who had heard it some years earlier in a lumber camp near Cadillac, Michigan. In Emelyn Elizabeth Gardner and Geraldine Jencks Chickering, *Ballads and Songs of Southern Michigan* (University of Michigan Press) Ann Arbor, 1939, p. 326. Laws, L20.

He was his father's only pride, his master's only joy,
And dearly did his parents love their wild Colloina boy.

When Jack was scarcely sixteen years, he left his native home,
And to Australia's sunny shore was much inclined to roam;
He robbed the wealthy squire; he stabbed Jack McCrory,
And trembling did they hand out their gold to the wild Colloina boy.

He bid the wealthy squires adieu and told them to beware,
For never to harm an honest lad while dealing on the square,
Or never deprive a mother of her pride and only joy,
For fear her mind would go wandering like the wild Colloina boy.

When Jack was scarcely eighteen years he began his wild career,
With a heart that knew no danger and a spirit that feared no fear.
He robbed the rich and helped the poor; the prairie he did destroy;
A terror to Australia was the wild Colloina boy.

One morning on the prairie as Jack he rode along,
A-listening to the mockingbirds as they sang a lofty song,
When up rode three mounted troopers, Kelly, David and Fitzroy,
They hollered, "Halt! Let's capture him, the wild Colloina boy!

"Surrender now, young Dolan, you are a plundering son,
Surrender now in the Queen's high name, for you see there's three to one."
He drew a pistol from each side and waved them up on high,
"I'll fight but never surrender," cried the wild Colloina boy.

He fired a shot at Kelly that brought him to the ground
And in return from David received a fatal wound;
Then a bullet pierced his proud young heart from the pistol of Fitzroy,
And that's the way they captured him, the wild Colloina boy.

BOLD JACK DONAHUE

> Come all you jolly highwaymen and outlaws of the land,
> Whose kind do live in slavery or wear a convict's brand;

"Bold Jack Donahue" was recorded by Charles L. Todd and Robert Sonkin from the singing of Cotton Davis, FSA camp, Shafter, California, 1940. Library of Congress AFS record 5103 B. Somewhat garbled text, reconstructed by reference to Robert W. Gordon, "Old Songs That Men Have Sung," *Adventure Magazine*, May 15, 1927, p. 190. Laws, L22.

Attention pay to what I say and value it if you do,
While I relate the natural fate of bold Jack Donahue.

This bold adopted highwayman, as you may understand,
Transported was by a cruel fate from Ireland's happy land,
From Dublin town of wide reknown where his first breath he drew,
His deeds of honor entitled him to "Bold Jack Donahue."

When he effected his escape, to rob he went straightway,
The people were afraid of him to travel night or day;
For every day in the newspapers they read of something new
Concerning this bold highwayman called Bold Jack Donahue.

Bold Donahue and his comrades rode out one afternoon,
Not thinking of the hands of death that might assail them soon;
But the cursed police to their surprise they quickly rode in view,
And in quick turn they did advance to take Bold Donahue.

Bold Donahue to his comrades: "If you prove true to me now,
Will Wright, McClellan, Bill Collins and also Winselow,
Be willing, be bold, be upright, be legally firm and true,
This day we'll gain our liberty," said Bold Jack Donahue.

"Oh, no," said cowardly Winselow, "to that we won't agree,
For, you see, there are fifteen of them and it's best for us to flee,
For if we stay we'll lose the day and the battle we will rue . . ."
"Be gone from me, you cowardly dog!" said Bold Jack Donahue.

The sergeant unto Donahue, "Put down your car-a-bine.
Do you intend to fight us, or unto us resign?"
"To surrender to such cowardly dogs is something I never would do,
I'll fight this day until I die," said Bold Jack Donahue.

The sergeant and the corporal their men they did divide,
While some rode in behind him and others at his side;
The sergeant fired at him and the people fired, too,
They fired a-many a round at Bold Jack Donahue.

Nine men he forced to bite the dust before the fatal ball
Had pierced the heart of Donahue which caused him for to fall;
And when he closed his trembling eyes, he bid this world adieu,
Dear Christians all, pray for the soul of Bold Jack Donahue.

BRENNAN ON THE MOOR

It is of a fearless Irishman a story I will tell,
His name was William Brennan, in Ireland he did dwell;
It was on the Calvert mountains he began his wild career,
Where many a wealthy gentleman he caused to shake with fear.

    Oh, young Brennan on the moor, young Brennan on the moor,
    Brave and undaunted stood young Brennan on the moor.

A brace of loaded pistols he carried with him each day,
He never robbed a poor man upon the king's highway;
For what he'd taken from the rich, like Turpin and Black Bess,
He always did divide it with a widow in distress.

One night he robbed an Irishman by the name of Jubr Bawn,
They traveled on together till the day began to dawn;
Then Jubr found his money gone, likewise his watch and chain,
Then he at once encountered him and robbed him back again.

When Willie found the packman was as good a man as he,
He took him on the highway his companion for to be;
The packman threw away his pack without any more delay,
And he proved a faithful comrade all on the king's highway.

One day upon the highway as Willie passed along,
He met the mayor of Cashel just one mile from the town;
The mayor knew his features, "I think, young man" said he,
"That your name is William Brennan, you must come along with me."

Now Willie's wife she being in town, provisions for to buy,
When she saw her Willie taken she began to weep and cry.
"Oh, hand to me the tenpenny," these words to her he spoke;
She handed him a blunderbuss from underneath her cloak.

"Brennan on the Moor" was recorded by Alan Lomax from the singing of Mrs. Carrie Grover of Gorham, Maine, at Washington, D.C., 1941. Library of Congress AFS record 4452 B3. Stanzas 8, 9, and 11 supplied from the singing of William J. Morgan, Berlin, Wisconsin, as collected by the University of Wisconsin Recording Project under the direction of Leland Coon. Library of Congress AFS record 8387 A. Mrs. Grover's version, with very slight textual variations from her oral recording, appears also in her *Heritage of Songs* (privately printed, Gould Academy, Bethel, Maine, n.d.), pp. 129–130. Laws, L7.

It's with a loaded blunderbuss, the truth I will unfold,
He made the mayor tremble and robbed him of his gold;
One hundred pounds he offered for his apprehension there,
And he with horse and saddle to the mountain did repair.

Now Brennan he's an outlaw all on the mountain side.
With infantry and cavalry to catch him they did try,
But he only laughed at them, until I've heard it said,
By a false-hearted female he was brutally betrayed.

It was on Tipperary, a place they called Shammore,
Where Brennan and his comrade that day did suffer sore;
They laid themselves down on the grass that grew amid the field,
And it's many a one received a wound before they did yield.

At length he was taken prisoner and in irons he was bound,
He was taken into Clonmore jail where strong walls did him surround;
The jury found him guilty, the judge made this reply,
"For robbery on the king's highway, young Brennan, you must die."

"Farewell, my little family, my wife and children three.
There is my poor old father who will shed tears for me,
Likewise my tender mother, as she wrung her hands and cried,
'Oh, would to God that Willie had within his cradle died!' "

Oh, young Brennan on the moor, young Brennan on the moor,
Brave and undaunted stood young Brennan on the moor.

CAPTAIN KIDD

Captain William Kidd was arrested in Boston in 1699, was returned to England for trial at the Old Bailey for murder and piracy on the high seas, and was hanged at Execution Dock, London, on May 23, 1701. The original broadside of twenty-two stanzas appeared in 1701, and was reprinted in C. H. Firth, *Naval Songs and Ballads* (Publications of the Navy Records Society, vol. 32), London, 1908. [Note from Laws, K35]

"Captain Kidd" was recorded by Sidney Robertson Cowell from the singing of Mrs. Carrie Grover of Gorham, Maine, at Teaneck, New Jersey, 1941. Library of Congress AFS record 4697 A1. Text supplemented with traditional stanzas. Laws, K35.

You captains brave and bold, hear our cries, hear our cries,
You captains brave and bold, hear our cries.
You captains brave and bold, though you seem uncontrolled,
Don't for the sake of gold lose your souls, lose your souls,
Don't for the sake of gold lose your souls.

Oh, my name was Robert Kidd as I sailed, as I sailed,
Oh, my name was Robert Kidd as I sailed.
My name was Robert Kidd and God's laws I did forbid,
And most wickedly I did as I sailed, as I sailed,
And most wickedly I did as I sailed.

Oh, my parents taught me well as I sailed, as I sailed,
Oh, my parents taught me well as I sailed.
Oh, my parents taught me well to shun the gates of hell,
But against them I rebelled as I sailed, as I sailed,
But against them I rebelled as I sailed.

I'd a Bible in my hand as I sailed, as I sailed,
I'd a Bible in my hand as I sailed.
I'd a Bible in my hand at my father's great command,
And I sunk it in the sand as I sailed, as I sailed,
And I sunk it in the sand as I sailed.

I murdered William Moore as I sailed, as I sailed,
I murdered William Moore as I sailed.
I murdered William Moore and left him in his gore,
Not many leagues from shore as I sailed.
Not many leagues from shore as I sailed.

And being cruel still as I sailed, as I sailed,
And being cruel still as I sailed,
And being cruel still, my gunner I did kill,
And his precious blood did spill as I sailed, as I sailed,
And his precious blood did spill as I sailed.

My mate took sick and died as I sailed, as I sailed,
My mate took sick and died as I sailed.
My mate took sick and died, which me much terrified,
When he called me to his bedside as I sailed, as I sailed,
When he called me to his bedside as I sailed.

And unto me did say, "See me die, see me die,"
And unto me did say, "See me die."
And unto me did say, "Take warning now by me,
There comes a reckoning day, you must die, you must die,
There comes a reckoning day, you must die."

I was sick and nigh to death as I sailed, as I sailed,
I was sick and nigh to death as I sailed.
I was sick and nigh to death, and I vowed at every breath
To walk in wisdom's ways as I sailed, as I sailed,
To walk in wisdom's ways as I sailed.

My repentance lasted not as I sailed, as I sailed,
My repentance lasted not as I sailed.
My repentance lasted not, my vows I soon forgot,
Damnation's my just lot as I sailed, as I sailed,
Damnation's my just lot as I sailed.

I steered from sound to sound as I sailed, as I sailed,
I steered from sound to sound as I sailed.
I steered from sound to sound, and many ships I found,
And most of them I burned as I sailed, as I sailed,
And most of them I burned as I sailed.

I spied three ships from Spain as I sailed, as I sailed,
I spied three ships from Spain as I sailed.
I spied three ships from Spain, I fired on the main
Till most of them were slain as I sailed, as I sailed,
Till most of them were slain as I sailed.

Then fourteen ships I saw as I sailed, as I sailed.
Then fourteen ships I saw as I sailed.
Then fourteen ships I saw and brave men they all were,
And they were too much for me as I sailed, as I sailed,
And they were too much for me as I sailed.

To Newgate I am cast, I must die, I must die,
To Newgate I am cast, I must die.
To Newgate I am cast with a sad and heavy heart,
To receive my just desert I must die, I must die,
To receive my just desert I must die.

To Execution Dock I must go, I must go,
To Execution Dock I must go,
To Execution Dock will many thousands flock,
But I must bear the shock, I must die, I must die,
But I must bear the shock, I must die.

Take warning now by me, I must die, I must die,
Take warning now by me, I must die.
Take warning now by me and shun bad company
Lest you come to hell with me, I must die, I must die,
Lest you come to hell with me, I must die.

SAM HALL

Tradition would have it that Sam Hall was in actuality a waif who had been
sold for a guinea to a chimney sweeper and who had worked for him until
some untimely adventure brought him to the gallows. (Let us remember
that boys of eleven were hanged in London for stealing a loaf of bread.) In
any event, the song, composed and promoted by a music hall "artist" in
the late eighteenth century, was extraordinarily well accepted and passed
into tradition. The text which follows is a composite of four drawn from
the Robert W. Gordon manuscript collection in the Archive of Folk Song,
the Library of Congress. Sandburg's and Lomax's texts are closely related.
For a classic study of "Samuel Hall's Family Tree" see the article by
Bertrand H. Bronson in the *California Folklore Quarterly*, 1 (1942): 47–
64, where he relates the stanzaic form to "Captain Kidd" and "Wondrous
Love" (both of them here) and otherwise traces the music and textual
forms.

My name is Samuel Hall, Samuel Hall,
My name is Samuel Hall, and I hate you one and all,
You're a bunch of muckers all, damn your hides, damn your hides.

I killed a man they said, so they said,
I killed a man they said when I hit him on the head,
And I left him there for dead, damn his hide, damn his hide.

They put me in the quod, in the quod,
They put me in the quod, and they left me there to rot,
That they did, so help me God, damn their hides, damn their hides.

The parson he did come, he did come,
The parson he did come, and he looked so god damn glum
When he talked of Kingdom Come, damn his hide, damn his hide.

The sheriff he came too, he came too,
The sheriff he came too, with his boys all dressed in blue,
They're a bunch of muckers, too, damn their hides, damn their hides.

To the gallows I must go, I must go,
To the gallows I must go, and I'll meet my friends below,
They'll say, "Sam, I told you so." Damn their hides, damn their hides.

And now I hear the bell, hear the bell,
And now I hear the bell, it's the signal for my knell,
So I'll meet you all in hell, damn your hides, damn your hides.

THE BOSTON BURGLAR

I was born in Boston, a city you all know well,
Brought up by honest parents, the truth to you I'll tell;
Brought up by honest parents, and reared most tenderly,
Till I became a sporting man, at the age of twenty-three.

My character was taken, and I was sent to jail,
My friends thought it was in vain to get me out on bail;
The jury proved me guilty, the clerk he wrote it down,
The judge he passed my sentence: it was off for Charles Town.

They put me on an east-bound train one cold December day,
And every station that I passed I heard the people say:
"There goes that Boston Burglar! for iron bars he's bound,
For some bad crime or other he's off for Charles Town."

If you could have seen my father, a-pleading at the bar,
Likewise my aged mother, a-pulling out her hair,
A-pulling out those old gray locks, while tears were streaming down:
"My darling boy, what have you done, that you're off for Charles Town?"

"The Boston Burglar" was collected by Mr. C. R. Bishop, Green Bank, Pocahontas County, West Virginia, 1917, from Miss Leone Oliver, who learned it from companions in high school. In John Harrington Cox, *Folk Songs of the South* (Harvard) Cambridge, Mass., 1925 (Dover reprint, 1967), pp. 296–297.

Young people who have your liberty, pray keep it as long as you can,
And don't go prowling round the streets to break the laws of man,
For if you do you'll surely lose, and find yourself like me,
Serving out twenty-one years in the penitentiary.

There lives a girl in Boston, a girl I love so well,
And e'er I gain my liberty, along with her I'll dwell;
And e'er I gain my liberty, bad company I'll shun;
Adieu to all bad company! adieu to all bad rum!

Frank James, *the Roving Gambler*

I was raised up in Louisville, a town you all knew well,
Raised up by honest parents, to you the truth I'll tell,
Raised up by honest parents most kind and tenderly,
Until I came a drinking man at the age of twenty-three.

'S I used to be a poor boy and I worked up on the square,
I learned to pocket money and I did not take it fair,
'S I worked out day by day and at night I'd rob and steal,
So when I'd make a great big haul, how happy I would feel.

As I used to ride a big bay horse and drive the buggy fine,
'S I courted a lady and I often called her mine,
'S I courted her for beauty and to me love was great,
For when she saw me coming she'd meet me at the gate.

One night when I lay sleeping, I dreamed a frightful dream,
'S I dreamed I was in Asheville on some clear (?) purple stream,
My friends had all forsaken me, no one to go my bail,
As I woke up broken-hearted in Hawthorne's County Jail.

Around came the jailer about ten o'clock,
The keys in his hands, he pressed them to the lock,
"Cheer up, cheer up, my prisoner," I thought I heard the old boss say,
"They'll send you 'round the mountain one 'leven long years to stay."

"Frank James, the Roving Gambler" was recorded by Artus M. Moser from the singing of
L. D. Smith at Swannanoa, North Carolina, 1946. Library of Congress record LP14. Laws,
L16B.

Then around came my sweetheart about eleven o'clock,
The novels in her hand, she pressed them to the lock,
"Cheer up, cheer up, my prisoner," I thought I heard the old boss say,
"They'll send you 'round the mountain one 'leven long years to stay."

Then around came my mother about twelve o'clock,
With a Bible in her hand she pressed it to the lock,
Says, "Turn to the 25th Chapter of Matthew, go read both night and day,
Remember your old mother and don't forget to pray."

They put me on a northbound train bound for the Frankfort town,
'S every station I passed through all people would seem to say,
"Yander goes Frank James the burglar for some big crime or other,
He's bound for the Frankfort Jail."

SAM BASS

An article by W. P. Webb, "The Legend of Sam Bass" (*Publications of the Texas Folklore Society*, III, 226–230), gives the pertinent facts relating to Sam Bass. The following is quoted from it:

Samuel Bass was from Indiana. He was born July 21, 1851, came to Texas, raced horses, made his headquarters in Denton County, participated in some bank robberies and train holdups. He became the recognized leader of his band and enjoyed a wide reputation, which he achieved before he was twenty-seven years old. In the summer of 1878, he left Denton County with the intention of robbing a bank or train. With him were Murphy, the man who had arranged to sell him out to the officers of the law, also Seaborn Barnes and Frank Jackson. The plan was made to rob the Round Rock Bank on Saturday, July 20, 1878. En route to Round Rock, Murphy sent a note to Major John B. Jones, adjutant general of Texas, giving their plan. The result was that when Bass reached Round Rock the town was full of Texas Rangers and other officers of the law. On Friday, Bass, with Jackson and Barnes, went into Round Rock to look over the ground before their attempt to rob. While purchasing tobacco in a store adjoining the bank, they were accosted by officers of the law, and a battle ensued. Barnes was killed on the spot, along with an officer. Bass escaped with a mortal wound, was found next day in the woods, and died the following day, Sunday, July 21, 1878. On that day he was twenty-seven. Frank Jackson made good his escape and has never been heard from since.

"Sam Bass" was recorded by Sam Eskin from the singing of Lannis F. Sutton, Palo Alto, California, 1949. Library of Congress record LP30. Laws, E4.

Sam Bass was buried at Round Rock and a rather elaborate monument was erected to him by friends. It bears simply his name, the dates of his birth and death, and age. Beside him, beneath a simpler sandstone marker, lies his companion, Seaborn Barnes, and on the marker are the words "He Was Right Bower to Sam Bass." Both Bass's monument and Barnes's gravestone have been mutilated and chipped by insensitive souvenir hunters. May they join Jim Murphy in his "scorching."

> Sam Bass was born in Indiana, that was his native home,
> When at the age of seventeen, young Sam begin to roam;
> He first came out to Texas a cowboy for to be —
> A kinder-hearted fellow than Sam you never see.
>
> Sam used to deal in race stock, one called the Denton mare,
> He matched her in scrub races and taken her to the fair;
> Sam used to coin the money and spend it very free,
> He always drank good liquor wherever he may be.
>
> Sam left the Collins ranch in the merry month of May
> With a herd of Texas cattle the Black Hills for to see,
> Sold out in Custer City and there got on a spree —
> A harder set of cowboys you hardly ever see.
>
> Sam had four companions, four bold and daring lads,
> There was Richardson, Jackson, Joe Collins, and Old Dad;
> A daring set of cowboys than Texas ever knew,
> They whipped the Texas Rangers and run the boys in blue.
>
> On their way back to Texas they robbed the U.P. train,
> And then split up in couples and started out again;
> Joe Collins and his partner was overtaken soon,
> With all of their good money they had to meet their doom.
>
> Sam had a good companion, called Arkansas for short,
> He was shot by a Texas Ranger by the name of Thomas Floyd;
> Old Tom's a tall six-footer and thinks he's mighty fly,
> Though I can tell his racket — he's a deadbeat on the sly.
>
> Sam got back to Texas all right-side-up with care,
> Rode into the town of Denton his friends all there to share;
> Sam's life was short in Texas for the robbery he did do,
> He robbed all off the passenger, mail, and express train, too.

Jim Murphy was arrested, and then released on bail,
He jumped his bond at Tyler and taken the train for Terrell;
Old Major Jones had posted Jim, and that was all a stall,
It was a plan to capture Sam before the coming fall.

Sam met his fate at Round Rock, July the twenty-first,
They pierced poor Sam with rifle ball and emptied out his purse;
Poor Sam is now a corpse and a-molding in the clay,
While Jackson's in the bushes a-trying to get away.

Jim borrowed Sam's good gold and did not want to pay,
The only way Jim thought to win was to give poor Sam away;
He give poor Sam away and left his friends to mourn —
Oh, what a scorching Jim will get when Gabriel blows his horn!

JESSE JAMES

Probably the most famous son of Missouri — after Mark Twain (and today Harry S. Truman) — is the bandit who, starting his career with Quantrill's bushwhackers, became the most notorious train- and bank-robber in the country. His career ended when, on April 4, 1882, he was shot treacherously by one of his own gang, Robert Ford, who was tempted by the $10,000 reward offered for the capture of James. The story goes that he was shot while hanging a picture on the wall of the house in St. Joseph in which he was living under the name of Howard. Most of the Jesse James songs seem to have sprung from one original, marked by the refrain about "that dirty little coward that shot Mr. Howard and laid poor Jesse in the grave." Robert Ford was shot and killed in Creede, Colorado, in his saloon and gambling house, by Ed Kelly, a friend of James's. [Basic note from H. M. Belden, *Ballads and Songs Collected by the Missouri Folk-Lore Society*, Columbia, 1940 (reprint edition, 1966), p. 401.]

Jesse James was a lad that killed many a man.
He robbed the Danville train.
But that dirty little coward that shot Mr. Howard
Has laid poor Jesse in the grave.

"Jesse James" was contributed to H. M. Belden in 1906 by George Williams of Bollinger County, Missouri, who said: "This song I heard a country boy named Jim Burton sing some eight years ago. Many people in the country know it. I had never seen it in print until lately." In Belden, *Ballads and Songs*, p. 402. Without music. Laws, E1.

It was Robert Ford, that dirty little coward,
I wonder how he does feel;
For he ate of Jesse's bread and slept in Jesse's bed
And laid poor Jesse in the grave.

    Poor Jesse had a wife to mourn for his life,
    His children they were brave;
    But that dirty little coward that shot Mr. Howard
    And laid poor Jesse in the grave!

It was his brother Frank who robbed the Gallatin bank
And carried the money from the town.
It was at this very place they had a little chase,
For they shot Capt. Sheets to the ground.

They went to the crossing not very far from here,
And there they did the same;
With the agent on his knees he delivered up the keys
To the outlaws Frank and Jesse James.

It was on Wednesday night, the moon was shining bright,
They robbed the Glenville train.
The people they did say, for many miles away,
It was robbed by Frank and Jesse James.

It was on Saturday night, Jesse was at home,
Talking with his family brave.
Robert Ford came along like a thief in the night
And laid poor Jesse in the grave.

The people held their breath when they heard of Jesse's death
And wondered how he ever came to die.
It was one of the gang called little Robert Ford,
He shot poor Jesse on the sly.

This song was made by Billy Gashade
As soon as the news did arrive.
He said there is no man with the law in his hand
Can take Jesse James when alive.

COLE YOUNGER

I am a bonded highwayman, Cole Younger is my name,
Through a many a depredation, I brought my friends to shame.
For the robbing of the Northfield bank they say I can't deny,
And now I am a poor prisoner; in the Stillwater jail I lie.

Come listen, comrades, listen, a story I will tell
Of a California miner on whom my fate befell;
We robbed him of his money, boys, and bid him go his way,
And that I'll always be sorry until my dying day.

We started then for Texas, that good old Lone Star state,
And on the Nebraska prairies the James boys we did meet.
With guns, cards, revolvers we all set down to play,
And drinking a lot of good whiskey to pass the time away.

We started then northward, and northward we did go
To the godforsaken country called Minnesot-e-o;
Our eyes being fixed on the Northfield bank, twin brother Bob did say,
"Cole, if you want to take that job, you'll surely curse the day."

We pointed out our pickets, up to the bank did go,
And there upon the counter we made our fatal blow;
Saying, "Hand us down your money, boys, and make no scarce delay.
We are the James and Younger boys and spare no time to pray."

THE ROWAN COUNTY CREW
(*Tolliver-Martin Feud Song*)

The Tolliver-Martin feud-shootings took place in 1884 when John Martin,
Floyd Tolliver, Sol Bradley, and a deputy sheriff named Baumgartner were
killed. The "war" continued beyond that date with further killings. Jean
Thomas, author of *Ballad Makin' in the Mountains of Kentucky*, New

"Cole Younger" was recorded by Charles Todd and Robert Sonkin from the singing of
Cotton Davis, Porterville, California, 1940. Library of Congress AFS record 5103 A.
Laws, E3.

"The Rowan County Crew" was collected by Duncan Emrich from Slim Haney (of
Kentucky) at Denver, Colorado, 1940. Laws, E20.

York, 1939, states that the author of the ballad was James William Day and that Day "sang his ballad for me in that same courthouse yard in Morehead, in the fall of 1936, standing in the self-same spot where he had stood as a young man the day the 'troubles' started." [Note condensed from Laws.]

Come all young men and ladies, fathers and mothers, too,
I'll relate to you the history of the Rowan County Crew,
Concerning bloody Rowan and many of her hideous deeds,
Dear friends, please give attention and remember how it reads.

'Twas in the month of August all on election day,
Young Martin he was wounded, they say by Johnny Day,
Although he did not believe it, he did not think it so,
He thought it was Floyd Tolliver that struck the fatal blow.

They shot and killed Sol Bradley, a sober and innocent man,
And left his wife and loving children to do the best they can.
They wounded young Ad Sizemore, although his life was saved,
He seems to shun the grog shop, since he stood so near the grave.

When Martin did recover, some months had come and passed,
While in the town of Morehead those men had met at last.
Tolliver and a friend or two about the streets did walk,
They seemed to be uneasy when no one wished to talk.

They stepped in Judge Carr's grocery and walked up to the bar,
But little did they think, dear friends, they'd met their fatal hour.
The sting of death was near him, Martin rushed in at the door
And a few words passed between them concerning their row before.

The people all were frightened and began to leave the room,
When a ball from Martin's pistol laid Tolliver in the tomb.
His friends all gathered around him, his wife to weep and wail,
Then Martin was arrested and soon confined in jail.

He was put in the jail of Rowan, there to remain a while,
In the hands of law and justice to bravely stand his trial.
The people talked of lynching him, at present though they fail,
For Martin was removed and placed in the Winchester jail.

Some people forged an order, their names I do not know,
But a plan was soon agreed upon, for Martin they did go.
Martin seemed to be discouraged, he seemed to be in dread,
"They've set a plan to kill me," to the jailor Martin said.

They placed the handcuffs on him, his heart was in distress,
They hurried to the station and stepped on the night express.
Along the line she lumbered at her usual speed,
There were but two in number to commit that dreadful deed.

Martin was in the smoking car accompanied by his wife,
They did not want her present when they took her husband's life.
When they arrived at Farmer's there was no time to lose,
A band approached the engineer and bid him not to move.

They stepped up to the prisoner with pistols in their hands,
In death he soon was sinking, he died in an iron band.
His wife was in another car all ready to retire,
And she cried, "Oh, God, they've killed him!" when she heard the pistols fire.

Now the death of these two men has caused great trouble in our land,
Caused men to leave their families and take a parting hand.
Retaliating is at war, and it may never cease,
I wish that I could see our land once more in peace.

They killed the deputy sheriff, Baumgartner was his name,
They shot him from the bushes after taking deliberate aim.
The death of him was dreadful and may not be forgot,
His body was pierced and torn with thirty-eight buckshot.

I composed this for a warning. Oh, be warned, you young men!
Your pistols will cause trouble, on this you may depend.
In the bottom of a whiskey glass a lurking devil dwells,
It burns the breasts of those who drink it and sends their souls to hell.

CLAUDE ALLEN

Professor Fletcher Collins of Elon College, North Carolina, has reported
that Claude Allen is still something of a local hero in the vicinity of Hills-
dale, Virginia, where, with his brother Sidney and several others, he was
arrested one Saturday night in 1912, "for drinking and carrying on in the
streets." At the trial following the arrest, the prisoners were fined one dollar

"Claude Allen" was recorded by Alan Lomax from the singing, with guitar, of Hobart
Smith at Saltville, Virginia, 1942. Library of Congress record LP7. Laws, E6.

each and sentenced to one day in jail. "Claude said right off he'd pay the fine but he was God damned if he'd take a sentence, 'No sir!' The Allens began shooting; so did the high sheriff and the other officials; and the Allens escaped through the windows. Claude was electrocuted for killing the sheriff; Sidney Allen was exiled from the state after his 35-year prison sentence had been commuted; and another brother was captured only years later when his sweetheart — to get a reward — told the police of his letters to her, written from somewhere out West."

For a historical note on the "courthouse massacre," see Arthur Palmer Hudson, *Folksongs of Mississippi and Their Background*, Chapel Hill, North Carolina, 1936, p. 242.

Claude Allen he and his dear old pappy
   Have met their fatal doom at last.
Their friends are glad their trouble's ended
   And hope their souls are now at rest.

Claude Allen was that tall and handsome,
   He still had hopes until the end
That he'll some way or other
   Escape his death from the Richmond pen.

The governor being so hard-hearted,
   Not caring what his friends might say,
He finally took his sweet life from him.
   In the cold, cold ground his body lay.

Claude Allen had a pretty sweetheart,
   She mourned the loss of the one she loved.
She hoped to meet beyond the river,
   Her fair young face in heaven above.

Claude's mother's tears was gently flowing,
   All for the one she loved so dear.
It seemed no one could tell her troubles,
   It seemed no one could tell but her.

How sad, how sad, to think of killin'
   A man all in his youthful years,
A-leaving his old mother weepin'
   And all his friends in bitter tears.

Look up on yonder lonely mountain,
    Claude Allen sleeps beneath the clay.
No more you'll hear his words of mercy
    Or see his face till Judgment Day.

Come all young boys, you may take warning.
    Be careful how you go astray,
Or you may be like poor Claude Allen
    And have this awful debt to pay.

WILD BILL JONES

One day as I was a-rambling around,
I met up with Wild Bill Jones;
He was walking and talking with my own true love,
And I bid him to leave her alone.

He says, "Young man, I'm twenty-one,
Too old for to be controlled."
And I drew my special from my side,
I destroyed that poor boy's soul.

He rolled, he struggled all over the ground,
And he gave one dying groan.
He looked right up at my darling's face,
Says, "Darling, you're left alone."

I'm bound for the walls of prison, little girls,
I'm bound for the walls of jail,
I'm bound for the walls of prison, little girls,
Oh, won't you go my bail?

When I am dead and in my grave,
With girls all a-crowding around,
Just push back the coffin lid,
Look down on a gambling man.

"Wild Bill Jones" was recorded by Herbert Halpert from the singing of Finley Adams, Dunham, Kentucky, 1939. Library of Congress AFS record 2797 A1. Stanza five supplied from the singing of the same song by Mrs. W. L. Martin, Hillsville, Virginia, 1939. Library of Congress AFS record 2746 B4. Laws, E10.

JOHN HARDY

John Hardy was a desperate little man,
He wore two guns every day,
He killed a man on the West Virginia line,
You should have seen John Hardy get away, poor boy,
You should have seen John Hardy get away.

John Hardy was standing in a dice-room door,
Not taking any interest in the game,
When a yellow girl threw ten dollars on the board,
Saying, "Deal John Hardy in the game, poor boy,
Deal John Hardy in the game."

John Hardy drew his pistol from his pocket,
And threw it down on the tray,
Saying, "The man that uses my yellow girl's money,
I'm going to blow him away, away,
I'm going to blow him away."

John Hardy drew to a four-card straight,
And the Chinaman drew to a pair,
John failed to catch, and the Chinaman won,
And he left him sitting back dead in his chair,
And he left him lying dead in his chair.

John started to catch the east-bound train,
So dark he could not see,
A police walked up and took him by the arm,
Saying, "John Hardy, come and go with me, poor boy,
John Hardy, come and go with me."

"I've been to the East and I've been to the West,
I've traveled this wide world round,
I've been to the river and I've been baptized,
And now I'm on my hanging-ground, oh Lord,
And now I'm on my hanging-ground."

"John Hardy" was recorded by Sidney Robertson Cowell from the singing of J. W. Russell, Marion, Virginia, 1936. Library of Congress AFS record 3163 A3. Stanza additions to Russell's brief text from John Harrington Cox, "John Hardy," *JAF*, 32 (1919):505ff. Laws, I2.

> They hung John Hardy in the old oak tree,
> Down beneath the blue,
> They told John Hardy when they swung him up,
> "John Hardy, that's the last of you, poor boy,
> John Hardy, that's the last of you."

DELIA HOLMES

According to Winn, who sings this song, "Delia" was composed about 1900 by a singer known as "Whistling Bill Ruff" of Dallas, Texas, following a murder in Georgia. There is no substantiation for this. Certain phrases relate to "Frankie and Johnny," but it is clearly an independent piece.

> Delia, Delia, why didn't you run?
> See that desperado and a forty-four smokeless gun.
> Crying, "All I had done gone."
>
>> All I had done gone!
>> All I had done gone!
>> Good-bye, Mother, friends and all,
>> All I had done gone!
>
> Now Coonie and his little sweetheart setting down talking low,
> Asked her would she marry him, she said, "Why sure."
> Crying, "All I had done gone."
>
> When the time come for marriage, she refused to go.
> "If you don't marry me, you cannot live no more."
>
> Shot her with a pistol, number fourty-four,
> "You did not marry me, you cannot live no more."
>
> Turned poor Delia over on her side very slow,
> She was crying, "Coonie, please don't shoot no more."
>
>> All I had done gone!
>> All I had done gone!
>> Good-bye, mother, friends and all,
>> All I had done gone!

"Delia Holmes" was collected by Chapman J. Milling from the singing of Will Winn, Columbia, South Carolina, 1937. See Chapman J. Milling, "Delia Holmes — A Neglected Negro Ballad," *SFQ*, 1 (December, 1937):3–8. Also the same song recorded and sung by Milling on Library of Congress AFS record 3789 A1, A2, A3. Laws, I5.

Death had proceeded. It wasn't so very long
Till her mother come running with a bucket on her arm.

"Tell me, my darling, what have you done wrong,
Caused Coonie to shoot you with that .44 smokeless gun?"

"Some give a nickel, some give a dime,
Help to bury this body of mine."

Threw down his pistol and tried to get away,
Officers picked him up in just a few days.

Placed him in the jail till his trial should come.
"Tell me now, officer, what have I done?"

They asked him did he remember this "A girl that you were in love,
And spoken things unto her that instantly taken her nerve?"

"She moved closely beside of me and threw her arms around."
"Do you remember little Delia Holmes and which you shot down?"

"Have I now any bond, or can I get one,
For the crime that I am charged, I plead guilty I have done?"

    All I had done gone!
    All I had done gone!
    Good-bye, mother, friends and all,
    All I had done gone!

The judge that tried him, handsome with the time,
Say, "Coonie, if I don't hang you, I'll give you ninety-nine.

"Ninety-nine years in prison working among the stone,
Hope that you'll get sorry that you have wrecked a home."

Coonie went to Atlanta, drinking from a silver cup,
Poor little Delia's in the cemetery, I hope to never wake up.

Delia's mother taken a trip out West,
Just to keep from hearing the talk of poor little Delia's death.

Everywhere the train would stop you could hear the people moan,
Singing that lonesome song, "Poor Delia's dead and gone."

Rubber-tired buggy, rubber-tired hack,
Take you to the cemetery, don't never bring you back.

> All I had done gone!
> All I had done gone!
> Good-bye, mother, friends and all,
> All I had done gone!

Coonie wrote to the Governor, asked, "Pardon me,
I was charged with murder in the first degree.

"The judge was liberal in giving me my time;
Happened that he didn't hang me, but he give me ninety-nine.

"I am now a murderer, serving a long, long time;
And if you will pardon me, I'll not be guilty of another crime.

"This is Coonie in Atlanta, working among the stone.
Have been here for forty-five years, and I'm now needed at home."
Crying all I had done gone.

> All I had done gone!
> All I had done gone!
> Good-bye, mother, friends and all;
> All I had done gone.

FRANKIE AND JOHNNIE

> Frankie and Johnnie were lovers.
> Oh, oh, how they did love!
> Swore to be true to each other
> As true as the stars up above.
> He was her man; he wouldn't do her wrong.

> Frankie went down to the corner.
> Just for a bucket of beer.
> Said, "Mr. Bartender,
> Has my loving Johnnie been here?
> He's my man; he won't do me wrong."

"Frankie and Johnnie" was collected by Mellinger E. Henry from Mrs. Ewart Wilson, Pensacola, North Carolina, 1930. In Henry, *Folksongs from the Southern Highlands*, New York, 1938, pp. 345–346. Without music.

"Frankie, I'll cause you no trouble;
Frankie, I'll tell you no lie;
Your lover left here about an hour ago
With a girl named Nellie Bly.
He's your man but he's doing you wrong."

Frankie looked over the transom;
There to her great surprise,
There on a couch sat her Johnnie
Making love to Nellie Bly.
He was her man, but he done her wrong.

Frankie pulled back her kimono,
Drew out her little .44;
Three times she shot
Right through that hard wood door,
Killed her man 'cause he done her wrong.

"Frankie, come, turn me over;
Come, turn me over slow;
Your bullet in my left side;
Oh, how it hurts me so!
You killed your man 'cause he done you wrong."

Bring on your rubber-tired hearses;
Bring on your rubber-tired hack.
Taking my man to the graveyard
And I'm not going to bring him back.
I killed my man 'cause he done me wrong.

Frankie went to the warden.
Said, "What are you going to do?"
The warden said to Frankie:
"It's the electric chair for you.
You've killed your man 'cause he done you wrong."

Frankie went to the policeman.
Said, "I don't want to live another day.
Lock me up in a dungeon
And throw the key away.
I've killed my man 'cause he done me wrong."

727

This story has no moral:
This story has no end;
This story goes right on to show
There's not no good in men.
She killed her man 'cause he done her wrong.

BAD MAN BALLAD

Late last night I was a-making my rounds,
Met my woman and I blowed her down,
I went on home, I went in to bed,
I put my hand cannon right under my head.

Early next morning 'bout the rising of the sun,
I gets up for to make-a my run.
I made a good run but I made it too slow,
I got overtaken in Mexico.

Standing on the corner, a-reading of a bill,
Up step a man name of Tom Medill:
"Look here," he asks, "if your name is Brown,
Believe you are the bully shot the woman down."

"Yes, oh, yes," I says, "this is him,
And if you got a warrant, just read it to me."
"Can't you see it? if you know what's best,
Come along with me — you're under arrest."

When I was arrested, I was dressed in black,
Put me on a train, and they brought me back.
Bound me over in the county jail,
Couldn't get a human for to go my bail.

Early next morning 'bout the rising of the sun,
I spied old judge dropping down the line.
I heared old jailer when he cleared his throat,
"Better get ready for the district court."

"Bad Man Ballad" was recorded by John A. Lomax from the singing of a Negro convict, Parchman, Mississippi, 1933. Library of Congress AFS record 1859 A1.

District court is now begin,
Twelve big jurymen, twelve honest men.
In his right hand he's holding the verdict,
Holding my verdict in his right hand.

"Forty-four years away under the ground,
'Member the night you shot the woman down?"
Then come the deputy, taken me away:
I'm loading the coal out every day.

TWENTY-ONE YEARS

The judge said "Stand up, boy, and dry up your tears,
You're sentenced to Nashville for twenty-one years."
So tell me good-bye, babe, say you'll be mine,
For twenty-one years, babe, is a mighty long time.

Go tell the Governor on your sweet soul,
If you can't get a pardon, try and get a parole.
If I had the Governor where the Governor's got me,
Before Tuesday morning the Governor'd be free.

I've counted on you, babe, to get me a break,
But I guess you've forgotten I'm here for your sake.
You know who is guilty, you know it too well,
But I'll rot in this jailhouse before I will tell.

So, all you young fellows with hearts brave and true,
Don't believe any woman, you're beat if you do.
Don't believe any woman — no matter what kind,
For twenty-one years, boys, is a mighty long time.

"Twenty-one Years" was collected by Duncan Emrich from a student informant, Denver, Colorado, 1941.

Hangings

Hang me, O hang me, and I'll be dead and gone,
Hang me, O hang me, and I'll be dead and gone,
I wouldn't mind the hangin', it's bein' gone so long,
It's layin' in the grave so long.

HANG ME, O HANG ME, AND I'LL BE DEAD AND GONE

Hang me, O hang me, and I'll be dead and gone,
Hang me, O hang me, and I'll be dead and gone,
I wouldn't mind the hangin', it's bein' gone so long,
It's layin' in the grave so long.

MCAFEE'S CONFESSION

The Trial of John McAfee for the murder of his wife lasted two days, March 2 and 3, 1825. He was found guilty and sentenced by Judge Joseph H. Crane to be hanged March 28. Monday morning, March 28, 1825, crowds began to come in from the country. At ten o'clock in the morning, McAfee was taken from the jail and seated in a carriage, attended by the Rev. Father Hill, a Catholic priest from Cincinnati, who had visited the prisoner on two previous occasions. Guarded by the militia, McAfee was conveyed to the gallows erected west of

"Hang Me, O Hang Me, and I'll Be Dead and Gone" is a refrain to a variant of "The Gambler," "secured by Miss Frances Barbour in 1917 from the singing of Minnie Doyel of Arlington, Phelps County, Missouri." In H. M. Belden, *Ballads and Songs Collected by the Missouri Folk-Lore Society*, Columbia (reprint edition 1966), p. 472.

"McAfee's Confession" was reported to H. M. Belden by Miss Lowry in 1905, as secured from an aunt who learned it (and set it down in her ballad book) in Indiana. In Belden, *Ballads and Songs Collected by the Missouri Folk-Lore Society*, Columbia (reprint edition, 1966), p. 318. Without music. Laws, F13.

Dayton, near the Miami River. He made a confession of his crime, and was hanged at 3:00 P.M.

— H. M. BELDEN

Draw near, young men, and learn of me
The sad and mournful history,
That you may never forgetful be
Of all this day I tell to thee.
I scarce had reached my fifth year
When Father and my mother dear
Were both laid in their silent grave
By him who did their being gave.

No more a mother's voice I heard,
No more a mother's love I shared,
No more was I a father's joy;
I was a helpless orphan boy.
But Providence, the orphan's friend,
A kind relief did quickly send
And snatched from want and poverty
Poor little orphan McAfee.

Beneath my uncle's friendly roof
From want and danger far aloof
Nine years was I kindly reared
And oft his good advice I heard.
But I was thoughtless, young, and gay
And often broke the Sabbath day;
In wickedness I took delight
And often done what was not right.

And when my uncle would me chide
I'd turn from him dissatisfied
And join again my wickedness
And Satan serve with eagerness.
At length arrived the fatal day
When from my home I ran away,
And to my sorrow now in life
I took unto myself a wife.

And she was kind and true to me
As any woman need to be;
And now alive would be, no doubt,
Had I ne'er seen Miss Hettie Shoup.
As well I mind the very day
When Hettie stole my heart away.
'Twas love for her controlled my will
And counseled me my wife to kill.

'Twas on one pleasant summer night
When all was still, the stars shone bright;
My wife was lying on her bed
When I to her approached and said:
"Dear wife, here's medicine I've brought
Which I this day for you have bought.
My dear, I'm sure it will cure you
Of those vile fits; pray take it, do."

She gave to me a tender look,
Then in her mouth the poison took;
Then with her baby on her bed
Down to her last long sleep she laid.
And, fearing she was not yet dead,
Upon her throat my hands I laid
And they such deep impression made
Her soul soon from her body fled.

Then was my heart filled full of woe;
I cried, "Oh, whither shall I go?
How shall I quit this lonesome place,
The world again how shall I face?
I'd freely give up all my store,
If I'd a thousand pounds or more,
If I could bring again to life
My dear, my darling murdered wife."

Her body's now beneath the sod,
Her soul, I hope, is with its God;
And soon into eternity
My guilty soul shall also be.
Young men, young men, be warned by me;

Pray shun all evil company,
Walk in the ways of righteousness,
And God your soul shall surely bless.

The moments now are drawing nigh
When from this world my soul shall fly
To meet Jehovah at his bar
And there my final sentence hear.
Dear friends, I bid you all adieu,
No more on earth shall I see you;
But on heaven's bright and flowery plain
I hope to meet you all again.

MUSGROVE

Oh, Musgrove, he persuaded me,
Persuaded me for to agree,
Persuading me, he thus did say,
Let's join and do some forgery.

My greedy heart deceivèd me;
The pride of wealth and property
Led me a captive, now, you see,
All in the bonds of misery.

Oh, now, in jail, where I do lay,
In heavy irons, cold as clay,
I soon the day shall shortly see,
That will land my soul in eternity.

JOHN ADKINS' FAREWELL

Poor drunkards, poor drunkards, take warning by me,
The fruits of transgression behold now I see;
My soul is tormented, my body confined,
My friends and dear children left weeping behind.

Much intoxication my ruin has been,
And my dear companion I've barbarously slain;
In yonder cold graveyard her body doth lie,
And I am confined, and must shortly die.

"Musgrove" comes from *The Social Harp*, 1855, p. 87.

"John Adkins' Farewell" is from *The Social Harp*, 1855, p. 200.

A solemn death warning to drunkards I leave,
While my poor body lies cold in the dark grave;
Remember John Adkins, his death and reform,
Lest justice o'ertakes you and sorrow comes on.

A whole life of sorrow can never atone,
For that cruel murder that my hands have done;
I am justly condemned, it's right that I should die,
Therefore let all drunkards take warning hereby.

Farewell, my dear children, wherever you be,
Though quite young and tender, and dear unto me;
I leave you exposed in nature's wide field,
In which God is able poor orphans to shield.

No mother to teach you, no father to guide
Your tender affections from sin's awful tide;
No portion to shun you from hunger or cold,
My poor little orphans are cast on the world.

When sorrows oppress you, and sickness comes on,
You'll cry for your mother, but, oh, she is gone;
Your father, in anger, struck her on the head,
She bled, groaned, and languished, and now she is dead.

My heart swells with sorrow, my eyes overflow,
Soon, oh, my dear children I'll bid you adieu;
Oh may my kind neighbors your guardians prove,
And heaven, kind heaven, protect you above.

My soul to His pleasure I humbly submit,
And with my last burthen fall down at His feet;
To plead for His mercy, that flows from above,
That pardons poor drunkards, and crowns them above.

FRANKIE SILVERS

Authenticated tradition has it that this song was composed in jail by Frances

"Frankie Silvers" was recorded by George W. Hibbitt and William Cabell Greet from the singing of Bascom Lamar Lunsford of South Turkey Creek, North Carolina, at Columbia University, 1935. Library of Congress AFS record 1817A and B1. Laws, E13.

(Frankie) Silvers and recited or sung by her on the scaffold before she was hanged at Morganton, North Carolina, on July 12, 1833, for the murder of her husband the preceding winter. The cause of the murder was considered to be jealousy, although it was also reported that Silvers mistreated his wife and that she killed him in protection of herself.

> This dreadful, dark and dismal day
> Has swept my glories all away,
> My sun goes down, my days are past,
> And I must leave this world at last.

Oh, Lord, what will become of me?
I am condemned, you all now see.
To heaven or hell my soul must fly
All in a moment when I die.

Judge Daniels has my sentence passed,
These prison walls I leave at last,
Nothing to cheer my drooping head
Until I'm numbered with the dead.

But, oh! that dreadful Judge I fear!
Shall I that awful sentence hear?
"Depart, ye cursèd, down to hell
And forever there to dwell."

I know that frightful ghosts I'll see
Gnawing their flesh in misery,
And then and there attended be
For murdering in the first degree.

There shall I meet that mournful face
Whose blood I spilled upon this place,
With flaming eyes to me he'll say,
"Why did you take my life away?"

His feeble hands fell gently down,
His cattering tongue soon lost its sound;
To see his soul and body part —
It strikes with terror to my heart.

I took his blooming days away,
Left him no time to God to pray,
And if sins fall on his head,
Must I not bear them in his stead?

The jealous thought that first gave strife
To make me take my husband's life;
For months and days I spent my time
Thinking how to commit that crime.

And on a dark and doleful night
I put his body out of sight,
With flames I tried him to consume,
But Death would not admit it done.

You all see me and on me gaze;
Be careful how you spend your days;
And never commit this awful crime,
But try to serve your God in time.

My mind on solemn subjects rolls.
My little child, God bless its soul!
All you that are of Adam's race,
Let not my faults this child disgrace.

Farewell, good people, all you see
What my bad conduct's brought to me:
To die of shame and of disgrace
Before this world of human race.

Awful deed to think of death,
In perfect health to lose my breath.
Farewell, my friends, I bid adieu;
Vengeance on me must now pursue.

Great God! How shall I be forgiven?
Not fit for earth — not fit for heaven!
But little time to pray to God,
For now I try that awful road.

TOM DOOLEY

This song is based on the murder by Tom Dula of Laura Foster in Wilkes
County, North Carolina, 1866. After a first trial and an appeal, the death
sentence was confirmed and Dula was hanged near Statesville "at 17 minutes past 2 o'clock P.M. on May 1st, 1868."

Oh, bow your head, Tom Dooley;
Oh, bow your head and cry;
You have killed poor Laury Foster
And you know you're bound to die.

You have killed poor Laury Foster;
You know you have done wrong;
You have killed poor Laury Foster,
Your true love in your arms.

"Tom Dooley" was collected by Mellinger E. Henry from Mrs. William Franklin, Crossnore,
Avery County, North Carolina, 1930. In Henry, *Folksongs from the Southern Highlands*,
New York, 1938, p. 325. Without music.

I take my banjo this evening;
I pick it on my knee;
This time tomorrow evening
It will be of no use to me.

This day and one more;
Oh, where do you reckon I be?
This day and one more,
And I'll be in eternity.

I had my trial at Wilkesboro;
Oh, what do you reckon they done?
They bound me over to Statesville
And there's where I'll be hung.

The limb being oak
And the rope being strong —
Oh, bow your head, Tom Dooley,
For you know you are bound to
     hang.

O Pappy, O Pappy,
What shall I do?
I have lost all my money,
And killed poor Laury too.

O Mammy, O Mammy,
Oh, don't you weep, nor cry;
I have killed poor Laury Foster
And you know I am bound to die.

Oh, what my mammy told me
Is about to come to pass:
That drinking and the women
Would be my ruin at last.

THE HANGING OF SAM ARCHER

Sam Archer was hanged in Shoals, Indiana, on July 9, 1886, before a crowd estimated at five thousand people for his part in the murder of Samuel A. Bunch. Prior to this, on March 9, 1886, his father, uncle, and brother — Tom, Martin V., and John Archer — had been hanged in the courthouse yard by a mob of men who first bound the sheriff to prevent his giving the alarm of the lynching. Two of the men, Tom and Martin V. Archer, were buried in a single grave in the little Jackman Cemetery, located near the French Lick Springs Hotel golf course. Tradition has it that they were buried in the clothes in which they were hanged, with their boots on, and with the ropes around their necks. The lynchings and the legal hanging, while based finally on the murder of Bunch, were the end result of an almost unbroken series of crimes by the Archers, including arson, burglary, torture, and other killings. Oddly enough, no ballad has been found of the lynching

"The Hanging of Sam Archer" was collected by Paul G. Brewster from Mrs. Ethel Hitchcock, Indian Springs, Indiana, 1946. Reported, with music, in *Hoosier Folklore*, 5 (1946): 130.

of the three Archers. The legal hanging alone is solemnized and the
sympathy of the author lies clearly with the unfortunate victim on the
scaffold.

Ye people who delight in sin,
I'll tell you what has lately been:
Come sympathize with our poor souls,
For this young man who died in Shoals.

It is so hard for us to say,
He was executed here today;
It was a gloomy sight to see,
Alas, too much for poor me.

We see him on the trapdoor,
So brave he views the crowd o'er;
The officer with his gray hairs,
In his eyes were standing tears.

Oh, see the sheriff pull down the cap,
And jerk the lever of the trap;
In Heaven I trust we'll meet,
Where he'll be loosed both hands and feet.

For the murder of Bunch he was arraigned,
In Shoals dungeon bound and chained;
Upon this he had to rely
Until the ninth day of July.

"Oh, mother, mother," he did cry,
"You're to blame because I die;
I was trained when I was young,
For which this day I'm to be hung.

"My brother Mart was shot and gone;
My father was hung and so was John.
I have one brother yet at home;
Have mercy, God, upon that one."

His little brother in wild despair,
He wrung his hands and tore his hair;
His little spirit seemed a wreck,
His quivering lip and burning cheek.

> Mourning friends with tearful eyes,
> To you all this may surprise;
> We fear the gallows now awaits
> For more of his associates.
>
> Come now, young men, be warned by me
> To shun all evil company;
> Upon your knees for mercy cry,
> Before, like Archer, bound to die.

THE CROPPY BOY

Lord Cornwallis was lord lieutenant with supreme military command.

Croppy Boy [with hair "cropped" short out of sympathy for the French revolutionaries] means one of the insurgents of the uprising in Wexford in 1798. Wearing the green means that he would not renounce his faith and become a Protestant.

The picture this song brings to mind is of myself as a small child sitting in my little splinter-bottomed rocker with my doll, while mother stood by her spinning wheel, spinning. It was a cold, windy day in October and the dreary whistle of the wind combined with the whir of mother's wheel as she drew the thread and sang this sad song to an inexpressibly sad tune was a combination I can never forget. Mother had a very sweet, sympathetic voice and I never have heard that tune since without feeling the cold shivers run up and down my spine just as they did on that dismal day.

— CARRIE GROVER

> It was early, early in the spring.
> The small birds they did sweetly sing,
> Sounding their notes from tree to tree,
> And the song they sang was old Ireland free.
>
> It was early, early last Thursday night,
> The yeoman cavalry gave me a fright.
> The yeoman cavalry was my downfall
> When I was taken to Lord Cornwall.

"The Croppy Boy" was recorded by Alan Lomax from the singing of Mrs. Carrie Grover of Gorham, Maine, at Washington, D.C., 1941. Library of Congress AFS record 4467 A2 and B1. Text with music also in Carrie B. Grover, *A Heritage of Songs* (privately printed, Gould Academy, Bethel, Maine, n.d.), pp. 38–39. Laws, J14.

It was in his guardhouse where I was laid,
And in his parlor where I was tried,
My sentence passed and my spirits low
When to New Guinea I was forced to go.

As I was marching through the street
The drums and fifes did play so sweet,
The drums and fifes did so sweetly play
As we were marching so far away.

As I was marching by my father's door,
My brother William stood on the floor,
My aged father did grieve full sore,
And my tender mother her hair she tore.

When my sister Mary heard the express,
She ran downstairs in her morning dress,
Saying, "Five hundred guineas I would lay down
To see you marching through Wexford town."

As we were marching through Wexford Street,
My sister Mary we chanced to meet;
That false young woman did me betray
And for one bare guinea swore my life away.

As we were marching o'er Wexford Hill,
Oh, who could blame me to cry my fill?
I looked behind and I looked before,
But my agèd mother I could see no more.

I wore the red and I wore the blue,
I wore the gray and the orange too,
I forsook all colors and did them deny.
I wore the green and for it I die.

When I was mounted on the gallows high,
My agèd father was standing by.
My agèd father did me deny,
And the name he gave me was the Croppy Boy.

When I am taken to my grave,
A decent funeral pray let me have.
Come, all good people, as you pass me by,
Say, "The Lord have pity on the Croppy Boy."

Blues

Give me my shoes and my Carhart overalls,
Let me step over yonder and blind the Cannon Ball;
That's the long train they call the Cannon Ball,
It makes a hundred miles and do no switchin' at all.

Train I ride doan burn no coal at all,
It doan burn nothin' but Texas Beaumont oil;
That's the long train they calls the Cannon Ball,
It makes a hundred miles and do no stoppin' at all.

If you ever had the blues, you know jus' how I feel,
Puts you on the wonder, and make you want to squeal;
When you take the blues and doan know what to do,
Jus' hunt you a train and ride the whole world through.

GONNA LAY MY HEAD DOWN ON SOME RAILROAD LINE

(*Spoken*): Gonna lay my head down on some railroad line.

Gonna lay my head down on some railroad line,
And take some train to satisfy my mind.
Honey, when I die, honey, don't you wear no black, hey, hey,
Honey, when I die, honey, don't you wear no black,
Then if you do my ghost come sneaking back.
Yonder comes a train, yonder comes a train,
Comin' down the railroad line,
Yonder comes a train, yonder comes a train,
Comin' down the railroad line, hey, hey, comin' through, buddy.
It takes some train to satisfy my mind.
My momma told me, my daddy told me too,
Says, "Son, everybody grin in your face,
You ain't no friend to you."

(*Spoken*): That's all.

"Gonna Lay My Head Down on Some Railroad Line" was recorded by Sidney Robertson Cowell from the singing of Will Wright at Clinton, Arkansas, 1936. Library of Congress record LP61.

THE RAILROAD BLUES

Every time you hear me sing this song
You may know I've caught a train and gone.
I get a letter, and this is how it read:
Stamped on the inside, "Yo' lover's sick in bed."

Give me my shoes and my Carhart overalls,
Let me step over yonder and blind the Cannon Ball;
That's the long train they call the Cannon Ball,
It makes a hundred miles and do no switchin' at all.

Train I ride doan burn no coal at all,
It doan burn nothin' but Texas Beaumont oil;
That's the long train they calls the Cannon Ball,
It makes a hundred miles and do no stoppin' at all.

If you ever had the blues, you know jus' how I feel,
Puts you on the wonder, and make you want to squeal;
When you take the blues and doan know what to do,
Jus' hunt you a train and ride the whole world through.

Big Four in Dallas done burned down,
Burned all night long, burned clean to the ground;
But give me my shoes, and press my overalls,
If you doan min' my goin', baby, I'll catch the Cannon Ball.

I'm worried now, but I won't be worried long,
This north-bound train will certainly take me home.
Number Nine is gone, Number Ten's switchin' in the yard,
But I'm goin' to see that girl if I have to ride the rods.

"The Railroad Blues" was collected by Walter Prescott Webb from the singing of Floyd Canada and reported in *JAF*, 28 (1915):290–299. Webb says that the song was "gathered around Beesville, Texas, in Bee County, 90 miles south of San Antonio and near the Nueces." His informant, Floyd Canada, gave him eighty stanzas of four lines each! Webb terms the whole a "Negro Iliad" (more properly: "Odyssey"). It is an incredible ballad-epic. "The Railroad Blues" is only a small portion of it. But a good portion. No music, but Webb states that it is sung to the tune of "Dallas Blues."

I got the railroad blues, but I haven't got the fare,
The company sho' ought to pay my way back there.
The train I ride is sixteen coaches long,
Dat's de train done take yo' baby home.

I'm a goin' away, it won't be long;
When I hit Houston, I'll call it gone.
When I git to Houston I'll stop and dry,
When I hit San Tone, I'll keep on by.

How I hate to hear the Monkey Motion* blow,
It puts me on the wonder, and makes me want to go.
Dat passenger-train got ways jus' lak a man,
Steal away yo' girl, and doan care where she land.

I may be right an' I may be wrong,
But it takes a worried woman to sing a worry song;
When a woman's in trouble, she wring her hands and cry,
But when a man's in trouble, it's a long freight-train and ride.

I RODE SOUTHERN, I RODE L. & N.

I've rode the Southern, I've rode the L. & N.,
I've rode the Southern, I've rode the L. & N.,
And the way I've been treated, I'm gonna ride them again.

The way I've been treated, sometime I wish I was dead,
The way I've been treated, sometime I wish I was dead,
But I've got no place to lay my weary head.

I've rode the Southern, I've rode the L. & N.,
I've rode the Southern and I've rode the L. & N.,
And the longest one I've ever rode is years now began.

I'm a rambling man, I ramble from town to town,
I'm a rambling man, I ramble from town to town,
Been looking for a-two blue eyes and now my baby's found.

* Name of train.

"I Rode Southern, I Rode L & N" was recorded by Charles L. Todd and Robert Sonkin from the singing, with guitar, of Merle Lovell at Shafter, California, 1940. Library of Congress record LP61.

I gave her my watch and I gave her my chain,
I gave her my watch and I gave her my chain,
I gave her all I had before she let me change her name.

THE TRAIN IS OFF THE TRACK

Oh, the train's off the track
And I can't get it back,
And I can't get a letter to my home,
To my home, to my home,
And I can't get a letter to my home.

If you like-a me
Like I like you,
We'll both like-a like the same.

If you say so
I'll railroad no more,
I'll sidetrack my train and go home,
And go home, and go home,
I'll sidetrack my train and go home.

Come on, my love,
This very day
I'd like for to change your name,
Your name, your name,
Oh I'd like for to change your name.

COAL LOADIN' BLUES

Here comes Old Man Adkins with a battle-ax,
Cuttin' everybody with a three-cent tax.
Lord, Lord, I got them coal loadin' blues.

Take up your bottom, lay down your track,
Shoot down your coal, boys, the motor's comin' back.
Lord, Lord, I got them coal loadin' blues.

Got my check in my pocket, I'm goin' to town.
Lord, Lord, I got them coal loadin' blues.

Hurry up, driver, give me two on a trip,
My wife's gone to the store for to draw some script.
Lord, Lord, I got them coal loadin' blues.

"The Train Is off the Track" was recorded by Herbert Halpert from the singing of Mrs. Esco Kilgore of Norton, Virginia, at Hamiltontown, near Wise, Virginia, 1939. Library of Congress record LP61.

"Coal Loadin' Blues" was recorded by George Korson from the singing of Joe Clancy, Harlan, Kentucky, 1940. Library of Congress record LP60.

COAL DIGGIN' BLUES

Fifteen years in the coal mine,
For 'taint a very long time.
Fifteen years in the coal mine,
'Course 'taint a very long time.
Some pullin' lifetime
Some pullin' ninety-nine.

Thought I heard a sea gull
'Way down on that ground;
Thought I heard a sea gull
'Way down on that ground.
Must've been those miners
A-turnin' that coal around.

When that train left Braeholm,
It sure was pullin' slow;
When that train left Braeholm,
It sure was pullin' slow;
My good girl said, "Honey,
I hate to see you go."

WORRIED LIFE BLUES

This and the succeeding seven blues were all recorded by Alan Lomax, Lewis Jones, and John W. Work in 1942 for a study jointly sponsored by the Library of Congress and Fisk University of Nashville, Tennessee. In the source note following each of the blues I have, therefore, given only the name of the performer or performers. All these blues appear on Library of Congress record LP59. None of the performers is identified with the exception of Son House, and the total knowledge we have of him is that his full name was Eugene House; he was born in Lyon, Mississippi, and was a "part-time preacher who wore a white cowboy hat." The rest of them are lost except as they appear here.

Oh lordy, lord, oh lordy, lord,
Hurt me so bad for us to part.
But someday, baby,
You ain't gonna worry my life anymore.

"Coal Diggin' Blues" was recorded by George Korson from the singing of Jerrel Stanley at Braeholm, West Virginia, 1940. Library of Congress record LP60.

"Worried Life Blues" was sung by David Edwards, with guitar, at Clarksdale, Mississippi, 1942.

So many nights since you been a gone,
How much I'm gonna worry myself along,
But someday, baby,
You ain't gonna worry my life anymore.

So many days since you went away,
How much I'm gonna worry both night and day.
But someday, baby,
You ain't gonna worry my life anymore.

So dat's my story,
All I have to say to you . . .
Bye bye, baby,
Don't care what you do.
But someday, baby,
You ain't gonna worry my life anymore.

So many nights since you been a gone,
How much I'm gonna worry myself along,
But someday, baby,
You ain't gonna worry my life anymore.

RAGGED AND DIRTY

(*Spoken*): Nothin' but a cryin' shame, you know that?

Lawd, I'm broke and hungry, ragged and dirty, too,
Broke and hungry, ragged and I'm dirty, too.
If I clean up, sweet mama,
Can I stay all night with you?

Lord, I went to my window, baby — I
Couldn't see through my blind,
Went to my window,
Couldn't see through my blind.
Heard my bedsprings uncovered,
I throwed down,
Heard my baby cryin'.

"Ragged and Dirty" was sung by William Brown, with guitar, at Clarksdale, Mississippi, 1942.

Now, if I can't come in, baby,
Just let me set down in your door.
I can't come in, baby,
Let me set down in your door.
Lord, I will leave so soon
That your man would never know.

Lord, how can I live here, baby,
Lord! and feel at ease?
How can I live here, baby,
Lord! and feel at ease?
'Cause that woman that I got me,
She do just what she please.

(*Spoken*): I can't help myself, you know that?

Lord, you shouldn't mistreat me, baby,
Because I'm young and wild,
Shouldn't mistreat me, 'cause I'm young and wild.
You must always remember, baby,
You was once a child.

Lord, I'm leavin' in the mornin', baby,
If I have to ride this line.
See ya' in the mornin',
Have to ride this line.
Mmm, mistreat me, baby,
And I swear I don't mind dying.

SPECIAL RIDER BLUES

Well, I'm goin' home,
I won't be back no more.
When I leave this time
I'm gon' hang grief on your door.

Now look a-here, honey,
I won't be your dog no more.

"Special Rider Blues" was sung by Son House, with guitar, at Robinsville, Mississippi, 1942.

Well, look a-here, honey,
I won't be your dog no more.
Excuse me, honey, for a-knockin' on your door.

I say your hair ain't curly,
And your doggone eyes ain't blue.
You know your hair ain't curly,
And your doggone eyes ain't blue.
Well, if you don't want me,
What the world I want with you?

Hey, look a-here, baby,
You ought not to dog me around.
I say, look a-here, honey,
You ought not to dog me around.
If I had my belongins',
I would leave this old bad-luck town.

You know that's a shame,
What a low down dirty shame,
Don't you know that's a shame,
What a low down old dirty shame!
You know, I'm sorry today
That I ever knowed your name.

DEPOT BLUES

Well look a-here, honey.
I ain't gonna cry no more.

I went to the depot, and I —
I looked up on the board.
I went to the depot,
I looked up on the board.
Well, I couldn't see no train,
I couldn't hear no whistle blow.

Engineer blow the whistle and the
Fireman he rung the bell.

"Depot Blues" was sung by Son House, with guitar, at Robinsville, Mississippi, 1942.

Oh oh oh, the fireman he rung the bell.
You know my woman's on board,
She's a waving back fare-you-well.

If I had the strength,
I would set this train off the track.
Mmmmmmmm, I would set this train off the track.
Yes, you make me a promise,
She gon' bring my baby back.

Mmmmmmmmm, she ain't comin' back no more.
I don't believe you evuh comin' back no mo'.
Mmmm, you leavin' now, baby,
But you hangin' grief on my door.

Mmmmmmmm, I'm gon' miss you from rollin' in my arms.
Oo-oo-oo, I'm gon' miss you from rollin' in my arms.
I can't get no sassin', baby, on the tele — telephone.

MISSISSIPPI BLUES

Goin' down to the delta,
Where I can have my fun.
Goin' down the delta,
Where I can have my fun.
Where I can drink my white lightnin', gamble —
I can bring my baby home.

Don't the delta look lonesome
When that evenin' sun go down?

(*Spoken*): Just 'bout good an' dark.

Don't this delta look lonesome
When that evenin' sun goes down?
Well, you been lookin' for your baby
Don't know where she could be found.

"Mississippi Blues" was sung by William Brown, with guitar, at Sadie Beck's Plantation, Arknasas, 1942.

(*Spoken*): Boy, I was lookin' all over town for her, you know dat?

Goin' back to my use-to-be,
Although that she have done me wrong.
Goin' back to my use-to-be,
Although that she have done me wrong.
Well, I think I'll have to forgive her
'Cause I'm tired o' driftin' through this world alone.

(*Spoken*): Ain't that a cryin' shame? 'Cause I started to think about her a
whole lot o' times. And she way down Mississippi, and here I am up here!

She treats me dirty,
But I love her just the same.
Well, she treats me dirty,
But I love her just the same.
Well, it just breaks my heart to hear —
Lord, some other men call her name.

(*Spoken*): They better not do that!

Now goodbye, I'm gon' leave you,
An' I won't be back no more.

(*Spoken*): I ain't gon' be gone all that long, you know —

Now goodbye, I'm gon' leave you,
An' I won't be back no mo'.
Man, my mind gets to ramblin' —
See you in nineteen and forty-fo'.

FOUR O'CLOCK FLOWER BLUES

Four o'clock flowers bloom out in the mornin'
And close in the afternoon.
Four o'clock flowers bloom out in the mornin'
And close in the afternoon.

Well, well, they are only summer beauties.
Hoo, hoo, Lord, boys, so have my little baby June.

"Four O'Clock Flower Blues" was sung by Willie Blackwell and William Brown, with guitar, at Sadie Beck's Plantation, Arkansas, 1942.

If you be a little more lovely,
And just a little more true.
If you'd only be a little more lovely,
And just a little more true.

Well, well, all the love I have to spare, hoo, hoo —
Lord, baby, then it would be for you.

I'm a hard-workin' man,
And I never gets my lovin' home.
I'm a hard-workin' man,
And it's true, I never gets my lovin' at home.
And when I think about it in the mornin',
Well, well, boys, it makes my heart ache in the afternoon.

(*Spoken*): Summertime is lovely.

I'm not jealous, but I'm superstitious;
The most workin' mens that way.
I'm not jealous, but I'm superstitious;
The most workin' mens is that way.
If I catch you playin' hookey,
Hoo, hoo, Lord, baby June, what a day, what a day!

EAST ST. LOUIS BLUES

I walked all the way from East St. Louis,
St. Louis to here.

Got nobody, Lawd,
No one to feel my pain.

Well, I had a sweet woman,
Called her Angeline.

Well, every time I looked, babe,
She'd be on my mind.

"East St. Louis Blues" was sung by William Brown, with guitar, at Sadie Beck's Plantation, Arkansas, 1942.

LOWDOWN DIRTY BLUES

Well, you know the sun is going down —
I said behind that old western hill.
Mmmmm, I said behind that old western hill.
You know I wouldn't do a thing,
Not against my baby's will.

Mmmmm, well, you know, that's bad,
I declare, that's too black bad.
Mmmmm, I declare, that's too black bad.
You know, my woman done quit me,
Hoo, man, look like the whole round world is bad.

You know, she stopped writin',
Wouldn't even send me no kind of word.
Ooo-hoo, I said, she wouldn't even sent me no kind of word.
She turned her little ole back on me,
'Bout some old lowdown thing she heard.

Mmmmm, well, I'm goin' away, baby,
I'm gon' stay a very long time.
Oooh, I say, I'm gon' stay a great long time.
You know I comin' back now, honey —
Whooo, babe, until you change you mind.

Mmmmm, I waked up every mornin', feelin' sick and bad.
I say, hoo-oo, every mornin', I been feelin' mighty sick and bad,
Thinkin' 'bout the old times, baby,
That I once had had.

Mmmmm, if I don't go crazy,
I say I'm goin' to lose my mind.
Mmmmm, I believe I'm gon' lose my mind.
'Cause I stay worried, hoohoo, baby,
Bothered, honey, all the time.

Mmmmm, lookah here, baby,
Set right here on my knee.

"Lowdown Dirty Blues" was sung by Son House, with guitar, at Robinsville, Mississippi, 1942.

753

Mmmmm, I said, set right down on my knee.
Well, I just want to tell you
Just how you been doin' me.

Mmmmm, what do you want for me to do?
Mmmmm, — hoo-ooo — I say, what do you want me to do?
I been doin' all I can, honey,
Just tryin' to get along with you.

Miscellaneous Pieces and Pieces Relating to the American Land and to Events on the American Land Regional and Historical

Come all ye Lewiston fact'ry girls,
I want you to understand,
I'm a-going to leave this factory
And return to my native land.

No more will I eat cold pudding,
No more will I eat hard bread,
No more will I eat those half-baked beans,
For I vow! They're killing me dead!

I'm going back to Boston town
And live on Tremont Street,
And I want all you fact'ry girls
To come to my house and eat!
  Sing dum de whickerty, dum de way.

THE DODGER

Yes, the candidate's a dodger, yes, a well-known dodger,
Yes, the candidate's a dodger, yes, and I'm a dodger, too.
He'll meet you and treat you and ask you for your vote,
But look out, boys, he's a dodging for a note!
  Yes, we're all dodging, a-dodging, dodging, dodging,
  Yes, we're all dodging out a way through the world.

Yes, the lawyer he's a dodger, yes, a well-known dodger,
Yes, the lawyer he's a dodger, yes, and I'm a dodger, too.

"The Dodger" was recorded by Sidney Robertson Cowell and Laurence Powell from the singing of Mrs. Emma Dusenbury, Mena, Arkansas, 1936. Library of Congress AFS record 3230 B2.

He'll plead you a case and claim you as a friend,
But look out, boys, he's easy for to bend!

Yes, the doctor he's a dodger, yes, a well-known dodger,
Yes, the doctor he's a dodger, yes, and I'm a dodger, too.
He'll doctor you and cure you for half you possess,
But look out, boys, he's a-dodging for the rest!

Yes, the preacher he's a dodger, yes, a well-known dodger,
Yes, the preacher he's a dodger, yes, and I'm a dodger, too.
He'll preach you a gospel and tell you of your crimes,
But look out, boys, he's a-dodging for your dimes!

Yes, the merchant he's a dodger, yes, a well-known dodger,
Yes, the merchant he's a dodger, yes, and I'm a dodger, too.
He'll sell you the goods at double the price,
But when you go to pay him, you'll have to pay him twice!

Yes, the farmer he's a dodger, yes, a well-known dodger,
Yes, the farmer he's a dodger, yes, and I'm a dodger, too.
He'll plow his cotton, he'll plow his corn,
He'll make a living just as sure as you're born!

Yes, the lover he's a dodger, yes, a well-known dodger,
Yes, the lover he's a dodger, yes, and I'm a dodger, too.
He'll hug you and kiss you and call you his bride,
But look out, girls, he's telling you a lie.
    Yes, we're all dodging, a-dodging, dodging, dodging,
    Yes, we're all dodging out a way through the world.

THE SONG OF COVE CREEK DAM

This is a personal cry against the coming TVA project, which would, of course, inundate thousands of acres of farmland, homes, cemeteries, and the like. It is a very good statement of what hundreds of those affected by the dam must have felt. There is resentment against the project on various counts, but also some reluctant understanding of what it would mean to the

"The Song of Cove Creek Dam," text, with music, is from "Miscellaneous Special Skills Songs" (Farm Resettlement Administration) collected by R. W. Hampton and others, 1936–1937. Manuscript from Tennessee in the collections of the Library of Congress.

country, as well as a final stanza of inevitable acceptance. It is not very good poetry, but it is sincere and demands reading from beginning to end. I like the restrained attack on Senator Norris: "If he's got a river up there, then why [in the hell] couldn't he have built him a dam of his own?"

When the old Cove Creek Dam first was started,
Most everyone said it would be so grand,
For they did not realize of the water
That was going to cover this land.

Many a time that old bill went through Congress,
To the Senate it would go,
Even if it was passed through the Senate,
It would only meet a president's veto.

But when Roosevelt was elected,
He come to Muscle Shoals,
"We will build a power plant here,
And at Cove Creek, a flood control."

So goodby to old Union County,
It's the dear sweet home of my birth,
There's no other place I'll put before her,
She's the sweetest place on earth.

Here we have our trials and our troubles,
But to each other we are kind and true;
What will we find in some other country,
Will the people be like me and you?

They say that this is just a project,
It's the best the South has ever owned.
If it's going to bring in so much money,
Why can't they pay us more for our homes?

There are people who have no land to sell,
And have nothing to fear or to dread;
But it will touch the hearts of ten thousand,
When they come to remove the dead,

For we all have folks that are buried,
It will bring remembrance back to our mind;
But we don't want to leave them a-sleeping
In this flooded water behind.

Of course it is bringing in some money,
For there our people are working night and day,
But just think of the fond hearts it's breaking,
For the ones that's old and gray.

The sad hour is yet to come,
When we leave our dear friends and our home,
For they say that the water will cover,
The dear place where we all love to roam.

The best land we have will be flooded,
In Union County, Tennessee,
But they say they will reforest all the wasteland,
By setting out black locust trees.

When this dam is fully completed,
And the wild beast takes our place,
I wish Senator Norris had to come here
And live by the sweat of his face.

If there's no such thing as a river
Up there at Norris's home;
If there is, then why couldn't he
Have built him a dam of his own?

It won't be long till we are scattered,
We'll be drifting in every way,
But if we will live true to Jesus,
He will gather us together some day.

ARIZONA

This is a song of the Dust Bowl and Depression, and would clearly seem to have been "made up" by one of the Okies — conceivably even the singer himself — on the way to California, or shortly after arrival there. Tempe is some thirty miles east of Phoenix.

"Arizona" was recorded by Charles Todd and Robert Sonkin from the singing of Jack Bryant, Firebaugh, California, 1940. Library of Congress AFS record 4148 A1.

We were out in Arizona, on the Painted Desert ground,
We had no place to call our home, and work could not be found.
Started to California, but our money it didn't last long,
I want to be in Oklahoma, be back in my old home.

Away out on the desert, where water is hard to find,
It's a hundred miles to Tempe and the wind blows all the time.
You will burn up in the daytime, yet you're cold when the sun goes down,
I want to be in Oklahoma, be back in my home town.

You people in Oklahoma, if you ever come West,
Have your pockets full of money, and you better be well dressed.
If you wind up on the desert, you're going to wish that you were dead,
You'll be longing for Oklahoma and your good old feather bed.

GO TO OLD IRELAND

Oh, go to old Ireland and then you will know
How dirty and filthy the Irish do go;
You go to the door, you're in mud to your knees,
You go to the bed and you're covered with fleas.
And it's down, down, down derry down.

Oh, go to old Ireland and there you will see
How ragged and half-starved the Irish do be;
You go to the cupboard, there's nothing but bones,
You go to the skillet, there's old husky pones,
And it's down, down, down derry down.

Oh, go to old Ireland and then you will know
How many it takes for to milk an old ewe,
There's two at the head and two at the hams
And six little devils to bang off the lambs.

I went to a tavern for to stay all the night,
I called for my supper, I thought it was right;
The cloth was laid down and the knicknacks were spread,
'Twas hoecake and hominy and a dead possum's head.

"Go to Old Ireland" was recorded by Alan Lomax from the singing of Mrs. Marianna
Schaupp, Washington, D.C., 1941. Library of Congress AFS record 6082 B1.

The straw was thrown down and the sheepskins were spread,
"And now," says the old man, "we'll all go to bed."
I laid myself down for to take all the ease,
Not a wink could I sleep for the graybacks and fleas.

"Oh, come pretty Patsy, and hang down your head,
Curse all your country and wish yourselves dead.
Your father's a wizard, your mother's a witch,
And you're a Scotch-Irish damn son-of-a-bitch."
And it's down, down, down derry down.

OH, IT'S NINE YEARS AGO I WAS DIGGING IN THE LAND

Oh, it's nine years ago I was digging in the land,
Me brogues on me feet and me spade in me hand;
Says I, "What a pity it is for to see
Such a gentleman as I digging turf by the lea."

    Darn tur-a-naddy, mish-n-darn tur-nan,
    A right tur-a-naddy, mish-n-darn tur-nan.

So I pulled off my brogues, shook hands with me spade,
And off to the war like a dashing Irish blade.
The sergeant and the captain asked me to enlist,
"By the great grafty greed, give me hold of your fist!"

Oh, the first thing they gave me it was an old gun,
Under the trigger I placed my thumb;
The gun being rusty went off with a shock,
Gave my poor shoulder a most darn devilish knock.

The next thing they gave me it was an old horse,
All saddled and bridled and two legs across;
He kicked up his heels and I held him a-level,
And the stiff-necked galligan, he ran to the devil.

"Oh, It's Nine Years Ago I Was Digging in the Land" was recorded from the singing of
Noble B. Brown, Millsville, Wisconsin, 1946, University of Wisconsin Recording Project
under the direction of Leland Coon. Library of Congress AFS record 8472 A2.

Oh, it's nine years ago, thank God it ain't ten,
I'm back in Ireland digging murphies again.
Success to the land, may God save the Queen,
And when the war's ended, I'll enlist again.

Darn tur-a-naddy, mish-n-darn tur-nan,
A right tur-a-naddy, mish-n-darn tur-nan.

THE DISHONEST MILLER

There was an old man who made his will
And all he had was a little old mill.

He called up his eldest son,
Says, "Son, oh, son, my race is run.
If you the miller I should make,
Tell me the toll you intend for to take?"
Sing fod-a-linky-day, sing fod-a-linky-day.

"Dad, you know my name is Heck,
From each bushel I'll take a peck;
If I the miller you should make,
That is the toll I intend for to take."
Sing fod-a-linky-day, sing fod-a-linky-day.

He then called up his second son,
Says, "Son, oh, son, my race is run.
If you the miller I should make,
Tell me the toll you intend for to take?"

"Dad, you know my name is Alf,
From each bushel I'll take a half;
If I the miller you should make,
That is the toll I intend for to take."

He then called up his youngest son,
Says, "Son, oh, son, my race is run.

"The Dishonest Miller" was recorded by George W. Hibbitt and William Cabell Greet from the singing of Bascom Lamar Lunsford of South Turkey Creek, North Carolina, at Columbia University, New York City, 1935. Library of Congress AFS record 1786 B2. Laws, Q21.

If you the miller I should make,
Tell me the toll you intend for to take?"

"Dad, you know I'm a darling boy,
Taking toll is all my joy.
It pleased you both to call me Jack,
I'll steal the corn and swear to the sack."

The old woman shouted "Hallelujah!" and cried,
The old man closed his eyes and died.
Sing fod-a-linky-day, sing, fod-a-linky-day.
Sing fod-a-linky-day, sing, fod-a-linky-day.

THE HORSE TRADER'S SONG

Where was you last winter, boys, when the ground was all covered in snow?
Where was you last winter, boys, when the ground was all covered in snow?
On the Blue Ridge Mountains, all wet, hungry and cold,
God knows I've been all way 'round this world.

Do you know these horse traders or do you know their plans?
Do you know these horse traders or do you know their plans?
Dragging around from town to town and pulling through the sand?
God knows I've been all way 'round this world.

Look ahead of your horses, boys, and yonder comes a man,
Look ahead of your horses, boys, and yonder comes a man,
And if we do snide him we'll none get narry a dram.

Look ahead of your horses, boys, and yonder comes a plug,
Look ahead of your horses, boys, and yonder comes a plug,
And if we do snide him we'll soon be out of grub.

Look ahead of your horses, boys, and yonder is a creek,
Look ahead of your horses, boys, and yonder is a creek,
We'll drive out for supper and hobble on the grass.

"The Horse Trader's Song" was recorded by Charles Todd and Robert Sonkin from the singing of Frank Pipkin, FSA camp, Arvin, California, 1941. Library of Congress AFS record 5122 A2.

We'll send our women from house to house to get whatever they can,
We'll send our women from house to house to get whatever they can,
Lord sakes, yonder comes a woman with a hog jaw in each hand.

We'll hook up our old snide horses and drive them out to town,
We'll hook up our old snide horses and take them out to town,
First old nester that comes along, he'll pay us to bring them back.

Come all you dido peddlers and let's go take a glass,
Come all you dido peddlers and let's go take a glass,
For I've swapped old Swagey, I've swapped old Swagey at last.

The new railroad is finished, boys, and the cars are on the track.
The new railroad is finished, boys, and the cars are on the track,
And if our women leaves us, money will bring them back.
God knows I've been all around this world —
                              And started around again.

THE CRANBERRY SONG

The author of this song is known to be Barney Reynolds, who created it at Mather, a town in the heart of the Wisconsin cranberry country. It has had considerable circulation in that region — with "the whole clutch." Mrs. Perry explains: "At each marsh every year, new verses are composed about the workers present at that season. Romances, accidents, humorous incidents are incorporated so that each year the song changes. I have sung, I believe, the Barney Reynolds original song. I think you could place the 'Cranberry Song' at about fifty years ago."

You ask me to sing, so I'll sing you a song,
I'll tell how in the marshes they all get along,
Bohemians and Irish and Yankees and Dutch —
It's down in the shanties you'll find the whole clutch.

Did you ever go to the cranberry bogs?
Some of the houses are hewed out of logs,

"The Cranberry Song" was recorded from the singing of Mrs. Frances Perry, Black River Falls, Wisconsin, 1946, by the University of Wisconsin Recording Project under the direction of Leland Coon. Library of Congress record LP55.

763

The walls are of boards, they are sawed out of pine
That grow in this country called "Cranberry Mine."

It's now then to Mather their tickets they'll buy,
And to all their people they'll bid them goodbye;
For fun and for frolic their plans they'll resign
For three or four weeks in the cranberry clime.

The hay is all cut and the wheat is all stacked,
Cranberries all ripe, so their clothes they will pack,
And away to the marshes to rake they will go
And dance to the music of the fiddle and bow.

All day in the marshes their rakes they will pull,
And feel the most gayest when the boxes are full;
In the evening they'll dance till they're all tired out,
And wish the cranberries would never play out.

LAKE CHEMO

The words of "Lake Chemo" were written by James Wilton Rowe of Great
Works, Maine, in 1871 to the tune of "Norah McShane," a pseudo-Irish
sentimental song by Eliza Cook, an English minor poetess, who published
her poem in *Melaia and Other Poems*, London, 1838. "Norah McShane" was
set to music in New York about 1850. Rowe not only used the air to the
song but parodied some of the lines as well. The relationship of the second
stanza of "Norah McShane" to the same stanza of "Lake Chemo" is obvious:

Oh, there's something so dear in the cot I was born in,
Though the walls are but mud and the roof is but thatch;
How familiar the grunt of the pigs in the morning —
What music in lifting the rusty old latch!

"Lake Chemo" is perhaps the only American ballad celebrating the joys of

"Lake Chemo" was recorded by Phillips Barry on dictaphone from the singing of Mrs.
Evie P. Chick, Clifton, Maine, 1932. Three stanzas, with three variant sets of music, reported
by Barry in *Bulletin of the Folksong Society of the Northeast*, Cambridge, Mass., 7
(1934):14–16. The remaining stanzas from Fannie Hardy Eckstorm and Mary Winslow
Smyth, *Minstrelsy of Maine*, Boston and New York, 1927, pp. 68–71.

summer vacationing, and appropriately enough comes from the resort state of Maine.

I left old Lake Chemo a long way behind me,
With many a tear back to Oldtown I came,
And if I but live till one year from this August,
I'll pack up my traps for old Chemo again.

> There pickerel are plenty, perch in abundance,
> Whiskey and new milk, they both flow like rain,
> And if I but live till one year from this August,
> I'll pack up my traps for Lake Chemo again.

'Tis pleasant to think of the shed-tent we slept in,
Though the walls were thin cloth and the roof was a pole;
How familiar the chirp of the birds in the morning,
And the Doctor digging the beans from the hole.

I think of fish-chowder, red-hot from the kettle,
And pork that we frizzled so nice on the fire;
With big, roaring Crawford a-raising the devil
Till three in the morning before he'd retire.

As the sun was setting in most royal splendor,
And the birds were singing their songs in the trees,
Then one of our number was seen without clothing
Promenading the beach and enjoying the breeze.

The name of this poor and unfortunate fellow
Is kept from the public just merely to show
The respect that we have for each one of the party,
The names of the most are here given below.

There was Rowe, Cushman, and Baker, and Douglass and Skinner,
With their wives and their sweethearts and others a score;
And last, but not least, came Miss Scott and Miss Nichols,
Two gushing young damsels from over the shore.

Now all you old fogies who want recreation,
Just go out to Chemo, if you want some fun;
There you'll find all our names engraved on a shingle,
Outshining in brilliance the rays of the sun.

THE FACTORY GIRL'S COME-ALL-YE

Phillips Barry states that "it is most probable that this song was current before 1850. In a series of articles on the 'Duties and Rights of Mill-Girls,' in the *New England Offering*, the [young girl] operatives are urged to spare the landlady's feelings 'if her bread is sometimes heavy and sour' (1848, p. 128), and to *cry*, but not to scold or pout if the overseer is discourteous. 'Your overseer is the better judge of what he can, and what he cannot, do in the way of repairing your disordered machinery, giving you the looms or frames you desire, allowing you to go when you wish. . . .' (1849, p. 57)." Times have changed. . . .

> Come all ye Lewiston fact'ry girls,
> I want you to understand,
> I'm a-going to leave this factory,
> And return to my native land.
>   Sing dum de whickerty, dum de way.
>
> No more will I take my Shaker* and shawl
> And hurry to the mill;
> No more will I work so pesky hard
> To earn a dollar bill.
>
> No more will I take the towel and soap
> To go to the sink and wash;
> No more will the overseer say
> "You're making a terrible splosh!"
>
> No more will I take the comb and go
> To the glass to comb my hair;
> No more the overseer will say
> "You're weaving your cloth too thin!"

* Bonnet.

"The Factory Girl's Come-All-Ye" was collected by Mrs. Susie Carr Young, Brewer, Maine, from Mrs. Mary E. Hindle, Bangor, Maine, n.d. Mrs. Hindle learned the song from Mrs. Sarah Green in 1875. Reported, with music, in *Bulletin of the Folksong Society of the Northeast*, Cambridge, Mass., 2 (1931):12–13.

No more will I eat cold pudding,
No more will I eat hard bread,
No more will I eat those half-baked beans,
For I vow! They're killing me dead!

I'm going back to Boston town
And live on Tremont Street;
And I want all you fact'ry girls
To come to my house and eat!
   Sing dum de whickerty, dum de way.

HARD TIMES

Come listen a while and give ear to my song
Concerning these hard times, it won't take you long;
How the people each other they try for to bite,
And in cheating each other they think they do right, they think they do right,
And so it is hard times wherever you go.

The baker he'll cheat you in the bread that you eat,
And so will the butcher in the weight of his meat;
He'll tip up his scales and make them go down,
And he'll swear it is weight when it lacks half a pound, it lacks half a pound,
And so it is hard times wherever you go.

The miller he'll tell you he'll grind for your toll,
And do the work as well as he can for his soul;
But when your back's turned, and the dish in his fist,
He'll give you the toll and himself keep the grist, himself keep the grist,
And so it is hard times wherever you go.

The landlord he'll feed your horse oats, corn, and hay,
And when your back's turned, he will take them away.
For oats he'll give chaff, and for corn he'll give bran,

"Hard Times" was collected, with music, from Mrs. Maude Simpson, Detroit, Michigan, 1934, who had it from the singing of her grandfather, Mr. Seth Evilsizer, who, in turn, had learned it from Mr. John Gibson, Alma, Michigan, during Grover Cleveland's administration. In Emelyn Elizabeth Gardner and Geraldine Jencks Chickering, *Ballads and Songs of Southern Michigan* (University of Michigan Press) Ann Arbor, 1939, p. 443.

And yet he will holler, "I'm too honest a man, too honest a man,"
And so it is hard times wherever you go.

The tinker he'll tell you he'll mend all your ware
For a little or nothing, some ale, or some beer;
Before he begins, he'll get half drunk or more
And in mending one hole he will punch twenty more, will punch twenty
   more,
And so it is hard times wherever you go.

Next is the ladies, the sweet little dears,
So fine at the balls and the parties appear,
With whalebones and corsets themselves they will squeeze
Till you'll have to unlace them before they can sneeze, before they can
   sneeze,
And so it is hard times wherever you go.

The doctor he'll tell you he'll cure all your ills
With his puffs and his powders, his syrups and squills;
He'll give you a dose that will make you grow fat,
Or he'll give you a dose that will leave you but your boots and your hat, your
   boots and your hat,
And so it is hard times wherever you go.

You've listened a while and give ear to my song,
Therefore you can't say I've sung anything wrong.
If there's anyone here from my song takes offense,
They can go to the devil and seek recompense, and seek recompense,
And so it is hard times wherever you go.

FREE SILVER

Laboring men, please all attend
While I relate my history,
Money it is very scarce;
Let's try and solve the mystery.

The question we will argue now
Has caused a great sensation;
It interests both old and young,
The welfare of our nation.

"Free Silver" was collected by the Federal Music Project, Works Progress Administration (WPA), Rowan County, Kentucky, ca. 1937. Lyda Messer Caudill, Supervisor for Rowan County. Ms., with music, in the Archive of Folk Song, Library of Congress.

The farmer is the cornerstone,
Though he is cruelly treated;
Bryan is the poor man's friend,
He wrongly was defeated.

You know our nation owes a debt,
'Tis true and I will say it:
The bonds they issued calls for
    gold,
And silver will not pay it.

You rascals in your easy chairs,
Your crime you are concealing,
We are sure to cut your salaries
    down
On you it's fastly stealing.

A few more years you'll hold the
    reins
Before our next great battle,
We'll arise, defend free silver's
    cause,
Regain our precious metal.

BRYAN'S LAST BATTLE
(*The Scopes Trial*)

Of all the tales of human struggle, hear this one from Tennessee,
The Holy Bible there on trial, its mighty truths must stricter be.
Its stubborn foe was evolution, the learned could not understand
How in its pages, white and holy, we surely read the fate of man.
Oh, who will go and end this struggle? Oh, who will go and be the man?
And face the foe so learned and mighty, and for the Holy Bible stand?

I see a man, though old in years, a strong and mighty man is he;
Amid the nation's sighs and tears, he starts for sunny Tennessee.
And when he reached the town of Dayton, he faced the foe, to them he said,
"I will not here deny my Maker, the Bible's good enough for me."
Yes, Bryan went to end the struggle, there was no greater man than he
To face the foe so learned and mighty, and give the Bible victory.

Evolution tried to take us back to live in monkeyland,
Bryan took the Holy Bible and stood for God-created man.
"I love this book my mother taught me, with pages pure and white as snow,
I'll place my faith in the Holy Bible, till all the world its riches know.
Oh, who will grieve those saints in glory, who struggle here for a brighter
    day,

"Bryan's Last Battle" was recorded by George W. Hibbitt and William Cabell Greet from the singing of Bascom Lamar Lunsford of South Turkey Creek, North Carolina, at Columbia University, New York City, 1935. Library of Congress AFS recording 1816 A.

And walk with faith and truth and virtue, and points us to a starlit way?"

Oh, Lord, keep the little town of Dayton; 'twas Bryan's last great cause to
    win.
He won with truth and love and virtue, when he struggled there with a world
    of sin.
Then let us cling to the Holy Bible, our rule of life, and faith our guide,
He proved its truth in every heartthrob, and upon its glorious faith he died.
The Bible shows me the Rose of Sharon, it points me to a perfect day,
And leads me to the Rock of Ages, my Saviour's love is a starlit way.

LINDBERGH

He was just a young aviator, and his nerves they were steady and true,
He took many chances and won them, so they called him the "Flying Fool."
He said to his friends, "I've a notion to pilot a trail o'er the sea,
I'll fly like a bird o'er the ocean, adventure is calling to me."
O'er the sea, o'er the sea like an eagle, alone he was making his flight,
And his loved ones behind him were praying for the Lord to protect him
    that night.

Alone in his airplane he speeded, he thought of his mother at home;
She gave him the courage he needed to fly 'neath the sky's starry dome.
Into the darkness he hurried, he passed through the sleet and the rain,
But this young human bird wasn't worried, his heart had a goal to obtain.
O'er the sea, o'er the sea like an eagle, there was no one to give him the cheer,
But he knew, as his eyes pierced the distance, that the goal he was seeking
    was near.

Thousands were waiting in Paris to see the young pilot alight,
The cheers reached the sky when they saw him come flying out of the night.
The news was sent back to his loved ones, the whole world went crazy with
    joy,
They acclaimed him the bravest of fliers, this darling young slip of a boy.
O'er the sea, o'er the sea like an eagle, he had answered adventure's great
    call,
And his name will go down through the ages, as the bravest hero of them all.

"Lindbergh" was recorded by Sidney Robertson Cowell from the singing of Clyde Spencer,
Crandon, Wisconsin, 1937. Library of Congress AFS record 3282 B2 and B3.

MOTHER'S ADVICE

Sit down by the side of your mother, my boy,
For only a moment, I know,
But you stay till I give you your parting advice,
It is all that I have to bestow.

 Hold fast to the light, hold fast to the right,
 Wherever your footsteps may roam,
 Oh, forsake not the way of salvation, my boy,
 That you learn from your mother at home.

You leave us to seek employment, my boy;
By the world you have never been tried,
But in all the temptation and struggle you meet
May you in your Savior confide.

You will find in this bundle a Bible, my boy,
It is the Book of all others the best,
It will teach you to live, and prepare you to die,
And will lead you to the gates of the blest.

I have prayed for you from the cradle, my boy,
I have taught you the best I know,
And as long as His mercy permits me to live,
I shall never cease praying for you.

Your father is coming to bid you good-bye,
Oh, how lonely and sad we shall be,
But far from your childhood and friends of your youth
You will think of your father and me.

I want you to feel every word that I've said,
For it comes from the depths of my love,
And, my boy, if we never behold you on earth,
Will you promise to meet us above?

"Mother's Advice" was collected by the Federal Music Project, Works Progress Administration (WPA), Rowan County, Kentucky. Lyda Messer Caudill, Supervisor for Rowan County. Ms., with music, in the Archive of Folk Song, Library of Congress.

Hold fast to the light, hold fast to the right,
Wherever your footsteps may roam,
Oh, forsake not the way of salvation, my boy,
That you learn from your mother at home.

THE ORPHAN GIRL

"No home, no home," cried an orphan girl
At the door of a prince's hall,
As trembling she stood on the marble step
And leaned on the polished wall.

Her clothes were thin and her feet were bare,
And the snow had covered her head.
"Oh, give me a home," she feebly cried,
"A home and a piece of bread.

"My father's face I have never seen,"
With tears in her eyes so bright,
"My mother sleeps in a new-made grave,
While her orphan begs tonight."

The night was dark and the snow fell fast
And the rich man closed his door.
His proud lips spurned as he proudly said,
"No room or bread for the poor."

The rich man slept on his velvet couch
And dreamed of his silver and gold,
While the orphan lay on a bed of snow
And murmured, "So cold, so cold."

The night rolled on like a midnight charm,
Rolled on like a federate knell.
The earth seemed wrapped in a winding sheet,
And the chilly snow still fell.

"The Orphan Girl" was collected by the Federal Music Project, Works Progress Administration (WPA), Floyd County, Kentucky, ca. 1937. Edith F. James, Supervisor for Floyd County. Ms., with music, in the Archive of Folk Song, Library of Congress.

When morning dawned the orphan girl
Still lay at the rich man's door,
But her soul had fled to her home on high
Where there's room and bread for the poor.

THE JOLLY THRESHERMAN

"Poor man, oh, poor man, come tell to me true,
How you maintain your family, and how you bring them through,
How you maintain your family, your children, who are small,
And nothing but your labor to maintain them at all?"

"When I get up in the morning, I'm always of good cheer;
With a flail in one hand and a bottle of good beer,
A flail in one hand and a bottle of good beer,
I live as happy as those who have ten thousand a year.

"My wife, she's always ready, sir, to haul in the yoke.
We live like lambs together, sir, we never do provoke.
Although it is quite possible that now we do live poor,
Yet we can feed a beggar who comes to our door."

When this nobleman did hear what this poor man did say,
He invited him to dine with him the very next day;
He invited him to dine with him, his children for to bring,
And in token of favor, he gave him a ring.

Early next morning this poor man arose,
He dressed up his children in the finest of their clothes;
This poor man, his wife, and his seven children small,
They all of them dined at this nobleman's hall.

Soon after dinner, this nobleman let him know
What he had in his heart on him for to bestow,
Saying, "Here are forty or fifty acres of good land."
He gave him a writing and signed his own hand.

"The Jolly Thresherman" was collected by John Harrington Cox and found in his *Traditional Ballads Mainly from West Virginia*, Works Progress Administration (WPA), American Folk-Song Publications Number 3, n.d. (1939), p. 70.

Saying, "Now you may be happy all of the days of your life,
And now I do entreat you, be kind to your wife;
Be kind to your wife, your children all around."
There are few such noblemen here to be found.

A BIBLIOGRAPHY OF AMERICAN FOLKSONG

in the English Language

Compiled by

Joseph C. Hickerson

Archive of Folk Song
Library of Congress

The first part of this listing is tied to the sections of this anthology. In some cases, the offering is sparse, suggesting one or two sources that in turn can lead the researcher to a full coverage. In other cases, a fuller listing is given, particularly for areas that have seen increased interest in recent years. Wherever possible, current reprintings are listed along with the first publication of each work.

The second part comprises an overall listing in four sections: general works on American folksong, general collections of American folksong, regional collections (with a summary by state), and general works on and collections of American Negro folksong.

The final section contains listings of book publishers with folk music series, specialized publishers of folk music recordings, and leading journals and magazines in the field.

LULLABIES AND SONGS FOR VERY SMALL CHILDREN, CUMULATIVE SONGS AND RHYMES, AND NONSENSE SONGS

Children's songs can be found scattered through most general and regional collections of American folksong. Anthologies of lullabies seem to be international in scope. The following two are representative:

Cass-Beggs, Barbara and Michael. *Folk Lullabies: 77 Traditional Folk Lullabies from Every Corner of the World.* New York: Oak Publications, 1969.
Commins, Dorothy Berliner. *Lullabies of the World.* New York: Random House, 1967.

The following are substantial general collections of American folksongs of or for children.

Cazden, Norman. *A Book of Nonsense Songs.* New York: Crown Publishers, 1961.
Cohen, Mike. *101 Plus 5 Folk Songs for Camp: Sea Shanties, Story Ballads, Work Songs, Animal Songs, Spirituals, Songs for Fun and Nonsense.* New York: Oak Publications, 1966. [Taken from the active repertoire of a Vermont children's camp.]
Jones, Bessie, and Bess Lomax Hawes. *Step It Down: Games, Plays, Songs, and Stories from the Afro-American Heritage.* New York: Harper & Row, 1972. [A collection from Georgia.]
Newell, William Wells. *Games and Songs of American Children.* New York: Harper & Bros., 1883, 1903. Reprint (introduction by Carl Withers). New York: Dover Publications, 1963.
Seeger, Ruth Crawford. *American Folk Songs for Children in Home, School, and Nursery School: A Book for Children, Parents and Teachers.* Garden City, N.Y.: Doubleday, 1948. [This and the next book contain materials transcribed from authentic, firsthand sources, particularly field recordings in the Library of Congress Archive of Folk Song.]
————. *Animal Folk Songs for Children: Traditional American Songs.* Garden City, N.Y.: Doubleday, 1950.

PLAY-PARTY, COURTING, AND KISSING GAMES AND SONGS

Game songs abound in many general and regional collections and in the children's collections mentioned above. Two important, comprehensive studies of the game (with and without song) are:

Avedon, Elliott M., and Brian Sutton-Smith. *The Study of Games.* New York: John Wiley & Sons, 1971. [Surveys, analyses, and bibliographies.]
Sutton-Smith, Brian. *The Folkgames of Children.* Austin: University of Texas Press, 1972. (Publications of the American Folklore Society, Bibliographic and Special Series, vol. 24.) [Collection of articles by the leading American game theoretician.]

The singing game or play party is well represented in the literature. The leading collection/study is:

Botkin, Benjamin A. *The American Play Party Song, with a Collection of Oklahoma Texts and Tunes.* Lincoln: University Studies of the University of Nebraska, vol. 38, nos. 1–4, 1937. Reprint. New York: Frederick Ungar, 1963. [Includes a comprehensive bibliography.]

Another substantial regional collection, with ample annotations:

Wolford, Leah Jackson. *The Play-Party in Indiana.* Indianapolis: Indiana Historical Commission, 1916. Edited and revised by W. Edson Richmond and William Tillson. Indianapolis: Indiana Historical Society Publications, vol. 20, no. 2, 1959.

Another standard reference:

McLendon, Altha Lea. "A Finding List of Play-Party Games." *Southern Folklore Quarterly* 8 (1944):201–234.

SQUARE-DANCE CALLS

Square dancing and related forms are discussed and documented in the following:

Burchenal, Elizabeth. *American Country Dance.* New York: G. Schirmer, 1918.
Damon, S. Foster. *The History of Square Dancing.* Barre, Mass.: Barre Gazette, 1957.
Handy Square Dance Book. Delaware, Ohio: Cooperative Recreation Service, 1955.
McNair, Ralph J. *Square Dance.* Garden City, N.Y.: Garden City Books, 1951.
Mayo, Margot. *The American Square Dance.* New York: Sentinel Books, 1943. Revised and enlarged, 1948. Reprint. New York: Oak Publications, 1964.
Putney, Cornelia F. *Square Dance U.S.A.* Dubuque, Iowa: W. C. Brown, 1955.
Ryan, Grace Laura. *Dances of Our Pioneers.* New York: A. S. Barnes, 1939.
Shaw, Lloyd. *Cowboy Dances: A Collection of Western Square Dances.* Rev. ed. Caldwell, Idaho: Caxton Printers, 1949.
————. *The Round Dance Book.* Caldwell, Idaho: Caxton Printers, 1948.
Smith, Frank H., with Rolf E. Hovey. *The Appalachian Square Dance.* Berea, Ky.: Berea College, 1955.
Sweet, Ralph. *Let's Create "Old Tyme" Square Dancing.* Hazardville, Conn.: Ralph Sweet, 1966.
Tolman, Beth, and Ralph Page. *The Country Dance Book.* New York: Farrar and Rinehart, 1937.
Wakefield, Eleanor Ely. *Folk Dancing in America.* New York: J. Lowell Pratt, 1966.

BANJO AND FIDDLE PIECES

Songs and texts associated with fiddle and banjo tunes can be found in numerous collections, especially from the South, the Appalachians, and the Ozarks.

LOVE

This universal subject permeates a large portion of the American folksong repertory. Ballads and lyric folksongs of love are found in every general and regional collection. One particular source for imported balladry on certain popular love themes is G. Malcolm Laws, Jr., *American Balladry from British Broadsides: A Guide for Students and Collectors of Traditional Song*, Philadelphia: American Folklore Society, Bibliographical and Special Series, vol. 8, 1957.

THE CHILD BALLADS

These English and Scottish ballads were anthologized, annotated and canonized during the latter half of the nineteenth century by Harvard Professor Francis James Child.

The Child ballad numbers from 1 to 305 are standard designations in most scholarly folksong collections. The ballad form attracted the strongest interest of folksong scholars for many years, as the following bibliography demonstrates. Aside from Child's original volumes, those by Bronson and Coffin are the most valuable reference and finding aids. The Leach and Coffin book reprints a number of ballad articles, including those in this list preceded by an asterisk.

Abrahams, Roger D. "Patterns of Structure and Role Relationships in the Child Ballad in the United States." *Journal of American Folklore* 79 (1966): 448–462.

Abrahams, Roger D., and George Foss. *Anglo-American Folksong Style*. Englewood Cliffs, N.J.: Prentice-Hall, 1968.

Barry, Phillips, Fannie Hardy Eckstorm, and Mary Winslow Smyth. *British Ballads from Maine: The Development of Popular Songs with Texts and Airs*. New Haven: Yale University Press, 1929. [Confined to Child ballads.]

Bayard, Samuel P. "Ballad Tunes and the Hustvedt Indexing Method." *Journal of American Folklore* 55 (1942):248–254.

Ben-Amos, Dan. "The Situation Structure of the Non-Humorous English Ballad." *Midwest Folklore* 13 (1963):163–176.

Boswell, George W. "Reciprocal Controls Exerted by Ballad Texts and Tunes." *Journal of American Folklore* 80 (1967):169–174.

―――――. "Shaping Controls of Ballad Tunes over Their Texts." *Tennessee Folklore Society Bulletin* 17 (1951):9–18.

Brewster, Paul G. *The Two Sisters*. Helsinki: Folklore Fellows Communications, vol. 62. no. 147, 1953.

Bronson, Bertrand H. *The Ballad as Song*. Berkeley and Los Angeles: University of California Press, 1969. [Anthology of the author's articles on the music of the ballad.]

*―――――. "The Interdependence of Ballad Tunes and Texts." *California Folklore Quarterly* 3 (1944):185–207.

―――――. *The Traditional Tunes of the Child Ballads*. Vols. 1–4. Princeton: Princeton University Press, 1959–1972. [Contains thousands of examples.]

Buchan, David. *The Ballad and the Folk*. London: Routledge & Kegan Paul, 1972.

Child, Francis James. "Ballad Poetry." In *Johnson's New Universal Cyclopaedia*. Vol. 1. New York: A. J. Johnson & Son, 1875.

―――――. *The English and Scottish Popular Ballads*. 5 vols. Boston and New York: Houghton Mifflin, 1882–1898. Reprint (hardbound). New York: Cooper Square Publishers, 1962. Reprint (paperbound). New York: Dover Publications, 1965.

―――――. *English and Scottish Popular Ballads*. Student's Cambridge Edition. Edited by Helen Child Sargent and George Lyman Kittredge. Boston: Houghton Mifflin, 1904.

Coffin, Tristram P. *The British Traditional Ballad in North America*. Philadelphia: American Folklore Society, Bibliographical and Special Series, vol. 2, 1950. Rev. ed., 1963.

*―――――. " 'Mary Hamilton' and the Anglo-American Ballad as an Art Form." *Journal of American Folklore* 70 (1957):208–214.

―――――. "Remarks Preliminary to a Study of Ballad Meter and Ballad Singing." *Journal of American Folklore* 78 (1965):149–153.

Davis, Arthur Kyle, Jr. *More Traditional Ballads of Virginia: Collected with the Co-operation of Members of the Virginia Folklore Society*. Chapel Hill: University of North Carolina Press, 1960. [Child ballads.]

————. "Some Problems of Ballad Publication." *Musical Quarterly* 14 (1928):283–296.

————. *Traditional Ballads of Virginia: Collected under the Auspices of the Virginia Folklore Society.* Cambridge: Harvard University Press, 1929. Reprint. Charlottesville: University Press of Virginia, 1969. [Child ballads.]

Entwistle, William J. *European Balladry.* Oxford: Clarendon Press, 1939.

Flanders, Helen Hartness. *Ancient Ballads Traditionally Sung in New England.* Vols. 1–4. Philadelphia: University of Pennsylvania Press, 1960–1965. [Child ballads.]

"Folksong and Ballad: A Symposium." *Journal of American Folklore* 70 (1957): 205–261.

Fowler, David C. *A Literary History of the Popular Ballad.* Durham, N.C.: Duke University Press, 1968.

Friedman, Albert B. *The Ballad Revival.* Chicago: University of Chicago Press, 1961.

————. *The Viking Book of Folk Ballads of the English-Speaking World.* New York: The Viking Press, 1961.

Gerould, Gordon Hall. *The Ballad of Tradition.* New York: Oxford University Press, 1932.

Goldstein, Kenneth S. "The Ballad Scholar and the Long-Playing Phonograph Record." In *Folklore and Society: Essays in Honor of Ben A. Botkin,* edited by Bruce Jackson, pp. 35–44. Hatboro, Pa.: Folklore Associates, 1966.

Gordon, Philip. "The Music of the Ballads." *Southern Folklore Quarterly* 6 (1942): 143–148.

Grieg, Gavin. *Last Leaves of Traditional Ballads and Ballad Airs.* Edited by Alexander Keith. Aberdeen: Aberdeen University Studies, no. 100, 1925. [Child ballads.]

Grundtvig, Svend, and Axel Olrik. *Danmarks Gamle Folkeviser.* 10 vols., Copenhagen: Samfundet Tilden Danske Literaturs Fremme, 1853–1965. Reprint. Copenhagen: Akademisk Forlag, 1966–1967. [Grundtvig greatly influenced the work of F. J. Child.]

Gummere, Francis B. *The Popular Ballad.* Boston and New York: Houghton Mifflin, 1907. Reprint. New York: Dover Publications, 1959.

Hart, Walter Morris. *Ballad and Epic: A Study in the Development of the Narrative Art.* Boston: Studies and Notes in Philology and Literature, vol. 11, 1907. Reprint. New York: Russell & Russell, 1967.

Henderson, Thomas F. *The Ballad in Literature,* Cambridge: University Press, 1912. Reprint. New York: Haskell, 1969.

Hendren, Joseph W. "The Scholar and the Ballad Singer." *Southern Folklore Quarterly* 18 (1954):139–146.

————. *A Study of Ballad Rhythm with Special Reference to Ballad Music.* Princeton: Princeton Studies in English, vol. 14, 1936. Reprint. New York: Gordian Press, 1966.

Hodgart, Matthew J. C. *The Ballads.* London: Hutchinson's University Library, 1950. 2nd ed. New York: Hillary House, 1962.

Hustvedt, Sigurd Bernhard. *Ballad Books and Ballad Men: Raids and Rescues in Britain, America, and the Scandinavian North since 1800.* Cambridge, Mass.: Harvard University Press, 1930. Reprint. New York: Johnson Reprint Corp., 1970.

————. *Ballad Criticism in Scandinavia and Great Britain during the Eighteenth Century.* New York: American-Scandinavian Foundation, 1916. Reprint. New York: Kraus Reprint, 1971.

————. "A Melodic Index of Child's Ballad Tunes." *Publications of the University of California at Los Angeles in Languages and Literatures* 1 (1936):51–78.

Hyman, Stanley Edgar. "The Child Ballads." In *The Promised End: Essays and Reviews, 1942–1962.* Cleveland and New York: World Publishing, 1963. Pp. 249–270. [Three essays.]

*James, Thelma G. "The English and Scottish Popular Ballads of Francis J. Child." *Journal of American Folklore* 46 (1933):51–68.

Jones, James H. "Commonplace and Memorization in the Oral Tradition of the English and Scottish Popular Ballads." *Journal of American Folklore* 74 (1961):97–112.

*Keith, Alexander. "Scottish Ballads: Their Evidence of Authorship and Origin." *Essays and Studies by Members of the English Association* 12 (1926):100–119.

Kinsley, James. *The Oxford Book of Ballads.* Oxford: Clarendon Press, 1969.

Laws, G. Malcolm, Jr. *The British Literary Ballad: A Study in Poetic Imitation.* Carbondale: Southern Illinois University Press, 1972; London and Amsterdam: Feffer & Simons, 1972.

————. "Stories Told in Song: The Ballads of America." In *Our Living Traditions: An Introduction to American Folklore*, edited by Tristram P. Coffin, pp. 83–93. New York: Basic Books, 1968.

Leach, MacEdward. "Ballad." In Funk & Wagnalls *Standard Dictionary of Folklore, Mythology, and Legend.* Edited by Maria Leach, vol. 1, pp. 106–111. New York: Funk & Wagnalls, 1949. Reprinted 1972.

————. *The Ballad Book.* New York: Harper & Bros., 1955.

————. "The Singer or the Song." In *Singers and Storytellers.* Edited by Mody C. Boatright et al., vol. 30, pp. 30–45. Dallas: Publications of the Texas Folklore Society, 1961.

Leach, MacEdward, and Tristram P. Coffin, eds. *The Critics and the Ballad.* Carbondale: Southern Illinois University Press, 1961.

List, George. "An Approach to the Indexing of Ballad Tunes." *Folklore and Folk Music Archivist* 6 (1963):7–16.

————. "Toward the Indexing of Ballad Texts." *Journal of American Folklore* 81 (1968):44–61.

Lloyd, A. L. *Folk Song in England.* London: Lawrence & Wishart, 1967; New York: International Publishers, 1967.

Long, Eleanor R. *"The Maid" and "The Hangman": Myth and Tradition in a Popular Ballad.* Berkeley: University of California Publications, Folklore Studies, vol. 21, 1971.

MacKenzie. M. L. "The Great Ballad Collectors: Percy, Herd, and Ritson." *Studies in Scottish Literature* 2 (1965):213–233.

MacKenzie, W. Roy. *The Quest of the Ballad.* Princeton: Princeton University Press, 1919. Reprint. New York: Haskell House, 1966.

McMillan, Douglas J. "A Survey of Theories Concerning the Oral Transmission of the Traditional Ballad." *Southern Folklore Quarterly* 28 (1964):299–309.

Miller, E. Joan Wilson. "The Rag-Bag World of Balladry." *Southern Folklore Quarterly* 24 (1960):217–225.

Miller, George M. "The Dramatic Element in the Popular Ballad." *University Studies of the University of Cincinnati*, series 2, 1 (1905):3–59.

Moore, Arthur K. "The Literary Status of the English Popular Ballad." *Comparative Literature* 10 (1958):1–20.

Morokoff, Gene E. "Whole Tale Parallels of the Child Ballads as Cited or Given by Child or in FFC 74." *Journal of American Folklore* 64 (1951):203–206.

Muir, Willa. *Living with Ballads.* New York: Oxford University Press, 1965.

Niles, John Jacob. *The Ballad Book of John Jacob Niles.* Boston: Houghton Mifflin, 1961. [A compilation of Child ballads by a noted composer/singer/collector.]

Nygard, Holger Olaf. "Ballad, Folkevise, Chanson Populaire." In *Folklore Studies in Honor of Arthur Palmer Hudson*, edited by Daniel Patterson, pp. 39–65. Chapel Hill: North Carolina Folklore Society, 1965.

————. *The Ballad of Heer Halewijn: Its Forms and Variations in Western Europe: A Study of the History and Nature of a Ballad Tradition.* Knoxville: University of Tennessee Press, 1958; Helsinki: Folklore Fellows Communications, vol. 67, no. 169, 1958.

————. "Popular Ballad and Medieval Romance." In *Folklore International: Essays in Traditional Literature, Belief, and Custom in Honor of Wayland Debs Hand.* Edited by D. K. Wilgus, pp. 161–173. Hatboro, Pa.: Folklore Associates, 1967.

Pound, Louise. *Poetic Origins and the Ballad.* New York: Macmillan, 1921. Reprint. New York: Russell & Russell, 1962.

Richmond, W. Edson. "Narrative Folk Poetry." In *Folklore and Folklife: An Introduction*, edited by Richard M. Dorson, pp. 85–98. Chicago: University of Chicago Press, 1972.

*————. "Some Effects of Scribal and Typographical Error on Oral Tradition." *Southern Folklore Quarterly* 15 (1951):159–170.

Roberts, Warren E. "Comic Elements in the English Traditional Ballad." *Journal of the International Folk Music Council* 3 (1951):76–81.

Seeger, Charles. "Versions and Variants of the Tunes of 'Barbara Allen.'" *Selected Reports: Publications of the Institute of Ethnomusicology of the University of California at Los Angeles* 1 (1966):120–163. [This also accompanies Library of Congress record LP54, *Versions and Variants of Barbara Allen.*]

Sidgwick, Frank. *The Ballad.* London: Martin Secker, 1914. Reprint. Folcroft, Pa.: Folcroft Library Editions, 1971.

Smith, Reed. *South Carolina Ballads: With a Study of Traditional Ballad To-Day.* Cambridge, Mass.: Harvard University Press, 1928. Reprints. Spartanburg, S.C.: Reprint Co., 1972; Freeport, N.Y.: Books for Libraries Press, 1972. [Child ballads.]

*Stewart, George R., Jr. "The Meter of the Popular Ballad." *Publications of the Modern Language Association* 40 (1925):933–962.

Streenstrup, J. C. H. R. *The Medieval Popular Ballad.* Translated from the Danish by Edward Godfrey Cox. Boston: Ginn, 1914. Reprint (foreword by David C. Fowler). Seattle: University of Washington Press, 1968.

Taylor, Archer. *"Edward" and "Sven i Rosengard": A Study in the Dissemination of a Ballad.* Chicago: University of Chicago Press, 1931.

————. The Parallels between Ballads and Tales." In *Festschrift zur 75. Geburtstag von Erich Seeman*, edited by Rolf Wilh. Brednich, Berlin: Walter de Greyter (*Jahrbuch für Volksliedforschung*, vol. 9), 1964. Pp. 104–115.

Thigpen, Kenneth A., Jr. "An Index to the Known Oral Sources of the Child Collection." *Folklore Forum* 5 (1972):55–69.

Toelken, J. Barre. "An Oral Canon for the Child Ballads: Construction and Application." *Journal of the Folklore Institute* 4 (1967):75–101.

Vargyas, Lajos. *Researches into the Mediaeval History of Folk Ballads.* Translated by Arthur H. Whitney. Budapest: Akademiai Kiado, 1967.

Wells, Evelyn Kendrick. *The Ballad Tree.* New York: Ronald Press, 1950.

White, Newman Ivey, general ed. *The Frank C. Brown Collection of North Carolina Folklore.* 7 vols. Durham, N.C.: Duke University Press, 1952–1964.
    Volume 2. *Folk Ballads.* Edited by Henry M. Belden and Arthur Palmer Hudson, 1952.
    Volume 4. *The Music of the Ballads.* Edited by Jan P. Shinhan, 1957.

Whiting, Bartlett Jere. *Traditional British Ballads*. New York: Appleton-Century-Crofts, 1955.

Wilgus, D. K. *Anglo-American Folksong Scholarship since 1898*. New Brunswick, N.J.: Rutgers University Press, 1959.

————. "Ballad Classification." *Midwest Folklore* 5 (1955):95–100.

————. "A Type-Index of Anglo-American Traditional Narrative Songs." *Journal of the Folklore Institute* 7 (1970):161–176.

Wimberly, Lowry C. *Folklore in the English and Scottish Ballads*. Chicago: University of Chicago Press, 1928. Reprints. New York: Frederick Ungar, 1959; New York: Dover Publications, 1965.

Winkelman, Donald M. "Musicological Techniques of Ballad Analysis." *Midwest Folklore* 10 (1960–1961):197–205.

————. "Poetic/Rhythmic Stress in the Child Ballads." *Keystone Folklore Quarterly* 12 (1967):103–117.

————. "Some Rhythmic Aspects of the Child Ballads." In *New Voices in American Studies*, edited by Ray B. Browne, Donald M. Winkelman, and Allan Hayman, pp. 151–162. Lafayette: Purdue University Studies, 1966.

CHILD BALLADS AVAILABLE ON LONG-PLAYING RECORDINGS FROM THE ARCHIVE OF FOLK SONG, LIBRARY OF CONGRESS

It may be noted that LPs 57 and 58 are given over exclusively to Child ballads, and that they are both edited by Professor Bertrand Harris Bronson. LP 54, edited by Charles Seeger, deals solely with versions and variants of "Barbara Allen," ballad no. 84. The other records that contain certain of the Child ballads also include other traditional Anglo-American songs and ballads outside the strict Child canon, but nonetheless within the mainstream of English-Scotch-Irish-American folksong. All are available at $4.95, postage and handling included, from the Recording Laboratory, Music Division, Library of Congress, Washington, D.C. 20540.

CHILD BALLAD NUMBER	TITLE	LIBRARY OF CONGRESS LONG-PLAYING RECORD NUMBER
1	The Devil's Nine Questions	LP 1
3	The False Knight upon the Road	LP 21
7	Sweet William	LP 12
10	The Two Sisters	LP 7
13	Edward	LP 12, LP 57
17	In Scotland Town	LP 65
18	Wild Boar	LP 57
	Bangum and the Boar	LP 57
45	The Bishop of Canterbury	LP 57
49	The Two Brothers	LP 7
53	Lord Bateman	LP 12, LP 57
	Lloyd Bateman	LP 57
54	The Cherry-Tree Carol	LP 12, LP 57

56	Lazarus	LP 57
68	Young Henerly	LP 66
73	Lord Thomas and Fair Ellender	LP 7
75	Lord Lovel	LP 55
79	The Three Babes	LP 7, LP 58
84	Barbara Allen	LP 1, LP 14, LP 51
	30 Versions and Variants of "Barbara Allen" (some incomplete)	LP 54
93	Bolakins	LP 7
167 250	Andrew Batann	LP 58
170	The Death of Queen Jane	LP 21
173	The Four Marys	LP 7
200	The Gypsy Davy	LP 1
208	The King's Love Letter	LP 58
243	The House Carpenter	LP 1
	Well Met, My Old True Love	LP 58
	The Ship Carpenter	LP 58
272	There Was an Old and Wealthy Man	LP 58
274	Our Goodman	LP 12
278	The Farmer's Curst Wife	LP 1
	Old Woman under the Hill	LP 51 (incomplete)
	The Devil and the Farmer's Wife	LP 58
283	The Oxford Merchant	LP 58
286	The Golden Willow Tree	LP 7
	A Ship Set Sail for North America	LP 58
289	The Mermaid	LP 58

HYMNS AND RELIGIOUS PIECES

The entire realm of white American folk hymnody has been studied at length in the following books by George Pullen Jackson (arranged chronologically):

White Spirituals in the Southern Uplands. Chapel Hill: University of North Carolina Press, 1933. Reprint (foreword by Don Yoder). Hatboro, Pa.: Folklore Associates, 1964. Reprint (without foreword). New York: Dover Publications, 1965.

Spiritual Folk-Songs of Early America: Two Hundred and Fifty Tunes and Texts with an Introduction and Notes. New York: J. J. Augustin, 1937. Reprint. New York: Dover Publications, 1964.

Down-East Spirituals and Others. New York: J. J. Augustin, 1943. 2nd ed., 1953.

White and Negro Spirituals: Their Life Span and Kinship. New York: J. J. Augustin, 1943.

Another Sheaf of White Spirituals. Gainesville: University of Florida Press, 1952. [Includes an overall song index to the five Jackson books listed here.]

Other books on American folk hymnody:

Andrews, Edward D. *The Gift to Be Simple: Songs, Dances and Rituals of the American Shakers.* New York: J. J. Augustin, 1940. Reprint. New York: Dover Publications, 1968.

Buchanan, Annabel Morris. *Folk Hymns of America*. New York: J. Fischer & Bros., 1938.
Horn, Dorothy O. *Sing to Me of Heaven: A Study of Folk and Early American Materials in Three Old Harp Books*. Gainesville: University of Florida Press, 1970.
McDowell, L. L. *Songs of the Old Camp Ground*. Ann Arbor, Mich.: Edwards Bros., 1937.

Three currently used books typify the genre of religious song used by Primitive Baptists and others, which frequently employs the "lining out" technique of song-leading or prompting:

Billips, Edward W. *The Sweet Songster: A Collection of the Most Popular and Approved Songs, Hymns and Ballads*. First published in 1854. Currently published by Arrowood Bros., Wayne, W. Va.
Ratliff, Foster. *The New Baptist Song Book, 1971: A Collection of Good Hymns, Songs and Ballads*. First published in 1957. Currently published by Foster Ratliff, Lookout, Ky.
Thomas, E. D. *A Choice Selection of Hymns and Spiritual Songs for the Use of the Baptist Church and All Lovers of Song*. First published in 1877. Currently published by Arrowood Bros., Wayne, W. Va.

From the nineteenth-century four- and seven-shape-note song traditions, the following songbooks are currently in use and in print (arranged by title):

The Christian Harmony, by William Walker. Revised 1958, by John Deason and O. A. Parris. John H. Deason, 161 Poydras Avenue, Mobile, Ala. 36606.
The Good Old Songs, by C. H. Cayce. 28th ed. 1967. Cayce Publishing, Thornton, Ark. 71766.
The New Harp of Columbia, by M. L. Swan. Nashville, Tenn: Publishing House of the M. E. Church, South, 1921. Available from House of Music, 732 Cherry Street, Chattanooga, Tenn. 37402.
Original Sacred Harp: Denson Revision: 1971 Edition. Sacred Harp Publishing Co., Hugh McGraw, Treasurer, P.O. Box 185, Bremen, Ga. 30110.
The Sacred Harp, by B. F. White and E. J. King. Facsimile of 3rd ed. (1859), 1968. Broadman Press, 127 9th Ave., North, Nashville, Tenn. 37234.
The Sacred Harp, revised by W. M. Cooper. 1950 printing. Sacred Harp Book Company, P.O. Box 46, Troy, Ala. 36081.
The Social Harp, by John G. McCurry. Facsimile reprint of 1855 ed. Daniel W. Patterson and John F. Garst, eds., 1973. University of Georgia Press, Athens, Ga. 30601.
The Southern Harmony, by William Walker. Facsimile reprint of 1854 ed. Glenn C. Wilcox, ed., 1966. Pro Musicamericana, Box 649, Murray, Ky. 42071.

THE NEGRO SPIRITUAL

For over a century, the Negro spiritual has been America's most popular folk music form to permeate the popular and art music of the world. The following are standard sources and discussions for this influential genre.

Allen, William Francis, Charles Pickard Ware, and Lucy McKim Garrison. *Slave Songs of the United States.* New York: A. Simpson, 1867. Reprints. New York: Peter Smith, 1951; Freeport, N.Y.: Books for Libraries Press, 1971. Rev. ed. New York: Oak Publications, 1965.

Ballanta (-Taylor), Nicholas George Julius. *Saint Helena Island Spirituals.* New York: G. Schirmer, 1925.

Barton, William E. *Old Plantation Hymns: A Collection of Hitherto Unpublished Melodies of the Slave and the Freedman, with Historical and Descriptive Notes.* Boston: Lamson, Wolffe, 1899. Reprint. New York: AMS Press, 1972.

Boatner, Edward, and Willa A. Townsend. *Spirituals Triumphant Old and New.* Nashville: National Baptist Convention, 1927.

Chambers, Henry Alban. *The Treasury of Negro Spirituals.* New York: Emerson Books, 1963.

Cone, James H. *The Spirituals and the Blues: An Interpretation.* New York: Seabury Press, 1972.

Courlander, Harold. "Anthems and Spirituals as Oral Literature." In *Negro Folk Music, U.S.A.* New York: Columbia University Press, 1963. Reprinted, 1970. Pp. 35–79.

Dett, R. Nathaniel. *Religious Folk-Songs of the Negro as Sung at Hampton Institute.* First published 1874. Rev. ed. Hampton, Va.: Hampton Institute Press, 1927. Reprint. New York: AMS Press, 1972.

Dixon, Christa. *Wesen und Wandel geistlicher Volkslieder: Negro Spirituals.* Wuppertal: Jugenddienst-Verlag, 1967.

Epstein, Dena J. "Slave Music in the United States before 1860: A Survey of Sources." Music Library Association *Notes* 20 (1963):195–212; 377–390.

Fenner, Thomas P., Frederic G. Rathburn, and Bessie Cleaveland. *Cabin and Plantation Songs as Sung by the Hampton Students.* New York: B. P. Putnam's Sons, 1901.

Fisher, Miles Mark. *Negro Slave Songs in the United States.* Ithaca: Cornell University Press for the American Historical Association, 1953. Reprint. New York: Russell & Russell, 1968.

Gordon, Robert Winslow. "The Negro Spiritual." In *The Carolina Low-Country*, by the Society for the Preservation of Spirituals, pp. 191–222. New York: Macmillan, 1931.

Grissom, Mary Allen. *The Negro Sings of a New Heaven.* Chapel Hill: University of North Carolina Press, 1930. Reprint. New York: Dover Publications, 1969.

Grossman, Stefan. *Rev. Gary Davis: The Holy Blues.* New York: Robbins Music Corp., 1970.

Hagen, Rochus A. M. "Abriss der Geschichte der Spiritualforschung." *Jahrbuch für Musikalische Volks- und Völkerkunde* 4 (1968):59–97.

Handy, William C. *W. C. Handy's Collection of Negro Spirituals.* 2 vols. New York: Handy Brothers Music, 1938.

Hays, Roland. *My Songs: Aframerican Folk Songs.* Boston: Little, Brown, 1948.

Jackson, Bruce. "The Glory Songs of the Lord." In *Our Living Traditions: An Introduction to American Folklore*, edited by Tristram P. Coffin, pp. 108–119. New York: Basic Books, 1968.

––––––. *Wake Up, Dead Man: Afro-American Worksongs from Texas Prisons.* Cambridge, Mass.: Harvard University Press, 1972.

Jackson, George Pullen. *White and Negro Spirituals.* New York: J. J. Augustin, 1944.

Johnson, Guy B. "The Negro Spiritual: A Problem in Anthropology." *American Anthropologist* 33 (1931):157–171.

Johnson, James Weldon, and J. Rosamond Johnson. *The Books of American Negro Spirituals: Including the Book of American Negro Spirituals and the Second Book of Negro Spirituals.* New York: Viking Press, 1940. Reprinted, 1969.

Katz, Bernard, ed. *The Social Implications of Early Negro Music in the United States.* New York: Arno Press, 1969. [Reprints of early articles.]

Kennedy, R. Emmet. *Mellows: A Chronicle of Unknown Singers.* New York: Albert & Charles Boni, 1925.

———. *More Mellows.* New York: Dodd, Mead, 1931.

Lehmann, Theo. *Negro Spirituals: Geschichte und Theologie.* Berlin: Echart-Verlag, 1965.

Locke, Alain. "The Negro Spirituals." In *The New Negro: An Interpretation.* Reprint (with a new introduction by Allan H. Spear). New York and London: Johnson Reprint Corp., 1968. Pp. 199–213.

Look Away: 56 Negro Folk Songs. Delaware, Ohio: Cooperative Recreation Service, 1960.

Lovell, John, Jr. *Black Song: The Forge and the Flame: The Story of How the Afro-American Spiritual Was Hammered Out.* New York: Macmillan, 1972; London: Collier-Macmillan, 1972.

———. "Reflections on the Origins of the Negro Spiritual." *Negro American Literary Forum* 3 (1969):91–97.

———. "The Social Implications of the Negro Spiritual." *Journal of Negro Education* 8 (1939):634–643. Reprinted in *The Social Implications of Early Negro Music in the United States,* edited by Bernard Katz, pp. 128–137. New York: Arno Press, 1969. Also reprinted in *Mother Wit from the Laughing Barrel: Readings in the Interpretation of Afro-American Folklore,* edited by Alan Dundes, pp. 452–464. Englewood Cliffs, N.J.: Prentice-Hall, 1973.

McIlhenny, E. A. *Befo' de War Spirituals.* Boston: Christopher Publishing House, 1933. Reprint. New York: AMS Press, 1973.

Odum, Howard W., and Guy B. Johnson. *The Negro and His Songs: A Study of Typical Negro Songs in the South.* Chapel Hill: University of North Carolina Press, 1925. Reprint (foreword by Roger D. Abrahams). Hatboro, Pa.: Folklore Associates, 1964. Reprint (without foreword). New York: Negro Universities Press, 1968.

Owens, J. Garfield. *All God's Chillun: Meditations on Negro Spirituals.* Nashville: Abingdon Press, 1971.

Parrish, Lydia. *Slave Songs of the Georgia Sea Islands.* New York: Creative Age Press, 1942. Reprint (foreword by Bruce Jackson). Hatboro, Pa.: Folklore Associates, 1965.

Thurman, Howard. *The Negro Spiritual Speaks of Life and Death.* New York and Evanston: Harper & Row, 1969.

White, Newman Ivey. *American Negro Folk-Songs.* Cambridge, Mass.: Harvard University Press, 1928. Reprint (foreword by Bruce Jackson). Hatboro, Pa.: Folklore Associates, 1965.

Wilgus, D. K. "The Negro White Spiritual." In *Anglo-American Folksong Scholarship since 1898.* New Brunswick, N.J.: Rutgers University Press, 1959. Pp. 345–364. Reprinted in *Mother Wit from the Laughing Barrel: Readings in the Interpretation of Afro-American Folklore,* edited by Alan Dundes, pp. 67–80. Englewood Cliffs, N.J.: Prentice-Hall, 1973.

CAROLS AND CHRISTMAS PIECES

In addition to scattered items contained in the general religious collections, there are two good books comprised solely of American Christmas folksongs:

Poston, Elizabeth. *The Second Penguin Book of Christmas Carols.* Harmondsworth, Middlesex, Eng., and Baltimore, Md.: Penguin Books, 1970.
Seeger, Ruth Crawford. *American Folk Songs for Christmas.* Garden City, N.Y.: Doubleday, 1953.

THE WARS

With the American Revolutionary Bicentennial approaching, a number of collections and studies of the music and song of that period can be expected. Meanwhile, the following sources are at hand:

Ames, Russell. *The Story of American Folk Song.* New York: Grosset & Dunlap, 1955. Reprinted, 1960. Pp. 31–41.
Barney, Samuel Eben. *Songs of the Revolution.* New Haven: Tuttle, Morehouse & Taylor, 1893.
Brand, Oscar. *Songs of '76: A Folksinger's History of the Revolution.* New York: M. Evans, 1972.
Coffin, Tristram P. *Uncertain Glory: Folklore and the American Revolution.* Detroit: Folklore Associates, 1971.
Dolph, Edward Arthur. *"Sound Off!" Soldier Songs from Yankee Doodle to Parley Voo.* New York: Cosmopolitan Book, 1929. Pp. 457–504.
Downes, Olin, and Elie Siegmeister. *A Treasury of American Songs.* New York: Howell, Soskin, 1940. 2nd ed. New York: Alfred A. Knopf, 1943. Pp. 53–81.
Eggleston, George Cary. *American War Ballads and Lyrics.* 2 vols. New York: G. P. Putnam's Sons, 1889. Pp. 21–104.
Engel, Carl. *Music from the Days of George Washington.* Washington, D.C.: United States George Washington Bicentennial Commission, 1931. 2nd, 3rd, 4th eds., 1932. Reprint. New York: AMS Press, 1970.
Fisher, William Arms. *The Music That Washington Knew.* Boston: Oliver Ditson, 1931.
Flanders, Helen Hartness. "Songs Alive from Revolutionary Times." *American Heritage* 2 (1951):48–49; 62–64.
Heintze, James R. "Music of the Washington Family: A Little-Known Collection." *Musical Quarterly* 56 (1970):288–293.
Ives, Burl. *The Burl Ives Song Book: American Songs in Historical Perspective.* New York: Ballantine Books, 1953. Pp. 81–126.
Luther, Frank. *Americans and Their Songs.* New York: Harper & Bros., 1942. Pp. 30–42.
Moore, Frank. *Songs and Ballads of the American Revolution.* New York: D. Appleton, 1856. New York: Hurst, 1905. Reprints. Port Washington, N.Y.: Kennikat Press, 1964; New York: New York Times, 1969.
Nesser, Robert W. *American Naval Songs and Ballads.* New Haven: Yale University Press, 1938; London: Oxford University Press, 1938. Pp. 3–50.

Newcomb, Lydia Bolles. "Songs and Ballads of the Revolution." *New England Magazine*, new series, 13 (1895):501–513.

Schlesinger, A. M. "A Note on Songs as Patriotic Propaganda, 1765–1776." *William and Mary Quarterly*, series 3, 11 (1954):78–88.

Scott, John Anthony. *The Ballad of America: The History of the United States in Song and Story.* New York: Bantam Books, 1966. Pp. 53–90.

————. "Ballads and Broadsides of the American Revolution." *Sing Out!* 16 (1966): 18–23.

Silber, Irwin. *Songs of Independence.* Harrisburg: Stackpole Books, 1973.

Sonneck, Oscar George Theodore. Report on "The Star-Spangled Banner," "Hail Columbia," "America," "Yankee Doodle." Washington, D.C.: Library of Congress, 1909. Reprint. New York: Dover Publications, 1972.

Sonneck, Oscar George Theodore, and William Treat Upton. *A Bibliography of Early Secular American Music.* Washington, D.C.: H. L. McQueen, 1905. Reprint (preface by Irving Lowens). New York: Da Capo Press, 1964.

Winstock, Lewis. *Songs and Music of the Redcoats: A History of the War Music of the British Army, 1642–1902.* London: Lee Cooper, 1970; Harrisburg, Pa.: Stackpole Books, 1970. Pp. 69–87.

The Civil War centennial period saw the appearance of four major musical works:

Bernard, Kenneth A. *Lincoln and the Music of the Civil War.* Caldwell, Idaho: Caxton Printers, 1966.

Glass, Paul, and Louis C. Singer. *Singing Soldiers (The Spirit of the Sixties): A History of the Civil War in Song.* New York: Grosset & Dunlap, 1968.

Heaps, Willard A. and Porter W. *The Singing Sixties: The Spirit of Civil War Days Drawn from the Music of the Times.* Norman: University of Oklahoma Press, 1960.

Silber, Irwin. *Songs of the Civil War.* New York: Columbia University Press, 1960. [Includes many songs from folk sources.]

A source of prime references, with synopses and discussions, to American war ballads can be found on pp. 118–131 and 257–259 of G. Malcolm Laws, Jr., *Native American Balladry: A Descriptive Study and a Bibliographical Syllabus*, Philadelphia: American Folklore Society, Bibliographical and Special Series, vol. 8, 1957; reprint edition, 1964.

The Dolph book cited in the American Revolution list is the only substantial anthology encompassing all American wars through World War I. (For seafaring war songs, see the Sea Song bibliography below.) The following are specialized collections:

Palmer, Edgar A. *G. I. Songs: Written, Composed and/or Collected by the Men in the Service.* New York: Sheridan House, 1944.

Wallrich, William. *Air Force Airs: Songs and Ballads of the United States Air Force: World War One through Korea.* New York: Duell, Sloan & Pearce, 1957.

THE ASSASSINATION OF PRESIDENTS

The best single source for assassination folksongs is an LP issued by the Library of Congress Archive of Folk Song, no. LP29, *Songs and Ballads of American History and of the Assassination of Presidents*, edited by Duncan Emrich. The five assassination ballads included are sung and played by Bascom Lamar Lunsford.

DISASTERS

The chief source for this subject is the chapter entitled "Ballads of Tragedies and Disasters" (pp. 212–228, 271–273) in G. Malcolm Laws, Jr., *Native American Balladry: A Descriptive Study and a Bibliographical Syllabus*, Philadelphia: American Folklore Society, Bibliographical and Special Series, vol. 1, 1950; revised edition, 1964. Further examples can be found in almost any general or regional American folksong collection. See especially the bibliographies for the following sections: Wars, Assassinations, Sea Songs, Lumbering, Coal, Railroading, Murders.

LUMBERING

Folksongs of lumbermen are common in many collections from the northern part of the United States and from Canada, as well as in several general collections. The following books are particularly important:

Barry, Phillips. *The Maine Woods Songster.* Cambridge, Mass.: Powell Publishing, 1939.

Beck, Earl Clifton. *Songs of the Michigan Lumberjacks.* Ann Arbor: University of Michigan Press, 1941. Rev. ed. *Lore of the Lumber Camps*, 1948.

Doerflinger, William M. *Shanteymen and Shanteyboys: Songs of the Sailor and Lumberman.* New York: Macmillan, 1951. Reprinted as *Songs of the Sailor and Lumberman*, 1972.

Eckstorm, Fannie Hardy, and Mary Winslow Smyth. *Minstrelsy of Maine: Folk-Songs and Ballads of the Woods and the Coast.* Boston and New York: Houghton Mifflin, 1927. Reprint. Ann Arbor, Mich.: Gryphon Books, 1971.

Fowke, Edith. *Lumbering Songs from the Northern Woods.* Austin: University of Texas Press, 1970. (Publications of the American Folklore Society, Memoir Series, vol. 55.) [Primarily from Ontario.]

Gray, Roland Palmer. *Songs and Ballads of the Maine Lumberjacks: With Other Songs from Maine.* Cambridge, Mass.: Harvard University Press, 1924. Reprint. Detroit: Singing Tree Press, 1969.

Ives, Edward D. *Larry Gorman: The Man Who Made the Songs.* Bloomington: Indiana University Press, 1964. [Study of a Maine lumberman/songwriter.]

Laws, G. Malcolm, Jr. *Native American Balladry: A Descriptive Study and a Bibliographical Syllabus.* Philadelphia: Publications of the American Folklore Society, Bibliographical and Special Series, vol. 1, 1950. Rev. ed., 1964. Pp. 146–160, 261–263.

Manny, Louise, and James Reginald Wilson. *Songs of Miramichi.* Fredericton, N.B.: Brunswick Press, 1968. [New Brunswick, Canada.]

Rickaby, Franz. *Ballads and Songs of the Shanty-Boy.* Cambridge, Mass.: Harvard University Press, 1926. [Wisconsin and Minnesota.]

THE '49ERS

Some songs engendered by the Western Gold Rush can be found in most anthologies of Western song. The following collection specializes in this subject:

Dwyer, Richard A., and Richard E. Lingenfelter. *The Songs of the Gold Rush.* Berkeley: University of California Press, 1964.

An older, smaller anthology:

Black, Eleanora, and Sidney Robertson. *The Gold Rush Song Book*. San Francisco: Colt Press, 1940.

Two of the more popular songsters of the Gold Rush era:

Stone, John A. *Put's Golden Songster*. San Francisco: D. & E. Appleton, 1858.
————. *Put's Original California Songster*. San Francisco: D. & E. Appleton, 1858. 4th ed., 1868.

Several texts appear in the following interesting treatise:

Howe, Octavius Thorndike. *Argonauts of '49: History and Adventures of the Emigrant Companies from Massachusetts, 1849–1850*. Cambridge, Mass.: Harvard University Press, 1923. Reprint. San Francisco: R & E Research Associates, 1970.

THE HARDROCK MEN

In addition to standard Western song anthologies, hard-rock miner song lore is treated in the following:

Emrich, Duncan. "Mining Songs." *Southern Folklore Quarterly* 6 (1942):103–106.
————. "Songs of the Western Miners." *California Folklore Quarterly* 1 (1942): 213–232.
Hand, Wayland D., Charles Cutts, Robert C. Wylder, and Betty Wylder. "Songs of the Butte Miners." *Western Folklore* 9 (1950):1–49.

COAL

The following are the important books on this subject:

Green, Archie. *Only a Miner: Studies in Recorded Coal-Mining Songs*. Urbana: University of Illinois Press, 1972.
Greenway, John. *American Folksongs of Protest*. Philadelphia: University of Pennsylvania Press, 1953. Reprint. New York: Octagon Books, 1970. Pp. 147–172, 252–275.
Korson, George. *Coal Dust on the Fiddle: Songs and Stories of the Anthracite Industry*. Philadelphia: University of Pennsylvania Press, 1938. Reprint (foreword by John Greenway). Hatboro, Pa.: Folklore Associates, 1964.
————. *Minstrels of the Mine Patch: Songs and Stories of the Anthracite Industry*. Philadelphia: University of Pennsylvania Press, 1938. Reprint (foreword by Archie Green). Hatboro, Pa.: Folklore Associates, 1964.

SEA SHANTIES, FORECASTLE SONGS OF THE SEA AND SAILORS, AND WRECKS AND DISASTERS AT SEA

In addition to the references in the following list, folksongs on these subjects are adrift in numerous general and regional collections, particularly those from the eastern seaboard. See the two Laws syllabi for further references.

Colcord, Joanna C. *Roll and Go: Songs of American Sailormen.* Indianapolis: Bobbs-Merrill, 1924. Revised as *Songs of American Sailormen.* New York: W. W. Norton, 1938. Reprint. New York: Oak Publications, 1964.

Doerflinger, William M. *Shanteymen and Shanteyboys: Songs of the Sailor and Lumberman.* New York: Macmillan, 1951. Reprinted as *Songs of the Sailor and Lumberman,* 1972.

Harlow, Frederick Pease. *Chanteying aboard American Ships.* Barre, Mass.: Barre Gazette, 1962.

Hugill, Stan. *Shanties and Sailors' Songs.* London: Jenkins, 1969; New York: Frederick A. Praeger, 1969.

————. *Shanties from the Seven Seas: Shipboard Work-Songs from the Great Days of Sail.* London: Routledge and Kegan Paul, 1961; E. P. Dutton, 1961. [The most definitive collection/study of this genre.]

Huntington, Gale. *Songs the Whalermen Sang.* Barre, Mass.: Barre Publishers, 1964. 2nd ed. New York: Dover Publications, 1970.

Laws, G. Malcolm, Jr. *American Balladry from British Broadsides: A Guide for Students and Collectors of Traditional Song.* Philadelphia: American Folklore Society, Bibliographical and Special Series, vol. 8, 1957. Pp. 140–163.

————. *Native American Balladry: A Descriptive Study and a Bibliographic Syllabus.* Philadelphia: American Folklore Society, Bibliographical and Special Series, vol. 1, 1950. Rev. ed., 1964. Pp. 161–174, 263–265.

Neeser, Robert W. *American Naval Songs and Ballads.* New York: Yale University Press, 1938; London: Oxford University Press, 1938.

Shay, Frank. *Iron Men and Wooden Ships: Deep Sea Chanties.* Garden City, N.Y.: Doubleday, Page, 1924. Also published as *Deep Sea Chanties: Old Sea Songs.* London: W. Heinemann, 1925. Reprinted as *American Sea Songs and Chanteys from the Days of Iron Men and Wooden Ships.* New York: W. W. Norton, 1948. Reprint. Freeport, N.Y.: Books for Libraries Press, 1969.

SONGS OF THE MORMONS

The following are the basic works on Mormon folksong:

Cheney, Thomas E. *Mormon Songs from the Rocky Mountains.* Austin: University of Texas Press, 1968. (Publications of the American Folklore Society, Memoir Series, vol. 53.)

Durham, Alfred. *Pioneer Songs.* Salt Lake City: Daughters of Utah Pioneers, 1932. 2nd rev. ed., 1940.

Fife, Austin and Alta S. *Saints of Sage and Saddle: Folklore among the Mormons.* Bloomington: Indiana University Press, 1956. Reprint. Gloucester, Mass.: Peter Smith, 1966.

Hubbard, Lester A. *Ballads and Songs from Utah.* Salt Lake City: University of Utah Press, 1961.

"WESTWARD THE COURSE . . ." AND THE COWBOY

All general folksong collections and those from Western states contain material germane to these subjects. The following are of particular note:

Allen, Jules Verne. *Cowboy Lore.* San Antonio: Naylor Printing, 1933. Reprints. 1950, 1971.

Belden, Henry M. *Ballads and Songs Collected by the Missouri Folk Song Society.* Columbia: University of Missouri Studies, vol. 15, no. 1, 1940. 2nd ed., 1955. Reprinted, 1966, 1973.

Botkin, Benjamin A. *A Treasury of Western Folklore.* New York: Crown, 1951. Pp. 728–792.

Fife, Austin E. and Alta S. *Ballads of the Great West.* Palo Alto, Calif.: American West Publishing, 1970.

——. *Cowboy and Western Songs: A Comprehensive Anthology.* New York: Clarkson N. Potter, 1969.

——. *Heaven on Horseback: Revivalist Songs in Verse in the Cowboy Idiom.* Logan: Utah State University Press, 1970. (Western Texts Society Series, vol. 1, no. 1.)

Finger, Charles J. *Frontier Ballads.* Garden City, N.Y.: Doubleday, Page, 1927.

Hubbard, Lester A. *Ballads and Songs from Utah.* Salt Lake City: University of Utah Press, 1961.

Larkin, Margaret. *Singing Cowboy: A Book of Western Songs.* New York: Alfred A. Knopf, 1931. Reprint. New York: Oak Publications, 1963.

Laws, G. Malcolm, Jr. *Native American Balladry: A Descriptive Study and a Bibliographic Syllabus.* Philadelphia: American Folklore Society, Bibliographical and Special Series, vol. 1, 1950. Rev. ed., 1964. Pp. 132–145, 259–261.

Lingenfelter, Richard E., Richard Dwyer, and David Cohen. *Songs of the American West.* Berkeley and Los Angeles: University of California Press, 1968.

Lomax, John. *Cowboy Songs and Other Frontier Ballads.* New York: Sturgis & Walton, 1910. Rev. eds., 1911, 1916 (reprinted by Macmillan, 1918). Rev. ed. (with Alan Lomax). New York: Macmillan, 1938. 13th printing, 1961.

——. *Songs of the Cattle Trail and Cow Camp.* New York: Macmillan, 1915. Reprint. New York: Duell, Sloan and Pearce, 1950.

Moore, Ethel and Chauncey O. *Ballads and Folk Songs of the Southwest.* Norman: University of Oklahoma Press, 1964.

Owens, William A. *Texas Folk Songs.* Austin: Publications of the Texas Folklore Society, no. 23, 1950.

Randolph, Vance. *Ozark Folksongs.* 4 vols. Columbia: State Historical Society of Missouri, 1946–1950.

Silber, Irwin, and Earl Robinson. *Songs of the Great American West.* New York: Macmillan, 1967; London: Collier-Macmillan, 1967.

Thorp, N. Howard. *Songs of the Cowboys*. Variants, commentary, notes and lexicon by Austin E. and Alta S. Fife. New York: Clarkson N. Potter, 1966. [Based on a collection originally published in 1908.]

WORK CHANTS

Songs of this genre are represented in a number of general collections of southern Negro folksong, as well as in the Lomax anthologies. See also references in the railroad section, which follows. One book concentrates on the subject:

Jackson, Bruce. *Wake Up, Dead Man: Afro-American Worksongs from Texas Prisons*. Cambridge, Mass.: Harvard University Press, 1972.

RAILROADING

The following deal with this special topic:

Botkin, Benjamin A., and Alvin F. Harlow. "Blues, Ballads, and Work Songs." In *A Treasury of Railroad Folklore*. New York: Crown Publishers, 1953. Pp. 434–466.

Carpenter, Ann Miller. "The Railroad in American Folk Song, 1865–1920." In *Diamond Bessie and the Shepherds*, edited by Wilson M. Hudson, pp. 103–119. Austin: Encino Press (Publications of the Texas Folklore Society, no. 36), 1972.

Cohen, Norman. " 'Casey Jones': At the Crossroads of Two Ballad Traditions." *Western Folklore* 32 (1973):77–103.

———. "Railroad Folksongs on Record — A Survey." *New York Folklore Quarterly* 26 (1970):91–113.

Donovan, Frank P., Jr. *The Railroad in Literature*. Boston: Railway and Locomotive Historical Society, 1940.

Ferris, William R., Jr. "Railroad Chants: Form and Function." *Mississippi Folklore Register* 4 (1970):1–14.

Hubbard, Freeman H. *Railroad Avenue: Great Stories and Legends of American Railroading*. New York: Whittlesey House, 1946. Rev. ed. San Marino, Calif.: Golden West Books, 1964.

Laws, G. Malcolm, Jr. "Ballads of Tragedies and Disasters." In *Native American Balladry: A Descriptive Study and a Bibliographic Syllabus*. Philadelphia: American Folklore Society, Bibliographical and Special Series, vol. 1, 1950. Pp. 211–228. Rev. ed., 1964.

Lomax, John A. and Alan. "Working on the Railroad." In *American Ballads and Folk Songs*. New York: Macmillan, 1934. Pp. 3–43.

———. "Railroaders and Hoboes." In *Our Singing Country*. New York: Macmillan, 1941. Pp. 254–270.

Manning, Ambrose. "Railroad Work Songs." *Tennessee Folklore Society Bulletin 32* (1966):41–47.

Milburn, George. *The Hobo's Hornbook, A Repertory for a Gutter Jongleur*. New York: Ives Washburn, 1930.

Sandburg, Carl. "Railroad and Work Gangs." In *The American Songbag*. New York: Harcourt, Brace, 1928. Pp. 355–386.

Sherwin, Sterling, and H. K. McClintock. *Railroad Songs of Yesterday*. New York: Shapiro, Bernstein, 1943.

MURDERS

Most American collections include murder ballads, and the subject warrants a special section of:

Laws, G. Malcolm, Jr. *Native American Balladry: A Descriptive Study and a Bibliographic Syllabus*. Philadelphia: American Folklore Society, Bibliographical and Special Series, vol. 1, 1950. Rev. ed., 1964. Pp. 190–210, 268–271.

The following book is given over to the topic:

Burt, Olive Wooley. *American Murder Ballads and Their Stories*. New York: Oxford University Press, 1958.

OUTLAWS, BAD MEN, AND HANGINGS

Another subject that is found in many American folksong collections. Specific references are in:

Laws, G. Malcolm, Jr. *Native American Balladry: A Descriptive Study and a Bibliographic Syllabus*. Philadelphia: American Folklore Society, Bibliographical and Special Series, vol. 1, 1950. Rev. ed., 1964. Pp. 176–189, 266–268.

BLUES

The blues have become the most influential American folk music form in the past few decades. For this reason, the following extensive bibliography would seem appropriate:

Albertson, Chris. *Bessie*. New York: Stein & Day, 1972. [Bessie Smith.]

Ames, Russell. "The Blues." In *The Story of American Folk Song*. New York: Grosset & Dunlap, 1955. Reprint, 1960. Pp. 249–268.

Bastin, Bruce. *Crying for the Carolines*. London: Studio Vista, 1971. [Bluesmen from North and South Carolina.]

Berendt, Joachim Ernst. *Blues*. Munich: Nymphenburger Verlagshandlung, 1957. 2nd ed., 1960.

Blesh, Rudi. "The Blues." In *Shining Trumpets: A History of Jazz*. New York: Knopf, 1946. Pp. 98–148.

Bluestein, Gene. "The Blues as a Literary Theme." *Massachusetts Review* 8 (1967): 593–617. Reprinted in *The Voice of the Folk: Folklore and American Literary Theory*. Amherst: University of Massachusetts Press, 1972. Pp. 117–140.

Bogaert, Karel. *Blues Lexicon: Blues, Cajun, Boogie Woogie, Gospel.* Antwerp: Standard Kitgeverij, 1971.

Bradford, Perry. *Born with the Blues.* New York: Oak Publications, 1965.

Broonzy, William, and Yannick Bruynoghe. *Big Bill Blues.* London: Cassell, 1955. Rev. ed. New York: Oak Publications, 1964.

Brown, Sterling A. "The Blues." *Phylon* 13 (1952):286–292.

———. "The Blues as Folk Poetry." In *Folk-Say, a Regional Miscellany: 1930*, edited by Benjamin A. Botkin, pp. 324–339. Norman: University of Oklahoma Press, 1930. Reprint. New York: Johnson Reprint Corp., 1971.

Campbell, E. Simms. "Blues." In *Jazzmen*, edited by Frederick Ramsey, Jr., and Charles Edward Smith, pp. 101–118. New York: Harcourt, Brace, 1939. Reprinted in *The Negro in Music and Art*, edited by Lindsay Patterson, pp. 53–63. Rev. ed. New York: Publishers Co., 1968.

Charters, Samuel B. *The Bluesmen: The Story and the Music of the Men Who Made the Blues.* New York: Oak Publications, 1967.

———. *The Country Blues.* New York: Rinehart, 1959.

———. *The Poetry of the Blues.* New York: Oak Publications, 1963.

———. *Robert Johnson.* New York: Oak Publications, 1973.

Chase, Gilbert. "Singin' the Blues." In *America's Music: From the Pilgrims to the Present.* 2nd ed. New York: McGraw-Hill, 1966. Pp. 448–464.

Clar, Mimi. "Folk Belief and Custom in the Blues." *Western Folklore* 19 (1960):173–189. Reprinted in *The Second Line* 11 [sic: 12] (1961):1–8; 12 (1962):23–30.

Cone, James H. *The Spirituals and the Blues: An Interpretation.* New York: Seabury Press, 1972.

Coolidge, Richard A. "The Blues in Theory." *NAJE Educator* (National Association of Jazz Educators) 3 (1971):13–16.

Courlander, Harold. "Blues." In *Negro Folk Music, U.S.A.* New York: Columbia University Press, 1963. Reprinted, 1970. Pp. 123–145.

Dane, Barbara. "The Meaning of the Blues." *Down Beat* 27 (1960):17–21.

Dauer, Alfons Michael. "Betrachtungen zur afro-amerikanischen Folklore, dargestellt an einem Blues von Lightnin' Hopkins." *Archiv für Völkerkunde*, 19 (1964–1965): 11–30.

Dixon, Robert M. W., and John Godrich. *Recording the Blues.* London: Studio Vista, 1970; New York: Stein & Day, 1970.

"Enigmatic Folksongs of the Southern Underworld." *Current Opinion* 67 (1919): 165–166.

Evans, David. "Africa and the Blues." *Living Blues* 10 (1972):27–29.

———. *Tommy Johnson.* London: Studio Vista, 1971.

Evans, David, and Bob Groom. *Charlie Patton.* Knutsford, Cheshire, Eng.: Blues World Booklet no. 2, 1969.

Fahey, John. *Charley Patton.* London: Studio Vista, 1970.

Ferris, William R. Jr. *Blues from the Delta.* London: Studio Vista, 1970.

———. "Blues." In *Mississippi Black Folklore: A Research Bibliography and Discography.* Hattiesburg: University and College Press of Mississippi, 1971. Pp. 24–32.

———. "Racial Repertoires among Blues Performers." *Ethnomusicology* 14 (1970): 439–449.

———. "Records and the Delta Blues Tradition." *Keystone Folklore Quarterly* 14 (1969):158–165.

Folk Blues. New York: Arc Music, 1965.

Fox, Mrs. Jesse W. "Beale Street and the Blues." *West Tennessee Historical Society Papers*, vol. 13, 1959. Pp. 128–147.

Garland, Phyl. *The Sound of Soul*. Chicago: Henry Regnery, 1969.

Garwood, Donald. *Masters of Instrumental Blues Guitar*. vol. 1. Laguna Beach, Calif.: Traditional Stringed Instruments, 1967. Reprint. New York: Oak Publications, 1968.

Gillet, Charlie. *The Sound of the City: The Rise of Rock & Roll*. New York: Outerbridge & Dienstfrey, 1970. Rev. ed. London: Souvenir Press, 1971.

Glover, Tony. *Blues Harp: An Instruction Method for Playing the Blues Harmonica*. New York: Oak Publications, 1965.

Godrich, John, and Robert M. W. Dixon. *Blues and Gospel Records 1902–1942*. Hatch End, Middlesex, Eng.: Brian Rust, 1964. Rev. ed. London: Storyville Publications, 1969.

Gombosi, Otto. "The Pedigree of the Blues." *Volume of Proceedings of the Music Teachers National Association*, 40th Series, 70th Year, 1946. Pp. 382–389.

Grainger, Porter, and Bob Ricketts. *How to Play and Sing the Blues like the Phonograph and Stage Artists*. New York: Jack Mills, 1926.

Green, Archie. "The Carter Family's 'Coal Miner's Blues.'" *Southern Folklore Quarterly* 25 (1961):226–237.

Groom, Bob. *Blind Lemon Jefferson*. Knutsford, Cheshire, Eng.: Blues World Booklet no. 3, 1970.

———. *The Blues Revival*. London: Studio Vista, 1971.

———. "The Library of Congress Blues and Gospel Recordings." Series in *Blues World*, beginning no. 38 (1971):8–11.

Groom, Bob, and Bob Yates. *Robert Johnson*. 4th ed. Knutsford, Cheshire, Eng.: Blues World Booklet no. 1, 1969.

Grossman, Stefan. *The Country Blues Guitar*. New York: Oak Publications, 1968.

———. *Delta Blues Guitar*. New York: Oak Publications, 1969.

———. *Ragtime Blues Guitarists*. New York: Oak Publications, 1970.

Grossman, Stefan, Stephan Calt, and Hal Grossman. *Country Blues Songbook*. New York: Oak Publications, 1973.

Gruver, Rod. "The Blues as Dramatic Monologues." *JEMF Quarterly* 5 (1970): 28–31.

———. "A Closer Look at the Blues." *Blues World* 26 (1970):4–10.

———. "The Funny Blues: Cryin' Just to Keep from Laughin.'" *Blues World* 33 (1970):19–20; 34 (1970):19–21; 35 (1970):20–21.

———. "Towards a Criticism of the Blues." *Jazz Monthly* 155 (1968):2–5.

Guralnik, Peter. "Blues as History." *Blues World* 22 (1968):5–13.

———. *Feel Like Going Home: Portraits in Blues & Rock 'n' Roll*. New York: Outerbridge & Dienstfrey, 1971.

Handy, William C. *Father of the Blues*. New York: Macmillan, 1941. Reprint. New York: Collier Books, 1970.

Handy, William C., and Myles A. Fellowes. "The Heart of the Blues." *Etude* 58 (1940):152, 193, 211.

Handy, William C., and Abbe Niles. *A Treasury of the Blues*. Rev. ed. of *Blues: An Anthology* (1926). New York: Charles Boni, 1949. Reprint. New York: Macmillan, 1972.

Haralambos, Michael. "Soul Music and Blues: Their Meaning and Relevance in Northern United States Black Ghettos." In *Afro-American Anthropology: Contemporary Perspectives*, edited by Norman E. Whitten, Jr., and John F. Szwed, pp. 367–384. New York: Free Press, 1970.

Hayakawa, S. I. "Popular Songs vs. the Facts of Life." *Etc.: A Review of General Semantics* 12 (1955):83–95. Reprinted in *Mass Culture: The Popular Arts in America*, edited by Bernard Rosenburg and David Manny White. Glencoe, Ill.: Free Press, 1957, pp. 393–403; in *Our Language and Our World*, edited by S. I. Hayakawa. New York: Harper & Bros., 1959, pp. 279–292; in *The Use and Misuse of Language*, edited by S. I. Hayakawa. Greenwich, Conn.: Fawcett Publications, 1962, pp. 150–163.

Hechman, Don. "Five Decades of Rhythm and Blues." *BMI: The Many Worlds of Music*. Summer 1969. Pp. 4–31.

Higgins, Steve. "Robert Johnson." *Seattle Folklore Society Newsletter* 2 (1970): 2–7; *Seattle Folklore Society Journal* 2 (1970):2–7, 22–23.

Hughes, Langston, and Arna Bontemps. "Blues." In *The Book of Negro Folklore*. New York: Dodd, Mead, 1958. Pp. 371–397.

Iglauer, Bruce et al. "David (Honeyboy) Edwards." *Living Blues* 1 (1970–1971): 19–24.

Jahn, Janheinz, and Alfons Michael Dauer. *Blues und Work Songs*. Frankfurt am Main: Fischer Bücherei, 1964.

Johnson, Guy B. "Double Meaning in the Popular Negro Blues." *Journal of Abnormal and Social Psychology* 22 (1927):12–20.

Jones, LeRoi. "Blues, Black & White America." *Metronome* 78 (1961):11–15.

———. *Blues People: Negro Music in White America*. New York: William Morrow and Company, 1963.

Jones, Max. "On Blues." In *PL Yearbook of Jazz 1946*, edited by Albert McCarthy, pp. 72–107. London: Editions Poetry London, 1946.

Keil, Charles. *Urban Blues*. Chicago: University of Chicago Press, 1966.

Kempf, Paul, Jr. "Striking the Blue Note in Music." *The Musician* 34 (1929):29.

Lang, Iain. *Jazz in Perspective: Background of the Blues*. London: Hutchinson, 1947.

Leadbitter, Mike. *Delta Country Blues*. Bexhill-on-Sea, Eng.: Blues Unlimited, 1968.

———. *Nothing But the Blues*. London: Hanover Books, 1971.

Leadbitter, Mike, and Neil Slaven. *Blues Records: January, 1943 to December, 1966*. London: Hanover Books, 1968.

Lehmann, Theo. *Blues and Toruble*. Berlin: Henschelverlag, 1966.

Locke, Alain. "Secular Folk Songs: The Blues and Work-Songs." In *The Negro and His Music*. Washington, D.C.: The Associates in Negro Folk Education, 1936. Reprint. Port Washington, N.Y.: Kennikat Press, 1968. Reprint (with *Negro Art: Past and Present*). New York: Arno Press, 1969. Pp. 28–35.

Lomax, Alan. "Blues." In *Folk Songs of North America*. London: Cassell, 1960; New York: Doubleday, 1960. Pp. 573–595.

Lomax, John A. and Alan. *Negro Folk Songs as Sung by Leadbelly*. New York: Macmillan, 1936.

Longini, Muriel Davis. "Folk Songs of Chicago Negroes." *Journal of American Folklore* 52 (1939):96–111.

McCarthy, Albert, Alun Morgan, Paul Oliver, and Max Harrison. *Jazz on Record: A Critical Review to the First 50 Years: 1917–1967*. London: Hanover Books, 1968.

Melnick, Mimi Clar. " 'I Can Peep through Muddy Water and Spy Dry Land': Boasts in the Blues." In *Folklore International: Essays in Traditional Literature, Belief, and Custom in Honor of Wayland Debs Hand*, edited by D. K. Wilgus, pp. 138–149. Hatboro, Pa.: Folklore Associates, 1967.

Middleton, Richard. *Pop Music and the Blues: A Study of the Relationship and Its Significance*. London: Victor Gollancz, 1972.

Mitchell, George. *Blow My Blues Away*. Baton Rouge: Louisiana State University Press, 1971.

Moore, Carman. *Somebody's Angel Child: The Story of Bessie Smith*. New York: Thomas Y. Crowell, 1969.

Napier, Simon. *Back Woods Blues*. Bexhill-on-Sea, Eng.: Blues Unlimited, 1968.

Nelson, Paul. "Country Blues Comes to Town." *Sing Out!* 14 (1964):14–24.

Newton, Francis. " 'Trouble Is a Man' (The Classic Blues Singers)." In *The Decca Book of Jazz*, edited by Peter Gammond, pp. 62–74. London: Frederick Muller, 1958.

Niles, Abbe. "Ballads, Songs and Snatches: Columbia Race Records." *Bookman* 67 (1928):422–424.

————. "Blue Notes." *New Republic* 45 (1926):292–293. Reprinted as "The Blues" in *Frontiers of Jazz*, edited by Ralph de Toledano, pp. 32–57. New York: Oliver Durrell, 1947. Reprint. New York: Frederick Ungar, 1962.

Odum, Howard W., and Guy B. Johnson. "The Blues: Workaday Sorrow Songs." In *Negro Workaday Songs*. Chapel Hill: University of North Carolina Press, 1926. Pp. 17–34. Reprint. New York: Negro Universities Press, 1969.

Oliver, Paul. "African Influence and the Blues." *Living Blues* 8 (1972):13–17.

————. "Blues as an Art Form." *Blue World* 21 (1968):1–7.

————. *Blues Fell This Morning: The Meaning of the Blues*. London: Cassell, 1960; New York: Horizon Press, 1961. Reprinted as *The Meaning of the Blues*. New York: Collier Books, 1963.

————. "Blues to Drive the Blues Away." In *Jazz*, edited by Nat Hentoff and Albert J. McCarthy, pp. 83–103. New York and Toronto: Rinehart, 1959.

————. *Conversation with the Blues*. New York: Horizon Press, 1965.

————. *Kings of Jazz: Bessie Smith*. London: Cassell, 1959; New York: Barnes, 1961.

————. *Savannah Syncopators: African Retentions in the Blues*. London: Studio Vista, 1970; New York: Stein & Day, 1970.

————. *Screening the Blues: Aspects of the Blues Tradition*. London: Cassell, 1968. Reprinted as *Aspects of the Blues Tradition*, New York: Oak Publications, 1970.

————. *The Story of the Blues*. Philadelphia: Chilton Book, 1969; London: Barre & Rockliff, 1969. Reprint. Harmondsworth, Eng.: Penguin Books, 1972.

Olsson, Bengt. *Memphis Blues and Jug Bands*. London: Studio Vista, 1970.

"Origin of 'Blues' Numbers." *Sheet Music News* 2 (1923):8–9, 41.

Osgood, Henry O. "The Blues." *Modern Music* 4 (1926):25–28.

————. "The Blooey Blues." In *So This Is Jazz*. Boston: Little, Brown, 1926. Pp. 63–75.

Oster, Harry. "Background of the Blues." In *Black America*, edited by John F. Szwed, pp. 143–157. New York and London: Basic Books, 1970.

————. "The Blues as a Genre." *Genre* 2 (1969):259–274.

————. *Living Country Blues*. Detroit: Folklore Associates, 1969.

The Paramount Book of the Blues. Port Washington, Wis.: New York Recording Laboratories, ca. 1926–1927. Reprint. Chicago: John Steiner, 1971.

Radcliffe, Charles. "Blues Walking like a Man." *Anarchy* 5 (1965):140–158.

Rooney, James. *Bossmen: Bill Monroe and Muddy Waters*. New York: Dial Press, 1971.

Roxin, Charles. *Aspects of the Blues*. Fairport, N.Y.: Space Age Printers, 1973.

Russell, Tony. *Blacks, Whites and Blues*. London: Studio Vista, 1970; New York: Stein & Day, 1970.

Sackheim, Eric, and Jonathan Shahn. *The Blues Line: A Collection of Blues Lyrics.* New York: Grossman Publishers, 1969. [A large collection of blues texts.]

Scarborough, Dorothy. "Blues." In *On the Trail of Negro Folk-Songs.* Cambridge, Mass.: Harvard University Press, 1925. Reprint (foreword by Roger D. Abrahams). Hatboro, Pa.: Folklore Associates, 1963. Pp. 264–280.

————. "The 'Blues' as Folk-Songs." *Publications of the Texas Folklore Society* 2 (1923). Reprinted as *Coffee in the Gourd*, edited by J. Frank Dobie, pp. 52–66. Dallas: Texas Folklore Society, 1935. Reprint. Dallas: Southern Methodist University Press, 1969.

Schuller, Gunther. *Early Jazz: Its Roots and Musical Development.* New York: Oxford University Press, 1968.

Sergeant, Winthrop. "The Derivation of the Blues." In *Jazz: Hot and Hybrid.* Rev. ed. New York: E. P. Dutton, 1946. Pp. 173–189.

Shaw, Arnold. *The Rock Revolution.* New York: Macmillan, 1969.

————. *The World of Soul: Black America's Contribution to the Pop Music Scene.* New York: Cowles Book, 1970.

Shirley, Kay, and Frank Driggs. *The Book of the Blues.* New York: Crown Publishers, 1963.

Silverman, Jerry. *Folk Blues: 110 American Folk Blues.* New York: Macmillan, 1958. Rev. eds. New York: Oak Publications, 1968; New York: Macmillan, 1971.

Stearns, Marshall W. "The Blues." In *The Story of Jazz.* New York: Oxford University Press, 1956. Pp. 99–108.

Stewart-Baxter, Derrick. *Ma Rainey and the Classic Blues Singers.* London: Studio Vista, 1970; New York: Stein & Day, 1970.

Strachwitz, Chris. "Blues from Coast to Coast." *American Folk Music Occasional* 1 (1964):20–37.

Summers, Lynn J. "African Influence and the Blues: An Interview with Richard A. Waterman." *Living Blues* 2 (1971):30–36.

Szwed, John F. "Musical Adaptation among Afro-Americans." *Journal of American Folklore* 82 (1969):112–121. Reprinted as "Afro-American Musical Adaptation" in *Afro-American Anthropology: Contemporary Perspectives*, edited by Norman E. Whitten, Jr., and John F. Szwed, pp. 219–228. New York: Free Press, 1970.

————. "Negro Music: Urban Renewal." In *Our Living Traditions: An Introduction to American Folklore*, edited by Tristram P. Coffin, pp. 272–282. New York: Basic Books, 1968.

Titon, Jeff. "Autobiography and Blues Texts: A Reply to 'The Blues as Dramatic Monologs.'" *JEMF Quarterly* 6 (1970):79–82.

Traum, Happy. "The Art of the Talking Blues." *Sing Out!* 15 (1966):53–59.

————. *The Blues Bag.* New York: Consolidated Music Publishers, 1968.

————. *Guitar Styles of Brownie McGhee.* New York: Oak Publications, 1971.

Ulanov, Barry. "The Blues." In *A History of Jazz in America.* New York: Viking Press, 1952. Reprint. New York: Da Capo Press, 1972. Pp. 26–34.

Van Vechten, Carl. "The Black Blues." *Vanity Fair* 24 (1925):57, 86, 92.

Welding, Peter. "The Rise of Folk-Blues." *Down Beat* 28 (1961):15–17.

————. "The Rise of the White Blues Performer." In *Down Beat: Music '65: 10th Yearbook.* Chicago: Maher Publications, 1965. Pp. 55–57, 85.

————. "Stringin' the Blues: The Art of the Folk Blues Guitar." *Down Beat* 32 (1965):22–24, 56.

White, Newman Ivey. "Blues and Miscellaneous Songs." In *American Negro Folk Songs.* Cambridge, Mass.: Harvard University Press, 1928. Reprint (foreword by Bruce Jackson). Hatboro, Pa.: Folklore Associates, 1963. Pp. 387–402.

Williams, Martin T. "The Blues." In *Where's the Melody? A Listener's Introduction to Jazz.* Rev. ed. New York: Pantheon Books, 1969. Pp. 17–32.

Wolfe, Charles K. "Where the Blues Is At: A Survey of Recent Research." *Popular Music and Society* 1 (1972):152–166.

Work, John W. "The Blues." In *American Negro Songs.* New York: Howell, Soskin, 1940. Pp. 28–36.

Addresses of English-Language Blues Periodicals

Blues Unlimited
38A Sackville Road
Bexhill-on-Sea, Sussex, England

Living Blues
P. O. Box 11303
Chicago, Illinois 60611

Blues World
22 Manor Crescent
Knutsford, Cheshire, England

Whiskey, Women, and . . .
39 Pine Avenue
Haverhill, Massachusetts 01830

GENERAL WORKS

Listings of general works, general collections, regional collections, and American Negro folk music materials, followed by book and record publishers and periodicals.

Abrahams, Roger D., and George Foss. *Anglo-American Folksong Style.* Englewood Cliffs, N.J.: Prentice-Hall, 1968.

Ames, Russell. *The Story of American Folk Song.* New York: Grosset & Dunlap, 1955. Reprinted, 1960.

Barry, Phillips. *Folk Music in America.* New York: WPA Federal Theater Project, National Service Bureau, pub. no. 805, June 1939. [Reprints of earlier articles.]

Bayard, Samuel P. "American Folksongs and Their Music." *Southern Folklore Quarterly* 17 (1953):122–139.

Brunvand, Jan Harold. *The Study of American Folklore: An Introduction.* New York: W. W. Norton, 1968. Pp. 128–177, 252–267.

Coffin, Tristram P. *An Analytical Index to the Journal of American Folklore.* Philadelphia: American Folklore Society, Bibliographical and Special Series, vol. 7, 1958. Pp. 179-238.

————. *The British Traditional Ballad in North America.* Philadelphia: American Folklore Society, Bibliographical and Special Series, vol. 2, 1950. Rev. ed., 1963.

————. *Our Living Traditions: An Introduction to American Folklore.* New York: Basic Books, 1968. Pp. 83–141.

Coffin, Tristram P., and Hennig Cohen. *Folklore in America.* Garden City, N.Y.: Doubleday, 1966. Reprinted 1970. Pp. 47–99.

Gordon, Robert Winslow. *Folk-Songs of America.* New York: National Service Bureau, Federal Theater Project, WPA, 1938. [Reprints of New York *Times* articles, 1927–1928.]

Greenway, John. *American Folksongs of Protest.* Philadelphia: University of Pennsylvania Press, 1953. Reprint. New York: Octagon Books, 1970.

Haywood, Charles. *A Bibliography of North America Folklore and Folksong.* New York: Greenberg, 1951. Rev. ed. 2 vols. New York: Dover Publications, 1962.

Lawless, Ray M. *Folksingers and Folksongs in America.* New York: Duell, Sloan & Pearce, 1960. Rev. ed., 1965.

Laws, G. Malcolm, Jr. *American Balladry from British Broadsides: A Guide for Students and Collectors of Traditional Song.* Philadelphia: American Folklore Society, Bibliographical and Special Series, vol. 8, 1957.

————. *Native American Balladry: A Descriptive Study and a Bibliographic Syllabus.* Philadelphia: American Folklore Society, Bibliographical and Special Series, vol. 1, 1950. Rev. ed., 1964.

Lomax, Alan, and Sidney Robertson Cowell. *American Folk Song and Folk Lore: A Regional Bibliography.* N.p.: Service Center of the Progressive Education Association (pamphlet number 8), 1942.

Lomax, John A. *Adventures of a Ballad Hunter.* New York: Macmillan, 1947. Reprint. New York: Hafner, 1971.

Nettl, Bruno. *Folk and Traditional Music of the Western Continents.* Englewood Cliffs, N.J.: Prentice-Hall, 1965. 2nd ed., 1973. Pp. 209–249.

————. *An Introduction to Folk Music in the United States.* Detroit: Wayne State University Press, 1960. Rev. ed., 1962.

Seeger, Charles. "Folk Music: U.S.A." In *Grove's Dictionary of Music and Musicians,* 5th ed., vol. 3, edited by Eric Blom, pp. 387–398. London: Macmillan, 1954; New York: St. Martin's Press, 1954. Reprinted, 1970.

Smith, Reed, et al. "Folk Music in America." In *The International Cyclopedia of Music and Musicians,* 9th ed., edited by Robert Sabin, pp. 698–721. New York: Dodd, Mead, 1964.

U.S. Library of Congress. *Check-List of Recorded Songs in the English Language in the Library of Congress Archive of American Folk Song to July, 1940.* Washington, D.C.: Library of Congress, 1942. Reprint. New York: Arno Press, 1971.

Wilgus, D. K. *Anglo-American Folksong Scholarship since 1898.* New Brunswick, N.J.: Rutgers University Press, 1959.

GENERAL COLLECTIONS

Botkin, Benjamin A. *A Treasury of American Folklore.* New York: Crown, 1944. Pp. 796–918.

Bronson, Bertrand H. *The Traditional Tunes of the Child Ballads.* Vols. 1–4. Princeton: Princeton University Press, 1959–1972. [Includes hundreds of examples from American sources.]

Burt, Olive Wooley. *American Murder Ballads and Their Stories.* New York: Oxford University Press, 1958.

Cohen, John, and Mike Seeger. *The New Lost City Ramblers Song Book.* New York: Oak Publications, 1964. [Transcribed from hillbilly recordings.]

Cray, Ed. *The Erotic Muse.* New York: Oak Publications, 1969. Published as *Bawdy Ballads.* London: Anthony Blond, 1970. [Annotated collection from American informants.]

Dolph, Edward Arthur. *"Sound Off!" Soldier Songs from Yankee Doodle to Parley Voo.* New York: Cosmopolitan, 1929.

Dunson, Josh, and Ethel Raim. *Anthology of American Folk Music.* New York: Oak Publications, 1973. [Transcribed from a Folkways reissue of race and hillbilly recordings.]

Emrich, Duncan. "Folksongs and Ballads." In *Folklore on the American Land.* Boston and Toronto: Little, Brown, 1972. Pp. 401–594.

Lomax, Alan. *Folk Songs of North America in the English Language.* London: Cassell, 1960; New York: Doubleday, 1960.

————. *The Penguin Book of American Folk Songs.* Harmondsworth, Middlesex, Eng. and Baltimore: Penguin Books, 1964.

Lomax, Alan, Woody Guthrie, and Pete Seeger. *Hard Hitting Songs for Hard-Hit People.* New York: Oak Publications, 1967. [Primarily transcribed from field recordings and race and hillbilly disks.]

Lomax, John and Alan. *American Ballads and Folk Songs.* New York: Macmillan, 1935. 20th printing, 1966.

————. *Folk Song: U.S.A.* New York: Duell, Sloan & Pearce, 1947. 4th ed. as *Best-Loved American Folk Songs.* New York: Grosset & Dunlap, 1954.

————. *Our Singing Country.* New York: Macmillan, 1941. [Transcribed from Library of Congress field recordings.]

Newell, William Wells. *Games and Songs of American Children.* New York: Harper & Bros., 1883, 1903. Reprint (introduction by Carl Withers). New York: Dover Publications, 1963.

Pound, Louise. *American Ballads and Songs.* New York: Charles Scribner's Sons, 1922. Reprinted, 1972.

Sandburg, Carl. *An American Songbag.* New York: Harcourt, Brace, 1927.

Scott, John Anthony. *Ballad of America: The History of the United States in Song and Story.* New York: Bantam, 1966.

Seeger, Ruth Crawford. *American Folk Songs for Children.* Garden City, N.Y.: Doubleday, 1948.

Silber, Irwin. *Songs of the Civil War.* New York: Columbia University Press, 1960.

REGIONAL COLLECTIONS

Abrahams, Roger D. *A Singer and Her Songs: Almeda Riddle's Book of Ballads.* Baton Rouge: Louisiana State University Press, 1970. [Arkansas.]

Arnold, Bryon. *Folksongs of Alabama.* University: University of Alabama Press, 1950.

Barry, Phillips. *Bulletin of the Folksong Society of the Northeast.* Cambridge, Mass.: Folk-Song Society of the Northeast, 1930–1936. Reprint (introduction by Samuel P. Bayard). Philadelphia: American Folklore Society, Bibliographical and Special Series, vol. 11, 1960.

————. *The Maine Woods Songster.* Cambridge, Mass.: Powell Publishing, 1939.

Barry, Phillips, Fannie Hardy Eckstorm, and Mary Winslow Smyth. *British Ballads from Maine.* New Haven: Yale University Press, 1929.

Beck, Earl Clifton. *Songs of the Michigan Lumberjacks.* Ann Arbor: University of Michigan Press, 1941. Rev. ed. *Lore of the Lumber Camps,* 1948.

Belden, Henry M. *Ballads and Songs Collected by the Missouri Folk Song Society.* Columbia: University of Missouri Studies, vol. 15, no. 1, 1940. 2nd ed., 1955. Reprinted, 1966, 1973.

Boette, Marie. *Singa Hipsy Doodle and Other Folk Songs of West Virginia.* Parsons, W. Va.: McClain Printing, 1971.

Botkin, Benjamin A. *The American Play-Party Song, with a Collection of Oklahoma Texts and Tunes.* Lincoln: University Studies of the University of Nebraska, vol. 38, nos. 1–4, 1937. Reprint. New York: Frederick Ungar, 1963.

Brewster, Paul. *Ballads and Songs of Indiana.* Bloomington: Indiana University Folklore Series, no. 1, 1940.

Burton, Thomas G., and Ambrose N. Manning. *The East Tennessee State University Collection of Folklore: Folksongs.* Johnson City: East Tennessee State University, Institute of Regional Studies, monograph no. 4, 1967.

————— .*The East Tennessee State University Collection of Folklore: Folksongs II.* Johnson City: Research Advisory Council of East Tennesee State University, 1969. [Northwestern North Carolina.]

Bush, Michael E. *Folk Songs of Central West Virginia.* Ripley, W. Va.: M. E. Bush, 1969.

—————. *Folk Songs of Central West Virginia.* Vol. 2. Glenville, W. Va.: Song Book, 1970.

Cambiaire, Celestin Pierre. *East Tennessee and Western Virginia Mountain Ballads.* London: Mitre Press, 1934.

Carey, George. *Maryland Folk Legends and Folk Songs.* Cambridge, Md.: Tidewater Publishers, 1971.

Cazden, Norman. *The Abelard Folk Song Book.* New York: Abelard Schuman, 1958. [Largely from the Catskill region of New York.]

Chappell, Louis W. *Folk-Songs of Roanoke and the Albemarle.* Morgantown, W. Va.: Ballad Press, 1939. [Coastal North Carolina.]

Chase, Richard. *American Folk Tales and Songs . . . as Preserved in the Appalachian Mountains.* New York: Signet, 1956. Reprint. New York: Dover Publications, 1971.

Cheney, Thomas E. *Mormon Songs from the Rocky Mountains: A Compilation of Mormon Folksongs.* Austin: University of Texas Press, 1968. (Publications of the American Folklore Society, Memoir Series, vol. 53.)

Colcord, Joanna C. *Roll and Go: Songs of American Sailormen.* Indianapolis: Bobbs-Merrill, 1924. Revised as *Songs of American Sailormen.* New York: W. W. Norton, 1938. Reprint. New York: Oak Publications, 1964.

Combs, Josiah H. *Folk-Songs of the Southern United States.* Edited by D. K. Wilgus. Austin: University of Texas Press, 1967. (American Folklore Society, Bibliographical and Special Series, vol. 19.)

Cox, John Harrington. *Folk-Songs of the South Collected under the Auspices of the West Virginia Folk-Lore Society.* Cambridge, Mass.: Harvard University Press, 1925. Reprint (foreword by Arthur Kyle Davis, Jr.). Hatboro, Pa.: Folklore Associates, 1963.

—————. *Traditional Ballads and Folk-Songs Mainly from West Virginia.* Published as two collections. New York: National Service Bureau, Federal Theater Project, WPA, 1939. Reprint (edited by George W. Boswell). Philadelphia: American Folklore Society, Bibliographical and Special Series, vol. 15, 1964.

Davis, Arthur Kyle, Jr. *Folk-Songs of Virginia. A Descriptive Index and Classification.* Durham, N.C.: Duke University Press, 1949. Reprint. New York: AMS Press, 1965.

—————. *More Traditional Ballads of Virginia.* Chapel Hill: University of North Carolina Press, 1960.

—————. *Traditional Ballads of Virginia.* Cambridge, Mass.: Harvard University Press, 1929. Reprint. Charlottesville: University Press of Virginia, 1969.

Dean, M. C. *Flying Cloud and One Hundred and Fifty Other Old-Time Songs and Ballads of Outdoor Men, Sailors, Lumber Jacks, Soldiers, Men of the Great Lakes, Railroadmen, Miners, etc.* Virginia, Minn.: Quickprint, 1922. Reprint. Norwood, Pa.: Norwood Editions, 1973.

Doerflinger, William M. *Shanteymen and Shanteyboys: Songs of the Sailor and Lumberman*. New York: Macmillan, 1951. Reprinted as *Songs of the Sailor and Lumberman*, 1972.

Eckstorm, Fannie Hardy, and Mary Winslow Smyth. *Minstrelsy of Maine: Folk-Songs and Ballads of the Woods and the Coast*. Boston and New York: Houghton Mifflin, 1927. Reprint. Ann Arbor: Gryphon Books, 1971.

Eddy, Mary O. *Ballads and Songs from Ohio*. New York: J. J. Augustin, 1939. Reprint (foreword by D. K. Wilgus). Hatboro, Pa.: Folklore Associates, 1964.

Fife, Austin E. and Alta S. *Cowboy and Western Songs: A Comprehensive Anthology*. New York: Clarkson N. Potter, 1969.

Finger, Charles, J. *Frontier Ballads*. Garden City, N.Y.: Doubleday, Page, 1927.

Flanders, Helen Hartness. *Ancient Ballads Traditionally Sung in New England*. 4 vols. Philadelphia: University of Pennsylvania Press, 1960–1965.

Flanders, Helen Hartness, Elizabeth Flanders Ballard, George Brown, and Phillips Barry. *The New Green Mountain Songster: Traditional Folk Songs of Vermont*. New Haven: Yale University Press, 1939. Reprint (introduction by Tristram P. Coffin). Hatboro, Pa.: Folklore Associates, 1966.

Flanders, Helen Hartness, and George Brown. *Vermont Folk-Songs & Ballads*. Brattleboro: Stephen Daye Press, 1932. Reprint (foreword by Horace P. Beck). Hatboro, Pa.: Folklore Associates, 1968.

Flanders, Helen Hartness, and Marguerite Olney. *Ballads Migrant in New England*. New York: Farrar, Straus, and Young, 1953. Reprint. Freeport, N.Y.: Books for Libraries Press, 1968.

Ford, Ira W. *Traditional Music of America*. New York: E. P. Dutton, 1940. Reprint (introduction by Judith McCulloh). Hatboro, Pa.: Folklore Associates, 1965. [Primarily from Missouri.]

Fuson, Harvey H. *Ballads of the Kentucky Highlands*. London: Mitre Press, 1931.

Gardner, Emelyn E., and Geraldine J. Chickering. *Ballads and Songs of Southern Michigan*. Ann Arbor: University of Michigan Press, 1939. Reprint (foreword by Albert B. Friedman). Hatboro, Pa.: Folklore Associates, 1967.

Gray, Roland Palmer. *Songs and Ballads of the Maine Lumberjacks: With Other Songs from Maine*. Cambridge, Mass.: Harvard University Press, 1924. Reprint. Detroit: Singing Tree Press, 1969.

Green, Archie. *Only a Miner: Studies in Recorded Coal-Mining Songs*. Urbana: University of Illinois Press, 1972.

Grover, Carrie B. *A Heritage of Songs*. N.p., n.d., Reprint. Norwood, Pa.: Norwood Editons, 1973. [Repertory of a Maine family.]

Harlow, Frederick Pease. *Chanteying aboard American Ships*. Barre, Mass.: Barre Gazette, 1962.

Henry, Mellinger Edward. *Folk-Songs from the Southern Highlands*. New York: J. J. Augustin, 1938.

————. *Songs Sung in the Southern Appalachians*. London: Mitre Press, 1934.

Hubbard, Lester A. *Ballads and Songs from Utah*. Salt Lake City: University of Utah Press, 1961.

Hudson, Arthur Palmer. *Folksongs of Mississippi and Their Background*. Chapel Hill: University of North Carolina Press, 1936.

Hugill, Stan. *Shanties from the Seven Seas: Shipboard Worksongs from the Great Days of Sail*. London: Routledge & Kegan Paul, 1961; New York: E. P. Dutton, 1961.

Huntington, Gale. *Folksongs from Martha's Vineyard*. Orono, Me.: Northeast Folklore, vol. 8, 1966.

————. *Songs the Whalermen Sang*. Barre, Mass.: Barre Publishers, 1964. 2nd ed. New York: Dover Publications, 1970.

Ives, Edward D. *Folksongs from Maine*. Orono, Me.: Northeast Folklore, vol. 7, 1965.

————. *Larry Gorman: The Man Who Made the Songs*. Bloomington: Indiana University Press, 1964.

Jackson, George Pullen. *Another Sheaf of White Spirituals*. Gainesville: University of Florida Press, 1952.

————. *Down-East Spirituals and Others*. New York: J. J. Augustin, 1943. 2nd ed., 1953.

————. *Spiritual Folk-Songs of Early America: Two Hundred and Fifty Tunes and Texts with an Introduction and Notes*. New York: J. J. Augustin, 1937. Reprint. New York: Dover Publications, 1964.

————. *White and Negro Spirituals: Their Life Span and Kinship*. New York: J. J. Augustin, 1943.

————. *White Spirituals in the Southern Uplands*. Chapel Hill: University of North Carolina Press, 1933. Reprint (foreword by Don Yoder). Hatboro, Pa.: Folklore Associates, 1964. Reprint (without foreword). New York: Dover Publications, 1965.

Joyner, Charles W. *Folk Song in South Carolina*. Columbia: University of South Carolina Press, 1971. (Tricentennial booklet no. 9.)

Korson, George. *Coal Dust on the Fiddle: Songs and Stories of the Bituminous Industry*. Philadelphia: University of Pennsylvania Press, 1943. Reprint (foreword by John Greenway). Hatboro, Pa.: Folklore Associates, 1965.

————. *Minstrels of the Mine Patch: Songs and Stories of the Anthracite Industry*. Philadelphia: University of Pennsylvania Press, 1938. Reprint (foreword by Archie Green). Hatboro, Pa.: Folklore Associates, 1964.

————. *Pennsylvania Songs and Legends*. Philadelphia: University of Pennsylvania Press, 1949. Reprint. Baltimore: Johns Hopkins Press, 1960.

Larkin, Margaret. *Singing Cowboy: A Book of Western Songs*. New York: Alfred A. Knopf, 1931. Reprint. New York: Oak Publications, 1963.

Lingenfelter, Richard E., Richard A. Dwyer, and David Cohen. *Songs of the American West*. Berkeley and Los Angeles: University of California Press, 1968.

Linscott, Eloise Hubbard. *Folk Songs of Old New England*. New York: Macmillan, 1939. Reprint. Hamden, Conn.: Archon Books, 1962.

Lomax, John. *Cowboy Songs and Other Frontier Ballads*. New York: Sturgis & Walton, 1910. Rev. ed., 1911, 1916 (reprinted by Macmillan, 1918). Rev. ed. (with Alan Lomax). New York: Macmillan, 1938. 13th printing, 1961.

————. *Songs of the Cattle Trail and Cow Camp*. New York: Macmillan, 1915. Reprint. New York: Duell, Sloan & Pearce, 1950.

Moore, Ethel and Chauncey O. *Ballads and Folk Songs of the Southwest*. Norman: University of Oklahoma Press, 1964.

Morris, Alton C. *Folksongs of Florida*. Gainesville: University of Florida Press, 1950.

Neely, Charles. *Tales and Songs of Southern Illinois*. Menasha, Wis.: George Banta Publishing, 1938.

Niles, John Jacob. *The Ballad Book of John Jacob Niles*. Boston: Houghton Mifflin, 1961. [Appalachia.]

Owens, William A. *Texas Folk Songs*. Austin: Publications of the Texas Folklore Society, no. 23, 1950.

Perrow, E. C. "Songs and Rhymes from the South." *Journal of American Folklore* 25 (1912):137–155; 26(1913):123–173; 28(1915):129–190.

Randolph, Vance. *Ozark Folksongs.* 4 vols. Columbia: State Historical Society of Missouri, 1946–1950.

Richardson, Ethel Park. *American Mountain Songs.* New York: Greenberg, 1927.

Rickaby, Franz. *Ballads and Songs of the Shanty-Boy.* Cambridge, Mass.: Harvard University Press, 1926. [Wisconsin and Minnesota.]

Ritchie, Jean. *Folk Songs of the Southern Appalachians.* New York: Oak Publications, 1965.

———. *Singing Family of the Cumberlands.* New York: Oxford University Press. Reprint. New York: Oak Publications, 1963.

Rosenberg, Bruce A. *The Folksong of Virginia: A Checklist of the WPA Holdings, Alderman Library, University of Virginia.* Charlottesville: University Press of Virginia, 1969.

Sackett, S. J., and William E. Koch. *Kansas Folklore.* Lincoln: University of Nebraska Press, 1961. Pp. 138–181 (chapters on folksong by Henry H. Malone and Joan O'Bryant).

Scarborough, Dorothy. *A Song Catcher in Southern Mountains: American Folk Songs of British Ancestry.* New York: Columbia University Press, 1937.

Sharp, Cecil J. *English Folk Songs from the Southern Appalachians.* 2 vols. Edited by Maud Karpeles. London and New York: Oxford University Press, 1932. Reprinted, 1952, 1960, 1966.

Shellans, Herbert. *Folk Songs of the Blue Ridge Mountains.* New York: Oak Publications, 1968. [Southern Virginia.]

Shoemaker, Henry W. *Mountain Minstrelsy of Pennsylvania.* Philadelphia: Newman F. McGirr, 1931. [3rd ed. of *North Pennsylvania Minstrelsy.*]

Silber, Irwin, and Earl Robinson. *Songs of the Great American West.* New York: Macmillan, 1967; London: Collier-Macmillan, 1967.

Smith, Reed. *South Carolina Ballads: With a Study of Traditional Ballad To-Day.* Cambridge, Mass.: Harvard University Press, 1928. Reprints. Spartanburg, S.C.: Reprint Co., 1972; Freeport, N.Y.: Books for Libraries Press, 1972.

Thomas, Jean. *Ballad Makin' in the Mountains of Kentucky.* New York: Henry Holt, 1939. Reprint. New York: Oak Publications, 1964.

———. *Devil's Ditties.* Chicago: W. Wilbur Hatfield, 1931. [Kentucky.]

Thomas, Jean, and Joseph A. Leeder. *The Singin' Gatherin': Tunes from the Southern Appalachians.* New York: Silver Burdett, 1939. [Kentucky.]

Thompson, Harold W., with Edith E. Cutting. *A Pioneer Songster: Texts from the Stevens-Douglas Manuscript of Western New York, 1841–1856.* Ithaca: Cornell University Press, 1958.

Thorp, N. Howard. *Songs of the Cowboys.* Variants, commentary, notes and lexicon by Austin E. and Alta S. Fife. New York: Clarkson N. Potter, 1966. [Based on a collection originally published in 1908.]

Treat, Asher E. "Kentucky Folksong in Northern Wisconsin." *Journal of American Folklore* 52(1939):1–51.

Welsch, Roger L. *A Treasury of Nebraska Pioneer Folklore.* Lincoln: University of Nebraska Press, 1966.

White, Newman Ivey, general ed. *The Frank C. Brown Collection of North Carolina Folklore.* 7 vols. Durham, N.C.: Duke University Press, 1952–1964.

Vol. 2. *Folk Ballads.* Edited by Henry M. Belden and Arthur Palmer Hudson, 1952.

Vol. 3. *Folk Songs.* Edited by Henry M. Belden and Arthur Palmer Hudson, 1952.

Vol. 4. *The Music of the Ballads.* Edited by Jan P. Shinhan, 1957.

Vol. 5. *The Music of the Songs.* Edited by Jan P. Shinhan, 1962.

Wolford, Leah Jackson. *The Play-Party in Indiana.* Indianapolis: Indiana Historical Commission, 1916. Edited and revised by W. Edson Richmond and William Tillson. Indianapolis: Indiana Historical Society Publications, vol. 20, no. 2, 1959.

SUMMARY BY STATE

[In addition, see the Western and Sailor portions of the bibliography. References are to the first author listed for each work. The first two entries are for regions covering more than one state.]

APPALACHIA: Chase, Green, Henry, Jackson, Korson, Niles, Perrow, Richardson, Scarborough, Sharp.
NEW ENGLAND: Barry, Flanders, Linscott.
ALABAMA: Arnold.
ARKANSAS: Abrahams, Randolph.
FLORIDA: Morris.
ILLINOIS: Neely.
INDIANA: Brewster, Wolford.
KANSAS: Sackett.
KENTUCKY: Combs, Fuson, Ritchie, Thomas, Treat (in Wisconsin).
MAINE: Barry, Eckstorm, Gray, Grover, Ives.
MARYLAND: Carey.
MASSACHUSETTS: Huntington.
MICHIGAN: Beck, Gardner.
MINNESOTA: Dean, Rickaby.
MISSISSIPPI: Hudson.
MISSOURI: Belden, Ford, Randolph.
NEBRASKA: Welsch.
NEW YORK: Cazden, Thompson.
NORTH CAROLINA: Burton, Chappell, White.
OHIO: Eddy.
OKLAHOMA: Botkin, Moore.
PENNSYLVANIA: Korson, Shoemaker.
SOUTH CAROLINA: Joyner, Smith.
TENNESSEE: Burton, Cambiaire.
TEXAS: Owens.
UTAH: Cheney, Hubbard.
VERMONT: Flanders.
VIRGINIA: Cambiaire, Davis, Rosenberg, Shellans.
WEST VIRGINIA: Boette, Bush, Combs, Cox.
WISCONSIN: Rickaby, Treat.

AMERICAN NEGRO

See the Negro Spiritual and Blues sections for more detailed treatment of these subjects.

Allen, William Francis, Charles Pickard Ware, and Lucy McKim Garrison. *Slave Songs of the United States.* New York: A. Simpson, 1867. Reprints. New York: Peter Smith, 1951; Freeport, N.Y.: Books for Libraries Press, 1971. Rev. ed. New York: Oak Publications, 1965.

Ballanta (-Taylor), Nicholas George Julius. *Saint Helena Island Spirituals.* New York: G. Schirmer, 1925.

Barton, William E. *Old Plantation Hymns: A Collection of Hitherto Unpublished Melodies of the Slave and the Freedman, with Historical and Descriptive Notes.* Boston: Lamson, Wolffe, 1899. Reprint. New York: AMS Press, 1972.

Boatner, Edward, and Willa A. Townsend. *Spirituals Triumphant Old and New.* Nashville: National Baptist Convention, 1927.

Chappell, Louis W. *John Henry: A Folk-Lore Study.* Jena: Fronmansche Verlag: Walter Biedermann, 1933. Reprint. Port Washington, N.Y.: Kennikat Press, 1968.

Charters, Samuel B. *The Bluesmen: The Story and the Music of the Men Who Made the Blues.* New York: Oak Publications, 1967.

———. *The Country Blues.* New York: Rinehart, 1959.

Cone, James H. *The Spirituals and the Blues: An Interpretation.* New York: Seabury Press, 1972.

Courlander, Harold. *Negro Folk Music, U.S.A.* New York: Columbia University Press, 1963. Reprinted, 1970.

———. *Negro Songs from Alabama.* New York: n.p., 1960. Rev. ed. New York: Oak Publications, 1963.

Epstein, Dena J. "Slave Music in the United States before 1860: A Survey of Sources." Music Library Association *Notes* 20 (1963):195–212; 377–390.

Fisher, Miles Mark. *Negro Slave Songs in the United States.* Ithaca: Cornell University Press for the American Historical Association, 1953. Reprint. New York: Russell & Russell, 1968.

Godrich, John, and Robert M. W. Dixon. *Blues and Gospel Records, 1902–1942.* Hatch End, Middlesex, Eng.: Brian Rust, 1964. Rev. ed. London: Storyville Publications, 1969.

Grissom, Mary Ellen. *The Negro Sings of a New Heaven.* Chapel Hill: University of North Carolina Press, 1930. Reprint. New York: Dover Publications, 1969.

Jackson, Bruce. *The Negro and His Folklore in Nineteenth-Century Periodicals.* Austin: University of Texas Press, 1967. (Publications of the American Folklore Society, Bibliographical and Special Series, vol. 18.)

———. *Wake Up, Dead Man: Afro-American Worksongs from Texas Prisons.* Cambridge, Mass.: Harvard University Press, 1972.

Johnson, Guy B. *Folk Culture of St. Helena Island, South Carolina.* Chapel Hill: University of North Carolina Press, 1930. Reprint (foreword by Don Yoder). Hatboro, Pa.: Folklore Associates, 1968. Pp. 63–130.

———. *John Henry: Tracking Down a Negro Legend.* Chapel Hill: University of North Carolina Press, 1929. Reprint. New York: AMS Press, 1969.

Johnson, J. Rosamond. *Rolling Along in Song: A Chronological Survey of American Negro Music.* New York: Viking Press, 1937.

Johnson, James Weldon, and J. Rosamond Johnson. *The Books of American Negro Spirituals: Including the Book of American Negro Spirituals and the Second Book of Negro Spirituals.* New York: Viking Press, 1940. Reprinted, 1969.

Jones, Bessie, and Bess Lomax Hawes. *Step It Down: Games, Plays, Songs, and Stories from the Afro-American Heritage.* New York: Harper & Row, 1972.

Katz, Bernard, ed. *The Social Implications of Early Negro Music in the United States.* New York: Arno Press, 1969. [Reprints of early essays.]

Kennedy, R. Emmet. *Mellows: A Chronicle of Unknown Singers.* New York: Albert & Charles Boni, 1925.

———. *More Mellows.* New York: Dodd, Mead, 1931.

Krehbiel, Henry Edward. *Afro-American Folksongs: A Study in Racial and National Music.* New York and London: G. Schirmer, 1914. Reprint. New York: Frederick Ungar, 1962.

Levine, Lawrence W. "Slave Songs and Slave Consciousness: An Exploration in Neglected Sources." In *Anonymous Americans: Explorations in Nineteenth-Century Social History,* edited by Tamara K. Harenen, pp. 99–130. Englewood Cliffs, N.J.: Prentice-Hall, 1971.

Lomax, Alan. *The Rainbow Sign: A Southern Documentary.* New York: Duell, Sloan & Pearce, 1959.

Lomax, John A. and Alan. *Negro Folk Songs as Sung by Leadbelly.* New York: Macmillan, 1936.

McIlhenny, E. A. *Befo' de War Spirituals.* Boston: Christopher Publishing House, 1933. Reprint. New York: AMS Press, 1973.

Odum, Howard W., and Guy B. Johnson. *The Negro and His Songs: A Study of Typical Negro Songs in the South.* Chapel Hill: University of North Carolina Press, 1925. Reprint (foreword by Roger D. Abrahams). Hatboro, Pa.: Folklore Associates, 1964. Reprint (without foreword). New York: Negro Universities Press, 1968.

———. *Negro Workaday Songs.* Chapel Hill: University of North Carolina Press, 1926. Reprint. New York: Negro Universities Press, 1969.

Oliver, Paul. *Blues Fell This Morning: The Meaning of the Blues.* London: Cassell, 1960; New York: Horizon Press, 1961. Reprinted as *The Meaning of the Blues.* New York: Collier Books, 1963.

———. *Conversation with the Blues.* New York: Horizon Press, 1965.

———. *Savannah Syncopators: African Retentions in the Blues.* London: Studio Vista, 1970: New York: Stein & Day, 1970.

———. *Screening the Blues: Aspects of the Blues Tradition.* London: Cassell, 1968. Reprinted as *Aspects of the Blues Tradition.* New York: Oak Publications, 1970.

———. *The Story of the Blues.* Philadelphia: Chilton Book, 1969; London: Barre & Rockliff, 1969. Reprint. Harmondsworth, Eng.: Penguin Books, 1972.

Oster, Harry. *Living Country Blues.* Detroit: Folklore Associates, 1969.

Parrish, Lydia. *Slave Songs of the Georgia Sea Islands.* New York: Creative Age Press, 1942. Reprint (foreword by Bruce Jackson). Hatboro, Pa.: Folklore Associates, 1965.

Ramsey, Frederic, Jr. *Been Here and Gone.* New Brunswick, N.J.: Rutgers University Press, 1960. [Photo-essay of southern Negro music and musicians.]

Sackheim, Eric, and Jonathan Shahn. *The Blues Line: A Collection of Blues Lyrics.* New York: Grossman Publishers, 1969. [A large collection of blues texts.]

Scarborough, Dorothy. *On the Trail of Negro Folk-Songs.* Cambridge, Mass.: Harvard University Press, 1925. Reprint (foreword by Roger D. Abrahams). Hatboro, Pa.: Folklore Associates, 1963.

Silverman, Jerry. *Folk Blues: 110 American Folk Blues.* New York: Macmillan, 1958. Rev. ed. New York: Oak Publications, 1968; New York: Macmillan, 1971.

Talley, Thomas W. *Negro Folk Rhymes: Wise and Otherwise.* New York: Macmillan, 1922. Reprint. Port Washington, N.Y.: Kennikat Press, 1968.

Waterman, Richard Alan. "African Influence on the Music of the Americas." In *Acculturation in the Americas: Proceedings and Selected Papers of the XXIXth International Congress of Americanists*, edited by Sol Tax, pp. 207–218. Chicago: University of Chicago Press, 1952. Reprint. New York: Cooper Square Publishers, 1967. Reprinted in *Anthropology and Art: Readings in Cross-Cultural Aesthetics*, edited by Charlotte M. Otten, pp. 227–244. Garden City, N.Y.: Natural History Press, 1971. Also reprinted in *Mother Wit from the Laughing Barrel: Readings in the Interpretation of Afro-American Folklore*, edited by Alan Dundes, pp. 81–94. Englewood Cliffs, N.J.: Prentice-Hall, 1973.

White, Newman Ivey. *American Negro Folk-Songs.* Cambridge, Mass.: Harvard University Press, 1928. Reprint (foreword by Bruce Jackson). Hatboro, Pa.: Folklore Associates, 1965.

Work, John Wesley. *American Negro Songs.* New York: Howell, Soskin; Bonanza Books, 1940.

———. *Folk Song of the American Negro.* Nashville: Press of Fisk University, 1915. Reprint. New York: Negro Universities Press, 1969.

AMERICAN BOOK PUBLISHERS WITH SPECIAL FOLK MUSIC SERIES OR CATALOGS

American Folklore Society Publications
See: University of Texas Press

Cooperative Recreation Service
Radnor Road
Delaware, Ohio 43105

Dover Publications
180 Varick Street
New York, New York 10014

Folklore Associates
See: Gale Research Company

Gale Research Company
Book Tower
Detroit, Michigan 48226
Includes Folklore Associates and Singing Tree Press

Indiana University Press
Tenth and Norton Street
Bloomington, Indiana 47401
Folklore Series

Johnson Reprint Corporation
111 Fifth Avenue
New York, New York 10003
Folklore and Society Series

Kraus Reprint Corporation
16 East 46th Street
New York, New York 10017

Norwood Editions
P.O. Box 38
Norwood, Pennsylvania 19074

Oak Publications
33 West 60th Street
New York, New York 10003

Singing Tree Press
See: Gale Research Company

University of California Press
2223 Fulton Street
Berkeley, California 94720
Folklore Studies

University of Texas Press
P.O. Box 7819
Austin, Texas 78712
    Publications of the American Folklore
    Society

For comprehensive listings of recent folk music books and their publishers, see appropriate headings in current issues of *Books in Print* and *Cumulative Book Index.*

RECORD COMPANIES SPECIALIZING IN AMERICAN FOLK MUSIC

Adelphi Records
P.O. Box 288
Silver Spring, Maryland 20907

American Heritage Music Corporation
1208 Everett Street
Caldwell, Idaho 83605

Archive of Folk Music
c/o Everest Record Group
10910 Wilshire Boulevard
West Los Angeles, California 90024

Arhoolie Records (Also: Blues Classics Records; Old-Timey Records; Folk-Lyric Records)
Box 9195
Berkeley, California 94719

Asch Records
    See: Folkways Records

Biograph Records (Also: Historical Records; Melodeon Records)
P.O. Box 109
Canaan, New York 12029

Blue Goose Records
    See: Yazoo Records

Blues Classics Records
    See: Arhoolie Records

County Records
307 East 37th Street
New York, New York 10016

Delmark Records
4243 North Lincoln Street
Chicago, Illinois 60618

F & W Records
Box 44
Plymouth Union, Vermont 05057

Fiddler's Grove Records
Box 11
Union Grove, North Carolina 28689

Folk-Legacy Records
Sharon Mountain Road
Sharon, Connecticut 06069

Folk-Lyric Records
    See: Arhoolie Records

Folkways Records (Also: Asch Records; RBF Records)
701 7th Avenue
New York, New York 10036

Fox Hollow Records
RD 1
Petersburg, New York 12138

Galax Old Fiddler's Convention
P.O. Box 655
Galax, Virginia 24333

Heirloom Records
RFD 2
Wiscasset, Maine 04578

Herwin Records
45 First Street
Glen Cove, New York 11542

Historical Records
    See: Biograph Records

JEMF Records
John Edwards Memorial Foundation
Folklore and Mythology Center
University of California
Los Angeles, California 90024

Kanawha Records
Box 2072
Dayton, Ohio 45429

Library of Congress (Archive of Folk
Song)
Recorded Sound Section
Music Division
Washington, D.C. 20540

Living Folk Records
65 Mount Auburn Street
Cambridge, Massachusetts 02138

Meadowlands Records
2301 Loring Place
Bronx, New York 10468

Melodeon Records
See: Biograph Records

Mountain Records
Rt. 3, Box 213-A
Galax, Virginia 24333

National Geographic Society
Recording Division
Washington, D.C. 20036

National Old Time Fiddlers' Contest
and Festival
Chamber of Commerce
Weiser, Idaho 83672

Northeast Fiddlers' Association
c/o Wayne Perry
R.F.D. No 1.
Stowe, Vermont 05672

Old-Timey Records
See: Arhoolie Records

Origin Jazz Library
(Also: Piedmont Records)
Box 863
Berkeley, California 94701

Philo Records
The Barn
North Ferrisburg, Vermont 05473

Piedmont Records
See: Origin Jazz Library

RBF Records
See: Folkways Records

Rounder Records
186 Willow Avenue
Somerville, Massachusetts 02144

Sacred Harp Publishing Company
P.O. Box 185
Bremen, Georgia 30110

Spivey Records
65 Grand Avenue
Brooklyn, New York 11205

Stinson Records
P.O. Box 3415
Granada Hills, California 91344

Stoneway Records
2817 Laura Koppe
Houston, Texas 77016

Takoma Records
P.O. Box 5403
Santa Monica, California 90405

Testament Records
577 Levering Avenue
Los Angeles, California 90024

Tradition Records
c/o Everest Record Group
10920 Wilshire Boulevard
West Los Angeles, California 90024

Traditional Records
P.O. Box 8
Cosby, Tennessee 37722

Union Grove Records
c/o J. Pierce Van Hoy
Box 38
Union Grove, North Carolina 28689

Vanguard Records
71 West 23rd Street
New York, New York 10010

Vetco Records
Jimmy Skinner Music Center
1300 Vine Street
Cincinnati, Ohio 45210

Voyager Recordings
424 35th Avenue
Seattle, Washington 98122

Yazoo Records (Also: Blue Goose
Records)
54 King Street
New York, New York 10014

AMERICAN FOLKLORE AND FOLK MUSIC PERIODICALS

AFFword
Arizona Friends of Folklore
Keith Cunningham
Box 4064
Northern Arizona University
Flagstaff, Arizona 86001

Abstracts of Folklore Studies
American Folklore Society
c/o University of Texas Press
P.O. Box 7819
Austin, Texas 78712

Country Dance and Song
The Country Dance & Song Society of
   America
55 Christopher Street
New York, New York 10014

Ethnomusicology
Society for Ethnomusicology
Room 513
210 South Main Street
Ann Arbor, Michigan 48108

Folklore Annual
Center for Intercultural Studies in
   Folklore and Oral History
University of Texas
Austin, Texas 78712

Folklore Forum
c/o The Folklore Institute
504 North Fess Street
Bloomington, Indiana 47401

Foxfire
Rabun Gap–Nacoochee School
Rabun Gap, Georgia 30568

Indiana Folklore
c/o The Folklore Institute
504 North Fess Street
Bloomington, Indiana 47401

JEMF Quarterly
John Edwards Memorial Foundation
Folklore and Mythology Center
University of California
Los Angeles, California 90024

Journal of American Folklore
America Folklore Society
c/o University of Texas Press
P.O. Box 7819
Austin, Texas 78712

Journal of Country Music
Country Music Foundation
700 16th Avenue, South
Nashville, Tennessee 37203

Journal of Popular Culture
101 University Hall
Bowling Green State University
Bowling Green, Ohio, 43403

Journal of the Folklore Institute
504 North Fess Street
Indiana University
Bloomington, Indiana 47401

*Journal of the Folklore Society of
Greater Washington*
P.O. Box 19303
20th Street Station
Washington, D.C. 20036

Journal of the Ohio Folklore Society
Professor Patricia Averill
Department of American Studies
Heidelberg College
Tiffin, Ohio 44883

Kentucky Folklore Record
Kentucky Folklore Society
Western Kentucky University
Bowling Green, Kentucky 42101

Keystone Folklore
Pennsylvania Folklore Society
Box 13, Logan Hall
University of Pennsylvania
Philadelphia, Pennsylvania 19104

Louisiana Folklore Miscellany
Louisiana Folklore Society
Department of English
Louisiana State University
New Orleans, Louisiana 70112

Mississippi Folklore Register
Mississippi Folklore Society
Southern Station
Box 418
Hattiesburg, Mississippi 39401

Mugwumps: The Magazine of Folk Instruments
Michael I. Holmes
Box 1171
Bowling Green, Kentucky 42101

New Mexico Folklore Record
c/o Mrs. Ernest W. Baughman
606 Vassar Drive
Albuquerque, New Mexico 87106

New York Folklore Quarterly
New York Folklore Society
c/o New York State Historical
Association
Cooperstown, New York 13326

North Carolina Folklore Journal
North Carolina Folklore Society
P.O. Box 5308
Raleigh, North Carolina 27607

Northeast Folklore
Edward D. Ives
South Stevens Hall
University of Maine
Orono, Maine 04473

Pennsylvania Folklife
Box 1053
Lancaster, Pennsylvania 17604

Popular Music and Society
Bowling Green State University
Bowling Green, Ohio 43403

Publications of the Texas Folklore Society
Francis E. Abernethy
Stephen F. Austin State University
Nacogdoches, Texas 75961

Seattle Folklore Society Journal
424 35th Avenue
Seattle, Washington 98122

Selected Reports
Institute of Ethnomusicology
University of California
Los Angeles, California 90024

Sing Out!
106 West 28th Street
New York, New York 10001

Southern Folklore Quarterly
University of Florida
Gainesville, Florida 32601

Tennessee Folklore Society Bulletin
Ralph W. Hyde
Middle Tennessee State University
Murfreesboro, Tennessee 37130

Viltis: A Folklore Magazine
P.O. Box 1226
Denver, Colorado 80201

Western Folklore
California Folklore Society
University of California Press
2223 Fulton Street
Berkeley, California 94720

Yearbook of the International Folk Music Council
Department of Music
Queen's University
Kingston, Ontario, Canada

INDEXES

Index of Titles

INDEX OF TITLES

INDEX OF TITLES

INDEX OF TITLES

Index of First Lines

825

INDEX OF FIRST LINES

INDEX OF FIRST LINES

INDEX OF FIRST LINES

DATE			
JUN 5 1980			
APR 8 '85			
MAY 8 '86			
APR 2 3 '86			
MAY 2 7 '91			
OCT. 30. 1991			
MAY 0 3 2004			